Beginning iPhone
Games Development

Peter Bakhirev
PJ Cabrera
Ian Marsh
Scott Penberthy
Ben Britten Smith
Eric Wing

Apress®

Beginning iPhone Games Development

ISBN-13 (pbk): 978-1-4302-2599-7

ISBN-13 (electronic): 978-1-4302-2600-0

Printed and bound in the United States of America 9 8 7 6 5 4 3 2 1

Publisher and President: Paul Manning
Lead Editor: Clay Andres
Developmental Editor: Jeffrey Pepper
Technical Reviewer: Peter Bakhirev, Eric Wing and Ben Britten Smith
Editorial Board: Clay Andres, Steve Anglin, Mark Beckner, Ewan Buckingham, Gary Cornell, Jonathan Gennick, Jonathan Hassell, Michelle Lowman, Matthew Moodie, Duncan Parkes, Jeffrey Pepper, Frank Pohlmann, Douglas Pundick, Ben Renow-Clarke, Dominic Shakeshaft, Matt Wade, Tom Welsh
Coordinating Editor: Kelly Moritz
Copy Editor: Marilyn Smith
Compositor: MacPS, LLC
Indexer: Potomac Indexers
Artist: April Milne
Cover Designer: Anna Ishchenko

Distributed to the book trade worldwide by Springer-Verlag New York, Inc., 233 Spring Street, 6th Floor, New York, NY 10013. Phone 1-800-SPRINGER, fax 201-348-4505, e-mail orders-ny@springer-sbm.com, or visit www.springeronline.com.

For information on translations, please e-mail rights@apress.com, or visit www.apress.com.

Apress and friends of ED books may be purchased in bulk for academic, corporate, or promotional use. eBook versions and licenses are also available for most titles. For more information, reference our Special Bulk Sales–eBook Licensing web page at www.apress.com/info/bulksales.

The source code for this book is available to readers at www.apress.com. You will need to answer questions pertaining to this book in order to successfully download the code.

Contents at a Glance

Contents

About the Authors

Peter Bakhirev is a longtime software developer, with over a decade of experience in Internet technologies and network programming, and an aspiring writer and entrepreneur. During the pre-iPhone era, he helped architect and implement one of the largest online poker sites. More recently, he participated in the creation of one of the first multiplayer games for the iPhone called Scramboni.

PJ Cabrera is a software engineer with more than 12 years of experience developing information systems in various industries, programming in C, C++, Java, PHP, Python, Ruby and Objective-C. He lives in the San Francisco Bay area and works as an iPhone and Rails developer for a stealth mode start-up in San Francisco.

Ian Marsh is the co-founder of the independent game studio NimbleBit based in San Diego, CA. He has been developing games for the iPhone since the advent of the App Store, with such successes as the #1 kids game "Scoops" and the #1 free game "Hanoi". When not developing games, Ian enjoys reading about science, tweeting about game development, and finger painting.

Scott Penberthy began coding shortly after the Apple II was launched in the 70's. His addiction to writing software fully bloomed with a scholarship to MIT, where he wrote a multiplayer online game that brought his school's antique computer to its knees. After graduating, Scott took a job at IBM Research, the birthplace of IBM's web products and services. After running up the corporate ladder in the 90's building massive web sites, he jettisoned in 2005 to return to his true love of coding. Now a successful entrepreneur, Scott runs an app studio in New York City.

Ben Britten Smith has been writing software on Apple platforms for 15 years. Most notably he was given an Academy Award for Technical Achievement for his feature film work with Mac-based suspended camera control systems. Lately he has switched his efforts from the big screen to the small screen.

His first iPhone game, "SnowDude" was published to the App Store a few months after the SDK became available. Since then he has written a dozen apps for various clients including the games: "Snowferno", The award winning: "Mole - A quest for the Terracore Gem", and the "Gambook Adventures" series of games. Ben lives in Melbourne, Australia with his wife Leonie and their pet bunnies.

Feeling he was living too extravagant of a lifestyle of ramen and subsidized bus passes, **Eric Wing** graduated (kicking and screaming) from the University of California at San Diego with a Masters degree in Computer Engineering just days before 9/11. In the following challenging world, he worked a wide range of jobs in the field from automated testing on satellite systems to scientific visualization with a variety of different operating systems and programming languages. But in a stroke of genius (actually, it was more likely just a stroke), he figured out how he could work even harder for no money and started working on open source projects. He has been a contributor to projects such as SDL (Simple DirectMedia Layer), OpenSceneGraph, and the Lua/Objective-C Bridge (and its successor LuaCocoa). And when he was offered a co-authorship of Beginning iPhone Games Development, how could he possibly refuse the idea of even more hard work for virtually no pay? It was a match made in heaven!

About the Technical Reviewer

The chapters of *Beginning iPhone Games Development* were peer-reviewed by the authors themselves. Peter Bakhirev reviewed chapters by Ian Marsh, PJ Cabrera, and Ben Britten Smith. Eric Wing reviewed the chapters written by Peter Bakhirev, and Ben Britten Smith was responsible for the tech review of Scott Penberthy's chapter.

Acknowledgments

Peter Bakhirev

Writing this book is part of a journey that started long time ago. Many better, kinder and smarter people than myself stood along the way and made this journey possible. Papa, thanks for putting that first computer together, for that tape with Basic on it, and for the wisdom (and all of the games, too). Mike, thanks for giving me a chance at that interview, for teaching me everything that I know about programming today, and for always being there ("We should do this again some time"). Lenny, thanks for believing that we could go from A to B (otherwise, I'd be going from 9 to 5 instead of writing this). Mama and Olya, thanks for the encouragement and asking about how the book is going almost every day. Lena, thanks for being and for believing, ILU and IWTHKWU. Thanks to Keith Shepherd for the introduction to Clay and Apress. Thanks to Clay Andres, Kelly Moritz, Douglas Pundick, Marilyn Smith and all of the wonderful people at Apress for pushing and pulling and making this happen.

PJ Cabrera

My gratitude goes out to Peter Bakhirev, Jeff Pepper, and Marilyn Smith for their help improving my chapters. Many thanks to Kelly Moritz and Dominic Shakeshaft for their patience. Kudos to Clay Andres and Douglas Pundick for their support. And last but not least, to my friends in the good ol' SNAP team, Kevin, Lenny, Ernesto, Cesar, Alejandro, Javier, Xavier, Edwin, thanks for keeping computing fun amidst a sea of chaos.

Ben Britten Smith

Ben would like to thank Neil from Tin Man Games for the use of his art assets.

Eric Wing

I want to acknowledge and give my everlasting thanks to a wonderful group of volunteers who reviewed my chapters.

First, my thanks to Daniel Peacock and Ryan Gordon for bringing to bear the full force of their technical expertise of OpenAL and audio in general to catch any mistakes and omissions. Also my thanks to Ian Minett for providing details about the Xbox implementations of OpenAL and Garin Hiebert for tracking down some obscure information concerning OpenAL for me.

Next, I wish to thank Josh Quick, Victor Gerth, Carlos McEvilly, and Wang Lam who reviewed my chapters from the perspective of the general audience for this book, thus enabling me to improve things before the book went to press.

Finally, there are several people who wish or need to stay anonymous. I wish to thank them nonetheless because their contributions were also significant.

And of course, my thanks to my co-authors and to the people at Apress for all their support.

Introduction

Hey there, curious reader! My name is Peter, and I'd like you to meet my fellow co-authors Ian, PJ, Scott, Ben and Eric. We are here for one simple reason: to help you learn how to make awesome iPhone games. You have probably noticed the word "beginning" in the title of this book. Here is what that means: you can develop games even if you have never thought of yourself as a "game developer" before. Even though it might seem like "rocket science" at first, in reality it is anything but (although one of the games that we will build in this book does have a rocket in it, along with spectacular explosions, out-of-this-world sounds and evil aliens.) We believe that anybody can learn the necessary skills, and we'll walk you through all of the steps and explain everything as we go along.

Speaking of ideas and games, we have a whole bunch of those for you to play with. This book includes half a dozen fully playable games that we will help you develop. In the process, you'll learn how to build 2D and 3D games with music, sound effects, support for multiple players and networking. But the question of "what to build" is at least as important as "how to build it", and you will find plenty of discussion about how to design something that's fun, as well.

In case you haven't developed for the iPhone before and need a crash course in how to use the tools of the trade, we have included a brief introduction to Objective-C and Xcode, but you can find a much more in-depth exploration of the iPhone development environment in "Beginning iPhone 3 Development" by Dave Mark and Jeff LaMarche, which we highly recommend. If you need a more thorough introduction to programming in general or C and Objective-C languages in particular, take a look at "Learn C on the Mac" by Dave Mark and "Learn Objective-C on the Mac" by Mark Darlymple and Scott Knaster.

Writing, coding and debugging this book was a lot of fun, and we hope that you will find it enjoyable and engaging. Good luck and see you in the App Store!

On behalf of the author team,

Peter Bakhirev

Chapter 1

A Revolutionary Gaming Platform: Games for Everyone, Anytime, Anywhere

The iPhone platform has drastically changed the landscape of next-generation mobile gaming. The iPhone is a device of many firsts, and its multifaceted nature is what pushes it above and beyond traditional mobile gaming platforms. The iPhone's ubiquity, connectivity, personal integration, popularity, and innovative interface make it one of the most potent and exciting platforms to develop for today.

The Ever-Present iPhone

Because the iPhone platform is first and foremost a mobile phone and/or digital music player, the vast majority of iPhone and iPod touch owners carry their devices around with them everywhere they go, every day. The combination of a phone, music player, and game player into a single, svelte package means that people no longer need to choose which devices to take with them each morning. This fact makes the iPhone a groundbreaking game platform.

For iPhone and iPod touch owners, any game is only seconds away—whether they're waiting at a gas pump or sitting on a trans-Atlantic flight. A quick glance around any public place illustrates the iPhone's proliferation and the quickly expanding market for iPhone games. For the gamer on the go, there's no better use of pocket space than the iPhone.

With games always within reach for players, developers can design either quick "pick-up-and-play" games or longer "appointment" games that may take 30 minutes or more to play. Great "time-waster" games, such as Veiled Game's Up There (see Figure 1–1), rarely last for more than a couple minutes and appeal to casual gamers who can't dedicate long spans of time to gaming. Others enjoy spending time in absorbing titles like Electronic Arts' SimCity (also shown in Figure 1–1). Either type of gamer can be an iPhone owner, and developers can even design a game that caters to both types. One thing is for certain: As an iPhone game developer, you can count on your game being carried around by your users every waking minute of their day.

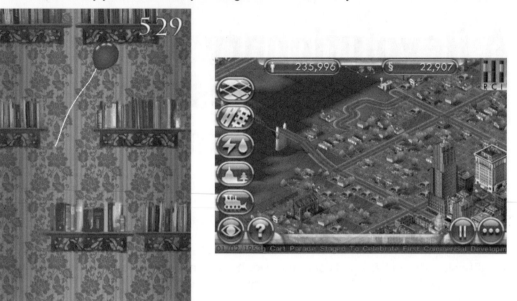

Figure 1–1. *Up There offers players a quick balloon-soaring game. Fans of simulation games can easily spend long stretches of time playing SimCity.*

Always having your game on hand not only means it will get more play time by your users, but it also helps to market your game. One of the best ways a high-quality iPhone game can be advertised is through word of mouth. iPhone users are likely to associate with other iPhone users. With their entire game collection right there in their pockets, gamers can show off their favorite games in an instant, and their friends can buy the game for themselves in a matter of seconds.

Mass Appeal—There's a Gamer Born Every Minute

Users are drawn to the iPhone for many reasons besides gaming. Some people are primarily interested in its web-browsing capabilities and multimedia features. But even those who have no history of playing video games find the App Store and its thousands of games very appealing.

The App Store's ease of use, combined with the availability of so many games, can turn anyone into a gamer, casual or otherwise. A developer can create games that will be enjoyed by all types of people—from a child on a car ride, to a Halo fan away from his Xbox, to a grandfather relaxing in his chair. The iPhone makes your games available to people who previously never considered gaming important enough to warrant buying one on any device.

The diversity of iPhone apps is actually blurring the definition of what a game is. Entertainment apps such as Snappy Touch's Flower Garden, The Blimp Pilots' Koi Pond (see Figure 1–2), and Bolt Creative's Pocket God are popular. These interactive experiences may not be games by literal definition, but they share many elements with games and can attract a huge fan base.

Figure 1–2. *Flower Garden lets users manage a virtual garden and send flowers to friends. Koi Pond presents users with an interactive virtual koi pond.*

Because many developers, rather than publishers, are deciding what kinds of apps to make, innovation and experimentation are running rampant. With so many potential customers and different types of gamers, there can be a market for almost any type of game—whether it's classic or something the world has never seen.

As an iPhone game developer, your customer base is growing every day and shows no sign of slowing down. Even when upgrading their iPhones or iPod touches, your customers can be sure to hang on to your games due to an easily supported standardized model lineup—a rarity in traditional cell phone gaming. Your game can target each and every iPhone and iPod touch gamer, regardless of which model they own. Even with a hugely successful title, it's impossible to saturate the market since there are new iPhone gamers born every minute.

User Interfaces—Death of the D-Pad

The iPhone's user interface is another part of the equation for this revolutionary platform. In the same way the Nintendo Wii made console gaming accessible to the general public's touch screen, accelerometer, camera, and microphone let game developers create intuitive natural interfaces to their interactive experiences.

With the tilt, touch, and microphone controls at their disposal, developers can make controls for their games transparent, creating an experience that is both immersive and easily comprehensible. Directly manipulating game objects with your finger or moving the physical device in your hands provides a visceral game interface to users. No longer is there a learning period of mentally mapping game buttons, pads, and joysticks to game actions. Interfaces on the iPhone must be immediately obvious to be usable at all.

Developers are utilizing these nontraditional control methods in new and unexpected ways. The iPhone's unique user interfaces have even spawned entirely new genres of games. Angling devices from side to side controls tilt games such as Lima Sky's Doodle Jump and NimbleBit's Scoops (see Figure 1–3). Multitouch games like Bed Bugs by Igloo Games put the players' concentration to the test by forcing them to manipulate multiple game objects at the same time. Entertainment apps Ocarina and Leaf Trombone by Smule allow users to play virtual instruments by blowing into the iPhone microphone.

Figure 1–3. *Scoops utilizes the iPhone's accelerometer to control a wobbling tower of ice cream scoops. Hanoi's natural interface lets players drag and drop game pieces.*

An iPhone game's interface can *be* the game, by presenting such a compelling and natural means of interaction that it becomes invisible to the user. A great example of the iPhone's capability for transparent user interfaces is NimbleBit's Hanoi (also shown in

Figure 1–3). Hanoi is the classic Towers of Hanoi puzzle used in many computer science algorithm classes. On most other platforms, this simple game would need to let users select a disk, perhaps with a directional pad and button, indicate on the screen which piece is selected, and then give users a way to drop the selected disk. When you think about it, this seems like a relatively complex interface to such a simple real-world task. In Hanoi for the iPhone, the user manipulates the pieces in a more natural manner: The user simply touches a disk, drags it to the correct position, and lets go. No directional pads, buttons, joysticks, or styluses are required.

Connectivity—Plays Well with Others

Another feature setting the iPhone apart from past mobile gaming platforms is its unprecedented connectivity. Developers targeting the iPhone (and iPod touch) can count on their game almost always having a data connection. This means that games on the iPhone can utilize Internet connectivity—whether it is a core part of the game play (multiplayer), a feature that improves an offline game (high score boards), or integration with social networks such as Facebook and Twitter. Games like Baseball Slugger by Com2uS (see Figure 1–4) pit you in a head-to-head contest against another player anywhere in the world from the comfort of your living room, a park bench, or a bus seat.

Figure 1–4. *Rolando 2 uses push notifications to challenge friends even when they aren't playing. Baseball Slugger lets you challenge players from around the world, anytime, anywhere.*

Even when devices are away from an Internet connection, a developer can use Bluetooth to connect players. With the addition of push notifications, you can keep your users involved and part of the game even when they're not playing. Games not designed for real-time multiplayer interaction, like Rolando 2 by ngmoco:) (also shown in Figure 1–4), utilize iPhone's connectivity by sending asynchronous challenges to other players. This type of technology is perfectly suited for things like notifying players when they're up in turn-based games, have been challenged by an opponent, or their record score has been dethroned.

Being a connected device not only improves games themselves, but also makes your games available to purchase and download at anytime and from anywhere. On traditional mobile platforms, gamers needed to visit retail stores and hope the game they wished to purchase was in stock. Previously, a good amount of time and effort stood between a customer's money and your games. With the live App Store only a tap away on the iPhone, it is easier and quicker than ever for developers to get their games on users' devices. Even with the recent arrival of digital distribution for some other mobile game platforms, the App Store's use of iTunes accounts avoids the need for purchasing or refilling points or credits to buy games; purchasing a game is as painless as buying a song. With the addition of support for paid downloadable content, developers also have multiple ways to monetize their creations.

The connectivity of the iPhone opens up a huge number of possibilities for game developers. They can create games that are dynamically updated with real-time data or new content. Not only can players play others across the world, but they can also voice chat with them in real time. A developer can integrate any number of Internet technologies into a game—be it social networking or streaming audio and video. Developers can even learn valuable things about how their games are being played by recording and retrieving usage data.

User Data—This Time It's Personal

The iPhone is the first gaming platform to have access to a wealth of personal information. Having the user's contacts, music, photos, videos, and location available for game developers to access opens the door for extremely personalized and customized experiences. How many other gaming platforms know who your friends are? With access to a user's contacts, iPhone games can use the names of friends and family for characters, contact them directly, or make multiplayer matchup a breeze. In ngmoco:)'s Dr. Awesome (see Figure 1–5), patients admitted to your hospital take the names of contacts from your address book, giving the game a very personal feel.

Figure 1–5. *Face Fighter players can customize their opponents with photos on their iPhone. The patients admitted in Dr. Awesome by ngmoco:) are the player's contacts.*

Not only can iPhone owners carry around their music collection in their pockets, but they can also choose their own game soundtracks from their favorite music. Players can customize their game's characters or environments with pictures or video taken or stored on their device.

In addition to all of this personal information, developers also have access to the device's physical location. While location-based games are still in their infancy, location can be used in more passive ways to match up nearby players or show maps of users worldwide.

Other devices have toyed with integrated or external cameras as a way to allow players to customize their games, but most fell short due to the fact you could use only pictures taken with that particular camera. Games and applications on the iPhone not only have access to the integrated camera, but also can use images saved from the browser, contained in an e-mail, saved to a contact, or sent in a multimedia message. This means that in games such as Appy Entertainment's Face Fighter (also shown in Figure 1–5), you can battle kung fu style against your best friend, a coworker, or a celebrity whose photo you saved from a web page.

With the ability to tap into an iPhone owner's music, photos, videos, friends, and location, game developers have unprecedented access to the personal lives of their players. In the right situations, iPhone games can allow customization or use fragments of personal information to evoke a more emotional response or give a greater feeling of ownership in the game. Used appropriately, access to this user data is another valuable tool in the inventive iPhone developer's toolbox.

Device Performance—A Multimedia Powerhouse

Most important to many developers is the power of the hardware. The processing power of a mobile gaming platform determines the extent that 3D graphics, physics simulations, and other technologies can be utilized in any game. Lucky for us, the iPhone is no slouch in this department. Veteran developers put the abilities of pre-3GS devices ahead of the Nintendo DS, and on par with the Sony PlayStation Portable (PSP). With the introduction of the 3GS model, the iPhone has advanced to the front of the pack in terms of hardware capability and performance.

With faster processers, more memory, and advanced 3D graphics support, future iPhone and iPod hardware will push the limits of what mobile games are capable of achieving. Each improved device will be able to create more polygons and simulate more physics. Established developers such as Electronic Arts, Gameloft, and Firemint have already produced iPhone titles that rival or surpass similar DS and PSP games (see Figure 1–6).

Figure 1–6. *Games like Firemint's Real Racing and Gameloft's Let's Golf show off the graphical power of the platform.*

With support for common game technologies such as OpenGL ES and OpenAL, experienced developers can make graphically rich experiences in no time. Since the iPhone Software Development Kit (SDK) supports C/C++ in addition to Objective-C, many existing libraries and a lot of game code can be reused or ported with little (or no) effort.

Along with the powerful hardware inside the devices, developers appreciate the presentation aspects. One glance at the crisp, high-resolution, glass-covered display will make developers forget the cheap, tiny screens of old mobile gaming. At 320 by 480 pixels, the screen is a wonderful canvas for high-quality game art and beautifully rendered 3D environments. The low response time of the display prevents any image ghosting, even with games running at 60 frames per second (fps). The smooth glass shield with the integrated capacitive touch screen makes tapping, dragging, pinching, and zooming a pleasure in any game.

To complete the package, the iPhone's hardware gives developers powerful audio capabilities. With hardware audio decoding, the CPU can concentrate on game play processing instead of background music. And when the highest quality lossless sounds are needed, there is plenty of disk space to hold them. While the single mono speaker might leave something to be desired, developers can count on most users having headphones on hand for truly immersive audio experiences.

Dev Kit? You're Holding It!

By far, the most revolutionary thing about the iPhone as a gaming platform is the fact that nearly anyone can develop for it. This fact alone dwarfs every other feature of the platform. A platform might have the most amazing groundbreaking features the gaming world has ever seen, but it's all for nothing if you're prevented from developing for it.

Traditionally, console manufacturers such as Nintendo, Sony, and Microsoft have put a huge number of restrictions on who can even purchase development kits. Developers must apply and provide detailed company information and design docs for the games they wish to make. It is then up to the manufacturers to decide whether the developers are competent enough and whether their game ideas are worthwhile. If you are lucky enough to become an authorized developer for one of these platforms, you're then hit with dev kit, licensing, testing, and certification fees—totaling thousands of dollars.

While some may complain that the iPhone's App Store is still a "walled garden," it is nowhere near as restrictive as the exclusive platforms of the past. All that Apple requires of its developers is a small annual fee. Apple doesn't care how many employees you have, how you're funded, or what kind of games you intend to make. Anyone—whether an experienced team or a single student just learning game development—can create games that will stand alongside titles made by huge developers like Electronic Art, Sega, and Gameloft. Shelf space is given to every developer free of charge, thanks to digital distribution, and any developer's game has the chance to be placed on the "end cap" of the App Store by being featured (see Figure 1–7).

Cost of development for the iPhone is significantly cheaper as well. Even if you don't already own an Intel-powered Mac, the total cost of computer, device, and developer fees would run around a thousand dollars or less. For most platforms, the development kits alone cost the same or more before adding fees for testing and certification.

Unlike traditional platforms, Apple is totally hands-off when it comes to the actual development itself. Apple doesn't require design docs or set milestones for you to meet. The only time Apple enforces its liberal requirements on your game is when it's finished and submitted to the App Store. The iPhone is the first popular gaming platform to be open to all developers.

Figure 1–7. *Games from small independent developers are in direct competition with those made by large and established developers and publishers.*

Innovation—Good Things Come from Small Developers

Innovation comes hand in hand with an open platform. The number and variety of people developing for the iPhone lead to the creation of things never before seen or even imagined. The iPhone is a wonderful new outlet for independent game developers to deliver their work to the world. Radical new games that would have a hard time seeing the light of day on a normal console face no such difficulty on the App Store.

Unique and innovative games such as Steph Thirion's Eliss and Mobigame's Edge (see Figure 1–8) can make it to market and start generating waves much quicker than would be possible on any other platform. Titles from relatively unknown developers can become hits overnight if they attract a large fan base that spreads news of the game by word of mouth, or have their games featured by Apple on iTunes or in a TV commercial. The App Store is one of the only platforms where games created by independent developers compete with the larger established developers and publishers, and even outnumber them.

Figure 1–8. *Eliss and Edge are two examples of unique and innovative games that have found success on the App Store.*

Chances are good that if you can dream it and build it, you can distribute it. While the large number of apps available for the iPhone can diminish the signal-to-noise ratio of high-quality games, consumers and Apple will continue to find ways of separating the wheat from the chaff.

Summary

The iPhone's ubiquity, mass appeal, user interface, connectivity, power, and low barrier to entry all combine to make it a game-changing, revolutionary new mobile gaming platform. Groundbreaking interactive experiences such as augmented reality are finding their way into people's hands. While still in its infancy, the iPhone and the App Store have already rewritten the rules of portable gaming. It's an exciting time to be a mobile game developer. In the next chapter, you'll get a better look at the tools and technologies you'll be using to get started.

Chapter **2**

Developing iPhone Games: Peeking Inside the iPhone Toolbox

Now that we've established the iPhone's platform credentials and described why you should be excited about developing for it, let's take a peek at some of the tools you'll be using. These technologies include Objective-C or C/C++, Xcode, UIKit, Quartz 2D, Core Animation, OpenGL, audio APIs, networking, and GameKit. This chapter provides a brief overview of these technologies, how they can be used when developing a game, and examples of how they are employed in existing games.

Development Tools and Environment

The language of iPhone development is Objective-C. As the name implies, Objective-C is an extension of the American National Standards Institute (ANSI) C language designed to give C simple and straightforward object-oriented capabilities. While most of the iPhone APIs have Objective-C interfaces, it is possible for the noninterfacing parts of an application to be written in C/C++, since Objective-C syntax is a superset of the GNU C/C++ syntax. You'll need at least some understanding of Objective-C and experience with C/C++.

Lucky for us, Apple prides itself on providing high-quality software to its developers. These tools have been enabling the creation of amazing software for the Mac for quite some time, and you'll be using nearly all the same tools for iPhone development. The foundation of iPhone development is Xcode, which allows for interface design, code editing, debugging, and performance analysis. All of this software is provided free of charge and will run on any Intel-based Mac computer.

The Xcode integrated development environment (IDE) is a full-featured code editor, project manager, and graphical debugger. Xcode contains all the amenities of a modern IDE, including robust syntax coloring, error reporting, code completion, and code folding. Compiling, installing, and launching your application requires a single click, and the on-device debugging is great for hunting down bugs. Make yourself comfortable with its user interface and shortcuts, because you'll be spending a lot of time writing your C/C++ and Objective-C inside Xcode.

Once your game is up and running, you can take advantage of the iPhone simulator. Able to simulate nearly every facet of the iPhone operating system apart from the accelerometer, the simulator is a quick and convenient way to test changes to your app. But make sure to test your app on a real device from time to time, since the simulator doesn't replicate device CPU performance or memory conditions.

Completing the package are a few other tools aimed at helping you design and optimize your iPhone apps. Interface Builder provides a graphical user interface (UI) editor, which automates the loading and positioning of UIKit elements such as buttons and labels. If you're not using OpenGL to build your game, Interface Builder can greatly simplify the creation of items like menus and other static elements. Once you've reached the optimization phase of development, Instruments will come in handy. A powerful profiling tool, Instruments collects and visualizes data such as disk, memory, and CPU usage, allowing you to quickly find the bottlenecks or memory hogs in your game.

UIKit

UIKit provides one of the simplest ways to draw images and other useful UI elements. Displaying and positioning bitmaps is very simple using UIKit, yet still remains relatively fast due to underlying hardware acceleration. UIKit is a great choice for games that don't have a large number of graphical elements or animations and don't need to run at the maximum of 60 fps. Aside from drawing bitmaps, UIKit makes it easy for developers to add other UI elements useful to games, such as alert boxes, text labels, and text-input fields. UIKit also gives access to user input, such as screen touches and accelerometer readings.

NimbleBit's Sky Burger (see Figure 2–1) is a tilt-controlled, burger-stacking game that was developed entirely in UIKit, without the direct use of OpenGL ES. While Sky Burger has a lot of graphics and animated elements, it is near the limit of what UIKit can do graphically with acceptable frame rates. If you wanted to add more graphical effects to a game like this, you would probably need to employ OpenGL ES to ensure that it runs quickly on all devices.

Textropolis by NimbleBit (also shown in Figure 2–1) is another example of a game that doesn't need the powerful graphical rendering provided by OpenGL ES. Because Textropolis is a word game with only small background animations, UIKit was a perfect fit for its development.

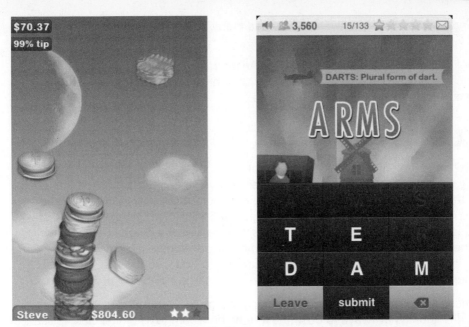

Figure 2–1. *Sky Burger and Textropolis by NimbleBit are examples of simple 2D games developed with UIKit.*

In Chapter 3, iPhone developer PJ Cabrera provides an in-depth look inside UIKit and tells you everything you need to know to get up and running with it. If you're planning to make a simple 2D game that doesn't need to run at 60 fps, consider building your game in UIKit.

Quartz 2D and Core Animation

Also known as Core Graphics, Quartz 2D provides developers with a more advanced, low-level drawing engine. While still a 2D technology, Quartz 2D provides useful and powerful features such as off-screen rendering, transparency layers, and advanced line drawing. These abilities come in handy for many game developers to do things like draw radar screens, mini maps, curved paths, and other UI elements. While it may be too slow to use for rendering the main elements of a game, Quartz 2D is another valuable tool in the iPhone developer's toolbox.

PJ Cabrera will give you all the details and more potential uses for Quartz 2D in Chapter 4. Be sure to read that chapter if you plan on doing any off-screen rendering or advanced drawing in your game.

What is a game without some animation? Core Animation gives developers a way to move and transform UIKit elements with a minimum amount of work. Using Core Animation, you can create hardware-accelerated, time-based animations using properties like position, rotation, transparency, and even matrix transformations. Core Animation is flexible enough for anything from animating game elements to adding a bit of flourish to game menus and UI elements. Core Animation can be used for transitioning between views as well; it provides many built-in transitions that are ready to use.

In Chapter 5, PJ goes over the basics of Core Animation, and even shows you how to use it to create particle-like effects. This isn't a chapter to skip, as uses for Core Animation can be found in just about any game.

OpenGL ES

Depending on the type of game you wish to make, OpenGL ES may be the single most important tool in your toolbox. OpenGL ES gives you powerful graphics rendering using a tried-and-true interface (see Figure 2–2). Whether your game draws in two or three dimensions, using OpenGL ES to render your graphics will almost always be the fastest option. Support for this rendering technology is what makes the iPhone competitive against other modern mobile platforms. With so many developers already versed in OpenGL and the huge amount of existing resources and code, support for OpenGL makes iPhone game development a familiar affair for a large number of programmers.

OpenGL makes it possible to render 3D graphics at high frame rates, and developers are constantly finding new ways to push the iPhone hardware to its limits. Games like Real Racing and Wild West Pinball by OOO Gameprom (see Figure 2–2) showcase the 3D graphics made possible with OpenGL. Casual games like Imangi Studios' Harbor Master (also shown in Figure 2–2) demonstrate the use of OpenGL for quick 2D rendering.

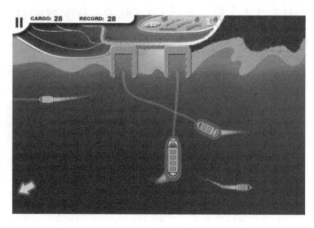

Figure 2–2. *OpenGL ES can provide speedy graphic rendering for both 2D and 3D games.*

OpenGL guru Ben Smith provides all the essentials in Chapters 6, 7, and 8. With the arrival of even more powerful 3D acceleration in the iPhone 3GS, this section of the book is bound to become dog-eared in no time.

Audio APIs

It is hard to make a compelling game on any platform without sound. Fortunately, iPhone developers have multiple choices when it comes to using sound in their games. You can use more advanced APIs such as OpenAL or simpler built-in services, depending on how much control you need over your game's audio.

Using the audio APIs, you can stream audio, play short sounds, or even simulate audio positioned in 3D space. You can give players the option to choose their own songs for a soundtrack or provide your own. Some games, like TAITO's Space Invaders Infinity Gene (see Figure 2–3), even generate game levels based on the player's song choice. Other games, such as Zen Bound by Secret Exit (also shown in Figure 2–3) use their soundtrack to immerse the player and set a mood for game play, even encouraging the user to use headphones for the complete experience.

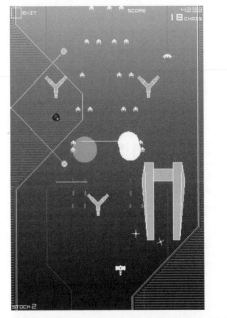

Figure 2–3. *Space Invaders Infinity Gene uses player song choice to generate levels. Zen Bound uses a beautiful and relaxing soundtrack to immerse players.*

Audio master Eric Wing will give you the ins and outs of audio on the iPhone in Chapters 9 through 12. After introducing the more basic audio APIs, Eric will take you on a detailed tour of OpenAL, including basic playback, positional audio, and streaming. Read these chapters so you'll be able to give your game the gift of sound!

Networking

Networked games are a natural fit for a platform as connected as the iPhone. Whether it's turn-based, real-time, worldwide, or local, your game can get added value with networked multiplayer and high-score capabilities. While there will always be a place for single-player games, more and more gamers are looking for networked features to make their gaming a more social experience.

Many technologies available to iPhone developers can help add connectivity to your game. Real-time multiplayer activities can be implemented through sockets and streams with servers and clients, or through GameKit's Bluetooth matchmaking. Simple things like global high scores can keep your players coming back again and again.

Games like Freeverse's Flick Fishing (see Figure 2–4) go beyond the simple score board. With Flick Fishing's Fish Net feature, any player can create a Net that others can join, which adds that player's successive catches to the Net. Using this group high-score mechanism, players can compete with people they know instead of anonymous players. Utilizing GameKit's Bluetooth matchmaking, Firemint's Flight Control (also shown in Figure 2–4) allows local players to play cooperatively by sending their aircraft across to each other's devices.

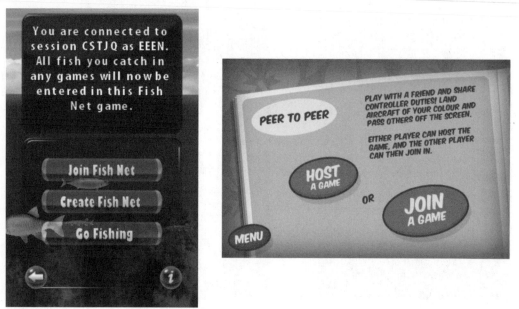

Figure 2–4. *Flick Fishing connects players through persistent group score boards. Flight Control offers local cooperative play through GameKit's Bluetooth matchmaking.*

With many different ways of networking available, nearly any type of player interaction is possible.

Networking ninja Peter Bakhirev gives you all the secrets to networking your iPhone game in Chapters 13 through 16. These chapters will get you familiar with sockets, streams, Bonjour, servers, clients, Bluetooth, and Wi-Fi connectivity. With your newfound networking knowledge, you'll be on your way to bringing your players together in new and exciting ways.

Summary

By this point, you should be hungry to get your hands dirty and start developing. Luckily, the real meat and potatoes lie just beyond this page, brimming with source code and real-world examples. Now that I (Ian Marsh) have given you some of the reasons you should be developing games for the iPhone and a quick look at the tools of the trade. I'll leave you in the very capable hands of PJ Cabrera, Ben Smith, Eric Wing, and Peter Bakhirev. Soak up all the information in the following chapters, get inspired, and start building something amazing!

Chapter 3

Moving Images on a Small Screen—UIKit Controls

You have already been introduced to the iPhone and iPhone gaming, and have seen an overview of its development environment. But what is iPhone development like? How complicated is it to learn Objective-C? How easy to use are the tools mentioned in the previous chapter? How do you get started making an iPhone game? This chapter begins the journey to answer these questions.

This chapter introduces you to the Cocoa Touch app environment, Objective-C, and UIKit framework. You will learn how to use the iPhone SDK's one-two-punch IDE and GUI design tool: Xcode and Interface Builder. We will build a simple iPhone game using Xcode, Interface Builder, and Cocoa Touch. Along the way, you will become acquainted with the essential APIs and get some important iPhone game design tips.

A Quick Introduction to Cocoa Touch

The Cocoa Touch app environment that powers the iPhone provides various C libraries, Objective-C frameworks, and associated design patterns that dictate how apps for the iPhone are built. This section introduces the iPhone app development environment. If you are already familiar with programming Cocoa Touch apps, feel free to skip to the next section.

The Cocoa Touch environment is composed of a number of Objective-C frameworks and C libraries that give the developer access to the iPhone's UI; technology such as geolocation through the GPS and compass; and input devices such as the touchscreen, accelerometer, and camera. Two frameworks are central to this environment:

- *Foundation framework*: Defines common classes such as NSObject and NSString that are used throughout Cocoa Touch.

■ *UIKit framework*: Provides classes for the creation of iPhone screens with buttons, labels, text fields, sliders, tables of data, and other UI components. Besides UI components, UIKit defines Objective-C classes that encapsulate app object properties and methods, and prototypes that define various app, view, and input events.

UIKit also dictates how developers should use these classes and prototypes by dividing functionality along the recommended guidelines of time-tested object-oriented programming (OOP) constructs, such as the Model-View-Controller (MVC) and Delegate design patterns. We will be discussing these classes, prototypes, and design patterns in the remainder of the chapter. But before we begin discussing UIKit, you need to get up to speed on Objective-C.

The Objective-C Language

Objective-C is an OO language invented in early 1980s by Brad Cox. Objective-C is a superset of the C language, and was invented independently of, but around the same time as, the more popular C++ language. Brad Cox's goal when he invented Objective-C was to bring the syntax and OO nature of the Smalltalk language to his C programming environment. He wanted to program in a Smalltalk-like environment and language. But as a C programmer of many years, he had developed and depended on a lot of C code he didn't want to rewrite. So he invented Objective-C to bridge the two languages together.

To properly understand and use Objective-C, you must know and have some experience with C programming, especially pointers and memory management. It also will help if you are familiar with OOP concepts such as classes, class instances (also called *objects*), inheritance, encapsulation, and polymorphism. If you already know Java, C#, or C++, it will be easier to learn Objective-C. Objective-C has different syntax for calling methods, and a few differences in how it treats null objects, undeclared methods, and memory management.

A Brief Objective-C Example

The first thing you will likely notice when looking at the Objective-C code of an iPhone project is that most code files end in *.m* (sometimes also *.mm*, which is used when you want to mix C++ and Objective-C). The *.m* stands for module. Like C and C++, Objective-C uses header files that end in *.h*. Header files are used for declaring types and method signatures.

Let's look at a short example of Objective-C code. Listing 3–1 shows a sample header file, named *SampleClass.h*.

Listing 3–1. *Sample header file (SampleClass.h)*

```
#import <Foundation/Foundation.h>

@interface SampleClass : NSObject
{
    float floatMember;
}
```

```
+ (void)classMethod;
+ (int)classMethodWithParameter:(int)intParam;
- (void)instanceMethod;
- (float)instanceMethodWithParam1:(float)floatParam andParam2:(int)intParam;
```

@end

The first line of code in Listing 3–1 is a framework import statement. In this case, we are importing a header file for a framework. #import works like the C and C++ #include statement. Objective-C uses #import instead of #include for various reasons, but one of them is that framework header files are stored in a separate place than standard C and C++ include files. One other difference is that #import reads the header file only once.

In the code in Listing 3–1, we import the Foundation framework. The significance of this is that the Foundation framework is the framework on which all other Objective-C frameworks are based. It's called Foundation because it's the foundation of all the other Objective-C frameworks.

The Foundation framework defines a few basic classes, which you will use very frequently in your iPhone programming. These classes represent typical data in an app, such as numbers, strings, arrays, sets, and implementations of many other computer science and OO concepts.

The following is the second line of code in Listing 3–1:

```
@interface SampleClass : NSObject
```

This is the start of a class interface declaration. Class declarations begin with @interface and end with @end.

The class being declared is called SampleClass. Unlike in Java and C#, the name of the class doesn't need to match the name of the file, but it is good practice to give them the same name. It simply makes it easier to find the right code.

In the class interface declaration, the class name is followed by a colon, then the name of the class from which the class being defined is derived. In this case, SampleClass is derived from NSObject. NSObject is the most important class in the Cocoa Touch environment. It is the class from which every class in Cocoa Touch is derived.

After the @interface line, we have three lines of code, which only make sense together:

```
{
    float floatMember;
}
```

The squiggly symbols are known as *curly brackets*, used in C and similar languages to group code together. In this case, we are declaring the list of instance variables for class SampleClass. In C++, these are called member variables. In Java, they are known as attributes. There is only one instance variable in this code. It is of type float, and its name is floatMember.

The next four lines of code consist of some method declarations:

```
+ (void)classMethod;
```

```
+ (int)classMethodWithParameter:(int)intParam;
- (void)instanceMethod;
- (float)instanceMethodWithParam1:(float)floatParam andParam2:(int)intParam;

@end
```

These look almost like method declarations in C and similar languages, except they don't have a list of parameters enclosed in parentheses, and they have plus and minus signs in front. The method declarations with the plus sign are class methods; the minus sign denotes instance methods. And there are methods with parameters, but they're declared differently than in C and similar languages.

In Objective-C, method parameters are denoted by a colon character before the parameter location in the method name, followed by the type and name of the parameter. So the class method `classMethodWithParameter:` has a parameter of type int called `intParam`. The instance method `instanceMethodWithParam1:andParam2:` has one parameter of type `float` called `floatParam` and a second parameter of type `int` called `intParam`.

Now the interface declaration of `SampleClass` ends, and we tell the compiler this by putting the @end symbol in the code. Typically, this goes at the end of the file.

With the interface declaration finished, we now move to the implementation of SampleClass, shown in Listing 3–2.

Listing 3–2. *Sample implementation file (SampleClass.m)*

```
#import "SampleClass.h"

@implementation SampleClass

static int intMember;

+ (void)classMethod
{
    NSLog(@"inside classMethod");
}
- (void)instanceMethod
{
    NSLog(@"inside instanceMethod");
}

+ (int)classMethodWithParameter:(int)intParam
{
    intMember = intParam;
    return intParam;
}
- (float)instanceMethodWithParam1:(float)floatParam andParam2:(int)intParam
{
    floatMember = floatParam;
    intMember = intParam;
    return floatParam * intParam;
}

@end
```

The first line of code in Listing 3–2 imports the *SampleClass.h* file. This lets us work with the `SampleClass` interface in the implementation file. This step should be familiar to C and C++ developers, as it is analogous to using #include to include a header file for a C++ class or a C module.

The next line of code starts the implementation block of `SampleClass`:

```
@implementation SampleClass
```

Similar to an `@interface` block, implementation starts with the `@implementation` symbol, followed by the name of the class, and ends with @end. In the implementation block of a class, you define the methods declared in the interface. The interface has only the name and parameters for the methods of the class. The implementation has the actual code for those methods, and for any other internal methods needed to complete the implementation of the class.

The next line of code immediately after the `@implementation` symbol, there is the definition of a `static int` module variable named `intMember`:

```
static int intMember;
```

This is going to be used in the code as if it were a class variable, because Objective-C doesn't have class variables. It's just a regular C module scope variable.

And now we come to the first of the method definitions:

```
+ (void)classMethod
{
    NSLog(@"inside classMethod");
}
```

The first method defined is a class method named `classMethod`, which does not take any parameters and does not return a value. It looks almost like a C method definition, except for the plus sign at the beginning of the line and the lack of parentheses for parameters.

Like any method definition in C and similar languages, the method body is contained inside a pair of curly brackets. This method makes a call to a C function called NSLog, which is provided by the Foundation framework. NSLog writes to the console log, and is useful when debugging. NSLog takes an Objective-C string object as its parameter. As you can see in the code, Objective-C string constants begin with the @ symbol. This is to differentiate them from C strings, which are a different beast. Objective-C strings are objects of Objective-C class NSString, whereas C strings are simply arrays of characters.

The next method definition is an instance method called `instanceMethod`:

```
- (void)instanceMethod
{
    NSLog(@"inside instanceMethod");
}
```

You can identify it's an instance method by the minus sign at the beginning of the line. Like the class method defined before it, it calls NSLog and passes a string object as a parameter to NSLog.

The next method definition is a class method named classMethodWithParameter:.

```
+ (int)classMethodWithParameter:(int)intParam
{
    intMember = intParam;
    return intParam;
}
```

The method takes one parameter, an integer named intParam, and returns an integer. In the method body, the value of intParam is assigned to the pseudo class variable intMember, and then it returns the value of intParam. Except for the first line of the method definition, this is pure C code.

The next method definition is an instance method named instanceMethodWithParam1:andParam2:.

```
- (float)instanceMethodWithParam1:(float)floatParam andParam2:(int)intParam
{
    floatMember = floatParam;
    intMember = intParam;
    return floatParam * intParam;
}
```

@end

This method takes two parameters and returns a float. The first parameter is a float named floatParam. The second method is an int named intParam. The code assigns floatParam to the instance variable floatMember, and also assigns intParam to intMember. Then it multiplies floatParam by intParam and returns the result.

With the last method definition, the implementation block ends with the @end symbol and the end of the file *SampleClass.m*.

So to recap, you learned how to declare the interface and define the implementation of Objective-C classes. You also learned how to declare method signatures in the interface, and how to define the code in these methods. Then you learned how to use method parameters in Objective-C. In the next few sections, you will learn how to use the SampleClass.

Using an Objective-C Class

Now let's look at how to allocate and initialize an instance, how to call class methods and instance methods, and how to call methods with parameters. Listing 3–3 shows the sample code that accomplishes this.

Listing 3–3. *The following Objective-C code shows how classes are allocated and initialized and how different kinds of methods are called and parameters are passed*

```
SampleClass *instance;

instance = [[SampleClass alloc] init];
```

```
[SampleClass classMethod];
[instance instanceMethod];
int result1 = [SampleClass classMethodWithParameter: 5];
float result2 = [instance instanceMethodWithParam1: 5.0 andParam2: 2];

[instance release];
```

The first line of code in Listing 3–3 declares a variable named instance, of type pointer to an object of a class type SampleClass. This syntax should be very familiar to C and C++ programmers, and other than the pointer symbol (the *), this code should also look familiar to C# and Java developers.

Now let's move on to the next line.

```
instance = [[SampleClass alloc] init];
```

If you have any knowledge of computer languages, you should be able to determine that the beginning of this line is storing something in the variable instance. But what is that to the right of the equal sign? What is that mess of brackets? This is certainly strange, because square brackets are usually employed in C and similar languages in the declaration of arrays and in the addressing of elements in arrays. But this looks different. In Objective-C, brackets are used to make method calls. This is to differentiate the Objective-C method calls from C function calls.

The method call always has two parts: the first part is an instance variable or a class name, and the second part is a method name and any parameters.

The brackets are nested, meaning that one pair of brackets is inside another. They kind of look like parentheses in a long math operation. In school, we learned that we should start with the stuff in the inner pair of parentheses and work our way out. In Objective-C, you use the same approach: inner brackets first.

The inner pair of brackets contains the code SampleClass alloc. Whenever you see a class name as the first part of the method call, you know that it is a call to a class method. In this case, we are calling the alloc method of class SampleClass.

But wait a minute! In the interface declaration of SampleClass, there is no method called alloc. That is correct. alloc is a method of class NSObject. Since everything derives from NSObject, all classes have a method called alloc. The alloc method creates an instance of a class and returns a pointer to this instance.

Because our brackets are nested, the result of [SampleClass alloc] is used as the first part of the second pair of brackets. So the instance returned by [SampleClass alloc] is used to make a call to an instance method named init. SampleClass does not declare a method named init. Once again, we are dealing with a method defined in the NSObject class—in this case, an instance method of NSObject called init.

The init method is used to initialize the instance variables of a class to a default, or initial, value. Classes typically override the init method when they have a lot of instance variables that must be initialized to safe and sensible default values. Besides overriding init, classes also define several init methods with one or more parameters, to set the initial values of several instance variables with a single method call.

The next four lines of code should be straightforward.

```
[SampleClass classMethod];
[instance instanceMethod];
int result1 = [SampleClass classMethodWithParameter: 5];
float result2 = [instance instanceMethodWithParam1: 5.0 andParam2: 2];
[instance release];
```

The first is a class method call to classMethod, which takes no parameters. Next is an instance call to instanceMethod, which also takes no parameters. Following that is a class call to a method named classMethodWithParameter:, which takes an integer parameter. In this case, we are passing the integer 2 into this method. This method returns an integer value, which we store in an int variable named result1. And finally, we have a call to an instance method named instanceMethodWithParam1:andParam2:, which takes a float parameter and an int parameter. We pass to this method the float 5.0 and the integer 2. This method returns a float value, which we store in float variable result2.

The last method call in Listing 3–3, [instance release], is an instance method call to another method inherited from class NSObject. The method release should be called whenever you are finished with an object instance you have created yourself with alloc. In this case, we allocated the instance, and we are finished using it, so it is released.

Memory Management in Objective-C

Memory management in Objective-C is different than in C and similar languages. In C and C++, you allocate memory with malloc or new, keep it in a pointer, pass it around to other code as needed, and free/delete it when you're finished. In C# and Java and some scripting languages, you only allocate objects; the language runtimes take care of freeing objects when there are no more references to them.

In Objective-C, release is not the same as free in C. Calling release decrements an internal reference counter inside the object. The memory held by an object is invalidated by the Objective-C runtime when this internal reference counter reaches 0.

When you first allocate an Objective-C object with alloc, its reference count is set to 1. You need to manage the reference counting yourself as you code, and remember to call release at the appropriate times, or the object will become a memory leak. When creating a class instance for a short time as in the example in Listing 3–3, it's simple to remember to release the object when you are finished. But when you have objects that stick around for a long time and get used by different sections of your code at different times, it can get quite complicated.

NSObject has another method called clone, which makes a new object that is a copy of another. The clone has its own reference counter and it is set to 1, regardless of the reference count of the original object from which the clone was made. As with any other kind of Objective-C object, you should call release on any clones once you are finished with them.

There are situations in Cocoa Touch programming when you don't allocate the objects yourself. The Cocoa Touch frameworks have a lot of convenient methods that allocate objects and return them to you. These objects are held in what is called an *autorelease pool*. If you are going to hold on to an object returned by these Cocoa Touch frameworks, Cocoa Touch might autorelease it and invalidate it before you are finished with it, leading to a crash. In situations like this, you need to increment the reference count of that object so that it is not invalidated. This is called *retaining the object*. It is done by calling a method named retain on the object. The method retain is another NSObject instance method, which every Objective-C class inherits. When you retain an object, you still must remember to call release on the object when you are finished with it, allowing the Cocoa Touch framework to autorelease and invalidate the object. Otherwise, you will have a memory leak.

You can use this automatic cleanup of objects in your own code by creating your own autorelease pool. An autorelease pool lets you control the release of objects in memory in an organized, reliable manner. To create an autorelease pool, you allocate an instance of the class NSAutoreleasePool and initialize it. Because NSAutoreleasePool instances are like any other Objective-C instance, when you are finished with the instance, you must release it. Listing 3–4 shows an example of creating and releasing an autorelease pool.

Listing 3–4. *Creating and releasing an autorelease pool*

```
NSAutoreleasePool * pool = [[NSAutoreleasePool alloc] init];
// other code here
[pool release];
```

You place objects in an autorelease pool by calling the autorelease method on the object. The method autorelease is another NSObject instance method. Calling autorelease on an object places the object in the most recently created autorelease pool. When the autorelease pool is released, all objects that were added to it are released.

So now that you've learned some Objective-C syntax and learned some things about how Objective-C and Cocoa Touch memory management works, you're ready to dive into the details of the Cocoa Touch environment and the UIKit framework.

> **NOTE:** To learn more about Objective-C syntax and memory management, see *Learn Objective-C on the Mac* by Mark Dalrymple and Scott Knaster (Apress, 2009). Apple also provides Objective-C tutorials on the iPhone Dev Center at http://developer.apple.com/iphone.

Cocoa Touch and the UIKit Framework

The UIKit framework is mainly used for the creation of the app's screens. The UIKit framework defines Objective-C classes for the various components that make up an iPhone app. UIKit has classes for the iPhone screen, views, scroll views, tables, table cells, text labels, buttons, images, and many kinds of controls that let developers create beautiful-looking iPhone apps.

An app's screens are created by laying out instances of UIKit classes, either programmatically using code or graphically through the Interface Builder design tool. The iPhone and iPod touch have a screen that is 320 pixels wide and 480 pixels tall when the device is held upright, in what is known as *portrait orientation*. Your job as a game developer is to fill that screen with exciting animations and other graphics to entertain the player. When programming with UIKit, you do this by placing graphic objects in a UIView.

Introducing UIView

A UIView is a container object. This means it can contain buttons, icons, labels, text fields, and any sort of UI components. You can even position UIView instances inside another UIView. In this chapter, we will mostly concern ourselves with placing image views inside a UIView and making them move according to a game's logic. Image views are a type of UIView that holds images.

A UIView is an Objective-C class representing a region of graphical real estate. A UIView has several properties, such as its position, size, background color, visibility, and whether it responds to touch events. Learning about these UIView properties is useful, not only because you use the UIView in iPhone programming, but also because all the other iPhone components derive from UIView. Buttons, labels, text fields, text views, and tables all are a kind of UIView. This means they also have all of these properties, and they behave the same way in regard to setting these properties.

The Frame Property

A UIView's screen position and size are expressed through a property called frame. The frame property is a C structure of type CGRect. This structure represents the specific properties of a rectangle. CGRect is used throughout iPhone UI development to specify the size and position of UI elements such as labels, buttons, and text fields.

The CGRect structure is made up of two elements:

- *Origin*: This first element is a C structure of type CGPoint. It holds the x and y coordinates of the rectangle's top-left corner.

- *Size*: This element is another C structure, of type CGSize. It holds the rectangle's width and height.

Figure 3–1 illustrates the concept of a UIView's frame. The dot at the upper-left corner of the iPhone's screen corresponds to position 0,0. The x axis extends from this corner toward the right side of the screen, such that an x value of 319 is at the right edge of the screen. The y axis extends toward the bottom of the screen, such that a y value of 479 is at the bottom of the screen. This means the dot at the bottom-right corner of the screen is at position 319,479. The view, represented by the rectangle in Figure 3–1, has its upper-left corner positioned at coordinates 100,100—that is, 100 pixels to the right of the top-left corner and 100 pixels from the top of the screen. This is its frame's origin. The view rectangle has a width of 100 pixels and a height of 40 pixels. This is its frame's size.

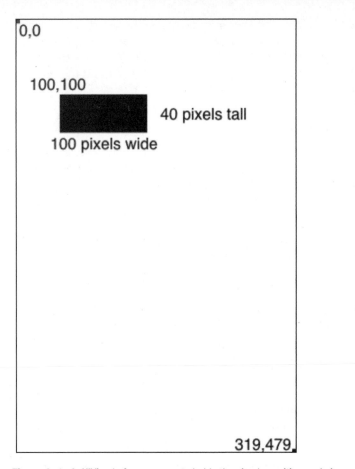

Figure 3–1. *A UIView's frame property holds the view's position and size.*

The following code fragment creates a view with the position and size illustrated in Figure 3–1:

```
CGRect newframe;
newFrame.origin = CGPointMake(100,100);
newFrame.size = CGSizeMake(100,40);
UIView *myView = [[UIView alloc] initWithFrame:newFrame];
```

> **NOTE:** You may notice that CGRect, CGPoint, and CGSize all start with the letters CG. They are C structures, rather than Objective-C classes. The CG stands for Core Graphics. Core Graphics, also known as Quartz 2D, is a low-level C library used internally by UIKit to draw lines, curves, gradients, and images. We will study Quartz 2D in more depth in the next chapter.

The x/y elements of the CGPoint structure and the height/width elements of the CGSize structure are C float values. That means that you can use a decimal number, such as 100.25, for any of the view's position coordinates or for the view's given width or height.

The iPhone screen is really made of 320 by 480 physical pixels, so how come you can specify fractions of a pixel? The iPhone and iPod touch are capable of what is called *subpixel rendering*. When given a position or size with a decimal number, it renders the graphic by interpolating between adjacent pixels, giving the appearance that the graphic was drawn partway between pixels.

The Background Color and Alpha Properties

Two other `UIView` properties are background color and alpha. *Alpha* (also known as *opacity*) is the opposite of transparency. The property is an unsigned `float`. It accepts values between 0.0 (no opacity) and 1.0 (fully opaque, or not transparent). Half transparency has an alpha value of 0.5. Any values higher than 1.0 are interpreted as meaning the same as 1.0.

When you set the `alpha` property of a view, all elements positioned within that view will be affected by the setting. So, if you have a button and a label inside the view, and you set the view's `alpha` property to partly transparent, these elements also will show as partly transparent.

Background color is a property of type `UIColor`. `UIColor` is an Objective-C class that is part of the UIKit framework. `UIColor` has a few color constants set for commonly used colors. You can use one of the built-in color constants for ease of programming of simple color choices. The following line of code sets the background color of a view to red:

```
myView.backgroundColor = [UIColor redColor];
```

Or you can assign a color with specific intensities of red, green, blue, and alpha.

```
myView.backgroundColor = [UIColor colorWithRed:1.0 green:0.5 blue:1.0 alpha:1.0];
```

For games, most of the time you will want your view to be totally transparent—to be seen through. You don't want the view to obscure what's behind it in any way. You can accomplish this in two ways:

- Set the alpha value of the `backgroundColor` property to 0.

- Use a convenient color constant called `clearColor`, like this:

```
myView.backgroundColor = [UIColor clearColor];
```

The Center Property

Another property of `UIView` is `center`, which lets you specify the coordinates for the center of the view. When you set the `center` property, the view uses the size element of the `frame` property to reset the frame's origin element.

```
myView.center = CGPointMake(15,25);
```

There are many other properties of `UIView` that can be useful in games programming, as you will see as we work through examples.

Now let's create our first game. Talking about stuff only gets you so far.

Building a Simple Game

We'll now build a game in which a ball bounces around the screen, making colored bricks disappear when the ball hits them. We'll begin with a quick introduction to creating a new Xcode project and using Interface Builder. If you're familiar with how to use Xcode and Interface Builder, you may want to skip directly to the "Snazzy Graphics Make the Grade" section.

Creating an Xcode Project

To create an iPhone game with UIKit, we'll start with a new View-based Application project in Xcode. Start Xcode and choose **File ➤ New Project**. This will open the New Project dialog box. Select Application under iPhone OS in the list on the left, and View-based Application in the right panel, as shown in Figure 3–2. Then click Choose.

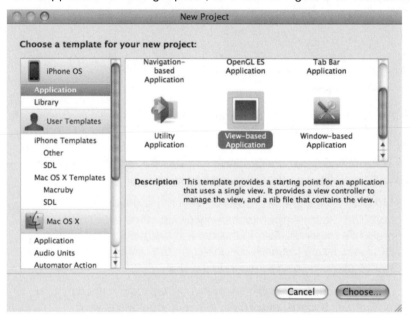

Figure 3–2. *Choose View-based Application from the New Project dialog box.*

In the next step, Xcode will prompt you for a name for your project and where to save it. We are making a brick-breaking game, so enter the name IVBricker and save it where you prefer (I saved the project in my user's Desktop folder). Xcode creates a folder named IVBricker where you specified, and then creates the project, as shown in Figure 3–3.

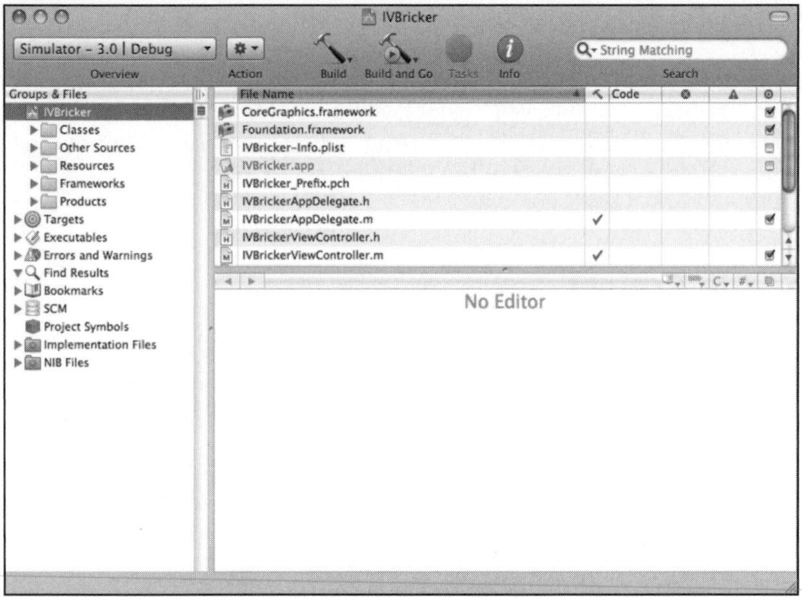

Figure 3–3. *The view-based application loaded in Xcode*

Once the project is loaded into Xcode, you see a panel named Groups & Files to the left, below the toolbar. The icon named IVBricker, highlighted in Figure 3–3, represents your project. When this icon is selected, the top-right panel, which is called the detail panel, shows all the files and frameworks that are used to create your application. Below the IVBricker icon in the left panel, you see the following folder icons:

- *Classes and Other Sources*: These groups contain the source code for your application. The Classes group is the only group in the default set that corresponds to a folder on disk. In this case, it has a matching folder named `Classes` inside the project's folder on the Desktop. Most of an app's source code will be located in this group.

- *Resources*: This group contains data files that your application needs to run, such as images, sounds, and so on. When Xcode builds your app, it bundles these data files along with your compiled code. You will drop data files into this group as you add new resources to your app. Besides data files, I also like to move my Interface Builder files to this group, for consistency.

- *Frameworks*: This group contains references to the different Cocoa Touch frameworks used by your code. The default frameworks specified by Xcode when it generated the project are fine for the sample projects in this chapter.

- *Products*: This group contains a reference to the built application bundle. This app bundle is what you will submit to the App Store when your app is ready to distribute.

These are the five standard groups of files that make up all newly created Xcode app projects. When you select one of these groups, only the files that belong within that group are shown in the detail panel. While these groups have folder icons, they don't necessarily correspond to folders on disk. They are aids provided by Xcode to help organize your files by function.

Now that we have looked at the organization of our project in Xcode, let's examine the UI of our new view-based application.

Creating the IVBricker User Interface

Select the Resources group in Xcode, and you will see three files there: *IVBricker-Info.plist*, *MainWindow.xib*, and *IVBrickerViewController.xib*. The two files that end in *.xib* are Interface Builder files.

Interface Builder is the iPhone SDK's GUI design tool. For games made with UIKit, you only need to know a few basic facts about Interface Builder. We'll start by taking a look at the main window file.

Examining the Main Window File

Select the file *MainWindow.xib* in Xcode and double-click it to open it in Interface Builder. The Interface Builder window offers three views, selectable from the View Mode icons on the upper left: an icon view mode, a list view mode that shows the component name and its type (see Figure 3–4), and a hierarchical view mode.

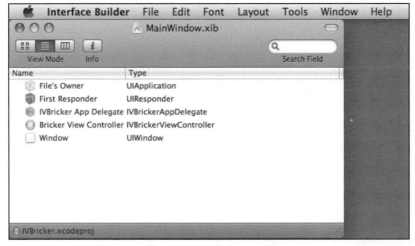

Figure 3–4. *The MainWindow.xib file contains the UI components that make up our application.*

When an iPhone app starts, Cocoa Touch looks in the app's *Info.plist* for a property called `Main nib file base name` and loads the file specified there. In an app created from Xcode templates, this property is hard-coded to the app's *MainWindow.xib* file.

Upon loading the *MainWindow.xib*, it starts processing the components and properties set in the file, as follows:

- *File's Owner*: Every Interface Builder file has a File's Owner component. The first thing Cocoa Touch does when loading an Interface Builder file is create an object of the type specified in the File's Owner. In the case of *MainWindow*, the File's Owner object is of type `UIApplication`. This is an important UIKit class, which starts setting up the Cocoa Touch environment for your app, and delivers events between the operating system and the rest of your application. This is the first UIKit object instantiated by an iPhone app.

> **NOTE:** For the purpose of game development, we can usually ignore the First Responder object in Interface Builder. You can learn more about this object in *Beginning iPhone 3 Development* by Dave Mark and Jeff LaMarche (Apress, 2009).

- *Application Delegate*: Every `UIApplication` instance needs an Application Delegate object, or else the app does nothing. Cocoa Touch loads *MainWindow* and creates an instance of the type specified in the application delegate. Once Cocoa Touch has finished loading *MainWindow* and processing all components and properties specified in the file, Cocoa Touch calls the application delegate to let the app know it has fully launched. Without an application delegate, this call wouldn't be delivered, and the app's components would just sit idle. The application delegate's job is to receive messages for the application's life-cycle events. We will discuss these application delegate messages in detail later in this chapter.

- *Window*: After the Application Delegate object, Cocoa Touch loads the Window component. In Cocoa Touch, the Window component holds the several different views that make up an app. This Window component is our app's main `UIWindow` instance.

- *View Controller*: The View Controller object represents the controller of the main view in the app. In this example, our main view controller is called `Bricker View Controller` and it is of type `IVBrickerViewController`. View controller classes respond to Cocoa Touch events that let the controller know the status of the view, such as whether the view has been loaded or whether Cocoa Touch will unload the view to reclaim memory. We will extend this class to respond to multitouch, accelerometer, and other type of events for this chapter's sample game.

So to recap, at application startup, Cocoa Touch loads the *MainWindow.xib* file and processes it. During processing of the *.xib* file, Cocoa Touch creates the `UIApplication` instance, the app delegate, the main window, the main view, and the view's view controller. Then it connects them together through the various components' properties.

Once this is done, Cocoa Touch notifies the application delegate that the application has finished launching.

We are finished examining the *MainWindow* file for now, so close that file and return to Xcode.

Examining the View Controller File

In your Xcode project, double-click the *IVBrickerViewController.xib* file in the Resources group. This will open the file in Interface Builder, as shown in Figure 3–5.

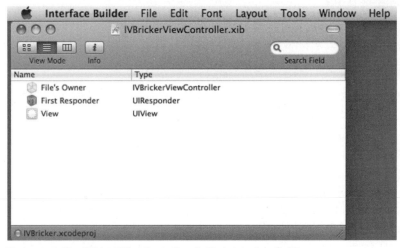

Figure 3–5. *The IVBrickerViewController.xib file in Interface Builder*

The *IVBrickerViewController.xib* file shows the Cocoa Touch components that make up the view controller for the app's main view. There is the view itself, represented by the component called View. And then there is *IVBrickerViewController.xib* File's Owner, which is an object of type IVBrickerViewController. You will note that this is the same type as the view controller in *MainWindow.xib*. This is no coincidence—they are the same object.

The View component in this Interface Builder file is where we will be placing the different UI components, such as text labels, that make up our main game screen.

Setting View Properties

Double-click the View component in Interface Builder to open a window with the visual layout of the view. Right now, it's empty and has a dark-gray background.

Bring up the Inspector window by pressing ⇧⌘I. We will use the Inspector window, shown in Figure 3–6, to change various properties of our view.

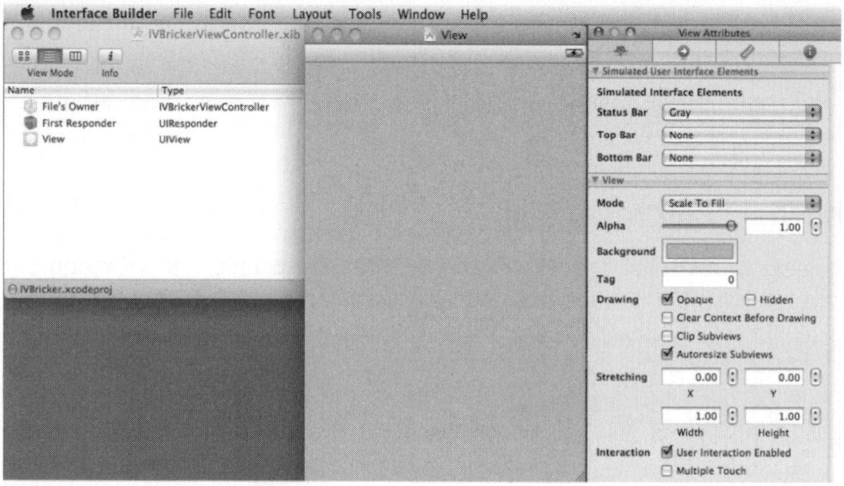

Figure 3–6. *The Inspector window (the one on the right) lets you change properties in your UI components. The View window (in the middle) is where you will place UI components.*

The Inspector window has four tabs along the top. The first tab from the left is called the Attributes tab, and it lets you modify various properties in the app's UI components.

Let's change the Background property to set our view's background color to some other color. Make sure the Attributes tab in the Inspector window is selected, and then click the color swatch of the Background property to open a color picker. Set the view's background color to black. Close the color picker once you've changed the color.

Adding Components to the View

Let's add other components to our view. Open the component library by pressing ⇧⌘L. This opens a window called Library, which displays the different types of components that can be laid out in a view in Interface Builder. At the top of the Library window, select the Objects half of the segmented button, and then select the Inputs & Values group in the Cocoa Touch library.

We will drag two labels to our view, to display the current score for our game in progress. Select Label from the component types shown in the Library window, and drag this to the View window. Place it close to the top and right border.

> **NOTE:** As you move UI components within the View window, keep an eye out for the blue dashed-line hint from Interface Builder. These dashed blue lines, which appear and disappear as you move components around the view, are hints to help you position components at a good distance from the borders of the view and from other components. They're there to help you; use them in your own designs.

With the new label selected, look for the Text property in the Inspector's Attributes tab. This property currently has a value of Label. Change the Text property of this label to five zeros: **00000**. This label will display the value of the score as it changes in our game.

The Font Size property has a check box called Adjust to Fit, which is currently selected. Deselect it to make the score display with a fixed font size. This will make the label truncate our five zeros, because it is not big enough to display the whole string. Change the Inspector to the third tab, the one with the ruler icon. This is the Size tab. Change the W (Width) property to **50**. Our label is now 50 pixels wide and displays our string of zeros comfortably. Now change the X and Y properties to **275** and **10**, respectively. Also, to the left of the coordinates there is a grid of points. Make sure the center dot is selected, so that a small red cross is centered on the grid. Throughout this chapter, the x and y coordinates represent the center of the component.

Drag a new label just to the left of the score label. Change the Text property to say **Score:**. Also, deselect the Font Size property's Adjust to Fit check box. Then switch to the Size tab. Change the W (Width) property to **50**, and the X and Y properties to **216** and **10**, respectively. Don't forget to select the center dot in the grid to the left if it's not already selected, or the position of the label won't be correct for these numbers.

Now our view has a score label and is starting to look more like a game in progress. Figure 3–7 shows the positioning of our labels.

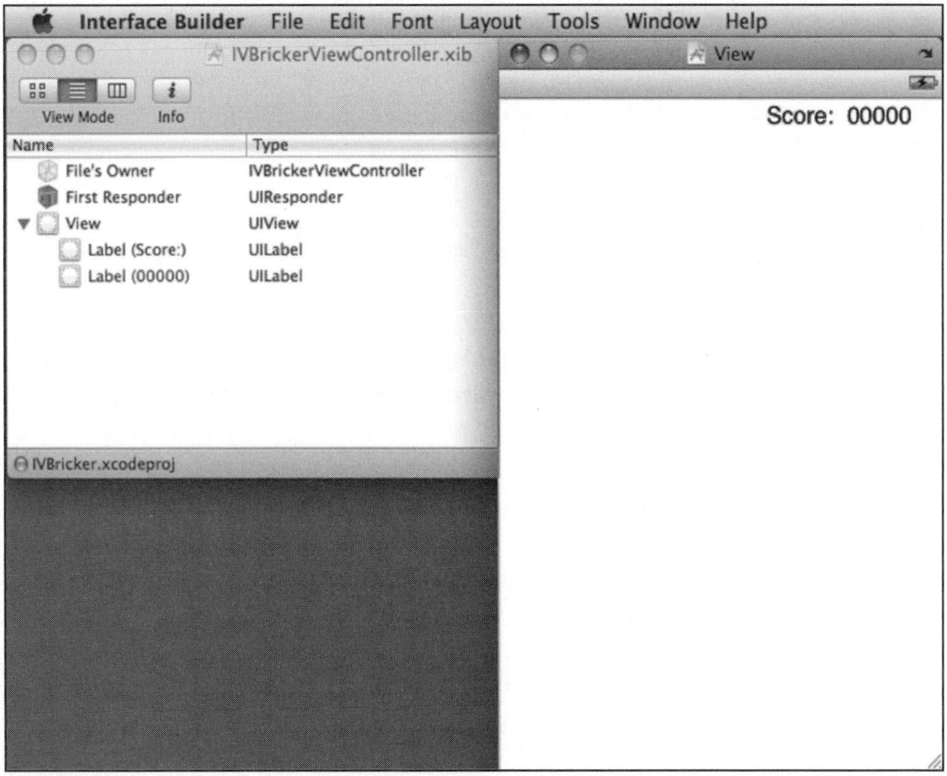

Figure 3–7. *The label components and their position in the view*

Now that we have added these labels, what's next? The score label with the zeros is going to be where the code displays the game's score. In our game code, every time the score changes, we will need to update the value displayed in the score label. To update the score label from our game code, we first need to add a property to the view controller. We will name this new property scoreLabel. After adding the property to the view controller, we will make a connection between the view controller's scoreLabel property and the score label component in Interface Builder.

Before continuing, save your changes to *IVBrickerViewController.xib* in Interface Builder.

Adding Code to the View Controller

Return to your Xcode project and select the Classes group in the project tree. In the detail panel at the top right, select the file *IVBrickerViewController.h*. The contents of the file will appear in the editor panel, below the detail panel.

Listing 3–5 shows the code for *IVBrickerViewController.h*. The lines of code in bold are the code that declares our scoreLabel instance variable (also called an *ivar*) and its matching property, and another instance variable for holding the score. Add these lines to your file and save the changes.

Listing 3–5. *The new code for IVBrickerViewController.h, which declares the scoreLabel instance variable and the property of the same name, as well as an integer instance variable called score.*

```
#import <UIKit/UIKit.h>

@interface IVBrickerViewController : UIViewController {
    UILabel *scoreLabel;
    int score;
}

@property (nonatomic, retain) IBOutlet UILabel *scoreLabel;
@end
```

Next, let's make the appropriate changes to *IVBrickerViewController.m*. Open this file in the editor panel, and add the code in bold from Listing 3–6.

Listing 3–6. *The new code for IVBrickerViewController.m synthesizes the scoreLabel property and releases it in the dealloc method.*

```
#import "IVBrickerViewController.h"

@implementation IVBrickerViewController

@synthesize scoreLabel;

- (void)dealloc {
    [scoreLabel release];

    [super dealloc];
}
```

I like to move the `dealloc` method definition from the end of the file to just after the last `@synthesize` statement. As you add `@synthesize` statements for your properties, you usually need to add matching `release` statements in the `dealloc` method. Moving the `dealloc` close to the `@synthesize` statements means less scrolling around as you code, and it also helps if you need a reminder to add the necessary `release` statements for the class's properties to the `dealloc` method definition.

Now that this code has been added to the class, we can connect the property to the label component in Interface Builder. Make sure you have saved your changes to *IVBrickerViewController.h* and *IVBrickerViewController.m* before continuing.

Connecting a Property with a Component

Switch back to Interface Builder and *IVBrickerViewController.xib*. Right-click the File's Owner. This will bring up a window that lists the File's Owner Outlets and Referencing Outlets. You will see `scoreLabel` listed first among the Outlets. Click and hold on the unfilled circle to the right of `scoreLabel` and drag to the Label (00000) component, as shown in Figure 3–8.

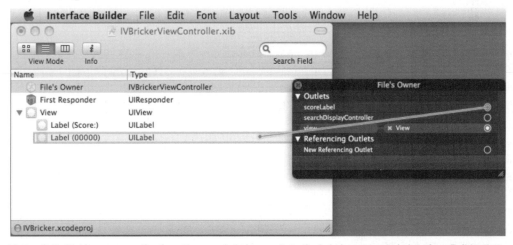

Figure 3–8. *Making a connection from the scoreLabel property to the Label component in Interface Builder that will display the score in the view*

> **NOTE:** Another way to connect the property to the label is to select the File's Owner, and switch tabs in the Inspector window to the second tab from the left, which is the Connections tab. Drag from the `scoreLabel`'s hollow circle to the corresponding label component.

Now that the connection is made, we can easily update the score label in our game with code like this in our view controller:

```
scoreLabel.text = [NSString stringWithFormat:@"%05d", score];
```

With the basic setup out of the way, you are now ready to learn about using UIKit specifically for making iPhone games.

> **NOTE:** If you would like to learn more about Cocoa Touch, Xcode, and Interface Builder, check out *Beginning iPhone 3 Development,* by Dave Mark and Jeff LaMarche (Apress, 2009).

Snazzy Graphics Make the Grade

For the brick-breaking game we're building, we need a ball to bounce around the screen. So to begin implementing this game, let's add a ball to our sample project.

> **NOTE:** If you skipped here because you already know Objective-C and how to use Xcode and Interface Builder, you can load the example project IVBricker first stage from the source code download. That will let you proceed where the previous section left off.

Adding the Image

In the source code download for this chapter, there is a folder named IVBricker finished version. In there, you will find a file named *ball.png*. Copy this file to your own project folder. Just copying the file to the project folder is not enough, though. Next, drag the file from the project folder to the Resources group in Xcode. When you build your project, Xcode will copy all the files in this group into your app.

With the file copied to the project Resources group, we can now add it to our view. Return to Interface Builder and the *IVBrickerViewController.xib* file. The View window should be open from when we added the two labels to the view. Open the Interface Builder Library window if it isn't open already (press ⇧⌘L). Select the Data Views group in the Library window. For displaying images, we will use the Image View component.

Image views are UIKit components of type UIImageView. They are used to display images. The iPhone SDK supports JPG, GIF, PNG, TIFF, BMP, ICO (Windows icon), and CUR (Windows cursor) files, and XBM file formats. Objects of the UIImageView class have various properties, such as height, width, x and y coordinates within the parent view, image transparency, image stretching ratios, background color, and so on.

Drag an image view from the Library window to the View window. With the new image view selected in the View window, look in the Attributes tab of the Inspector window for a property called Image. In the drop-down list, you should see *ball.png*. Choose this as the image, and the image view will change to show the ball graphic, as shown in Figure 3–9.

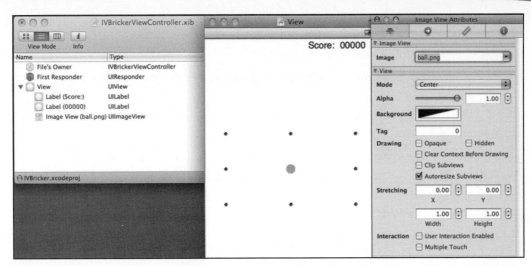

Figure 3–9. *The image view is now displaying the ball graphic. We need to resize the Image View component to make it better fit the dimensions of the ball.*

Now select the Size tab in the Inspector window, set the width and height of the image view to **16** by **16** pixels, and X and Y to **159** and **239**, respectively. This places the ball in the middle of the view. (Don't forget the center dot on the position grid needs to be selected to have the red cross displayed; otherwise, the ball will not be positioned correctly.)

Save your work and return to Xcode. Build and run your project. When the app launches in the simulator, you should see the black background, the red ball, and the score displayed, but they all just sit there. Let's make the ball do something.

To access the ball programmatically in our game code, we need to add it as a property in the view controller, in the same fashion that we added `scoreLabel` to the view controller earlier. In Xcode, open the file *IVBrickerViewController.h* and add the code in bold in Listing 3–7, which declares the ball instance variable and the property of the same name.

Listing 3–7. *The new code for IVBrickerViewController.h, which declares the ball ivar and the property of the same name.*

```
#import <UIKit/UIKit.h>

@interface IVBrickerViewController : UIViewController {
    UILabel *scoreLabel;
    int score;

    UIImageView *ball;
}

@property (nonatomic, retain) IBOutlet UILabel *scoreLabel;

@property (nonatomic, retain) IBOutlet UIImageView *ball;

@end
```

Next, let's change the file *IVBrickerViewController.m*. Open this file in the editor panel, and add the code in bold from Listing 3–8, which synthesizes the ball property and releases it in the dealloc method.

Listing 3–8. *The new code for IVBrickerViewController.m synthesizes the ball property and releases it in the dealloc method.*

```
#import "IVBrickerViewController.h"

@implementation IVBrickerViewController

@synthesize scoreLabel;
@synthesize ball;

- (void)dealloc {
    [scoreLabel release];

    [ball release];

    [super dealloc];
}
```

Once you have added the new code to *IVBrickerViewController.h* and *IVBrickerViewController.m*, you need to connect the image view in Interface Builder to the properties in the view controller. The steps to follow are the same as connecting the score label with the scoreLabel property (described earlier in the "Connecting a Property with a Component" section). After the ball property is connected to the ball image view, we can start making the ball do something on the screen.

The Illusion of Motion

To create the illusion of motion on a screen, movies and TV use still frames presented in quick succession, one after the other, within a short lapse of time. This is the origin of the term *frames per second* used in video performance. In games programming, the display logic is ideally performed at least 30 times per second, to give the illusion of smoothly moving images on the screen.

On the iPhone, a class called NSTimer, provided by Foundation framework, lets you schedule a method to be called repeatedly, several times per second. We will now write a method to modify the ball's position over time, to make it bounce around the screen, using NSTimer.

> **NOTE:** There is a new way to create a timer in iPhone SDK 3.1, called CADisplayLink, which is more appropriate for games. CADisplayLink synchronizes with the iPhone display, which is guaranteed to refresh 60 times per second. We will continue this game example using NSTimer, but switch the code to use CADisplayLink at the end of the chapter.

Go back to Xcode and open *IVBrickerViewController.h* in the editor panel. Add the code in bold in Listing 3–9.

Listing 3–9. *Add the ivar ballMovement to the view controller's interface.*

```
@interface IVBrickerViewController : UIViewController {
        UILabel *scoreLabel;
        int score;

        UIImageView *ball;

        CGPoint ballMovement;
}

@property (nonatomic, retain) IBOutlet UILabel *scoreLabel;

@property (nonatomic, retain) IBOutlet UIImageView *ball;

- (void)initializeTimer;

- (void)animateBall:(NSTimer *)theTimer;

@end
```

This code adds another instance variable to the view controller, called ballMovement, which holds the number of pixels that the ball will move per frame. CGPoint is a C structure provided by the Core Graphics framework. It has X and Y attributes, which let us specify different rates of movement vertically and horizontally. We also declare the signature for the methods initializeTimer and animateBall:.

Next, open the file *IVBrickerViewController.m*. Remove the comments around the viewDidLoad method, and then apply the changes shown in bold in Listing 3–10. Note the code for the methods initializeTimer and animateBall:.

Listing 3–10. *Here are the implementations of the viewDidLoad, initializeTimer, and animateBall: methods in the view controller.*

```
- (void)viewDidLoad {
    [super viewDidLoad];

    ballMovement = CGPointMake(4,4);

    [self initializeTimer];
}
- (void)initializeTimer {
    float theInterval = 1.0/30.0;
    [NSTimer scheduledTimerWithTimeInterval:theInterval target:self
        selector:@selector(animateBall:) userInfo:nil repeats:YES];
}
- (void)animateBall:(NSTimer *)theTimer {
    ball.center = CGPointMake(ball.center.x+ballMovement.x,
        ball.center.y+ballMovement.y);

    if(ball.center.x > 300 || ball.center.x < 20)
        ballMovement.x = -ballMovement.x;
    if(ball.center.y > 440 || ball.center.y < 40)
        ballMovement.y = -ballMovement.y;
```

```
}
```

This implements the `viewDidLoad`, `initializeTimer`, and `animateBall:` methods in the view controller. `viewDidLoad` sets an initial value to the `ballMovement` instance variable, of 4 pixels vertically by 4 pixels horizontally. Next, it calls the `initializeTimer` method. The `initializeTimer` method creates an `NSTimer` instance, initializing it to call the `animateBall:` method 30 times per second.

The `animateBall:` method begins by taking the ball center coordinates and adjusting it by the values of the corresponding `ballMovement` coordinates. This effectively moves the ball by 4 pixels vertically and horizontally every frame. The remaining lines of code in `animateBall:` check whether the ball has reached any of the four edges of the screen. If it has, the code reverses the direction of ball movement by changing the value of the coordinate from 4 to -4 and vice versa. For example, if the ball is moving left to right and it reaches the right edge, the ball "bounces" off the edge and starts moving to the left.

You may notice the current code within `animateBall:` does not make use of the `NSTimer` object that is passed in as a parameter. This object will come in handy later on in the chapter. For example, we will add code to stop the timer when the player loses a life and when the game is over.

Save your work. Now build and run the project, and behold the greatness of iPhone animated 2D graphics on the simulator.

Now that we have some motion going on, let's add some user interaction.

> **NOTE:** In this simple example, I am putting game state and game logic code in the view controller. When designing large games with a lot of enemies, obstacles, and many other game elements to keep track of, it is more organized to create several classes to contain a model of what is happening on the screen and to separate the game logic code from game model code. The view controller's job then becomes simpler, as it just needs to send input events to the game logic and update the view according to the game model. Separating model code, view code, and controller code is called the Model-View-Controller design pattern.

Rocking and Grooving with User Input

The iPhone platform provides very advanced input technologies for games. Besides just touching the screen, the iPhone can track multiple touches separately, allowing for the creation of complex UIs with multiple touch areas on the screen at once. All devices in the iPhone platform family have an accelerometer built in, allowing applications to track movement, which can make for a very interesting gaming experience.

Now let's add a paddle to our fledgling game, and experiment with adding input handling to our code. Look in the source code download for this chapter, in the folder named IVBricker finished version, for a file called *paddle.png*. Copy it to your project folder, and add this to your project's Resources group in the same manner as you did with the *ball.png* file.

Next, load *IVBrickerViewController.xib* in Interface Builder (if it isn't open already) and add an image view from the Cocoa Touch component library. Specify the *paddle.png* as the image you want to use for the new image view. Set the width and height of the paddle image view as **60** and **16**, respectively, and the x and y coordinates as **159** and **399**, respectively. Don't forget the center dot on the position grid needs to be selected to have the red cross displayed, so the paddle will be positioned correctly.

Now return to Xcode. We'll add another instance variable and property to the view controller, to let us control the paddle from our code. Let's give the instance variable and property the more than appropriate names of `paddle`. Listing 3–11 shows the code changes to the view controller's interface in bold.

Listing 3–11. *Adding an ivar and property called paddle to the view controller's interface.*

```
#import <UIKit/UIKit.h>

@interface IVBrickerViewController : UIViewController {
    UILabel *scoreLabel;
    int score;

    UIImageView *ball;

    CGPoint ballMovement;

    UIImageView *paddle;
}

@property (nonatomic, retain) IBOutlet UILabel *scoreLabel;

@property (nonatomic, retain) IBOutlet UIImageView *ball;

@property (nonatomic, retain) IBOutlet UIImageView *paddle;

- (void)initializeTimer;

- (void)animateBall:(NSTimer *)theTimer;

@end
```

Listing 3–12 shows the changes to the view controller's implementation in bold.

Listing 3–12. *Synthesizing and releasing paddle in the view controller's implementation.*

```
#import "IVBrickerViewController.h"

@implementation IVBrickerViewController

@synthesize scoreLabel;

@synthesize ball;

@synthesize paddle;

- (void)dealloc {
    [scoreLabel release];

    [ball release];
```

```
    [paddle release];

    [super dealloc];
}
```

Now that these changes have been made in the code, go back to Interface Builder and connect the `paddle` property to the paddle image view. Once that is done, we can use code to move the paddle on the screen.

Handling Accelerometer Input

Let's add accelerometer control to the code to see how that works. In Listing 3–13, you can see the code to enable this support in our example project. Add the code in bold to the *IVBrickerViewController.m* file.

Listing 3–13. *The code in bold adds accelerometer support to the view controller.*

```
- (void) accelerometer:(UIAccelerometer *)accelerometer
    didAccelerate:(UIAcceleration *)accel
{
    float newX = paddle.center.x + (accel.x * 12);
    if(newX > 30 && newX < 290)
        paddle.center = CGPointMake( newX, paddle.center.y );
}

- (void)viewDidLoad {
    [super viewDidLoad];

    UIAccelerometer *theAccel = [UIAccelerometer sharedAccelerometer];
    theAccel.updateInterval = 1.0f / 30.0f;
    theAccel.delegate = self;

    ballMovement = CGPointMake(4,4);
```

The first method in Listing 3–13 takes the accelerometer reading for left to right movement, multiplies it by 12, and adds this to the current location of the paddle. The paddle location is updated only if the paddle is not moving past the right or left edge of the view.

The next section of new code is within the `viewDidLoad` method, and it configures the accelerometer to take readings 30 times per second. It also sets up the view controller as the accelerometer delegate. This means that the accelerometer will call the method named `accelerometer:didAccelerate:` defined at the beginning of the listing.

If you were to build this code, you would find that there is a compiler warning in the line of code that sets the accelerometer delegate. The code compiles and runs properly, but I find compiler warnings annoying. To get rid of that warning, open *IVBrickerViewController.h* and change this line:

```
@interface IVBrickerViewController : UIViewController {
```

to read like this instead:

```
@interface IVBrickerViewController : UIViewController
```

```
    <UIAccelerometerDelegate>
{
```

> **NOTE:** If you were to run this latest version of the example project in the simulator, you would find it does nothing. This is because the simulator doesn't support accelerometer readings. You will need to set up the project to run on your device to test this code. This requires signing up as a registered iPhone developer. You can find how to do this at the Apple iPhone Developer Connection site (`http://developer.apple.com/iphone`).

To play the game, hold your device upright, and tilt it left or right to move the paddle. The more you tilt the device, the faster the paddle moves.

Once you run this code on your development device, you will find that the paddle moves, but the ball does not reverse direction when it collides with the paddle. Bear with me—we will fix this in the next section.

You will also perhaps not be too thrilled with using the accelerometer with this type of game. It's not very precise, and moving fast requires tilting the device fast, which makes keeping your eye on the ball a difficult task. But the purpose of this example was to show you how to set up the accelerometer. This game will actually use the touchscreen for input. So, remove the accelerometer code we just added from the project, and let's see how to add touch support next.

Handling Touchscreen Input

The view created by the Xcode template is already enabled for touch support when the project was created. All we need to add to the view code are the methods to process touch events. These methods are called touchesBegan:withEvent:, touchesMoved:withEvent:, and touchesEnded:withEvent:. Cocoa Touch calls these methods when the user touches a component that is touch-enabled, such as our view.

Before we begin adding these methods, we need to add an instance variable to our view controller to track how the users drag their finger on the screen. Listing 3–14 shows the code to be added to the header file. Add the line of code in bold to *IVBrickerViewController.h*.

Listing 3–14. *Adding touchOffset to the view controller's header file.*

```
#import <UIKit/UIKit.h>

@interface IVBrickerViewController : UIViewController {
    UILabel *scoreLabel;
    int score;

    UIImageView *ball;

    CGPoint ballMovement;

    UIImageView *paddle;
    float touchOffset;
```

```
}
```

I'll explain the use of touchOffset in context in a second.

Now that we have modified the header file, we can add the touch event handling code to the view controller implementation, as shown in Listing 3–15.

Listing 3–15. *Implementing touch handling in the view controller.*

```
- (void)touchesBegan:(NSSet *)touches withEvent:(UIEvent *)event {
    UITouch *touch = [[event allTouches] anyObject];
    touchOffset = paddle.center.x -
        [touch locationInView:touch.view].x;
}

- (void)touchesMoved:(NSSet *)touches withEvent:(UIEvent *)event {
    UITouch *touch = [[event allTouches] anyObject];
    float distanceMoved =
        ([touch locationInView:touch.view].x + touchOffset) -
        paddle.center.x;
    float newX = paddle.center.x + distanceMoved;
    if (newX > 30 && newX < 290)
        paddle.center = CGPointMake( newX, paddle.center.y );
    if (newX > 290)
        paddle.center = CGPointMake( 290, paddle.center.y );
    if (newX < 30)
        paddle.center = CGPointMake( 30, paddle.center.y );
}
```

The first method in Listing 3–15, touchesBegan:withEvent:, is called when the user touches the screen. This code stores in the touchOffset instance variable the distance in horizontal pixels between the user's touch of the screen and the paddle's center position. This tells us where the user first touched the screen to begin moving the paddle.

The second method, touchesMoved:withEvent:, is called when the user drags a finger following a touchesBegan:withEvent:. This code takes the touchOffset value that was stored by the first method, adds it to the horizontal position of the current touchesMoved event, and then subtracts the paddle's center position. This effectively lets us track the finger's movement left to right relative to the initial touch event. Next, we apply this horizontal distance to the paddle's position. This code makes for very smooth movement of the paddle.

Run this latest version of the code. You'll see that it is possible to move the paddle from one edge of the screen to the other very quickly, without taking your eyes off the ball. It's a marked improvement over the accelerometer version.

When Objects Collide

So far in our game, the ball just keeps moving right through the paddle as if it were not there. The reason is simple: the ball doesn't know about the paddle. The animation code for the paddle checks only for the edge of the view. So let's add more code to make the animateBall: method check the paddle's position and act properly when the ball touches the paddle. Add the code in bold in Listing 3–16 to *IVBrickerViewController.m*.

Listing 3–16. *Adding collision-detection code between paddle and ball in the animateBall: method*

```
- (void)animateBall:(NSTimer *)theTimer {
    ball.center = CGPointMake(ball.center.x+ballMovement.x,
        ball.center.y+ballMovement.y);

    BOOL paddleCollision = ball.center.y >= paddle.center.y - 16 &&
        ball.center.y <= paddle.center.y + 16 &&
        ball.center.x > paddle.center.x - 32 &&
        ball.center.x < paddle.center.x + 32;

    if(paddleCollision) {
        ballMovement.y = -ballMovement.y;

        if (ball.center.y >= paddle.center.y - 16 && ballMovement.y < 0) {
            ball.center = CGPointMake(ball.center.x, paddle.center.y - 16);
        } else if (ball.center.y <= paddle.center.y + 16 && ballMovement.y > 0) {
            ball.center = CGPointMake(ball.center.x, paddle.center.y + 16);
        } else if (ball.center.x >= paddle.center.x - 32 && ballMovement.x < 0) {
            ball.center = CGPointMake(paddle.center.x - 32, ball.center.y);
        } else if (ball.center.x <= paddle.center.x + 32 && ballMovement.x > 0) {
            ball.center = CGPointMake(paddle.center.x + 32, ball.center.y);
        }
    }

    if(ball.center.x > 310 || ball.center.x < 16)
        ballMovement.x = -ballMovement.x;
    if(ball.center.y > 444 || ball.center.y < 32)
        ballMovement.y = -ballMovement.y;
}
```

The code in Listing 3–16 checks whether the ball has touched the paddle, and makes the ball bounce away in the opposite direction. Because the ball moves 4 pixels at a time in any direction, there is code, from line 13 to line 21 of the listing, to check that the ball has not gotten stuck inside the paddle.

With these latest changes, our program is now fully interactive, but it's still missing something. It's a graphics demo, not a game. We need to add more code to make this example into a game.

Besides animation and interaction, a game consists of a goal or goals the player must achieve. We need a set of failure conditions, which eventually lead to the game being over for the player, and a set of winning conditions, which eventually lead to the completion of the game's goals.

Failure Conditions

The only failure condition in a typical brick-breaking game is missing the ball and letting it reach the bottom edge of the screen. When the ball reaches the bottom of the screen, the game logic stops the ball and informs the player he lost. Then it resets the ball to the center of the screen and starts the ball moving again.

Games typically give the player a set number of lives at the beginning of a game session. In our brick-breaking game, the code must subtract one of these lives every time the ball reaches the bottom of the screen. Once the player has run out of lives, the game is over.

To implement the logic to count and display the number of lives, we need to add an instance variable to hold the current amount of lives, an integer we will simply call `lives`, and a property of type `UILabel` for displaying this value. We also need another `UILabel` property, to display the "Game Over" message and any other messages for the user. We will code this first, and deal with points and winning conditions in a later section. Listing 3–17 shows the class interface changes needed to begin implementing these game-play improvements. Add the code in bold to the file *IVBrickerViewController.h*.

Listing 3–17. *The view controller header file changes for adding support for game lives and user messages to our example program*

```
    UIImageView *paddle;
    float touchOffset;

    int lives;
    UILabel *livesLabel;
    UILabel *messageLabel;

    BOOL isPlaying;
    NSTimer *theTimer;
}

@property (nonatomic, retain) IBOutlet UILabel *scoreLabel;

@property (nonatomic, retain) IBOutlet UIImageView *ball;

@property (nonatomic, retain) IBOutlet UIImageView *paddle;

@property (nonatomic, retain) IBOutlet UILabel *livesLabel;
@property (nonatomic, retain) IBOutlet UILabel *messageLabel;

- (void)startPlaying;
- (void)pauseGame;
```

The code in Listing 3–17 adds four instance variables to the view controller. I've already discussed the meaning of `lives` and the two labels. `isPlaying` will be used in the touch event handling to determine if the game play is paused. Another instance variable is added for the timer instance.

At the end of the listing are two new properties for the labels. We have also added declarations for two methods, named `startPlaying`, and `pauseGame`, which will be used to clean up and organize some of the code that's starting to clutter the method `viewDidLoad`.

Now that we've changed the view controller interface, let's change the view controller implementation. Open *IVBrickerViewController.m* and modify the code as shown in bold in Listing 3–18.

Listing 3–18. *Modify IVBrickerViewController.m to match these changes in the code.*

```
@synthesize paddle;

@synthesize livesLabel;
@synthesize messageLabel;

- (void)dealloc {
    [scoreLabel release];

    [ball release];

    [paddle release];

    [livesLabel release];
    [messageLabel release];

    [super dealloc];
}
```

As in our previous changes to the code, we synthesize the properties from the header file, and we release them in the `dealloc` method. These synthesized properties can now be used in Interface Builder to connect the UI components to the code.

Open the *IVBrickerViewController.xib* file in Interface Builder to add these new labels to the UI. Drag each label from the Library window to the view, and configure them as follows:

- Place a label against the top and left borders. On the Attributes tab in the Inspector, set the Text property to **Lives:**. Deselect the Font Size attribute's option Adjust to Fit. On the Size tab, change the X and Y attributes to **45** and **10**, respectively. Then change the width to **44**.

- Position another label to the right of the Lives: label. On the Attributes tab, set the Text property to **3**. Deselect the Font Size attribute's option Adjust to Fit. On the Size tab, change the X and Y attributes to **83** and **10**, respectively. Then change the width to **20**.

- Postion a third label just above the paddle. On the Attributes tab, set the Text property to **Game Over**. Set the Alignment property to Centered (the middle button next to Layout, just below the Line Breaks selector). Deselect the Font Size attribute's option Adjust to Fit. Click the Font property (where it currently says "Helvetica, 17.0") to open a font picker window. Select English for Collections, Helvetica for Family, Oblique for Typeface, and 36 for Size. Close the font picker. On the Size tab, change the X and Y attributes to **159** and **353**, respectively. Then change the width to **310** and the height to **43**.

Once these three labels are placed and sized, connect them to the properties in the view controller. Right-click the File's Owner to open the Outlets and Referencing Outlets window. Make a connection from the `livesLabel` property to the component named Label (3), and then make a connection from the `messageLabel` property to the component named Label (Game Over). Figure 3–10 shows the three labels and their relative positions.

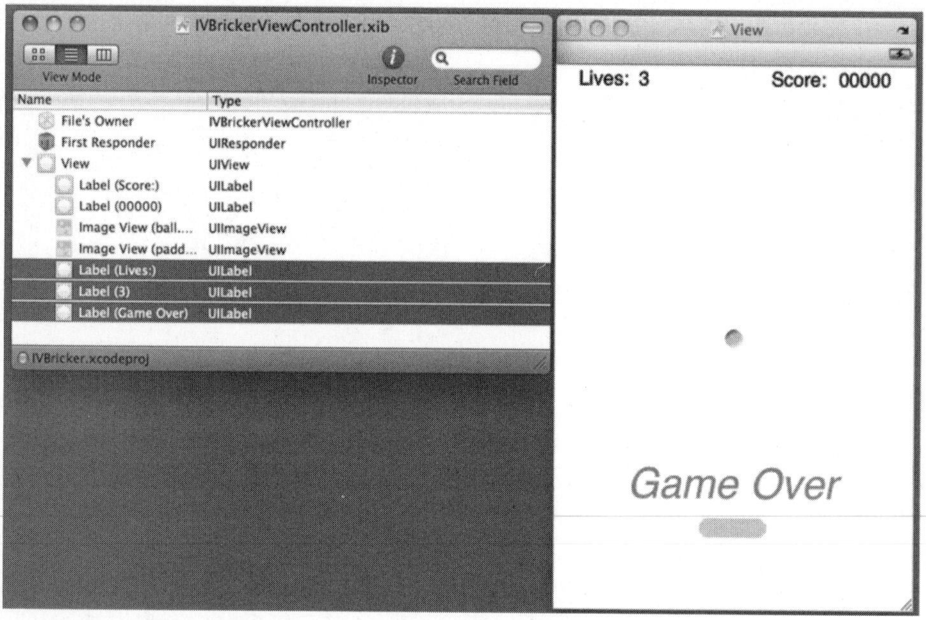

Figure 3–10. *The three new labels in the view: a placeholder for the text "Lives:", one to display the number of lives the player has, and another for user messages like "Game Over"*

Now that we've made changes to the view controller class and to the UI, let's make the other changes to the implementation, to start bringing the game to life. The changes are extensive, so I've broken them up into two listings. Listing 3–19 shows the changes (in bold) to the first half of the *IVBrickerViewController.m* file.

Listing 3–19. *Changes to the viewDidLoad method in IVBrickerViewController.m*

```
- (void)viewDidLoad {
    [super viewDidLoad];

    [self startPlaying];
}

- (void)startPlaying {
    if (!lives) {
        lives = 3;
        score = 0;
    }
    scoreLabel.text = [NSString stringWithFormat:@"%05d", score];
    livesLabel.text = [NSString stringWithFormat:@"%d", lives];

    ball.center = CGPointMake(159, 239);
    ballMovement = CGPointMake(4,4);
    // choose whether the ball moves left to right or right to left
    if (arc4random() % 100 < 50)
        ballMovement.x = -ballMovement.x;
```

```
        messageLabel.hidden = YES;
        isPlaying = YES;

        [self initializeTimer];
}

- (void)pauseGame {
        [theTimer invalidate];
        theTimer = nil;
}

- (void)initializeTimer {
        if (theTimer == nil) {
            float theInterval = 1.0f/30.0f;
            // I've renamed animateBall: to gameLogic
            theTimer = [NSTimer scheduledTimerWithTimeInterval:theInterval target:self
                selector:@selector(gameLogic) userInfo:nil repeats:YES];
        }
}
```

The first major change from the earlier versions is in the viewDidLoad method. Previously, most of the initialization code was in this method. We've refactored it into a new method called startPlaying. The rationale for this is that the initialization code needs to be called from more than one place now. The game-play initialization code needs to be called when any of the following happen:

■   When the player first starts the app

■   When play is restarted after the player loses one life

■   When starting a new game after losing three lives

It is better to factor out the initialization code into a method that can be called from several places, rather than copy and paste this code into several places. When you copy and paste code, you increase the chances of bugs happening every time you need to change the copied code.

The startPlaying method starts by resetting the number of player lives to 3, and it resets the score to 0 if the number of lives has reached 0. Then it updates the score and lives labels on screen. As in earlier versions of the initialization code, it sets the ballMovement instance variable to 4 pixels vertically and horizontally, and positions the ball in the center of the screen. As an extra twist, the code picks a number randomly and decides whether the ball will move left to right or right to left when animation starts.

The initialization code then hides the message label and sets the isPlaying flag to YES. Finally, we initialize the **NSTimer** instance by calling initializeTimer. Note that the animateBall: method has been renamed to gameLogic, as explained after the next listing.

Listing 3–20 contains the rest of the changes to the view controller implementation.

Listing 3–20. *The remaining changes to IVBrickerViewController.m*

```objc
- (void)touchesBegan:(NSSet *)touches withEvent:(UIEvent *)event {
    if (isPlaying) {
        UITouch *touch = [[event allTouches] anyObject];
        touchOffset = paddle.center.x -
            [touch locationInView:touch.view].x;
    } else {
        [self startPlaying];
    }
}

- (void)touchesMoved:(NSSet *)touches withEvent:(UIEvent *)event {
    if (isPlaying) {
        UITouch *touch = [[event allTouches] anyObject];
        float distanceMoved =
            ([touch locationInView:touch.view].x + touchOffset) -
                paddle.center.x;
        float newX = paddle.center.x + distanceMoved;
        if (newX > 30 && newX < 290)
            paddle.center = CGPointMake( newX, paddle.center.y );
    }
}

// I've renamed animateBall: to gameLogic
- (void)gameLogic {
    ball.center = CGPointMake(ball.center.x+ballMovement.x,
        ball.center.y+ballMovement.y);

    BOOL paddleCollision = ball.center.y >= paddle.center.y - 16 &&
        ball.center.y <= paddle.center.y + 16 &&
        ball.center.x > paddle.center.x - 32 &&
        ball.center.x < paddle.center.x + 32;

    if(paddleCollision)
        ballMovement.y = -ballMovement.y;

    if (ball.center.x > 310 || ball.center.x < 16)
        ballMovement.x = -ballMovement.x;

    if (ball.center.y < 32)

        ballMovement.y = -ballMovement.y;

    if (ball.center.y > 444) {
        [self pauseGame];
        isPlaying = NO;
        lives--;
        livesLabel.text = [NSString stringWithFormat:@"%d", lives];

        if (!lives) {
            messageLabel.text = @"Game Over";
        } else {
            messageLabel.text = @"Ball Out of Bounds";
        }
        messageLabel.hidden = NO;
    }
```

```
}
```

The touch event handling code in Listing 3–20 checks the isPlaying flag to determine whether the ball is in play. When isPlaying is set to YES, the touch event handling code performs the same steps as before. When isPlaying is set to NO, the touchesBegan event handling restarts game play. In contrast, the touchesMoved event handling ignores the touch event when isPlaying is set to NO.

As noted earlier, another change made in the code is the renaming of the method animateBall: to gameLogic. This method now does a few more things than just animate the ball. The ball now bounces back only when it touches the paddle or when it touches the top, right, or left border of the screen. When the ball reaches the bottom of the screen, the code stops the game by invalidating the game logic timer in the pauseGame method, sets the isPlaying flag to NO, decrements the lives counter, and displays the number of lives left. It also checks whether the player has any lives left and displays a "Game Over" message if not. Otherwise, it tells the player the ball is out of bounds. The game continues once the user taps the screen.

Now that we have finished adding the code to handle failure conditions, let's discuss what we need to do to implement winning conditions.

Winning Conditions

In a brick-breaking game, you earn points by bouncing the ball against colored bricks of different colors. Typically, each different color earns you different points. You also get bonus points for bouncing the ball on more than one brick in a row—the more bricks in a row, the higher the bonus. You win by removing all the colored bricks before running out of lives.

Right now, our game example lacks all of these winning conditions. First, we will need to add a grid of bricks to our screen. We will use a different image view object for each brick. Next, we need to add code to the game logic, to detect when the ball bounces off one of these bricks, and it needs to increment our score appropriately.

Let's look first at an efficient way to display a grid of image views.

Loading and Displaying Images Programmatically

So far in our sample program, we've added image views to our view by dragging components in Interface Builder. This is convenient in that it saves us from typing a lot of boilerplate code. But if your game were made of hundreds of different images, it would be quite impractical to add them all to the view in Interface Builder. You would need to carefully place the image views, and make connections to your properties in your code so that you could manipulate the image views as needed in your game.

Creating and manipulating UIImage and UIImageView in code is another way to load and display images in an iPhone application. We've been using UIImage and UIImageView in this chapter all along, but not in pure code. We had the help of Interface Builder.

A UIImage instance is a representation of image data loaded from files in a variety of image formats. You typically create a UIImage instance by loading a file from the iPhone's flash disk or downloading it from a URL. The code in Listing 3–21 shows how to load an image from your application bundle.

Listing 3–21. *Loading an image from the application bundle*

```
UIImage* myImageObj;
NSString* imagePath = [[NSBundle mainBundle]
    pathForResource:@"myImage" ofType:@"png"];

// load it like this
myImageObj = [[UIImage alloc] initWithContentsOfFile:imagePath];
// or like this
myImageObj = [UIImage imageNamed:imagePath];
```

> **NOTE:** Whether you use [[UIImage alloc] initWithContentsOfFile:] or [UIImage imageNamed:] is up to you, but be aware that [UIImage imageNamed:] tends to retain images longer than necessary sometimes. I'll demonstrate how to code and document a UIImage cache with a loadImage: method in the "Managing Memory with a Custom Image Loader" section later in this chapter. This cache will provide a method to release the images if memory use becomes an issue.

A UIImage instance is immutable, meaning the object does not have methods for changing the image properties, such as height, width, opacity, and so on; you can only get the image's properties. The object also does not provide direct access to the image data. This means you cannot draw on a UIImage object and change any of its pixels. (The iPhone does support drawing onto a view's graphics context and turning this drawing into a UIImage object. You can use other APIs for drawing, which we will examine in the next chapter.)

The image object itself is not displayable. To display an image, you create an instance of the UIImageView class, initializing it with an instance of UIImage. Once your UIImageView object is created, you can add it to a view to display it. Listing 3–22 shows how to initialize a UIImageView instance with an instance of UIImage and add it to a view (named mainView in the example).

Listing 3–22. *Initializing an image view with a previously loaded image object, then adding it to a view*

```
UIImageView* myImgView = [[UIImageView alloc]
    initWithImage:myImageObj];
[mainView addSubview:myImgView];
```

While this example stores the image view instance in a variable, you can store the object anywhere, such as in an array, set, or any other collection objects available in Cocoa.

A downside to creating image views programmatically is that you can manipulate these image views only in code. You lose all the visual design comforts of Interface Builder. But with the lack of comfort comes an increase in flexibility. Along with being able to have as many image views as memory allows, you can change the properties of your image views, including their size, position, transparency, and visibility (whether it is hidden or shown). These properties are the same as the attributes shown in Interface Builder.

Now that we have learned a little about how to create image views through code, we can start putting together the different parts we need to finish our sample game.

Creating the Grid of Bricks

First, we need to store our rows of bricks. To do that, we need to know how many bricks to allocate. For this example, we will use bricks of the same width as the paddle: 64 pixels. The iPhone screen is 320 pixels wide, which means we can fit five bricks side to side across the screen. The bricks are about three times as tall as the paddle image. We can fit four rows of bricks on screen, if we place our bricks just a little below where the score and lives counter are displayed, and extend downward toward the center of the screen just above where the ball is displayed when the game begins.

To store our grid of bricks, we'll use a C array to keep things simple. We need to allocate a 5-by-4 array of pointers to image views. By now, you should know the drill: open *IVBrickerViewController.h* and copy the code in bold in Listing 3–23.

Listing 3–23. *Allocating an array of pointers to image view objects in image view.*

```
    UILabel *messageLabel;

    BOOL isPlaying;
    NSTimer *theTimer;

#define BRICKS_WIDTH 5
#define BRICKS_HEIGHT 4
    UIImageView *bricks[BRICKS_WIDTH][BRICKS_HEIGHT];
    NSString *brickTypes[4];
}

@property (nonatomic, retain) IBOutlet UILabel *scoreLabel;
@property (nonatomic, retain) IBOutlet UIImageView *ball;
@property (nonatomic, retain) IBOutlet UIImageView *paddle;
@property (nonatomic, retain) IBOutlet UILabel *livesLabel;
@property (nonatomic, retain) IBOutlet UILabel *messageLabel;

- (void)initializeTimer;
- (void)pauseGame;
- (void)startPlaying;

- (void)initializeBricks;

@end
```

The code in Listing 3–23 declares two constants, BRICK_WIDTH and BRICKS_HEIGHT, and then declares an array of pointers to image views using these constants to specify the array's size. The code proceeds to declare an array of strings to hold the file names of the brick images. The code changes end with the declaration of a method named initializeBricks.

For this example, I have created brick images in four different colors. You can find these in the code download, in the IVBricker finished version folder, as the files named *bricktype1.png* through *bricktype4.png*.

Once we have declared our array of bricks, we need to fill it with image view instances. This is accomplished by looping through the bricks array and selecting a different image name from the brickTypes list as we instantiate each image view. Besides instantiating the image view and assigning it to the array, we need to assign each image view a position on screen and add it to the main view. As you've done for the previous updates, open *IVBrickerViewController.m* and copy the code in bold shown in Listing 3–24.

Listing 3–24. *Filling the bricks image view array when the view first loads*

```
- (void)viewDidLoad {
    [super viewDidLoad];

    [self initializeBricks];

    [self startPlaying];
}

- (void)initializeBricks
{
    brickTypes[0] = @"bricktype1.png";
    brickTypes[1] = @"bricktype2.png";
    brickTypes[2] = @"bricktype3.png";
    brickTypes[3] = @"bricktype4.png";

    int count = 0;
    for (int y = 0; y < BRICKS_HEIGHT; y++)
    {
        for (int x = 0; x < BRICKS_WIDTH; x++)
        {
            UIImage *image = [UIImage imageNamed:
                brickTypes[count++ % 4]];
            bricks[x][y] = [[[UIImageView alloc] initWithImage:image]
                autorelease];
            CGRect newFrame = bricks[x][y].frame;
            newFrame.origin = CGPointMake(x * 64, (y * 40) + 100);
            bricks[x][y].frame = newFrame;
            [self.view addSubview:bricks[x][y]];
        }
    }
}

- (void)startPlaying {
```

In the code in Listing 3–24, we call a new method named initialzeBricks from the viewDidLoad method. Then in the initializeBricks method, we assign a different file name to each element of the brickTypes array.

The rest of the code in Listing 3–24 loops through our 5-by-4 grid of bricks, and then allocates an image view and assigns one of the four different color brick images to the image view. Then it computes a position on screen in pixels, based on the position of the image view in the grid. The calculation stems from the fact the brick images are sized 64 by 40 pixels. The code multiplies the x grid coordinate by 64 and multiplies the y grid coordinate by 40, to arrive at their pixel positions. We add an extra 100 pixels to the vertical position, to place the first row of bricks below the Score and Lives labels and provide some room for the ball to bounce between the labels and the first row of bricks. Figure 3–11 shows the game displaying the grid of bricks.

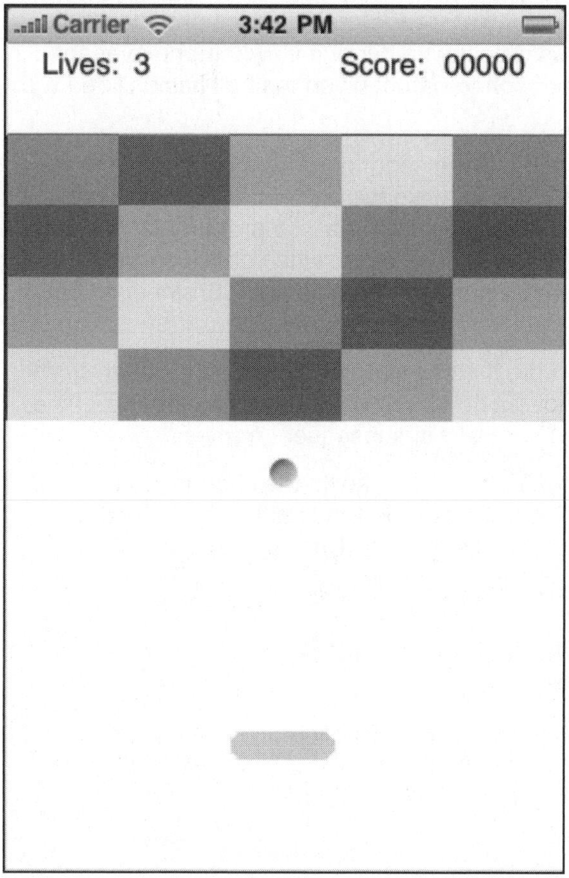

Figure 3–11. *The game now displays a grid of bricks above the center of the screen.*

Detecting image View Collisions

So now the game has a grid of bricks, a ball and a paddle, but if you run it, you will see that there is still no way of earning points and winning the game. We need to add code to the gameLogic: method to handle scoring and game-winning conditions. The code needs to do the following:

- Detect when the ball collides with one of the bricks.

- Bounce the ball in the opposite direction it was heading before the collision.

- Add points to the score.

- Remove the brick from the grid.

- Once all the bricks have been removed, stop the gameLogic: timer and display a message to the player indicating she has won the game.

As explained earlier in the chapter, the frame property of a view holds the coordinates and size of the rectangular area occupied by that view. Core Graphics provides the function CGRectIntersectsRect to help us detect whether one view's frame overlaps another view's frame. We will use this function to detect when the ball has collided with a brick.

Once we have detected a collision with a brick, we need to remove the brick from the view. Rather than just remove it, it looks nicer to make the brick fade out over time, such as half a second. We can do this by decreasing the brick's alpha property by 0.1 each time we run through the collision detection code. Therefore, when checking for a collision, the code should ignore bricks that don't have an alpha of 1.0, since the ball has already hit these bricks in previous frames.

Besides having the bricks fade out when hit, the ball also needs to bounce away from the side of the brick it hit. If the ball is moving down vertically and it hits the top of the brick, the ball should react by moving up vertically in subsequent frames.

Let's look at the code to detect collisions. Listing 3–25 shows the changes to the gameLogic: method and other functions added to support these changes. The code in bold shows the modifications to be made to *IVBrickerViewController.m*.

Listing 3–25. *This listing shows the code added to gameLogic: to detect when bricks are hit.*

```
- (void)gameLogic:(NSTimer *) theTimer {
        ball.center = CGPointMake(ball.center.x+ballMovement.x,
                ball.center.y+ballMovement.y);

        BOOL paddleCollision = ball.center.y >= paddle.center.y - 16 &&
        ball.center.y <= paddle.center.y + 16 &&
        ball.center.x > paddle.center.x - 32 &&
        ball.center.x < paddle.center.x + 32;

    if(paddleCollision)
        ballMovement.y = -ballMovement.y;

    BOOL there_are_solid_bricks = NO;

    for (int y = 0; y < BRICKS_HEIGHT; y++)
    {
        for (int x = 0; x < BRICKS_WIDTH; x++)
        {
            if (1.0 == bricks[x][y].alpha)
            {
                there_are_solid_bricks = YES;
                if ( CGRectIntersectsRect(ball.frame, bricks[x][y].frame) )
                {
                    [self processCollision:bricks[x][y]];
                }
```

```
            }
            else
            {
                if (bricks[x][y].alpha > 0)
                    bricks[x][y].alpha -= 0.1;
            }
        }
    }

    if (!there_are_solid_bricks) {
        [theTimer invalidate];
        isPlaying = NO;
        lives = 0;

        messageLabel.text = @"You Win!";
        messageLabel.hidden = NO;
    }

    if (ball.center.x > 310 || ball.center.x < 16)
        ballMovement.x = -ballMovement.x;
    if (ball.center.y < 32)
        ballMovement.y = -ballMovement.y;

    if (ball.center.y > 444) {
        [theTimer invalidate];
        isPlaying = NO;
        lives--;
        livesLabel.text = [NSString stringWithFormat:@"%d", lives];

        if (!lives) {
            messageLabel.text = @"Game Over";
        } else {
        messageLabel.text = @"Ball Out of Bounds";
        }
        messageLabel.hidden = NO;
    }
}

- (void)processCollision:(UIImageView *)brick
{
    score += 10;
    scoreLabel.text = [NSString stringWithFormat:@"%d", score];

    if (ballMovement.x > 0 && brick.frame.origin.x - ball.center.x <= 4)
        ballMovement.x = -ballMovement.x;
    else if (ballMovement.x < 0 && ball.center.x - (brick.frame.origin.x +
brick.frame.size.width) <= 4)
        ballMovement.x = -ballMovement.x;

    if (ballMovement.y > 0 && brick.frame.origin.y - ball.center.y <= 4)
        ballMovement.y = -ballMovement.y;
    else if (ballMovement.y < 0 && ball.center.y - (brick.frame.origin.y +
brick.frame.size.height) <= 4)
        ballMovement.y = -ballMovement.y;
```

```
        brick.alpha -= 0.1;
}
```

The code changes start by declaring a variable to determine whether if there are any solid bricks left on the screen. This variable, named there_are_solid_bricks, is initially set to NO. As the code loops over each of the bricks in the grid, it checks whether the brick is solid. If the code finds a nonsolid brick, it decreases the brick's alpha property once per frame until it is totally transparent.

Once we find a solid brick, we set there_are_solid_bricks to YES. This variable essentially lets the code determine if the player has won the game. The player wins when there are no solid bricks left.

When the code finds a solid brick, it also checks whether the ball has hit a brick, by using the Core Graphics function CGRectIntersectsRect to determine if any part of the ball is within the brick's area. If there is a collision, the code calls the method processCollision, passing in the brick object as a parameter.

The processCollision method increases the score by ten points and displays the new score. It also checks which side of the brick the ball hit, and bounces the ball in the appropriate direction. And last but not least, it decreases the brick's alpha property, to mark the brick as nonsolid.

Changing the Timer to CADisplayLink

Earlier in the chapter, I mentioned that iPhone SDK 3.1 added the CADisplayLink class, a new way of scheduling a method to be called periodically. It is similar to NSTimer, but runs more precisely. It is synchronized to the iPhone's screen logic, which refreshes itself 60 times per second. Listings 3–26 and 3–27 show the modifications needed to change the game logic code to use CADisplayLink.

Listing 3–26. *This listing shows the changes that need to be made to IVBrickerViewController.h*

```
#import <UIKit/UIKit.h>
#import <QuartzCore/CADisplayLink.h>

@interface IVBrickerViewController : UIViewController {
    UILabel *scoreLabel;
    int score;

    UIImageView *ball;

    CGPoint ballMovement;

    UIImageView *paddle;
    float touchOffset;

    int lives;
    UILabel *livesLabel;
    UILabel *messageLabel;

    BOOL isPlaying;
    CADisplayLink *theTimer;
```

```
#define BRICKS_WIDTH 5
#define BRICKS_HEIGHT 4
```

Listing 3–27. *This listing shows the changes that need to be made to IVBrickerViewController.m*

```
- (void)pauseGame {
    [theTimer invalidate];
    theTimer = nil;
}

- (void)initializeTimer {
    if (theTimer == nil) {
        theTimer = [CADisplayLink displayLinkWithTarget:self
            selector:@selector(gameLogic)];
        theTimer.frameInterval = 2;
        [theTimer addToRunLoop: [NSRunLoop currentRunLoop]
            forMode: NSDefaultRunLoopMode];
    }
}
```

Listing 3–26 changes the instance variable named theTimer to the correct type, from NSTimer to CADisplayLink. Llisting 3–27 shows the changes in the way theTimer is initialized. The NSTimer initializer took as one of its parameters a time interval between calls to the game logic. CADisplayLink defaults to running at 60 frames per second, and doesn't need this time interval to be set. But our game logic is meant to run at 30 frames per second, so we set the CADisplayLink property named frameInterval to a value of 2. This tells CADisplayLink to run every other frame, effectively making the game logic run at 30 times per second.

CADisplayLink also differs from NSTimer in that NSTimer takes another parameter to set whether the timer repeats. CADisplayLink is set to repeat until it is invalidated. Another difference is that the display link needs to be added to a run loop, a Cocoa Touch construct for handling system events. NSTimer started running as soon as it was initialized.

Before using this version of IVBricker, you need to include in your project the Quartz Core framework. To add it to your project, right-click the Frameworks group in the Groups and Files panel and select **Add ➤ Existing Frameworks** from the pop-up menu. You will see a drop-down list of all the different iPhone frameworks, as shown in Figure 3–12. Choose QuartzCore.framework and click the **Add** button.

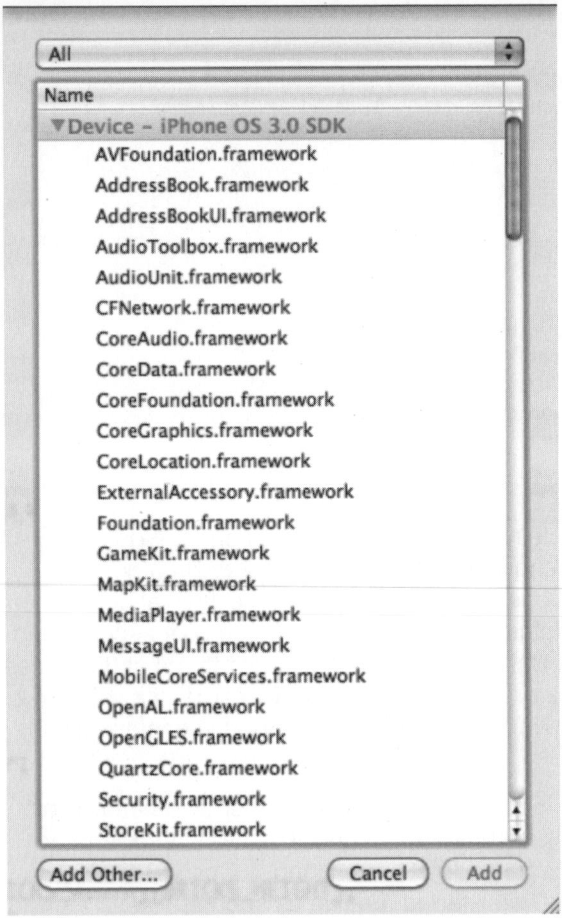

All	

Name

▼ Device – iPhone OS 3.0 SDK

AVFoundation.framework
AddressBook.framework
AddressBookUI.framework
AudioToolbox.framework
AudioUnit.framework
CFNetwork.framework
CoreAudio.framework
CoreData.framework
CoreFoundation.framework
CoreGraphics.framework
CoreLocation.framework
ExternalAccessory.framework
Foundation.framework
GameKit.framework
MapKit.framework
MediaPlayer.framework
MessageUI.framework
MobileCoreServices.framework
OpenAL.framework
OpenGLES.framework
QuartzCore.framework
Security.framework
StoreKit.framework

Add Other...   Cancel   Add

Figure 3–12. *Choose QuartzCore.framework and click the Add button.*

The End?

We now have all the code for a complete game. It handles scoring, losing the game, and winning the game. But there are still some things to cover that are very important in iPhone programming. The rest of the chapter is focused on these important topics in iPhone game development.

In the next section, we tackle what to do in your game when players lock their iPhone, or are interrupted by a phone call or text message. Sometimes they need to quit your app temporarily, but they'll be back later. How do you handle that kind of thing?

After that, we cover some tips and tricks in the area of memory handling involving images.

And last but not least, we will look at different ways of implementing animated image views.

Application Delegate Events

Earlier in this chapter, I alluded to the fact that a Cocoa Touch application is made up of several objects. When we created our sample game, we based it on a template that comes with Xcode, the View-based Application template. This template has a *MainWindow.xib* file, which is automatically loaded and processed by Cocoa Touch at application startup. By loading and processing *MainWindow.xib*, Cocoa Touch creates the main `UIWindow` instance, the `IVBrickerViewController` and its view with the paddle and ball image views, the `UIApplication` instance, and the `IVBrickerAppDelegate` instance.

Once these instances are created, Cocoa Touch is able to start our application code rolling by sending messages to methods in the application delegate and in the view controller. In the code template we used to begin coding our game, the app begins its life cycle with a call to the method `applicationDidFinishLaunching:` in the app delegate. In this method, we assign the `IVBrickerViewController`'s view to the `UIWindow` instance and make the window visible. Then Cocoa Touch proceeds to message the `viewDidLoad` method in `IVBrickerViewController`, where the code creates the grid of bricks, initializes score and lives counters, and starts the timer to animate the ball and process the game logic.

Besides messaging these two methods in the app delegate and the view controller, there are many more messages that UIKit sends the application delegate during the lifetime of an app. These messages can be classified as low memory warnings, user interruption warnings, messages to allow resuming from interruptions, and application termination messages.

Application Termination

The `UIApplicationDelegate` class defines a method called `applicationWillTerminate:`, which is typically called when users quit your application through the iPhone's home button, or when they quit your game to answer a phone call, respond to a text message, or respond to any other kind of notification from the operating system. You can use this delegate method to save your game's state, to allow the user to resume your game at a later time.

You don't need to worry about closing windows, deallocating views, or releasing memory in the `applicationWillTerminate:` method. iPhone OS cleans up after your application shortly after this method is called. You should close any open files and release database handles, though. SQLite databases can become corrupt if they are not closed properly.

You'll learn more about saving the game state in the "Saving and Loading Game State" section later in this chapter. The important thing to keep in mind is that you have at most two to three seconds to do what you need to save your game's current state. You should save your game state as quickly and efficiently as possible, or else the operating system will kill your app before it's finished saving all the data, leading to data corruption.

Application Interruptions

The app delegate also defines a method called `applicationWillResignActive:`, which is called when the user is interrupted, such as when the user receives a phone call or text, or when the device is locked. The `applicationWillResignActive:` message allows you to pause your game while the user decides whether to answer that call or reply to the text message. You should invalidate any timers, effectively pausing your game. You should also use this method to save the user's progress in your game.

If the user decides to close the notification message without answering the phone call or replying to the text message, Cocoa Touch resumes the game by calling the method `applicationDidBecomeActive:`. Use this method to initialize any timers in your game that were invalidated in the `applicationWillResignActive:` method.

Listing 3–28 shows sample implementations of `applicationWillResignActive:` and `applicationDidBecomeActive:` for our IVBricker game. These methods go in the *IVBrickerAppDelegate.m* file.

Listing 3–28. *These are example implementations of the methods applicationWillResignActive: and applicationDidBecomeActive:*

```
- (void)applicationWillResignActive:(UIApplication *)application
{
    [viewController pauseGame];
    [viewController saveGameState];
}

- (void)applicationDidBecomeActive:(UIApplication *)application
{
    [viewController loadGameState];
    [viewController startPlaying];
}
```

In Listing 3–28, when the game is interrupted by a phone call or when the phone is locked and the `applicationWillResignActive:` method is called, the code pauses the game and saves the game state. When the app is ready to resume after an interruption, and the `applicationDidBecomeActive:` method is called, the code reloads the game state and continues the game.

Low Memory Warnings

One thing to keep in mind when developing for iPhone is that your game's available RAM is limited. Typically, iPhone OS uses about 40MB of RAM. This leaves you with less than 24MB of RAM available when running your game on an iPhone 2G or 3G. The situation with iPod touch models is a bit better. Because the iPod touch doesn't need to receive phone calls or text messages, the operating system uses less RAM than on an iPhone. You have about 32MB of RAM available when running your game on an iPod touch.

The important thing to remember is that your game will be forcibly shut down by the operating system if it uses too much of the available RAM. If the operating system kills your app, it's too late to start worrying about why it happened. It is likely you have a memory leak somewhere, and you will need to spend some time debugging the problem.

Cocoa Touch does try to help, though. There is a message received by the app delegate that lets you try to free up memory before it's too late. The message calls a method named `applicationDidReceiveMemoryWarning:`. You should use the `applicationDidReceiveMemoryWarning:` method to release any cached data your application may hold in the app delegate.

For example, if your game uses data from a web service, you can cache that data the first time you retrieve it from the web service. Subsequent uses of the web service data can access the cache, rather than hitting the web service every time. The app delegate is an ideal place to hold this data, and the `applicationDidReceiveMemoryWarning:` method should release this cache when memory is low. If your app needs the web service data again, it can reload it from the web service and cache it until memory is low again.

View controllers also receive a similar message, with call to the method named `viewDidUnload`. Over the course of a game, you are likely to load several views, one for each screen in your game. As you navigate from one screen to the other, it is likely the other screens don't need to take up RAM while they are not visible. Cocoa Touch calls the `viewDidUnload` method after a view is removed from the screen. If your view allocates any objects in memory, it should release them in the `viewDidUnload` method.

Saving and Loading Game State

In Listing 3–28, you saw code for pausing the game when the iPhone gets an interrupting notification or when it is locked, and code for resuming the game. This code also called the `saveGameState` and `loadGameState` methods in the view controller. This section will examine these methods and explain one technique for saving and loading game state with the Cocoa Touch frameworks.

Cocoa Touch provides the class `NSUserDefaults` for saving data and looking it up at a later time. You obtain an instance to the default data store with the `NSUserDefaults` class method `standardUserDefaults`. Then you use this instance with methods like `setObject:forKey:`, `setInteger:forKey:`, and `setDouble:forKey:`, to assign each piece of data you want to save a key and a value. Later on, you use the key to read the data, using the default data store instance with a method such `objectForKey:`, `stringForKey:`, `integerForKey:`, or `doubleForKey:`. Listing 3–29 shows an implementation of the methods `saveGameState` and `loadGameState` using `NSUserDefaults`.

Listing 3–29. *Implementing saveGameState and loadGameState using NSUserDefaults*

```
NSString *kLivesKey = @"IVBrickerLives";
NSString *kScoreKey = @"IVBrickerScore";

- (void)saveGameState {
    [[NSUserDefaults standardUserDefaults] setInteger:lives forKey:kLivesKey];
    [[NSUserDefaults standardUserDefaults] setInteger:score forKey:kScoreKey];
}

- (void)loadGameState {
    lives = [[NSUserDefaults standardUserDefaults] integerForKey:kLivesKey];
    livesLabel.text = [NSString stringWithFormat:@"%d", lives];
```

```
score = [[NSUserDefaults standardUserDefaults] integerForKey:kScoreKey];
scoreLabel.text = [NSString stringWithFormat:@"%d", score];
}
```

Besides using saveGameState and loadGameState in the app delegate app termination, inactivate and reactivate notification methods, you should save game state when the user loses or wins a game. Just insert a call to saveGameState in the gameLogic method in the code sections for winning or losing. Listing 3–30 has the necessary changes to the code in bold.

Listing 3–30. *The changes to the game logic code.*

```
if (!there_are_solid_bricks) {
    [self pauseGame];
    isPlaying = NO;
    lives = 0;
    [self saveGameState];

    messageLabel.text = @"You Win!";
    messageLabel.hidden = NO;
}

if (ball.center.x > 310 || ball.center.x < 16)
    ballMovement.x = -ballMovement.x;
if (ball.center.y < 32)
    ballMovement.y = -ballMovement.y;

if (ball.center.y > 444) {

    [self pauseGame];
    isPlaying = NO;
    lives--;
    livesLabel.text = [NSString stringWithFormat:@"%d", lives];

    if (!lives) {
        [self saveGameState];
        messageLabel.text = @"Game Over";
    } else {
        messageLabel.text = @"Ball Out of Bounds";
```

The viewDidLoad method should also be changed to load the game state at game launch time. Listing 3–31 shows the changes to the viewDidLoad method in bold.

Listing 3–31. *The changes made to the viewDidLoad method to load the game state at game launch.*

```
- (void)viewDidLoad {
    [super viewDidLoad];

    [self loadGameState];

    [self initializeBricks];

    [self startPlaying];
}
```

By including the code in Listing 3–31, the game state gets loaded from previous runs of the app.

When designing your game, you should determine what kind of state it makes sense to save in your game when the user is interrupted. In this chapter's trivial game example, we save the score and the number of lives, by way of example. We could also save the ball position and the current alpha value of the bricks.

A more complex arcade game with multiple levels would also save the current game level. In a real-time combat strategy game, you could choose to save the state of each game unit at different checkpoints in the current mission. The point is to try as much as possible to allow the player to resume play without needing to start the game or the current level from the beginning.

Managing Memory with a Custom Image Loader

When we're dealing with development of a game, it is likely loading too many images or other resources is causing the memory problem. There are ways to architect your image loading so that you can release memory taken up by your images. Listings 3–32 and 3–33 show a simple implementation of a caching image loader you can use in your apps.

Listing 3–32. *The interface to the custom image loader, named ImageCache.h*

```
#import <Foundation/Foundation.h>

@interface ImageCache : NSObject {
}

+ (UIImage*)loadImage:(NSString*)imageName;
+ (void)releaseCache;

@end
```

Listing 3–33. *The implementation to the custom image loader, named ImageCache.m*

```
#import "ImageCache.h"

@implementation ImageCache

static NSMutableDictionary *dict;

+ (UIImage*)loadImage:(NSString*)imageName
{
    if (!dict) dict = [[NSMutableDictionary dictionary] retain];

    UIImage* image = [dict objectForKey:imageName];
    if (!image)
    {
        NSString* imagePath = [[NSBundle mainBundle]
                                        pathForResource:imageName
                                        ofType:nil];

        image = [UIImage imageWithContentsOfFile:imagePath];
        if (image)
        {
            [dict setObject:image forKey:imageName];
```

```
        }
    }
    return image;
}

+ (void)releaseCache {
    if (dict) {
        [dict removeAllObjects];
    }
}
```

@end

To use the caching image loader, call the `loadImage:` class method of the `ImageCache` class, passing in the image file name as a parameter. To release all the images held in the cache, call the `releaseCache` class method.

This basic code gets the job done, but it is an all-or-nothing approach. You cache every image, and when the operating system complains memory is low, you unload every image from the cache. You could easily modify this code to let you keep several different caches rather than one universal cache. That way, you could use a different cache for each view in your app, and unload images only from views that are no longer on screen.

Animating Images

In the previous sections of this chapter, you learned how to create a basic game using `UIView`, `UIImage`, `UIImageView`, and `NSTimer`. The image views used in previous sections were static. They changed position and transparency depending on events processed by the game logic, but the `UIImage` instance displayed by any particular `UIImageView` was always the same throughout the game.

But there are many types of games in which you need to display different images several times per second. For example, if the game features a robot walking and jumping around the screen, the game needs to display a different image of the robot as it takes each step or as it jumps.

In this section, we will examine different techniques to display a sequence of images several times per second, using `UIImageView`.

Using the UIImageView Animation Properties

The first technique available to do animation with image views is actually built in to the `UIImageView` class. Image views have a property called `animationImages`. This property is an `NSArray` of `UIImage` instances. You can create an array of images, each image a different frame of your animation, and assign the array to this property. Then you use the image view's `animationDuration` property to set how long the animation will last. The `animationDuration` property accepts fractions of a second.

To play the animation once and stop immediately after the last frame is displayed, you can set the image view property `animationRepeatCount` to 1. The default value of this property is 0, which makes the animation repeat indefinitely. You can also call the method `stopAnimating` at any time to stop the animation, regardless of the `animationRepeatCount` or `animationDuration`.

One important point to remember is that the animation doesn't start immediately once the `animationImages` property is set; you must call the image view method `startAnimating` to display the animation. Once you call the `startAnimating` method, Cocoa Touch will automatically display a different image in the `animationImages` array every 1/30 second, until the time interval set in `animationDuration` property or until you call the `stopAnimating` method, whichever happens first.

Listing 3–34 demonstrates how to use `UIImageView` animations.

Listing 3–34. *Using image view animations*

```
NSMutableArray *images = [NSMutableArray alloc] initWithCapacity: 30];

// load the images into the array
for (int i = 1; i <= 30; i++) {
    NSString *imageName = [NSString stringWithFormat: @"animation1_f%0d.png", i ];
    UIImage *image = [ImageCache loadImage: imageName ];
    [images addObject: image];
}

// set the animations property on the image view
imageView.animationImages = images;
[images release];

imageView.animationDuration = 1;
imageView.animationRepeatCount = 1;
[imageView startAnimating];
```

The code in Listing 3–34 assumes that a variable named `imageView` holds a `UIImageView` instance and that it has been set up properly to display somewhere on the screen. The code creates an array of `UIImage` instances by loading 30 different images, named *animation1_f01.png* through *animation1_f30.png*.

The code proceeds to set the `animationImages` property of the image view. The `animationImages` property holds its own copy of the array, meaning our array is no longer needed, so we release it immediately. The code sets the `animationDuration` and `animationRepeatCount` properties and starts the animation with a call to the `startAnimating` method.

One limitation of using this animation technique built in to `UIImageView` is that Cocoa Touch changes the image displayed only every 1/30 second, and you cannot change this rate. You will need to use another technique if you want your animation to run faster or slower than 30 frames per second. Another limitation is that it is not very precise. Cocoa Touch doesn't guarantee that it will start animating immediately or that each image change will happen at precise 1/30-second intervals. Cocoa Touch does the best it can to run the animation, but there can be slight delays of a few fractions of a second.

Using NSTimer for Animation

Another animation technique available with UIKit is setting up an NSTimer to change the image property several times per second. One benefit of using this technique is that runs more precisely, and you're not limited to animation intervals 1/30 second. Listings 3–35 and 3–36 show the interface and the implementation of a class that derives from UIImageView and overrides the startAnimation and stopAnimation methods to use NSTimer.

Listing 3–35. *The interface of a class derived from UIImageView that uses NSTimer to improve the precision of animations*

```
#import <UIKit/UIKit.h>

@interface BetterAnimations : UIImageView {
    int _frameCounter;
    int _repeatCounter;
    NSTimeInterval _animationInterval;
    NSTimeInterval _timeElapsed;
    NSTimer *_theTimer;
}

@property (nonatomic, readwrite) NSTimeInterval animationInterval;

@end
```

Listing 3–36. *The implementation of a class derived from UIImageView that uses NSTimer to improve the precision of animations*

```
#import "BetterAnimations.h"

@implementation BetterAnimations

@synthesize animationInterval = _animationInterval;

- (BetterAnimations*)init {
    if (self = [super init]) {
        _animationInterval = 1.0 / 30.0;
        _frameCounter = 0;
        _repeatCounter = 0;
        _timeElapsed = 0;
        _theTimer = nil;
    }
    return self;
}

- (void)setAnimationInterval:(NSTimeInterval)newValue {
    if ( (1.0 / 15.0) < newValue) {
        _animationInterval = 1.0 / 15.0;
    } else if ( (1.0 / 60.0) > newValue) {
        _animationInterval = 1.0 / 60.0;
    } else {
        _animationInterval = newValue;
    }
}

- (void)stopAnimating {
    if (_theTimer) {
```

```
            [_theTimer invalidate];
            _theTimer = nil;
        }
    }

- (void)startAnimating {
    if (self.animationDuration > 0 && self.animationImages &&
                [self.animationImages count] > 0) {
        _frameCounter = 0;
        _repeatCounter = 0;
        _timeElapsed = 0;

        _theTimer = [NSTimer timerWithTimeInterval:_animationInterval
                target:self
                selector:@selector(changeAnimationImage)
                userInfo:nil
                repeats:(self.animationRepeatCount > 0)];
    }
}

- (void)changeAnimationImage {
    self.image = [self.animationImages objectAtIndex:frameCounter++];
    _timeElapsed += _animationInterval;

    if ( (_timeElapsed >= self.animationDuration ||
                frameCounter >= self.animationImages.length) &&
                (0 < self.animationRepeatCount   &&
                _repeatCounter <= self.animationRepeatCount) ) {
        _repeatCounter++;
        _frameCounter = 0;
    }
    if (_repeatCounter >= self.animationRepeatCount) {
        [self stopAnimating];
    }
}

@end
```

The class in Listing 3–36 can be used exactly like UIImageView, but animations run more precisely by virtue of using NSTimer. It also adds a new property named animationInterval, which lets you specify the time between image changes. It defaults to 1/30 second, but can be changed to any fraction of a second less than 1/60 second and up to 1/15 second. Any values less than 1/60 get rounded up to 1/60; values greater than 1/15 get rounded down to 1/15.

Using CADisplayLink for Animation

A third animation technique is using CADisplayLink. As you learned earlier, CADisplayLink runs very precisely at 60 times per second, thanks to being triggered by the iPhone's display circuits. This solution also derives from UIImageView, which means you use it in the same way as you would use the UIImageView animation feature. This solution defaults to running at 60 frames per second, rather than UIImageView's 30 frames per second. Listings 3–37 and 3–38 show the interface and implementation of this class.

Listing 3–37. *The interface of a class derived from UIImageView that uses CADisplayLink to improve the precision of animations*

```objc
#import <UIKit/UIKit.h>
#import <QuartzCore/CADisplayLink.h>

@interface MoreBetterAnimations : UIImageView {
    int _frameCounter;
    int _repeatCounter;
    NSTimeInterval _timeElapsed;
    CADisplayLink *_displayLink;
}

@property (nonatomic, readwrite) NSInteger frameInterval;

@end
```

Listing 3–38. *The implementation of a class derived from UIImageView that uses CADisplayLink to improve the precision of animations*

```objc
#import "MoreBetterAnimations.h"

@implementation MoreBetterAnimations

@synthesize frameInterval;

- (MoreBetterAnimations *)init {
    if (self = [super init]) {
        _frameCounter = 0;
        _repeatCounter = 0;
        _timeElapsed = 0;
        _displayLink= [CADisplayLink displayLinkWithTarget:self
                selector:@selector(changeAnimationImage) ];
    }
    return self;
}

- (NSInteger)frameInterval {
    if (!_displayLink)   {
        _displayLink= [CADisplayLink displayLinkWithTarget:self
                selector:@selector(changeAnimationImage) ];
    }
    return _displayLink.frameInterval;
}

- (void)setFrameInterval:(NSInteger)newValue {
    if (!_displayLink)   {
        _displayLink= [CADisplayLink displayLinkWithTarget:self
                selector:@selector(changeAnimationImage) ];
    }
    if ( 1 > newValue) {
        _displayLink.frameInterval = 1;
    } else if ( 4 < newValue) {
        _displayLink.frameInterval = 4;
    } else {
        _displayLink.frameInterval= newValue;
    }
}
```

```
- (void)stopAnimating {
    if (_displayLink) {
        [_displayLink invalidate];
        _displayLink= nil;
    }
}

- (void)startAnimating {
    if (self.animationDuration > 0 && self.animationImages &&
                [self.animationImages count] > 0) {
        _frameCounter = 0;
        _repeatCounter = 0;
        _timeElapsed = 0;

        if (!_displayLink)   {
            _displayLink= [CADisplayLink displayLinkWithTarget:self
                    selector:@selector(changeAnimationImage) ];
        }
        [_displayLink addToRunLoop: [NSRunLoop currentRunLoop]
                                    forMode: NSDefaultRunLoopMode];
    }
}

- (void)changeAnimationImage {
    self.image = [self.animationImages objectAtIndex:frameCounter++];
    _timeElapsed += _displayLink.duration;

    if ( (_timeElapsed >= self.animationDuration ||
                _frameCounter >= self.animationImages.length) &&
            (0 < self.animationRepeatCount  &&
            _repeatCounter <= self.animationRepeatCount) ) {
        _repeatCounter++;
        _frameCounter = 0;
    }
    if (_repeatCounter >= self.animationRepeatCount) {
        [self stopAnimating];
    }
}

@end
```

You use this code in a manner similar to the BetterAnimations class shown in the previous section. But instead of setting an animationInterval property that takes fractions of a second between frames, this one uses a property called frameInterval, which takes an integer between 1 and 4. This property tells the CADisplayLink at what ratio of 60 frames per second to display the animation. The frameInterval property defaults to 1, which means 60 frames per second. A frameInterval of 2 means the animation will display at 60/2, or 30 frames per second, and so on for the other values.

To use the MoreBetterAnimations class, you will need to add the Quartz Core framework to your project, as we did when we switched IVBricker from NSTimer to CADisplayLink (see Figure 3–12).

Summary

This chapter lays the foundation for what is to follow in this book. In this chapter, you learned the basics of Objective-C programming. You learned a little about how to use Xcode to make an iPhone view with labels and other UI components. And you learned how to make a basic game using UIKit and other Cocoa Touch technologies like NSTimer.

The chapter also introduced you to some of the different application life-cycle notifications Cocoa Touch sends to applications as they launch, load views, unload views, terminate, and get interrupted by other device functions. You learned how to save game state to allow the player to terminate your game and resume playing at a later time. The chapter concluded by examining image caching and animation techniques.

The sample project called IVBricker final version contains all the game code in this chapter, all the way to the section on saving game state and use of the image cache. Take a look at that project to see how it all comes together.

With the knowledge gained in this chapter, you should be able to get started programming basic iPhone games. These skills will help you apply the contents in the rest of this book for more advanced game-programming technologies.

Chapter 4

She Shoots, She Hits, She Scores!

In the previous chapters, you've been introduced to gaming on the iPhone and taken a trip through the world of UIKit. This can be considered GUI-level development. You use the Apple-supplied tools, dragging and dropping icons, and assembling the logic with bits of code here and there. If you're lucky, you get to stay in the world of Objective-C, tossing messages back and forth. It's a wonderful world. Apps can be built in a single day!

Soon, though, you'll want more. You might want to draw your own characters or import vector art from popular programs such as Adobe Illustrator. You may want your graphics to shrink and grow, fade, twirl, and change color. Static text can be much more interesting when it, too, changes size, rotates about the screen, and bounces off other objects. Fixed graphics become animated, flipbook movies, allowing your characters to come to life. Characters should jump, laugh, wiggle, and entertain. Games should be fun.

This chapter introduces you to the world of Quartz 2D games on the iPhone. Quartz 2D is a powerful API that simplifies the inner workings of the iPhone, allowing you to draw vector art, play with images, and manipulate fonts. As you leave the world of UIKit and enter the land of Quartz 2D, you'll write code to position and manipulate these items. There is a bit of math involved. We'll do our best to keep it simple.

To give you insight into how popular games are built, we'll walk though the construction of a Quartz 2D implementation of Atari's Asteroids. Let's begin with an overview of how we'll build the game.

Quartz 2D Game Overview

The iPhone SDK includes copious documentation on Quartz 2D, as well as sample code for numerous Quartz 2D-powered apps. Our goal here is to make sense of it all, and to help you understand how to use Quartz 2D to build games. We'll skip over a lot of Quartz's capabilities, such as the ability to generate Adobe PDF documents or work on standard Mac OS X platforms. You won't need those for your games. Instead, we'll choose the tasty bits and assemble them into a framework.

We begin by organizing the rich capabilities of Quartz 2D into Objective-C classes called *sprites*. The English definition of a sprite is a small or elflike supernatural being, an elflike person, a ghost. In the gaming world, a sprite can be the main character, an animated scoop of ice cream, a space rocket, or the tiny dust particles that appear after something has exploded. Sprites move; they do stuff. Our classes provide general methods for moving, rotating, scaling, and coloring sprites in a game world. The guts of our classes are functional calls into the Quartz 2D API.

With sprites out of the way, we introduce a Quartz 2D game loop, depicted in Figure 4–1. As you saw in Chapter 3, timers are an effective tool for making changes 30 times a second. We call each iteration of the loop a "tic," like the ticking of a clock. The game loop organizes the changes to sprites during a tic into three steps: *update*, *render*, and *persist*.

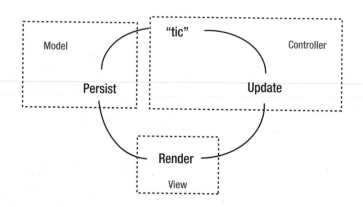

Figure 4–1. *A Quartz 2D game loop with the MVC model*

At the beginning of every tic of the timer clock, the update step adds or deletes items from the game, and then moves each sprite just a hair. The render step places visible sprites on the screen. The persist step records shared information on a common "blackboard," while capturing external changes to the UI (such as a finger touch or accelerometer movement). The loop repeats, 30 times a second, giving the illusion of movement and interactivity.

We implement the game loop with a set of classes, following the Model-View-Controller (MVC) design pattern introduced in Chapter 3. The blackboard is our *model*, holding information that persists beyond each game loop. The *controller* manipulates sprites during the update step with custom game logic. The controller also records changes to the UI and iPhone events in the model. Finally, the *view* places sprites on the screen during the render step. Quartz 2D plays a heavy role in the views, and is only a bit player in the controller and model.

With sprites and the game loop in hand, we dive into an implementation of Atari's Asteroids, as shown in Figure 4–2. This game is a set of sprites with one model. The buttons are implemented as image sprites, using frame animation to emulate button presses. The core and status displays are simple text sprites. The ship, rocks, and bullets are sprites made with shaded vector art. Sound effects, button presses, scoring, and lives are all kept in a centralized model. Game logic, from exploding asteroids to firing missiles, is kept in a controller class.

Figure 4–2. *A version of Atari's Asteroids in Quartz 2D*

The source code provided for this chapter includes two projects: *figures.tar.gz* and *asteroids.tar.gz*. The *figures.tar.gz* project contains all the sample code through the "Heads-Up Displays" section. One of the files, *Defs.h,* contains documentation on how to build the code for each figure in a live project. You may find it helpful to keep a window open with the source code, this book at your side, going back and forth between the text and the Xcode project.

The *asteroids.tar.gz* project covers the more detailed Asteroids game which is described in the "Asteroids Game Architecture" section. This is a complete game with sound effects, animation, levels, and scoring, built and extended from the classes we'll cover here. A lot of the logic and effects are particular to Asteroids and will not be covered in the chapter text. However, the code contains copious documentation to take your learning further.

Let's get started.

Every Artist Needs a Canvas

Quartz 2D paints and draws on a *graphics context*. The context is essentially the canvas for your game, and you'll need it when calling the various functions in the Quartz 2D API. It's an internal data structure associated with a UIView. Let's create one now. Luckily, you need to do this only once.

Open Xcode and start a new project. Select View-based Application, as shown in Figure 4–3. Then name the project Asteroids, as shown in Figure 4–4.

Figure 4–3. *Starting a new view-based application*

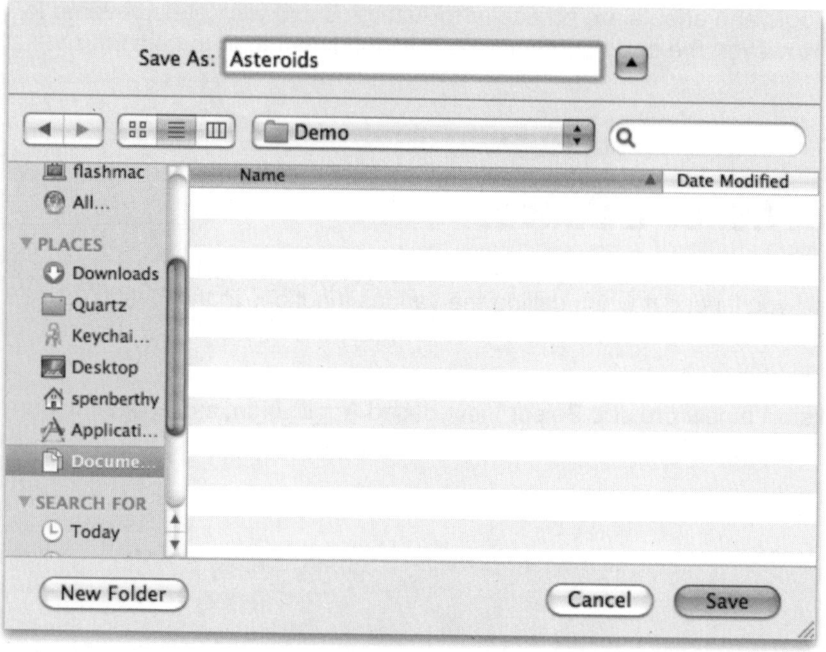

Figure 4–4. *Naming the application Asteroids*

Open `Asteroid`'s project settings in Xcode (select Project ➤ Edit Settings). Look toward the bottom of the window, where Xcode prompts you for the organization name. Enter your company name (shown as Acme Games in the example). Next, choose the iPhone Device 3.0 platform, as shown in Figure 4–5. Close the window.

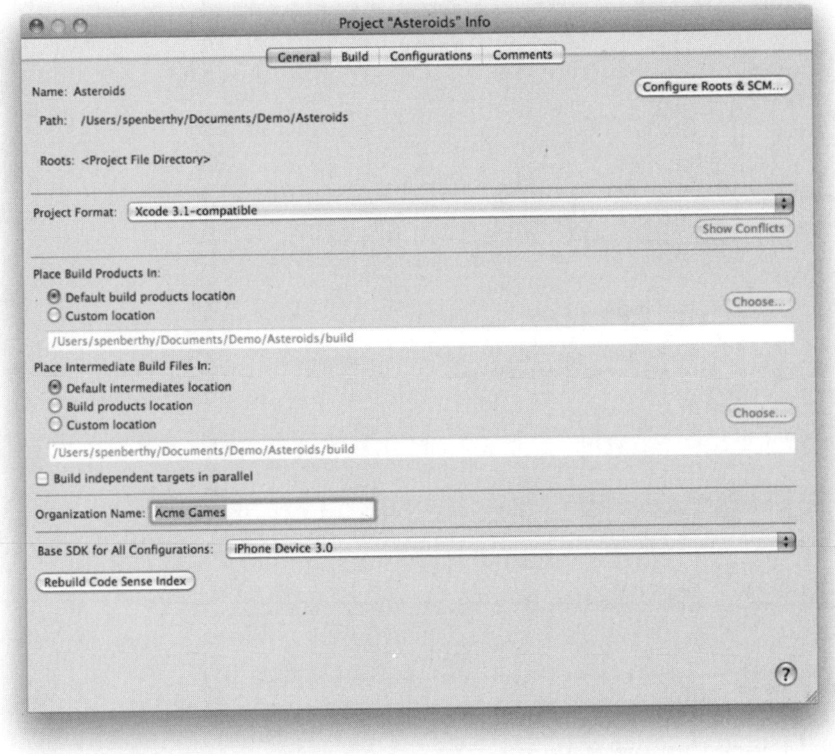

Figure 4–5. *Changing the company name and iPhone version for project files*

Now let's create a `UIView` subclass to hold our Quartz canvas. Add a new file to the Classes group in Xcode, choosing Cocoa Touch Class, and then selecting `UIView` as its superclass. Name it *AsteroidsView.m*, as shown in Figure 4–6. Click Finish. The window shows generated text for *Asteroids.m*, using your name and company name, as shown in Figure 4–7.

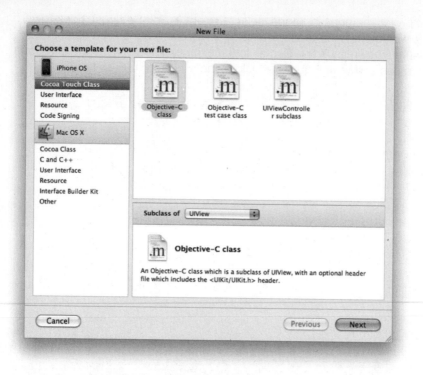

Figure 4–6. *Creating a new AsteroidsView subclass of UIView in Xcode*

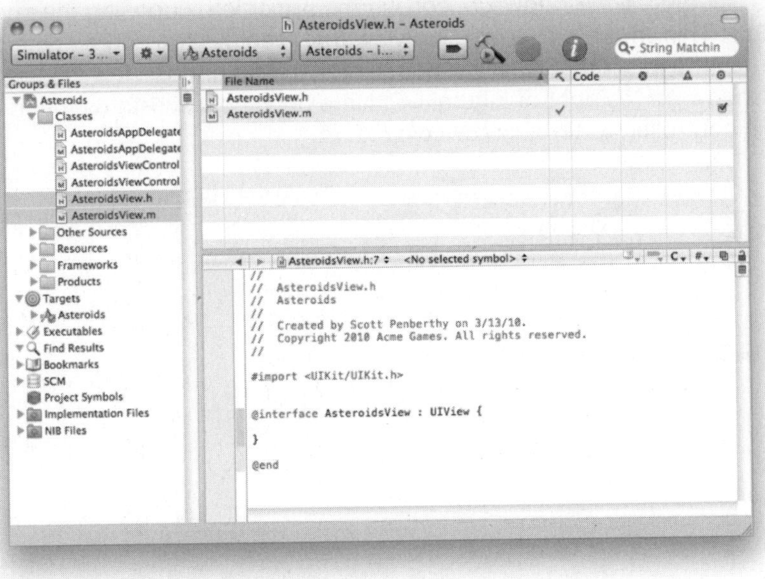

Figure 4–7. *Prepopulated files for AsteroidsView.m and AsteroidsView.h*

We now have a skeletal class for the main view of our game. We need to connect this view to the default controller, telling the iPhone we want total control over how the view is drawn. To do this, open the Resources group in the Xcode navigator and double-click *MainWindow.xib* to launch Interface Builder (as you did in Chapter 3), as shown in Figure 4–8.

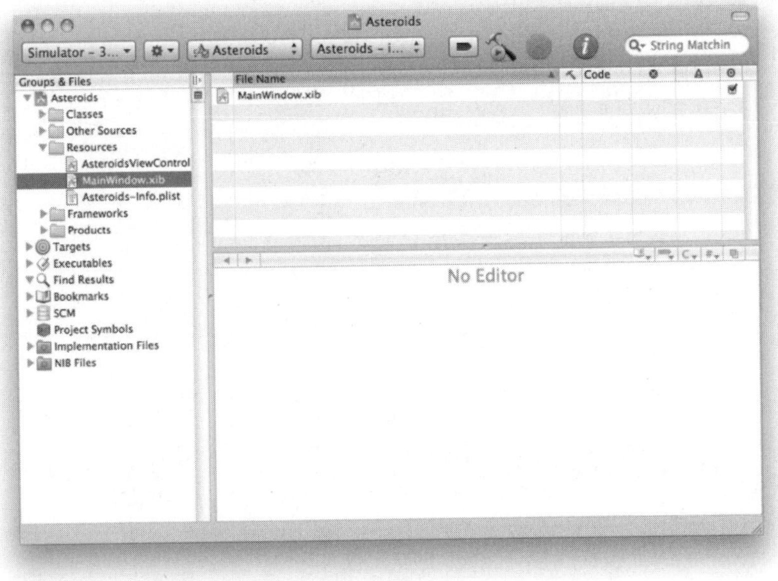

Figure 4–8. *The bare Asteroids app and its MainWindow.xib resource*

In Interface Builder, click the *MainWindow.xib* icons in the upper left, choosing the one with lines in the middle. This will shift to a detailed view that displays the entire name of each object, as seen on the left in Figure 4–9. Double-click the Asteroids View Controller entry to reveal the window on the right of Figure 4–9. Note how the view states that it is loaded from our main controller, `AsteroidsViewController`.

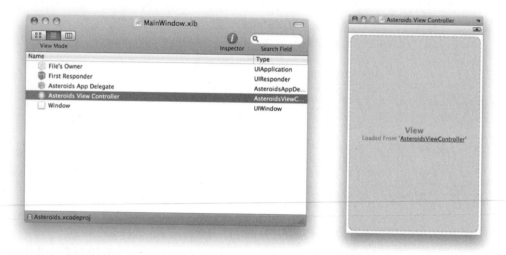

Figure 4–9. *Interface Builder in detail mode, showing the Asteroids view controller*

Click the blue underlined text `AsteroidsViewController`. This will reveal the underlying view object, shown on the left of Figure 4–10. We'll now tell Interface Builder that this view should use `AsteroidsView`, versus the default `UIView`. Double-click View to reveal the View window on the right of Figure 4–10.

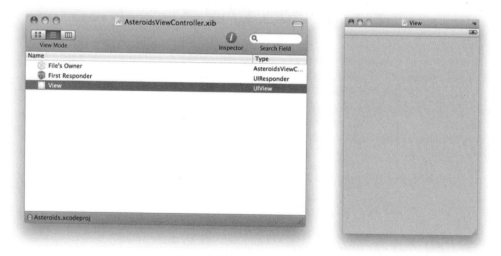

Figure 4–10. *The view controller in detail mode, with its view highlighted*

Click the View window. Carefully press ⌘4 while the View window is selected. This will open the Inspector window for the view, as shown in Figure 4–11. The Class selector at the very top of the Inspector window tells the iPhone which class will control display of the view. Since we already created AsteroidsView, it should be one of the choices available. Navigate to it and select it, as shown on the left in Figure 4–11.

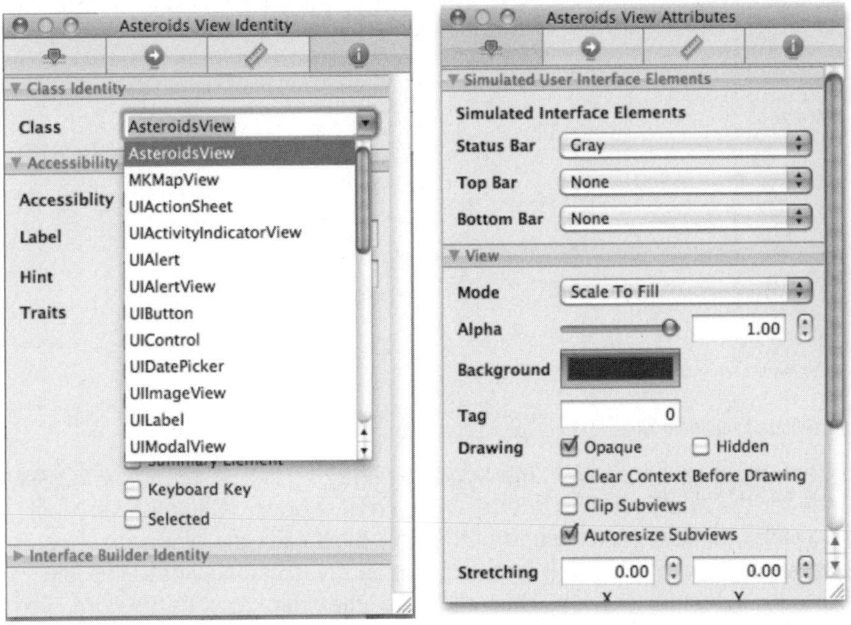

Figure 4–11. *Connecting our AsteroidsView class to the main view in Interface Builder, then changing the background color to Licorice (solid black)*

Our Asteroids game occurs in space. We'll need a black background. While we're here, let's change that as well. Click the icon in the upper left of the Inspector window—the one that looks like a slider. The window will change to look like the one on the right in Figure 4–11. The current color will be a default gray. Click the color, changing it to Licorice, a solid black color. The view window will also change to black.

Press ⌘Q to exit Interface Builder, answering Yes when you're asked whether to save your changes to Asteroids.

Return to Xcode, and then compile and run Asteroids in the simulator. The simulator should start fine, showing a completely black view, as shown in Figure 4–12. At the top of the view, you'll see a gray status bar. Let's get rid of it.

Figure 4–12. *A black iPhone canvas for Quartz, containing a status bar.*

Navigate to the Resources group again in the Xcode navigator. Click *Asteroids-Info.plist*, revealing attributes for the application in Xcode's property list editor. Click the very last entry, which will create a plus sign at the end of the row. Now click the plus sign. This will create a new property, prompting you to select from a given list. Navigate this list and choose Status Bar is Initially Hidden. Then click the little check box to the right. You should see a window similar to that in Figure 4–13.

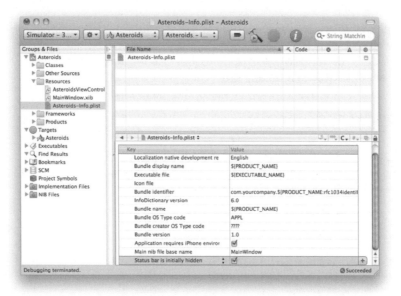

Figure 4–13. *Hiding the status bar*

Compile and run your application in Xcode (⇧⌘↵). The simulator should now be completely black, as in Figure 4–14. We're ready to write some code.

Figure 4–14. *A blank canvas, ready for Quartz 2D*

Your First Graphic with Quartz 2D

At this point, you're probably itching to play with graphics. The steps we just completed set up our main view, connected the view controller to this view, turned off the status bar, and gave us total control over drawing.

Open the AsteroidsView class and change the content of the drawRect method to the following code. This method is called whenever AsteroidsView needs updating.

```
- (void)drawRect:(CGRect)rect {

 // Get a graphics context, saving its state
  CGContextRef context = UIGraphicsGetCurrentContext();
  CGContextSaveGState(context);

  // Reset the transformation
  CGAffineTransform t0 = CGContextGetCTM(context);
  t0 = CGAffineTransformInvert(t0);
  CGContextConcatCTM(context,t0);

  // Draw a green rectangle
  CGContextBeginPath(context);
  CGContextSetRGBFillColor(context, 0,1,0,1);
  CGContextAddRect(context, CGRectMake(0,0,100,200));
  CGContextClosePath(context);
  CGContextDrawPath(context,kCGPathFill);

  CGContextRestoreGState(context);
}
```

Save your project and compile. A green rectangle will appear on the canvas, as shown in Figure 4–15. The rectangle is painted at the lower left (0,0), and proceeds 100 units to the right in the x direction and 200 units to the top in the y direction. The rectangle demonstrates the default coordinate system of Quartz 2D. On the iPhone and iPod touch, the x axis extends from 0 to 320 pixels. The y axis extends from 0 to 480 pixels.

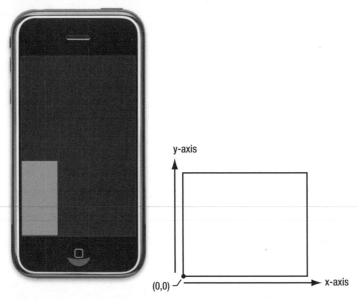

Figure 4–15. *A 100-by-200 green rectangle painted at (0,0) by Quartz 2D. The default Quartz 2D coordinate system is shown on the right.*

Saving and Restoring the Context

The iPhone provides a single call to retrieve the Quartz 2D graphics context during a draw operation:

```
// Get a graphics context, with no transformations
CGContextRef context = UIGraphicsGetCurrentContext();
```

All Quartz 2D data structures and API calls have a CG prefix, which stands for Core Graphics. CGContextRef is a pointer to a Quartz data structure for the artist canvas. UIGraphicsGetCurrentContext asks the iPhone for the current view. Unlike with desktop operating systems, there is only one window within the phone, and thus one context.

You can think of the context as a physical canvas. Like a canvas, the context can be moved, rotated, shrunk, and stretched, and then covered in layers of paint. Imagine you are an artist with a large canvas in front of you, perhaps several feet on a side. If you have a complex scene you're trying to paint, you can rotate and move the canvas to make things easier to draw. For example, after you paint birds in the sky, you can move the canvas again, and paint the grass or ocean waves.

So, when you sit down at a canvas, the first thing you need to do is to get your bearings. You may have left it in an odd state the day before, when the birds were being painted. Today, you're painting the ocean. Time to move the canvas.

But first, we need to be good citizens by calling `CGContextSaveGState`. This remembers the current state of the canvas for us, which we can later restore with a single call to `CGContextRestoreGState`.

In a large program, multiple classes and artists will be painting on the canvas. As a rule of thumb, we should always leave the canvas in the same state that we found it. With the canvas state stowed away, we can safely move it into place.

Quartz 2D describes the shifts of the canvas with matrix transformations. These are mathematical relationships that tell how to position points in space. In 2D games, we're typically interested in *affine transformations*. An affine transformation does what you expect in the real world. If you scale or move an object, edges that started straight remain straight. Affine transformations are reversible. If you scale an object down, then scale it back up, it doesn't change. If you move an object from one point to another, then back, it doesn't change.

It's important to follow one simple algorithm whenever drawing with Quartz 2D:

1. Save the context state.

2. Perform a single, combined matrix transformation.

3. Draw your graphics that need this transformation.

4. Restore the context.

> **NOTE:** I found that trying to be smart or tricky—combining multiple transformations within a single draw or trying to figure out the math when multiple items need to be on the screen in various scales and rotations—is rarely worth the effort. Once you finally get the math right, your design may change. Worse, looking at the complex code weeks or months later will lead to confusion, making the code brittle.

Let's tell Quartz 2D to put our canvas back in the default or (0,0) position. We do this by asking for the current transformation, a mathematical matrix describing how the canvas was moved from its original location, orientation, and scale. The canvas could be in any state. We then calculate the exact opposite motion, which in mathematics is called the *inverse matrix*. Finally, we ask Quartz 2D to apply the inverse matrix to the current transformation. Since the transformations are affine, and since all affine transformations are reversible, this will place our canvas back to the default location.

We need three lines of code:

```
CGAffineTransform t0 = CGContextGetCTM(context);
t0 = CGAffineTransformInvert(t0);
CGContextConcatCTM(context,t0);
```

CGContextGetCTM returns the graphic context's transformation matrix or CTM, as a matrix data structure. We call CGAffineTransformInvert to create the inverse matrix. We then call CGContextConcatCTM, which will concatenate our new matrix t0 with the existing matrix. *Concatenation* is the act of multiplying the matrix you supply (t0 in this case) with the current drawing matrix. When any matrix is multiplied by its inverse, we get the *identity matrix*. The identity matrix restores the canvas to its original, native state, as though no transformations were performed.

> **NOTE:** More details on matrices and transformations can be found online at http://bit.ly/cmwg7D, a shortened URL to relevant sections of Apple's *Quartz 2D Programming Guide.*

Adding Color

Let's throw some paint on the canvas. Like any good artist, Quartz 2D likes to paint outlines before it fills in a scene. These outlines are called *paths*. The following lines of code create a rectangular path (the lines are numbered on the right for clarity).

```
CGContextBeginPath(context);                              (1)
CGContextSetRGBFillColor(context, 0,1,0,1);               (2)
CGContextAddRect(context, CGRectMake(0,0,100,200));       (3)
CGContextClosePath(context);                              (4)
```

As before, the API functions begin with the letters CG. Most calls require the graphics context, which we went through great pains to create. CGContextBeginPath, on line 1, starts a fresh, new path in Quartz 2D. The Quartz 2D engine is like an artist with just one pair of hands. At any time, only one path is being created.

CGContextSetRGBFillColor, on line 2, specifies the color we would like to use in our path. Colors in Quartz 2D are specified in three unit values—a floating-point number between 0 and 1—for each of red, green, and blue. A value of 0 means to use no color for the given color component, 0.5 means to use 50% of that color, and 1.0 means to use 100% of the color. A fourth unit value represents the opacity, where 0 means the graphic is invisible, 0.5 means make the graphic 50% transparent, and 1 means the graphic is completely opaque. Quartz has numerous, powerful ways to combine these colors for interesting effects. For now, we'll use the default, which just adds the components together to create a single green, completely opaque color:

(0 x red) + (1.0 x green) + (0.0 x blue) at an opacity of 1.0

CGContextAddRect, on line 3, adds a single rectangle to the current path. We describe our rectangle using the CGRectMake macro. The macro is passed an origin (0,0), a width (100), and a height (200).

CGContextClosePath, on line 4, tells Quartz 2D that we're finished with the current path, and ready to paint with it on the canvas. The following call tells Quartz to take the current path, fill it in with the current color, and add it to the canvas. The first argument is the context. The second argument is a drawing mode, one of several available.

```
CGContextDrawPath(context,kCGPathFill);
```

Finally, being good citizens, we restore the state of the canvas with a single call:

```
CGContextRestoreGState(context);
```

Sprites

Our Quartz 2D API calls for drawing the green rectangle can be generalized, then reused for all kinds of graphical items on the screen. Instead of hard-coding the location, size, and attributes of our rectangle, we create a class to store these values as instance variables. As noted earlier in the chapter, the common name used in the industry for an object that comes alive is the *sprite*.

Creating the Sprite Class

Let's create a new class, Sprite, as a subclass of NSObject. Add a new file to the Classes group in Xcode, naming it Sprite. Replace the default @interface definition in *Sprite.h* to that shown in Listing 4–1.

Listing 4–1. *The Sprite interface in Sprite.h*

```
@interface Sprite : NSObject {
        CGFloat x;              // x location
        CGFloat y;              // y location
        CGFloat r;              // red tint
        CGFloat g;              // green tint
        CGFloat b;              // blue tint
        CGFloat alpha;          // alpha value, for transparency
        CGFloat speed;          // speed of movement in pixels/frame
        CGFloat angle;          // angle of movement in degrees
        CGFloat rotation;       // rotation of our sprite in degrees, about the center
        CGFloat width;          // width of sprite in pixels
        CGFloat height;         // height of sprite in pixels
        CGFloat scale;          // uniform scaling factor for size
        int frame;              // for animation

        CGFloat cosTheta;       // precomputed for speed
        CGFloat sinTheta;
        CGRect box;             // our bounding box

        BOOL render;            // true when we're rendering
        BOOL offScreen;         // true when we're off the screen
        BOOL wrap;              // true if you want the motion to wrap on the screen
}

@property (assign) BOOL wrap, render, offScreen;
@property (assign) CGFloat x, y, r, g, b, alpha;
@property (assign) CGFloat speed, angle, rotation;
@property (assign) CGFloat width, height, scale;
@property (assign) CGRect box;
@property (assign) int frame;
```

The Sprite class captures the 2D geometry and color of a graphic that we would like to place on the iPhone. x and y capture the desired location of our graphic on the screen. The variables r, g, b, and alpha capture the Quartz 2D color and transparency (floating-point values ranging from 0.0 to 1.0, as described earlier).

We store two different angles for each sprite. Figure 4–16 demonstrates these two angles on a rectangle. The original or starting position is shown in thinner gray lines, and the modified position is shown with thicker black lines.

rotation captures the number of degrees we've rotated our object (about its center). We follow standard geometry, where increasing angles represent counterclockwise rotations. An angle of 0 means no rotation. A 90-degree rotation turns the graphic counterclockwise a quarter turn. A 180-degree rotation turns the graphic counterclockwise a half turn. A 360-degree rotation is a complete spin, back to the original orientation. Figure 4–16 shows a rectangle rotated 45 degrees.

Quartz 2D uses radians to measure angles. You might recall that a 360-degree circle is equal to 2π radians and that π is approximately 3.1415926. Let's add convenience functions to the sprite, so that we can work in degrees, while the math is stored natively inside the sprite. We do this by overriding the default methods for getting and setting the rotation instance variable, as shown in Listing 4–2.

Listing 4–2. *Convenience functions for working in degrees vs. radians*

```
- (void) setRotation: (CGFloat) degrees
{
        rotation = degrees*3.141592/180.0;
}

- (CGFloat) rotation:
{
        return  rotation*180.0/3.141592;
}

- (void) setAngle: (CGFloat) degrees
{
        rotation = degrees*3.141592/180.0;
        cosTheta = cos(rotation);
        sinTheta = sin(rotation);
}

- (CGFloat) angle:
{
        return  rotation*180.0/3.141592;
}
```

angle describes movement of sprites on the canvas. An angle of 0 represents a straight movement to the right, parallel to the x axis. An angle of 90 is straight up and parallel to the y axis, 180 is to the left, and 270 is straight down. Figure 4–16 shows a rectangle that has a movement angle of 45 degrees. The amount a sprite moves during each tic of the game loop is represented as its speed.

Two variables save processing time during the update cycle of a game loop. costheta stores the cosine of the movement angle, and sintheta stores the sine of the movement angle. These trigonometry functions are expensive and best computed once, when the angle of movement changes.

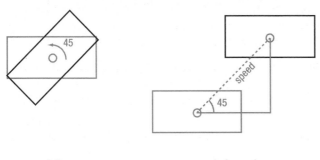

rotation   angle & speed

Figure 4–16. *A sprite's rotation, angle, and speed*

box stores the bounding box for our sprite. A *bounding box* is the smallest rectangle that completely covers all parts of our sprite, rotated if necessary. Games use these all the time to determine whether two sprites might collide. In Asteroids, we'll use the bounding box of rocks and bullets to determine when a rock should explode. The bounding box for our ship is compared against the bounding box for rocks to determine if our ship should die. Figure 4–17 shows the bounding box for a rock and ship at different rotations.

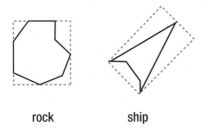

rock   ship

Figure 4–17. *A sprite's bounding box (dashed line)*

scale tells us how big to draw the sprite. A scale of 1.0 means to draw it at default size, 0.5 at half the size, 4.0 at four times the size, and so on. width and height capture the dimensions of our sprite, before any rotations or scaling are done.

We keep three Boolean switches for every sprite: render, offscreen, and wrap. render determines whether our sprite should be drawn on the screen. This is a handy switch for taking sprites on and off the canvas. This can be useful for things like space aliens that suddenly appear, pop-up menus, destroyed rocks, and alert messages. offscreen records whether the sprite has moved out of sight. In the Asteroids game, an off-screen bullet just disappears, assuming it continues to fire off into the ether. wrap tells the update loop what to do when a sprite goes off the screen. Rocks don't disappear. They come back to haunt the main ship, wrapping around the screen. Your ship doesn't disappear, either. As you thrust across the screen, your ship wraps from one side to the next.

Finally, we keep an integer value frame to represent the current "frame" for the sprite's own movie. Some sprites are composed of multiple images or drawings, one for each frame of a small animation. This enables a sprite to appear to walk, emit fire, and so on.

It's time to put our Sprite class to work. Open the *Sprite.m* file in Xcode. Quartz likes to generate paths first, before filling them in. Add the following outlinePath: method to the Sprite class:

```
- (void) outlinePath: (CGContextRef) context
{
        // By default, just draw our box outline, assuming our center is at (0,0)

        CGFloat w2 = box.size.width*0.5;
        CGFloat h2 = box.size.height*0.5;

        CGContextBeginPath(context);
        CGContextMoveToPoint(context, -w2, h2);
        CGContextAddLineToPoint(context, w2, h2);
        CGContextAddLineToPoint(context, w2, -h2);
        CGContextAddLineToPoint(context, -w2, -h2);
        CGContextAddLineToPoint(context, -w2, h2);
        CGContextClosePath(context);
}
```

We use two new Quartz 2D functions: CGContextMoveToPoint and CGContextAddLineToPoint. Paths in Quartz 2D have the notion of the "current point" for sketching. The CGContextMoveToPoint function moves the current point to an (x,y) location, shown here as (-w2,-h2), where w2 is half the width of the bounding box and h2 is half the height. The CGContextAddLineToPoint function tells Quartz 2D to draw a line from the current point to a new (x,y) location, moving the current point to (x,y) as well. We make four such calls, drawing a rectangle centered at the origin, as shown in Figure 4–18.

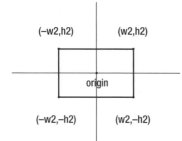

Figure 4–18. *The outline path of a sprite*

The outline path is the shape of the sprite's bounding box. It doesn't yet have the scale, rotation, or location information. Transformations do the math for us. We'll add color later, too. We do this in two steps, one draw method to set up the canvas and current color, invoking a second drawBody to do the actual drawing. First, let's add the method for drawBody, which will fill the path with our chosen r,g,b color and transparency alpha:

```
- (void) drawBody: (CGContextRef) context
{
        CGContextSetRGBFillColor(context, r, g, b, alpha);
        [self outlinePath: (context)];
        CGContextDrawPath(context,kCGPathFill);
}
```

This method uses the outline path and the Quartz 2D call CGContextDrawPath to fill it with the current color, just as we did with our green rectangle. Add just one more method to the Sprite class, draw:

```
- (void) draw: (CGContextRef) context
{
        CGContextSaveGState(context);

        // Position the sprite
        CGAffineTransform t = CGAffineTransformIdentity;
        t = CGAffineTransformTranslate(t,x,y);
        t = CGAffineTransformRotate(t,rotation);
        t = CGAffineTransformScale(t,scale,scale);
        CGContextConcatCTM(context, t);

        // Draw our body
        [self drawBody: context];

        CGContextRestoreGState(context);
}
```

Here, we encounter a bit of math and some peculiarities with Quartz 2D. Let's walk through it.

We first make a copy of the identity matrix CGAffineTransformIdentity in the local variable t. Think of this as the number 1 in multiplication. If you concatenate (multiply) the current matrix by the identity matrix, it leaves the current transformation unchanged—any number times 1 equals that number.

Next, we pass the matrix t to CGAffineTransformTranslate, creating a new matrix that will translate the canvas x units in the x direction, and our y units in the y direction. *Translate* is the mathematical term for movement along a given axis. We store the result of this translation back in our matrix t. This technique is called *chaining*, where we chain together multiple matrix transformations into one.

We chain the matrix t again, calling CGAffineTransformRotate, rotating our canvas by our sprite's rotation.

We chain the matrix one final time, calling CGAffineTransformScale, scaling our canvas by the scale of our sprite. This will ensure that a unit movement (1 pixel on our path) equals the appropriate units on our canvas.

Now here's the peculiar part. Our code executes three transformations in a row: a translation, a rotation, and a scale. The underlying mathematics, however, capture these in reverse order, much like a last-in-first-out stack in computer science. When Quartz applies the transformation matrix to drawing operations, the math essentially applies the transformations in the reverse order that we specified. Thus, our drawing operations will conduct the following transformations, in order:

1. Scale the drawing by the scale property.

2. Rotate the drawing by the rotation property.

3. Translate the drawing to the specified (x,y) location.

We write the code in reverse, first translating (step 3), then rotating (step 2), then scaling (step 3). We've conveniently located our outline path so that it centers at (0,0) of the canvas. In fact, all drawBody methods should center their drawing at (0,0). This way, when the canvas is spun in one direction or another by Quartz, our graphic spins about its center.

Quartz performs the affine transforms of draw as shown in Figure 4–19, correctly positioning the desired graphic on our iPhone screen.

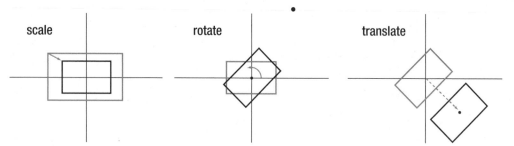

Figure 4–19. *The transformation sequence of the Sprite draw method*

Before we try out our sprite, let's tidy up the Sprite class by adding @synthesize definitions for all these attributes, and changing the init method to use some default values. Change the beginning of your Sprite class definition so that it looks like this, at the top of *Sprite.m*:

```
@implementation Sprite
@synthesize x,y,speed,angle,width,height,scale,frame,box,rotation,wrap,render;
@synthesize r,g,b,alpha,offScreen;
```

Objective-C will create methods that allow us to access sprite attributes with the dot syntax; for example, mySprite.speed becomes shorthand for [mySprite speed].

Next, replace the init method with the code shown in Listing 4–3.

Listing 4–3. *The Sprite init method, which chooses default values*

```
- (id) init
{
        self = [super init];
        if (self) {
                wrap = NO;
```

```
                x = y = 0.0;
                width = height = 1.0;
                scale = 1.0;
                speed = 0.0;
                angle = 0.0;
                rotation = 0;
                cosTheta = 1.0;
                sinTheta = 0.0;
                r = 1.0;
                g = 1.0;
                b = 1.0;
                alpha = 1.0;
                offScreen = NO;
                box = CGRectMake(0,0,0,0);
                frame = 0;
                render = YES;
        }
        return self;
}
```

Using the Sprite Class

Now we can see how our sprite works. Return to the definition of the AsteroidsView class. Update the header file (*AsteroidsView.h*), adding a new Sprite instance variable named test:

```
#import <UIKit/UIKit.h>
#import "Sprite.h"

@interface AsteroidsView : UIView {
        Sprite *test;
}

@end
```

Let's change the init routine of AsteroidsView so that we create a single sprite, just like the green rectangle from earlier. Open *AsteroidsView.m* and add the following initWithCoder method. This is the init method for windows created by Interface Builder.

```
- (id)initWithCoder: (NSCoder *) coder {
    if (self = [super initWithCoder: coder]) {
                // Initialization code
        test = [[Sprite alloc] init];
        test.x = 50;
        test.y = 100;
        test.width = 100;
        test.height = 200;
        test.r = 0.0;
        test.g = 1.0;
        test.b = 0.0;
    }
    return self;
}
```

We can use the drawing routines of our `Sprite` class, ditching the hard-coded routines from earlier. Change the `drawRect` of our `AsteroidsView` class in *AsteroidsView.m* to reflect this (the changes are shown in bold).

```
- (void)drawRect:(CGRect)rect {
    // Get a graphics context, saving its state
    CGContextRef context = UIGraphicsGetCurrentContext();
    CGContextSaveGState(context);

    // Reset the transformation
    CGAffineTransform t0 = CGContextGetCTM(context);
    t0 = CGAffineTransformInvert(t0);
    CGContextConcatCTM(context,t0);

    // Draw a green rectangle
    [test updateBox];
    [test draw: context];

    CGContextRestoreGState(context);
}
#
```

Don't forget to clean up after yourself, changing the `dealloc` method of the `AsteroidsView` class as follows:

```
- (void)dealloc {
    [test release];
    [super dealloc];
}
```

Compile and run `AsteroidsView`. You should see something familiar if all went well (see Figure 4–20).

Figure 4–20. *A Sprite version of our green rectangle*

It looks like nothing has changed! However, to the contrary, we have significantly more power at our disposal.

Let's change the drawRect routine of our AsteroidsView class. After the first rectangle is drawn, we'll move the test sprite, rotate it by 90 degrees, change its color to purple, scale it by 50%, and set its alpha transparency to 25%. We draw it a second time, using the sprite like a rubber stamp to produce another rectangle on our screen.

See Listing 4–4 for the new source code of drawRect, and Figure 4–21 for the resulting display. Quartz layers the sprites onto the canvas using the *painter's model* of 2D graphics. Basically, this means that items are layered in the order they're drawn, like painting with oils on a canvas. The green rectangle is drawn first; the purple, semitransparent purple rectangle is drawn second. You can see the green underneath the purple, creating a combined color.

Listing 4–4. *An updated drawRect routine*

```
- (void)drawRect:(CGRect)rect {
    // Get a graphics context, saving its state
    CGContextRef context = UIGraphicsGetCurrentContext();
    CGContextSaveGState(context);

    // Reset the transformation
    CGAffineTransform t0 = CGContextGetCTM(context);
    t0 = CGAffineTransformInvert(t0);
    CGContextConcatCTM(context,t0);

    // Draw a green rectangle
    [test updateBox];
    [test draw: context];

    // Draw it again, in purple, rotated
    test.x = 75;
    test.y = 100;
    test.r = 1.0;
    test.g = 0.0;
    test.b = 1.0;
    test.alpha = 0.25;
    test.scale = 0.5;
    test.rotation = 90;
    [test updateBox];
    [test draw: context];

    CGContextRestoreGState(context);

}
```

Figure 4–21. *Quartz 2D's painter's model demonstrated by the new drawRect code*

Which Way Is Up?

Our sprites look great in portrait mode, where the screen is vertical. Many games prefer landscape mode, providing a wider area for scrolling backgrounds, card tables, and two thumbs. Asteroids is one such game.

Changing to Landscape Orientation

Let's turn our iPhone into a landscape application and see what happens. Make the following change to the applicationDidFinishLaunching method of our AsteroidAppsDelegate class (see the source code in *AsteroidAppsDelegate.m*):

```
- (void)applicationDidFinishLaunching:(UIApplication *)application {

        [application setStatusBarOrientation: UIInterfaceOrientationLandscapeRight
animated:NO];
        [application setStatusBarHidden:YES animated:NO];
        [window addSubview:viewController.view];
        [window makeKeyAndVisible];
}
```

We call the setStatusBarOrientation method on our main application, specifying that we want landscape mode. We also make sure the status bar doesn't pop back up, asking that it remain hidden.

Compile and run the Asteroids application. Your screen should look like Figure 4–22.

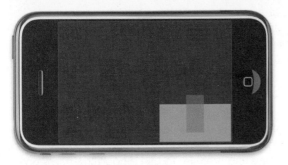

Figure 4–22. *The iPhone in landscape mode, with no changes*

If you look at this sideways, you'll see that nothing has changed. The green and purple rectangles are drawn as they were before, along the left edge, above the iPhone button. This is not what we want. Instead, we expect to see the green rectangle in the lower left of the display, regardless of orientation. We can fix this with transformations on the Quartz context. We keep the same coordinates for our objects. We turn the virtual canvas to suit our needs.

Replace the draw method in *Sprite.m* with the following code:

```
- (void) draw: (CGContextRef) context
{
        CGContextSaveGState(context);

        // Position the sprite
        CGAffineTransform t = CGAffineTransformIdentity;
        t = CGAffineTransformTranslate(t,y,480-x);
        t = CGAffineTransformRotate(t,rotation - 3.141592*0.5);
        t = CGAffineTransformScale(t,scale,scale);
        CGContextConcatCTM(context, t);

        [self drawBody: context];

        CGContextRestoreGState(context);
}
```

Compile and run the application. Your screen should now look like Figure 4–23.

Figure 4–23. *Landscape mode, corrected through affine transformations*

We left the scale the same. That doesn't change when we shift from landscape to portrait mode. We decrease the rotation angle by -90 degrees, to offset the iPhone landscape rotation of +90 degrees. Finally, we reverse the y and x values, offsetting x from 480 to make everything line up.

Centering the Origin

So far, we've been using the lower-left corner of the display as the origin of our game coordinate system. The Asteroids game starts with a ship in the center, fending off rocks and ships that come from all angles. You may find it easier to use a coordinate system where the origin is in the center of the display, with x increasing to the right and y increasing toward the top, as shown in Figure 4–24.

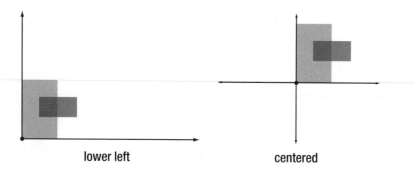

lower left   centered

Figure 4–24. *Centering the origin in landscape mode*

We accomplish this by adjusting our transform. Here is a version of the Sprite draw method that centers the origin in landscape mode:

```
- (void) draw: (CGContextRef) context
{
        CGContextSaveGState(context);

        // Position the sprite
        CGAffineTransform t = CGAffineTransformIdentity;
        t = CGAffineTransformTranslate(t,y+160,240-x);
        t = CGAffineTransformRotate(t,rotation - 3.141592*0.5);
        t = CGAffineTransformScale(t,scale,scale);
        CGContextConcatCTM(context, t);

        [self drawBody: context];
        CGContextRestoreGState(context);
}
```

Change the draw method in *Sprite.m*, recompile, and run the application. You'll see the rectangles shift to the center, as indicated by the "centered" coordinate system in Figure 4–24. A sample output is shown in Figure 4–25.

Figure 4–25. *Two sprites on a landscape coordinate system centered in the display*

If this seems confusing, don't worry. It is! We just have to get it right once, add the transforms to our core `Sprite` class, and then forget about it. I usually add methods to my game controller to sense the device orientation, as follows:

```
UIDeviceOrientation orient = [[UIDevice currentDevice] orientation];
```

The value of `orient` will be one of the following:

- `UIDeviceOrientationUnknown`: Unknown, assume no rotation
- `UIDeviceOrientationPortrait`: No rotation
- `UIDeviceOrientationPortraitUpsideDown`: 180 degree rotation
- `UIDeviceOrientationLandscapeLeft`: 90 degree rotation
- `UIDeviceOrientationLandscapeRight`: –90 degree rotation
- `UIDeviceOrientationFaceUp`: Unknown rotation
- `UIDeviceOrientationFaceDown`: Unknown rotation

Good interface designs are simple and intuitive. I recommend that you only use two orientations for drawing, the ones included in this chapter: portrait and landscape right. It's up to you whether to place the origin at the lower left or use the center. I prefer the center. The math is cleaner in code.

If you have made it this far, congratulations! The bulk of the math is behind us. We'll now look at three subclasses of `Sprite`: one for vector art, another for images, and a third for text.

Vector Art

Our green and purple rectangles can also be called *vector art*. In fact, a popular display at the Museum of Modern Art in New York City shows just that: large green, purple, and red rectangles. It's an acquired taste.

Vector art uses the drawing routines of Quartz 2D to draw lines, curves, and polygons. These shapes can be filled with color using other Quartz 2D API calls. Vector art scales nicely, producing smooth edges and curves regardless of the scale.

Creating the VectorSprite Class

Figure 4–26 shows vector art for a spaceship suitable for Asteroids. Let's figure out how to make these come alive with a new class, VectorSprite. We'll keep the drawings simple to focus on the use of Quartz 2D.

Figure 4–26. *Vector art for a spaceship*

Return to your Asteroids project in Xcode. Create a new class named VectorSprite as a subclass of NSObject (see Figure 4–27), placing it in the Classes group.

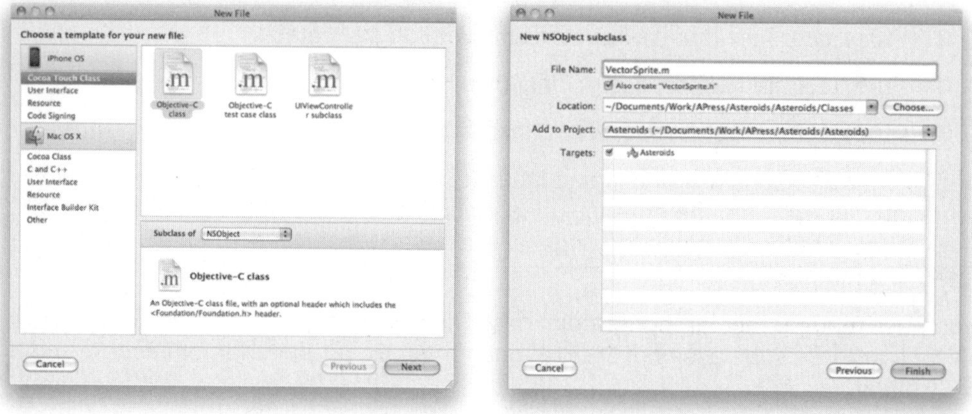

![New File dialog screenshots showing template selection and NSObject subclass options]

Figure 4–27. *Creating a new VectorSprite class*

Change the contents of *VectorSprite.h* to the following:

```
#import <Foundation/Foundation.h>
#include "Sprite.h"

@interface VectorSprite : Sprite {
        CGFloat *points;
        int count;
        CGFloat vectorScale;7
}
```

```
@property (assign) int count;
@property (assign) CGFloat vectorScale;
@property (assign) CGFloat *points;
+ (VectorSprite *) withPoints: (CGFloat *) rawPoints count: (int) count;
- (void) updateSize;
@end
```

The VectorSprite class is a subclass of the Sprite class we just created. It will inherit the drawing operations, transformations, and all those nifty parameters to describe how a sprite moves and positions itself in space.

We add a few new instance variables to capture the vector art:

```
CGFloat *points;
int count;
```

We're going to assume that art is quite simple—just a set of connected lines in 2D that form one polygon. The points variable is an array of floating-point values, stored in a compact array in memory. The edges of our line segments are stored in order, (x0, y0), (x1, y1), ..., , (xn, yn) for all n points. The integer count records the number of point pairs. Figure 4–28 shows an example of how points are laid out in memory with a count of 4.

We then make points an assignable property rather than a retained property, assuming someone else will worry about managing their memory usage:

```
@property (assign) CGFloat *points;
@property (assign) int count;
```

Why? We could have dozens of sprites that all share the same design. There's no sense duplicating this data and wasting precious memory on the iPhone.

We can vary the size of the art by paying attention to the scale property in our parent Sprite class. This introduces the last instance variable, vectorScale. Often, we'll want art to get small or large, but keep the lines the same size. Think of multiple rocks within an Asteroids game, floating in space, all of various sizes. If we relied on the canvas to scale our art, the line thickness would scale just as well. Multiplying the size of our art by five would produce lines that are five times thicker! That's clearly not what we want. To keep our interface clean, we'll override the default scale routines in Sprite. Let's do that now.

Add the setScale and updateSize methods shown in Listing 4–5 to the VectorSprite class in *VectorSprite.m*. The first of these overrides the dot-method for size in Sprite. We intercept the attempt to change the native size. We store the value in vectorScale instead, calling an updateSize routine to figure out our sprite's new width and height.

Listing 4–5. *Overriding changes to scale in VectorSprite.m*

```
@synthesize points, count, vectorScale;

- (void) setScale: (CGFloat) s
{
        self.vectorScale = s;
        scale = 1.0;
        [self updateSize];
}

- (void) updateSize
```

```
{
        CGFloat w,h,minX,minY,maxX,maxY;
        w = h;
        minX = minY = maxX = maxY = 0.0;
        for (int i=0; i < count; i++) {
                CGFloat x1 = points[i*2]*vectorScale;
                CGFloat y1 = points[i*2+1]*vectorScale;
                if (x1 < minX) minX = x1;
                if (x1 > maxX) maxX = x1;
                if (y1 < minY) minY = y1;
                if (y1 > maxY) maxY = y1;
        }
        width = ceil(maxX - minX);
        height = ceil(maxY - minY);
}
```

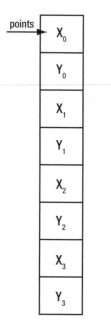

Figure 4–28. *An array of points within a VectorSprite*

Every vector sprite will need a set of points, and these are often shared. Let's create a class-wide method that will take a constant array of points and return a VectorSprite that uses them. Add the following withPoints:count: method to the VectorSprite class in *VectorSprite.m*:

```
+ (VectorSprite *) withPoints: (CGFloat *) rawPoints count: (int) count
{
        VectorSprite *v = [[VectorSprite alloc] init];
        v.count = count;
        v.points = rawPoints;
        v.vectorScale = 1.0;
```

```
        [v updateSize];
        return v;
}
```

With a set of points, scale, width and height, we're ready to draw something on the screen. We'll replace the default Sprite method for creating a path with our own. Add the following outlinePath method to the VectorSprite class in *VectorSprite.m*:

```
- (void) outlinePath: (CGContextRef) context
{
        CGContextBeginPath(context);
        CGContextSetRGBStrokeColor(context, r, g, b, alpha);
        for (int i=0; i < count; i++) {
                CGFloat x1 = points[i*2]*vectorScale;
                CGFloat y1 = points[i*2+1]*vectorScale;
                if (i == 0) {
                        CGContextMoveToPoint(context, x1, y1);
                }
                else {
                        CGContextAddLineToPoint(context, x1, y1);
                }
        }

        CGContextClosePath(context);
}
```

You've seen these Quartz 2D API calls before, when we created our green and purple rectangles. This time, we're generalizing our code to use an arbitrary set of points, connecting them together into a single polygon, and then filling them as before. It's time to test it.

Using the VectorSprite Class

Open the definition for our view, *AsteroidsView.m*. Make sure to import the definition for our newly created VectorSprite class, and then change the initWithCoder routine to use a VectorSprite instead of the default Sprite. Leave everything else unchanged. Remember that our VectorSprite is a subclass of Sprite, and should behave just as our rectangles did. All we've done is change how the sprite is stored and how its outline is drawn. See Listing 4–6 for the changes to the top of *AsteroidsView.m*.

Listing 4–6. *A revised AsteroidsView class that uses a VectorSprite to draw rectangles*

```
#import "AsteroidsView.h"
#import "VectorSprite.h"

@implementation AsteroidsView

#define kVectorArtCount 4
static CGFloat kVectorArt[] = {
        -50,100,  50,100,  50,-100,  -50,-100,
};

- (id) initWithCoder: (NSCoder *) coder {
        if (self = [super initWithCoder: coder]) {
                test = [VectorSprite withPoints: kVectorArt count: kVectorArtCount];
```

```
            test.scale = 1.0;
            test.x = 50;
            test.y = 100;
            test.r = 0.0;
            test.g = 1.0;
            test.b = 0.0;
            test.alpha = 1.0;
        }
        return self;
    }
```

With these changes, you should see our familiar rectangles in the centered coordinate system, as shown in Figure 4–29.

Figure 4–29. *A VectorSprite version of our dual rectangles*

The rectangles display as before. We've moved the hard-coded points into an external array of data. Note how the data is arranged so that the VectorSprite points are centered at (0,0). We have specified the first point as (-50,100), or the upper left of our green rectangle, centered at (0,0). The second point is (50,100), moving to the right on the x axis, but staying at the top of the y. We drop down to the lower right (50,-100), and then back to the lower left (-50,-100). Quartz 2D closes the path for us.

The data for *every* shape in our game must be centered at (0,0). This enables us to share common matrix transformations with all sprites. We use the x, y, rotation, and scale attributes to position them on the display. We *do not* use points for this. Instead, the points are like a Quartz 2D path—a generalized version of the vector art that we can reposition, scale, and rotate to our heart's content.

Let's put our first pair of asteroids on the screen. Change the points in the kVectorArt array to the following, then compile. You should see two asteroids in place of the rectangles, as shown in Figure 4–30.

```
#define kVectorArtCount 12
static CGFloat kVectorArt[] = {
        -7,12, 1,9, 8,12, 15,5, 8,3, 15,-4, 8,-12,
        -3,-10, -6,-12, -14,-7, -10,0, -14,5
};
```

Figure 4–30. *Tiny green and purple asteroids courtesy of VectorSprite*

The source code for Asteroids (in *asteroids.tar.gz*) demonstrates other tricks you can do with a VectorSprite. Here, we've used a simple, solid fill color. The Asteroids code includes a gradient fill, outlining the objects in white. I'll spare you the details of creating a gradient, which is the subject of a more advanced book on Quartz 2D. Instead, let's peek at the drawBody method for VectorSprite within the full Asteroids game:

```
- (void) drawBody:(CGContextRef)context
{
        [self outlinePath: context];                      (1)
        CGContextDrawPath(context,kCGPathFillStroke);

        [self outlinePath: context];                      (2)
        CGContextClip(context);                            (3)
        [self gradientFill: context];                      (4)
}
```

As labeled in the listing, this code works as follows:

1. We draw the outline path, but tell Quartz 2D to just fill the stroke of the path. Think of the stroke as a pen, following along the points of the path.

2. We create another copy of the outline path.

3. We turn the current path into a *clipping region.* Once a clipping region has been set in Quartz 2D, all subsequent draw operations are *clipped* if they fall outside the path area. Clipping cuts off a drawing at the edges of the path.

4. We call a routine to draw a large splotch of gradient color. This gives rocks with a bit more texture, as shown in Figure 4–31.

Figure 4–31. *Vector sprites for a ship and rocks, drawn with a gradient fill and white edges*

A production game will use more elaborate vector graphics—potentially multiple polygons in several colors, each with a particular shading technique. Still, the basic design is the same as the one shown here. VectorSprite instances are subclasses of Sprite, referring to a set of shared data points.

Some art can be quite complicated, with hundreds of polygons and dozens of layers, plus shading effects like dropped shadows, gradients, and blends. Drawing these 30 times a second in Quartz 2D is just not possible. In these cases, we need to use bitmap images for our sprites. We'll cover that next.

> **NOTE:** In Chapters 6 through 8, Ben Smith will introduce OpenGL, a layer in the iPhone beneath Quartz 2D, closer to the metal of the graphics processor. OpenGL is happy to draw polygons with hundreds of points at game speed.

Flipbook Animations

Over two centuries ago, flipbook animations were an inspiration for the original motion picture. Figure 4–32 contains two flipbooks, where the individual pages are laid out in a grid. The animation on the left mimics what we're doing here – app construction. It depicts a construction worker walking in four different directions, one direction per row. Let's call him Mario. The flipbook on the right shows a two-frame animation for buttons in our Asteroids app: a thrust button, a button for rotating left, a button for rotating right, and a final button for firing missiles. Since buttons can get a tad dull, we'll instead create a small diversion and make Mario come alive. We'll have him walk about our screen, as if on break from hours of coding. The Asteroids game we review at the end of the chapter will animate the buttons, a simpler version of what we'll now describe.

Figure 4–32. *The modern flipbook: a sprite atlas*

Creating the AtlasSprite Class

Let's first dispense with some basic terminology common to all games. A single image that contains multiple frames of an animation is called a *sprite atlas*. The simplest atlas uses a fixed size for each frame, arranging them neatly into rows and columns. Frames are numbered from 0 at the upper left, reading from left to right, and then down the atlas, as shown in Figure 4-32 and illustrated in Figure 4–33.

0	1	2	3	4	5
6	7	8	9	10	11
12	13	14	15	16	17
18	19	20	21	22	23

frame numbering

Figure 4–33. *Frame numbering within a grid*

Time to cut some code.

Return to the Asteroids project in Xcode. Create a new file in the Classes group, a subclass of NSObject. Call it *AtlasSprite.m*, as shown in Figure 4–34.

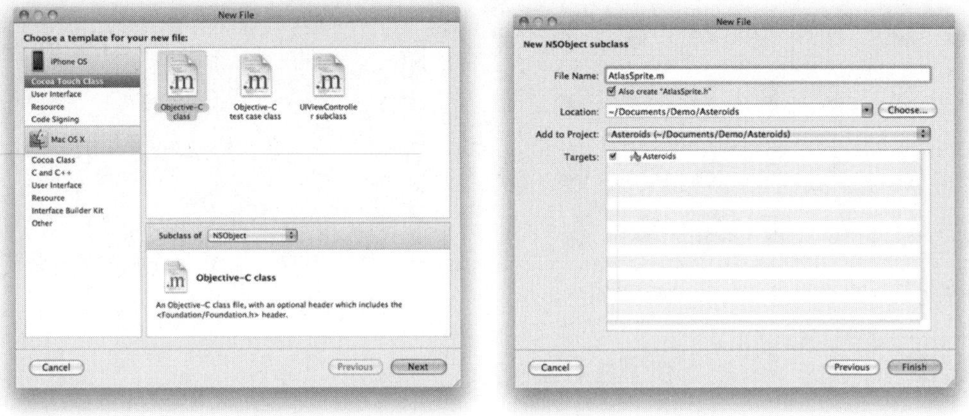

Figure 4–34. *Creating a new AtlasSprite class*

Replace the contents of *AtlasSprite.h* with the class definition shown in Listing 4–7.

Listing 4–7. *The AtlasSprite class definition in AtlasSprite.h*

```
#import <Foundation/Foundation.h>
#import "Sprite.h"

@interface AtlasSprite : Sprite {
        CGFloat w2;                     // half width, for caching
        CGFloat h2;                     // half height, for caching
        CGFloat atlasWidth;             // as it says
        CGFloat atlasHeight;
        UIImage *atlas;                 // atlas containing all images of this sprite
        CGImageRef image;               // a Quartz reference to the image
        CGRect clipRect;                // a clip rectangle
        int rows;                       // how many rows are in the atlas
        int columns;                    // how many columns are in the atlas
}

@property (assign) CGFloat w2, h2, atlasWidth, atlasHeight;
@property (assign) CGRect clipRect;
@property (assign) int rows, columns;
@property (retain, nonatomic) UIImage *atlas;
@property (assign) CGImageRef image;

+ (AtlasSprite *) fromFile: (NSString *) fname withRows: (int) rows withColumns: (int)
columns;
+ (NSMutableDictionary *) sharedSpriteAtlas;
+ (UIImage *) getSpriteAtlas: (NSString *) name;

@end
```

Here, you see a few new items from Quartz 2D. CGImageRef is a pointer to an internal structure in Quartz that holds all the display information for an image. You used UIImage in the previous chapter, where images were created in Interface Builder. We'll be using UIImage to quickly read from a file, digging inside the structure to pull out a CGImageRef.

We'll build a convenience function at the class level, `fromfile:withRows:withColumns`, for building an atlas sprite from a single image. This method will take an input file name, plus the number of rows and columns in the sprite image. The class figures out all the rest.

The class will assume that a single image is shared by multiple sprites, much like the `VectorSprite` class assumed vector data was shared.

Open the *AtlasSprite.m* file. We'll create a shared dictionary to store all the images needed by our sprites. Add the following methods to the `AtlasSprite` implementation, plus the Objective-C directives to expose our data, at the top of *AtlasSprite.m*.

```
@implementation AtlasSprite
@synthesize rows,columns;
@synthesize image, atlas, atlasWidth, atlasHeight, clipRect, w2, h2;

+(NSMutableDictionary *) sharedSpriteAtlas
{
        static NSMutableDictionary *sharedSpriteDictionary;
        @synchronized(self)
        {
                if (!sharedSpriteDictionary) {
                        sharedSpriteDictionary = [[NSMutableDictionary alloc] init];
                        return sharedSpriteDictionary;
                }
        }
        return sharedSpriteDictionary;
}
```

The `sharedSpriteAtlas` method synchronizes access to a static variable, which we use to store a common NSMutableDictionary. If the dictionary doesn't exist, we create it— once. This is a common technique for implementing singletons, object-oriented-speak for (gasp) global variables.

Now we need a class method to look up an image by its short file name. Add the following method to your `AtlasSprite` class:

```
+ (UIImage *) getSpriteAtlas: (NSString *) name
{
        NSMutableDictionary *d = [AtlasSprite sharedSpriteAtlas];
        UIImage *img = [d objectForKey: name];
        if (!img) {
                img = [[UIImage alloc]
                        initWithContentsOfFile: [[NSBundle mainBundle]
                                pathForResource:name ofType:nil]];
                [d setObject: img forKey: name];
        }
        return img;
}
```

The class method `getSpriteAtlas` takes a file name as an argument. It first checks whether the file name has an associated UIImage pointer in the shared dictionary. If so, the pointer is returned. If not, the method looks for the file name in the global application bundle, creating a UIImage and storing it in the dictionary, and then returns it. This is referred to as *image caching* in the previous chapter.

Let's create the main convenience function of our `AtlasSprite` class:

```
+ (AtlasSprite *) fromFile: (NSString *) fname withRows: (int) rows withColumns: (int)
columns
{
        AtlasSprite *s = [[AtlasSprite alloc] init];
        s.atlas = [[AtlasSprite getSpriteAtlas: fname] retain];
        CGImageRef img = [s.atlas CGImage];
        s.image = img;

        int width = CGImageGetWidth(s.image);
        int height = CGImageGetHeight(s.image);
        if (rows < 1) rows = 1;
        if (columns < 1) columns = 1;
        s.atlasWidth = width;
        s.atlasHeight = height;
        s.rows = rows;
        s.columns = columns;
        s.width = round(width/s.columns);
        s.height = round(height/s.rows);
        s.w2 = s.width*0.5;
        s.h2 = s.height*0.5;
        s.clipRect = CGRectMake(-s.width*0.5,-s.height*0.5,s.width,s.height);
        return s;
}
```

The first two lines allocate an `AtlasSprite` and retrieve the atlas image from the shared dictionary. The first bold line sends the `CGImage` message to the `UIImage` object, giving us a `CGImageRef` handle. This is a C structure and cannot receive Objective-C messages. We store it locally.

The next few lines extract the dimensions of the image, using the Quartz methods `CGImageGetWidth` and `CGImageGetHeight`. Note that we don't need a context in these API calls, as we did for other Quartz 2D calls. That indicates that we're asking for data or activities that are unaffected by transformations. We want the raw, original size of our image.

After we extract the atlas's width and height, we use a bit of arithmetic to calculate the width and height of a single sprite image. We store these values in the newly created `AtlasSprite` image. We cache splitting the dimensions in half, as we'll need these values for every draw operation. Pay close attention to this line:

```
s.clipRect = CGRectMake(-s.width*0.5,-s.height*0.5,s.width,s.height);
```

Recognize this? We're creating a rectangle, centered at (0,0). The upper left is (-w/2,-h/2) and it extends the full width and height of a single sprite. This rectangle has the same dimensions as the default outline path in our `Sprite` class, shown in Figure 4–17. We're going to use this rectangle to clip out a section of the sprite atlas. The magic occurs in the `drawBody` method of `AtlasSprite`. Add that now to *AtlasSprite.m*:

```
- (void) drawBody: (CGContextRef) context
{
        int r0 = floor(frame/columns);
        int c0 = frame-columns*r0;
        CGFloat u = c0*width + w2;                              // (u,v) center of sprite frame
```

```
        CGFloat v = atlasHeight - (r0*height + h2);        // within the atlas

        // clip our image from the atlas
        CGContextBeginPath(context);
        CGContextAddRect(context, clipRect);
        CGContextClip(context);

        // draw the atlas
        CGContextDrawImage(context, CGRectMake(-u,-v,atlasWidth,atlasHeight), image);
}
```

The drawBody method first computes the center of our current frame within the sprite atlas. We label its x coordinate u and its y coordinate v. You'll learn more about (u,v) coordinates in the chapters on OpenGL.

Next, we set up the path centered at (0,0). We tell Quartz that we want to clip everything that falls outside this smaller rectangle.

Finally, we draw the image using CGContextDrawImage. This method expects an image reference, which we have, as well as a rectangle on which to draw the image.

We need to be careful. Quartz will scale the existing image to fit the rectangle. Since we have all the scaling we need in the base Sprite class, we draw the entire sprite atlas at the given width and height. The trick here is to *shift* the sprite atlas to (-u,-v). That centers the frame we want at (0,0). Figure 4–35 shows this technique for the (u,v) coordinates of frame 16 in the construction worker atlas. The clipping path is also centered at (0,0).

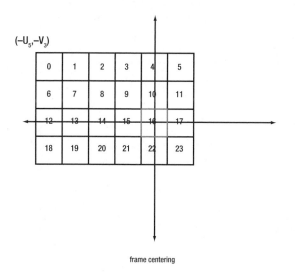

frame centering

Figure 4–35. *AtlasSprite centers a frame, clipping to the rectangular area*

Now for some housekeeping. Change the init method of AtlasSprite to set some default values, and clean up after ourselves in the dealloc method in *AtlasSprite.m*:

```
- (id) init
{
        self = [super init];
        if (self) {
                rows = 0.0;
                columns = 0.0;
        }
        return self;
}

- (void) dealloc
{
        [atlas release];
        CGImageRelease(image);
        [super dealloc];
}
```

The dealloc method introduces CGImageRelease, the Quartz 2D API call for releasing a
CGImageRef handle. Images can eat up a lot of memory, so it's important to make sure
you allocate and release images carefully. That's all we need for the atlas sprite. Now
let's animate one, making Mario run around our iPhone screen.

Modifying the Sprite Class

We'll need to upgrade the base Sprite class, finally using those angle, speed, cosTheta
and sinTheta values with simple trigonometry in the tic method (see Listing 4–8). This
method will be called with every tick of the game clock. We'll upgrade the bounding box
calculations as well, checking whether the sprite has moved off the screen, wrapping it
across edges if necessary (also in Listing 4–8).

Listing 4–8. *Changes to the Sprite class in the Sprite.m file*

```
#define kScreenWidth 320
#define kScreenHeight 480

- (void) updateBox
{
        CGFloat w = width*scale;
        CGFloat h = height*scale;
        CGFloat w2 = w*0.5;
        CGFloat h2 = h*0.5;
        CGPoint origin = box.origin;
        CGSize bsize = box.size;
        CGFloat left = -kScreenHeight*0.5;
        CGFloat right = -left;
        CGFloat top = kScreenWidth*0.5;
        CGFloat bottom = -top;

        offScreen = NO;
        if (wrap) {
                if ((x+w2) < left) x = right + w2;
                else if ((x-w2) > right) x = left - w2;
                else if ((y+h2) < bottom) y = top + h2;
                else if ((y-h2) > top) y = bottom - h2;
        }
```

```
        else {
                offScreen =
                ((x+w2) < left) ||
                ((x-w2) > right) ||
                ((y+h2) < bottom) ||
                ((y-h2) > top);
        }

        origin.x = x-w2*scale;
        origin.y = y-h2*scale;
        bsize.width = w;
        bsize.height = h;
        box.origin = origin;
        box.size = bsize;
}

- (void) tic: (NSTimeInterval) dt
{
        if (!render) return;

        CGFloat sdt = speed*dt;
        x += sdt*cosTheta;
        y += sdt*sinTheta;
        if (sdt) [self updateBox];
}
```

> **NOTE:** The updateBox method as shown handles only landscape mode on the iPhone. It's left as an exercise for the reader to upgrade this method for portrait mode or other coordinate systems.

With this code in place, *all* sprites know how to move themselves. We send the sprite a tic message, along with an interval of time in seconds. The default action advances the x and y position along the angle of motion, and then updates the bounding box for later collision or off-screen detection.

Using the AtlasSprite Class

The final changes we need are a timer and an atlas sprite, updating the atlas sprite at each tic, rendering it on screen. We start with Mario at the center, facing right. We choose a random angle and send Mario along his way. When he hits an edge (offscreen becomes true), we calculate the angle back to the center of the screen. We then add a random bounce angle, back in the general direction of the screen center, +/- a few degrees. This logic normally sits in a game controller. We'll cheat for now and make the changes in *AsteroidsView.m*, as shown in Listing 4–9. We'll also change the background color of our view to white, creating a sense of being "behind the scenes" of our app. Mario will be walking back and forth in this white wasteland.

Listing 4–9. *Changes to AsteroidsView.m to demonstrate animation with AtlasSprite*

```
#define RANDOM_SEED() srandom(time(NULL))
#define RANDOM_INT(__MIN__, __MAX__) ((__MIN__) + random() % ((__MAX__+1) - (__MIN__)))
```

```
// Some constants for our motion
#define kSteps 8
#define kSpeed 300
#define kFPS 20.0
#define kBounce 30
#define kDirForward 0
#define kDirBackward 1
#define kDirUp 2
#define kDirDown 3

// Some Mario walking animations, using frame numbers
static int kForward[]  = {0,1,2,3,4,5,6,7};
static int kUpward[]   = {8,9,10,11,12,13,14,15};
static int kDownward[] = {16,17,18,19,20,21,22,23};
static int kBackward[] = {24,25,26,27,28,29,30,31};

- (id) initWithCoder: (NSCoder *) coder {
        if (self = [super initWithCoder: coder]) {
                test = [AtlasSprite fromFile: @"mario.png" withRows: 4 withColumns: 8];
                test.angle = 0;
                test.speed = kSpeed;
                direction = kDirForward;
                self.backgroundColor = [UIColor whiteColor];
                timer = [NSTimer scheduledTimerWithTimeInterval: 1.0/kFPS
                                                target:self
                                                selector:@selector(gameLoop)
                                                userInfo:nil
                                                repeats:YES];
        }
        return self;
}

- (void) gameLoop
{
        frame = (frame+1)%kSteps;
        [test tic: 1.0/kFPS];

        // If we run offscreen, head back to the center of the screen
        // +/- kBounce degrees. Pick our new animation using the angle of walk.
        if (test.offScreen) {
                RANDOM_SEED();
                int toCenter = round(atan2(-test.y,-test.x)*180.0/3.141592);
                if (toCenter < 0) toCenter += 360;
                int bounce = (toCenter+RANDOM_INT(-kBounce,kBounce))%360;
                if (bounce <= 60 || bounce >= 300) direction = kDirForward;
                else if (bounce > 60 && bounce < 120) direction = kDirUp;
                else if (bounce >= 120 && bounce <= 240) direction = kDirBackward;
                else direction = kDirDown;
                test.angle = bounce;
                test.scale = 0.4+1.6*RANDOM_INT(0,10)/10.0;
                while (test.offScreen) [test tic: 1.0/kFPS];
        }

        // Choose the appropriate frame for our motion.
        switch (direction) {
```

```
                case kDirForward:                     test.frame = kForward[frame];
break;
                case kDirBackward:          test.frame = kBackward[frame]; break;
                case kDirUp:                test.frame = kUpward[frame]; break;
                case kDirDown:              test.frame = kDownward[frame]; break;
        }
        [self setNeedsDisplay];  // We need to be rendered, please.
}

- (void)drawRect:(CGRect)rect {
        // Get a graphics context, saving its state
        CGContextRef context = UIGraphicsGetCurrentContext();
        CGContextSaveGState(context);

        // Reset the transformation
        CGAffineTransform t0 = CGContextGetCTM(context);
        t0 = CGAffineTransformInvert(t0);
        CGContextConcatCTM(context,t0);

        [test draw: context];

        CGContextRestoreGState(context);

}

- (void)dealloc {
        [test release];
        [timer invalidate];
    [super dealloc];
}
```

The code in Listing 4–9 requires a new instance variable, holding the current animation state and frame number. Make the following changes to *AsteroidsView.h*:

```
@interface AsteroidsView : UIView {
        Sprite *test;
        NSTimer *timer;
        int frame;
        int direction;
}
```

The source for the Mario sprite image (*mario.jpg*) is found in both the *asteroids.tar.gz* and *figures.tar.gz* source code for this chapter. You will need to add this to the Resources group in Xcode.

The code describes motion with an array of frame values, tracking the motion name with a state variable, direction. Four such motions are defined:

```
#define kDirForward 0
#define kDirBackward 1
#define kDirUp 2
#define kDirDown 3

static int kForward[] =  {0,1,2,3,4,5,6,7};
static int kUpward[] =   {8,9,10,11,12,13,14,15};
static int kDownward[] = {16,17,18,19,20,21,22,23};
static int kBackward[] = {24,25,26,27,28,29,30,31};
```

The forward (kForward) motion starts at frame zero (0), with Mario standing straight. It advances to frame 7,showing Mario walking to the right as he swings his hammer back and forth. The frames are drawn by Reiner "Tiles" Prokein, a generous character animator in Germany with numerous free animations. See http://bit.ly/PzclV for many more.

Reiner has carefully designed the last frame of each animated walk so that it flows seamlessly back to the initial frame (0). We advance frames in the app by incrementing a frame counter, using modulo (%) arithmetic to wrap the number between 0 and kSteps – 1.

```
frame = (frame+1)%kSteps;
```

The code also changes Mario's size every time he runs off screen. The size starts at 40% of the sprite size and scales randomly up to 200%. Since this can move him quite a bit, and we don't want the offscreen flag to keep firing, we run a while loop, waiting for him to reappear before continuing:

```
test.scale = 0.4+1.6*RANDOM_INT(0,10)/10.0;
while (test.offScreen) [test tic: 1.0/kFPS];
```

The sprite's speed is specified in pixels per second. We want him moving rather quickly, so we set this to 300 pixels per second:

```
#define kSpeed 300
```

To summarize, here's what we did in the last several pages:

■ Created a sprite atlas and stored it in the project's Resources group.

■ Added AtlasSprite as a subclass of Sprite. The drawBody method extracts the current frame through clipping and translation.

■ Upgraded Sprite to support motion at every tic, updating the bounding box, setting the offscreen flag or wrapping around edges.

■ Upgraded AsteroidsView by adding a timer, an AtlasSprite, and a gameLoop method that causes Mario to bounce around the screen.

That gives us Mario, as shown in Figure 4–36!

Figure 4–36. Mario walks aimlessly around the iPhone, bouncing off edges and changing size, all courtesy of AtlasSprite and an updated AsteroidsView class.

Atlas sprites are powerful. They pick up where vector sprites fall short. However, sometimes you'll need to display text to the user. Most games have heads-up displays that show the current score, the number of lives or time left, and other critical statistics. Creating all these with atlas sprites is possible yet tedious. Quartz 2D provides a rich set of libraries for drawing text from local fonts. We might as well use it. In the next section, you'll learn how to use Quartz fonts within the sprite framework we've begun to build.

Heads-Up Displays

Quartz 2D has rich font support—on the desktop. The iPhone is limited to a small set of preloaded fonts, probably to keep the local storage to a minimum and to stay within tight design constraints. Designers are passionate about fonts. Spend a few minutes Googling for "Comic Sans" to get a taste. The simple font shown in Figure 4-37 seems to drive designers batty, with font-hating groups, t-shirts, and hilarious cartoons that humiliate fans of Comic Sans. Will we ever see Comic Sans on the iPhone? You must be crazy.

ABCDEFGHIJKLMNO
PQRSTUVWXYZÀÅÉ
ÎÕØÜabcdefghijklmn
opqrstuvwxyzàåéîõøü
&1234567890($£.,!?)

Figure 4–37. Fonts are limited on the iPhone. And there's no Comic Sans.

I've found it safe to stick with Arial and Helvetica—nice clean fonts without messy serifs at the edges. We'll wrap the Quartz 2D font API in a nice little sprite, enabling us to rotate, scale, colorize, and move the text around on the screen.

Ready? Let's cut some code.

Creating the TextSprite Class

Use Xcode to create a new class, TextSprite, as a subclass of NSObject. Place it in the Classes group as you've done with our other sprite classes. Figure 4–38 should look familiar.

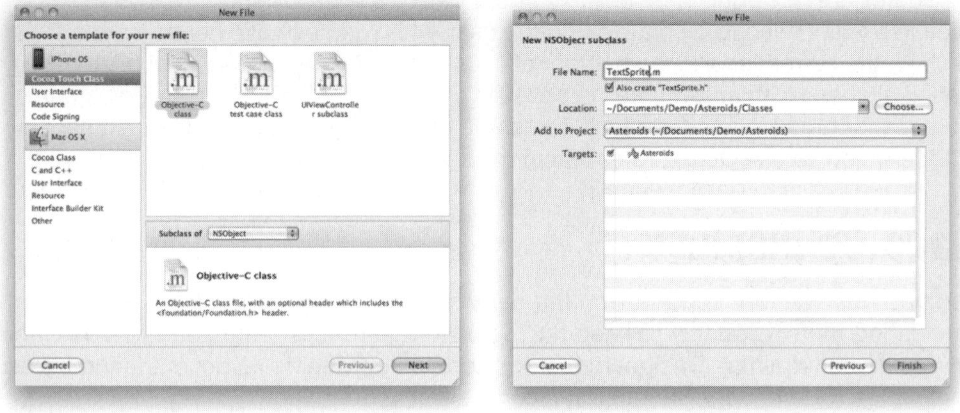

Figure 4–38. *Creating a new TextSprite class*

Replace the generated code in *TextSprite.h* with the following class definition for our TextSprite class:

```
#import <Foundation/Foundation.h>
#import "Sprite.h"

@interface TextSprite : Sprite {
        NSString *text;
        NSString *font;
        uint fontSize;
        uint textLength;
}

@property (assign) NSString *text;
@property (assign) NSString *font;
@property (assign) uint fontSize;

+ (TextSprite *) withString: (NSString *) label;
- (void) moveUpperLeftTo: (CGPoint) p;
- (void) newText: (NSString *) val;

@end
```

TextSprite is a subclass of Sprite, as are AtlasSprite and VectorSprite. Here, we store two strings: text will contain the string we want to display, and font will contain the name of the Quartz 2D font we want to use. The iPhone allows the following font names, which I've shown here as NSString constants you can use for the font instance variable:

- @"Arial"
- @"Helvetica"
- @"Georgia"
- @"Courier New"
- @"Marker Felt"

- @"Times New Roman"

- @"Trebuchet MS"

- @"Verdana"

- @"Zapfino"

TextSprite retains the desired fontSize in points, and caches the number of characters in the current text as textLength. Both of these values are used every time text is rendered, so we cache them to prevent needless calls to the length method of NSString.

We support a convenience class function, TextSprite withString: @"", for creating text sprites directly from an NSString resource. Since the text is often used for heads-up displays, where values change frequently, we supply a newText method for changing the underlying string. Finally, we provide a moveUpperLeftTo: method for positioning the upper-left corner of a text string on the display. All the other sprites were positioned at the center. I find text is easier to grab onto the left edge and move it around in code.

Let's jump to the implementation of the TextSprite class. Open *TextSprite.m* and replace the generated code with a new init routine and our convenience method for creating text sprites. Here, we'll set some default values.

```
#import "TextSprite.h"
#define kDefaultFont      @"Helvetica"
#define kDefaultFontSize       14

@implementation TextSprite
@synthesize text, font, fontSize;

- (id) init
{
        self = [super init];
        if (self) {
                font = [kDefaultFont retain];
                fontSize = kDefaultFontSize;
                text = nil;
                width = height = 0.0;
        }
        return self;
}

+ (TextSprite *) withString: (NSString *) label
{
        TextSprite *ts = [[TextSprite alloc] init];
        if (ts) {
                ts.text = [label retain];
        }
        return ts;
}

- (void) newText: (NSString *) val
{
        if (text) [text release];
        text = [val retain];
        width = 0;
        height = 0;
```

```
        }

@end
```

TextSprite makes a habit of retaining every NSString that it receives, to prevent memory issues in future renderings. The init and withString methods are no different. We make sure to clean this up in the dealloc method, also part of *TextSprite.m*:

```
- (void) dealloc
{
        [text release];
        [font release];
        [super dealloc];
}
```

The newText method appears to be doing something peculiar. After storing a copy of the NSString in the text variable, it sets the width and height of the sprite to zero. The drawBody method of newText watches for a zero width and height, indicating that it needs to step aside and calculate the overall string size and bounding box. These change with every new string or font change. Copy the code from Listing 4–10 and place it in *TextSprite.m* as well.

Listing 4–10. *The core routines of the TextSprite class*

```
- (void) computeWidth: (CGContextRef) context
{
        textLength = [text length];

        CGFontRef fref = CGFontCreateWithFontName((CFStringRef) font);
        if (!fref) {
                width=0.0;
                height=0.0;
                printf("Warning: missing font %s\n",[font UTF8String]);
                return;
        }
        CGRect bbox = CGFontGetFontBBox(fref);
        int units = CGFontGetUnitsPerEm(fref);

        // Convert from glyph units, multiply by fontSize to get our height
        height = ( ((float) bbox.size.height) / ((float) units)) * fontSize;

        // Draw the text, invisibly, to figure out its width
        CGPoint left = CGContextGetTextPosition(context);
        CGContextSetTextDrawingMode(context, kCGTextInvisible);
        CGContextSetTextMatrix(context, CGAffineTransformIdentity);
        CGContextSelectFont(context,[font UTF8String],
                                fontSize, kCGEncodingMacRoman);
        CGContextShowText(context, [text UTF8String], textLength);
        CGPoint right = CGContextGetTextPosition(context);
        width = right.x - left.x;

        // Figure out our new bounding box and release
        [self updateBox];
        CGFontRelease(fref);
```

```
            return;
}

- (void) drawBody: (CGContextRef) context
{
        if (!text) return;
        if (!width) [self computeWidth: context];

        CGContextSelectFont(context, [font UTF8String],
                                 fontSize, kCGEncodingMacRoman);
        CGContextSetTextDrawingMode (context, kCGTextFillStroke);
        CGContextSetRGBFillColor(context, r,g,b,alpha);
        CGContextSetRGBStrokeColor(context,r,g,b,alpha);
        CGContextShowTextAtPoint(context, 0,0, [text UTF8String], textLength);
}
```

Recall that drawBody is called whenever a sprite is sent a draw message. TextSprite first checks if it has any text. If not, there's no reason to do anything, so it just returns without affecting the screen. Next, it checks whether the current width is zero. If so, the computeWidth method is invoked for the current context.

You may wonder why we don't calculate the string's dimensions at the time it's changed. The reason is that fonts differ in size based on the context in which they're drawn. Quartz 2D was designed to let us manipulate graphics, images, and fonts without worrying about the underlying hardware or printer. If we really need to know how big something is going to be on a device, we must wait until we have a handle on the context (our canvas).

The computeWidth method is chock-full of Quartz 2D API calls. We first call CGFontCreateWithFontName and hand it a Quartz string (known as a CFStringRef) that represents the name of the font we want to use. Luckily, CFStringRef and NSString use the same data structure. Casting from one to the next is a free operation. The API function gives us a CGFontRef data structure. As with CGImageRef, this is a C structure and cannot receive Objective-C messages.

We first check to see the CGFontRef (fref) is nonzero. This means we have a valid pointer, and Quartz was able to find the font for us. If not, we just print an error. If the font can't be found, the app can't really do anything, so it should exit gracefully. In this case, we just do nothing and print something to the console for debugging.

Assuming that our font reference fref is valid, we call CGFontGetFontBBox, which returns a bounding box that is big enough any character in the font. While some characters are clearly smaller than others (think a period versus a capital W), the bounding box is still useful for determining the maximum height of our string. But there's still a problem.

The CGFont class works in "glyph units." We don't care what they are; we just need to convert them to device units. We do that by first calling CGFontGetUnitsPerEm, which tells us how many of those glyph units are equal to one point. Remember our pointSize? The next line computes the height, multiplying pointSize times the size of a single point in the given font.

Calculating width is more involved. We actually need to draw the font on the screen—invisibly—and watch as Quartz advances its hand. We then measure the distance from when Quartz started and when it finished, giving us the width in device units. Obviously, we want to do this as few times as possible. Quartz 2D draws a font with five steps:

1. Pick a drawing mode with `CGContextSetTextDrawingMode` to know how characters will hit the canvas.

2. Specify any font transformations you want with `CGContextSetTextMatrix`.

3. Select a font with `CGContextSelectFont`, passing in a font name as an `UTF8String` and the font size as a floating-point value.

4. Optionally, set a stroke color with `CGContextSetRGBStrokeColor` and a fill color with `CGContextSetRGBFillColor`.

5. Display the text, either at the current point with `CGContextShowText` or at a specific point on the canvas with `CGContextShowTextAtPoint`.

You can see these steps in action, both in `computeWidth` as we draw the text invisibly, and then again in `drawBody`. We position the font at (0,0). Quartz 2D draws the string of characters, placing the baseline of the first character at (0,0). This is the imaginary line on which all characters in a string "sit" so that they line up properly. See Figure 4–39 for a description of the various parts of a font.

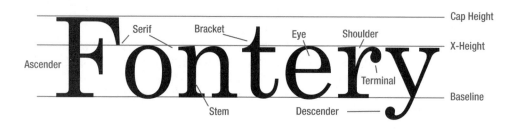

Figure 4–39. *Various parts of a CGFont. We care about the baseline.*

We can simplify all this fontery by adding another method to our `TextSprite` class. Add the following to *TextSprite.m*:

```
- (void) moveUpperLeftTo: (CGPoint) p
{
        CGPoint p2 = CGPointMake(0,0);
        p2.x = p.x;
        p2.y = p.y + height;
        [self moveTo: p2];
}
```

That's it for our `TextSprite`. Let's draw some text.

Using the TextSprite Class

Open our overworked view, *AsteroidsView.m*. Assuming you've kept up with this, you should now have a routine that moves Mario around the screen. First, add the following import statement to the top *of AsteroidsView.m*:

```
#import "TextView.h"
```

We're going to leave the drawRect routine in place, but replace the initializer in *AsteroidsView.m*:

```
- (id) initWithCoder: (NSCoder *) coder {
        if (self = [super initWithCoder: coder]) {
                test = [TextSprite withString: @"Hello World!"];
                test.r = 0;
                test.g = 1.0;
                test.b = 1.0;
                test.x = -85;
                test.y = -30;
                test.rotation = 20;
                [(TextSprite *) test setFontSize: 36];
        }
        return self;
}
```

The new initWithCoder creates a text sprite, passing in the string "Hello World!". We change its color to cyan, a combination of green (1.0) and blue (1.0). Next, we move the string a bit to the left in the x direction, and then down a bit in the y direction. We rotate the text 20 degrees counterclockwise. Finally, we set the font size to a large 36 points.

Compile and run the result. You should see the bright cyan words "Hello World" in the center of the iPhone, as shown in Figure 4–40. Note how the rotations are different from our earlier sprites. We've written the code to rotate the text from the lower left, along the baseline of the first character. This is typical convention in many graphics programs. A 90-degree rotation is useful for labeling y axes, with the words moving up, from bottom to top. A -90-degree rotation has the words reading from top to bottom.

Figure 4–40. *"Hello World" rotated 15 degrees with a TextSprite*

At this point, we've created basic sprites, vector sprites, atlas sprites, and text sprites. You can see the pattern forming. We create a new subclass of Sprite, adding a few instance variables to track the data we need. We override the outlinePath or drawBody method, drawing our sprite centered at (0,0). We respond to the `tic` method, taking a time interval and updating our internal model accordingly.

We packed a lot of functionality into the `drawRect:` method of `AsteroidsView` that really should be pulled into an outside controller. The data in the view should also be extracted, and kept in a separate model class. As you'll see, many games are just a set of sprites and a shared model, plus a bit of programming for game logic, audio, special effects, and networking—just a tad.

We're now going to leap ahead and move quickly to cover game architecture.

Asteroids Game Architecture

The companion source code for this chapter includes an entire game of Asteroids in *asteroids.tar.gz*, built from the sprite classes discussed here. We'll now step through the basic game architecture and highlight interesting bits.

> **NOTE:** This version of Asteroids does include a basic audio system, keying off state changes in a shared model. Audio systems are described by Eric Wing in Chapters 9 through 12.

The Asteroids Game Loop

You saw many of the parts of a game loop in the earlier part of this chapter. The Asteroids code extends it a bit in Figure 4–41, and organizes the work into an MVC design pattern.

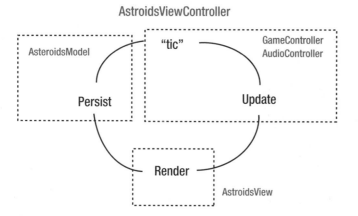

Figure 4–41. *The Asteroids implementation of a Quartz game loop*

When the app first launches, the iPhone invokes the `AsteroidsViewController`. This class creates the model and controllers, places the phone in landscape mode, creates a timer as we did earlier, and then calls the `tic` method of the game controller until the app is terminated by a user. Here's the complete source of its `gameLoop` method:

```
- (void)gameLoop
{
        // we use our own autorelease pool so that we can control when garbage gets
collected
        NSAutoreleasePool * apool = [[NSAutoreleasePool alloc] init];

        self.timeSinceLevelStart = [levelStartTime timeIntervalSinceNow];
        self.deltaTime =  lastFrameStartTime - timeSinceLevelStart;
        self.lastFrameStartTime = timeSinceLevelStart;

        [game tic: self.deltaTime];

        [apool release];
}
```

As shown in Figure 4–41, the primary purpose of `AsteroidsViewController` is to run the
tic loop. All of the sprites and game state are stored in `AsteroidsModel`, a class that
really doesn't do much other than keep things in one place. I like to treat the model as a
database of sorts. I may occasionally add routines to this, much like someone would
add stored procedures to a database, when accessing local data is much faster and
cleaner than doing it "over the wire" to an external class.

The Asteroids Model

Let's take a peek inside a real game model. Here's the complete interface definition of
`AsteroidsModel`:

```
@interface AsteroidsModel : NSObject {
        NSMutableArray *rocks;
        NSMutableArray *bullets;
        NSMutableArray *deadSprites;
        NSMutableArray *newSprites;
        NSMutableDictionary *fingers;
        Sprite *ship;
        Sprite *saucer;

        AtlasSprite *thrust;
        AtlasSprite *left;
        AtlasSprite *right;
        AtlasSprite *fire;
        TextSprite *status;
        TextSprite *lives;

        NSMutableDictionary *state;
        int lastBullet;
        CGFloat time;
}
```

The mutable arrays store all rocks and bullets that fly around the screen. We also
synchronize the addition or creation of sprites. During a single tic, sprites may die and
sprites may be born. We push all new sprites into one array and all dead sprites into
another. After the rendering is complete, we clean up the sprite lists in the persist cycle,
before the next tic occurs.

The model points to several atlas sprites, which are used as buttons in the interface. Two text sprites form the heads-up display: one to show our score and status, and another to show the number of lives left.

What I find most useful is the central dictionary, state. Two convenience methods are defined and used throughout the game:

```
+ (int) getState: (NSString *) indicator
{
        AsteroidsModel *game = [AsteroidsModel sharedModel];
        if (game.state == nil) game.state = [[NSMutableDictionary alloc] init];
        NSNumber *n = [game.state objectForKey: indicator];
        if (n) {
                return [n intValue];
        }
        return kUnknown;
}

+ (void) setState: (NSString *) indicator to: (int) val
{
        AsteroidsModel *game = [AsteroidsModel sharedModel];
        if (game.state == nil) game.state = [[NSMutableDictionary alloc] init];
        NSNumber *n = [NSNumber numberWithInt: val];
        [game.state setObject: n forKey: indicator];
}
```

The various controllers and views can get any information about the game by referring to these methods. This forms the heart of the persist step, for keeping information in between tic cycles. We define several constants for the state variable names, and also use constants for their values. This helps us by letting the compiler catch state errors, where we're using an unknown value for some state variable.

For example, we use the following constants to track the major state of the game:

```
#define kGameState              @"gameState"
#define kGameStatePlay          0
#define kGameStateLevel         1
#define kGameStateNewLife       2
#define kGameStateDone          3
```

Other classes can query the game state with this call:

```
 uint state = [AsteroidsModel getState: kGameState];
```

They change the state value with another call:

```
uint state = [AsteroidsModel setState: kGameState to: kGameStatePlay];
```

Following in this convention, we also keep a list of the current finger state in an array of Fingers. This doesn't have much to do with Quartz graphics, so we won't go into the details here. Suffice it to say that we keep the current location of fingers on the display. During an update cycle, the game controller tests whether these finger points intersect with the atlas sprite buttons. If they do, their frame is changed.

The Asteroids View

Remember how we kept changing `AsteroidsView` to demonstrate each new sprite that we created? In a real game, the view should be kept nice and clean. Though this game was put together rather quickly (and therefore could use some optimization), here's the entire interface:

```
@interface AsteroidsView : UIView {
    AsteroidsModel *model;
    BOOL ready;
}
```

The ready flag is used to delay display until the game and audio controllers are running. The view maintains a reference to the common, underlying model, `AsteroidsModel`. The model will hold the position of all our elements, their colors, and so forth with `Sprite` instances. Our view will sift through the items and figure out how to display them quickly on the phone. For this simple application, we need only a single `drawRect` method:

```
- (void)drawRect: (CGRect)rect {
    if (!ready) return;

    // Get a graphics context, with no transformations
    CGContextRef context = UIGraphicsGetCurrentContext();            (1)
    CGContextSaveGState(context);
    CGAffineTransform t0 = CGContextGetCTM(context);                 (2)
    t0 = CGAffineTransformInvert(t0);
    CGContextConcatCTM(context,t0);

    [model.status draw: context];                                    (3)
    [model.lives draw: context];

    // Draw
    if (![AsteroidsModel getState: kGameOver]) {
        [[model myShip] draw: context];
    }

    NSMutableArray *rocks = [model rocks];
    for (Sprite *rock in rocks) {
        [rock draw: context];
    }

    NSMutableArray *bullets = [model bullets];
    for (Sprite *bullet in bullets) {
        [bullet draw: context];
    }

    [model.left draw: context];
    [model.right draw: context];
    [model.thrust draw: context];
    [model.fire draw: context];

    CGContextRestoreGState(context);                                 (4)

}
```

Other than the typical initialization and teardown routines, this is the bulk of AsteroidsView. It should look familiar. We grab the context (1) and save its state for later. We reset the transformation (2). We call the draw method of all our items (3). Finally, we restore the context state (4).

As the number of sprites grows, you may find your application bogging down. The clean abstractions we've introduced here are common in object-oriented programming. Each sprite sets up its own transformations, displays itself, returning control to the view for the next item. At scale, this can get expensive. Each change to the transformations, colors, and so on requires a context switch within the rendering chips on the phone. These switches are expensive, slowing down the graphics pipeline.

Production applications are not as pretty. The views often optimize the display loop, combining multiple operations into one, minimizing the number of calls into the graphics chip. These techniques are called *pipeline optimization*. Although we won't go into the details of these techniques here, just remember that when you find yourself needing to break the sprite abstraction, or feeling like you need to bunch things together for speed, have no fear—this is typical.

Let's move on to the heart of our game, the game controller.

The Asteroids Game Controller

Practically all of the game logic for Asteroids is kept in a single class, GameController. Yet the MVC design pattern allows us to keep a clean structure. Here is the interface definition:

```
@interface GameController : NSObject {
        AsteroidsModel *model;
        AsteroidsView *view;
        AudioController *audio;
        BOOL start;
        int restartDelay;
}
```

You've seen AsteroidsModel and AsteroidsView. We'll save AudioController for later in the book. The Boolean, start, is a flag to let us know if this is the very first tic, so that we can initialize our model state. The integer restartDelay is a countdown timer. When a life or level ends, the game controller sets this variable to a set number of frames. As long as the restartDelay is nonzero, the game controller will ignore the buttons and keep the ship hidden from view.

Let's take a look at how GameController starts up and handles the tic message:

```
- (id) initWithView: (AsteroidsView *) theView
{
        self = [super init];
        if (self) {
                AsteroidsModel *m = [AsteroidsModel sharedModel];
                self.audio = [[AudioController alloc] init];
                self.model = m;
                self.view = theView;
```

```
                self.start = YES;
                [m initState];
                [theView useModel: m];
        }
        return self;
}

- (void) tic: (NSTimeInterval) dt
{
        if (start) {
                start = NO;
                model.time = 0;
        }
        else {
                [self updateModel: dt];
                [self updateView: dt];
                [audio tic: dt];
        }
}
```

The initializer is passed a view by the `AsteroidsViewController`. We then tap into the singleton `AsteroidsModel` and create the audio controller. We wire up the view, model, audio, and call the `initState` of `AsteroidsModel`, which initializes state values for our game::

```
- (void) initState
{
        [AsteroidsModel setState: kThrust to: kThrustOff];
        [AsteroidsModel setState: kLeft to: kLeftOff];
        [AsteroidsModel setState: kRight to: kRightOff];
        [AsteroidsModel setState: kFire to: kFireOff];
        [AsteroidsModel setState: kReload to: 0];
        [AsteroidsModel setState: kGameOver to: 0];
        [AsteroidsModel setState: kLife to: kLives];
        [AsteroidsModel setState: kScore to: 0];
        [AsteroidsModel setState: kLevel to: 0];
        [AsteroidsModel setState: kGameState to: kGameStatePlay];
}
```

The `tic` method is surprisingly simple. We update the model, and then update the view. Updating the model uses a divide-and-conquer approach. During `updateBullets`, we check whether the bullets on the screen are hitting any rocks, increasing score, dividing a rock in half, setting the new fragments on their way. During `updateShip`, we check whether rocks have smashed into our side. We also check the state of the buttons (e.g. fire, left, right, and thrust), and then adjust the sprite values for speed, rotation, and angle. If the fire button is depressed, we emit small sprites into the ether as "bullets." These bullet sprites copy the rotation of the ship as their initial, angular motion, appearing to fire out of the tip of the ship.

```
- (void) updateModel: (NSTimeInterval) dt
{
        model.time += dt;
        [self moveRocks: dt];
        [self updateShip: dt];
        [self updateFingers: dt];
        [self updateBullets: dt];
```

```
        [model updateButtons];
        [model unleashGrimReaper];
}
```

The last method call is my favorite, `unleashGrimReaper`. This cleans up the model, moving all dead sprites back into a common pool (such as bullets and rock fragments). They, too, will live another day.

Conclusion

This chapter began by creating a blank canvas, which Quartz 2D calls a *context*. We jumped through menus and configuration panels to put Quartz 2D in total control over our main view. We then defined our first sprite, an elfish creature that captures the basics of motion and position for all objects in a game. Sprites tap into the Quartz 2D API and provide a clean abstraction, hiding much of the complexity.

Sprites introduced a bit of math. You learned about affine transformations, which convert the (x,y) position of a sprite into a physical location on the iPhone screen. These transformations are done once a cycle, during the `draw` method. We showed affine transformations for successfully rotating, scaling, and translating sprites, both in portrait and landscape modes.

Then we created three types of sprites: vector sprites, atlas sprites, and text sprites. Vector sprites are helpful in turning an array of points into filled shapes, which form things like rocks, spaceships, and bullets. Atlas sprites extend this capability, allowing arbitrarily complex images to be displayed in a single call through images. An atlas sprite pulls its image from a matrix of frame images stored on a single, larger image called a *sprite atlas*. We used an antique frame atlas to animate a character wandering around our iPhone. Text sprites hide the complexity of Quartz 2D fonts and enable us to position and colorize text anywhere on the screen. We promised not to use Comic Sans.

Finally, we took a quick tour of the game loop and classes within an Asteroids game, built from the sprites covered in this chapter. The game loop followed the three steps of update, render, and persist, all run by the tick of a clock set up by our main `AsteroidsViewController`.

I encourage you to play with the source code of Asteroids. I also hope you have as much fun building derivatives of the game, and using pieces of the code in your own wonderful creations, as I did building this game. Feel free to follow me on Twitter, at @drjsp173. Send me a direct message anytime to chat.

Chapter 5

Flipping Out and Sweeping Away with Core Animation

In previous chapters, you learned about displaying moving graphics with the `UIImageView`, and about drawing lines, shapes, paths, and gradients on a `UIView` with Quartz 2D. These technologies pack a lot of functionality and are essential to making 2D games on the iPhone. You will be using them a lot in your games.

Quartz 2D is actually a Mac OS X technology that has made its way unchanged to the iPhone. Like the Core Foundation and Foundation frameworks, Quartz 2D is a fundamental API in both Mac OS X and iPhone OS. UIKit, while very central to iPhone programming, is a simplified version of Mac OS X's AppKit.

Another iPhone technology with a lot of functionality is Core Animation. Unlike Quartz 2D and UIKit, Core Animation was invented just for the iPhone, and made its way into Mac OS X Leopard after the iPhone was developed. Core Animation's power for making dynamic effects on the iPhone's UI is what gives the iPhone its personality.

Core Animation is the technology behind the slick way views slide as you navigate around in many iPhone apps. It's used to make an application's loading image grow and fade in once you touch the app's icon. It's also behind the application screen shrinking and fading to nothingness once you quit with the home button.

To be clear, the animation part of the name Core Animation has nothing to do with displaying a sequence of images in rapid succession. Core Animation is used for the movement of components across the screen, such as the sliding of photos on and off the screen as you navigate through a photo album in your favorite photo app. It is also used for special effects, such as the curling page in the Maps application. You will use Core Animation to add cool animated effects to your game's UI, or to make a terrific intro screen.

In this chapter, you will learn how to unleash the power of Core Animation in your own games.

Core Animation Sample Project Overview

To get started with Core Animation as soon as possible, we will begin coding from an existing project. This will get us to the important code faster than walking through creating the project in Interface Builder, which is covered in Chapter 3.

To begin, open the sample project called CoreAChicken first stage (provided with this book's source code) in Xcode. Select the Resources group in the Groups and Files pane. Double-click the CoreAChickenViewController.xib file to open it, as shown in Figure 5–1.

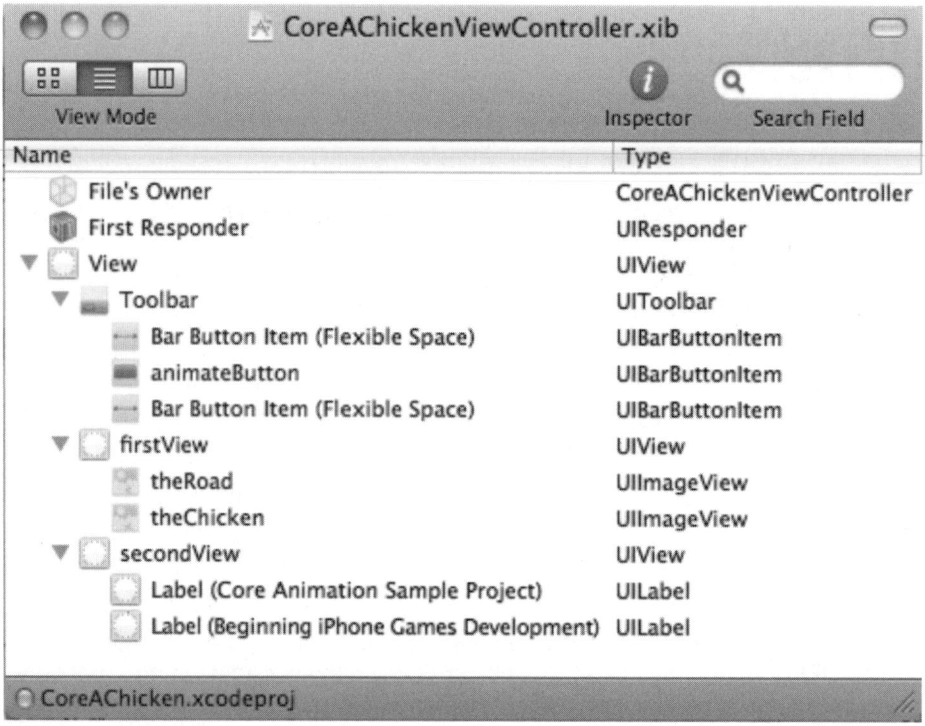

Figure 5–1. *The CoreAChickenViewController.xib file opened in Interface Builder, in list view mode, with view and toolbar objects expanded to show their components*

Figure 5–1 shows the logical composition of the sample app's only view controller. It is composed of a view, which contains a toolbar and two views. The views are called firstView and secondView. The toolbar has a button called animateButton. The firstView is composed of two image views, called theRoad and theChicken. The secondView contains two labels.

Let's look now at the visual composition of the same view controller. If you don't see the window shown in Figure 5–2, double-click the component called View to open it.

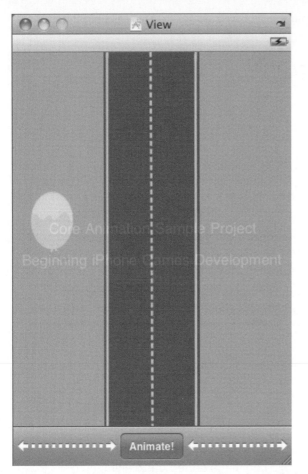

Figure 5–2. *The visual layout of the app's main screen as displayed in Interface Builder's view editing window*

In Figure 5–2, you can see the toolbar at the bottom of the screen, with the animateButton component. Above the toolbar are two views stacked on top of one another. The secondView is laid out on top of firstView, but secondView actually has its hidden property set. This makes Interface Builder show secondView as half transparent in this window. Because secondView is shown half transparent, you can see firstView behind it, and the image views called theChicken and theRoad laid out in firstView.

Keep in mind that even though secondView is shown half transparent in Interface Builder, when the app runs, it will not be visible because the hidden property is set. When the app first runs, firstView will be visible, and the first animations will be run on it. We will change secondView's hidden property and animate it in some of the code we will write in this chapter, to create fades and other types of animated transitions between the two views.

The code we'll be concerned with in this chapter is an animate method, which will demonstrate Core Animation routines. It's in the *CoreAChickenViewController.m* file, which you can open in Xcode, from the Classes group. Listing 5–1 shows the code, which is appears around line 20 in the file.

Listing 5–1. *The code that powers the animateButton in the sample app (in CoreAChickenViewController.m)*

```
- (IBAction)animate {
    static int counter = 0;

    switch (++counter) {
        default:
            counter = 0;
            break;
    }
}
```

The code begins by defining an IBAction method named animate. IBAction methods are connected to a UI component in Interface Builder. They are called when a button gets clicked or when the user triggers some other event. The animate method is connected to the animateButton displayed on the toolbar at the bottom of the app's main view.

In this first stage of the code, the method doesn't do much. It declares a static integer variable called counter, increments it, and checks it in a switch statement. There's only one case in the switch, the default case, which resets the counter back to 0.

In the course of this chapter, we will code the animate method to play through a sequence of Core Animation routines—a different routine each time the animateButton is clicked. When the last routine plays, the counter is reset to start again from the first routine.

You will be adding switch cases and animation routines to this method throughout this chapter. I will walk you through the code and explain the Core Animation APIs used.

Animating UIViews

The easiest way to use Core Animation is to take advantage of its close integration with UIKit on the iPhone. In creating UIKit, Apple engineers added basic animation functionality that uses Core Animation behind the scenes, simplifying its application for the most common use cases. We will examine the simpler APIs in this section, and explore the more complex (and more flexible) APIs in later sections.

The UIView class provides class methods for the programming of animated transitions between different property values in your UI components. You use these class methods to begin an animation block, to set animation properties such as animation duration, and to commit the animation block.

You begin an animation block by calling the UIView class method named beginAnimations:context:. This method takes two parameters: an NSString instance used to identify the animation block and a context. Both parameters are optional, but their purpose is to help you identify which animation block called your animation delegate methods (as you'll see in the examples throughout this chapter).

The context parameter is a void pointer, meaning that you can pass anything you want in this parameter. You can use this context pointer to pass a data structure or instance of a class that your animation delegate may need to analyze or modify in regard to the animation starting or finishing.

Once you have begun an animation block, you close it by calling the `UIView` class method named `commitAnimations`. Committing the animation block will make Core Animation play the animation in a separate thread from your UI event handling.

Animation blocks can be nested, which means you can begin one animation block within another. Each animation block can have its own animation properties, such as its own animation identifier and duration. But the nested animation blocks won't start playing until the outer animation block is committed. Here's how animation blocks can be nested:

```
[UIView beginAnimations:@"animation1" context:nil];

// component1 properties animated here

[UIView beginAnimations:@"animation2" context:nil];

// component2 properties animated here

[UIView commitAnimations];

[UIView commitAnimations];
```

As you may remember from Chapter 3's introduction to UIKit, UIKit components such as `UIImageView`, `UILabel`, and `UIButton` are derived from `UIView`. By deriving from a common class, they have many properties in common, such as `position`, `size`, and `alpha`. Core Animation can animate the following five `UIView` properties:

- `frame`: The component's frame rectangle, in terms of its superview.
- `center`: The coordinates of the component's center point, in terms of its superview.
- `bounds`: The view's bounding rectangle, in coordinates inside the component.
- `transform`: The transform applied to the component, relative to the center of the bounding rectangle.
- `alpha`: The component's alpha value, which represent its opacity.

Changing any of these properties within an animation block will make Core Animation play an animation in which the value of the property or properties change from their initial value just before the start of the animation block to the final value set within the animation block.

For example, let's say we have a `UIImageView` component with an initial `alpha` property value of 1. We start an animation block, set the value of the component's `alpha` property to 0, and then commit the animation to close the animation block. This will make Core Animation play an animation in which the opacity of the component changes from fully opaque to fully transparent.

That's enough talk, let's look at some code to make these concepts become more concrete. Listing 5–2 shows the `animate` method, expanded to support a total of ten animations. Replace the current version of the `animate` method in the *CoreAChickenViewController.m* file with this one.

Listing 5–2. *The expanded animate method, with ten animations (in CoreAChickenViewController.m)*

```
- (IBAction)animate {
    static int counter = 0;

    switch (++counter) {
        case 1:
            [self viewAnimation1];
            break;
        case 2:
            [self viewAnimation2];
            break;
        case 3:
            [self viewAnimation3];
            break;
        case 4:
            [self viewAnimation4];
            break;
        case 5:
            [self viewAnimation5];
            break;
        case 6:
            [self viewAnimation6];
            break;
        case 7:
            [self viewAnimation7];
            break;
        case 8:
            [self viewAnimation8];
            break;
        case 9:
            [self viewAnimation9];
            break;
        default:
            [self viewAnimation10];
            counter = 0;
            break;
    }
    animateButton.enabled = NO;
}
```

In Listing 5–2, the `animate` method's `switch` statement has been modified with nine new `case` statements. Each `case` statement, including the default one, calls a different method. The methods are called `viewAnimation1` through `viewAnimation10`.

You may note that at the end of the `animate` method, the `animateButton` is disabled. This is so that the user cannot trigger another animation before the current animation is completed. Animation blocks cancel each other out unless they are nested. If the `animationButton` is not disabled between animations, and the user clicks the button while one animation is playing, the current animation will be canceled as the next animation starts, and this will look wrong. As you'll see in the rest of the code to follow, the `animateButton` is enabled again at the end of each animation.

Let's now walk through these view animation methods.

Simple Movement

Listing 5–3 shows the code for method `viewAnimation1`.

Listing 5–3. *The viewAnimation1 method*

```
- (void)viewAnimation1 {
    // Reset properties to default values
    theChicken.transform = CGAffineTransformIdentity;
    theChicken.frame = CGRectMake(15, 144, 62, 90);

    [UIView beginAnimations:@"viewAnimation1" context:theChicken];
    [UIView setAnimationDelegate:self];
    [UIView setAnimationDidStopSelector:
        @selector(animationDidStop:finished:context:)];

    theChicken.frame = CGRectMake(15, 330, 62, 90);

    [UIView commitAnimations];
}
```

The first line of code in the `viewAnimation1` method resets `theChicken`'s properties to default values. The `transform` property controls rotation, scaling (size changes), and translation (position changes) using a set of functions that will be discussed in the "UIView Transforms" section later in this chapter. The `CGAffineTransformIdentity` constant resets the property to a value that essentially means "no transform." After resetting the transform, the code sets `theChicken`'s `frame` property to the starting position for this animation.

The next line of code starts an animation block with the animation identifier `viewAnimation1` and `theChicken` image view as the context parameter.

Following that, the code sets the animation delegate:

```
[UIView setAnimationDelegate:self];
[UIView setAnimationDidStopSelector:@selector(animationDidStop:finished:context:)];
```

The animation delegate receives notifications when the animation is about to start and when the animation has stopped through two selectors you can assign. We assign the selector named `animationDidStop:finished:context:` to be called when the animation stops. Setting the delegate and selectors is optional. But in this sample project, we must always set a delegate and delegate method for stopping the animation, because we need to reenable the `animateButton` at the end of each animation. You can also assign a selector to be notified when the animation is about to start, if you need that functionality, by calling the `UIView` class method `setAnimationWillStartSelector:` and passing the appropriate selector.

In the next line of code in the `viewAnimation1` method, we change the frame of the image view `theChicken`:

```
theChicken.frame = CGRectMake(15, 330, 62, 90);
```

The initial position of theChicken's in the Interface Builder *.xib* file is at coordinates 15 and 144 for the x and y values. Its initial size is a width of 62 and a height of 90. So this line of code simply moves theChicken down the screen to y coordinate 330.

The last line of code in the viewAnimation1 method commits the animation, closing the animation block:

```
[UIView commitAnimations];
```

This makes Core Animation play an animation that moves theChicken down the screen in 0.2 second, to stand at the top of the toolbar. The duration of 0.2 second is the default of a UIView animation, unless you set a different duration using the UIView method setAnimationDuration:.

Once the animation stops, Core Animation calls the method we set earlier for notifications that the animation ended. Listing 5–4 shows the code for this delegate method.

Listing 5–4. *The animationDidStop:finished:context: animation delegate method*

```
- (void)animationDidStop:(NSString *)theAnimation finished:(BOOL)flag
context:(void *)context
{
    animateButton.enabled = YES;
}
```

The signature for this method is the standard signature for the animationDidStop delegate. You can call the method anything you want, but if the method takes parameters, the parameter types must match this signature, or the method may cause a crash.

The first parameter must be a pointer to an NSString instance. It will be set to the value you passed for the animation name in the beginAnimations:context: call for this animation. The second parameter, if there is one, must be a Boolean flag. The value passed will be YES if the animation ran to completion or NO if it was interrupted. The current animation can be interrupted by another animation block being committed before the current animation plays out.

The last parameter to the delegate method must be a void pointer. It will be set to the value of the context parameter passed in the beginAnimations:context: for the current animation calling the animation delegate.

Animation Curves

Listing 5–5 shows the method viewAnimation2 and its animation stop delegate method.

Listing 5–5. *The viewAnimation2 method and its animation stop delegate method*

```
- (void)viewAnimation2 {
    [UIView beginAnimations:nil context:nil];
    [UIView setAnimationDuration:1];
    [UIView setAnimationDelegate:self];
    [UIView setAnimationDidStopSelector:@selector(animationDidStop)];
```

```
    theChicken.frame = CGRectMake(15, 144, 62, 90);

    [UIView commitAnimations];
}

- (void)animationDidStop {
    animateButton.enabled = YES;
}
```

In this listing, the animation block begins with no parameters set for the animation identifier and for the context. In the next line of code, we set the animation duration to 1 second by calling the setAnimationDuration: class method.

Rather than set the animationDidStop selector to the standard signature, we pass in a selector with no parameters. This has no danger of causing a crash, as any parameters passed by the caller will be ignored.

After setting the delegate and animation stop selector, the code sets the frame for theChicken image view back to the original x and y coordinates of 15 and 144. Then we commit the animation to close the animation block.

When this animation plays, theChicken image view slides back up to the original coordinates over the length of 1 second. If you look carefully, you will see the animation starts moving the image view slowly, picks up speed as it progresses, and then slows down as the animation is about to end. This is the default *animation curve* used by Core Animation.

When making an animation, the result can look rather mechanical if the animator just changes the movement of the animated component in an evenly spaced manner between frames. Through decades of study and practice in the art of animation, professional animators have learned that there are ways to animate a scene and add a touch of variation to their work. These variations make the animation look more interesting than just moving something from position A to B in a straight line.

Animation curves are a property of an animation you can set to tell Core Animation to apply the changes to the component you want to animate in an uneven manner, to add these variations to the animated result. These curves modify how Core Animation processes the animation. For example, it may begin slowly and pick up acceleration as the animation progresses, or it might start by moving rapidly and then slow down as it reaches the end.

You set the animation curve by calling the UIView class method setAnimationCurve:, passing one of the following curve constants:

- UIViewAnimationCurveEaseInOut: The default animation curve. The animation begins slowly, accelerates until the middle of the animation's duration, and then slows down again until completion.

- UIViewAnimationCurveEaseIn: The animation begins slowly and accelerates until the end.

- UIViewAnimationCurveEaseOut: The animation begins fast but slows down until it reaches the end.

■ UIViewAnimationCurveLinear: The animation runs at a constant speed.

So far, you've learned that animations have a default duration of 0.2 second and that they have a default animation curve that makes the animation start slowly, pick up speed for about half the duration, and then slow down until it stops for the other half of the duration. You also learned you can set delegate methods to be notified when the animation is about to start and when it has come to an end.

Reverse and Repeat

The viewAnimation3 method, shown in Listing 5–6, demonstrates a few more animation properties.

Listing 5–6. *The viewAnimation3 method and its animation stop delegate method*

```
- (void)viewAnimation3 {
    [UIView beginAnimations:@"viewAnimation3" context:theRoad];
    [UIView setAnimationCurve:UIViewAnimationCurveLinear];
    [UIView setAnimationDuration:0.5];

    [UIView setAnimationRepeatAutoreverses:YES];
    [UIView setAnimationRepeatCount:2];
    [UIView setAnimationDelegate:self];
    [UIView setAnimationDidStopSelector:
        @selector(theRoadAnimationDidStop:finished:context:)];

    theRoad.alpha = 0.0;
    [UIView commitAnimations];
}

- (void)theRoadAnimationDidStop:(NSString *)theAnimation finished:(BOOL)flag
context:(void *)context
{
    ((UIView *)context).alpha = 1.0;
    animateButton.enabled = YES;
}
```

The viewAnimation3 method begins by starting an animation block, passing in the string "viewAnimation3" as the animation identifier and the image view called theRoad as the context parameter.

The next method sets the animation curve to linear:

```
[UIView setAnimationCurve:UIViewAnimationCurveLinear];
```

This means the animated properties will change at constant speed, from the current value to the value set within the animation block.

The next line of code sets the animation duration to half a second:

```
[UIView setAnimationDuration:0.5];
```

The following lines of code set the animation to autoreverse and to play twice:

```
[UIView setAnimationRepeatAutoreverses:YES];
[UIView setAnimationRepeatCount:2];
```

The animation will play forward for the duration set in the previous line, play backward for the same duration, and then repeat. This means that the animation plays forward once for half a second, then plays backward for half a second, then plays forward again for half a second, and once again backward for half a second. The animation's total play time will be 2 seconds.

By default, animations don't autoreverse and the repeat count is set to 0, which means there is no repetition. The autoreverse setting is ignored if the repeat count is 0.

The repeat count can be fractional, which means the animation will not play all the way through. If you set the repeat count to 0.5, for example, the animation will stop at the exact halfway point of the duration setting. If you set the repeat count to 6.5, the animation will repeat six times, then stop halfway through a seventh repetition.

The next two lines of code set the animation delegate object and the name of the method that will be called when the animation stops:

```
[UIView setAnimationDelegate:self];
[UIView
setAnimationDidStopSelector:@selector(theRoadAnimationDidStop:finished:context:)];
```

The selector's signature matches the standard signature for this delegate method. In this particular delegate method, it means the animation context will be passed as the third parameter to the method. We will make use of the context parameter in the animation delegate method to set the object's property to its final value.

This next line identifies the object and property being changed in the animation:

```
theRoad.alpha = 0.0;
```

The image view named theRoad has a current alpha value of 1, making theRoad fully opaque. In this animation, it is being changed to 0, fully transparent.

In the last line of code in this method, the animation block is closed with the committing of the animation to the Core Animation queue.

```
[UIView commitAnimations];
```

In essence, the viewAnimation3 method makes theRoad fade out and fade back in twice over a length of 2 seconds.

The next section of code is the animation stop delegate method:

```
- (void)theRoadAnimationDidStop:(NSString *)theAnimation finished:(BOOL)flag
context:(void *)context
{
    ((UIView *)context).alpha = 1.0;
    animateButton.enabled = YES;
}
```

In this method, we use the context parameter, which was set to theRoad at the start of the animation block in viewAnimation3. So the delegate method is setting theRoad's alpha property back to 1 now that the animation has ended.

Delay, Ease-In, and Ease-Out

The next view animation methods introduce a few new animation settings. Let's continue with Listing 5–7, which shows viewAnimation4.

Listing 5–7. *The viewAnimation4 method and its animation stop delegate method*

```
- (void)viewAnimation4 {
    [UIView beginAnimations:nil context:nil];
    [UIView setAnimationDelay:0.5];
    [UIView setAnimationDuration:1];
    [UIView setAnimationCurve:UIViewAnimationCurveEaseIn];

    [UIView setAnimationRepeatAutoreverses:YES];
    [UIView setAnimationRepeatCount:2];
    [UIView setAnimationDelegate:self];
    [UIView setAnimationDidStopSelector:
        @selector(resetTheChickenProperties)];

    theChicken.frame = CGRectMake(15, 330, 62, 90);
    [UIView commitAnimations];
}

- (void)resetTheChickenProperties {
    theChicken.transform = CGAffineTransformIdentity;
    theChicken.frame = CGRectMake(15, 144, 62, 90);
    animateButton.enabled = YES;
}
```

The viewAnimation4 method introduces the concept of the animation delay. You can set a delay for the start of the animation by calling the UIView class method setAnimationDelay:. The animation delay defaults to a value of 0, and the setting accepts a fraction. In this code sample, the animation delay is set to 0.5 second.

The animation curve is set to ease-in. This curve is what you should use for animations simulating bouncing. This animation makes theChicken bounce on the toolbar a couple of times.

Listing 5–8 shows the code for viewAnimation5, which uses the ease-out animation curve.

Listing 5–8. *The viewAnimation5 method*

```
- (void)viewAnimation5 {
    [UIView beginAnimations:nil context:nil];
    [UIView setAnimationDuration:1];
    [UIView setAnimationCurve:UIViewAnimationCurveEaseOut];
    [UIView setAnimationDelegate:self];
    [UIView setAnimationDidStopSelector:@selector(animationDidStop)];

    theChicken.frame = CGRectMake(235, 144, 62, 90);
    [UIView commitAnimations];
}
```

The ease-out animation curve is perfect for simulating throwing an object up in the air and seeing gravity slow it down over time. It's the opposite of the bouncing effect.

UIView Transforms

The next three animations introduce the transform property. The transform property is used to affect the size (scale), position (translation), and/or rotation of a UIKit component, using the following Core Graphics functions:

- CGAffineTransformMakeScale: Changes the size of the component. You pass a scale for the width and height of the component. The value of the parameters can be fractions.

- CGAffineTransformMakeTranslation: Changes the position of the component relative to its original position. You pass units of relative movement along the x and y axes. The x and y units can be fractions.

- CGAffineTransformMakeRotation: Rotates the component about its center coordinates. You pass the number of radians by which to rotate. The value of the parameter can be a fraction.

- CGAffineTransformIdentity: Resets the transform property (no transformation).

> **NOTE:** *Radians* are the metric equivalent to the degree of rotation of the English system. 180 degrees equal 3.14159 radians. A positive value means clockwise rotation. A negative value means counterclockwise rotation. To convert from degrees to radians, apply the formula degrees * pi / 180.

Listing 5–9 shows the viewAnimation6 and viewAnimation7 methods. These two methods demonstrate scaling and rotation transforms.

Listing 5–9. *The viewAnimation6 and viewAnimation7 methods*

```
- (void)viewAnimation6 {
    [UIView beginAnimations:nil context:nil];
    [UIView setAnimationDuration:1];
    [UIView setAnimationCurve:UIViewAnimationCurveLinear];
    [UIView setAnimationDelegate:self];
    [UIView setAnimationDidStopSelector:@selector(animationDidStop)];

    theChicken.transform = CGAffineTransformMakeScale(1.25, 1.25);
    [UIView commitAnimations];
}

- (void)viewAnimation7 {
    [UIView beginAnimations:nil context:nil];
    [UIView setAnimationDuration:1];
    [UIView setAnimationCurve:UIViewAnimationCurveLinear];
    [UIView setAnimationDelegate:self];
    [UIView setAnimationDidStopSelector:@selector(animationDidStop)];

    CGAffineTransform transform1 = CGAffineTransformMakeScale(1, 1);
    CGAffineTransform transform2 =
        CGAffineTransformMakeRotation(179.9 * M_PI / 180.0);
```

```
    theChicken.transform = CGAffineTransformConcat(transform1,
                                                    transform2);
    [UIView commitAnimations];
}
```

In the `viewAnimation6` method, we are scaling `theChicken` to 1.25 times its original size. In the `viewAnimation7` method, `theChicken` is scaled back down to original size. And at the same time, it rotates `theChicken` clockwise by 179.9 degrees. (Remember that a positive value means clockwise rotation; a negative value means counterclockwise rotation.)

NOTE: The rotation applied is 179.9 degrees rather than 180 degrees, because Core Animation misinterpreted my intention when I specified 180 degrees. When I specified 180 degrees for the transform, Core Animation interpreted this as a counterclockwise rotation of 180 degrees. Using 179.9 made Core Animation apply the animation as I intended.

The `viewAnimation7` method shows that transforms can be combined. The result of two `CGAffineTransformMake*` functions can be used as inputs to the `CGAffineTransformConcat` function. This result can be concatenated with a third, and the result concatenated with a fourth, and so on. In this case, we combine two transforms and assign them to the component's `transform` property.

The `viewAnimation8` method, presented in Listing 5–10, shows another way of combining transforms.

Listing 5–10. *The viewAnimation8 method*

```
- (void)viewAnimation8 {
    [UIView beginAnimations:nil context:nil];
    [UIView setAnimationDuration:1];
    [UIView setAnimationCurve:UIViewAnimationCurveEaseInOut];
    [UIView setAnimationDelegate:self];
    [UIView setAnimationDidStopSelector:
        @selector(resetTheChickenProperties)];

    CGAffineTransform transform1 =
        CGAffineTransformMakeTranslation(-220, 0);
    theChicken.transform =
        CGAffineTransformRotate(transform1, 359.9 * M_PI / 180.0);
    [UIView commitAnimations];
}
```

In the `viewAnimation8` method, the code creates a transform, which applies a translation of 220 pixels to the left of the current position. When applied to `theChicken` at this point in the animations, this transform essentially moves it to the original frame coordinates set in the *CoreAChickenViewController.xib* file. Before applying this transform, though, we call the function `CGAffineTransformRotate`, and apply to the translation transform a clockwise rotation transform of 359.9 degrees. This completes the half circle rotation started in `viewAnimation7`. These combined transforms are applied to `theChicken`, and then the animation block is closed and the animation committed.

NOTE: The rotation applied is 359.9 degrees rather than 360 degrees, because Core Animation misinterpreted my intention when I specified 360 degrees. Using 359.9 made Core Animation apply the animation as I intended.

If you want to see a finished working version of the code up to this part of the chapter, you can check out the Xcode project in the folder called `CoreAChicken UIView animations`, in the source code for this chapter.

UIView Transitions

Besides animating the movement and opacity of UI components such as image views, UIKit's integration of Core Animation also has the ability to animate transitions that occupy the whole screen. These work well to swap areas of the screen out and replace that area with other components.

The API for using `UIView` transitions is called `setAnimationTransition:forView:cache:`. This API takes as parameters a transition type, the superview of the components to be transitioned, and a Boolean describing whether you want Core Animation to cache the look of the superview before and after the animation. This caching improves Core Animation's performance.

Four transition types are used by `UIView` transitions:

- `UIViewAnimationTransitionFlipFromRight`: Makes the view contents flip from the right to the left, revealing another view on the other side of the screen. You can see this transition type in the Weather app, when you click the Info disclosure icon at the lower-right corner of the screen.

- `UIViewAnimationTransitionFlipFromLeft`: Makes the view contents flip from the left to the right, revealing another view on the other side of the screen. This animation is the opposite of the previous one. In the Weather app, it hides the "back" of the Weather app when you click the Done button.

- `UIViewAnimationTransitionCurlUp`: Makes the current view curl up and away like a page on a notepad, revealing another view underneath. You can see this animation play only 50% of the way in the Maps app, when you click the curling page icon to the lower left on the toolbar.

- `UIViewAnimationTransitionCurlDown`: Takes the current view and covers it as if a page were uncurling from the top of the screen and revealing another view. This animation is the opposite of the previous one. You can see this by clicking the curling page icon again after revealing the view beneath.

The `viewAnimation9` and `viewAnimation10` methods use view transitions to hide `firstView` and show `secondView` and vice versa. Listing 5–11 shows these methods.

Listing 5–11. *The viewAnimation9 and viewAnimation10 methods*

```
- (void)viewAnimation9 {
    [UIView beginAnimations:nil context:nil];
    [UIView setAnimationDuration:1];
    [UIView setAnimationCurve:UIViewAnimationCurveEaseIn];
    [UIView setAnimationTransition:UIViewAnimationTransitionCurlUp
        forView:self.view cache:YES];
    [UIView setAnimationDelegate:self];
    [UIView setAnimationDidStopSelector:@selector(animationDidStop)];

    firstView.hidden = YES;
    secondView.hidden = NO;
    [UIView commitAnimations];
}

- (void)viewAnimation10 {
    [UIView beginAnimations:nil context:nil];
    [UIView setAnimationDuration:1];
    [UIView setAnimationCurve:UIViewAnimationCurveEaseInOut];
    [UIView setAnimationTransition:UIViewAnimationTransitionFlipFromLeft
        forView:self.view cache:YES];
    [UIView setAnimationDelegate:self];
    [UIView setAnimationDidStopSelector:@selector(animationDidStop)];

    firstView.hidden = NO;
    secondView.hidden = YES;
    [UIView commitAnimations];
}
```

The code for `viewAnimation9` should look familiar by now. It starts an animation block, sets an animation duration and animation curve, sets delegates and delegate selectors, and commits the animation to close the animation block. The main difference is the use of the `setAnimationTransition:forView:cache:` method.

```
[UIView setAnimationTransition:UIViewAnimationTransitionCurlUp
    forView:self.view cache:YES];
```

This line of code sets the animation transition type to curl up. We specify the transition is for the view controller's view, which contains both `firstView` and `secondView`. We also specify that Core Animation should cache the animation for the best performance.

The next relevant lines of code are the hiding and showing of the views:

```
firstView.hidden = YES;
secondView.hidden = NO;
```

We simply hide `firstView` and show `secondView`. When the animation is committed, Core Animation whisks `firstView` away with a page-curl animation about a second long, with `secondView` shown as `firstView` animates away.

In the `viewAnimation10` method, the relevant code is the line that sets the animation transition type:

```
[UIView setAnimationTransition:UIViewAnimationTransitionFlipFromLeft
```

```
                forView:self.view cache:YES];
```

Here, we specify the transition type that flips the view, with the new view coming from the left side of the screen.

In this view animation, we show the `firstView` and hide the `secondView`:

```
firstView.hidden = NO;
secondView.hidden = YES;
```

We are essentially undoing the work of the previous animation, but with a different transition type. When this animation is committed, Core Animation flips the screen from the left, hiding `secondView` behind `firstView`, which is again the only visible view.

There are other transition animations the iPhone can do, but these require coding directly with Core Animation APIs. Our exploration of `UIView` animation methods concludes, and we move on to the more complex APIs offered by Core Animation itself.

Animating Core Animation Layers

I mentioned at the beginning at the `UIView` animations section that the animation methods provided by `UIView` were a convenience—a gentle façade provided by the designers of the iPhone SDK to hide the complexity of Core Animation from developers for the most common types of animation effects. In this section, we'll look at how to create animations with Core Animation APIs to do many of the same things you can do with UIView animations.

Core Animation operates on instances of the class `CALayer`. Every UIKit component has a `CALayer` instance, accessible through the `layer` property of the component. It is on this layer that UIKit components draw, and it is the UIKit component's layer that is displayed on screen. When working with UIKit components to create your UI, you typically don't need to concern yourself with the Core Animation layer, unless you want to use the Core Animation APIs directly.

Core Animation layers have many of the same properties as `UIView`, such as `frame`, `bounds`, `backgroundColor`, and `hidden`. Like `UIView`, many of the layer's properties can be animated, including the following (a partial list):

- position
- bounds
- anchorPoint
- backgroundColor
- hidden

Implicit Animations

You can trigger an animation on a layer simply by changing one of the layer properties that can be animated. For a UIKit component, you reference the `layer` property, and then change the property on the layer, as in this example:

```
theChicken.layer.position = CGPointMake(225, 144);
```

This is called an *implicit animation*, and does not require the creation of an animation block. Just change one or several properties, and an animation will be played on the layer, changing the property or properties from the current value to the new value.

Implicit animations have a default duration of 0.25 seconds. You can change the duration of an implicit animation by setting the duration value in the implicit Core Animation transaction, as follows:

```
[CATransaction setValue:[NSNumber numberWithFloat:1.0]
                 forKey:kCATransactionAnimationDuration];
```

You change the animation duration value before you modify the property you want to animate. Once changed, the animation will play for the specified duration.

Implicit animations are played with a linear animation curve. Core Animation calls animation curves *timing functions* (covered in the next section). Here is an example of changing to the ease-in, ease-out timing function:

```
[CATransaction setValue:kCAMediaTimingFunctionEaseInEaseOut
                 forKey:kCATransactionAnimationTimingFunction];
```

One thing to remember is that the animation duration and timing function are reset back to default values after the implicit animation plays to the end. Unless you create an explicit transaction and retain it for reuse at later points, the values you give these settings are lost once the implicit transaction is finished playing.

Timing Functions

The Core Animation term *timing function* seems like an important distinction, but it's just another name for animation curve. You assign the timing function by calling the class method `functionWithName:` in the `CAMediaTimingFunction` class. This class method takes as a parameter the type of timing function you want to use. The Core Animation timing functions are as follows:

- `kCAMediaTimingFunctionDefault`: Approximates a Bézier timing function with control points (0.0,0.0), (0.25,0.1), (0.25,0.1), (1.0,1.0). It's a curve similar to ease-in, ease-out, but the start and stop slowdowns are not as pronounced.

- `kCAMediaTimingFunctionEaseInEaseOut`: Equivalent to UIViewAnimationCurveEaseInOut.

- `kCAMediaTimingFunctionEaseIn`: Equivalent to UIViewAnimationCurveEaseIn.

- kCAMediaTimingFunctionEaseOut: Equivalent to UIViewAnimationCurveEaseOut.

- kCAMediaTimingFunctionLinear: Equivalent to UIViewAnimationCurveLinear. This is the default timing function for transitions.

kCAMediaTimingFunctionDefault is the default timing function for all Core Animation classes, *except* transitions. As noted, the default timing function for transitions is kCAMediaTimingFunctionLinear.

Layer Animation Transitions

Now that we've covered the basics of implicit animations on Core Animation layers, let's cover one explicit animation class in the Core Animation arsenal: layer animation transitions. Core Animation provides four transition types:

- kCATransitionFade: Fades in or out the layer content as it becomes visible or hidden (the default).

- kCATransitionMoveIn: The layer content slides over the layers underneath.

- kCATransitionPush: The layers underneath are pushed out by the layer as it slides over.

- kCATransitionReveal: The layer content is revealed gradually, covering the layers underneath.

Let's expand the animate method to demonstrate these transitions, as shown in Listing 5–12. The code in bold represents the code you need to add or change.

Listing 5–12. *New code for the animate method in CoreAChickenViewController.m*

```
case 10:
    [self viewAnimation10];
    break;
case 11:
    [self transition1];
    break;
case 12:
    [self transition2];
    break;
case 13:
    [self transition3];
    break;
default:
    [self transition4];
    counter = 0;
    break;
```

This code adds four new switch case statements and animation methods to the animate method, called transition1 through transition4. Let's look at each of these methods.

Fade

Listing 5–13 shows the transition1 method.

Listing 5–13. *The transition1 method*

```
- (void)transition1 {
    CATransition *transition = [CATransition animation];
    transition.duration = 0.75;
    transition.timingFunction = [CAMediaTimingFunction
        functionWithName:kCAMediaTimingFunctionLinear];
    transition.delegate = self;

    transition.type = kCATransitionFade;

    [self.view.layer addAnimation:transition forKey:@"transition1"];

    firstView.hidden = YES;
    secondView.hidden = NO;
}
```

The method begins by creating an instance of a class called CATransition. This is class derived from CAAnimation, the base class for all Core Animation animation APIs. You instantiate a CATransition instance by calling the class method named animation:

```
    CATransition *transition = [CATransition animation];
```

The CATransition instance has properties for specifying how a transition is going to play—its type and its duration, and other important aspects such as its delegate. The properties of the CATransition instance are similar in nature to the animation settings in UIView, although they may be called differently in Core Animation.

One similarity to a UIView animation is that creating the CATransition instance is like beginning a UIView animation block. One difference is that there is no animation identifier and no context. The class instance itself is used as the identifier in the Core Animation delegate.

One major difference between animations and transitions is that transitions work on the whole screen. UIView animations and Core Animation implicit animations work at the more granular level of properties.

The next lines of code set the animation duration and the timing function:

```
    transition.duration = 0.75;
    transition.timingFunction = [CAMediaTimingFunction
        functionWithName:kCAMediaTimingFunctionLinear];
```

The duration property and timing functions were discussed earlier. As in UIView animation, transitions play for 0.25 second unless you specify a value.

The next line of code sets the delegate for the transition:

```
    transition.delegate = self;
```

Unlike the UIView animation delegate, you don't need to set a selector. The transition expects the delegate to have methods named animationDidStart: and animationDidStop:finished:.

The next line of code sets the transition type:

```
transition.type = kCATransitionFade;
```

As noted earlier, kCATransitionFade fades in or out the layer content as it becomes visible or hidden.

The next line of code adds the animation to the layer property of the view controller's view.

```
[self.view.layer addAnimation:transition forKey:@"transition1"];
```

Until it is removed, this layer will play this transition every time a subview of the view controller's view is animated. If firstView or secondView is hidden, shown, or removed from the superview, or if one of these or another view is added to the superview, Core Animation will trigger this transition. You can remove an animation from a layer by calling the CALayer instance method removeAnimationForKey: and passing in the key with which it was added to the layer.

Adding the animation to the layer is similar in concept to committing a UIView animation block. The exception is that the animation does not begin playing immediately upon being added to the layer. Core Animation transitions and other animation types begin playing when the event handler loop goes idle. The animate method that calls the various animation and transition methods is called by Cocoa Touch to handle the touch event for the animateButton. Therefore, the Cocoa Touch event handler is busy while the animate method processes the touch event. The transition will play once the animate method ends and the flow of execution returns to the Cocoa Touch event handler.

Now that the transition has been added to the layer, the next lines of code tell the fade transition what to operate on:

```
firstView.hidden = YES;
secondView.hidden = NO;
```

The transition will hide the firstView and show the secondView.

In summary, the transition1 method creates a Core Animation transition to hide the firstView and show the secondView using the fade transition type and the linear timing function over a period of 1 second.

In line 6 of Listing 5–13, we set the delegate for this transition. As noted earlier, we don't need to specify a selector for the notification methods. Core Animation expects the delegate to provide at least one of two methods: animationDidStart: and animationDidStop:finished:. Listing 5–14 shows the transition delegate method implemented in the sample project.

Listing 5–14. *The transition delegate method animationDidStop:finished:*

```
- (void)animationDidStop:(CAAnimation *)theAnimation finished:(BOOL)flag {
    animateButton.enabled = YES;
}
```

As I mentioned earlier, Core Animation passes the transition object as the first parameter of the delegate methods, in a similar fashion to how it passes the animation identifier as first parameter in a UIView animation delegate method.

Move In, Push, and Reveal

Let's examine the other transition methods in our example, shown in Listing 5–15.

Listing 5–15. *The transition2, transition3, and transition4 methods*

```
- (void)transition2 {
    CATransition *transition = [CATransition animation];
    transition.duration = 0.75;
    transition.timingFunction = [CAMediaTimingFunction
                        functionWithName:kCAMediaTimingFunctionEaseIn];
    transition.delegate = self;

    transition.type = kCATransitionMoveIn;
    transition.subtype = kCATransitionFromRight;

    [self.view.layer addAnimation:transition forKey:@"transition2"];

    firstView.hidden = NO;
    secondView.hidden = YES;
}

- (void)transition3 {
    CATransition *transition = [CATransition animation];
    transition.duration = 0.75;
    transition.timingFunction = [CAMediaTimingFunction
                        functionWithName:kCAMediaTimingFunctionEaseOut];
    transition.delegate = self;

    transition.type = kCATransitionPush;
    transition.subtype = kCATransitionFromLeft;

    [self.view.layer addAnimation:transition forKey:@"transition3"];

    firstView.hidden = YES;
    secondView.hidden = NO;
}

- (void)transition4 {
    CATransition *transition = [CATransition animation];
    transition.duration = 0.75;
    transition.timingFunction = [CAMediaTimingFunction
                        functionWithName:kCAMediaTimingFunctionEaseInEaseOut];
    transition.delegate = self;

    transition.type = kCATransitionReveal;
    transition.subtype = kCATransitionFromRight;

    [self.view.layer addAnimation:transition forKey:@"transition4"];

    firstView.hidden = NO;
    secondView.hidden = YES;
}
```

These other transition methods are nearly identical to transition1. They differ by setting different timing functions and transition types. Another key difference is that these methods also set a subtype property on the transition. Whereas in the UIView transitions, we had transition types of curl up/curl down and flip left/flip right, in these Core Animation transitions types, we have only types of move in, push, and reveal. The subtype specifies a direction for the transition. as follows:

- kCATransitionFromTop
- kCATransitionFromBottom
- kCATransitionFromLeft
- kCATransitionFromRight

The fade transition type ignores the subtype because there is only one fade transition. You fade one view out and fade another one in. There is no movement involved.

Core Animation transitions are a cool way to make your UI stand out, by adding interesting animations every time you change screens. UIKit already provides animated transitions as part of the UINavigator functionality, but with Core Animation, you can choose to add your own interesting twist with four types and four subtypes of transitions.

Summary

In this chapter, you learned how to animate UIView instances by changing their properties within an animation block. You learned how to customize the playback of your animations by changing animation block settings such as animation duration, repetition count, and animation delay. The chapter also covered UIView transition effects. You then learned how to use implicit Core Animation animations to perform similar techniques by modifying the Core Animation layer present in all UIKit components. The chapter concluded with examples of Core Animation transitions.

The code for the full implementation of this chapter's example project is provided in a folder called CoreAChicken finished version. I have also provided a version of the brick-breaking game from Chapter 3 that integrates Core Animation, in a folder named IVBricker CoreAnim. When the ball hits a brick in this version of the game, the brick doesn't just fade out to nothing—it also falls off the screen. The fading out of the brick and its falling to the bottom of the screen are implemented using UIView animations.

Core Animation provides a tool set for adding slick transition effects and animations to your game. With the knowledge acquired in this chapter, you can create cool screens, animated intros, cutscenes, and other great game features.

Many more Core Animation APIs are available. If you're interested, you can refer to Apple's excellent iPhone SDK documentation to learn more about Core Animation.

OpenGL Basics: Wrapping Your Head Around the OpenGL API

If you have played any 3D games or worked on any programs that involve graphics, you may have heard of OpenGL. You may have read the term on a game box or on a web site, or had some other programmer suggest to you that you might want to check out OpenGL. What is this OpenGL thing and how do you use it for your own purposes?

Whether you are totally new to OpenGL programming or you already know a bit about it, this and the next two chapters will bring you up to speed with developing in OpenGL ES for the iPhone.

What Is OpenGL ES and Why Do I Care?

There are a few main ways that you can draw graphics onto the iPhone screen:

- You can make a custom UI view and put some Quartz 2D drawing code in the `drawRect:` method.

- You can use Core Animation layers and provide their graphics content via their delegate methods.

- You can render your graphics with OpenGL ES.

If you have been doing graphics on the iPhone without OpenGL, then you have either been drawing directly with Quartz 2D or providing images to views or layers and using Core Animation. OpenGL is a very different beast. With OpenGL ES, you are setting up a scene, which the OpenGL engine will draw for you. This is known as *rendering*. Whereas using the UIKit and Quartz 2D is like drawing a sketch on a pad of paper, using OpenGL is more like putting a bunch of objects on a table and taking a picture.

OK, but what is OpenGL?

OpenGL stands for Open Graphics Language, and as the name implies, it is open and free for anyone to use. Due to OpenGL's openness, it is used on many platforms. OpenGL ES is the embedded system version, which is a smaller subset of the OpenGL API that you might use if you wanted to do graphics on the desktop. From here on out, I am going to use the term *OpenGL* to collectively refer to both the OpenGL ES implementation that is on the iPhone and more generic OpenGL concepts.

Why would you want to use OpenGL?

If you need some extra speed, or want to move into the exciting world of 3D, then you may want to have a look at building your game with OpenGL. Moving to OpenGL is not terribly hard, but it will definitely add some extra complexity to your game application, so it is good to know when to use OpenGL and when you can get away without it.

If you are planning on a 3D game, you are most likely going to want to use OpenGL. However, many 2D games can also benefit from the added performance that you get from OpenGL. If your game is fast-paced and requires that extra bit of performance, or if your game has a lot of moving images on the screen at one time, you might want to consider moving your code over to OpenGL.

In this chapter, I am going to focus on the basics of OpenGL on iPhone, covering what it takes to build a 2D game in OpenGL. The techniques used to build a high-performance 2D game are very similar to those for building a 3D game, and in later chapters, I will talk about making the jump to 3D.

If you've been using the UIKit and Quartz 2D, you know that they are designed to make it very easy to draw stuff—all the complicated underlying hardware concerns are abstracted away from your code, and you never need to worry about them. OpenGL is a lower-level API. In order for OpenGL to be able to perform well, the programmer needs to do some harder work to get the data into a format that OpenGL can use. This means you will need to do some things in a way that is better for the hardware and more complicated for your program. This may sound daunting, but the trade-off is greatly enhanced performance and more control over your graphics output.

Understanding the 3D World

Having OpenGL render a scene is very much like taking a picture. So, before we get into any technical jargon, let's step back and take a look at what you need to do take a photograph of something.

Let's pretend we want to take a picture of some solid shapes on a table. How do we do that?

First, we need a table and some shapes. Great! That's easy. The table and the shapes are the subjects of the photograph. They are the stuff we want to see in the final photo. Let's call whatever it is we want to see in the final photo the *scene* that we want to capture.

OK, we have our scene set with our shapes on the table. Now we need a camera. Our camera will have two main parts: a lens and a recorder. The recorder can be a bit of film, a digital CCD, or magical pixies that paint whatever they see very quickly. The important thing is that the recorder makes an image of whatever it can see through the lens, and that image is our rendering.

We have almost everything we need to take a photo, but there is one more requirement: a perspective. We need to decide where we want to put the camera to take the photo. Do we want to look straight down on the objects? Maybe view them from the side? This is our camera position.

Once we have these four parts: a scene, a lens to look through, something that will record what it sees, and a position to put the camera, we can finally take our photo (check out Figure 6–1).

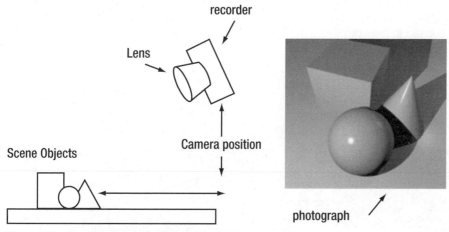

Figure 6–1. *The basic items needed to take a photograph*

Now we can start to think about how OpenGL works. As I mentioned earlier, you don't draw your scenes— you build them and OpenGL renders them. Unfortunately, OpenGL does not have a table to put things on, so you need to build that. You also need to build the objects that go on that table. This can sound a bit difficult, but once you get used to it, you might find you prefer this build-and-render method over explicit drawing.

Matrix Basics: Taking the Red Pill

In order to be able to tell OpenGL where our objects are and what they look like, we need to figure out how to specify things in 3D space. To do this, we use a *matrix*.

A matrix is actually a fairly complex mathematical concept, and you could spend a whole semester at a university learning about matrixes and still not understand them fully (as I did). Luckily for us, OpenGL will handle all of the hard math, so we just need to understand the basics.

A matrix is composed of three components: a position (also known as the translation), a rotation, and a scale. These things are probably exactly what you think they are. The *translation* is where in space the object is placed. The *rotation* defines how the object is oriented. The *scale* is how big the object is. Take a look at Figure 6–2 to see these three components in action.

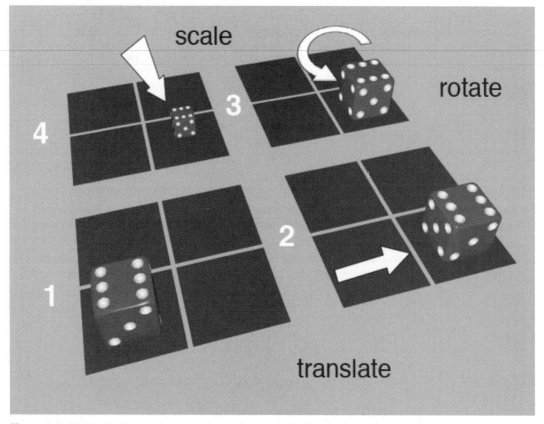

Figure 6–2. *If we start at image 1 and we change the translation of our die, we get image 2. We then rotate the die and get image 3. Finally, we scale down the die and get image 4.*

NOTE: I want to give a quick shout-out to Neil from Tin Man Games for allowing me to use one of their lovely dice models from their iPhone Gamebook Adventures applications (`http://GamebookAdventures.com`).

In Figure 6–2, our die gets translated to the right by one square, then rotated counterclockwise by 90 degrees, then scaled down to half its original dimensions (which is an eighth of its original size). If we put all three of those operations together in one blob, that blob is the matrix for that object.

How do we specify these three things? We need to define a frame of reference. This sounds complicated, but it's really easy. If you have done some 2D graphics, you already know about the x and y axes. The x axis is basically left and right across the screen, and the y axis is up and down. We just need one more axis, which we will call z, and that will be into the screen and out of the screen (see Figure 6–3).

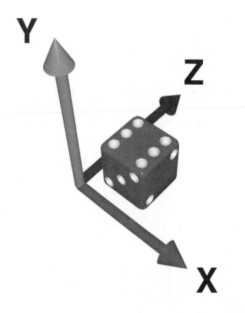

Figure 6–3. *The three axes: x goes across, y goes up and down, and z goes in and out.*

So, if we want to specify the position of some object, we now have a frame of reference. We can say that an object is x units from the left, y units up, and z units back. Easy!

Scaling is similarly simple. We define the scale multiplier for each axis. So, if we wanted to make our object half its length in the x direction, we would scale it by 0.5 times x, 1 times y, and 1 times z. We multiply y and z by 1 so that they don't change (see Figure 6–4).

Figure 6–4. *We are scaling our die by half in the x direction.*

Rotations are only slightly more complicated. We need to define a rotation angle and then an axis to rotate around. It is easiest if you imagine that we are always rotating around one of the axes we defined earlier—the x, y, or z axis.

What does it mean to rotate around the y axis? Imagine that we have the y axis from Figure 6–3. We take that and spear it through our object, right in the center. This will be the pivot of the rotation. Using that pivot, we spin our object however many degrees we want (see Figure 6–5).

Figure 6–5. *Rotation around the y axis. From left to right, we see the die rotate counterclockwise 90 degrees in three steps.*

Now, if we combine a couple of different rotations, we can define any arbitrary orientation we want. Just imagine that we rotate first around the y axis and then around the x axis, as in Figure 6–6. We could then go on and do some rotation around the z axis as well. These three axes allow us to build any arbitrary orientation for our object.

rotate around Y   rotate around X

Figure 6–6. *Compound rotations. Technically speaking, we can actually get from the leftmost orientation to the rightmost with a single rotation around a vector, but it is much simpler to think in terms of compound rotations.*

Bringing It All Together

So, we have these three bits: the translation, the rotation, and the scale. Put them together, and we get a matrix. Matrixes are actually super helpful, as they can be multiplied together. How does this work? Let's look at a real-world example.

If you have some dice sitting on a table, and you move the table, the dice will go with it. If you take the house that the table is in and move it, the table goes with the house, and the dice go with the table. (If we pretend for a moment that moving a house would not smash everything inside it.)

If you wanted this to work the same way in OpenGL, then you would simply multiply the matrix of the table with the matrix of the house. That way, the table would be in the same place relative to the house. Then you take that new table matrix (house times table) and multiply it by the dice matrix, and no matter how you rotate or move the house and the table, the dice will stick to it like glue. If you did not multiply the house matrix and the table matrix, then the house would move, and the table would stay where it was, probably in the empty space left by the house.

So, now we have looked at the basics of an OpenGL rendering: the objects in the scene, the lens, the recorder, and the camera position. We have also looked at how to define a matrix for an object, and you have seen that matrixes can be used to keep objects oriented and positioned relative to one another. We are ready to get technical.

Matrix Types

In OpenGL there are four main matrixes, called the *model*, the *view*, the *viewport*, and the *projection*. Don't let the jargon fool you—these four matrixes are exactly equivalent to our scene objects, camera position, recorder, and lens. Let's take a quick look at each matrix type.

The Model and the Model Matrix

The model is the stuff we are looking at. In our camera analogy, the model is everything in the scene: the table, the house, the dice … everything. This is what you spend most of your time building in your code.

Each object has its own matrix, and when it is time to render the object, the model matrix is calculated for each object. To render the dice, we get the house matrix multiplied by the table matrix multiplied by the dice matrix. Then to render the table, we get just the house matrix multiplied by the table matrix, and so on. In other words, the model matrix tells OpenGL exactly where your object is, how it is oriented, and how big it is.

The View Matrix

The view matrix is where our camera is positioned and where it is facing. Just like the die, our camera has a position in space, and a rotation to figure out where it is pointing. If we hold the camera low down, close to the die, then the die will be very big in the frame. If we stand back and hold the camera far away from the die, it will be very small in the frame. This camera position is known as the view matrix.

The Projection

The projection view is named a bit confusingly. The projection is the lens that we put on our camera. If we put a big fish-eye lens on our camera, we will see more objects then if we put on a very long telephoto lens.

The projection is different from the view or model matrix in that you don't specify a translation, rotation, and scale, since those values don't make much sense for a lens.

The Viewport

The viewport is where the image is recorded. It is our photograph. The viewport matrix specifies how big that photograph will be and its aspect ratio.

As with the projection matrix, we don't specify a translation, rotation, and scale for the viewport. There are special function calls to define the size and position of the viewport.

Stateful API

The final important piece of the puzzle is that OpenGL is a stateful API. This means that there are a whole bunch of variables that you can change about the engine, and those variables will affect everything you render until you change them again.

For instance, in our camera analogy, if we turn off the lights in the house, then no matter where we move our camera or how we rearrange the scene objects, the images will be dark. OpenGL works the same way. It will remember any state changes you make.

In addition, each part of OpenGL has its own state. So, the model matrix will remember its own state, the projection will remember its own state, and so forth.

Even the API itself has its own state. In other words, whenever you make an OpenGL method call, you are talking to a particular part of the engine. So, if you want to move the models around, you need to change the state to the model view state. If you want to change the viewport, you first need to change to the viewport state before making any function calls. Some of the systems have their own special method calls; others use the same calls. So, it is very important to keep track of which system you are talking to, and make sure you don't do something like rotate your entire model off the screen when you really meant to just turn the camera a bit.

Now, all this might seem like a great deal of stuff to know just to draw some 2D graphics faster. This is somewhat true. For 2D stuff, what we are basically doing is pointing the camera directly down at our table, and then just moving some simple 2D shapes around, almost like arranging little pieces of paper. To do this, you will just need to set up your projection and viewport, and forget about it. Then you will deal mostly with the view and model matrixes. But it is important to know about these high-level concepts before we dive into the code. So, now you know!

Rendering Basics

Just like every other application on the iPhone, OpenGL-based applications need to display their contents in a UIView of some sort. Since OpenGL does the rendering for us, and we don't draw things directly to the screen, we need a special type of view to be able to see the OpenGL renderings. This is the recorder from our analogy—it is the place where the user will see the final image.

Apple provides us with a very handy object to work with: the CAEAGLLayer. The CAEAGLLayer is the basis for all OpenGL content on the iPhone. Getting the CAEAGLLayer set up and ready to go for rendering is a nontrivial process, so we will step through it and go over all the parts.

But before we get to the specifics, let's step back and have a look at how OpenGL rendering really works. Up till now, we have been talking about OpenGL rendering a single image, and all the work that goes into making that single image. Generally, what we want is a moving image. So, after having OpenGL render a static image of our scene, we change the scene slightly, then render it, change it, render it, and so on (see Figure 6–7).

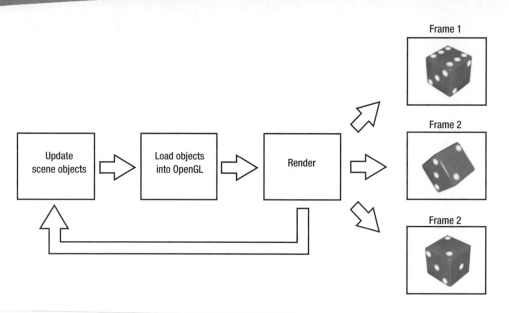

Figure 6–7. *A basic render loop. Update the objects by changing the scene in some way, then load those objects into OpenGL, and then render. This creates the illusion of motion.*

We are going to try to render our scene a whole bunch of times every second, and between each frame rendering, we will move our objects a bit. This is very similar to stop-motion animation.

Our job as programmers is to make code that updates the scene objects and loads them into OpenGL. All the rendering is done by OpenGL—in our case, by the CAEAGLLayer. The CAEAGLLayer works just like all the other Core Animation layers, and it needs a view to display it. In this chapter's example, we will make a wrapper for our CAEAGLLayer and call it the EAGLView.

The Basic Game Template

This is a good time to open the sample code for this chapter. You have a project called BBOpenGLGameTemplate. If you build it and run it in the simulator, you should be able to tap the screen and have the box spin around (see Figure 6–8).

What you see here is the CAEAGLLayer, which is inside our EAGLView. We have added a single, square object to the scene. Every frame step, we are rotating the Technicolor-dream square by a few degrees and rerendering the entire scene. This will be the basis for our OpenGL game.

We have six objects in our template: the app delegate, scene controller, input view controller, scene objects, meshes, and EAGLView. Figure 6–9 provides a simple overview of all the objects and what they do.

Figure 6–8. *The game template in action—not too exciting just yet*

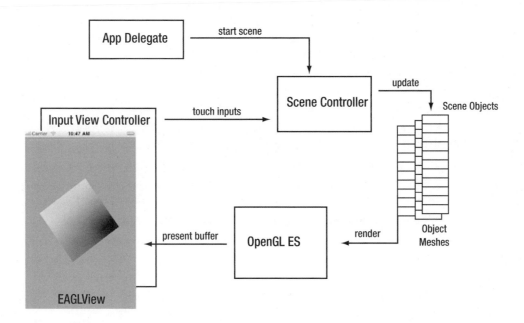

Figure 6–9. *Our basic game template design*

At the top, we have the app delegate. This sets up all our views and controllers. Once everything is ready, the delegate tells the scene controller to start the scene.

The scene controller is the main traffic control object. It handles the game loop. In the game loop, the scene controller first handles any touch inputs from the input view controller, then it updates all of the scene objects, and finally, it tells the objects to render themselves.

The scene objects represent all of the things we might want to render in our scene. They have all the basic state information, such as their position, rotation, and scale. They also contain a mesh object.

Mesh objects define how an object looks. The mesh's job is to load itself into the OpenGL engine.

At the end of the render loop, the OpenGL engine renders the scene and sends it to the EAGLView.

Our game design is nice and simple. Now let's look at the code. We are going to start with the most complicated bit first: the EAGLView.

Wrapping the CAEAGLLayer in a View: EAGLView

The EAGLView is our handy wrapper for the CAEAGLLayer, which actually provides the low-level layer that renders our OpenGL scene into its own contents. It is important to understand how the EAGLView works, which is why we are looking at it first. It is a bit low level and technical, but don't let that worry you, as we won't need to change much of this low-level code. Astute readers may notice that our EAGLView object looks quite a bit like the Xcode OpenGL ES template, especially the older OS 2.x version. This EAGLView is based on that older template, with some minor modifications.

> **NOTE:** In case you are wondering, EAGL is Apple's version of the EGL, an OpenGL specification for embedded graphics language, which is the interface between OpenGL and the iPhone hardware. The EGL specification is an even lower-level API that we don't really need to worry about, because the CAEAGLLayer takes care of all of that stuff for us.

Let's begin! Here's the very first method we see in the *EAGLView.m* file:

```
+ (Class)layerClass {
    return [CAEAGLLayer class];
}
```

This tells the UIView that its main layer is going to be a CAEAGLLayer. The CAEAGLLayer is where the OpenGL content will be ultimately rendered. Without a CAEAGLLayer, we can't do any OpenGL, so it is pretty important. No matter what else you do with this template, you need to have a CAEAGLLayer to render your OpenGL content.

First Steps: The Init Method

Next up is the `initWithCoder:` method. We are going to be specifying some of the esoteric `CAEAGLLayer` settings here. These settings define how the final image will look.

```
- (id)initWithFrame:(CGRect)rect {

    if ((self = [super initWithFrame:rect])) {
        // get the layer
        CAEAGLLayer *eaglLayer = (CAEAGLLayer *)self.layer;

        eaglLayer.opaque = YES;
        eaglLayer.drawableProperties = [NSDictionary dictionaryWithObjectsAndKeys:
        [NSNumber numberWithBool:NO], kEAGLDrawablePropertyRetainedBacking,
                    kEAGLColorFormatRGBA8, kEAGLDrawablePropertyColorFormat, nil];

        context = [[EAGLContext alloc] initWithAPI:kEAGLRenderingAPIOpenGLES1];

        if (!context || ![EAGLContext setCurrentContext:context]) {
            [self release];
            return nil;
        }
    }
    return self;
}
```

The first thing that we do is grab a reference to our `CAEAGLLayer` so we can set some basic parameters.

```
eaglLayer.opaque = YES;
```

This is basically a hint for the rendering system that we do not plan to have any transparent pixels in our layer content. This is a good habit to get into for any layers you are using that do not require transparency, but doubly so for `CAEAGLLayer`. You can use OpenGL to render a semitransparent scene and overlay that on top of some other UIKit views, but your game's performance will suffer greatly. The OpenGL rendering pipeline is a fickle beast, and on the iPhone, it performs optimally when it is the bottom layer. So, unless you have a very good reason, be sure to set the layer to be opaque.

Next up, we are going to set the drawing properties on our layer. These specify to OpenGL how the final output will behave.

```
eaglLayer.drawableProperties = [NSDictionary dictionaryWithObjectsAndKeys:
        [NSNumber numberWithBool:NO], kEAGLDrawablePropertyRetainedBacking,
        kEAGLColorFormatRGBA8, kEAGLDrawablePropertyColorFormat, nil];
```

We are specifying some things that affect the viewport—specifically, the memory that represents the viewport. `kEAGLDrawablePropertyRetainedBacking` refers to how the memory is handled after it has been displayed. Generally, we do not want to retain the backing buffer.

Wait, what is a backing buffer, and why don't we want to keep it around?

Think back to our basic render loop (Figure 6–7), and remember that we are rendering each frame individually and then showing it to the user. This means that we actually need to have a few screen-sized chunks of memory. We need a chunk of memory to render our new frames into, a chunk of memory that we can hand off to the CAEAGLLayer, and a chunk of memory that is used to store the frame the user is looking at right now. The chunk of memory that holds the current frame is the backing buffer for the CAEAGLLayer. That backing buffer is the final resting place for our pixels.

For the most part, you will always be rendering new frames and will have no need to access the current frame, so you tell the CAEAGLLayer that it does not need to keep it around any longer than absolutely necessary. Those pixels get pushed out to the display, and you never need to deal with them again. This helps with performance, so unless you have a very good reason to keep it, you should not retain the backing buffer.

Next, we need to specify the format of the final image. kEAGLDrawablePropertyColorFormat tells OpenGL how the memory is formatted. The default of RGBA8 means that our output buffer will be full quality, 1 byte of memory for red, green, blue, and alpha for each pixel. Now, we just told the renderer that our layer is opaque, so the alpha byte is kind of wasted here. Unfortunately, the only other option is kEAGLColorFormatRGB565. RGB565 means that we get 5 bits for red, 6 bits for green, and 5 bits for blue. What does this mean in terms of your scene? kEAGLColorFormatRGBA8 gives you millions of colors, whereas kEAGLColorFormatRGB565 gives you only tens of thousands of colors. Figure 6–10 is an example of the two different color formats. They look very similar, but the RGB565 format will tend to make chunkier gradients. We will leave it full quality for our game template.

Figure 6–10. *kEAGLColorFormatRGBA8 (left) and kEAGLColorFormatRGB565 (right). RGB565 is slightly chunkier.*

TIP: The only time I really notice the difference between kEAGLColorFormatRGBA8 and kEAGLColorFormatRGB565 is if my textures have very subtle gradients. My advice is to leave it at kEAGLColorFormatRGBA8 for now, and then later when you are optimizing, try it at kEAGLColorFormatRGB565 and see if the image quality suffers. I find that for most of my projects, I end up using kEAGLColorFormatRGB565, but it all depends on your specific game.

Next, we set up the context.

```
context = [[EAGLContext alloc] initWithAPI:kEAGLRenderingAPIOpenGLES1];
```

The context basically handles the rendering to the EAGLLayer. It is exactly like a CGContextRef in Quartz 2D. It is important to note the API constant we are providing: kEAGLRenderingAPIOpenGLES1. This tells the context that we are going to be using OpenGL ES 1.1 style commands and structures. With the introduction of the new iPhone 3GS, we can now take advantage of OpenGL ES 2.0 features on that specific device. OpenGL ES 2.0 is quite a bit different from OpenGL ES 1.1, and it is difficult to get a good handle on the 2.0 API without a firm grasp of the basics of OpenGL, so we are going to stick mainly to the 1.1 API. This will give you a good understanding of OpenGL basics, and then the step to the 2.0 API will be a small one.

TIP: If you start a new project with Xcode's OpenGL ES template, you can get a nice starting point for OpenGL ES 2.0 applications, and also see some of the differences between OpenGL ES 1.1 and OpenGL ES 2.0. There are a few other little things that you may want to do if you are going to be moving up to OpenGL ES 2.0, and I will note them as they come up. If you make it through these three introductory chapters on OpenGL ES 1.1, you will be in a good position to take the next step into the world of shaders and programmable pipelines.

Frame Buffers, Render Buffers, and Depth Buffers

The next method in *EAGLView.m* we are going to look at is createFrameBuffer. Frame buffers are similar to the backing buffer discussed in the previous section. They are the chunks of memory that OpenGL needs to be able to do its work.

```
- (BOOL)createFramebuffer {
    glGenFramebuffersOES(1, &viewFramebuffer);
    glGenRenderbuffersOES(1, &viewRenderbuffer);

    glBindFramebufferOES(GL_FRAMEBUFFER_OES, viewFramebuffer);
    glBindRenderbufferOES(GL_RENDERBUFFER_OES, viewRenderbuffer);

    [context renderbufferStorage:GL_RENDERBUFFER_OES
fromDrawable:(CAEAGLLayer*)self.layer];
    glFramebufferRenderbufferOES(GL_FRAMEBUFFER_OES, GL_COLOR_ATTACHMENT0_OES,
GL_RENDERBUFFER_OES, viewRenderbuffer);
```

```
    glGetRenderbufferParameterivOES(GL_RENDERBUFFER_OES, GL_RENDERBUFFER_WIDTH_OES,
&backingWidth);
    glGetRenderbufferParameterivOES(GL_RENDERBUFFER_OES, GL_RENDERBUFFER_HEIGHT_OES,
&backingHeight);

    if (USE_DEPTH_BUFFER) {
        glGenRenderbuffersOES(1, &depthRenderbuffer);
        glBindRenderbufferOES(GL_RENDERBUFFER_OES, depthRenderbuffer);
        glRenderbufferStorageOES(GL_RENDERBUFFER_OES, GL_DEPTH_COMPONENT16_OES,
backingWidth, backingHeight);
        glFramebufferRenderbufferOES(GL_FRAMEBUFFER_OES, GL_DEPTH_ATTACHMENT_OES,
GL_RENDERBUFFER_OES, depthRenderbuffer);
    }

    if(glCheckFramebufferStatusOES(GL_FRAMEBUFFER_OES) != GL_FRAMEBUFFER_COMPLETE_OES) {
        NSLog(@"failed to make complete framebuffer object %x",
glCheckFramebufferStatusOES(GL_FRAMEBUFFER_OES));
        return NO;
    }

    return YES;
}
```

The important concepts to take away from this method are the three basic buffers: the frame buffer, the render buffer, and the depth buffer. The other side effect of this method is that the instance variables backingWidth and backingHeight are set based on the size of the view. These are just the width and height of the view bounds in pixels.

The frame, render, and depth buffers are all instance variables. The frame buffer is basically the big chunk of memory that will be used to hold the various bits of data needed to render a single frame. The render buffer is where the frame will be rendered before it is copied into the CAEAGLLayer backing buffer and ultimately ends up on the display. The depth buffer requires a bit more explanation.

Notice the if (USE_DEPTH_BUFFER) block in the createFrameBuffer method. Way up at the top of the *EAGLView.m* file, you see this define:

#define USE_DEPTH_BUFFER 0

For the template code, we are not going to use the depth buffer. If you want to use the depth buffer, just change the define's 0 to a 1.

OK, so that's how you turn on a depth buffer. But what is it?

OpenGL, like most every other graphics display API, uses what is known as the painter's algorithm to draw things to the screen. This means that the first thing that you send to the engine gets drawn first, and the second thing will get drawn second; if they occupy the same screen space, then the second thing will be on top of the first thing. This makes a great deal of sense, and it is also how a painter would paint a picture. However, we have a problem once we move into a 3D space. What if the second object drawn is actually farther away than the first object? Well, if you do not use the depth buffer, then the second object will get drawn on top of the first object, even though it should technically be behind it. This can look very odd, especially if the scene is fairly complex (see Figure 6–11). How do you fix it? One solution is to make sure that you always draw things that are farther away from the camera first. Another option is to let the engine figure out what is in front, and that is what the depth buffer is for.

Figure 6–11. *Sometimes you need to use the depth buffer to sort out more complicated rendering situations.*

When you set USE_DEPTH_BUFFER to 1, this method will also generate a depth buffer that the engine can use for depth sorting. (To use depth sorting, you also need to turn it on in the engine like so: glEnable(GL_DEPTH_TEST).) When depth sorting is active, the engine will take all your draw calls and sort the various vertexes based on how far away they are from the camera, and render them in the proper order.

How great! Just turn on the depth sort, make sure there is a depth buffer, and the engine will do all this hard sorting for you! Well, unfortunately, nothing comes without a price. In this case, the price is performance. If you can architect your code in such a way that you can guarantee that the objects will get drawn to the screen in the correct order, then you will get better performance out of your system. In our example, we will be dealing mostly with 2D scenes, so it will be fairly easy to keep everything in the right order, and we won't need to use the depth buffer.

The next method, layoutSubviews, is responsible for creating the frame buffers and setting up the view for the first time.

```
- (void)layoutSubviews
{
    [EAGLContext setCurrentContext:context];
    [self destroyFramebuffer];
    [self createFramebuffer];
    [self setupView];
}
```

The first thing we do is set the EAGLContext. We got the context way back in the init method. Next, we destroy the frame buffer if there is one, which allows us to make a new one.

```
- (void)destroyFramebuffer {
    glDeleteFramebuffersOES(1, &viewFramebuffer);
    viewFramebuffer = 0;
    glDeleteRenderbuffersOES(1, &viewRenderbuffer);
    viewRenderbuffer = 0;

    if(depthRenderbuffer) {
        glDeleteRenderbuffersOES(1, &depthRenderbuffer);
        depthRenderbuffer = 0;
    }
}
```

This is the exact opposite of the createFrameBuffer method. We are cleaning up our buffers. Just destroy each buffer and set the reference to 0.

Our next stop is the setupView method, where all the interesting stuff starts to happen.

Seeing into the OpenGL World

Near the beginning of the chapter, I talked about the idea of a table with some objects, a camera, a lens, and a camera position. In order to see into our 3D world, we will need the camera and the lens. In OpenGL, these are called the *viewport* and the *projection matrix*.

With that in mind, let's have a look at the setupView method in the *EAGLView.m* file:

```
- (void)setupView
{
    // set up the window that we will view the scene through
    glViewport(0, 0, backingWidth, backingHeight);

    // switch to the projection matrix and set up our 'camera lens'
    glMatrixMode(GL_PROJECTION);
    glLoadIdentity();
    glOrthof(-1.0f, 1.0f, -1.5f, 1.5f, -1.0f, 1.0f);

    // switch to model mode and set our background color
    glMatrixMode(GL_MODELVIEW);
    glClearColor(0.5f, 0.5f, 0.5f, 1.0f);
}
```

This looks like a very simple method, and it is, but it covers a few concepts that are very important.

The viewport is the place where the final image is ultimately displayed to the user. All we really need to specify about the viewport is how big it is. We do that in the first line of the method:

```
// set up the window that we will view the scene through
glViewport(0, 0, backingWidth, backingHeight);
```

This is simply defining the rectangle that will be the viewport. For our purposes, we will have it fill the entire view, so we tell it to start at 0,0 and use the backing width and height for its own size. This seems a bit redundant though. Why do we need to define the viewport if we already have a view size defined, and we have already defined the size of our frame and render buffers?

Remember how we talked about OpenGL being stateful? Well, that means that once you set some values into the engine, they stay set until you decide to change them. The viewport is one of those things. If you wanted to render two separate scenes to the same frame, you could set the viewport to the left half of the view and draw some objects, and then set the viewport to the right half of the view and draw some other objects. When you rendered that scene, it would look like a split screen. For our purposes, we just want to render a single scene, so we set it to take up the whole view.

Next up is the projection matrix:

```
// switch to the projection matrix and set up our 'camera lens'
glMatrixMode(GL_PROJECTION);
glLoadIdentity();
glOrthof(-1.0f, 1.0f, -1.5f, 1.5f, -1.0f, 1.0f);
```

The first line here is a very important one. By calling glMatrixMode(), we are telling OpenGL to change modes to GL_PROJECTION. So now any OpenGL function calls will apply to the projection matrix.

The next thing we do is call glLoadIdentity(). This clears whatever might have been in the projection matrix and sets it back to the identity matrix. The identity matrix is a matrix that, when multiplied by any other matrix, makes no changes. It is the blank slate of matrixes.

But what is the projection matrix? You may recall that I described the projection matrix as similar to the lens of the camera through which you are viewing your scene. This is a fairly apt analogy, except that the projection matrix can do so many more things than any camera lens can do.

There are two main modes of the projection matrix: perspective mode and orthographic mode. In perspective mode, your models are foreshortened. The farther away they are from the camera, the smaller they get. In orthographic mode, you do not have this property, so no matter how far something is from the camera, it will always render the same size. You can see the difference in Figure 6–12.

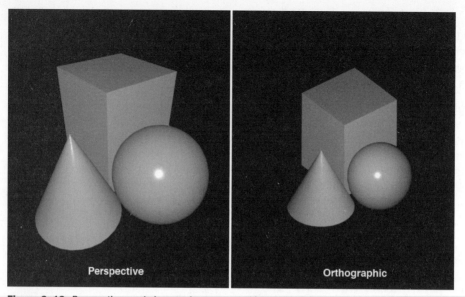

Figure 6–12. *Perspective mode is more how we see things with the naked eye (or though a camera lens). Orthographic mode is good for 2D work as well as technical 3D work, where being able to tell the relative sizes of objects is necessary.*

For our template, we will use orthographic mode.

```
glOrthof(-1.0f, 1.0f, -1.5f, 1.5f, -1.0f, 1.0f);
```

The orthographic mode defines a simple box shape that is our visible space. We specify the leftmost value, the rightmost value, the upper bounds, the lower bounds, and the near and far bounds.

```
glOrthof(left, right, bottom, top, near, far);
```

The resulting box is what is visible on screen. Any scene objects that are inside that volume will be rendered. This is a simple way of doing 2D work. This way, any objects we place on the xy plane at z = 0 will be rendered—well, as long as the objects do not stray too far away from xy = 0,0.

Orthographic mode does not fit neatly into terms of real-world cameras and clever analogies. It is very hard to take a photograph that is truly orthographic. The closest analogy is a very long lens shooting subjects that are very far away. Luckily for us, we have no similar limitations in the virtual world!

Slightly more complicated in OpenGL, but easier to imagine, is the perspective mode. The perspective mode renders images the way that you might actually see them through a camera lens. The downside is that it can be a bit complicated to set up. In this mode, you are defining a view frustrum. A *view frustrum* is the shape of the field of view of a lens. This is sort of a truncated pyramid shape, and it is defined in the same way as the orthographic viewing volume.

```
glFrustrum(left, right, bottom, top, near, far);
```

However, you do not get a nice box shape, but something more like Figure 6–13.

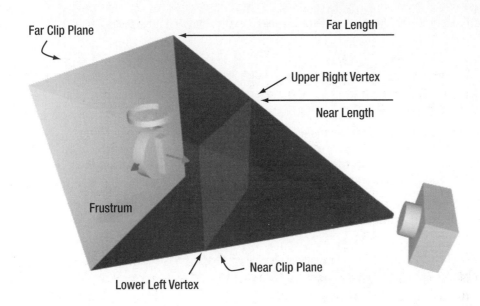

Figure 6–13. *A perspective mode view frustrum. Anything that is in the frustrum between the near plane and the far plane will be rendered.*

The lower left vertex is defined by the values (left, bottom, -near), and the upper right is defined by (right, top, -near). The shape of the frustrum, roughly equivalent to the focal length of a camera lens, is defined by the relationship between the near clip plane and the far clip plane. This is a simple model, but in practice, it is quite hard to use.

A very handy utility that comes with the desktop version of OpenGL is called gluPerspective(). It allows you to specify the view frustrum as an aspect ratio and a viewing angle, which is much easier for most people to do. Unfortunately, that handy function is not part of the smaller OpenGL ES API. However, gluPerspective() is so useful that it is worthwhile to rewrite this function. You can find this in the *EAGLView.m* file:

```
-(void)perspectiveFovY:(GLfloat)fovY aspect:(GLfloat)aspect zNear:(GLfloat)zNear
zFar:(GLfloat)zFar
{
    const GLfloat pi = 3.1415926;

    // - halfWidth = left, halfWidth = right
    // - halfHeight = bottom, halfHeight = top

    GLfloat halfWidth, halfHeight;
    //    use the fovy and some trig to find the height
    halfHeight = tan( (fovY / 2) / 180 * pi ) * zNear;

    //    use the height and the aspect ratio to calc the width
    halfWidth = halfHeight * aspect;
```

```
//    now call glFrustum with our new values
glFrustumf( -halfWidth, halfWidth, -halfHeight, halfHeight, zNear, zFar );
}
```

> **NOTE:** Any functions you come across in OpenGL code that start with `glu` or `glut` are not part of the OpenGL ES specification. You will need to implement them yourself.

Here, we are just taking some easier-to-handle values and then calculating the vertex values that `glFrustrum()` requires. `fovY` is the vertical angle of the field of view. The aspect ratio is the width of the view over the height. `zNear` and `zFar` are the z positions of the near and far clipping planes.

So, the projection matrix defines what slice of 3D space we will actually see in our rendering, and how those objects will be drawn.

> **CAUTION:** Be sure you are in the right mode when you are setting or changing the projection matrix! Don't forget to go into `glMatrixMode(GL_PROJECTION)` before making calls to `glFrustrum()` or `glOrtho()`.

Whether you're using the perspective or orthographic mode, make sure that your near and far plane are set properly. A common mistake is to not realize that any objects or vertexes that fall outside the view frustrum will not be rendered. You may find that your camera and objects are in the right place, but nothing is rendering. Check to make sure that your objects are not closer than your near clipping plane or farther than your far clipping plane. Unlike with real cameras, if you build a brick wall between the camera and your model, if it is between the camera and the near clip plane, it will not show up. Similarly, you might build a complex and lovely mountain range with a setting sun to show behind your model, but if it is farther away than your far clip plane, you will never see it.

We have gone off on a few tangents, but we are still talking about the `setupView` method in the `EAGLView` object. Let's look at the last two lines:

```
// switch to model mode and set our background color
glMatrixMode(GL_MODELVIEW);
glClearColor(0.5f, 0.5f, 0.5f, 1.0f);
```

Again, you see the `glMatrixMode()` call. This time, we are telling OpenGL that any further calls need to apply to the model view matrix. In this case, that call is to set the clear color. The clear color is basically the background color of the view. When you wipe your view clean to get ready to render the next frame, this is the color you get.

Drawing and Rendering

We are nearly finished with the EAGLView. Our final methods are beginDraw and finishDraw. These are the beginning and the end of our rendering loop. We call beginDraw, and then we make all of our OpenGL calls to build our scene. Finally, we call finishDraw, which tells OpenGL to render our scene to the display.

```
-(void)beginDraw
{
    // make sure that you are drawing to the current context
    [EAGLContext setCurrentContext:context];
    glBindFramebufferOES(GL_FRAMEBUFFER_OES, viewFramebuffer);

    // make sure we are in model matrix mode and clear the frame
    glMatrixMode(GL_MODELVIEW);
    glClear(GL_COLOR_BUFFER_BIT);
    // set a clean transform
    glLoadIdentity();
}
```

The first thing we do is set the context. This informs the hardware that our EAGLView is going to be doing the rendering for the time being. Next, we bind the frame buffer. We do quite a bit of binding in OpenGL, but all that really means is that we tell OpenGL to use our frame buffer to draw into. Binding is simply making a connection between OpenGL and some bit of data or memory space that you control.

The next bit looks familiar:

```
    glMatrixMode(GL_MODELVIEW);
    glClear(GL_COLOR_BUFFER_BIT);
    // set a clean transform
    glLoadIdentity();
```

You have already seen a few of these functions. glMatrixMode() tells OpenGL that we are going to be dealing with the model matrix; that is, we are going to be drawing objects. The call to glClear() cleans the view with whatever color we have defined for the clear color. Finally, we load the identity matrix, which we know is the clean slate of matrixes.

So, beginDraw basically sets us up a blank page to work on. The finishDraw method does the opposite.

```
-(void)finishDraw
{
    glBindRenderbufferOES(GL_RENDERBUFFER_OES, viewRenderbuffer);
    [context presentRenderbuffer:GL_RENDERBUFFER_OES];
}
```

finishDraw finalizes the draw process by handing the render buffer over to the context to push to the screen. This is where the actual rendering happens. After this method returns, you will have a new frame on the display.

Now you understand the basics of how the OpenGL scene is rendered out to the display, and you know how to set up the CAEAGLLayer. But we still haven't drawn anything yet! Next, we'll look at the scene objects and meshes, and how to actually get objects into OpenGL.

How to Draw Stuff with OpenGL

You have seen the EAGLView now, up close and personal. Now we are going to explore how to actually send information about your objects into OpenGL. The two building blocks for this are the scene object and the mesh object.

The scene object holds all the state for your object, and the mesh object holds the information for how your object looks. Let's begin by looking at the basic functionality of each of these objects.

The Scene and Mesh Objects

The scene object has three main methods: awake, update, and render. These can be seen in the *BBSceneObject.m* file. I will move pretty quickly through them here, and provide more details in the next sections. The intent is to give you the big picture before we get into the specifics.

First up is the awake method:

```
static CGFloat spinnySquareVertices[8] = {
-0.5f, -0.5f,
0.5f,  -0.5f,
-0.5f,  0.5f,
0.5f,   0.5f,
};

static CGFloat spinnySquareColors[16] = {
1.0, 1.0,   0, 1.0,
0,   1.0, 1.0, 1.0,
0,     0,   0,   0,
1.0,   0, 1.0, 1.0,
};

-(void)awake
{
    mesh = [[BBMesh alloc] initWithVertexes:spinnySquareVertices
            vertexCount:4
            vertexSize:2
            renderStyle:GL_TRIANGLE_STRIP];
    mesh.colors = spinnySquareColors;
    mesh.colorSize = 4;
}
```

The awake method is allocating a mesh object, and sending in those two ugly lists of numbers: spinnySquareVertices and spinnySquareColors, along with the OpenGL constant GL_TRIANGLE_STRIP. We will look at all of this in more detail when we get to the mesh, but for now, just remember that the mesh is holding all of the data that tells us what the object looks like.

Next, let's look at the update method:

```
-(void)update
{
    // check the inputs, have we gotten a touch down?
    NSSet * touches = [[BBSceneController sharedSceneController].inputController
touchEvents];
    for (UITouch * touch in [touches allObjects]) {
        // then we toggle our active state
        if (touch.phase == UITouchPhaseEnded) {
            active = !active;
        }
    }
    // if we are currently active, we will update our zRotation by 3 degrees
    if (active)    zRotation += 3.0;
}
```

This simple update method checks to see if there has been any touch activity, and if so, it toggles the active flag. If we are active, then increase zRotation by 3. This gets called every frame, and if we have tapped the screen and activated the object, then it will spin at 3 degrees per frame.

NOTE: Remember that we are spinning around the z axis. The z axis is like an arrow pointing straight out of the screen, which is why the square looks like it is pivoting around its center.

Finally, the render method in the scene object looks like this:

```
 // called once every frame
-(void)render
{
    // clear the matrix
    glPushMatrix();
    glLoadIdentity();

    // move to my position
    glTranslatef(x, y, z);

    // rotate
    glRotatef(xRotation, 1.0f, 0.0f, 0.0f);
    glRotatef(yRotation, 0.0f, 1.0f, 0.0f);
    glRotatef(zRotation, 0.0f, 0.0f, 1.0f);

    //scale
    glScalef(xScale, yScale, zScale);

    [mesh render];

    //restore the matrix
    glPopMatrix();
}
```

The render method provides a clean slate to draw itself onto. It also saves whatever state the engine was in before it got to this object. It then moves to where it is meant to be drawing, rotates to the correct orientation, and scales itself to the desired size. Then it calls the [mesh render] method, which will actually build our object. Finally, we restore the saved state.

Basically, the scene object render method controls where your object will be drawn, what orientation it is in, and how big it is.

Now, let's look at the mesh render method in the *BBMesh.m* file:

```
// called once every frame
-(void)render
{
    // load arrays into the engine
    glVertexPointer(vertexSize, GL_FLOAT, 0, vertexes);
    glEnableClientState(GL_VERTEX_ARRAY);
    glColorPointer(colorSize, GL_FLOAT, 0, colors);
    glEnableClientState(GL_COLOR_ARRAY);

    //render
    glDrawArrays(renderStyle, 0, vertexCount);
}
```

We are close to having all the pieces to the puzzle. You can see we are doing some things with the arrays of ugly numbers passed in earlier. This is defining the shape and color of our object to OpenGL. Finally, we call glDrawArrays(), which sounds suspiciously like it should actually draw something!

OK, let's step back and have a look at the rendering. We start in the scene object render method and we do this:

- ■ Save the state of the engine.

- ■ Clean the slate in preparation for drawing.

- ■ Move our object to its position in space.

- ■ Rotate our object to its orientation in space.

- ■ Scale our object to its size.

Then, in our mesh object, we do the following:

- ■ Define our object shape and color.

- ■ Draw our object.

And back in the scene object, we do this:

- ■ Restore the saved state.

This is the basic technique for drawing an object in OpenGL. Let's look at each bit in detail.

Pushing and Popping Matrixes

As you now know, OpenGL is a stateful system. You may recall that back in our `beginDraw` method in the `EAGLView`, the last thing we did was to set the model matrix as the current matrix. This means that all the calls we are making in these render methods are affecting the model matrix.

Remember that the model matrix state defines things like position and rotation. Before this scene object's `render` method is called, some other process might have translated, rotated, and scaled. We have no idea if this has happened, so we want to make sure that our object shows up in the correct spot. To do this, we make the following call:

```
// clear the matrix
glPushMatrix();
glLoadIdentity();
```

`glPushMatrix()` takes the current state of the model matrix and pushes a copy of it onto a stack, effectively saving it for later. You have seen `glLoadIdentity()` a few times now, and you know that it clears the current matrix. This leaves us with a fresh matrix to start with.

We then go on to put all of our object's data into the matrix and render it. But the last thing we want to do is restore the saved matrix, so we make the following call:

```
//restore the matrix
glPopMatrix();
```

This takes whatever matrix was at the top of the stack—in this case, the one we saved just a moment ago—and makes it the current matrix. This means that whatever is happening to the engine outside our object, we won't change it.

Putting Your Objects in the Scene

We talked earlier about matrixes and that they specify a position, rotation, and scale. But how do we tell OpenGL about these things? Recall from the beginning of the chapter the discussion of the three axes, and rotating and scaling things. These are just the OpenGL-specific methods for setting those values. There are actually several different ways to apply a matrix to your model, and we will cover a few of them in the chapters to come. Here, we'll look at the simplest method of moving your model around in space: using `glTranslate()`, `glRotate()`, and `glScale()`.

Moving Objects

`glTranslate()` is a simple method. It takes in x, y, and z values, and moves your model the specified amounts in the specified directions. The only thing to remember is that `glTranslate()` moves your model relative to where it currently resides. Consider the following call:

```
glTranslatef( 1.0, 1.0, 1.0);
```

This method call will not move your model to 1,1,1; instead, it will move it one unit in x, one unit in y, and one unit in z from wherever it is now.

In our case, we have cleared the matrix with a `glLoadIdentity()`, so our objects start at 0,0,0. Later, when we start parenting objects together, it will become more important to remember that `glTranslate()` is always relative to the current matrix position.

You might be wondering about that f on the end of the preceding function call. Most all the functions in OpenGL that take numerical values can be called with more than one data type. You will see suffixes like vi, fv, f, and x—just to name a few. There are many good reasons for sending your data to OpenGL as a float vector (fv, which is just an array of floats), but mostly they have to do with wringing every last bit of performance out of the system. We will touch on a few of these in the chapters to come, but for the most part, I am going to stick to the float (f) versions of most functions to keep things simple.

Scaling Objects

`glScale()` behaves exactly like `glTranslate()`. You pass in x, y, and z values, and it will scale your model by the specified amounts in the specified directions. Again, this is fairly straightforward.

The same caveats apply as those for `glTranslate()`: `glScale()` applies the scale multipliers to what you already have. The following call will make your model twice as tall without affecting the other axes:

```
glScale( 1.0, 2.0, 1.0);
```

The only gotcha with `glScale()` is that it is a multiplier, so if you don't want it to affect one of your axes, then pass in `1.0`.

Spinning Objects

Finally, we have `glRotate()`. `glRotate()` takes four values: the first is the rotation angle in degrees, and the next three specify a vector to rotate around. The simplest of these is to rotate around the unit vectors, like so:

```
// rotate
glRotatef(xRotation, 1.0f, 0.0f, 0.0f);
glRotatef(yRotation, 0.0f, 1.0f, 0.0f);
glRotatef(zRotation, 0.0f, 0.0f, 1.0f);
```

Earlier, I mentioned compound rotations. That is what we are doing here. The `glRotate` command can rotate your object around any arbitrary vector, but to keep things simple, we are doing three separate rotations using the major axes as the vectors.

This is a good time for a minor diversion to talk about unit vectors. In our first rotation in the preceding example, we are rotating some amount around the vector 1,0,0. This is a unit vector. A unit vector is any vector whose length is 1. This unit vector is a special one, in that all of its length is in one axis. This means that this unit vector is equivalent to the x axis. So in the preceding code, we first rotate around the x axis, then the y axis, and finally the z axis.

Rotations can be confusing, and it is worth repeating a figure from earlier in the book, which I will now call Figure 6–14. Breaking down your rotations into angles about the main axes is a decent way to keep the rotations simple. If you aren't doing complex things, then this is a fine way to deal with rotations.

Figure 6–14. *A reminder about how rotations work. We pick an axis, then we use that axis as a pivot to spin our object.*

NOTE: The art and mathematics behind rotating things in 3D space, as well as the specification of said rotations, are actually very complex. I could easily spend a whole chapter just talking about rotations—possibly even a whole book. However, I don't have that kind of space, so we will keep it very simple.

It is important to note that if you do the exact same rotations, but in a different order, then your model will end up in very different orientations. In Figure 6–15, we start with our die and we rotate it by 90 degrees around the y axis. Then we rotate it 90 degrees around the z axis. Excellent, we rolled a 4! But if we take those exact same rotations, but apply them in the reverse order, our die is in the wrong orientation, and our 4 is now a 5. So, remember that the order of your rotations matter.

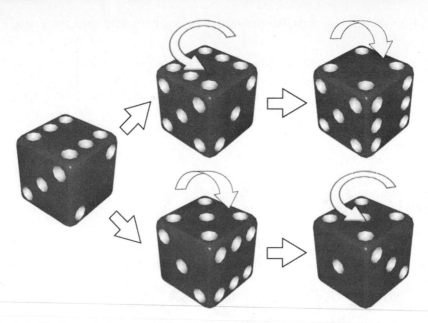

Figure 6–15. *If we apply the same rotations, but in a different order, we do not get the same resulting orientation.*

In fact, any time you are adjusting any matrix with glRotate(), glTranslate(), and glScale(), the order is always important. If you perform the functions in one order, you will almost never get the same result if you apply them in another order.

Defining Your Object in 3D Space

You now know how to move our object, set its orientation, and set its size. But how do you define its shape? You may have figured this out by the name of the object: mesh. We will use a mesh of vertexes to define the shape of our object.

Vertex and Color Information

A vertex is simply a single point in space. This single point is defined by its x, y, and z coordinates. However, in order to draw a vertex, we need to know at least one more thing about it: its color.

Recall our two ugly lists of numbers from *BBSceneObject.m*. We took those arrays and loaded them into the mesh object as the vertex array and the color array.

```
static CGFloat spinnySquareVertices[8] = {
-0.5f, -0.5f,
0.5f, -0.5f,
-0.5f, 0.5f,
0.5f, 0.5f,
};

static CGFloat spinnySquareColors[16] = {
1.0, 1.0, 0, 1.0,
```

```
0,    1.0, 1.0, 1.0,
0,     0,   0,   0,
1.0,   0, 1.0, 1.0,
};
```

Also recall the mesh render method from *BBMesh.h*:

```
// load arrays into the engine
glVertexPointer(vertexSize, GL_FLOAT, 0, vertexes);
glEnableClientState(GL_VERTEX_ARRAY);
glColorPointer(colorSize, GL_FLOAT, 0, colors);
glEnableClientState(GL_COLOR_ARRAY);
```

How does this work? For each vertex you want to send to OpenGL, you need to tell it how many coordinates and what kind of values they are. So, in our template we are calling this:

```
glVertexPointer(vertexSize, GL_FLOAT, 0, vertexes);
```

The first number is the size of each vertex. In this case, we are sending only x and y, so our size is 2. In OpenGL, if you specify only two vertexes, they are always the x and y vertexes, and the z is considered to be 0. Later on, we will be doing 3D stuff, and we will be including the z value.

The next value is telling OpenGL what type of value to expect—in this case, floats. The size and the variable type allow OpenGL to quickly and easily get to any vertex in your array. The third value is the index from where you want to start drawing. If you have a huge array full of vertexes, then you might not want to start right at the beginning, but instead draw some subset of vertexes. In our case, we are starting at index 0, or the beginning. Lastly, we pass in the actual vertex data, as a C-style array.

For colors, we are doing basically the same thing:

```
glColorPointer(colorSize, GL_FLOAT, 0, colors);
```

Here, the size is 4, because we have red, green, blue, and alpha coordinates for each color. Looking at the arrays of numbers, you can see that our vertex array is in groups of two, and the color array is in groups of four. This makes it easy to visualize which colors go with which vertexes. Our first vertex is at x,y,z = -0.5,-0.5,0.0, and the color is RGBA = 1.0, 1.0, 0.0, 1.0, which is yellow.

We are also using these cryptic enable client state calls:

```
glEnableClientState(GL_VERTEX_ARRAY);
glEnableClientState(GL_COLOR_ARRAY);
```

These inform the engine which arrays we are bothering to define. Vertex position and color are not the only arrays of information that we could be passing to OpenGL; there are quite a few different types of information we could be sending into the engine. Here, we are passing only vertex and color, so we also need a way to tell OpenGL which types of information we are providing it, and glEnableClientState() is how that's done.

Regarding the color array, when you specify a color change between one vertex and the next, OpenGL will render a smooth gradient between those two vertexes by default. If you are rendering triangles with three different colors on the three corners, it will blend them all together. This is how the spinning square gets its Technicolor appearance.

Understanding Triangles

Once the data is loaded into the renderer, and you have enabled the bits you are interested in, you need to tell OpenGL how you want all that data converted into images. Basically, the renderer will go through the vertex data one vertex at a time and build an image. You have the choice of whether you want to simply connect all the vertexes with lines or use the vertexes to create triangles.

In OpenGL ES, you have seven choices of how you want your vertex data turned into images, You can see in Figure 6–16 that each rendering style will produce very different results given the input vertexes, so it is up to you to pick the one that suits your geometry.

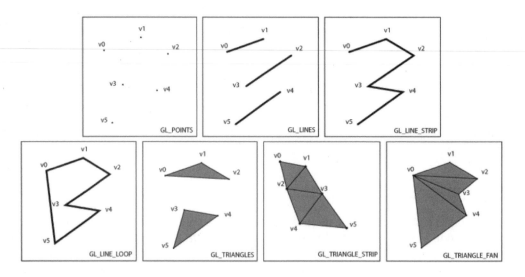

Figure 6–16. *The seven ways we can convert our points into solid objects in OpenGL ES*

The three styles that draw triangles (GL_TRIANGLES, GL_TRIANGLE_STRIP, and GL_TRIANGLE_FAN) mean that OpenGL will fill each triangle with whatever colors are specified for the three vertexes that make up that triangle.

```
glDrawArrays(GL_TRIANGLE_STRIP, 0, 4);
```

In our template code, we are using the GL_TRIANGLE_STRIP style. The next value in that method is the index of the vertex array that we want to start with, and the last value is the number of vertexes that we want to render in this draw call.

Our vertex array is the array of reference, and it has a size of two 2. We have also activated and supplied a color array, with a size of 4. Then we said we wanted to render these arrays as a triangle strip. That's simple enough. But what is going on here?

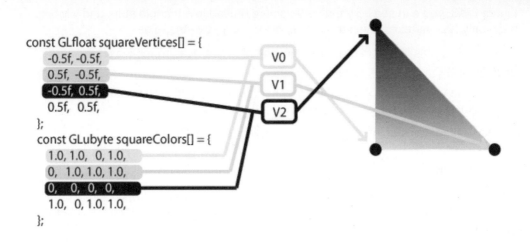

Figure 6–17. *How the first three vertexes are drawn*

You can see in Figure 6–17 that for each vertex, the engine grabs values from the array based on the size—in this case, two values. It assigns those to x and y, and makes z = 0 by default.

Since we supplied a color array also, the engine knows to go to that array, and get out a color based on the size. In this case, it grabs four values off the array and builds a color from them. Once it has all this information for that single vertex, it moves onto the next vertex. Since we have specified to draw them in a triangle strip, it will collect three vertexes and then render that triangle, smoothly blending the colors of the vertexes.

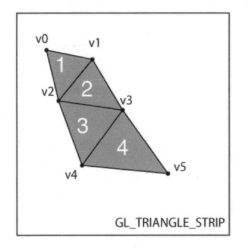

Figure 6–18. *The triangles in a strip share vertexes. Triangle 1 is made of v0, v1, v2. Triangle 2 is made of v2, v1, v3.*

To complete our square, the engine drops the first vertex but keeps the second and third. This is because we specified GL_TRIANGLE_STRIP as the rendering style. In

Figure 6–18, you can see how the vertexes are reused in a triangle strip, and why we need only four vertexes, even though we are drawing two triangles.

So the crux of this is that in order to draw anything, we need to tell the engine three things:

- The vertex positions and all other information about each vertex, in the form of ordered lists of values

- Which types of information we are giving to OpenGL, using `glEnableClientState()`

- Which rendering style to use when drawing those vertexes

This is the foundation of all drawing in OpenGL ES. Once you wrap your brain around this seemingly convoluted way to draw, everything you learn in the following chapters will come very easily.

Well, there is one last thing that can be quite confusing. We have two sets of positions. The vertex array specifies an x, y, and z value for every point in our object. And we also specify an x, y, and z translation for the scene object. What is that about?

Way back at the beginning of the chapter, we talked about matrixes and how they can be multiplied together. There was discussion of a house matrix multiplied by a table matrix and so on. Well, the way this actually works is that each and every point you pass into OpenGL as part of a vertex array gets multiplied by the current model matrix. When you multiply a point with a matrix, what you get is a new point that has been transformed by whatever translation, rotation, and scale that the matrix specified. This is why we specified our scene object's translation, rotation, and scale before we had the mesh render the vertexes. Every point in our vertex arrays is transformed into this new position by the model matrix.

By now, you should be beginning to see the power that this gives you as a developer. You can create an arbitrarily complicated mesh of points that represents your object, like a spaceship. And all you need to do to render it from any crazy angle is to pass in a few translation, rotation, and scale parameters. What if you want to draw two spaceships? Render one, change the model matrix to a new position and orientation, and then render the other one.

All of this code infrastructure can seem very daunting, but once it is in place, you will have so much fun you won't know how you lived without OpenGL.

The Game Loop and the Timer

So far, you have learned about how to set up the OpenGL system to render to the screen. You have seen how to define objects, move them around, and render them. Now it's time to look at the glue that holds this game code together: the game loop.

In Core Animation, you can just tell a layer, "Move over there, over 2 seconds," and it does all the work for you. In OpenGL, we need to handle all the motion ourselves. In order to do this, we need to be constantly updating the objects and rendering them so that they animate properly. To animate the objects, we need to render a whole bunch of new frames every second, and for this, we need a timer. However, it's not quite as simple as that.

On the iPhone hardware, the screen refresh rate is 60 Hz. The OpenGL render engine can swap the buffers to the screen only 60 times a second. On top of that, the buffer-swapping code will wait for the screen to be completely refreshed before it swaps to the next buffer. This means that 60 fps is the highest frame rate you can achieve on the iPhone. If you can get your code to finish all the processing for each frame in under 1/60 second, your animations will be very smooth.

The other effect of the rendering being tied to the hardware refresh rate is that if your code takes just slightly longer than 1/60 second and you miss the refresh window, you will need to wait until the next one before your buffer will be displayed. This means that in reality, you can get only a few frame rates out of the renderer: 60 fps, 30 fps (60/2), 20 fps (60/3), 15 fps (60/4), and so on.

So, there are actually two separate frame rates in your code: the rate at which your game code executes and the rate at which the user actually sees the frames. Practically speaking, if your code is executing slightly slower than 60 fps (say 58 fps), you will be getting only 30 fps actual performance from the renderer (because you are just missing every other screen refresh). This is not necessarily a bad thing, as long as the actual achieved frame rate is consistent. However, if your code is very close to the cutoff rate (i.e. it slides between 59 fps and 61 fps), then you will be moving from 60 fps actual render performance to 30 fps and back again, which can cause stuttering and jittery animation. It is better to have smooth animation at 30 fps than to have stuttery animation that is sometimes 60 fps and sometimes 30 fps. Therefore, it is a good idea to measure your game loop performance and pick the appropriate animation interval so that you are never dropping below your desired frame rate.

There are a few ways to approach this timer issue. The simplest is to simply use an NSTimer that calls your game loop every 1/60 second. The upside of this method is that it is very easy. The downside is that if you take too long to render, you can get out of sync with the display refresh rate, and your frames per second will suffer.

A more complicated approach is to simply run the game loop as fast as possible. As soon as you are finished rendering a frame, you start rendering the next—you don't wait for any timers to fire or anything. This is generally how high-end 3D games work. This method allows you to squeeze every last bit of performance out of your graphics hardware. However, since the iPhone graphics are pegged at 60 Hz, generating frames faster than that will not make your game any smoother. The only thing it will do is drain your battery faster.

Finally, in iPhone OS 3.1, Apple introduced the idea of a display link. A *display link* is a hardware-triggered callback that will call a specified method on your object every time the screen refreshes. This object is called the CADisplayLink. Setting it up is very similar to setting up a timer. If you were to use a display link for your code, it might look a bit like this:

```
displayLink = [CADisplayLink displayLinkWithTarget:self selector:@selector(gameLoop)];
```

```
[displayLink setFrameInterval:animationFrameInterval];
[displayLink addToRunLoop:[NSRunLoop currentRunLoop] forMode:NSDefaultRunLoopMode];
```

This will call the gameLoop method every 1/60 second, every time the screen refreshes.

We are not going to use the display link for the example in this chapter, because it is for OS 3.1 only, and we want to make sure this code will run on any old iPhone. Also, we are not doing anything that is very processor-heavy, so we don't really need to worry so much about frames per second until we get into the 3D stuff in the next chapters.

In our template, both the game loop and the timer are the responsibility of the scene controller. Here is our timer start code, from the *BBSceneController* file:

```
- (void)startAnimation
{
    self.animationTimer = [NSTimer scheduledTimerWithTimeInterval:animationInterval
        target:self selector:@selector(gameLoop) userInfo:nil repeats:YES];
}
```

It's very simple. There are a few other methods in there to deal with changing the timer and stopping the timer, which are all pretty self-explanatory.

This brings us to the game loop, in the same file:

```
- (void)gameLoop
{
    // apply our inputs to the objects in the scene
    [self updateModel];
    // send our objects to the renderer
    [self renderScene];
}
```

Every 1/60 second, we update the model, and then we render. It's that simple. Let's take a closer look at the updateModel and renderScene methods.

```
- (void)updateModel
{
    // simply call 'update' on all our scene objects
    [sceneObjects makeObjectsPerformSelector:@selector(update)];
    // be sure to clear the events
    [inputController clearEvents];
}
```

You may recall from our scene objects that the update method checked to see if there was a tap, and also incremented the rotation. Later on, our update methods will become more complicated, but this controller code will stay the same.

The last line calls [inputController clearEvents]. We will talk about the input controller next, but this is basically just clearing out any touch events that were used during this frame, and getting ready to look for any more that might show up before the next frame.

```
- (void)renderScene
{
    // turn openGL 'on' for this frame
    [openGLView beginDraw];
    // simply call 'render' on all our scene objects
    [sceneObjects makeObjectsPerformSelector:@selector(render)];
    // finalize this frame
```

```
    [openGLView finishDraw];
}
```

renderScene calls the beginDraw method on the EAGLView. Recall that this clears the OpenGL state, giving us a blank slate to work from. Then it tells all the scene objects to render themselves. Finally, it tells the EAGLView to finish the drawing, which completes the rendering and pushes the final image to the display.

Our last two methods in *BBSceneController.m* are the ones that are called to set up our scene:

```
// this is where we initialize all our scene objects
-(void)loadScene
{
    // this is where we store all our objects
    sceneObjects = [[NSMutableArray alloc] init];

    // add a single scene object just for testing
    BBSceneObject * object = [[BBSceneObject alloc] init];
    [object awake];
    [sceneObjects addObject:object];
    [object release];
}
```

Here, you add any objects you want to be in your scene to your list of scene objects. In this case, it is a single BBSceneObject, which is our spinning square. Note that we call the awake method on our scene object. For the way our design works, we need to be sure to call the awake method before the first time the object is updated or rendered.

```
-(void) startScene
{
    self.animationInterval = 1.0/60.0;
    [self startAnimation];
}
```

Finally, startScene is called when you are ready to start the game loop. It sets the animation frame interval and kicks off the timer.

The scene controller is the heart of the game template. Its game loop drives all the objects and keeps the rendered frames flowing to the display.

In our design, there should only ever be one scene controller. This is known as a *singleton*.

Why use a singleton? The scene controller is responsible for the game loop, and the game loop is responsible for telling OpenGL when it is time to render. We have only one OpenGL system, so we should have only one object controlling that system. Using a singleton enforces that one-to-one relationship.

In order to make a singleton, we need to do a bit of funky code magic.

```
// Singleton accessor.  This is how you should ALWAYS get a reference
// to the scene controller.  Never init your own.
+(BBSceneController*)sharedSceneController
{
  static BBSceneController *sharedSceneController;
  @synchronized(self)
```

```
{
  if (!sharedSceneController)
    sharedSceneController = [[BBSceneController alloc] init];
}
return sharedSceneController;
}
```

This is our singleton accessor method. Instead of allocating a scene controller, you call this class method, like so:

```
BBSceneController * sceneController = [BBSceneController sharedSceneController];
```

How does this work? Well, the most important part of this is the static variable declaration on the first line.

```
static BBSceneController *sharedSceneController;
```

The `static` keyword tells the compiler that we want to clear out a space in memory to hold this object, and we don't want that space to ever change. The means that when we put something there, the next time we look for that object, it will still be there. This can seem a bit strange if you have never used static declarations before. The basic functionality is that when the `sharedSceneController` method is first called, the memory location that is referenced by the variable `sharedSceneController` will be `nil`.

Then we get to the next bit of code:

```
@synchronized(self)
{
  if (!sharedSceneController)
    sharedSceneController = [[BBSceneController alloc] init];
}
```

The `if` branch will come back true (since the variable is `nil`), and we will allocate and initialize a new scene controller, and put it into our static location. We want to do this in a synchronized block because we could, in theory, get two method calls at the same time from two different threads, and we only ever want a single scene controller. In our sample code, this cannot happen, because we are not doing anything multithreaded. But this code could definitely be upgraded to use background threading, and we want to be smart about keeping it thread-safe.

So that is what happens the first time through this code. Then, a while later, another object might call this method. This is where the magic of the static declaration comes in. Suppose this line is called a second time:

```
static BBSceneController *sharedSceneController;
```

The very same memory location as before is returned, and our previously allocated and initialized scene controller is waiting there. This means that our scene controller is not `nil`, and it flows right through to the return call. This way, any object that calls this method will always get the same scene controller back.

We will use this singleton accessor quite a bit in the coming chapters, as it will make accessing the scene controller much simpler for our scene objects.

The Input Controller

The input controller is a standard view controller subclass, and its main view is the `EAGLView`. This means that the input controller will get all the touch events from the `EAGLView`. This is a good time to talk about how we are going to be handling the touch events.

In the Cocoa API, the main thread is responsible for all of the user input detection, as well as all the user interface rendering. In a normal application, you just sit around and wait until there is some external event; your app is meant to process that event and then go back to waiting. This works very well for a great deal of applications. However, when you are on a tight schedule, trying to render as many frames per second as you possibly can, the order of events and the timing are very important.

For the most part, you will want touch events to be used during your update phase. You want the scene objects to be able to see if there were any events in the last frame and then make use of them. In the case of our template so far, we are checking to see if there was a touch-down event; if there was, then we toggle our active state.

Since touch events can occur at any time, we want to be able to hold onto them for a short while, so that the events can be used by the scene objects in the next update cycle of the game loop. So, we will want place to store the events until we can use them. We will use an `NSSet`. This makes it nice and easy. We just take the touches as they come in, and we put them right into our set. Then later, during the update phase, our scene objects can check to see if there are any touches. You may recall this from earlier in our discussion of the scene objects.

Now take a look at the code in *BBInputController.m*:

```objc
- (void)touchesBegan:(NSSet *)touches withEvent:(UIEvent *)event
{
    // just store them all in the big set
    [touchEvents addObjectsFromArray:[touches allObjects]];
}

- (void)touchesMoved:(NSSet *)touches withEvent:(UIEvent *)event
{
    // just store them all in the big set
    [touchEvents addObjectsFromArray:[touches allObjects]];
}

- (void)touchesEnded:(NSSet *)touches withEvent:(UIEvent *)event
{
    // just store them all in the big set
    [touchEvents addObjectsFromArray:[touches allObjects]];
}


// just a handy way for other object to clear our events
- (void)clearEvents
{
    [touchEvents removeAllObjects];
}
```

The code is pretty simple. We have our three standard touch event handling methods. We take all of the touch events and put them into a storage set so that our scene objects will be able to get at them. Lastly, we put in a method to allow the scene controller to clear out all our events at the end of the game loop.

Our input controller will become much more complicated as we start to add some more specialized input processing in the coming chapters, but for now, this will do fine.

The App Delegate

The last object we are going to look at in this chapter is actually the first object to get used in our application: the *app delegate*. The app delegate is responsible for setting up all of our various controllers and views, making sure everything is wired up properly, and finally setting the scene in motion.

Open *BBOpenGLGameTemplateAppDelegate.m* and look at the applicationDidFinishLaunching: method:

```
- (void)applicationDidFinishLaunching:(UIApplication *)application
{
    BBSceneController * sceneController = [BBSceneController sharedSceneController];

    // make a new input view controller, and save it to the scene controller
    BBInputViewController * anInputController = [[BBInputViewController alloc]
initWithNibName:nil bundle:nil];
    sceneController.inputController = anInputController;
    [anInputController release];

    // init our main EAGLView with the same bounds as the window
    EAGLView * glView = [[EAGLView alloc] initWithFrame:window.bounds];
    sceneController.inputController.view = glView;
    sceneController.openGLView = glView;
    [glView release];

    // set our view as the first window view
    [window addSubview:sceneController.inputController.view];
    [window makeKeyAndVisible];

    // begin the game
    [sceneController loadScene];
    [sceneController startScene];
}
```

We use our handy singleton accessor to grab a pointer to our scene controller, attach a new input controller and EAGLView to it, add them to our window, and finally start up the game!

Summary

Our game so far consists of a spinning, rainbow-colored square. This is really great, but it does not have a whole lot of replay value. In the next chapters, we are going to add some actual game functionality to our budding game engine.

This chapter has been packed to the rafters with information. Let's have a quick review of what we covered.

We talked about the 3D world, and how to specify positions, rotation, and scales in OpenGL. We explored the analogy of the objects, the camera, the lens, and the camera position, and how that relates to the model matrix, the viewport, and the projection matrix.

We specified a simple square object with an array of vertexes and colors. We saw how we can move the square around using its matrix values. We had a look at how to set up OpenGL ES rendering for the iPhone using the CAEAGLLayer.

Then we took all this new knowledge about OpenGL and built a small game engine that we will be able to expand upon in the coming chapters. Our engine has a standard game loop that updates the game objects every frame and then renders them.

This is a bit of information overload. If some of these concepts are still fuzzy, rest assured that we will be covering them again and again in the next two chapters. For now, I encourage you to go in and play around with the scene object. Adjust the vertex values or the colors and see what happens. Set the scene object's translation values to something other than 0,0,0, and see where the square moves. But don't make the numbers very big! Remember that the square is only one unit across, so if you set its x translation to 2, it will probably be out of your viewing volume. Maybe add two scene objects, or three or four. Experimenting in this way will give you a good feel for how the OpenGL system works.

The most important things to take away from this chapter are a basic understanding of how to get information into OpenGL and how to get OpenGL to show you your scene. Once you understand these basics, everything else is just different shades of the same ideas. How do we get different kinds of information into OpenGL? How do we get OpenGL to render our objects in different ways? We will be looking at these techniques in the coming chapters.

Chapter 7

Putting It Together: Making a Game in OpenGL

Now for the exciting part. We get to take all that fairly dry stuff about OpenGL function calls from Chapter 6 and turn it into a game about blowing stuff up!

This chapter guides you through an iterative game design. We will start with our humble game template and add bits and pieces to it until our game is finished.

Our first version of the game is going to look the simplest. It is intended to demonstrate how to draw lines and effectively "sketch" with OpenGL. The biggest thing we are going to do in this chapter is to build the actual game mechanics. We will define how all the objects interact and how we control them. Then, when we build the other versions in the next chapter, we can just alter the way the interface is being displayed, without needing to change the underlying game code.

Before we jump into the code, we need to start where every good game should start: with a game design.

Space Rocks! Game Design

I've decided that we should re-create a classic arcade game—one that I spent countless hours of my early youth playing on the Atari 2600. I am speaking, of course, of Asteroids. Now, our game is not going to be exactly like Asteroids—it's more like a homage to Asteroids. We will call it Space Rocks!.

Here are our development specifications:

- Our spaceship can be rotated right and left relative to its current heading. This is done with interface buttons.

- Our spaceship can apply thrust to move it in its current heading. This will be done via interface buttons.

- Our spaceship will drift at whatever speed and heading it has.

- Our spaceship can fire missiles via an interface button.

- If an asteroid hits our ship, then game over.

- The asteroids have some drift speed and rotational speed.

- If a missile hits an asteroid, then that asteroid gets smashed.

- A smashed asteroid will break into smaller asteroid fragments, which will have their own drift speed and rotation.

- If a missile hits an asteroid fragment, it is destroyed.

We'll go through a few different looks for the game, as shown in Figure 7–1. The first one will be the retro, replicating the look and feel of the very old arcade games. Then we will move into a textured mode, where the objects will get a bit of an upgrade and have some nicer textures applied to them. Finally, we will develop a 2.5D mode, where the objects will all be 3D models but will still be limited to the 2D game-play world. We'll create the retro version in this chapter, and the other two versions in the next chapter.

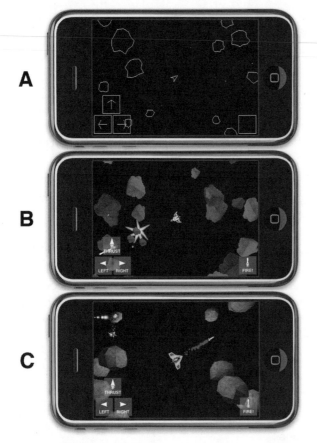

Figure 7–1. *Our three visual styles. A is a retro line-drawn look, B is a simply 2D sprite style, and C uses 3D models and lighting.*

Now that we have a game idea, a nice title, and some requirements, let's define our interface. I find the classic ways are still the best, so I will break out my trusty Dungeons & Dragons mapmaking graph paper, and impart upon it some very artistic sketches, as shown in Figure 7–2.

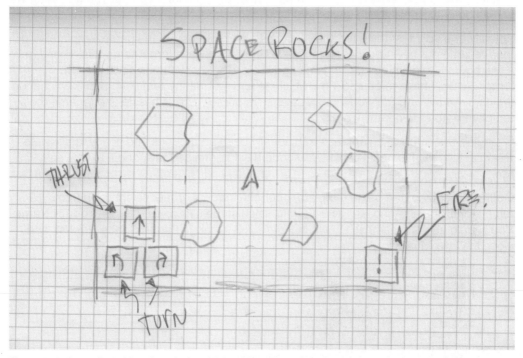

Figure 7–2. *Space Rocks! interface design. All the objects that will be in our scene are shown here.*

As you can see in the figure, we have some rocks, a few buttons, and a spaceship. The only things missing from our lovely sketch are the missiles that we will fire to smash the rocks.

Where do we start?

Luckily, we have this handy game template. Let's start there.

Getting Started with the Template

Our template already has the main view set up. We don't need to rebuild that, although it's oriented in portrait mode, and our game is going to be in landscape orientation, so we will need to sort that out. We already have a scene controller, so that is where all of our game control code will go. We have an input controller, so it should be responsible for handling the button inputs. And we have a nice generic scene object and a mesh object that we can use to start making our game pieces.

What don't we have? Well, I can see right now that we are going to need some way to figure out if a rock has hit the ship or if a missile has hit a rock. We will do this by setting up a collision-detection system (later in the chapter).

OK, it's time to start modifying our template and turning it into a game. The first thing we should do is to rotate the interface into landscape mode. No, wait.

Actually, the very first thing we should do is to make a copy of the game template, and then rename our new application to Space Rocks!. I always forget to do this. Then I get a few hours into developing the game and realize that I have been saving over my template. So, I have to go into Time Machine and restore the template, and then change the name of the app I'm working on. Let's save ourselves that hassle and rename the template before doing any work.

Changing the name of an app has traditionally been an arduous and nearly impossible task. Luckily, the last few versions of Xcode have addressed this, and it is very easy now.

Open your copy of the game template, open the Targets group, select the game template target, and choose **File ➤ Get Info**. Then in the search field, type **Product Name**. You should see one item, as shown in Figure 7–3. Change that to **Space Rocks!**, and close the Info window.

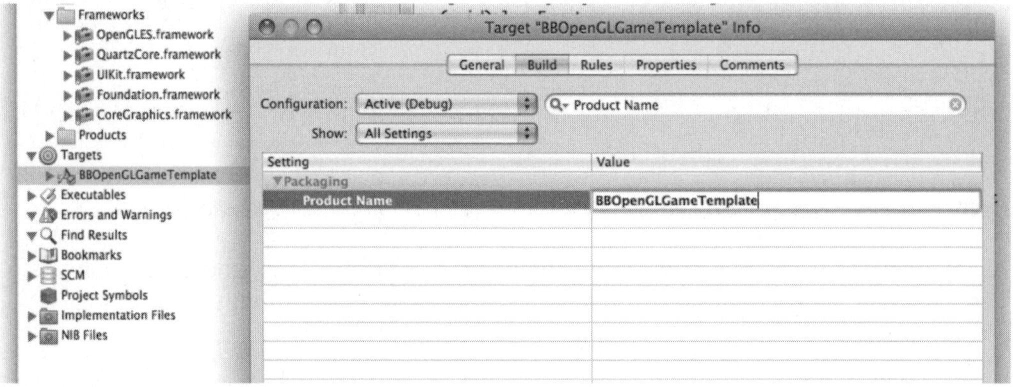

Figure 7–3. *Changing the name of our game so something less boring*

Now that the renaming is taken care of, we can actually start.

Rotation Makes the World Go 'Round

We need our OpenGL view to be in landscape mode. The simplest way to do this is to use the built-in `viewController` functionality to spin our view for us. However, when using OpenGL, Apple recommends that for the best performance, we should instead rotate our projection matrix. Much like the other aspects of Core Animation and the UIKit, the simplest way is usually not the best way in terms of performance. But in this case, it is almost just as easy.

In our EAGLView, we are setting up our view in the appropriately named method: setupView. It might be handy to be able to pick which kind of view we would like, so instead of overwriting the setupView method, we will rename it to setupViewPortrait, and we will add a new method called setupViewLandscape.

```
- (void)setupViewLandscape
{
    // set up matrices and transforms for OpenGL ES
    glViewport(0, 0, backingWidth, backingHeight);
    glMatrixMode(GL_PROJECTION);
    glLoadIdentity();
    glRotatef(-90.0f, 0.0f, 0.0f, 1.0f);
    // set up the viewport so that it is analogous to the screen pixels
    glOrthof(-backingHeight/2.0, backingHeight/2.0, -backingWidth/2.0, backingWidth/2.0,
-1.0f, 1.0f);

    glMatrixMode(GL_MODELVIEW);

    // clear the view with black
    glClearColor(0.0f, 0.0f, 0.0f, 1.0f);
}
```

What are we doing here? Remember that we will perform all the rotation of the interface inside our OpenGL view, so we will define the viewport exactly the same as if we were going to be displaying in portrait mode. Then we switch into projection mode so that we are talking to the projection matrix.

The next command is glLoadIdentity(). As noted in Chapter 6, this is a simple function that just clears out whatever matrix transforms might be stored and effectively gives you a clean slate. We do this here just in case this method is ever called a second time, or if it is called after we have applied some other transforms to the projection matrix.

Next, we have a standard rotate function call, rotating 90 degrees in reverse around the z axis. This will make it so that "up" is the right edge of the phone, and it will be oriented correctly when the home button is on the right.

With our glOrtho call, we are doing something a bit differently than previously in the template.

```
glOrthof(-backingHeight/2.0, backingHeight/2.0, -backingWidth/2.0, backingWidth/2.0, -
1.0f, 1.0f);
```

Since we get to arbitrarily define the view space with our glOrtho call, we are going to keep the origin at the center of the screen. However, unlike in the template code where we defined the view to be 2 units wide and 3 units high, in this case, we will make our viewing area more analogous to the pixels on the screen. So our coordinate system will be 480 pixels wide and 320 pixels tall. The lower-left corner will be at location (-240,-160) and the upper right will be at (240,160).

The last difference is that we are going to set our background to black—after all, this is a space game.

```
- (void)layoutSubviews
{
```

```
    .
    .
    .
    [self setupViewLandscape]; // used to be setupView
}
```

We are going to be using setupViewLandscape for Space Rocks!, so be sure to change the call in layoutSubviews to our new method.

If you build and run the project right now, you will notice that it seems like it is totally black. Where did our square go? It is still there, but it is very small. You might be able to see a single pixel being rendered in the center of the screen. Remember we just changed our view settings from 2 by 3 to 480 by 320. Our square is only a single pixel big now, and it happens to actually be between pixels. If it is rotated, you won't be able to see it at all.

Go into your scene controller and set the scale of our single scene object to something like 100 in both x and y, as follows:

```
-(void)loadScene
{
    .
    .
    .
    //Add a single scene object just for testing
    BBSceneObject * object = [[BBSceneObject alloc] init];
    object.xScale = 100.0;
    object.yScale = 100.0;
    .
    .
    .
}
```

Now you will be able to see the square (and spin it!), as shown in Figure 7–4.

Figure 7–4: *The spinny square, landscape style*

The next thing to do is to get rid of the pesky status bar. To do this, you just need to add a new entry into your *info.plist* document. Open the *info.plist* (if you are following along with the provided projects, it is called *BBOpenGLGameTemplate-Info.plist*).

Select any current entry, and a little + icon will show up at the end of the line. Click that, and you will get a new blank entry. Select "Status bar is initially hidden." Then once that is locked in, be sure to check the check box, as shown in Figure 7–5. And that's it!

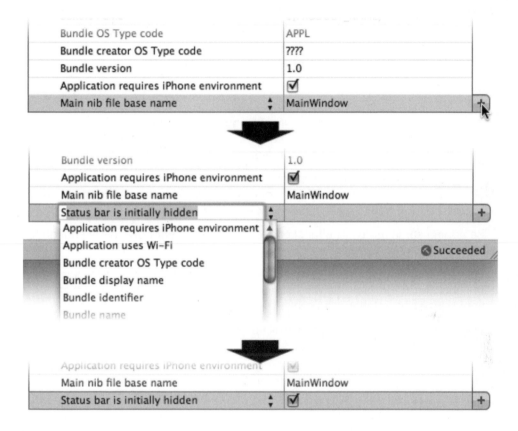

Figure 7–5. *Adding an entry to your info.plist to turn off the status bar*

3D Point Upgrade

In the scene object of our template project, we are defining our translation, scale, and rotation with a swath of CGFloat settings.

```
CGFloat x,y,z;
CGFloat xRotation,yRotation,zRotation;
CGFloat xScale,yScale,zScale;
```

However, in most any OpenGL program, you will want to be passing these variables around quite a bit. It would be handy to have a nice type definition that would hold three values, like a CGPoint, but with z. So, we are going to define our own 3D point type.

Make a new, empty header file, call it *BBPoint.h*, and define our point:

```
// A 3D point
typedef struct {
    CGFloat         x, y, z;
} BBPoint;

 typedef BBPoint* BBPointPtr;

static inline BBPoint BBPointMake(CGFloat x, CGFloat y, CGFloat z)
{
    return (BBPoint) {x, y, z};
}
```

If you are new to Objective-C or the C family of languages, this might look a bit odd. First, we are defining a C structure that contains our point information. A struct is like the predecessor to object—just a holder for some other variables.

Next, we are defining a static inline function. This is a way to make a function easily accessible by any object anytime—well, any object that includes this file. This particular method is just a handy way to make a new BBPoint struct.

We will be adding some more inline functions to this file later. For now, this is enough to get started.

In our original game template, we stored the transforms in nine variables, like xRotation, yRotation, and zRotation. Now we will just have three BBPoint structs to hold that information: translation, rotation, and scale.

Now we need to update our BBSceneObject files. Let's start with *BBSceneObject.h*:

```
@interface BBSceneObject : NSObject {
    // transform values
     BBPoint translation; // add in BBPoints
    BBPoint rotation; // take out x,y,z etc..
    BBPoint scale;


    .

    .

}
@property (assign) BBPoint translation;
@property (assign) BBPoint rotation;
@property (assign) BBPoint scale;
```

Then we move to the *BBSceneObject.m* file. First, we will change the properties at the top and the init method.

```
@synthesize translation,rotation,scale;

- (id) init
{
```

```
    self = [super init];
    if (self != nil) {
        translation = BBPointMake(0.0, 0.0, 0.0);
        rotation = BBPointMake(0.0, 0.0, 0.0);
        scale = BBPointMake(1.0, 1.0, 1.0);
    }
    return self;
}
```

Next, change the render method:

```
// called once every frame
-(void)render
{
    .
    .

    .
    glTranslatef(translation.x, translation.y, translation.z);
    // rotate
    glRotatef(rotation.x, 1.0f, 0.0f, 0.0f);
    glRotatef(rotation.y, 0.0f, 1.0f, 0.0f);
    glRotatef(rotation.z, 0.0f, 0.0f, 1.0f);
    //scale
    glScalef(scale.x, scale.y, scale.z);
    .
    .

}
```

Finally, we want the scene object to be our root object, so we don't want it to rotate our objects on a tap anymore. For now, we will just clear out the update method so our subclasses can override it.

```
-(void)update
{
    // subclasses can override this for their own purposes
}
```

That is going to make things much simpler.

OK, enough fiddling about. Let's render something!

Adding Buttons

Next, we want to add buttons to our interface so that our players can control the action.

You have two options for adding buttons: You can use UIKit buttons and simply lay them over your OpenGL view, or you can draw your own buttons. Using UIKit buttons works fine and is probably the easiest way to add buttons to your game. However, if you are trying to achieve the best performance possible, you should avoid putting a UIView on top of your OpenGL view. This is especially true if you want to use the controls in the game.

In other words, you might have a view that slides over your main game view to change some preferences, or something similar. In that case, you can simply use UIKit views. They will impact your OpenGL rendering performance, but with the game in the background, this is OK. However, for game controls that are always visible and in constant use during the game, I highly recommend that you draw your own buttons.

Because our controls are right on the main game screen, we want to draw our own. We will make them scene objects and add them to the rendering pipeline.

This is a good solution for rendering, but it is a slight conundrum in regard to good design. In theory, our input controller object should own and control the buttons, since they are inputs. It doesn't make much design sense to have the scene controller own the button objects. This means that we will need to separate our rendering pipeline into two sections: the main scene and the interface objects. It turns out that this is going to be very helpful to us down the road (good design always is), so we will pursue this design decision.

Creating a Button Object

Before we can think about where to load the buttons and where to store them, we need a button object. We will subclass the scene object, and make a new class called BBButton.

```
@interface BBButton : BBSceneObject {
    BOOL pressed;
    id target;
    SEL buttonDownAction;
    SEL buttonUpAction;
    CGRect screenRect;
}

@property (assign) id target;
@property (assign) SEL buttonDownAction;
@property (assign) SEL buttonUpAction;
```

Since it is a scene object, it will inherit all the positioning and rotating and rendering methods, so we don't need to worry about those just yet. We do need at least two states: pressed and not pressed. A BOOL will do nicely for that.

We will model our buttons roughly on the UIKit buttons, in that we will have a target object and a couple action selectors.

Finally, we will need to do hit testing. We will cache a screen rectangle, so we will be able to see whether our touches have hit our button.

In our implementation file, we will want to override the awake method and the update method.

In the awake method, we will define our mesh:

```
-(void)awake
{
    pressed = NO;
    mesh = [[BBMesh alloc] initWithVertexes:BBSquareOutlineVertexes
vertexCount:BBSquareOutlineVertexesCount
                    vertexStride:BBSquareVertexStride
```

```
                    renderStyle:BBSquareOutlineRenderStyle];
    mesh.colors = BBSquareOutlineColorValues;
    mesh.colorStride = BBSquareColorStride;
}
```

Mostly, we just pass a few static array variables into the mesh. Where do all those come from? Before I get into that, let me digress for a moment and talk about all the ways you can use your vertex data.

Working with Vertex Data

OpenGL does not provide any built-in mechanism for storing your vertex data. Ultimately, your vertex data will be quite complex, even with the simplest of models. There are literally dozens of decent open file formats that you can choose for your data, each with its own advantages and disadvantages.

The sample code has the vertex data simply spliced right into it as static variables. The only advantage to this method is that the vertexes are right there, and you can see them and easily edit them. This is nice when you are just starting with OpenGL, but I would suggest that as a long-term solution, it is not so good.

All the 3D modeling tools that I am aware of will export the models into a flat, text-based, human-readable file format. I suggest that you start with that file, and write a quick parser to load the vertex data from the file into the mesh. Then, as your 3D modeling needs progress, you can switch to more complicated file formats. I could go on for the rest of the chapter talking about the various formats and why you might want to use them or avoid them, but I would rather talk about how to use the vertex data once you have it in your program.

As I mentioned, for the sample code, we are going to just jam the vertex data directly into the file as a static variable declaration, like so:

```
#pragma mark square

static NSInteger BBSquareVertexStride = 2;
static NSInteger BBSquareColorStride = 4;
static GLenum BBSquareOutlineRenderStyle = GL_LINE_LOOP;
static NSInteger BBSquareOutlineVertexesCount = 4;
static CGFloat BBSquareOutlineVertexes[8] = {-0.5f, -0.5f, 0.5f, -0.5f, 0.5f,   0.5f, -
0.5f,  0.5f};

static CGFloat BBSquareOutlineColorValues[16] = {1.0,1.0,1.0,1.0, 1.0,1.0,1.0,1.0,
1.0,1.0,1.0,1.0, 1.0,1.0,1.0,1.0};

static GLenum BBSquareFillRenderStyle = GL_TRIANGLE_STRIP;

static NSInteger BBSquareFillVertexesCount = 4;
static CGFloat BBSquareFillVertexes[8] = {-0.5,-0.5, 0.5,-0.5, -0.5,0.5, 0.5,0.5};
```

So what do we have here? We are actually specifying two sets of vertexes and colors: one for an outlined rendering and one for a filled rendering. We are going to use the outline for the unpressed state of the button, and then use the filled version for when the button is pressed. We talked about the various rendering styles in Chapter 6, which are shown again in Figure 7–6.

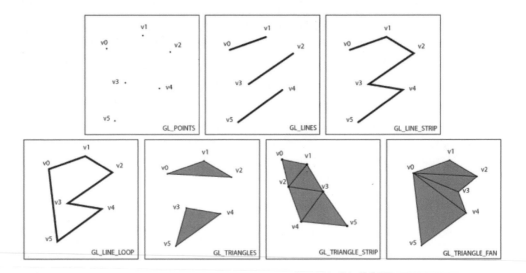

Figure 7–6. *The seven rendering styles available to us in OpenGL ES*

We will use GL_LINE_LOOP to draw the unfilled button and GL_TRIANGLE_STRIP to draw the filled one.

I know what you're thinking: "Hey, the vertex information for the outlined vertexes and the fill vertexes are the exact same thing, only in a slightly different order!" You are exactly right. There is actually a way that we can reuse the vertexes in one array by specifying only the indexes of the vertexes we want to use. We'll take a look at that approach in the next chapter. For now, we will just repeat ourselves a bit.

Let's take a closer look at these vertexes, and talk a bit about how to build a good set of vertex data.

First, notice that even though we have changed our screen coordinates to be 480 by 320, we are still defining a square that is only a single pixel wide. Why is that? It is really mostly personal preference, but if you do any amount of 3D work, you will find that building your models in some sort of uniform unit scale is very useful. In the case of this simple button, we are making it a single pixel wide so that we can easily scale it to whatever size we want. So, for example, if we want to make our button 50 pixels wide, we just set the x scale to 50.

The other very important thing—probably more important than using a unit scale—is to consistently register your models. By register, I mean that you should always build them so that either the center is at 0,0,0 or a corner is at 0,0,0 (see Figure 7–7). And if you use a corner, it should always be the same corner for all your objects.

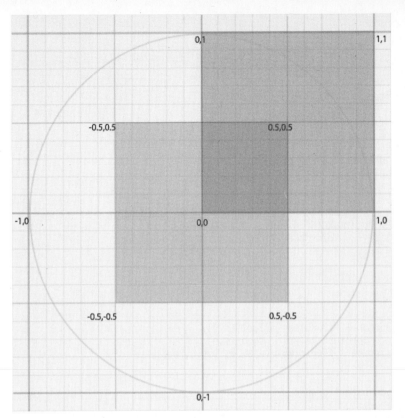

Figure 7–7. *The middle square and the circle are center-registered, and the square in the upper right is corner-registered.*

If you don't do this, then all your code to manipulate your models will become very inconsistent, and you will be constantly shifting things around to keep everything lined up. The other reason to register all your models is because it allows for very easy reuse. Simply reset the translation, scale, and rotation and redraw the object.

I generally center-register everything, and try to keep things in nice easy units.

We have been getting off track a bit, so let's get back to the button code. We have defined our button mesh, and now we just need to instantiate a few of them and see how they look.

Storing Buttons

We decided earlier that the input controller would own the buttons, so we will need somewhere to store them.

Now we are going to jump to our `BBInputViewController` object. First, add a mutable array instance variable called `interfaceObjects` to the *BBInputViewController.h* file. Next, we will build a new method called `loadInterface` in the *BBInputViewController.m* file:

```
-(void)loadInterface
{
    // lazy init
    if (interfaceObjects == nil) interfaceObjects = [[NSMutableArray alloc] init];

    // right arrow button
    BBButton * rightButton = [[BBButton alloc] init];
    rightButton.scale = BBPointMake(50.0, 50.0, 1.0);
    rightButton.translation = BBPointMake(-155.0, -130.0, 0.0);
    rightButton.active = YES;
    [rightButton awake];
    [interfaceObjects addObject:rightButton];
    [rightButton release];

    // left arrow
    BBButton * leftButton = [[BBButton alloc] init];
    leftButton.scale = BBPointMake(50.0, 50.0, 1.0);
    leftButton.translation = BBPointMake(-210.0, -130.0, 0.0);
    leftButton.active = YES;
    [leftButton awake];
    [interfaceObjects addObject:leftButton];
    [leftButton release];

    // forward button
    BBButton * forwardButton = [[BBButton alloc] init];
    forwardButton.scale = BBPointMake(50.0, 50.0, 1.0);
    forwardButton.translation = BBPointMake(-185.0, -75.0, 0.0);
    forwardButton.active = YES;
    [forwardButton awake];
    [interfaceObjects addObject:forwardButton];
    [forwardButton release];

    // fire button
    BBButton * fireButton = [[BBButton alloc] init];
    fireButton.scale = BBPointMake(50.0, 50.0, 1.0);
    fireButton.translation = BBPointMake(210.0, -130.0, 0.0);
    fireButton.active = YES;
    [fireButton awake];
    [interfaceObjects addObject:fireButton];
    [fireButton release];
}
```

A few more little methods, and we can finally see what our buttons look like. In the input controller, add two more methods, one to update our buttons and one to render them:

```
-(void)updateInterface
{
    [interfaceObjects makeObjectsPerformSelector:@selector(update)];
}

-(void)renderInterface
{
    // simply call 'render' on all our scene objects
    [interfaceObjects makeObjectsPerformSelector:@selector(render)];
}
```

Now all we need to do is insert the update and render methods into the rendering pipeline in our scene controller object:

```
- (void)updateModel
{
    // simply call 'update' on all our scene objects
    [inputController updateInterface]; //<-- add this new line
    [sceneObjects makeObjectsPerformSelector:@selector(update)];
    // be sure to clear the events
    [inputController clearEvents];
}

- (void)renderScene
{
    // turn OpenGL 'on' for this frame
    [openGLView beginDraw];
    // simply call 'render' on all our scene objects
    [sceneObjects makeObjectsPerformSelector:@selector(render)];
    // draw the interface on top of everything
    [inputController renderInterface]; // <-- also a new line
    // finalize this frame
    [openGLView finishDraw];
}
```

We want the buttons to update before the other objects so that our scene objects will be able to catch input events as quickly as possible. When we render, we want to render the interface last, so that it lies over the top of all of our other rendering.

Build and run! Wait...nothing. Oh, right! We will need to call our new loadInterface method from somewhere. Probably at the end of the loadScene method in the *BBSceneController.m* file is the best place:

```
-(void)loadScene
{
    .
    .
    [inputController loadInterface];
}
```

Now build and run the game.

Excellent! We have buttons. Your app should look like Figure 7–8. Our buttons don't do anything yet, so it is a very bad game so far.

Figure 7–8. *Our buttons are not very interesting. Later, we will make them look better.*

Detecting Touches

Now that we can draw our buttons, we need to detect if there are touches in our rectangle. In order to do this, we need to know what our on screen coordinates are. How can we do that? We will have to find our bounds in our OpenGL coordinates, and then convert them to screen coordinates.

Let's start with our own coordinates. The object that keeps track of our vertex data is the BBMesh object, so we should add this new code to the *BBMesh.m* file:

```
+(CGRect)meshBounds:(BBMesh*)mesh scale:(BBPoint)scale
{
    if (mesh == nil) return CGRectZero;
    // need to run through my vertexes and find my extremes
    if (mesh.vertexCount < 2) return CGRectZero;
    CGFloat xMin,yMin,xMax,yMax;
    xMin = xMax = mesh.vertexes[0];
    yMin = yMax = mesh.vertexes[1];
    NSInteger index;
    for (index = 0; index < mesh.vertexCount; index++) {
        NSInteger position = index * mesh.vertexStride;
        if (xMin > mesh.vertexes[position] * scale.x) xMin = mesh.vertexes[position] *
scale.x;
        if (xMax < mesh.vertexes[position] * scale.x) xMax = mesh.vertexes[position] *
scale.x;
        if (yMin > mesh.vertexes[position + 1] * scale.y) yMin = mesh.vertexes[position
+ 1] * scale.y;
        if (yMax < mesh.vertexes[position + 1] * scale.y) yMax = mesh.vertexes[position
+ 1] * scale.y;
    }
```

```
    CGRect meshBounds = CGRectMake(xMin, yMin, xMax - xMin, yMax - yMin);
    if (CGRectGetWidth(meshBounds) < 1.0) meshBounds.size.width = 1.0;
    if (CGRectGetHeight(meshBounds) < 1.0) meshBounds.size.height = 1.0;
    return meshBounds;
}
```

This simply runs through the vertexes and finds the extremes. We use the scale to scale the mesh up to our current size. Note that this method will work with 3D objects, but it will return only the 2D bounding box. The bounding box is the smallest box that will enclose all the points in our mesh.

The meshBounds method is not terribly slow, but we don't want to be calling it every time we need the bounds, so let's keep a cached copy of that in our BBSceneObject:

```
@interface BBSceneObject : NSObject {
    .
    .
    CGRect meshBounds;
    .
    .
}
```

```
@property (assign) CGRect meshBounds;
```

In the implementation file (don't forget to add a @synthesize meshBounds), we want to add a line to the init method:

```
meshBounds = CGRectZero;
```

This is just to make sure that our mesh bounds are initialized. Then override the synthesized accessor for meshBounds:

```
-(CGRect) meshBounds
{
    if (CGRectEqualToRect(meshBounds, CGRectZero)) {
        meshBounds = [BBMesh meshBounds:mesh scale:scale];
    }
    return meshBounds;
}
```

We check to see if our current meshBounds are zero; if so, we run our bounds utility, and then save that for later. If our meshBounds are already defined, then this returns them directly. This is a good way to do a lazy initialization of meshBounds. Not all scene objects will need to ever define the mesh bounds, so we will save them from running that code.

All that code was in the scene object, so our button object will inherit all this functionality.

Once we have the mesh bounds, we are going to need a way to convert them to screen bounds.

In our *BBInputViewController.m* file, we will add another handy utility method:

```
-(CGRect)screenRectFromMeshRect:(CGRect)rect atPoint:(CGPoint)meshCenter
{
    // find the point on the screen that is the center of the rectangle
    // and use that to build a screen-space rectangle
```

```
    CGPoint screenCenter = CGPointZero;
    CGPoint rectOrigin = CGPointZero;
    // since our view is rotated, then our x and y are flipped
    screenCenter.x = meshCenter.y + 160.0; // need to shift it over
    screenCenter.y = meshCenter.x + 240.0; // need to shift it up

    rectOrigin.x = screenCenter.x - (CGRectGetHeight(rect)/2.0); // height and width
    rectOrigin.y = screenCenter.y - (CGRectGetWidth(rect)/2.0); // are flipped

    return CGRectMake(rectOrigin.x, rectOrigin.y, CGRectGetHeight(rect),
CGRectGetWidth(rect));
}
```

We call this method with our mesh bounds and a center point. Since our OpenGL coordinates are the same scale as our screen coordinates, all we need to do is some simple shifting to get a screen rectangle.

Let's go back to our BBButton object. We have all the pieces of the puzzle now. First, we store the screenRect at the end of the awake method:

```
-(void)awake
{
          .
          .
          .
    screenRect = [[BBSceneController sharedSceneController].inputController
                          screenRectFromMeshRect:self.meshBounds
                          atPoint:CGPointMake(translation.x, translation.y)];
}
```

We will need some method to deal with the touch events from the input controller:

```
-(void)handleTouches
{
    NSSet * touches = [[BBSceneController sharedSceneController].inputController
touchEvents];
    // if there are no touches then return early
    if ([touches count] == 0) return;

    BOOL pointInBounds = NO;
    for (UITouch * touch in [touches allObjects]) {
        CGPoint touchPoint = [touch locationInView:[touch view]];
        if (CGRectContainsPoint(screenRect, touchPoint)) {
            pointInBounds = YES;
            if (touch.phase == UITouchPhaseBegan) [self touchDown];
        }
    }
    if (!pointInBounds) [self touchUp];
}
```

Since we are effectively polling the touch events from the input controller, we need to deal with them slightly differently than we would in a standard UIView touch event type setting. For any give frame, we will get all the events that occurred during that frame. If there are no events during that frame, then we return early, since there will be no state change.

Next, we set up the flag pointInBounds and set it to NO. Then we use our screenRect to check if any of the touch events occurred inside our bounds. If we get a touch began event that occurs inside our bounds, we call touch down.

If we get to the end of the method and have not found any points inside our screenRect, we know that we need to toggle to the touch up position.

```
-(void)touchUp
{
    if (!pressed) return; // we were already up
    pressed = NO;
     [self setNotPressedVertexes];
    [target performSelector:buttonUpAction];
}

-(void)touchDown
{
    if (pressed) return; // we were already down
    pressed = YES;
     [self setPressedVertexes];
    [target performSelector:buttonDownAction];
}
```

Our touchUp and touchDown methods will change our vertexes so that we render the proper state. These methods also allow for the parent object to specify the methods to be called when the events happen. This is crucial for reuse.

In the case of our simple buttons, we are calling the setPressedVertexes and setNotPressedVertexes methods:

```
-(void)setPressedVertexes
{
    mesh.vertexes = BBSquareFillVertexes;
    mesh.renderStyle = BBSquareFillRenderStyle;
    mesh.vertexCount = BBSquareFillVertexesCount;
    mesh.colors = BBSquareOutlineColorValues;
}

-(void)setNotPressedVertexes
{
    mesh.vertexes = BBSquareOutlineVertexes;
    mesh.renderStyle = BBSquareOutlineRenderStyle;
    mesh.vertexCount = BBSquareOutlineVertexesCount;
    mesh.colors = BBSquareOutlineColorValues;
}
```

Recall that early on, we had the two different sets of information: one for the GL_LINE_LOOP rendering style and one for the GL_TRIANGLE_STRIP style. Our normal state for the button is to be not pressed, and that is using the outline values, which will render the buttons as a line loop. The pressed vertexes will render with the fill values, which use the triangle strip to render a filled square.

The last thing we need in our BBButton is to override the update method, which gets called every frame. We handle any touch events, and then call our super:

```
// called once every frame
```

```
-(void)update
{
    // first, check to see if there is a touch that is hitting our bounds
    [self handleTouches];
    [super update];
}
```

At the moment, the [super update] calls an empty method, but we will be filling that in later, so don't forget to add it in here.

If you build now, you should be able to tap your buttons and have them light up (see Figure 7–9). You may notice that you can't press two buttons at once. We need to tell the EAGLView that we want it to be multitouch-enabled. This is a single line, and it goes into the initWithFrame: method in the EAGLView:

```
self.multipleTouchEnabled = YES;
```

Anywhere is fine, but I usually put it at the end of the if block.

Figure 7–9. *Our buttons respond to touches now. How exciting!*

Now when you build and run the program, you should be able to press the fire button at the same time as one of the movement buttons.

Great! Now our buttons are working, but they aren't calling any methods yet. For this, we will revisit the input controller. We are bouncing back and forth quite a bit here, and there will be quite a bit of this until we get our main game functioning, so bear with me.

Wiring Up the Buttons

We will need somewhere to store our button state so that any scene objects that are interested can find it. We will add a few instance variables to our BBInputViewController.

```
@interface BBInputViewController : UIViewController {
    NSMutableSet* touchEvents;
    NSMutableArray * interfaceObjects;

    CGFloat forwardMagnitude; // <-- add some new state variables
    CGFloat rightMagnitude;
    CGFloat leftMagnitude;
    BOOL fireMissile;
}
```

We will make them properties too, just to make it easier for external objects to access them.

In the input controller implementation, we need to add a bunch of very simple methods. These will be the action methods that are called by the buttons:

```
#pragma mark Input Registers

-(void)fireButtonDown { self.fireMissile = YES; }

-(void)fireButtonUp { }

-(void)leftButtonDown {    self.leftMagnitude = 1.0; }

-(void)leftButtonUp { self.leftMagnitude = 0.0;    }

-(void)rightButtonDown { self.rightMagnitude = 1.0;    }

-(void)rightButtonUp {    self.rightMagnitude = 0.0; }

-(void)forwardButtonDown {   self.forwardMagnitude = 1.0;    }

-(void)forwardButtonUp {   self.forwardMagnitude = 0.0;    }
```

The last thing we need to do here is connect our buttons to our actions.

```
    // right arrow button
    BBButton * rightButton = [[BBButton alloc] init];
    rightButton.scale = BBPointMake(50.0, 50.0, 1.0);
    rightButton.translation = BBPointMake(-155.0, -130.0, 0.0);
    // add some new lines to connect our buttons to actions
    rightButton.target = self;
    rightButton.buttonDownAction = @selector(rightButtonDown);
    rightButton.buttonUpAction = @selector(rightButtonUp);

    rightButton.active = YES;
    [rightButton awake];
    [interfaceObjects addObject:rightButton];
    [rightButton release];
```

I am showing only the first button here, but I am sure that you can figure out the rest.

Building a Better Spaceship

If we are going to be smashing rocks in space, we will need a spaceship. But first, we need to stop and think for a moment. If we have a look at our scene object and also have a look at our requirements, we might notice that we are lacking the ability to provide one fundamental mechanic to our game: movement. Don't get me wrong—we know that we can spin the square, and it will be quite easy to add movement to a child of the scene object. However, we have three things that will need to be moving: our ship, the rocks, and the missiles.

Going Mobile

Wouldn't it be nice if we needed to implement movement only once, and all those objects that need to move would just get it for free? Yes, it would. So let's do that now.

We will make an abstract child class of the scene object called BBMobileObject:

```
@interface BBMobileObject : BBSceneObject {
    BBPoint speed;
    BBPoint rotationalSpeed;
}

@property (assign) BBPoint speed;
@property (assign) BBPoint rotationalSpeed;
```

We could also add scale speed, but I don't think we need that just yet.

Inside our object, we have a single overridden update method:

```
-(void)update
{
    translation.x += speed.x;
    translation.y += speed.y;
    translation.z += speed.z;

    rotation.x += rotationalSpeed.x;
    rotation.y += rotationalSpeed.y;
    rotation.z += rotationalSpeed.z;
    [super update];
}
```

That was easy! Now, if we set a speed vector and a rotation vector, our object will automatically move and spin. With just a bit of up-front work, we have given ourselves the gift of motion to be used on all our other scene objects.

Great! Can we finally build a spaceship? Yes! Off to the drawing board (literally).

Adding the Spaceship

We will need a new object. We'll call it BBSpaceShip. It will need to be a child of the BBMobileObject so that we can move it easily. And it will have one thing it can do other than move: fire missiles.

```
@interface BBSpaceShip : BBMobileObject {

}

-(void)fireMissile;

@end
```

And that's all there is to creating our BBSpaceShip object.

We need to design our spaceship model now. I prefer the old ways, with a pencil and graph paper (see Figure 7–10), but that's just me.

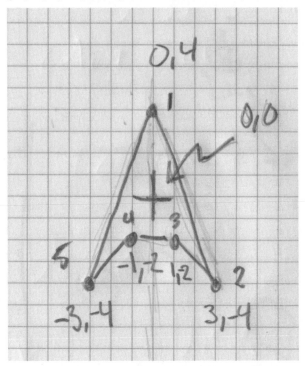

Figure 7–10. *A very high-tech spaceship design, registered at 0,0 in the center*

Once we have a nice design, we will convert it into vertex arrays.

```
#pragma mark Space Ship

static NSInteger BBSpaceShipVertexStride = 2;
static NSInteger BBSpaceShipColorStride = 4;

static NSInteger BBSpaceShipOutlineVertexesCount = 5;
static CGFloat BBSpaceShipOutlineVertexes[10] = {0.0, 4.0,    3.0, -4.0, 1.0, -2.0,    -
1.0, -2.0, -3.0, -4.0};

static CGFloat BBSpaceShipColorValues[20] = {1.0,1.0,1.0,1.0, 1.0,1.0,1.0,1.0,
1.0,1.0,1.0,1.0, 1.0,1.0,1.0,1.0, 1.0,1.0,1.0,1.0};
```

For now, we will make everything white, for that nice retro beam-trace look. We put our vertex data at the top of our implementation file, and override the standard awake and update methods. We will even stub out a fire method that we will fill in later when we have some missiles to fire.

```
@implementation BBSpaceShip
// called once when the object is first created.
-(void)awake
{
    mesh = [[BBMesh alloc] initWithVertexes:BBSpaceShipOutlineVertexes
                          vertexCount:BBSpaceShipOutlineVertexesCount
                        vertexStride:BBSpaceShipVertexStride
                          renderStyle:GL_LINE_LOOP];
    mesh.colors = BBSpaceShipColorValues;
    mesh.colorStride = BBSpaceShipColorStride;
}

-(void)update
{
    [super update];
    CGFloat rightTurn = [[BBSceneController sharedSceneController].inputController
rightMagnitude];
    CGFloat leftTurn = [[BBSceneController sharedSceneController].inputController
leftMagnitude];

    rotation.z += ((rightTurn * -1.0) + leftTurn) * TURN_SPEED_FACTOR;

    if ([[BBSceneController sharedSceneController].inputController fireMissile]) [self
fireMissile];


    CGFloat forwardMag = [[BBSceneController sharedSceneController].inputController
forwardMagnitude] * THRUST_SPEED_FACTOR;
    if (forwardMag <= 0.0001) return; // we are not moving so return early

    CGFloat radians = rotation.z/BBRADIANS_TO_DEGREES;
    // now we need to do the thrusters
    // figure out the components of the speed
    speed.x += sinf(radians) * -forwardMag;
    speed.y += cosf(radians) * forwardMag;
}

-(void)fireMissile
{
    // shoot!
    [[BBSceneController sharedSceneController].inputController setFireMissile:NO];
}
```

Our awake method is simple, with just the standard mesh initialization. The update method is far more interesting.

We call the super update method so that we get all the benefits of the mobile object.

Next, we check the input controller for the right and left turn magnitudes, and apply them to our rotation. We multiply the turn magnitude by a constant multiplier, and we do the same with the forward magnitude. Those constants, like TURN_SPEED_FACTOR, will go in a new file called *BBConfiguration.h*. This new header file will be a handy place to store any constants that we might want to tweak later.

Then we check to see if we are shooting, and we call the appropriate method. For now, we don't have any missiles, but we do know that we want to fire only a single missile every time the button gets hit, so we will need to toggle the missile launch flag back to NO.

Lastly, we will use some basic trigonometry to figure out what our heading is in terms of x and y, and add that thrust to our speed vector.

We're finished with the spaceship. Now all we need to do is add it to our scene.

Back in our BBSceneController, in the loadScene method, we should remove the lines that add the spinny square to our game, since we don't need that behavior anymore. Instead, add an instance of the spaceship.

```
// this is where we initialize all our scene objects
-(void)loadScene
{
    // this is where we store all our objects
    sceneObjects = [[NSMutableArray alloc] init];

    BBSpaceShip * ship = [[BBSpaceShip alloc] init];
    ship.scale = BBPointMake(2.5, 2.5, 1.0);
     [self addObjectToScene:ship];
    [ship release];

    [inputController loadInterface];
}
```

We are calling a new method here: addObjectToScene.

Adding and Removing Scene Objects

Why don't we just add the spaceship object to the sceneObjects array directly? The big reason is that we are iterating across that array during the update phase of the game loop. During that phase, objects may want to add new objects or remove objects from the scene. For instance, if the spaceship wants to fire a missile, it will need to add an object to the scene. Similarly, if a missile smashes a rock, it will want to remove itself and the rock from the scene.

Since we are iterating across the sceneObjects array, we can't add or remove objects from that array. If we change the underlying array while iterating across it, we can cause a crash. So, we don't want to do that. Similarly, if we need to remove objects from the scene, we can't do that directly.

We will need to add in a few more NSMutableArrays to our BBSceneController: one called objectsToAdd and one called objectsToRemove.

```
// we don't actually add the object directly to the scene.
// this can get called anytime during the game loop, so we want to
// queue up any objects that need adding and add them at the start of
// the next game loop
```

```objc
-(void)addObjectToScene:(BBSceneObject*)sceneObject
{
    // lazy init
    if (objectsToAdd == nil) objectsToAdd = [[NSMutableArray alloc] init];
    // activate and wake up our object
    sceneObject.active = YES;
    [sceneObject awake];
    [objectsToAdd addObject:sceneObject];
}

// similar to adding objects, we cannot just remove objects from
// the scene at any time; we want to queue them for removal
// and purge them at the end of the game loop
-(void)removeObjectFromScene:(BBSceneObject*)sceneObject
{
    if (objectsToRemove == nil) objectsToRemove = [[NSMutableArray alloc] init];
    [objectsToRemove addObject:sceneObject];
}
```

Now that we have these two new methods, we need to alter our game loop so that we can add in the new objects at the beginning of the loop and remove any objects after.

```objc
- (void)gameLoop
{
    // we use our own autorelease pool so that we can control
    // when garbage gets collected
    NSAutoreleasePool * apool = [[NSAutoreleasePool alloc] init];

    // add any queued scene objects
    if ([objectsToAdd count] > 0) {
        [sceneObjects addObjectsFromArray:objectsToAdd];
        [objectsToAdd removeAllObjects];
    }

    // update our model
    [self updateModel];
    // send our objects to the renderer
    [self renderScene];

    // remove any objects that need removal
    if ([objectsToRemove count] > 0) {
        [sceneObjects removeObjectsInArray:objectsToRemove];
        [objectsToRemove removeAllObjects];
    }

    [apool release];
}
```

We have not only added two new phases to the game loop, but we also added an autorelease pool. It is good practice to use autorelease pools whenever you are trying to maintain the highest performance. Using a pool allows you to specify the time you want any autoreleased objects to be collected. If you don't specify your own pool, then objects are put into the big application-wide pool. The application-wide pool empties whenever it gets full, which might be right in the middle of a very high-performance part of your app. By defining our own pool, any transitory objects that might be defined in the game loop will be released at a good time for us.

OK, now back to the ship! If you build and run it, you should be able to not only see your ship, but also fly it around the screen (See Figure 7–11). However, you'll notice one problem very quickly: You can fly off the screen and never come back. Since this is a retro remake, we should make it so that if you fly off the left side of the screen, you fly back in from the right.

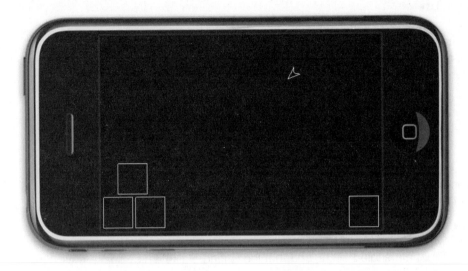

Figure 7–11. *We can now see our ship, and we can fly it around, too!*

Falling Off the Edge of the Screen

We want any object that flies off the screen to come back in the other side, so it would make sense to add this functionality to the mobile object, since any moving object will be a child.

Let's add a single method to our `BBMobileObject`:

```
-(void)checkArenaBounds
{
    if (translation.x > (240.0 + CGRectGetWidth(self.meshBounds)/2.0)) translation.x -= 480.0 + CGRectGetWidth(self.meshBounds);
    if (translation.x < (-240.0 - CGRectGetWidth(self.meshBounds)/2.0)) translation.x += 480.0 + CGRectGetWidth(self.meshBounds);

    if (translation.y > (160.0 + CGRectGetHeight(self.meshBounds)/2.0)) translation.y -= 320.0 + CGRectGetHeight(self.meshBounds);
    if (translation.y < (-160.0 - CGRectGetHeight(self.meshBounds)/2.0)) translation.y += 320.0 + CGRectGetHeight(self.meshBounds);
}
```

It may look complicated, but it is very simple. If our object is fully off the screen in any direction, we simply move it to the other side of the screen.

We call this from the update method in the BBMobileObject:

```
-(void)update
{
    .
    .
    [self checkArenaBounds];
    [super update];
}
```

And that's it. Now any object that inherits from the mobile object will not only get the benefits of motion, but will also be automatically transported from one side of the screen to the other if it goes out of bounds.

We have a spaceship. Now let's make some rocks.

Space Rocks!

For our rocks, we will make a new class of scene objects called BBRock, and it will be very similar to the process we took to make the spaceship and the buttons. But this time, we will make a randomly generated mesh, so that each space rock will be unique.

We will start with an ideal rock, which is a circle; in other words, every vertex is 1 unit from 0,0. However, if we modulate that radius by a small random amount for every vertex, we will get a mangled circle, and that looks kind of like a nice space rock. You can see how this will work in Figure 7–12.

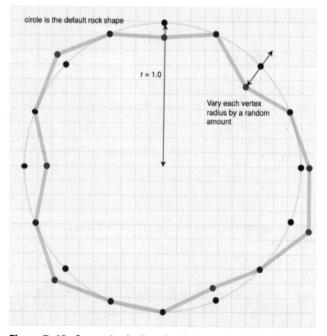

Figure 7–12. *Our randomization of a circle to get a space rock. All we need to do is vary the radius of each vertex by a small random amount.*

For this, we will need something that will generate random numbers. We will define a few macros:

```
#define RANDOM_SEED() srandom(time(NULL))
#define RANDOM_INT(__MIN__, __MAX__) ((__MIN__) + random() % ((__MAX__ +1) - (__MIN__)))
```

Let's put them in our *BBConfiguration.h* file. The first macro is just a quick way to seed the random number generator. The second one is a bit more complicated, but basically just returns a random integer between MAX and MIN.

Now let's make our new BBRock object. It will also be a subclass of the mobile object.

```
@interface BBRock : BBMobileObject {
    CGFloat * verts;
    CGFloat * colors;
}
```

Since we are going to be generating our vertexes, as opposed to just using static arrays, we will need some place to store them, hence the CGFloat pointers.

As with the other scene objects, we will have a few static variables in our implementation file:

```
#pragma mark Rocks mesh
// the rocks are going to be randomly generated
// so we just need some basic info about them
static NSInteger BBRockVertexStride = 2;
static NSInteger BBRockColorStride = 4;
static NSInteger BBRockOutlineVertexesCount = 16;
```

Now the big, scary awake method. Let's take this in pieces.

```
-(void)awake
{
    // pick a random number of vertexes, more than 8, less than the max count
    NSInteger myVertexCount = RANDOM_INT(8,BBRockOutlineVertexesCount);

    // malloc some memory for our vertexes and colors
    verts = (CGFloat *) malloc(myVertexCount * BBRockVertexStride * sizeof(CGFloat));
    colors = (CGFloat *) malloc(myVertexCount * BBRockColorStride * sizeof(CGFloat));

    // we need to use radians for our angle since we will
    // be using the trig functions
    CGFloat radians = 0.0;
    CGFloat radianIncrement = (2.0 * 3.14159) / (CGFloat)myVertexCount;
```

In this first part, we are just doing some setup. We get a random vertex count, allocate some memory for our vertexes, and finally set up our angle counter and angle step.

```
    // generate the vertexes
    NSInteger vertexIndex = 0;
    for (vertexIndex = 0; vertexIndex < myVertexCount; vertexIndex++) {
        NSInteger position = vertexIndex * BBRockVertexStride;
        // random radial adjustment
        CGFloat radiusAdjust = 0.25 - (RANDOM_INT(1,100)/100.0 * 0.5);
        // calculate the point on the circle, but vary the radius
        verts[position] = cosf(radians) * (1.0 + radiusAdjust);
        verts[position + 1] = sinf(radians) * (1.0 + radiusAdjust);
```

```
        // move on to the next angle
        radians += radianIncrement;
    }
```

This part is the most interesting. If we simply multiplied the cosine and sine functions by 1.0, we would get a circle with radius 1.0. Instead, we are adjusting the radius by +/- 0.25. This way, we retain the roughly circular shape, but get a nice randomization.

```
    // now the colors, just make it white for now, all 1's
    for (vertexIndex = 0; vertexIndex < myVertexCount * BBRockColorStride;
vertexIndex++) {
        colors[vertexIndex] = 1.0;
    }

    // now alloc our mesh with our random verts
    mesh = [[BBMesh alloc] initWithVertexes:verts
                                vertexCount:myVertexCount
                                vertexStride:BBRockVertexStride
                                renderStyle:GL_LINE_LOOP];

    mesh.colors = colors;
    mesh.colorStride = BBRockColorStride;
```

```
}
```

This last bit is just finishing up. For now, all our colors will be white. We do a standard mesh initialization, but with our freshly minted vertexes, and we are ready to go. Since the only thing rocks do is drift about, and we get all that functionality from the superclass, we are basically finished here.

However, it might be nice to have a quick and easy way to get a single randomized rock. We can do this with a class method (or two).

```
+(BBRock*)randomRock
{
    return [BBRock randomRockWithScale:NSMakeRange(15, 20)];
}

+(BBRock*)randomRockWithScale:(NSRange)scaleRange
{
    BBRock * rock = [[BBRock alloc] init];
    CGFloat scale = RANDOM_INT(scaleRange.location,NSMaxRange(scaleRange));
    rock.scale = BBPointMake(scale, scale, 1.0);
    CGFloat x = RANDOM_INT(100,230);
    NSInteger flipX = RANDOM_INT(1,10);
    if (flipX <= 5) x *= -1.0;
    CGFloat y = RANDOM_INT(0,320) - 160;
    rock.translation = BBPointMake(x, y, 0.0);
    // the rocks will be moving either up or down in the y axis
    CGFloat speed = RANDOM_INT(1,100)/100.0;
    NSInteger flipY = RANDOM_INT(1,10);
    if (flipY <= 5) speed *= -1.0;
    rock.speed = BBPointMake(0.0, speed, 0.0);

    CGFloat rotSpeed = RANDOM_INT(1,100)/200.0;
    NSInteger flipRot = RANDOM_INT(1,10);
    if (flipRot <= 5) rotSpeed *= -1.0;
```

```
    rock.rotationalSpeed = BBPointMake(0.0, 0.0, rotSpeed);
    return [rock autorelease];
}
```

Our random rock generator picks a scale between the specified scale range, picks a random x position either above 100 or below -100, and a random y position. It also adds a random speed and spin to our rock. And since we inherit from BBMobileObject, our rocks will never drift off the screen (well, not without coming back in on the other side).

To see how the rocks look, we need to add them to our loadScene in the scene controller. We will actually make a method call for this:

```
// generate a bunch of random rocks and add them to the scene
-(void)generateRocks
{
    NSInteger rockCount = 10;
    NSInteger index;
    for (index = 0; index < rockCount; index ++) {
        [self addObjectToScene:[BBRock randomRock]];
    }
}
```

Now we add that to our loadScene, and we might as well seed the random number here, too, since we call it only once.

```
// this is where we initialize all our scene objects
-(void)loadScene
{
    RANDOM_SEED();
    .
    .
    .
    [self generateRocks];
    [inputController loadInterface];
}
```

If you build and run it (see Figure 7–13), you will see our rocks drifting around either side of the screen, and you can fly around using our controls. Now we need to be able to smash stuff. We need weapons!

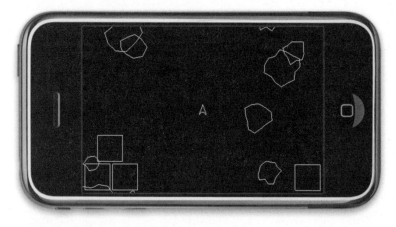

Figure 7–13. *This is starting to look like a real game.*

Adding Missiles

You may have noticed a pattern here. For our missiles, we need to add a new scene object, so we will make a new subclass of the mobile object and call it BBMissile:

```
@interface BBMissile : BBMobileObject {

}

@end
```

Our missiles will be pretty simple; they don't need anything extra. They do, however, need a model. Let's just make them very skinny triangles:

```
#pragma mark Missile mesh

static NSInteger BBMissileVertexStride = 2;
static NSInteger BBMissileColorStride = 4;

static NSInteger BBMissileOutlineVertexesCount = 3;
static CGFloat BBMissileOutlineVertexes[6] =
{-0.2, 0.0,  0.2,0.0,  0.0, 2.0};

static CGFloat BBMissileColorValues[12] =
{1.0,1.0,1.0,1.0, 1.0,1.0,1.0,1.0, 1.0,1.0,1.0,1.0};
```

Add a standard awake method referencing our vertex data:

```
-(void)awake
{
    mesh = [[BBMesh alloc] initWithVertexes:BBMissileOutlineVertexes
                    vertexCount:BBMissileOutlineVertexesCount
                    vertexStride:BBMissileVertexStride
                    renderStyle:GL_TRIANGLES];
    mesh.colors = BBMissileColorValues;
    mesh.colorStride = BBMissileColorStride;
}
```

Firing Missiles

Now we need some way to generate missiles. For that, we go back to our stubbed out fireMissile method in the BBSpaceShip object:

```
-(void)fireMissile
{
    // need to spawn a missile
    BBMissile * missile = [[BBMissile alloc] init];
    missile.scale = BBPointMake(5.0, 5.0, 1.0);
    // we need to position it at the tip of our ship
    CGFloat radians = rotation.z/BBRADIANS_TO_DEGREES;
    CGFloat speedX = -sinf(radians) * 3.0;
    CGFloat speedY = cosf(radians) * 3.0;

    missile.speed = BBPointMake(speedX, speedY, 0.0);
```

```
    missile.translation = BBPointMake(translation.x + missile.speed.x * 3.0,
translation.y + missile.speed.y * 3.0, 0.0);
    missile.rotation = BBPointMake(0.0, 0.0, self.rotation.z);

    [[BBSceneController sharedSceneController] addObjectToScene:missile];
    [missile release];

    [[BBSceneController sharedSceneController].inputController setFireMissile:NO];
}
```

Here, we are doing some pretty standard stuff. We allocate a missile object. We then get the angle of our current heading in radians. This way, we can build a speed vector that is going in the right direction. It turns out the direction of the speed vector is also the direction we want to translate the missile from our center point to make it look like it is coming out of the tip of our ship. Lastly, we set the missile rotation to be the same as our current heading.

Once our missile is ready, we want to add it to our scene, so we call addObjectToScene on the BBSceneController. This will queue up this missile to be added to the scene at the start of the next game loop.

If you build and run the game now, you can fire missiles to your heart's content! The problem is that after a very short while, the missiles start to clutter the screen (see Figure 7–14).

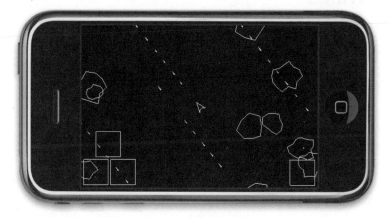

Figure 7–14. *We need to be careful or we might shoot ourselves in the back.*

Removing Unwanted Missiles

Once we have added a way for the objects to interact, many of these missiles will be used up when they smash the rocks. Ultimately though, we probably need to change it so that they reach only as far as the edge of the screen.

You may recall that back into our mobile object, we added a method called checkArenaBounds, which handles keeping all our objects on the screen. In order to fix the missile issue, all we need to do is override that method in our BBMissile class, and we will be good to go!

```
-(void)checkArenaBounds
{
    BOOL outOfArena = NO;
    if (translation.x > (240.0 + CGRectGetWidth(self.meshBounds)/2.0)) outOfArena = YES;
    if (translation.x < (-240.0 - CGRectGetWidth(self.meshBounds)/2.0)) outOfArena =
YES;

    if (translation.y > (160.0 + CGRectGetHeight(self.meshBounds)/2.0)) outOfArena =
YES;
    if (translation.y < (-160.0 - CGRectGetHeight(self.meshBounds)/2.0)) outOfArena =
YES;

    if (outOfArena) {
        [[BBSceneController sharedSceneController] removeObjectFromScene:self];
    }
}
```

This looks very similar to the checkArenaBounds that is in the BBMobileObject class. We
are doing basically the same thing, except in this case, if we find ourselves outside the
screen bounds, we need to remove ourselves from the scene. This is easily
accomplished by calling the scene controller method removeObjectFromScene. This will
queue up the missile for removal at the end of this game loop.

Making Nicer Buttons

Our buttons are very bland squares. Since this is the retro version, we want to stick to
the retro look, but it would be nice if the buttons had some sort of marking on them. But
we just need to change the nonpressed look of the buttons, since when they are
pressed, not only is your finger in the way of seeing them, but they already fill with white,
which is fine.

For our nicer buttons, we will make a new subclass for the type of button we want,
called BBArrowButton:

```
@interface BBArrowButton : BBButton {

}
```

We will keep it very simple. We just want a button with an arrow on it.

```
#pragma mark arrow button mesh
static NSInteger BBArrowButtonOutlineVertexesCount = 14;
static CGFloat BBArrowButtonOutlineVertexes[28] = {-0.25, 0.0, 0.25, 0.0,
0.25, 0.0, 0.1, 0.25,0.25, 0.0, 0.1,-0.25, -0.5,-0.5,-0.5, 0.5, -0.5, 0.5,
0.5, 0.5, 0.5, 0.5, 0.5,-0.5, 0.5,-0.5,-0.5,-0.5};
static GLenum BBArrowButtonOutlineRenderStyle = GL_LINES;
static CGFloat BBArrowButtonOutlineColorValues[56] =
{1.0,1.0,1.0,1.0, 1.0,1.0,1.0,1.0, 1.0,1.0,1.0,1.0, 1.0,1.0,1.0,1.0,
1.0,1.0,1.0,1.0, 1.0,1.0,1.0,1.0, 1.0,1.0,1.0,1.0, 1.0,1.0,1.0,1.0,
1.0,1.0,1.0,1.0, 1.0,1.0,1.0,1.0, 1.0,1.0,1.0,1.0, 1.0,1.0,1.0,1.0,
1.0,1.0,1.0,1.0, 1.0,1.0,1.0,1.0};


@implementation BBArrowButton
-(void)setNotPressedVertexes
```

```
{
    mesh.vertexes = BBArrowButtonOutlineVertexes;
    mesh.renderStyle = BBArrowButtonOutlineRenderStyle;
    mesh.vertexCount = BBArrowButtonOutlineVertexesCount;
    mesh.colors = BBArrowButtonOutlineColorValues;
}
```

Our new button is mostly just new vertexes. The only code we are running is to override the setNotPressedVertexes method, so that when the button is in the up position, it displays our new look. In case you can't render vertexes in your head, this will be an arrow pointing to the right.

Now, in the input controller, where we instantiate our buttons, just change the class from BBButton to BBArrowButton. Oh, and unless you want all your buttons to point to the right, don't forget to rotate them as well.

```
-(void)loadInterface
{
    .
    .
    .
    // right arrow button
    BBArrowButton * rightButton = [[BBArrowButton alloc] init];
    .
    .
    // left arrow
    BBArrowButton * leftButton = [[BBArrowButton alloc] init];
    leftButton.rotation = BBPointMake(0.0, 0.0, 180.0);
    .
    .
    // forward button
    BBArrowButton * forwardButton = [[BBArrowButton alloc] init];
    forwardButton.rotation = BBPointMake(0.0, 0.0, 90.0);
    .
    .
}
```

If you build and run this, you can fly around with the arrow buttons, fire missiles, and watch the rocks drift by (see Figure 7–15).

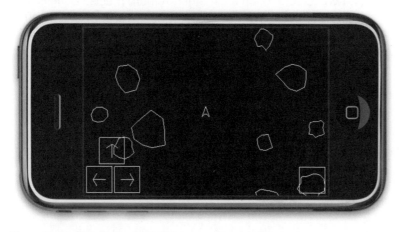

Figure 7–15. *Nicer buttons with little arrows drawn in them.*

Now all we need to do is add object interaction so that our missiles can smash rocks and rocks can smash the spaceship. In order for our objects to interact, we need collision detection.

Collision Detection

You may be tired of reading this, but like many subtopics of OpenGL game design, collision detection is it's own huge area of content. Again, I could write whole chapters on this subject alone. Here, I am going to skim the surface to give you just enough understanding of the issues involved to implement your own simple collision-detection system.

In a well-designed OpenGL game, the part of the game loop that takes the most time is the actual rendering. However, when you start to add dozens and dozens of objects to your scene, the collision-detection code can quickly take over your processor, and is often the cause of slowdown and poor performance. Without this subsystem, however, you have no game, because your objects cannot interact. Therefore, it is vitally important that you design the collision system to be efficient.

The next hurdle is that most OpenGL games are in 3D, so you have the added dimension that makes fast and efficient collision detection an order of magnitude more difficult. Space Rocks! is all in 2D, but I am also going to cover some techniques that apply to 3D as well.

We are going to start with some broad concepts, and then narrow the focus to our specific game domain.

We will begin with the most basic question, because we need to define exactly what a collision is in order to design a system to find collisions.

What Is a Collision?

Simply put, a collision is when two objects touch each other. A more precise definition is that in any given frame of the game, if two object meshes overlap after they have been updated, that is a collision.

OK, now you know what a collision is. But how do you figure out if two object meshes overlap?

The simplest way is to test all of the primitive structures of one mesh and see if any of them intersect the primitives of another mesh. By primitives, I mean the triangles or lines that make up the mesh.

In our case, a missile is composed of triangle primitives, and rocks are made of line primitives. And they are both made of vertexes. In order to see if we have a collision, we need to check all the line segments in the rock mesh to see if they intersect with the triangles of the missile mesh.

Now let's do some quick estimation. If we have 20 rocks on the screen, which all have roughly 16 line segments, and we need to check them against a single missile, that is 320 possible line-triangle intersections we need to perform. But we can fire 5, 10, or even 15 missiles into the scene, so we are looking at possibly 4800 checks in a single frame. Now what if we smashed all of the rocks at once, and they have all broken into 3 smaller rocks? This gives us 60 rocks to check against, say, 15 missiles. That tops out at nearly 15,000 line-triangle intersection checks! This would bring our iPhone CPU to its knees. We need to find a better way.

Collision-Detection Techniques

There are many collision-detection methods we could use. Figure 7–16 shows just a few of the easier ones.

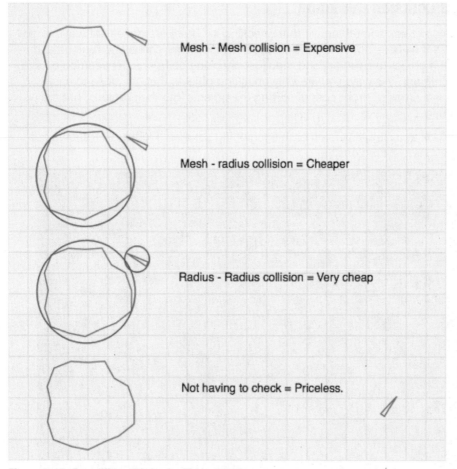

Mesh - Mesh collision = Expensive

Mesh - radius collision = Cheaper

Radius - Radius collision = Very cheap

Not having to check = Priceless.

Figure 7–16. *Four different kinds of collision detection*

If we pretend that each rock is really a circle, then we just need to do a single radius-triangle check to see if the missile has collided with the rock. If it has collided, we could do a more complicated mesh-to-mesh collision check.

Along those same lines, if we pretend that both objects are like circles, then our initial check becomes even cheaper.

Even better, we can figure out a clever way to tell if the objects are not even close enough to each other to even check. This idea of not checking is the best and most widely used approach to collision detection. It can get kind of complicated, so we won't implement it in Space Rocks!. However, it is very important to at least understand the theory behind this approach, so we will go over the simplest version. Then we will take one step back and implement the "very cheap" method illustrated in Figure 7–16.

Optimized Collision Detection

So, how do you check something without checking it? There are dozens of ways to go about this, but it all boils down to a simple idea: dividing your scene into regions and assigning each object to a region, and then just checking collisions between objects in that specific region. This way, you are only checking objects that are close to each other. There is a small up-front cost of sorting the objects into their regions, but the savings are huge.

Let's take a look at a simple version of this regioning scheme. Figure 7–17 shows our scene sliced up into 24 regions.

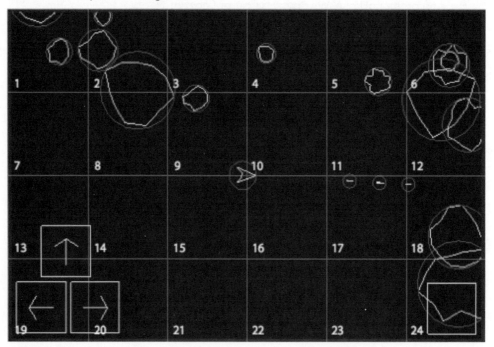

Figure 7–17. *Our scene, sliced into 24 regions for collision-detection optimization*

First, we need to make an array of 24 buckets. Then we go through all our objects and put them into the buckets based on where they are in the scene. In some cases, this is easy, such as for the single rock that is fully inside bucket 4. Other objects span multiple regions, so they must be put into multiple buckets (like our spaceship, which is in four regions).

In order to quickly sort the objects, we can define a simple hashing formula. It could be anything that is quick to calculate. In our case, we might use the radius and center of each object to figure out the minimum and maximum points, and then sort the objects based on in which bins those points reside. Once we have sorted all our objects into buckets, we simply find the objects that we care about—in this case. the ship and the missiles—and see if they collide with any objects in their buckets.

In our example in Figure 7–17, we need to check our ship against the two rocks in bucket 9, the rightmost missile against the rocks in bucket 18, and the leftmost missile against the rocks in bucket 11. If were we doing a straight radius check against all the objects, we have 4 colliders (the ship and 3 missiles) and 14 collidees (the rocks). The result is 56 checks. But using our bucket method, we have 18 checks to get everything into the buckets, and then 6 checks to find the collisions. That is roughly half as many checks as required the previous method. A 50% reduction is good, but our scene is also very simple.

If we go back to our worst-case scenario of 15 missiles and 60 rocks (plus the ship!), we are looking at about 1000 checks if we don't segment our space into regions. For our worst-case scenario, let's pretend that each missile is in a different region with 5 rocks (which would be pretty unlikely). We have an up-front cost of 76 objects to put into the buckets, and then 75 checks for collisions. The result is 150 total checks, which is 15% of the checks required for the nonsegmented algorithm—a huge savings.

You can see how this segmenting approach is very efficient for large and complicated scenes. And this method is only the simplest of the segmenting schemes. The next most complicated methods involve binary search trees, where the 3D space is cut in half, those halves are cut in half, and so forth. The collision-detection segmenting algorithms only get more complex from there.

Radius-to-Radius Collision Check

For our game, we are going to do a simple radius-to-radius brute-force check, with a secondary mesh check. This will be adequate for our game needs. Where do we begin?

In all but the most expensive version of collision checking, you do not check collisions against the actual vertexes of the object, but instead against some approximation of that object. In our case, we are using a circle to approximate a rock—well, actually a sphere.

This secondary object is not our mesh, but it is a simpler approximation. We will need a new object to hold this simpler model, and we will call it a collider. (It is often referred to as a collision mesh, but I like to call them colliders, since referring to the collision mesh and the render mesh can get confusing.)

You can use anything as a collider, but there are a few tried-and-true shapes that make the calculations fast and easy:

- Spheres are the cheapest to check against. You just need to do a single distance check against the radius. If you are within the radius of the sphere, you collide.

- Boxes are slightly more complicated, but similarly easy to calculate. An axis-aligned bounding box (also known as an AABB) is the simplest of the boxes. Being axis-aligned means that all of the box's faces are parallel to the main x, y, and z axes. Since two opposing faces of the box define a range for a single axis, it takes only three simple range checks to see if a point lies within the box. For instance, the top and bottom of the box define the maximum and minimum y values. If the y value of the point you are checking is not within that range, then it is not in the box. If it is within the range, then check the x axis, and so on.

Problems arise when your model objects are not the right shape to be well approximated by a sphere or a box. In order to solve this problem, you segment your model into smaller boxes or spheres. You can chop up your model into smaller and smaller bits until the approximation is close enough for the game mechanic you care about.

For instance, the iPhone game Snow Dude has a fairly complex 2D character (see Figure 7–18). The single circle is a bad approximation, but would work well for a first-pass collision test. The bounding box is a bit better, and depending on what you are colliding with, it might be enough. If you want finer-grained collisions, you will need to segment the character into a compound collider, using a series of boxes or circles, or a mix of both.

Naturally, the more segments of the collider you have, the more expensive it is to check against. You will need to balance the complexity of your collider with you required performance and game needs. It is important to make the collider system that you use as simple and fast as possible for your game. Don't use complex compound colliders or expensive collision schemes if you don't need them.

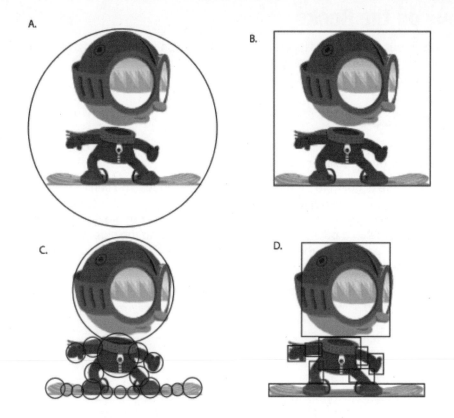

Figure 7–18. *The main character from the iPhone game Snow Dude showing various ways of representing a collider. A shows a simple radius collider. B shows an axis-aligned bounding box (commonly referred to as an AABB). C and D show compound colliders.*

In the actual Snow Dude game, players are actually concerned only with avoiding obstacles with their snowboard. For its collision detection, we were able to get away with a very simple collider that was just two small bounding boxes at the edges of the snowboard (see Figure 7–19).

Figure 7–19. *The actual Snow Dude colliders were much simpler—just two bounding boxes.*

Collisions on the Rocks

For our first pass in our game, we will start out with simple spherical colliders. Most of our objects will be fine approximated as circles. If we find a collision in the first pass, we will refine our collision test with a more detailed check.

Centroid and Radius

For our needs, we will define two things: the radius that we are going to be checking against and the center of our collider sphere.

The center of the sphere is going to be the centroid of your model. The centroid is basically the average of all the vertexes. If your vertexes are fairly evenly spaced throughout the model, then the centroid is very close to the center of gravity. In some cases, as with our spaceship model, the centroid will be biased to the side with the most vertexes. That is fine. We are using the radius and centroid as a first pass, so the most important thing is that it fully covers our model.

In our mesh object, we will add the centroid and the radius as properties:

```
@interface BBMesh : NSObject {
    .
    .
    .

    BBPoint centroid;
    CGFloat radius;
}
    .

    .

    .

@property (assign) BBPoint centroid;
@property (assign) CGFloat radius;
```

Then, inside the object, we will build two new methods: calculateCentroid and calculateRadius. calculateCentroid simply adds up all the vertex points, and then divides by the total:

```
-(BBPoint)calculateCentroid
{
    CGFloat xTotal = 0;
    CGFloat yTotal = 0;
    CGFloat zTotal = 0;
    NSInteger index;
    // step through each vertex and add them all up
    for (index = 0; index < vertexCount; index++) {
        NSInteger position = index * vertexStride;
        xTotal += vertexes[position];
        yTotal += vertexes[position + 1];
        if (vertexStride > 2) zTotal += vertexes[position + 2];
    }
```

```
        // now average each total over the number of vertexes
        return BBPointMake(xTotal/(CGFloat)vertexCount, yTotal/(CGFloat)vertexCount,
zTotal/(CGFloat)vertexCount);
}
```

The calculateRadius method requires the centroid in order to work properly, so be sure to call calculateCentroid first. We will build this method so that it works on both 3D models as well as 2D models.

```
-(CGFloat)calculateRadius
{
    CGFloat rad = 0.0;
    NSInteger index;
    // simply iterate across al vertexes, and find the maximum radius
    // from the centroid
    for (index = 0; index < vertexCount; index++) {
        NSInteger position = index * vertexStride;
        BBPoint vert;
        if (vertexStride > 2) {
            vert = BBPointMake(vertexes[position], vertexes[position + 1],
vertexes[position + 2]);
        } else {
            vert = BBPointMake(vertexes[position], vertexes[position + 1], 0.0);
        }
        CGFloat thisRadius = BBPointDistance(centroid, vert);
        if (rad < thisRadius) rad = thisRadius;
    }
    return rad;
}
```

Finding the radius is also quite easy. We just need to find the smallest circle that will encompass all of our vertexes. We will just check every vertex, and the furthest one out will become the radius. We need to be able to calculate the distance between two points in order to check the radius. This is a fairly common requirement, so we will add a new inline function called BBPointDistance() to the *BBPoint.h* file:

```
static inline float BBPointDistance(BBPoint p1, BBPoint p2)
{
    return sqrt(((p1.x - p2.x) * (p1.x - p2.x)) +
                ((p1.y - p2.y)  * (p1.y - p2.y)) +
                ((p1.z - p2.z) * (p1.z - p2.z)));
}
```

The final touch in our BBMesh object is to add these two lines to the init method:

```
        self.centroid = [self calculateCentroid];
        self.radius = [self calculateRadius];
```

Now our mesh will automatically calculate its own centroid and radius when it is initialized.

Colliders and Collidees

Earlier, we talked about how we want to keep the number of collision checks to a bare minimum. Along these lines, we can save a whole bunch of collision checks if we limit the types of objects that we are checking. Let's define three types of scene objects with respect to collisions:

- A collider is an object that we need to check against all the collidee objects. These include missiles and the spaceship.

- A collidee is an object that can be hit, but does not check to see if it is hitting anything. This includes all the rocks.

- Noncolliders are things that don't collide, like the buttons.

With these objects in mind, we will embark upon our journey of building a simple collision-detection system. We already have part of the information that we need: the centroid and radius of our meshes. However, when checking for collisions, we will need to take that centroid and move it to wherever the object happens to be at the time, and scale the radius to whatever scale the object has at the time.

As noted, we need to define a collider object for our system. This object is similar to a standard scene object, except instead of carrying around a model that has been scaled and transformed to the correct position each frame, it will carry around our collision mesh (which, in this case, is a simple circle).

The idea is to create a "shadow" object that is similar in some way to our rendered object and has the same position, scale, and rotation. This is a powerful concept, and you will use it quite often if you build many 3D games. However, there is a small issue. We now have two sets of information that need to be translated, scaled, and rotated in the same way. We want to keep our calculations to a minimum, so it would make sense to do this calculation only once. How do we get OpenGL to apply a transform to our non-OpenGL object?

Take the Red Pill: The Transform Matrix

In our code at the moment, all of our translating, rotating, and scaling is happening in the render method. This doesn't really make too much sense, since we should be rendering in the render method, and doing all that other stuff in the update method. By moving that stuff into update, we could apply our transformations to any shadow objects that need it, like the collider.

When you call methods like glTranslate and glRotate, OpenGL is simply building a matrix behind the scenes. OpenGL then uses this matrix and multiplies it by all your vertexes to get the actual points in space that it will use to render your object.

As noted in Chapter 6, technically, a matrix is an abstract mathematical concept, and there are many types. However, in terms of OpenGL, we are talking specifically about a single kind of matrix: a four-by-four transform matrix. Matrixes in OpenGL are generally represented visually like this:

```
m[0]   m[4]   m[ 8]   m[12]
m[1]   m[5]   m[ 9]   m[13]
m[2]   m[6]   m[10]   m[14]
m[3]   m[7]   m[11]   m[15]
```

Note that this convention is slightly different from the usual programmer convention of having the first four indexes along the top row. Matrixes are usually shown this way because mathematicians like them this way. If you have learned how to manipulate matrixes by hand, you will also appreciate them being laid out in this way.

For our purposes, we don't really care about the layout. A four-by-four matrix is just a list of 16 numbers:

```
CGFloat * matrix = (CGFloat *) malloc(16 * sizeof(CGFloat));
```

These 16 numbers are what you need to define the position, scale, and rotation of a model.

Basically, you generate a matrix with your position, scale, and rotation, then multiply all your vertexes by that matrix to get new points in space that have been transformed by that matrix.

OK, but how do we make these matrixes? Fortunately, OpenGL makes them for us. We just need to save them.

We will add a matrix property to our top-level `BBSceneObject`. Then we will be kind of clever, and move all the matrix-manipulation methods into the `update` method:

```
-(void)update
{
    glPushMatrix();
    glLoadIdentity();

    // move to my position
    glTranslatef(translation.x, translation.y, translation.z);

    // rotate
    glRotatef(rotation.x, 1.0f, 0.0f, 0.0f);
    glRotatef(rotation.y, 0.0f, 1.0f, 0.0f);
    glRotatef(rotation.z, 0.0f, 0.0f, 1.0f);

    //scale
    glScalef(scale.x, scale.y, scale.z);
    // save the matrix transform
    glGetFloatv(GL_MODELVIEW_MATRIX, matrix);
    //restore the matrix
    glPopMatrix();
}
```

This looks a great deal like our old `render` method. What we are doing here is simply using OpenGL to build a matrix for us. `glPushMatrix()` saves whatever matrix OpenGL is currently holding. Then we call `glLoadIdentity()`, which gives us a clean slate. After that, we simply make our translations, rotations, and scale calls, just as before. The big difference is that at the end of that, we make this call:

```
glGetFloatv(GL_MODELVIEW_MATRIX, matrix);
```

This asks OpenGL to take the matrix we just built and put it into our local matrix array. Then we call popMatrix, and OpenGL is restored to whatever state it was in before it got to our method.

Once we have our own transform matrix, our `render` method becomes very simple:

```
-(void)render
{
    if (!mesh || !active) return; // if we do not have a mesh, no need to render
    // clear the matrix
    glPushMatrix();
    glLoadIdentity();
    // set our transform
    glMultMatrixf(matrix);
    [mesh render];
    glPopMatrix();
}
```

We are simply handing our matrix back to OpenGL to use when our mesh renders. The `glMultMatrixf()` method tells OpenGL to apply that matrix to the current state. This is the equivalent of calling all of the individual glTranslate, glRotate, and glScale methods. Now we have our own transform matrix in a place that is easy to get to, and we can move on to building our collider object.

The Collider Object

Our new collider object is going to be pretty simple. It will need to be the transformed version of the centroid and radius from our mesh, so we want to hold on to the `transformedCentroid`, the `transformedRadius`, and whether we are a collider or a collidee.

```
@interface BBCollider : BBSceneObject {
    BBPoint transformedCentroid;
    BOOL checkForCollision;
    CGFloat maxRadius;
}

@property (assign) BOOL checkForCollision;
@property (assign) CGFloat maxRadius;
```

checkForCollision will tell any objects that will be handling this one whether it is a collider or a collidee. (Colliders check; collidees don't.)

The maxRadius is a version of the transformed radius. Since our object can be scaled asymmetrically, we will need to scale based on the largest scale axis, so it is more than just the transformed radius.

Here, we are making the collider a subclass of BBSceneObject. This is not strictly necessary, but it makes it so that we can render the collidees and see what is going on. If you are following along in the code sample, you will notice that there are some scene object method overrides to render the colliders. By now, you should be familiar with the scene object render code, so I won't go over it again for the collider.

In our collider implementation, we will define an updateCollider method that takes a sceneObject. Our collider will use that scene object to generate its own dimensions and get ready to check for collisions.

```
-(void)updateCollider:(BBSceneObject*)sceneObject
{
    if (sceneObject == nil) return;
    transformedCentroid = BBPointMatrixMultiply([sceneObject mesh].centroid ,
[sceneObject matrix]);
    maxRadius = sceneObject.scale.x;
    if (maxRadius < sceneObject.scale.y)      maxRadius = sceneObject.scale.y;
    if ((maxRadius < sceneObject.scale.z) && ([sceneObject mesh].vertexStride > 2))
maxRadius = sceneObject.scale.z;
    maxRadius *= [sceneObject mesh].radius;

    // scene object iVars
    translation = transformedCentroid;
    scale = BBPointMake([sceneObject mesh].radius * sceneObject.scale.x, [sceneObject
mesh].radius * sceneObject.scale.y,0.0);
}
```

First, we get the transformed centroid. Then we find the maximum radius. But wait, how did we transform that point?

We grabbed the transform matrix (the one we coded in the previous section), and then multiplied it with a point, which gives us a new point. How do you multiply a point by a matrix? In our *BBPoint.h* file, we will need to add another inline function:

```
static inline BBPoint BBPointMatrixMultiply(BBPoint p, CGFloat* m)
{
    CGFloat x = (p.x*m[0]) + (p.y*m[4]) + (p.z*m[8]) + m[12];
    CGFloat y = (p.x*m[1]) + (p.y*m[5]) + (p.z*m[9]) + m[13];
    CGFloat z = (p.x*m[2]) + (p.y*m[6]) + (p.z*m[10]) + m[14];

    return (BBPoint) {x, y, z};
}
```

That is how you multiply a matrix with a point and get a new point. If you understand the math behind matrixes, then this makes sense to you already. If not, then just trust me that this works.

For the collider, the last thing we need is a way to check its position and radius against another collider to see if we hit.

```
-(BOOL)doesCollideWithCollider:(BBCollider*)aCollider
{
    // just need to check the distance between our two points and
    // our radius
    CGFloat collisionDistance = self.maxRadius + aCollider.maxRadius;
    CGFloat objectDistance = BBPointDistance(self.translation, aCollider.translation);
    if (objectDistance < collisionDistance) return YES;
    return NO;
}
```

Now we have these collider objects, but where do they fit into the code? We actually need yet another object. We also will need a new phase for our game loop.

The Collision Controller Object

We will use a collision controller object to check the colliders with the collidees and act accordingly. In order to do this, we need three sets of information at our disposal:

- All the scene objects

- All the scene objects in the current frame that are colliders

- All the scene objects in the current frame that are collidees

With that in mind, let's start to make our collision controller:

```
@interface BBCollisionController : BBSceneObject {
    NSArray * sceneObjects;
    NSMutableArray * allColliders;
    NSMutableArray * collidersToCheck;
}
```

Again, we are making this a scene object so that we can render the colliders. This is handy, but not strictly necessary.

We have our three arrays: sceneObjects contains—you guessed it—the scene objects, allColliders contains any object that has an attached collider, and collidersToCheck contains any object that has an attached collider whose checkForCollision is set to YES. Well, they will contain this information once we write the code to generate the arrays:

```
-(void)handleCollisions
{
    // two types of colliders
    // ones that need to be checked for collision and ones that do not
    if (allColliders == nil) allColliders = [[NSMutableArray alloc] init];
    [allColliders removeAllObjects];
    if (collidersToCheck == nil) collidersToCheck = [[NSMutableArray alloc] init];
    [collidersToCheck removeAllObjects];

    // first build our separate arrays
  for (BBSceneObject * obj in sceneObjects) {
        if (obj.collider != nil){
            [allColliders addObject:obj];
            if (obj.collider.checkForCollision) [collidersToCheck addObject:obj];
        }
    }

    // now check to see if anything is hitting anything else
    for (BBSceneObject * colliderObject in collidersToCheck) {
        for (BBSceneObject * collideeObject in allColliders) {
            if (colliderObject == collideeObject) continue;
            if ([colliderObject.collider
doesCollideWithCollider:collideeObject.collider]) {
                if ([colliderObject respondsToSelector:@selector(didCollideWith:)])
[colliderObject didCollideWith:collideeObject];
            }
        }
    }
}
```

This method is basically the entirety of the collision controller. First, we clear out any old objects from our last frame. Next, we go through all the scene objects and load any with an attached collider into our `allColliders`. Then we do a second check to see if any of them need to be checked.

Once we have our arrays, we can do the actual checking. We go through our (hopefully) smaller `collidersToCheck` array (our colliders) and check them against the `allColliders` array (the collidees). If they do hit, then we see if they implement the `didCollideWith:` method, and if so, we send them that message. When we run this, any objects that collide will get notified, and they will need to handle the collision.

We have a few more things to do before we can turn on our collision system. We need to hook it up in the scene controller, add the colliders to the scene objects, and implement some `didCollideWith:` methods in the scene objects that will be colliding.

Back to the Scene Controller

First, let's look at the `BBSceneController`. We will need to add a collision controller instance variable:

```
@interface BBSceneController : NSObject {
    .
    .
    BBCollisionController * collisionController;
    .
    .
}
```

There is no need to make it a property, because it should be used only from within the scene controller.

In our `loadScene` method in the `BBSceneController`, we will instantiate our new controller instance variable:

```
// this is where we initialize all our scene objects
-(void)loadScene
{
    .
    .
    collisionController = [[BBCollisionController alloc] init];
    collisionController.sceneObjects = sceneObjects;
    if (DEBUG_DRAW_COLLIDERS)    [self addObjectToScene:collisionController];
    .
    .
}
```

We need to add the collision controller to our scene objects only if we are debugging and want to draw the collider objects (see Figure 7–20). DEBUG_DRAW_COLLIDERS is another configuration constant that is defined in the *BBConfiguration.h* file. This way, we can turn the collider rendering on and off as needed.

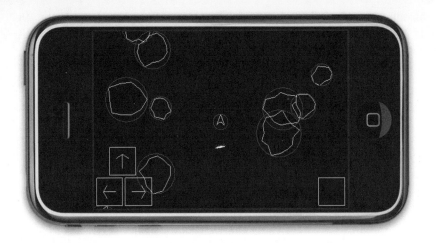

Figure 7–20. *Our collider meshes rendered around our objects*

Next, we will need to add a phase to our game loop:

```
- (void)gameLoop
{
    .
    .
    .
    // update our model
    [self updateModel];
    // deal with collisions
    [collisionController handleCollisions]; //<-- add in collisions

    // send our objects to the renderer
    [self renderScene];
    .
    .
    .
}
```

We put it immediately after we update and before we render. This way, our collisions are handled immediately after the objects have updated their positions.

If you build and run the code now, it should work fine, but there are no collider objects being instantiated yet.

Scene Object Updates

Let's look at the top-level BBSceneObject.

```
@interface BBSceneObject : NSObject {
    // transform values
    .
    .
    BBCollider * collider;
}
    .
    .
@property (retain) BBCollider * collider;
```

.
.

We add a `collider` instance variable and make it a property. In our `update` method, we just need to add a single line, at the end of the method:

```
// called once every frame
-(void)update
{
    .
    .
    if (collider != nil) [collider updateCollider:self];
}
```

We call the `updateCollider` method, and pass in ourselves. This will keep the collider object up to date with our scene object's transform matrix.

We still haven't instantiated any colliders. This should happen only in the objects that we want to be able to hit or be hit—rocks, missiles, and ships. We are going to be making a lot of colliders, so it will be handy to create a factory class method to generate them for us:

```
+(BBCollider*)collider
{
    BBCollider * collider = [[BBCollider alloc] init];
    if (DEBUG_DRAW_COLLIDERS) {
        collider.active = YES;
        [collider awake];
    }
    collider.checkForCollision = NO;
    return [collider autorelease];
}
```

This will be in the collider implementation file. It just provides a handy way to allocate colliders. And it gives us a central place to deal with the rendering debug code. Don't forget that `DEBUG_DRAW_COLLIDERS` is defined in the *BBConfiguration.h* file, so be sure to include that file.

Where do we instantiate these colliders? The same place we build our meshes, in the scene object `awake` method. Let's look at `BBSpaceShip`.

```
-(void)awake
{
    .
    .
    .
    self.collider = [BBCollider collider];
    [self.collider setCheckForCollision:YES];
}
```

In these two lines, we grab a new collider from the factory method, and then set our `checkForCollision` to YES.

We also need to implement the `didCollideWith:` method in the `BBSpaceShip` class.

```
- (void)didCollideWith:(BBSceneObject*)sceneObject;
{
```

```
    // if we did not hit a rock, then get out early
    if (![sceneObject isKindOfClass:[BBRock class]]) return;
    // we did hit a rock! smash it!
    [(BBRock*)sceneObject smash];
    // now destroy ourself
    [[BBSceneController sharedSceneController] removeObjectFromScene:self];
}
```

For now, we don't care if we shoot ourselves. We only care if we hit a rock. We tell the rock to smash itself, and then we tell the scene controller to remove us from the scene (which would be the end of that game).

We'll do the same thing in our BBMissile class: add the two lines to the awake method and add a didCollideWith: method that is exactly like the one in the spaceship object.

Our rocks are collidees, so they are just a bit different. We just need to add the collider to the awake method in the BBRock class, but we don't need to set checkForCollision to YES.

```
-(void)awake
{
    .

    .
    self.collider = [BBCollider collider];
}
```

Since we want the rocks to just be collidees, and not colliders, we do not need to implement didCollideWith:. But we do need to add the smash method that we called in the ship and missile classes when we hit the rocks.

What does smash do? Well, according to our specifications, a hit rock will turn into three smaller rock fragments, and if they are hit, they are gone. We will need to introduce a smash counter to our rock objects to keep track of whether they are original rocks or they have been hit once.

```
-(void)smash
{
    smashCount++;
    // queue myself for removal
    [[BBSceneController sharedSceneController] removeObjectFromScene:self];

    // if we have already been smashed once, then that is it
    if (smashCount >= 2) return;

    // need to break ourself apart
    NSInteger smallRockScale = scale.x / 3.0;

    BBRock * newRock = [[BBRock alloc] init];
    newRock.scale = BBPointMake(smallRockScale, smallRockScale, 1.0);
    // now we need to position it
    BBPoint position = BBPointMake(0.0, 0.5, 0.0);
    newRock.translation = BBPointMatrixMultiply(position , matrix);
    newRock.speed = BBPointMake(speed.x + (position.x * SMASH_SPEED_FACTOR), speed.y +
(position.y * SMASH_SPEED_FACTOR), 0.0);
    newRock.rotationalSpeed = rotationalSpeed;
    newRock.smashCount = smashCount;
```

```
    [[BBSceneController sharedSceneController] addObjectToScene:newRock];
    [newRock release];

    newRock = [[BBRock alloc] init];
    newRock.scale = BBPointMake(smallRockScale, smallRockScale, 1.0);
    // now we need to position it
    position = BBPointMake(0.35, -0.35, 0.0);
    newRock.translation = BBPointMatrixMultiply(position , matrix);
    newRock.speed = BBPointMake(speed.x + (position.x * SMASH_SPEED_FACTOR), speed.y +
(position.y * SMASH_SPEED_FACTOR), 0.0);
    newRock.rotationalSpeed = rotationalSpeed;
    newRock.smashCount = smashCount;
    [[BBSceneController sharedSceneController] addObjectToScene:newRock];
    [newRock release];

    newRock = [[BBRock alloc] init];
    newRock.scale = BBPointMake(smallRockScale, smallRockScale, 1.0);
    // now we need to position it
    position = BBPointMake(-0.35, -0.35, 0.0);
    newRock.translation = BBPointMatrixMultiply(position , matrix);
    newRock.speed = BBPointMake(speed.x + (position.x * SMASH_SPEED_FACTOR), speed.y +
(position.y * SMASH_SPEED_FACTOR), 0.0);
    newRock.rotationalSpeed = rotationalSpeed;
    newRock.smashCount = smashCount;
    [[BBSceneController sharedSceneController] addObjectToScene:newRock];
    [newRock release];
}
```

Although this is a big, ugly method, all it does is queue the rock for removal from the
scene, and queue up three new, smaller rocks to be added to the scene (see Figure 7–21).

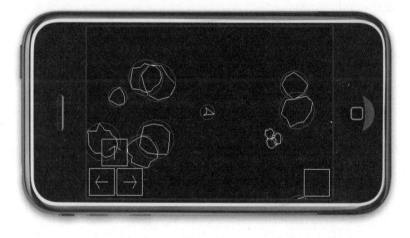

Figure 7–21. *Three rock fragments appear right after you smash a big rock.*

Collision Checking Redux

Our game play is basically done. We have satisfied all of our requirements, but there is a
small but frustrating problem with our game. Our collision checking is very fast, but it's

not very accurate. The way that the rocks and ship are shaped causes false positives during the collision checking.

Figure 7–22 shows an example. The ship and rock are not actually colliding, but the radiuses of the collision mesh circles will generate a positive collision. How do we deal with that?

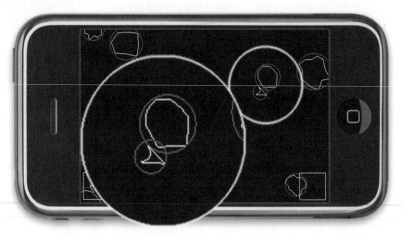

Figure 7–22. *Our ship and the rock are not actually colliding, but our simple collision-detection system will flag this as a collision, and our ship will be destroyed. This is very frustrating, and we need to fix it.*

We need to define a secondary collision check that we call only after we have had one of these general collisions. In this case, we will do a fairly simple secondary check and see if any of the spaceship's vertexes are within the collision circle of the rock. It is still not perfect, and will return some false positives. However, collision checking is always a balance between a perfect collision check, which is expensive, and an approximate check, which is fast. This secondary check will make the missiles and ship behave more appropriately, and it is good enough for the purposes of our game.

In our BBCollider object, we are going to define another method called doesCollideWithMesh:

```
-(BOOL)doesCollideWithMesh:(BBSceneObject*)sceneObject
{
    NSInteger index;
    // step through each vertex of the scene object
    // transform it into real space coordinates
    // and check it against our radius
    for (index = 0; index < sceneObject.mesh.vertexCount; index++) {
        NSInteger position = index * sceneObject.mesh.vertexStride;
        BBPoint vert;
        if (sceneObject.mesh.vertexStride > 2) {
            vert = BBPointMake(sceneObject.mesh.vertexes[position],
sceneObject.mesh.vertexes[position + 1], sceneObject.mesh.vertexes[position + 2]);
        } else {
            vert = BBPointMake(sceneObject.mesh.vertexes[position],
sceneObject.mesh.vertexes[position + 1], 0.0);
        }
```

```
        vert = BBPointMatrixMultiply(vert , [sceneObject matrix]);
        CGFloat distance = BBPointDistance(self.translation, vert);
        if (distance < self.maxRadius) return YES;
    }
    return NO;
}
```

We grab every vertex in the mesh, transform it by the scene object's matrix transform to get the spatial location of the vertex, and then check it against the radius of the collider. If the vertex lies within the radius, then we call it a hit.

Great! We have this new secondary checking system. But how do we use it?

Both our BBMissile and our BBSpaceShip have a didCollideWith: method. In this method, we will call this secondary check just to make sure we hit the rock.

In the *BBSpaceShip.m* file, our revisions look like this:

```
- (void)didCollideWith:(BBSceneObject*)sceneObject;
{
    // if we did not hit a rock, then get out early
    if (![sceneObject isKindOfClass:[BBRock class]]) return;
    // OK, we really want to make sure that we were hit,
    // so we are going to do a secondary check to make sure one of our vertexes is
inside the
    // collision radius of the rock
    if (![sceneObject.collider doesCollideWithMesh:self]) return;

    // we did hit a rock! smash it!
    [(BBRock*)sceneObject smash];
    // now destroy ourself
    [[BBSceneController sharedSceneController] removeObjectFromScene:self];
}
```

After we make sure that it is a rock we are hitting, we call the new secondary doesCollideWithMesh: method. If that does not return a positive, then we return from the method early. If it does return a positive, we go ahead and deal with the collision as before.

Similarly, we need to add the exact same check to our BBMissile object.

If you build and run the game now, you should be able to fly around, smash rocks, and get smashed in return. Our game is lacking nice user interface options, like restarting after you die, so it could still use some extra work.

Summary

We have done quite a bit in this chapter:

- We took our very simple game template, which was little more than a wrapper for an OpenGL view initialization, and added a simple system for making scene objects.

- We added those objects to the scene to be rendered every frame.

- We built some simple touch interface items to get input from the player.

- We built a rough collision-detection system that allowed our objects to interact.

This is a whole lot to take in, so let's review the process at a high level. Revisiting a diagram presented in Chapter 6 (see Figure 7–23), we can see our basic template design. Let's consider what we have added to the various steps. It hasn't changed much at all. We have just fleshed out our game using the same basic structure.

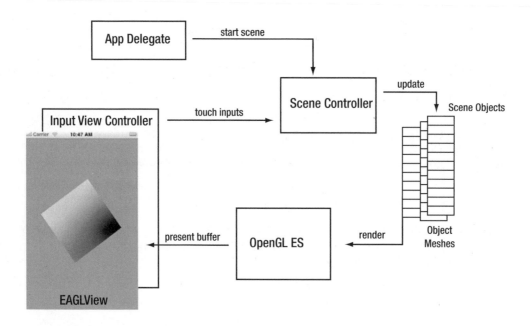

Figure 7–23. *The basic flow of a game engine*

Now, when the app delegate starts the scene, the scene controller adds a spaceship and some rocks to the scene. It also tells the input view controller to set up the GUI elements.

Then, in every frame of the game loop, the scene controller tells the spaceship and the rocks, and any other objects, to update themselves. During the update phase, each object can ask to see if the input view controller has any touches that they might be interested in, and can act accordingly. The input view controller also stores the various movement state variables that the spaceship object can access to decide where it is flying and how fast.

After the update loop, the collision controller checks to see if there are any objects that are hitting each other. If there are, it tells them to handle those events.

The next step in the game loop is to tell every visible object in the scene to render itself into the OpenGL engine.

Finally, we tell OpenGL that we are finished sending it objects to render, and it presents the finished image to the user.

In the next chapter, we will iterate this process two more times. We will add two more different rendering styles to Space Rocks!, and even look at some new features, like particle effects.

Chapter 8

The Next Steps: Atlases, Sprites, and Particles— Oh My!

So far, we have looked at very simple 2D rendering. While this is fine for our game's retro version, you generally will want your graphics to look a bit cooler than just white lines.

In this chapter, we are going to first upgrade our rendering to be able to handle textures, and take a look at a 2D game that is based entirely on simple textured quads. After that, we will delve into the third dimension. We will look at how to build 3D models, and light them and texture them. Finally we will dip briefly into a bit more advanced code with a simple particle system. Figure 8–1 gives you a preview of both versions.

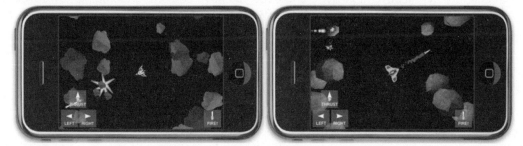

Figure 8–1. *On the left, our 2D simple texture game; on the right, our 3D model based game with some simple particle systems*

Textures and Texture Atlases

We will build on the code we finished in the previous chapter, creating a textured version called SpaceRocksTextured. The only real difference between Space Rocks! and SpaceRocksTextured is that instead of white outlines, we will be rendering actual images into the 3D OpenGL space.

To get started, make a copy of your Space Rocks! project and rename it **SpaceRocksTextured**. If you want to follow along instead of building from your earlier projects, I've supplied it as a sample code project for this chapter.

In the previous chapters, I have tried to include every line of code and comment on even the most mundane commands. From here on out, I am going to presume that you can follow along, and I won't point out every @property declaration and dealloc method.

What Is a Texture Anyway, and Why Do I Care?

A texture is just a fancy name for an image. Once we take that image and apply it to a polygon, then we generally refer to it as a texture (see Figure 8–2). Images are generally known as *materials* before they become loaded into the rendering engine, and then *textures* after they have been loaded.

In the vast majority of cases, you will want to use textures in your OpenGL applications. Because of this, OpenGL has been designed to be incredibly efficient at drawing textures into polygons—not just flat polygons like the one in Figure 8–2, but polygons that have been turned every which way in 3D space. In fact, OpenGL is so fast at pushing texture pixels that it is almost always quicker to use OpenGL to do 2D drawing than any other option on the iPhone. (Of course, this is why we are even bothering to talk about OpenGL—if it were not the fastest way to get graphics onto the screen, we wouldn't care so much, now would we?)

However, the downside to this great speed is added complexity. Using a UIImageView, we can load and display an image on screen in just a few simple UIKit calls. In OpenGL, it is much more complicated.

But don't fret! We'll cover it all here, and once you have come to understand how to load and use textures in OpenGL, you'll wonder why you ever did it any other way!

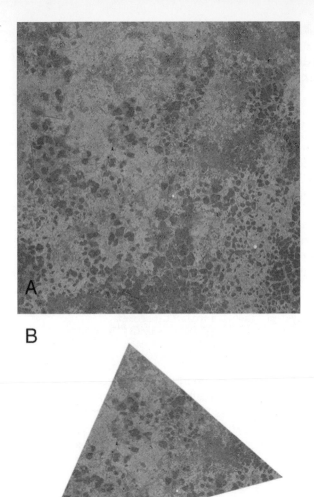

Figure 8–2. *A: Our rock texture; B: Our rock texture applied to a polygon*

Getting Image Data into OpenGL

In order to render an image into an on-screen texture, we need to get it into the
rendering pipeline somehow. I think that this calls for a new singleton controller object.
We should call it `BBMaterialController`. Open the `BBMaterialController` files and let's
have a look.

```
@interface BBMaterialController : NSObject {
    NSMutableDictionary * materialLibrary;
}
```

We want to have a place to store our materials so that we can reference them later. We
will use a dictionary so we can use readable strings as keys to pull out our materials.

We are going to need a way to get an image that is in our bundle and put it into a format that OpenGL can deal with, and then assign it a texture ID. This will be the heart of the material controller, and it is a very big and ugly method, so let's take it one piece at a time. This is in the *BBMaterialControler.m* file.

```
// does the heavy lifting for getting a named image into a texture
// that is loaded into OpenGL; it is roughly based on Apple's Sample Code
-(CGSize)loadTextureImage:(NSString*)imageName materialKey:(NSString*)materialKey
{
        CGContextRef spriteContext; //context ref for the UIImage
        GLubyte *spriteData; // a temporary buffer to hold our image data
        size_t width, height;
        GLuint textureID; // the ultimate ID for this texture
```

Here, we will take a UIImage that we load from the bundle, and then draw it into a CGContextRef. This will change the UIImage into an uncompressed 32-bit RGBA block of raw data. This is what OpenGL wants. Well, actually this is one of a handful of ways you can format texture data, but it is the simplest, and we'll stick to the simplest for now.

Next, we will get the image:

```
        // grab the image off the file system, jam it into a CGImageRef
        UIImage*        uiImage = [[UIImage alloc] initWithContentsOfFile:[[NSBundle ↵
mainBundle] pathForResource:imageName ofType:nil]];
        CGImageRef spriteImage = [uiImage CGImage];
```

We are using initWithContentsOfFile here, instead of the much simpler imageNamed: method. This is because imageNamed: does some automatic caching of the image data, which we don't want. We are going to have two copies of this image in memory for a little while already, and if we are loading a lot of textures, we want to be able to control just how much image data is in memory at any given time. This way, we can explicitly release the UIImage when we are finished with it.

So far, we have loaded the UIImage from the file system and then grabbed the CGImageRef that points to that raw data. Now, let's find out about its size:

```
width = CGImageGetWidth(spriteImage);
height = CGImageGetHeight(spriteImage);

CGSize imageSize = CGSizeMake(width, height);

if (spriteImage) {
        // allocated memory needed for the bitmap context
        spriteData = (GLubyte *) malloc(width * height * 4);
```

We find the height and width of the image, and we make a memory buffer that is big enough to hold 32 bits per pixel—1 byte for each color and 1 byte for alpha.

It is important to note that all textures must have dimensions that are a power of 2 and can be no bigger than 1024 on a side. What does that mean? Your image can have a dimension of 2, 4, 8, 16, 32, 64, 128, 256, 512, or 1024—and that's it. Your images do not need to be square, however; for example, you can have a texture that is 8 by 512 or 128 by 256. We are going to make sure that our images are the correct dimensions, but if you plan on being able to load in any old image, you need to check to make sure your images meet this requirement.

Let's continue with the crux of this method:

```
// create a context that is the right size and format
spriteContext = CGBitmapContextCreate(spriteData, width, height, 8, width * 4, ↵
CGImageGetColorSpace(spriteImage), kCGImageAlphaPremultipliedLast);
// draw our image into the context
CGContextDrawImage(spriteContext, ↵
            CGRectMake(0.0, 0.0, (CGFloat)width, (CGFloat)height), cgImage);
// get rid of the context, it has served its purpose
CGContextRelease(spriteContext);
```

We make a context that is the correct format for OpenGL, and then we draw our image into that context. This guarantees that no matter what kind of image we had before, we now have an uncompressed RGBA image, and it is in our `imageData` variable. Once we have done that, we can get rid of the context, since we only needed it to draw the data into our `imageData` memory buffer.

Now we get to the OpenGL-specific part of this method:

```
// use OpenGL ES to generate a name for the texture
glGenTextures(1, &textureID);
// bind the texture name
glBindTexture(GL_TEXTURE_2D, textureID);
```

First, we call `glGenTextures`, which simply asks OpenGL to make room for another texture and tell us what ID that texture will have. Then we call `glBindTexture`, which basically tells OpenGL to make that texture ID the active texture. Any texture-specific calls we make now will apply to that texture ID.

```
// push the image data into the OpenGL video memory
glTexImage2D(GL_TEXTURE_2D, 0, GL_RGBA, width, height, 0, GL_RGBA, GL_UNSIGNED_BYTE, ↵
imageData);

// release the image data
free(imageData);
```

By calling `glTexImage2D`, we are effectively handing that image data over to OpenGL. We need to tell OpenGL the size, format, and data type for the image data so it can handle it properly. After that call, OpenGL now "owns" that data, so we should get rid of our copy.

```
// set the texture parameters
glTexParameteri(GL_TEXTURE_2D, GL_TEXTURE_MIN_FILTER, GL_LINEAR);
glTexParameteri(GL_TEXTURE_2D, GL_TEXTURE_MAG_FILTER, GL_NEAREST);
```

These two lines tell OpenGL how to handle pixels in this texture when they do not match up exactly. Since you can scale, rotate, and transform your surfaces in so many ways, OpenGL needs to know how to deal with translating your texture onto that surface. Almost never will the surface be a nice multiple of the pixel size of your image, so OpenGL will need to smush the colors somehow to make the texture fit.

Passing in GL_LINEAR will do a weighed blend of the surrounding colors, and is probably what you are generally used to seeing if you have ever scaled an image down in any image editor. GL_NEAREST just takes the nearest color and replicates that. GL_NEAREST is much faster than GL_LINEAR. If you are trying to fill a huge amount of polygons on screen, you may find that it is necessary to switch to GL_NEAREST to get the performance you want. Figure 8–3 shows examples of both filters.

> **NOTE:** I tend to think of GL_LINEAR as a blurring filter and GL_NEAREST as a sharper filter. I generally set my maximum filter to nearest, so that my objects still look sharp at large sizes, but I'll use linear for smaller sizes, so that the various features can blend together.

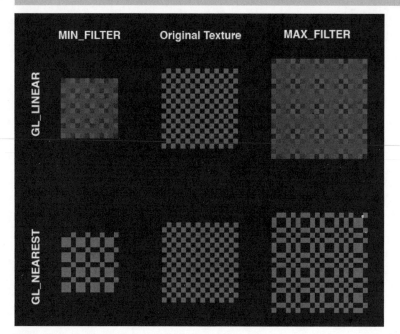

Figure 8–3. *Texture minimum and maximum filters. Here is a very hard-to-scale texture, which has been scaled to the least flattering sizes to show how the filters behave.*

Finally, we will make sure that 2D textures are enabled and set up a blending function.

```
        // enable use of the texture
        glEnable(GL_TEXTURE_2D);
        // set a blending function to use
        glBlendFunc(GL_ONE, GL_ONE_MINUS_SRC_ALPHA);
        // enable blending
        glEnable(GL_BLEND);
} else {
        NSLog(@"no texture");
        return CGSizeZero;
}
```

The blending function tells OpenGL how to handle semitransparent textures. In this case, we are telling it to allow the textures behind to show through the transparent pixels based on the alpha value, which is pretty standard.

And here's the final stretch:

```
    [uiImage release];

    if (materialLibrary == nil) materialLibrary = [[NSMutableDictionary alloc]
init];

    // now put the texture ID into the library
    [materialLibrary setObject:[NSNumber numberWithUnsignedInt:textureID] ↵
forKey:materialKey];
    return imageSize;
}
```

We release our `UIImage` and get back all that memory. Then we store the texture ID as an `NSNumber` in our material library, keyed to our material key.

Well, this method is mildly disappointing, since all it really does is push bytes around the system. How do we use these newly loaded textures?

Binding Textures

Just as we do for everything else in OpenGL, we need to tell the renderer when we are going to be using a certain texture and make sure that texturing is enabled. This is known as *binding* a texture.

We will add a simple method to our material controller to bind textures. This is also in the *BBMaterialController.m* file.

```
// grabs the openGL texture ID from the library and calls the openGL bind texture method
-(void)bindMaterial:(NSString*)materialKey
{
    NSNumber * numberObj = [materialLibrary objectForKey:materialKey];
    if (numberObj == nil) return;
    GLuint textureID = [numberObj unsignedIntValue];

    glEnable(GL_TEXTURE_2D);
    glBindTexture(GL_TEXTURE_2D, textureID);
}
```

This is a very simple method. We grab the stored ID with our material key, and we just tell OpenGL, "Hey, bind this ID!" Until we bind a new texture, whenever we draw a triangle that requires texturing, this is the texture that will be used. It is important to note that binding textures can be expensive, so group all your objects that use the same textures together when rendering, if possible.

Then to render, we will need to do something like this:

```
-(void)render
{
    glVertexPointer(vertexSize, GL_FLOAT, 0, vertexes);
    glEnableClientState(GL_VERTEX_ARRAY);
    glColorPointer(colorSize, GL_FLOAT, 0, colors);
    glEnableClientState(GL_COLOR_ARRAY);

    if (materialKey != nil) {
```

```
                 [[BBMaterialController sharedMaterialController] bindMaterial:↵
materialKey];

                 glEnableClientState(GL_TEXTURE_COORD_ARRAY);
                 glTexCoordPointer(2, GL_FLOAT, 0, uvCoordinates);
           }
           //render
           glDrawArrays(renderStyle, 0, vertexCount);
}
```

What are `GL_TEXTURE_COORD_ARRAY` and uvCoordinates? They are how we map the texture images onto surfaces, with a new set of numbers—fun, right?

And that's it! Now you can texture all your polygons.

UV Is Not Bad for Your Skin

In the previous chapters, we talked about the various rendering styles that we have available to us on the iPhone. There were a handful of points and lines, and then a few based on triangles: `GL_TRIANGLES`, `GL_TRIANGLE_STRIP`, and `GL_TRIANGLE_FAN`.

In order to draw a texture, we need to have some place to put it. In the case of OpenGL ES on the iPhone, this will always be a triangle of some sort. Don't feel slighted, however. Even though the more powerful versions of OpenGL allow you to draw quads and arbitrary polygons, almost everyone just uses triangles anyway. It turns out that if you make all you models from a single type of primitive, you can really optimize your pipeline.

Now we have these triangles that need to be filled in, and we have these rectangular images in our texture memory. How do we get the two to play nice together?

Well, we need a new set of numbers. We need to be able to map a vertex in space to a vertex on the texture. Generally, on images, we would use x to define how far across some point is from the corner and y to tell us how far up from the corner. That might get just a bit confusing, since we are already using an x and a y to define the vertex positions in our model. Instead, let's call the ones on a texture U and V (in the olden days these were sometimes referred to as S and T as well).

UV coordinates are pretty straightforward. There are just a few things to keep in mind about them:

- *Normalization*: UVs should generally be normalized between 0.0 and 1.0. So the UV1 in Figure 8–4 might be something like 0.3, 0.8 if the lower-left corner is 0,0. This UV coordinate maps to the V1 vertex. You will notice that the mapped texture on the right of Figure 8–4 is a warped version of the texture. OpenGL is very good at squishing your textures to fit into whatever triangles you give it.

- *Order*: When texturing your models, the order in which you send your vertexes is important. This becomes very relevant when you deal with lighting and back-face culling. For now, just keep in mind that you need to be careful when specifying vertexes to make sure they are in the correct order.

- *Range*: If you pass in a UV that is less than 0 or greater than 1, strange things will happen. If you pass a UV point that is not in the range of 0 to 1, OpenGL checks to see what you have set for the texture wrapping mode. For now, just be sure to send UVs between 0 and 1.

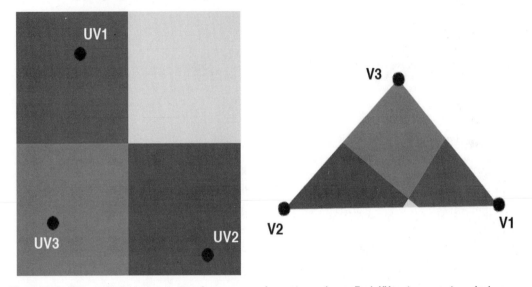

Figure 8–4. *UV coordinates map a texture from a square image to a polygon. Each UV vertex maps to a single xyz vertex in the model.*

Having the UVs be normalized between 0.0 and 1.0 can make figuring out your UVs a bit tedious, but it is super handy when you want to make your textures half the size or twice the size. This is known as the level of detail (LOD), and you can actually give OpenGL multiple copies of each of your textures to use at various sizes. For example, if your textured surface is very close, you might use the 1024-by-1024 texture, because you want to be able to see every little detail. On the other hand, if the surface is really far away, then go ahead and use that 32-by-32 version, because you can barely see it anyway. Providing multiple LODs is known as *mipmapping*.

You Get a Textured Quad!

Wait! Just a few pages ago, I said that we cannot render quads, only triangles. What am I talking about?

Well, a textured quad is just a common concept in 2D (and even 3D) game design. In our case, a textured quad is really a textured pair of triangles (see Figure 8–5), but that doesn't roll trippingly off the tongue as well as "textured quad."

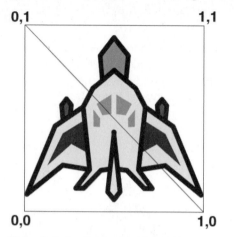

Figure 8–5. *Our fancy new ship graphic as a textured quad*

Textured quads are a great way to get your 2D images to the screen very fast. When doing a lot of 2D work, you can use textured quads for everything. This makes texture handling very simple, since every object has the same vertexes. For example, the images in Figure 8–6 have different textures, but they have the same vertexes as our ship quad.

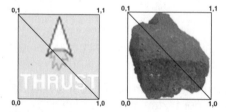

Figure 8–6. *Button as a quad, rock as a quad…everything as a quad!*

Each object had a very simple model, consisting of just four vertexes that form a square, like our button objects. Then all we need to do is specify four UV coordinates—one for each vertex—and a scale and a position, and we have our object. We need only four vertexes because we are going to be drawing the quads as a GL_TRIANGLE_STRIP, just as we drew the buttons in the previous chapter.

For our new textured Space Rocks! version, we will need a new mesh subclass, which we'll call BBTexturedQuad:

```
@interface BBTexturedQuad : BBMesh {
        GLfloat * uvCoordinates;
        NSString * materialKey;
}
```

This is just like our old mesh, but with a place to store the UV coordinates and a handle to a material key.

```
static CGFloat BBTexturedQuadVertexes[8] = {-0.5,-0.5, 0.5,-0.5, -0.5,0.5, 0.5,0.5};
static CGFloat BBTexturedQuadColorValues[16] = {1.0,1.0,1.0,1.0, 1.0,1.0,1.0,1.0, ↵
1.0,1.0,1.0,1.0, 1.0,1.0,1.0,1.0};

@implementation BBTexturedQuad

@synthesize uvCoordinates,materialKey;

- (id) init
{
        self = [super initWithVertexes:BBTexturedQuadVertexes
                                vertexCount:4
                                  vertexSize:2
                       renderStyle:GL_TRIANGLE_STRIP];
        if (self != nil) {
                // 4 vertexes
                uvCoordinates = (CGFloat *) malloc(8 * sizeof(CGFloat));
                colors = BBTexturedQuadColorValues;
                colorSize = 4;
        }
        return self;
}
```

Again, this is like our other mesh, but we are hard-coding our vertexes as a square centered on 0,0.

We will use this render method to override the simpler mesh rendering and add in our texture coordinates. These are the new lines of code:

```
[[BBMaterialController sharedMaterialController] bindMaterial:materialKey];

glEnableClientState(GL_TEXTURE_COORD_ARRAY);
glTexCoordPointer(2, GL_FLOAT, 0, uvCoordinates);
```

We call to the material controller to bind our material. Then we make sure that texture arrays are enabled, similar to how we enabled colors and vertex arrays to be able to draw lines. Finally, we pass in our UV coordinates.

There is one small step missing here. We don't have a good way to specify our UV coordinates. We could simply make a static uvCoordinates array that specifies the UVs as I have shown in the figures.

```
static CGFloat BBTexturedQuadUVs[8] = {0.0,0.0, 1.0,0.0, 0.0,1.0, 1.0,1.0};
```

Then we just set our UVs for every textured quad to those values and have a separate image for each object. This is actually how many 2D games are built. However, we are in a bit of a special situation on the iPhone. We need to be very careful of things that will crush our performance. And material changes are expensive. That's where the texture atlas comes in.

Say Hello to the Texture Atlas

Every time we bind a new material, OpenGL must move a bunch of memory around so that it can get ready to paint the new pixels all over the next bunch of surfaces. This is absolutely unavoidable, and it is not a very fast operation. We want to do this as few times as possible.

Even in our simple game, if we used a single image for each item, we would have about 20 material changes for every frame drawn. This isn't too terrible, and we could probably get away with it in our sample game. However, in real life, you will probably have dozens, if not hundreds, of small textures you want to render at one time. That many material changes will bring OpenGL to its knees.

How do we avoid this crushing cost? We combine a whole bunch of little textures into one big texture and use the UV coordinates to render just the bit that we want. This big sheet of smaller images is known as a *sprite sheet* or a *texture atlas* (see Figure 8–7).

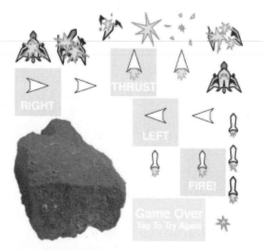

Figure 8–7. *A single 256-by-256 atlas contains all the individual textures that we need for SpaceRocksTextured*

Of course, as you would expect, this extra added goodness comes at the price of a bit of added complexity. We have this single atlas image, but we need to know where every individual image starts and ends. This means we will need some sort of metadata file alongside our actual atlas image.

Earlier, we talked about the minimum and maximum filters (MIN_FILTER and MAX_FILTER). Keep in mind that those filters will bleed out of your UV quad by a pixel or so, looking for extra pixel information to properly filter your textures. This is usually a great thing, but with atlases, it will cause problems. The filter algorithm will grab pixels from the image next to the one you are trying to display, and you will get strange artifacting. To avoid this problem, you need to guarantee that there is a minimum of 2 pixels between each image in the atlas.

NOTE: For this example, I generated the atlas and the metadata from another program that I wrote for this very function. You don't need to do anything so complicated. Typically, simple texture atlases will contain many images of a similar size, arranged in a grid. In this way, you can define a simple rule for finding the UV coordinates of any given "cell" in the texture atlas. Since this example has a lot of images that are dissimilar in size, I used a program to pack the atlases for me.

Figure 8–8 shows three packed texture atlases that we used for the Snow Dude game mentioned in the previous chapter. If we had used individual images for each sprite, then Snow Dude's performance would have been terrible.

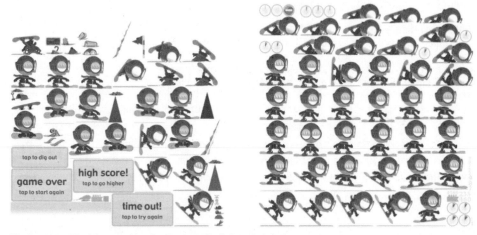

Figure 8–8. *All of the graphics for Snow Dude fit into three atlases.*

CAUTION: If you are mipmapping your atlases, make sure to arrange your images so that there is at least a 2-pixel gap between them.

For SpaceRocksTextured, I have generated an atlas and a *.plist* file that contains the information we need for each image.

```
<plist version="1.0">
<array>
        <dict>
                <key>height</key>
                <real>128</real>
                <key>name</key>
                <string>rockTexture</string>
                <key>width</key>
                <real>128</real>
                <key>xLocation</key>
                <real>1</real>
                <key>yLocation</key>
```

```
                    <real>127</real>
        </dict>
<dict>
                    <key>height</key>


    .
    .

    .
</array>
</plist>
```

The property list is just an array of items that have the name of the texture, the height and width of the texture, and the position of the lower-left corner.

In our BBMaterialController, we will need a few new methods to deal with our atlas:

```
-(void)loadAtlasData:(NSString*)atlasName
{
        NSAutoreleasePool * apool = [[NSAutoreleasePool alloc] init];
        if (quadLibrary == nil) quadLibrary = [[NSMutableDictionary alloc] init];

        CGSize atlasSize = [self loadTextureImage:[atlasName ↵
stringByAppendingPathExtension:@"png"] materialKey:atlasName];

        NSArray * itemData = [NSArray arrayWithContentsOfFile:[[NSBundle mainBundle] ↵
pathForResource:atlasName ofType:@"plist"]];
```

We are going to use the atlas name (SpaceRocksAtlas) as the material key, as well as the name of the PNG image and the *.plist* file (*SpaceRocksAtlas.png* and *SpaceRocksAtlas.plist*). We first load the image using our loadTextureImage: method.

Now we step through our atlas metadata one record at a time and build a new quad for each texture.

```
    for (NSDictionary * record in itemData) {
                BBTexturedQuad * quad = [self texturedQuadFromAtlasRecord:record ↵
atlasSize:atlasSize materialKey:atlasName];
                [quadLibrary setObject:quad forKey:[record objectForKey:@"name"]];
        }
        [apool release];
}
```

Similar to how we handled the materials, we are going to preload all the quads and store them in a quad library to be easily retrieved by name. This central storage is very handy. This way, your objects need to know only what their texture key is, and they can use that to retrieve their quad data.

Now let's have a look at our texturedQuadFromAtlasRecord: method:

```
-(BBTexturedQuad*)texturedQuadFromAtlasRecord:(NSDictionary*)record
                                    atlasSize:(CGSize)atlasSize
                                    materialKey:(NSString*)key;
{
        BBTexturedQuad * quad = [[BBTexturedQuad alloc] init];

        GLfloat xLocation = [[record objectForKey:@"xLocation"] floatValue];
        GLfloat yLocation = [[record objectForKey:@"yLocation"] floatValue];
```

```
GLfloat width = [[record objectForKey:@"width"] floatValue];
GLfloat height = [[record objectForKey:@"height"] floatValue];

// find the normalized texture coordinates
GLfloat uMin = xLocation/atlasSize.width;
GLfloat vMin = yLocation/atlasSize.height;
GLfloat uMax = (xLocation + width)/atlasSize.width;
GLfloat vMax = (yLocation + height)/atlasSize.height;
```

We grab all the information we need from the *.plist* record, and use it to build our UV minimum and maximum. Note this is all based on texture size. This is handy, because we can use the same metadata for all our texture sizes.

```
quad.uvCoordinates[0] = uMin;
quad.uvCoordinates[1] = vMax;

quad.uvCoordinates[2] = uMax;
quad.uvCoordinates[3] = vMax;

quad.uvCoordinates[4] = uMin;
quad.uvCoordinates[5] = vMin;

quad.uvCoordinates[6] = uMax;
quad.uvCoordinates[7] = vMin;
quad.materialKey = key;

return [quad autorelease];
}
```

Lastly, we set the UV coordinates in our textured quad. Astute readers will notice that these are in a strange order. Our first pair, which should map to the lower-left corner of our quad, is actually the upper-left corner. This is because of the way that Core Graphics renders images into contexts. All of our textures are flipped upside down. However, we can rectify this by modifying the order in which we map our UVs. This is much simpler and faster than trying to flip the image upright as we load it.

The other odd thing that we are doing here is preloading everything. Every third line in the Apple documentation suggests that you lazy-load all your resources, building them only at the time you need them. This is great advice, as long as you're not trying to maximize performance. We want to do all of this heavy loading before the game starts, so that we don't have major slowdowns while we load textures.

With that in mind, we should add two more things to our material controller:

```
- (id) init
{
        self = [super init];
        if (self != nil) {
                [self loadAtlasData:@"SpaceRocksAtlas"];
        }
        return self;
}
```

Now, as soon as anyone asks for the material controller, it will load our atlas, and all the quads will be ready.

The last thing we need is a handy way to get our newly built quads out to the objects that need them.

```
-(BBTexturedQuad*)quadFromAtlasKey:(NSString*)atlasKey
{
        return [quadLibrary objectForKey:atlasKey];
}
```

Now we are ready to change over our objects to the new universe of textures.

Switching the Old and Busted for the New Hotness

We have created a very simple mechanism for getting a prebuilt textured quad. All we need to do is go through each of our scene objects and change their mesh over from the old static retro style to the new textured quads.

We will start with our spaceship:

```
// called once when the object is first created
-(void)awake
{
    // old
        //       mesh = [[BBMesh alloc] initWithVertexes:BBSpaceShipOutlineVertexes
        //                        vertexCount:BBSpaceShipOutlineVertexesCount
        //                             vertexSize:BBSpaceShipVertexSize
        //                             renderStyle:GL_LINE_LOOP];
        //      mesh.colors = BBSpaceShipColorValues;
        //      mesh.colorSize = BBSpaceShipColorSize;

        // new hotness: mesh uses prebuilt textured quad
        self.mesh = [[BBMaterialController sharedMaterialController]
quadFromAtlasKey:@"ship"];
        self.scale = BBPointMake(40, 40, 1.0);

        self.collider = [BBCollider collider];
        [self.collider setCheckForCollision:YES];
}
```

I left in the old code just for comparison.

By standardizing on quads and adding a bit of boilerplate quad-building code in our material controller, building new objects is much simpler. If your game is primarily 2D, this is most definitely one of the quickest and simplest ways to handle your art assets and get them onto the screen. Snow Dude uses textured quads exclusively.

A Nicer User Interface

Quads are super handy for 2D game objects, but they are even handier for user interface items. Even in a 3D game, your buttons, scores, and heads-up displays will generally be 2D, so why not use quads?

Our retro buttons need to be spruced up a bit, so let's make a new button subclass, called BBTexturedButton.

```
@implementation BBTexturedButton

- (id) initWithUpKey:(NSString*)upKey downKey:(NSString*)downKey
{
        self = [super init];
        if (self != nil) {
                upQuad = [[BBMaterialController sharedMaterialController] ↵
quadFromAtlasKey:upKey];
                downQuad = [[BBMaterialController sharedMaterialController] ↵
quadFromAtlasKey:downKey];
                [upQuad retain];
                [downQuad retain];
        }
        return self;
}
```

First, since using the named images from the atlas makes things so much simpler, let's make an init method that builds the up state quad and the down state quad.

```
// called once when the object is first created
-(void)awake
{
        [self setNotPressedVertexes];
        screenRect = [[BBSceneController sharedSceneController].inputController
                                screenRectFromMeshRect:self.meshBounds
                                atPoint:CGPointMake(translation.x,
                                translation.y)];
}
```

Our awake method is quick and simple. We just set our default state to up, and then build our screen rectangle so we can properly handle touch events.

Then we override the setPressed and setNotPressed methods, and we are finished!

```
-(void)setPressedVertexes
{
        self.mesh = downQuad;
}

-(void)setNotPressedVertexes
{
        self.mesh = upQuad;
}
```

Since we are a Button subclass, we inherit all the touch handling code functionality, making this object very simple.

Now to take advantage of this new class, all we need to do is go into the input controller and change the object type for all our buttons.

Here is the old code:

```
// right arrow button
        BBArrowButton * rightButton = [[BBArrowButton alloc] init];
        rightButton.scale = BBPointMake(50.0, 50.0, 1.0);
        rightButton.translation = BBPointMake(-155.0, -130.0, 0.0);
        .
        .
```

And here is the new code:

```
// right arrow button
        BBTexturedButton * rightButton = [[BBTexturedButton alloc] initWithUpKey:↵
@"rightUp" downKey:@"rightDown"];
        rightButton.scale = BBPointMake(50.0, 50.0, 1.0);
        rightButton.translation = BBPointMake(-155.0, -130.0, 0.0);
        .
        .
```

Everything else stays the same—same location, same scale, and same callbacks.

If you build and run the game now, you should see our new ship in all its 2D textured glory, and some nicer buttons (see Figure 8–9).

Figure 8–9. *SpaceRocksTextured so far. Next, we need to add our rocks back in.*

Colors with Textures

Even though we are now using textured quads, we still have this array of color information that we are passing in. How does this affect our textures?

Astute readers will have noticed that we made white the default color for our quad. This keeps the quad looking just as it does in the atlas. If we want to tint our quad a different color, all we need to do is change the color values that we are passing in, and OpenGL will happily render a purple ship, a red ship, or whatever. This is very handy if you want to reuse some graphics for different sides of a conflict in your game. For instance, if you have a tank model, you can tint it red for one side and blue for the other, thus saving yourself from needing two sets of different colored textures in your atlas.

We are now going to make our rocks more interesting. Let's go into the BBRock object and update it to use the new textured quads. While we are there, we will add some random color tint to each new rock.

```
-(void)awake
{
        // new quad for our mesh
    self.mesh = [[BBMaterialController sharedMaterialController] quadFromAtlasKey:↵
@"rockTexture"];

        // malloc some memory for our vertexes and colors
        verts = (CGFloat *) malloc(4 * BBRockVertexSize * sizeof(CGFloat));
        colors = (CGFloat *) malloc(4 * BBRockColorSize * sizeof(CGFloat));

    // pick some random values between 0.0 and 1.0
        CGFloat r = (CGFloat)RANDOM_INT(1,100)/100.0;
        CGFloat g = (CGFloat)RANDOM_INT(1,100)/100.0;
        CGFloat b = (CGFloat)RANDOM_INT(1,100)/100.0;

        NSInteger vertexIndex = 0;
        for (vertexIndex = 0; vertexIndex < 16; vertexIndex += 4) {
                colors[vertexIndex] = r;
                colors[vertexIndex + 1] = g;
                colors[vertexIndex + 2] = b;
                colors[vertexIndex + 3] = 1.0;
        }

        self.collider = [BBCollider collider];
}
```

The next thing we need to do is actually use these colors in our render method.

```
// called once every frame
-(void)render
{
    mesh.colors = colors; // set my colors into the mesh for rendering
    mesh.colorSize = 4;
    [super render];
}
```

Here, we are just jumping in right before our super's render method is called and setting our custom colors. You might think that it would be better to set the colors once in the awake method. However, we are actually sharing the mesh with all the other textured quads. This means that we need to set our colors every frame.

We need to make one more adjustment here. In the previous version, our rocks had a rough radius of 1 unit. Our rocks here are about half that size, since our quads are 1 unit on a side. We will want to make our textured rocks slightly bigger to compensate.

```
+(BBRock*)randomRock
{
    return [BBRock randomRockWithScale:NSMakeRange(35, 55)];
}
```

We make the space rocks just over twice as big as their retro predecessors.

Now when you build and run the game, you get a Technicolor storm of rocks, all textured to look like a bad photo of a rock I have in my backyard (Figure 8–10).

NOTE: I am mixing my art styles here. Generally, I would stick with either graphic art style or photographic style, but I wanted to have an example of both. So that is why the rocks are a bit odd-looking.

Figure 8–10. *SpaceRocksTextured with more rocks. Now it looks a bit like the gravel at the bottom of a fish tank.*

Sprite Animation

I have been using the term *textured quad* quite a bit in the previous sections. Another term that you will come across quite frequently means basically the same thing: *sprite*. When we start to talk about animating quads, we generally refer to them as *sprites* or *sprite animations*.

Now that we have this easy way to swap graphics in and out, we can start to think about how to add some life to our game using some simple animations. In the Space Rocks! atlas, I have included three very simple and quick animations:

- A three-frame animation for the missile
- A three-frame animation for an explosion
- A four-frame animation for the ship exploding

Sprite animation is just like most any other animation. We have a different image for each frame we want to show. If we show enough images fast enough, then it looks like actual motion. Figure 8–11 shows the images for our missile animation. We will loop these three frames over and over to give the illusion that there is a thrust exhaust coming from the missiles.

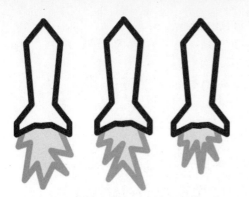

Figure 8–11. *A few frames of animation to make our missiles a bit livelier*

Luckily, doing animations is pretty easy. We will just subclass our new textured quad and make a new class called BBAnimatedtQuad.

```
@interface BBAnimatedQuad : BBTexturedQuad {
        NSMutableArray * frameQuads;
        CGFloat speed;
        NSTimeInterval elapsedTime;
        BOOL loops;
        BOOL didFinish;
}
```

Our new animated quad needs a few instance variables to keep track of which frame we are on and whether this animation loops indefinitely or it is finished.

```
- (id) init
{
        self = [super init];
        if (self != nil) {
                self.speed = 12; // 12 fps
                self.loops = NO;
                self.didFinish = NO;
                elapsedTime = 0.0;
        }
        return self;
}
```

We just set a few defaults in this simple `init` method.

We will also need to store our frames, provide a simple way to add frames to our animation, and provide a way to set the current frame to be displayed.

```
-(void)addFrame:(BBTexturedQuad*)aQuad
{
        if (frameQuads == nil) frameQuads = [[NSMutableArray alloc] init];
        [frameQuads addObject:aQuad];
}

-(void)setFrame:(BBTexturedQuad*)quad
{
        self.uvCoordinates = quad.uvCoordinates;
        self.materialKey = quad.materialKey;
}
```

Then we need a mechanism to switch between the frames.

```
-(void)updateAnimation
{
        elapsedTime += 1.0/60.0;
        NSInteger frame = (int)(elapsedTime/(1.0/speed));
        if (loops) frame = frame % [frameQuads count];
        if (frame >= [frameQuads count]) {
                didFinish = YES;
                return;
        }
        [self setFrame:[frameQuads objectAtIndex:frame]];
}
```

All the other code in the object is pretty straightforward, but here we are doing something a bit different. If we play back our animations at the same rate that the game is running (in this case, about 60 fps), our three or four frames will play back too fast to even notice. So, instead, we give each animation its own frame rate. This is great, except now we need to have some idea of how much time has passed between each frame. There are a few ways to do this.

The simplest way to get the timing information would be to just divide the frame rate by some integer, and have a counter that counts how many times we run the update method; then, every sixth one, we change the frame. In the case of SpaceRocksTextured, this approach would probably be fine. We aren't going to be pushing the OpenGL rendering engine very hard, so we should stay pretty close to the 60 fps mark at all times. However, in most gaming situations (and later when we move to 3D models), this is not the case, and the frame rate can jump all over the place. In this case, we need to introduce a new concept: the delta time.

Frame Rate Independence

So far, Space Rocks! runs right at the maximum frame rate of 60 fps (at least on my 3G test phone). Everything that governs movement in the game is based on that frame rate. For instance, a new missile has a speed of 3.0 because that speed looks good at 60 fps.

However, in a more typical game, you would want to push the rendering capabilities of the iPhone much harder, and so your frame rate will tend to fluctuate (sometimes quite radically), based on how many objects are on screen, whether you are firing missiles, and so on.

The problem is that our missiles, which move at 3 pixels per frame, will slow down and speed up depending on how fast we can render a single frame of our game. This is not usually what you want. What we want is our speed in terms of seconds. In the case of our missiles, we want it to move 180 pixels per second (3 times 60 frames).

We could just increment the position once a second, but that would be unbearably choppy. To keep the movement smooth, we need to update the position every frame, but only as much as we need to total an average of 180 pixels per second.

The way to do this is to introduce a new state variable known as the deltaTime. This is the actual amount of time that the last frame took to render. We then use that to calculate the speed of our objects in the current frame.

But before we can look at calculating our speed with this new deltaTime, we need to figure out how to find it in the first place. The best place to measure the time between frames is right at the beginning of the game loop in our *BBSceneController.m* file.

```
- (void)gameLoop
{
        // we use our own autorelease pool so that we can control when garbage gets ⏎
collected
        NSAutoreleasePool * apool = [[NSAutoreleasePool alloc] init];

         thisFrameStartTime = [levelStartDate timeIntervalSinceNow];
        deltaTime =  lastFrameStartTime - thisFrameStartTime;
        lastFrameStartTime = thisFrameStartTime;
        .
        .
        .
```

We have three new instance variables: levelStartDate, lastFrameStartTime, and thisFrameStartTime. levelStartDate is an NSDate, and we will reset that to now at the beginning of every scene.

```
// makes everything go
-(void) startScene
{
        self.animationInterval = 1.0/60.0;
        [self startAnimation];
        // reset our clock
        self.levelStartDate = [NSDate date];
        lastFrameStartTime = 0;
}
```

The instance variable lastFrameStartTime is the time interval since our level start for the last time we went through the game loop. thisFrameStartTime is the time interval since the level started for the current frame.

Finally, deltaTime is the time between our last frame time and this frame time. To get the actual frame rate of our game was, we simply need to take the inverse of that delta time:

```
NSLog(@"current frame rate: %f",1.0/deltaTime);
```

So, now that we have this handy time measurement, how do we use it?

Well, if we go into our high-level class BBMobileObject, the update method is where the speeds are all applied to the actual position of each moving object.

```
-(void)update
{
        CGFloat deltaTime = [[BBSceneController sharedSceneController] deltaTime];
        translation.x += speed.x * deltaTime;
        translation.y += speed.y * deltaTime;
        translation.z += speed.z * deltaTime;

        rotation.x += rotationalSpeed.x * deltaTime;
```

```
        rotation.y += rotationalSpeed.y * deltaTime;
        rotation.z += rotationalSpeed.z * deltaTime;
        [self checkArenaBounds];
        [super update];
}
```

Now our moving objects will move smoothly no matter the frame rate. However, if you build and run this, you will notice that everything is moving very slowly. Don't forget that up until now, all of our speeds were in pixels per frame. So, we need to go back and change them all to pixels per second. This means that we need to find every place where we specified a speed—rotational or translational—and multiply that speed by 60.

For instance, in the *BBSpaceShip.m* file, in our `fireMissile` method, the changes look like this:

```
-(void)fireMissile
{
        // need to spawn a missile
        BBMissile * missile = [[BBMissile alloc] init];
        missile.scale = BBPointMake(5, 5, 5);
        // we need to position it at the tip of our ship
        CGFloat radians = rotation.z/BBRADIANS_TO_DEGREES;
         CGFloat speedX = -sinf(radians) * 3.0 * 60; // speed in pixels per
        CGFloat speedY = cosf(radians) * 3.0 * 60; // second
            .
            .
            .
```

OK, so all the objects need to have their speeds updated. But how does this apply to our animations?

In our animation `update` method, we are looking at the delta time, keeping track of the total elapsed time, and setting our frame rate based on that time and how fast we should be changing our frames.

```
        elapsedTime += [BBSceneController sharedSceneController].deltaTime;
            NSInteger frame = (int)(elapsedTime/(1.0/speed));
```

In this case, our animation is running at a speed of 12 fps, so whenever the elapsed time increments enough to equal 1/12 second, our frame will change to the next in the sequence. Now, in our *BBAnimatedQuad.m* file, the `updateAnimation` would look something like this:

```
-(void)updateAnimation
{
    // use the delta time so we can animate smoothly
    elapsedTime += [BBSceneController sharedSceneController].deltaTime;
    NSInteger frame = (int)(elapsedTime/(1.0/speed));
    if (loops) frame = frame % [frameQuads count];
    if (frame >= [frameQuads count]) {
        didFinish = YES;
        return;
    }
    [self setFrame:[frameQuads objectAtIndex:frame]];
}
```

The last thing we need to complete the animated quad picture is an easy way to build the quads. For this, just as with the textured quad, we will return to the material controller and add another factory method to our *BBAnimatedQuad.m* file:

```
-(BBAnimatedQuad*)animationFromAtlasKeys:(NSArray*)atlasKeys
{
        BBAnimatedQuad * animation = [[BBAnimatedQuad alloc] init];
        for (NSString * key in atlasKeys) {
                [animation addFrame:[self quadFromAtlasKey:key]];
        }
        return [animation autorelease];
}
```

This is a very quick way to generate an animated quad. Now we can put this to good use in our missile object.

```
-(void)awake
{
        self.mesh = [[BBMaterialController sharedMaterialController] ↵
animationFromAtlasKeys:[NSArray
arrayWithObjects:@"missile1",@"missile2",@"missile3",nil]];
        self.scale = BBPointMake(12, 31, 1.0);

        [(BBAnimatedQuad*)mesh setLoops:YES];
        self.collider = [BBCollider collider];
        [self.collider setCheckForCollision:YES];
}
```

We simply set our mesh to be an animated quad, pass in a series of atlas keys, and we are ready to go. Don't forget to turn on looping, since we want the missile animation to loop until the missile is destroyed.

```
// called once every frame
-(void)update
{
        [super update];
        if ([mesh isKindOfClass:[BBAnimatedQuad class]]) [(BBAnimatedQuad*)mesh ↵
updateAnimation];
}
```

And, lastly, we need to make sure our animation is being updated properly. We will add a quick check to make sure we have the right mesh, and if so, send it an update. Figure 8–12 shows the missile animation in action, as well as the rock-exploding animation we are about to add.

Figure 8–12. *Animating our missiles and rock explosions adds excitement to the game.*

Animations for Everything

Now we have two more animations in our atlas: one for when the ship is destroyed and one for when a rock is smashed. We have a small problem, however: When our rock or ship is destroyed, it is removed from the scene and released. This means that it can no longer send updates to the animation to tell it to change frames. To fix this, we will need yet another object—a self-contained animation that can remove itself from the scene when it has finished playing. Let's call it a BBAnimation object and make it a BBSceneObject subclass.

```
- (id) initWithAtlasKeys:(NSArray*)keys loops:(BOOL)loops speed:(NSInteger)speed
{
        self = [super init];
        if (self != nil) {
                self.mesh = [[BBMaterialController sharedMaterialController] ↵
animationFromAtlasKeys:keys];
                [(BBAnimatedQuad*)mesh setSpeed:speed];
                [(BBAnimatedQuad*)mesh setLoops:loops];
        }
        return self;
}
```

The init method passes the keys, the speed, and the looping flag directly to the animated quad that is our mesh.

```
-(void)awake
{
}
```

Override the awake method; we don't need to do anything here.

```
// called once every frame
-(void)update
{
        [super update];
        [(BBAnimatedQuad*)mesh updateAnimation];
        if ([(BBAnimatedQuad*)mesh didFinish]) {
                [[BBSceneController sharedSceneController] removeObjectFromScene:self];
```

```
            }
    }
```

In our update method, all we need to do is to update the animation. Once it has finished, we queue ourselves for removal from the scene.

Let's have a look at how we would use this in our BBRock object:

```
-(void)smash
{
        smashCount++;
        // queue myself for removal
        [[BBSceneController sharedSceneController] removeObjectFromScene:self];

        // your rock asplode!
        BBAnimation * splodey = [[BBAnimation alloc] initWithAtlasKeys:[NSArray ↵
arrayWithObjects:@"bang1",@"bang2",@"bang3",nil] loops:NO speed:6];
        splodey.active = YES;
        splodey.translation = self.translation;
        splodey.scale = self.scale;
        [[BBSceneController sharedSceneController] addObjectToScene:splodey];
        [splodey release];
        .
        .
        .
```

At the top of the smash method, immediately after we queue ourselves for removal from the scene, we build an explosion animation (see Figure 8–13). We put it right where we used to be, and then hand it off to the scene controller. That's it!

Figure 8–13. *Our ship A-splode!*

From 2D to 3D

We've moved pretty quickly in the chapter so far. We converted our game from a very retro-looking 2D game that was all white outlines to fully textured graphics. We talked about texture atlases, how to get better performance by bundling your images into a single file, and how to quickly and easily build animations into your game. And we talked about how to keep your motion smooth, even if your frame rate is chunky.

You now have a simple but easily expandable game template that has all the bits and pieces you need to build full 2D games in OpenGL. The Snow Dude game uses roughly this same engine. The follow-on games—Skate Dude and BMX Dude—will use almost this same engine as well.

However, as you are probably aware, while OpenGL is really good at rendering 2D content, it is also quite good for building 3D content! So, let's move into the next dimension and talk about how to handle full 3D models. We'll do some basic lighting and get you on the path to building fully 3D immersive games.

It's Only One More D—What's the Big Deal?

So what does it really mean to move from 2D to 3D? Technically speaking, our 2D Space Rocks! was in a 3D world; we were just very stingy with our z coordinates. But moving into the next dimension is a bit more complicated than just adding a third axis.

Textured quads are great, and we will still be using them for our user interface items, but all of our scene objects need to get 3D models.

So far, we haven't even worried about lighting, since it doesn't matter too much with 2D (although you can do some very cool effects with 2D and lighting…). We could just render our 3D objects with the default ambient lighting, but then they won't actually look 3D. Humans tend to perceive the shape of things they see based on the contrast between the light and shadow. Without shadow, there is no perceived shape. So moving into 3D also means we need to figure out how to light our models.

As soon as we turn on the (nondefault) lights in OpenGL, we open a big can of worms. In order to light a surface, OpenGL needs to know a lot of things about how that surface reacts to light. We will need to define the properties of that surface, such as how shiny it is and how the light reflects off the surface. This requires a whole new set of numbers, called *normal vectors*, which we will need to provide to the engine along with our vertexes, UVs, and colors.

I mention all this to prepare you for the rest of this chapter. I am going to be moving a bit more quickly now, and I want you to be ready for it. I will cover more high-level concepts and show only a few code snippets here and there. You will want to have the sample code handy to be able to get the big picture.

For this version, make a copy of your project and rename it **SpaceRocks3D**. (If you are following along with the sample projects, use the project of the same name.)

Where Do 3D Models Come From?

For our retro version of Space Rocks!, I built all the models by hand by drawing them on a bit of graph paper. In the textured version, all of our models were the same four vertexes. Once we move into the next dimension, building models by hand becomes quite difficult.

The solution is to use a 3D modeling program to build the objects. Plenty of 3D modeling programs are available, most costing thousands of dollars. But there are a few really good modelers that are quite affordable, and some are even free.

Blender is an open source modeling tool that you can find for most any platform out there. If your budget is zero, then this is a great place to start, since it is free. Even if you have a big budget, Blender (http://www.blender.org) is worth a look. It is a very capable and advanced 3D tool.

When I worked in visual effects, I used Maya, which is a fantastic commercial modeler. However, it is quite expensive. These days, I generally rely on Cheetah3D (http://cheetah3d.com) for my modest modeling needs (see Figure 8–14). It is cheap (around $150 at the time of this writing), easy to learn, and very advanced for the price.

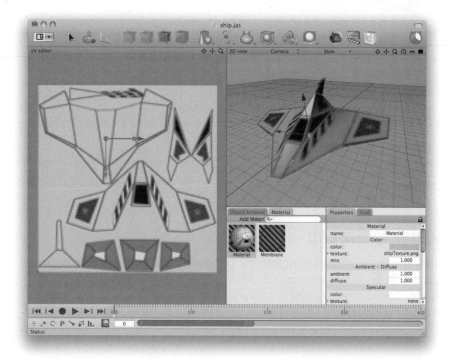

Figure 8–14. *Our new spaceship model created in Cheetah3D*

All the models for SpaceRocks3D were made in Cheetah3D and exported as *.h* files. Figure 8–15 shows the three main models we will be playing with in the rest of the chapter.

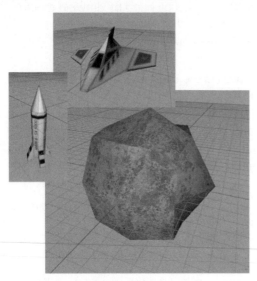

Figure 8–15. *Our new cast of characters*

The other handy thing about Cheetah3D is its active and helpful community of users who can provide help. When I needed to get my Cheetah3D models to work on the iPhone, a quick Google search lead me right to a script called *c3d_to_iphone_h.pl* by Rob Bajorek (`http://cocoaswirl.com/2009/05/09/cheetah3d-header-file-converter-for-iphone/`). I used this script to get my models from Cheetah3D into my Xcode project.

Suffice it so say that you will need a 3D modeler, or at least the services of an artist who has one. Let's get to the real subject here: how to use your 3D models in your iPhone games.

From Modeler to Screen

There are literally dozens and dozens of formats for storing 3D model information. We are going to stick with the simplest route possible: embedding the models as static arrays in the code. This method has its advantages and disadvantages. On the plus side, it requires zero code to load these files (well, it does require an `#include` command). On the downside, there is no good way to dynamically load models this way, and once the code is compiled, you cannot alter the models easily.

If you want to be able to store and load your models from some sort of file, you will need to figure out which file format has the appropriate properties for your game, and then either write or find a library that parses that file into some usable format for your code.

What Is Normal?

Before we jump in and start loading textures, we need to talk about normals. A *normal* is the vector that is perpendicular to a surface (see Figure 8–16). It is the vector that sticks straight out.

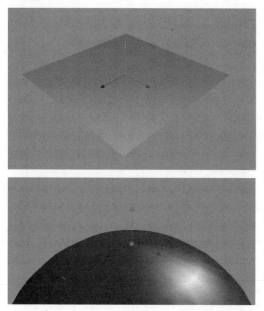

Figure 8–16. *In both examples, the normal is the arrow pointing up.*

Normals are important because they tell OpenGL how to have the lights interact with the object surfaces. The normal basically tells OpenGL which direction that vertex is facing. OpenGL uses this data to calculate the angles of all the incoming light sources and decide how bright that vertex will be.

Luckily, calculating normals is not very hard. Even luckier, most 3D modeling packages do it for you.

Our models come complete with precalculated normals, so we don't need to do much. But we do need to know about them, because we will need to pass them as yet another big array of numbers into the renderer.

```
glEnableClientState(GL_NORMAL_ARRAY);
glNormalPointer(GL_FLOAT, 0, OBJ_normal_vectors);
```

Standardizing on GL_TRIANGLES

Let's have a quick look at how we are getting all of this information. In the sample code, you will notice a few *.h* files, with names like *rock_iphone.h* and *missile_iphone.h*. These are the data files that hold our 3D model data. Here is a snippet of the *ship_iphone.h* file:

```
#define Ship_vertex_count              115
#define Ship_polygon_count             82
#define Ship_vertex_array_size         Ship_polygon_count * 3

float Ship_texture_coordinates [] = {
        0.53796, 0.93502, 0.54236, 0.87917, 0.60727, 0.89044,
        .
        .
        .
        0.77903, 0.41658, 0.73596, 0.37100, 0.75723, 0.23776,
};

float Ship_normal_vectors [] = {
        0.18593, -0.96722, 0.17293, 0.19288, -0.95849, -0.20998, -0.19077, -0.95848, -⏎
0.21194,
        .
        .
        .
        0.91313, 0.04440, 0.40523, 0.91313, 0.04440, 0.40523, 0.76904, 0.09214, 0.63253,
};

float Ship_vertex_coordinates [] = {
        -0.07586, -0.22036, -0.07558, -0.07586, -0.22036, 0.07497, 0.07470, -0.22036, -⏎
0.07497,
        .
        .
        .
        0.02790, -0.35827, 0.30770, 0.00559, -0.21063, 0.38461, 0.05856, 0.11942,
0.24730,
};
```

To save some paper, I have chopped out roughly nine pages of numbers, which you can see in the full source code. However, from this excerpt, it evident that these files have our UVs (texture coordinates), the normals, and the vertexes.

It is important to note that these vertex arrays are meant to be rendered with the GL_TRIANGLES style. This is pretty standard for most basic modeler exports. It is a fairly complicated process to try to get all your triangles into one long GL_TRIANGLE_STRIP, so most modelers don't even bother. However, if you could get all your triangles in strip form, then you would be saving quite a bit of data space, since you would not be resending so many vertexes.

This brings us to our last thought about model data: How much is too much? This very simple ship model has 115 vertexes. Each vertex is 3 floats, each UV is 2 floats, and each normal is 3 floats. That is 8 floats per vertex, and a float on the iPhone is 4 bytes, so each vertex is 32 bytes of data. My calculator tells me that means this ship is 3680 bytes—not too bad. The rock model is 2592 bytes, and there are 20 rocks, so that's 51,840 bytes, and we haven't even started thinking about how many missiles we might be firing. But probably the entire scene will be under 2500 total vertexes, which is about 80,000 bytes.

Remember that we want to run at 60 fps, which means we are trying to push about 4.8 million bytes of data every second. Don't forget this is just the vertex data; we haven't even considered the texture data.

I am trying to make this sound like a big amount of data, and it is. However, the iPhone is a pretty amazing bit of hardware, and you should be able to process around 7000 and

12,000 vertexes and between 20 and 30 `drawArray` calls, and still hit 30 fps on the 3G and older devices.

Do keep in mind that your vertex count can go up very quickly. Make sure your models are as simple as you can make them. Even with our very simple scene and seemingly simple models, we easily found ourselves at a third of the maximum capacity. Later in the chapter, when we get to particle systems, we will push the vertex count right up to the limit.

Also note that we are using floats for all of our data. If you are trying to push the limit, you can instead use ints or shorts for all of your vertex data, cutting down on the total number of bytes flowing into OpenGL for each frame.

Textures Plus Models

We already have all the data we need to render our models. Now we just need to make sure that we have the correct material loaded when we render. We already have a method to do this in the material controller:

```
[self loadTextureImage:@"shipTexture.png" materialKey:@"shipTexture"];
```

We call this in the `init` method of our `BBMaterialController` to make sure that our ship texture is available. Then when we render, we can bind to that material. In order to make it even easier, let's make a new mesh subclass: `BBTexturedMesh`. This will be very similar to the textured quad, but instead of hard-coded vertexes, we will allow the vertexes and UV coordinates to be set. Don't forget that we also need the normals, or our lights won't work correctly.

```
@interface BBTexturedMesh : BBMesh {
        GLfloat * uvCoordinates;
        GLfloat * normals;
        NSString * materialKey;
}

@property (assign) GLfloat * uvCoordinates;
@property (assign) GLfloat * normals;
@property (retain) NSString * materialKey;
```

We are just adding on to the `BBMesh` object. Now we can store UVs, normals, and a material key.

```
-(void)render
{
  [[BBMaterialController sharedMaterialController] bindMaterial:materialKey];

  glEnableClientState(GL_VERTEX_ARRAY);
  glEnableClientState(GL_TEXTURE_COORD_ARRAY);
  glEnableClientState(GL_NORMAL_ARRAY);

  glVertexPointer(vertexSize, GL_FLOAT, 0, vertexes);
  glTexCoordPointer(2, GL_FLOAT, 0, uvCoordinates);
  glNormalPointer(GL_FLOAT, 0, normals);
  glDrawArrays(renderStyle, 0, vertexCount);
}
```

In our implementation, we override the render method and provide our own. Now we are ready to add the 3D models to our scene objects.

Let's begin, as we always do, with the spaceship:

```
-(void)awake
{
        mesh = [[BBTexturedMesh alloc] initWithVertexes:Ship_vertex_coordinates
                                    vertexCount:Ship_vertex_array_size
                                                    vertexSize:3
                                                renderStyle:GL_TRIANGLES];
        [(BBTexturedMesh*)mesh setMaterialKey:@"shipTexture"];
        [(BBTexturedMesh*)mesh setUvCoordinates:Ship_texture_coordinates];
        [(BBTexturedMesh*)mesh setNormals:Ship_normal_vectors];

        self.collider = [BBCollider collider];
        [self.collider setCheckForCollision:YES];
        dead = NO;
}
```

Again, we simply need to alter our awake method to take advantage of the new mesh object. Don't forget to include *ship_iphone.h*.

That's it. We can update the rocks and the missiles in the same way. Once we do that, we can build our game and see the glory of 3D (see Figure 8–17).

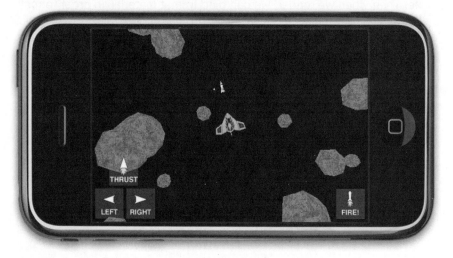

Figure 8–17. *3D models, but without lighting effects, they're pretty dull*

Well, it really is not all that glorious yet. Everything looks very flat. At this point, we could have just stuck with textured quads and 2D.

Shadows Define Shape

In order to be able to define a shape in our minds, our eyes need to be able to compare how the light falls across a surface. This creates light areas and shady areas. It is this contrast that helps us see shapes.

So far, our game has plenty of light. What we want is some shadow. Currently. we are just using the default "no defined lights" state in OpenGL. When you do not define any specific lighting, the renderer happily makes all the textures the same brightness, no matter how the surfaces are oriented. This is like having a big set of work lights on, and after you are finished with the construction, you want to be able to adjust the lighting.

To change this, we need to define at least one light. Once we enable lighting effects, the boring "work lights" constant lighting will go away, and we will get our shadows.

OpenGL is a very clever API. It knows how to simulate light hitting a surface, and it will figure out how the light hitting that surface will reflect back to the viewer. If that sounds complicated, it is.

Luckily, we don't need to know the esoteric ins and outs of optics and refraction theory. But we do need to know a few fairly complicated things, such as what kind of light sources we want to make.

We can look at the code while we talk about these things. In the BBSceneController, let's add a new method called setupLighting.

```
-(void)setupLighting
{
  // light features
  GLfloat light_ambient[]= { 0.2f, 0.2f, 0.2f, 1.0f };
  GLfloat light_diffuse[]= { 80.0f, 80.0f, 80.0f, 0.0f };
  GLfloat light_specular[]= { 80.0f, 80.0f, 80.0f, 0.0f };
  // set up light 0
  glLightfv (GL_LIGHT0, GL_AMBIENT, light_ambient);
  glLightfv (GL_LIGHT0, GL_DIFFUSE, light_diffuse);
  glLightfv (GL_LIGHT0, GL_SPECULAR, light_specular);
```

The first thing that we want to do is tell OpenGL what kind of light we want. Each light generates three types of lighting (see Figure 8–18):

- *Diffuse light* is what makes our shadows look real. When diffuse light hits a surface, it is applied based on the normal of the surface and the angle that the light is hitting it. (Remember the normal from a few pages ago? This is why we care about normals.)

- *Specular light* is the light you see in the shiny spot of an object. It is the most reflective light.

- *Ambient light* comes from everywhere. If you turned on full ambient light and turned off diffuse and specular light, you would basically have the default lighting. Every pixel will receive the same amount of ambient light.

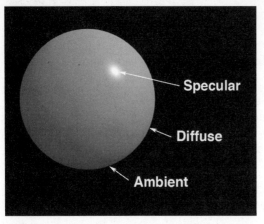

Figure 8–18. *Visualizing the three parts of a light source, and how it falls onto a sphere.*

If we think of light shining on a ball, then the ambient light would be noticed on the dark side, away from our light source. The diffuse light would define the shape of the ball, and the specular light would show up at the point of greatest reflective intensity.

For our light, we have picked a pretty low level of ambient light and equally intense diffuse and specular light.

We can also define the material properties for our lighting. Our new light source will look very different reflecting off fuzzy red velvet than it would when reflecting off smooth red plastic.

```
GLfloat mat_specular[] = { 0.5, 0.5, 0.5, 1.0 };
GLfloat mat_shininess[] = { 120.0 };
glMaterialfv(GL_FRONT_AND_BACK, GL_SPECULAR, mat_specular);
glMaterialfv(GL_FRONT_AND_BACK, GL_SHININESS, mat_shininess);
```

glMaterial and all the associated concepts and code that go along with it could fill yet another chapter. I added these few lines of material definition code just to whet your appetite. Using materials, you can make surfaces that are transparent, surfaces that glow with their own inner light, and surfaces that are shiny and reflective. As typical with OpenGL, this material will be applied to any models you draw until you change it. This allows you to have dozens of different material types in your scene if you want. However, in SpaceRocks3D we can get away with using the default material, so I have commented out the glMaterial commands in the sample code.

```
glShadeModel (GL_SMOOTH);
```

The glShadeModel tells OpenGL how to apply all of its light and shadow information to each surface. You have two choices (see Figure 8–19):

- GL_SMOOTH: This is the default setting, which you have already seen. For our original Technicolor spinning box, the colors from each corner were smoothly interpolated inside the box. This is the GL_SMOOTH shade model at work.

- GL_FLAT: This makes the color of the entire triangle the same. GL_FLAT is much faster than GL_SMOOTH, but the effect is generally less than desirable. Similarly, whereas GL_SMOOTH will blend light across each triangle in an attempt to replicate a real lighting situation, GL_FLAT will show each triangle as either light or dark. GL_FLAT is not generally used unless you really need that last tiny bit of performance and are willing to take the visual degradation that comes along with it.

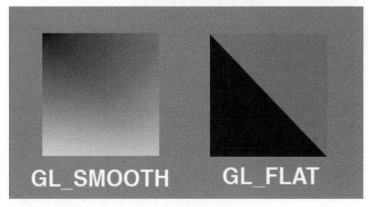

Figure 8–19. *Smooth shading versus flat shading*

Next, we need to place our light source somewhere.

```
// place the light up and to the right
GLfloat light0_position[] = { 50.0, 50.0, 50.0, 1.0 };
 glLightfv(GL_LIGHT0, GL_POSITION, light0_position);
```

In this case, we position the light source up and to the right of our ship. This should give us some pleasing shadows and add some depth to the scene.

Now we can turn on the lights.

```
// Enable lighting and lights
glEnable(GL_LIGHTING);
glEnable(GL_LIGHT0);
```

A constant that you have seen a few times now is GL_LIGHT0. OpenGL provides you with eight possible light sources, GL_LIGHT0, GL_LIGHT1...GL_LIGHT7. For each source you use, you need to define all the various light properties, as we have done here for GL_LIGHT0. Then, after all that, you need to make sure that lighting is enabled, and that the light source you care about is also enabled.

The next thing we are going to do is a bit funky, and is only tangentially related to lighting. If you build the app now, you will notice that the rocks and the ship are rendering oddly, as if some of the back of the rocks were being rendered in front of the rocks (see Figure 8–20). This is not at all pleasing.

Figure 8–20. *Something is not right here. You can see the backs of the rocks!*

Depth Buffer and Face Culling

You may recall the depth buffer, introduced in Chapter 6. It is true that the depth buffer will kind of solve the problem we are having with our rocks by sorting the triangles and drawing the ones that are closer to the camera on top of the ones that are farther away. However, the depth buffer comes with a few problems.

On the plus side, the way the iPhone graphics hardware renders your models makes the use of the depth buffer a very inexpensive process. On the minus side, depth buffers in general are very bad at handling transparent textures. I won't go into the technical details, but suffice it to say you have to be very careful of the order in which you send you objects to the renderer if you have any textures that might have transparent or semitransparent pixels. This is not to say that the depth buffer and semitransparent objects cannot be used together—they absolutely can, but it takes some clever prerenderer sorting.

I really enjoy using transparent textures. I think they add a great deal of character to some scenes (usually in the form of particles, which we will be discussing shortly). But I don't like to add extra sorting code if I don't have to, so I try to avoid using the depth buffer whenever I can.

So then what is our option? Our best bet is to simply not draw the offending triangles. We do this by using the OpenGL function glCullFace.

> **NOTE:** Although I'm showing the culling code after the lighting code here, it is before the lighting code in the sample project. What gives? Well, since OpenGL is a stateful API, the order of most of the calls doesn't really matter. We are just flipping all of the switches to the positions we want them before we do a drawArrays call.

```
    // cull the unseen faces
    glEnable(GL_CULL_FACE);
    // we use 'front' culling because Cheetah3d exports our models to be compatible
    // with this way

    glCullFace(GL_FRONT);
}
```

What does this do? The renderer actually throws out vertexes that do not match the culling filter. Since each triangle is a flat surface, depending on the orientation of that triangle in relation to the camera, it is either facing toward the camera or facing away from the camera. But wait! How can we tell which side is the front and which side is the back?

Each triangle has three vertexes, and the order in which these vertexes are handed to the renderer is known as the *winding* of the triangle. You can pass your three vertexes in clockwise order or in counterclockwise order, if you are facing the front of the triangle. If you flip that triangle over, then the vertexes will now be in the opposite winding from your perspective. By looking at this winding, we can tell whether a triangle is facing us. We just need to pick one and say counterclockwise is front-facing (or we could say clockwise is front-facing; it doesn't matter as long as we are consistent). It is generally accepted that counterclockwise winding is front-facing (see Figure 8–21).

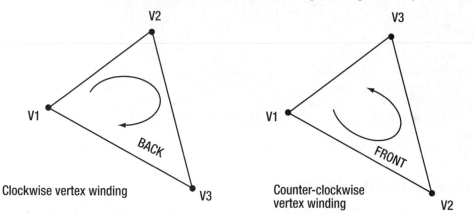

Figure 8–21. *Vertex winding determines whether the face you are looking at is the front or the back of the surface.*

Generally, OpenGL will just fill in the triangle irrespective of how it is facing the camera. However, this is a bit wasteful, since there are many hidden surfaces. Instead, we tell OpenGL to simply ignore the set of faces that is facing away from us.

The default front-face winding in OpenGL is counterclockwise, and the default culling face is the back face. However, sometimes your modeler will provide you with your triangles in a different order, and back-face culling makes your scene look strange. You can do one of two things:

- Tell OpenGL that front faces should be defined as clockwise windings:
  glFrontFace(GL_CW);

■   Tell OpenGL to remove the front faces instead of the back faces.

OK, our lighting is set up. Now we need to add the setupLighting call to into our renderScene method in the scene controller:

```
- (void)renderScene
{
        // turn openGL 'on' for this frame
        [openGLView beginDraw];

        [self setupLighting];
        .
        .
        .
```

If you build and run the game now, you will see our game in 3D (see Figure 8–22)!

Figure 8–22. *Finally, Space Rocks! in 3D*

Collision Detection Tweaks

In both the textured and 3D versions of Space Rocks!, I have glossed over a few things as we upgraded. The biggest piece is the collision-detection code. I covered it decently when we first encountered it in Chapter 7, and it really has not changed much since the retro game. I have tweaked it slightly to be compatible with the textured quads and again with the 3D models. But, in each case, the basic idea has held true: Keep the initial collision detection as simple as possible.

In the case of the retro game, we used circles and checked the distance between our objects against the radius of their collision circles. In SpaceRocksTextured, this was modified to manually adjust the radius of the collider to more closely match the artwork. I also added a half-dozen collision points to the spaceship in order to be able to do the secondary check against the mesh.

In SpaceRocks3D, our collision circles become collision spheres. I used the same code that is in the retro version for a secondary collision check.

You can examine all of these changes in the source code for the textured and 3D versions. Now, let's see how to add particle effects.

Particle Systems Add Life to Your Game

If you have played any games in the past few years, I can pretty much guarantee that you have seen a particle effect in one of them. Particle effects are generated by a particle system.

What Is a Particle System?

Particle systems are amazingly versatile. At their simplest, particles can simulate simple fluid systems, like a water spurt or exhaust flames from a rocket. Particle systems can be used to great effect as explosions or heavy weather. With some clever use, a particle system can become a magical energy field or a crackling laser blast. With a well-designed particle system class, you will find that you can do all of these things just by tweaking a few parameters.

OK, that all sounds very exciting, but doesn't really explain what a particle system is or how it works. At its core, a particle system is just a collection of textured quads. Each quad has its own state, much like any other scene object.

What generally makes particle systems unique is that their visual appearance is made up of many smaller images. Each tiny image is a single particle, and when all of the particles are rendered at once, they give the appearance of very fluid, living, organic effects. Figure 8–23 shows some examples of simple particle effects.

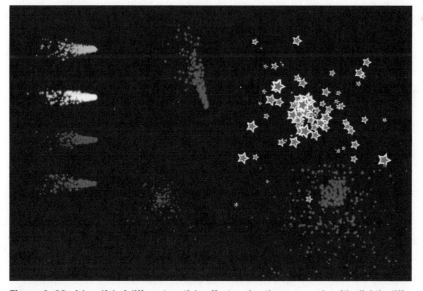

Figure 8–23. *A handful of different particle effects using the same code with slightly different parameters and textures*

Often, the textures used to make up a particle system will be blurry, translucent textures. These tend to be very good at mimicking smoke and fire. The overall effect is that the half-opaque particles, when seen in concentration, will be very bright and intense, but as they drift apart, they become dimmer and more transparent. Figure 8–24 shows a closeup of the red particle from the example in Figure 8–23. You can see how this particle is mostly transparent. However, you can just as easily use hard-edged graphics to produce very interesting effects, such as comical stars coming off a character's head after being hit by an anvil, or coins streaming out of a slot machine.

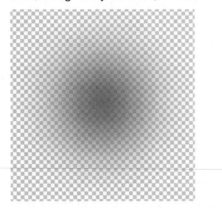

Figure 8–24. *Particles are generally very simple little blobs of color.*

OpenGL is one of those APIs that makes particle systems feasible. OpenGL is so incredibly efficient at pushing textures out onto the screen that you can easily have hundreds or even thousands of individual particles on the screen at once, and still maintain incredibly high frame rates. This is something that is nearly impossible to achieve with the other graphics APIs on the iPhone. That said, in order to render a few thousand individual particles at the same time, we need to be a bit clever about how we design our system.

A Lot of Random Numbers

As I mentioned earlier, one of the defining characteristics of a particle system is that each particle has unique properties. In other words, each particle should have slightly different velocity vectors and a slightly different lifetime. This variety is what gives the particle system its organic feel.

How do we give our particles a unique state? One way is to actually simulate the real-life system you are trying to portray. So if you wanted to have a particle system that looked like a stream of water jetting out of a fountain, then you could build a numeric simulator that took into account the water pressure, shape of the nozzle, viscosity of the water, and a whole host of other things that would require a degree in fluid dynamics to know.

Or you can take the easy way out (my preference) and just assign a handful of random numbers to all the state variables, and then tweak them until your effect looks good.

Much earlier, we added a handy macro for grabbing random ints. We could use that (and we will), but what we ultimately want is a bit more granular numbers. We want a random float. This means we need some new code. This will end up in our particle system, but this particular method will go into *BBPoint.h* with all the rest of the inline methods.

```
static inline CGFloat BBRandomFloat(BBRange range)
{
        // return a random float in the range
        CGFloat randPercent = ( (CGFloat)(random() % 10001) )/10000.0;
        CGFloat offset = randPercent * range.length;
        return offset + range.start;
}
```

This is pretty simple. But it does require a new structure—a range that can be negative and floating point (unlike NSRange).

```
typedef struct {
        CGFloat                         start, length;
} BBRange;

static inline BBRange BBRangeMake(CGFloat start, CGFloat len)
{
        return (BBRange) {start,len};
}
```

Great! Now we have a nice, easy way to get random floats in whatever range we desire. We are ready to build our system.

The Nitty-Gritty of a Particle System: Particles

Particle systems have two main components: the particle controller, often called the *emitter*, and the particles themselves.

Just like all the other scene objects, each particle is updated once a frame, and each particle has some basic state associated with it—like position and speed.

So far, this is not any different than most other scene objects, but our particles will need just a bit more information. Our emitter will be making new particles and adding them to the system, but we also need to know when to remove them. In order to do this, we need to know how long a particle will stay in the system. Let's call this the particle's life. If we give each particle some amount of life and remove a bit of life every frame, then once our life gets to zero, we will know to remove it.

How much life do we take each frame? Let's call that the decay of the particle.

Finally, it would be nice if our particles could change size during their life. We will need two more state variables: size and grow. Since we want our particles to be simple, we will make size both the height and width of our quad. The grow variable will be the amount that we change each particle's size every frame, much like decay.

Position, speed, life, decay, size, and grow states should be enough to get us started.

```
@interface BBParticle : NSObject {
```

```
    BBPoint position;
        BBPoint velocity;
        CGFloat life;
        CGFloat decay;
        CGFloat size;
        CGFloat grow;
}

@implementation BBParticle

@synthesize position,velocity,life,decay,size,grow;

-(void)update
{
        position.x += velocity.x;
        position.y += velocity.y;
        position.z += velocity.z;

        life -= decay;
        size += grow;
        if (size < 0.0) size = 0.0; // otherwise we will still render, just flipped
}
```

Our particle is a very simple object. It has a bit of state, and during each update, it moves itself based on its speed and then decrements its life. More advanced particle systems allow for dozens of various changing states. Things like rotation and color animation will add excitement to your particle system.

Our emitter is a bit more complicated.

Particle Emitters and You

Before we start on the emitter code, we need to figure out a few things about our particle system. First, why don't we just make each particle a textured quad and have the particles render themselves? It seems like making a new object that is so similar to a scene object is duplicating our efforts.

This is somewhat true, but the problem with using normal scene objects as particles is the sheer volume of them. Each scene object requires its own draw call. If we have, say, 3000 particles and we called glDrawArrays 3000 times, we would probably be lucky to be getting 2 or 3 fps. We need to figure out a better way to draw our particles.

If we keep our particles fairly simple, and they all use the same material, then we can draw them all in the same draw call. In order to do this, we need to use GL_TRIANGLES and provide two separate triangles for each quad, and send them all as a single draw call.

Also be aware that allocating new objects takes an order of magnitude longer than reusing preallocated objects. We should plan to have a large pool of prebuilt particles available.

We will have some big array of currently active particles. We will iterate across that list and update each particle, and then add its vertexes to our model data.

Since we won't be able to remove particles from the active array as we are iterating across it, we will need a dead particle queue to hold the particles that are no longer active and should be returned to the pool. Figure 8–25 shows this circle of particle life.

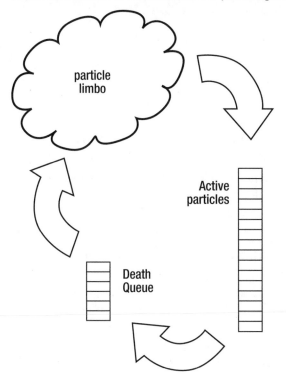

Figure 8–25. *The circle of particle life. New particles are pulled from the big pool. Once they are out of life, they are queued for removal and put back into the big pool of inactive particles, shown here as particle limbo.*

Once we are finished building our OpenGL data arrays, we will render them out in a single draw call.

Let's look at some code. We need a new object, the BBParticleSystem, which will be a subclass of BBSceneObject.

```
@interface BBParticleSystem : BBSceneObject {
        NSMutableArray * activeParticles;
        NSMutableArray * objectsToRemove;
        NSMutableArray * particlePool;
        GLfloat * uvCoordinates;
        GLfloat * vertexes;
        NSString * materialKey;
        NSInteger vertexIndex;
        BOOL emit;
        CGFloat minU;
        CGFloat maxU;
        CGFloat minV;
        CGFloat maxV;
```

```
        NSInteger emitCounter;

        BBRange emissionRange;
        BBRange sizeRange;
        BBRange growRange;

        BBRange xVelocityRange;
        BBRange yVelocityRange;

        BBRange lifeRange;
        BBRange decayRange;
}
```

The particle system has a lot of instance variables. We need to store all the particles in their various states. We need to hold onto the OpenGL vertex and UV data. And we also need to know what our particle property ranges will be.

In our awake method, we will build a whole bunch of particles and put them into the pool. Also, we will allocate some space for our vertexes and UV coordinates.

```
-(void)awake
{
        // alloc some space for our particles
        if (activeParticles == nil) activeParticles = [[NSMutableArray alloc] init];

        // we are going to prealloc a whole bunch of particles so
        // we don't waste time during gameplay allocing them
        particlePool = [[NSMutableArray alloc] initWithCapacity:BB_MAX_PARTICLES];
        NSInteger count = 0;
        for (count = 0; count < BB_MAX_PARTICLES; count++) {
                BBParticle * p = [[BBParticle alloc] init];
                [particlePool addObject:p];
                [p release];
        }

        // finally make some space for our final particle mesh
        // our vertexes will be all 3 axes, and we need 6 axes per particle
        vertexes = (CGFloat *) malloc(3 * 6 * BB_MAX_PARTICLES * sizeof(CGFloat));
        uvCoordinates = (CGFloat *) malloc(2 * 6 * BB_MAX_PARTICLES * sizeof(CGFloat));
}
```

Note that we are making our vertex and UV arrays big enough to hold every single particle. Most of the time, we will be using only a fraction of that memory space, but allocating new space is expensive, so we want to make sure we have enough to start out with. Also notice that we have set BB_MAX_PARTICLES to 100. That means that every single particle emitter we allocate will have enough space for 100 particles.

Next, we will need a method to define the texture that we will use for our particles.

```
-(void)setParticle:(NSString*)atlasKey
{
        // ok, here we are going to go and get the quad that will be our particle image
        // however, we do not want to keep the mesh, we just want to get some information ↵
from it
        BBTexturedQuad * quad = [[BBMaterialController sharedMaterialController] ↵
quadFromAtlasKey:atlasKey];
```

```
    // get the material key so we can bind it during render
    self.materialKey = quad.materialKey;
```

We grab a quad from the material controller, but unlike the other scene objects, we are not going to keep it as our mesh. Instead, we just want to find out what the material key is and what the UVs are.

```
    // now we need to find the max/min of the UV coordinates
    // this is the location in the atlas where our image is, and we are
    // going to be applying it to every particle
    CGFloat u,v;
    NSInteger index;
    minU = minV = 1.0;
    maxU = maxV = 0.0;
    CGFloat * uvs = [quad uvCoordinates];
    for (index = 0; index < quad.vertexCount; index++) {
            u = uvs[index * 2];
            v = uvs[(index * 2) + 1];
            if (u < minU) minU = u;
            if (v < minV) minV = v;
            if (u > maxU) maxU = u;
            if (v > maxV) maxV = v;
    }
}
```

Since we are a subclass of the BBSceneObject, we will override the update method to do our main chunk of work.

```
-(void)update
{
    // update active particles, they will move themselves
    [super update];

    // build arrays
    [self buildVertexArrays];

    // generate new particles and queue them for addition
    [self emitNewParticles];

    // remove old particles
    [self clearDeadQueue];
}
```

The first thing we will do is build the vertex arrays for our existing particles. Then we will add any new particles to the system. Finally, we will clear out the dead particles and return them to the pool.

```
-(void)buildVertexArrays
{
    // go through all our individual particles and add their triangles
    // to our big mesh
    vertexIndex = 0;
    for (BBParticle * particle in activeParticles) {
            [particle update]; // first, update each particle before we use its data

            // check to see if we have run out of life, or are too small to see
            // and if they are, then queue them for removal
            if ((particle.life < 0) || (particle.size < 0.3)) {
```

```
                    [self removeChildParticle:particle];
                    continue; // skip to the next particle, no need to add this one
        }
```

This is the first part of our buildArrays method. We first reset our vertexIndex. We will need this to be able to keep track of where we are in the new arrays.

We call update on the particle, and it updates its state variables. If we have sucked the last bit of life from the particle in this update, then we queue it for death and move on to the next particle.

This next bit is fairly important. Since we are culling faces, we need to make sure that we build our triangles in the proper order, or they will simply be culled and we won't ever see them.

```
        // for each particle, need 2 triangles, so 6 verts
        // first triangle of the quad.  Need to load them in clockwise
        // order since our models are in that order
        [self addVertex:(particle.position.x - particle.size)
            y:(particle.position.y + particle.size)
            u:minU
            v:minV];
        [self addVertex:(particle.position.x + particle.size)
            y:(particle.position.y - particle.size)
            u:maxU
            v:maxV];
        [self addVertex:(particle.position.x - particle.size)
            y:(particle.position.y - particle.size)
            u:minU
            v:maxV];

        // second triangle of the quad
        [self addVertex:(particle.position.x - particle.size)
            y:(particle.position.y + particle.size)
            u:minU
            v:minV];
        [self addVertex:(particle.position.x + particle.size)
            y:(particle.position.y + particle.size)
            u:maxU
            v:minV];
        [self addVertex:(particle.position.x + particle.size)
          y:(particle.position.y - particle.size)
          u:maxU
          v:maxV];

    }
}
```

The addVertex: method is a simple method that just constructs the vertex and UV arrays one vertex at a time.

```
// add a single vertex to our arrays
-(void)addVertex:(CGFloat)x y:(CGFloat)y u:(CGFloat)u v:(CGFloat)v
{
        // our position in the vertex array
        NSInteger pos = vertexIndex * 3.0;
        vertexes[pos] = x;
```

```
        vertexes[pos + 1] = y;
        vertexes[pos + 2] = self.translation.z;

        // the UV array has a different position
        pos = vertexIndex * 2.0;
        uvCoordinates[pos] = u;
        uvCoordinates[pos + 1] = v;
        // increment our vertex count
        vertexIndex++;
}
```

Next, we emit new particles.

```
-(void)emitNewParticles
{
        if (!emit) return;
        if (emitCounter > 0) emitCounter --; // if emitCounter == -1, then emit forever
        if (emitCounter == 0) emit = NO; // this will be our last time through the emit ↵
method

        NSInteger newParticles = (NSInteger)BBRandomFloat(emissionRange); // grab a random ↵
number to be emitted

        NSInteger index;
        CGFloat veloX,veloY;
        for (index = 0; index < newParticles; index++) {
                if ([particlePool count] == 0) {
                        // if we are out of particles, then just get out early
                        return;
                }
                // grab a premade particle and set it up with some new random numbers
                BBParticle * p = [particlePool lastObject];
                p.position = self.translation;
                veloX = BBRandomFloat(xVelocityRange);
                veloY = BBRandomFloat(yVelocityRange);
                p.velocity = BBPointMake(veloX, veloY, 0.0);

                p.life = BBRandomFloat(lifeRange);
                p.size = BBRandomFloat(sizeRange);
                p.grow = BBRandomFloat(growRange);
                p.decay = BBRandomFloat(decayRange);

                // add this particle
                [activeParticles addObject:p];
                // remove this particle from the unused array
                [particlePool removeLastObject];
        }
}
```

There is one thing of note here (well, there are a lot of things of note, but only one I haven't talked about yet): the variable emitCounter. Generally, this particle system will just emit particles forever and ever, until you release it. However, sometimes we just want a short burst of particles, say, for an explosion. To be able to handle this case, we have added this emitCounter so that the emitter will shut itself off after a certain number of frames. This way, we can set your emissionRange fairly high, set our emitCounter to 3 or 4, and get some fantastic explosion effects.

The last thing we do in our update method is to clear out the dead particles.

```
-(void)clearDeadQueue
{
        // remove any objects that need removal
        if ([objectsToRemove count] > 0) {
                [activeParticles removeObjectsInArray:objectsToRemove];
                [particlePool addObjectsFromArray:objectsToRemove];
                [objectsToRemove removeAllObjects];
        }
}
```

Here, we are simply moving particles from the active array into the pool. The reason we are doing this here instead of in the build array method is that you cannot alter an array while you are iterating across it.

So we now have a possibly huge array of vertexes and UV coordinates. We will need to override the render method since we have a bit of a special case.

```
// we want to override the super's render because
// we dont have a mesh, but instead are holding onto all the array data
// as instance vars
-(void)render
{
        if (!active) return;

        // clear the matrix
        glPushMatrix();
        glLoadIdentity();

        // bind our texture
        [[BBMaterialController sharedMaterialController] bindMaterial:materialKey];

        glEnableClientState(GL_VERTEX_ARRAY);
        glEnableClientState(GL_TEXTURE_COORD_ARRAY);
        glDisableClientState(GL_NORMAL_ARRAY);

        // send the arrays to the renderer
        glVertexPointer(3, GL_FLOAT, 0, vertexes);
    glTexCoordPointer(2, GL_FLOAT, 0, uvCoordinates);
        //draw
    glDrawArrays(GL_TRIANGLES, 0, vertexIndex);

        glPopMatrix();
}
```

Notice we are disabling the GL_NORMAL_ARRAY. We don't have normals for our particles, and we don't want the renderer thinking that the normal arrays that are resident in memory are valid for our particles, so we disable it for this draw call. This is not to say that you cannot or should not have normals for your particles. You can, and should if you want your lighting to affect them. However, for our simple system, we will go without normals.

Tuning Our System

Now we have our particle system. We will add one to our scene objects and tune it so it looks right. Let's start with the missile.

In the awake method in our BBMissile object, add this code:

```
particleEmitter = [[BBParticleSystem alloc] init];
particleEmitter.emissionRange = BBRangeMake(3.0, 0.0); // 3 per frame
particleEmitter.sizeRange = BBRangeMake(8.0, 1.0); // roughly the same size
particleEmitter.growRange = BBRangeMake(-0.8, 0.5); // shrinking

particleEmitter.xVelocityRange = BBRangeMake(-0.5, 1.0); //emit slowly
particleEmitter.yVelocityRange = BBRangeMake(-0.5, 1.0); //all directions

particleEmitter.lifeRange = BBRangeMake(0.0, 2.5);
particleEmitter.decayRange = BBRangeMake(0.03, 0.05);

[particleEmitter setParticle:@"redBlur"];
particleEmitter.emit = YES;
```

Remember that our range structure is the start of the range and the length of the range. This can be slightly confusing, especially with negative numbers. Keep in mind that BBRangeMake(-0.8, 0.5) will generate a number between -0.8 and -0.3, not -0.8 and 0.5.

We will need to move the particle system along with us as we move. And we will want it to be near the back of the missile, so we will shift it down just a bit.

```
-(void)update
{
        .
        .
        particleEmitter.translation = BBPointMatrixMultiply(BBPointMake(0.0, -2.0, 0.0), ↵
matrix);
        .
        .
}
```

We're almost there, but before we can try this out, we need one more bit of code in our BBMissile object:

```
- (void) dealloc
{
        if (particleEmitter != nil) [[BBSceneController sharedSceneController] ↵
removeObjectFromScene:particleEmitter];
        [particleEmitter release];
        [super dealloc];
}
```

We don't want the particle system to hang around after our missile has been destroyed!

If you build and run the game now, you will see our missiles have groovy red exhaust trails (see Figure 8–26).

Figure 8–26. *Missiles are so much more fun to shoot now! Pew—Pew!*

Particle Systems for Everything

With our textured version of Space Rocks!, once we had built our animated quads, we wanted to add them for everything. Similarly, you will want to do the same with the particle effects.

Since I don't have enough hands to be able to fire missiles, thrust, and avoid the enemy UFO while simultaneously taking a screenshot, I employed a bit of Photoshoppery in Figure 8–27 to make this last figure. The thrusters on the ships and the exhaust of the missiles look fairly good in a still image, but the green rock explosion is less exciting when looking at only a single frame. To fully appreciate all the explosions, you will need to compile the app yourself and smash some rocks! (Did I mention I added an enemy UFO for you? Yeah, they shoot missiles too, and they can destroy you, so look out! I know—it is pretty awesome.)

Figure 8–27. *The final game, with a lot of particles*

What the Future Holds: Shaders

As part of iPhone SDK 3.0 and the new iPhone 3GS, Apple upgraded the OpenGL hardware on the new devices to be able to take advantage of the newer OpenGL 2.0 specification.

Probably the largest difference between 1.1 and 2.0 that you will hear about is the ability to implement shaders (there are tons of other differences as well, but that is the one that most people are excited about).

What is a *shader*? Shading is the process by which OpenGL takes your texture and combines it with the vertex positions, the light and color information, and a handful of other variables, and eventually ends up with a color value for every pixel on your screen. There is a mathematical function that governs how all those variables react to each other and finally come up with a color for that pixel that lands on your screen.

OpenGL ES 1.1 is a fixed pipeline, so there is no way to alter the way your triangles get shaded. This doesn't mean that you cannot do some amazing things with OpenGL ES 1.1, but it is a bit more complicated.

OpenGL ES 2.0 is a programmable pipeline. This means that you can define your own functions for how pixels get painted into your triangles. There is a whole language devoted to shaders known as the OpenGL Shading Language (GLSL). You use that to define shaders. You can then hand them to the rendering pipeline, just as you would hand it a texture, so you can have multiple shaders for all your various materials and objects.

GLSL, OpenGL ES 2.0, and shaders are yet another topic that could (and has) filled entire books, so I won't say much more about it here. The topics and concepts covered in this and previous two chapters put you well on your way to being able to pick up shaders and all the new stuff in OpenGL ES 2.0.

Summary

These chapters about OpenGL have been pretty dense with information. This chapter went especially quickly. It may be worth a second read if all the concepts have not fully seated in your brain.

And if you have grown as attached to Space Rocks! as I have, then you will be pleased to know that in the next few chapters, Eric Wing will take the 3D version to the next level and add some sound using OpenAL (and he may even give you some more advanced tips on OpenGL as well).

For more information about OpenGL ES, see the OpenGL ES Specification, header files, EGL, and manuals (`http://khronos.org/opengles/spec`). I know it will sound like I am joking, but the ES specification is really quite interesting, and it is not so huge that reading it constitutes a daunting task.

As always, the Apple documentation is a good place to find the platform specifics:

- The iPhone OS Reference Library
  (`http://developer.apple.com/iphone/library/documentation/O penGLES/Reference/OpenGLES_Framework/`)

- The OpenGL Introduction
  (`developer.apple.com/iphone/library/documentation/3DDrawin g/Conceptual/OpenGLES_ProgrammingGuide/Introduction/Introd uction.html`)

Also, if you have any questions about my code or these chapters, don't hesitate to stop by my blog (`http://benbritten.com`) and drop me an e-mail or a comment.

Chapter 9

Introduction to Core Audio

As you have seen with the graphics APIs on the iPhone, you are given multiple choices, each with its own unique strengths and weaknesses, allowing you to select the solution that best addresses your particular problem. Audio follows this pattern.

This chapter introduces Core Audio, Apple's fundamental technology for dealing with audio.

Audio Services Provided by Core Audio

Core Audio is quite a large topic, made up of various services that specialize in different areas. To make it more palatable, it is typically broken down into smaller pieces. Figure 9–1 shows a breakdown based on application service layers. At the very bottom of the application stack is the underlying hardware, followed by the driver layer. All the layers built on top of the drivers are application-level services that Apple provides for us, in the form of APIs and frameworks to use in our applications.

The good news is that for most games, you won't need to use all of the Core Audio services in depth. The trick is to identify the ones that best meet the needs for your game. Here, I will present a quick introduction to all of these services. Then, in the remainder of this chapter and the next three chapters, we will cover the most important ones for games in more detail and demonstrate how to use them.

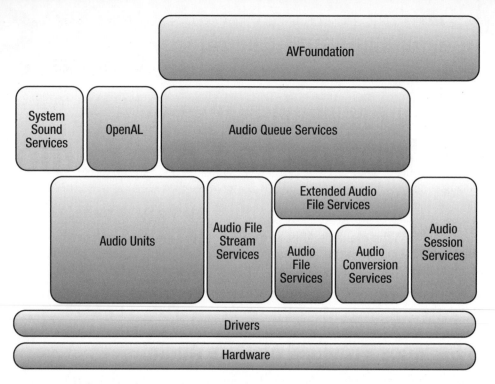

Figure 9–1. *An overview of the application-level services in Core Audio. A box above another box indicates that the higher-level service in the upper box is built on top of the lower-level service in the lower box.*

Audio Units

Audio units compose the lowest level service for Core Audio at the application-level. If there were no other services available on iPhone OS, you would use this service to play or record a sound. Audio units are software objects that process audio samples in specific ways. They may be combined to create more complex effects, and you may create your own.

iPhone OS comes with seven built-in audio units:

- 3D Mixer unit
- Multichannel Mixer unit
- Converter unit
- I/O unit
- iPod Equalizer unit
- Voice Processing I/O unit (new in iPhone OS 3.0)
- Generic Output unit

Audio units provide the lowest latency[1] and the most flexibility among all the APIs. But the trade-off is that using audio units is complicated. We won't be using audio units directly in the upcoming audio examples. But don't worry—we will cover plenty of other APIs to help you play and record sound in much easier ways, and they all ultimately go through audio units under the hood.

Audio File Services

Audio File Services helps you read and write files stored on disk. Audio File Services supports many popular file formats and insulates you from needing to know all the specific differences between them. For example, you may have an audio file bundled with your application that you want to play in your game. The APIs provided with this service will help you open the file and read it.

Audio File Stream Services

Audio File Stream Services is the corollary service to Audio File Services. What Audio File Services does for audio files stored on disk, Audio File Stream Services does for audio data (streams) that is not necessarily connected to a file.

Audio File Stream Services supports many popular streamed-based formats, insulating you from needing to know the implementation details. Typically, Audio File Stream Services is helpful for network-based audio applications.

Audio Conversion Services

Audio Conversion Services lets you convert data to and from pulse-code modulation (PCM) format (the raw uncompressed data format for audio, discussed in more detail in the "Codecs and File Formats" section a little later in the chapter). For example, you may have an MP3 file you want to use in your game. This service can decode an MP3 so it can be played.

Extended Audio File Services

You can think of Extended Audio File Services as Audio File Services plus Audio Conversion Services. Extended Audio File Services is an API built on top of Audio File Services and Audio Conversion Services. This makes it a little easier to load and convert files directly, without needing to do the extra work of using the two underlying APIs yourself.

---

[1] *Latency* is the delay time between when you tell the computer to start playing a sound and when you actually start hearing it. Less latency is better.

Audio File Services and Extended Audio File Services are fairly uninteresting to talk about without a specific usage need, so they will be discussed in the context of OpenAL and Audio Queue Services in Chapters 10 and 12.

Audio Session Services

Audio Session Services is a very important service to iPhone OS. However, it is easy for first-time iPhone OS developers to overlook it, because Audio Session Services is not focused directly on the fundamentals of audio. Instead, Audio Session Services focuses on how your application will interact with competing audio needs on the device. We'll take a closer look at Audio Session Services in the "Setting Policies for Your Audio: Introducing Audio Session Services" section later in this chapter.

System Sound Services

System Sound Services is a basic service that allows you to play short sounds and alerts. Apple defines "short" as less than 30 seconds, and preferably less than 5 seconds. System Sound Services also has the unique ability to invoke vibration on devices that support vibration (i.e., not the iPod touch). Sound playback also does not obey the same rules that all the other audio services must follow (controlled by Audio Session Services). The reason for both vibration and not obeying the same rules is that this API is intended to be used as an alert API to notify the user of special events.

You may notice from Figure 9–1 that the System Sound Services box hangs out slightly above only drivers/hardware. This represents the fact that there is nothing else in Core Audio that provides access to the vibration system. I'll talk more about System Sound Services in the "Alerts and Vibration: Introducing System Sound Services" section later in this chapter.

Audio Queue Services

Audio Queue Services is suited for dealing with playback and recording that lasts a long time. "Long" is roughly defined as anything that is 30 seconds or more. Audio Queue Services also gives you finer control over how audio is played, such as pausing, resuming, looping, and synchronizing audio.

You can see from Figure 9–1 that Audio Queue Services is one of the more encompassing services, dealing with playback and recording (audio units), files and streams, and conversion of formats. Thus, its box in the figure extends over the Audio Units, Audio File Stream Services, and Extended Audio File Services boxes.

For gaming purposes, Audio Queue Services is best for music or long files like narration (speech). It is covered in Chapter 12, and contrasted with other APIs suitable for music: AVFoundation, OpenAL, and the Media Player framework.

AVFoundation

The AVFoundation framework provides a high-level API in Objective-C for your audio needs. It also happens to be the only Objective-C–based framework in Core Audio. It provides the `AVAudioPlayer` class for playback, the `AVAudioRecorder` class for recording, and the `AVAudioSession` class for setting up an audio session.

As you can see in Figure 9–1, AVFoundation is built on top of multiple services, similar to Audio Queue Services. But AVFoundation also includes a wrapper class to Audio Session Services. so the AVFoundation box extends over the Audio Session Services box as well. But even though AVFoundation is drawn above a service, it does not mean you, as a developer, will be able to directly access all the features and capabilities of the lower-level services from within this higher-level service. As with any higher-level API, there are always trade-offs between ease of use and functionality. You may find that it does not provide some features and capabilities you need, so you must drop down to a lower-level service and use it directly.

> **NOTE:** There is a slight inaccuracy in Figure 9–1: AVFoundation currently does not really work with Audio File Stream Services or support anything with nonfile-based data (streams). AVFoundation provides some APIs that use NSURLs, which, in theory, make AVFoundation stream-capable, but as of OS 3.1, URLs must be of the `file://` type; other types, such as `http://`, are not supported. But, in theory, Apple could change its back-end implementation to support this, so maybe one day Figure 9–1 will be perfectly accurate.

If AVFoundation can meet you requirements, you are strongly encouraged to use this API, as you will be able to accomplish things in significantly fewer lines of code. You'll see an example of using AVFoundation in the "Easy Audio Playback in Objective-C with AVFoundation" section later in this chapter.

OpenAL

Unlike Apple's other proprietary audio APIs on the device, OpenAL is a cross-platform industry standard for playing and capturing audio. OpenAL's specialty is playing *spatialized sound*, also known as *positional sound*. You may think of this as sound in 3D space. Sounds may have properties such as position, and OpenAL will apply effects to make distant sounds sound fainter than closer sounds.

The design of OpenAL was heavily influenced by OpenGL and tends to complement applications written in OpenGL very well. Performance was also another design focus for OpenAL, so it provides low latency as well. Games are the primary users of OpenAL.

OpenAL is probably the framework of most interest to game developers. Because of this, OpenAL will be covered in detail in the subsequent audio chapters. Chapters 10 and 11 are exclusively dedicated to OpenAL; Chapter 12 also covers additional Core Audio frameworks.

TIP: While Apple tends to describe AVFoundation and OpenAL as part of Core Audio, it might be helpful to think of these as higher-level APIs that are implemented on top of Core Audio. They don't necessarily provide any functionality you couldn't implement yourself using Apple's other services, but they save you the time and difficulty of having to do so. In fact, Apple's desktop implementation of OpenAL is open source, and you can see for yourself how it was implemented. (OpenAL is built on top of the 3D Mixer unit and the I/O unit.)

The Core Audio Frameworks

Now that we have reviewed the services provided by Core Audio, it may be helpful to see how they map to the SDK frameworks, as there isn't a one-to-one correspondence. The application-level services are actually broken down into five different frameworks:

- Core Audio
- Audio Toolbox
- Audio Unit
- AVFoundation
- OpenAL

To help you visualize this, Figure 9–2 illustrates the mapping of the frameworks to the services illustrated in Figure 9–1.

You might be a little confused by seeing a Core Audio framework when I have just described all of these services as part of Core Audio. Just keep in mind that the Core Audio framework is a distinct entity from Core Audio the system technology. The Core Audio framework simply provides the headers and data types used by all the other frameworks.

The Audio Unit, AVFoundation, and OpenAL frameworks are very straightforward and map directly to their services by the same name (though keep in mind that AVFoundation is composed of three Objective-C classes: AVAudioPlayer, AVAudioRecorder, and AVAudioSession).

The Audio Toolbox framework provides all the other remaining application-level services listed in the previous section, including the all-important Audio Session Services.

Another framework worth introducing is the Media Player framework. Though not considered part of Core Audio, the Media Player framework allows you to access and play songs, audiobooks, and podcasts that are installed in the user's iPod library. However, there are limitations on what you can do with this framework. Perhaps the most significant limitation is that you cannot access the audio files themselves, their raw data, or their decoded audio streams. This limitation makes it impossible to interact with anything in Core Audio. But if you just want to play back files from the user's iPod library, this is the framework you need to use. The Media Player framework is covered in Chapter 12.

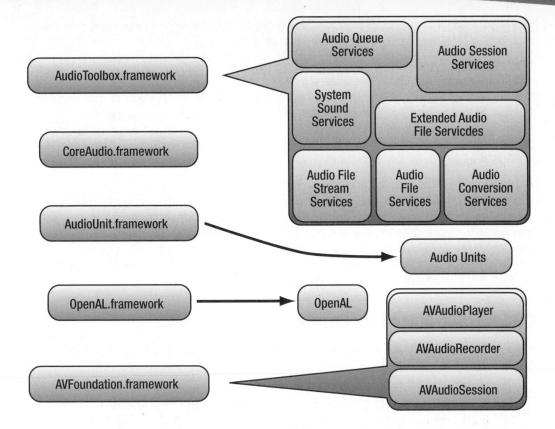

Figure 9.2. *A mapping of the individual frameworks provided by Core Audio (left side) to the services illustrated from Figure 9–1. For explicitness, the AVFoundation service is broken down into the three major Objective-C classes that make up the service.*

Codecs and File Formats

To deal with audio data, we need a common convention to represent audio as computer bits. Most things in Core Audio use linear PCM format. Linear PCM is the most commonly used uncompressed digital audio data format. It works by measuring the amplitude of an (analog) audio signal at regular intervals (also known as the *sampling rate*) and converting each sample to a numerical value. The numerical value is then expressed as bits to the computer.

The number of bits and how the bits are expressed can differ. The most common numbers of bits used to represent a single sample are 8, 16, and 32, which you might also recognize as 1 byte, 2 bytes, and 4 bytes. In addition, the bytes may be used to represent integers or floating-point values, and they may be signed or unsigned. In the multibyte cases, the endian[2] order can differ as well.

While Mac OS X has moved to 32-bit floating-point linear PCM, iPhone OS uses integer and fixed-point audio data. The iPhone and iPod touch want their linear PCM data to be in little-endian, 16-bit integers. If you are intimidated by this talk of endianness, don't be. For our purposes, we won't need to deal with the low-level details of endianness. We just need to make sure all the audio files we use are already in 16-bit little-endian format, or pass the correct constant flags to Core Audio APIs to tell it to treat everything as 16-bit little-endian.

Because linear PCM is bulky and can be represented different ways, there are assortments of file formats and compression algorithms. A compression algorithm or scheme is often referred to as a *codec*, which can be short for coder-decoder or compressor-decompressor. File formats are just containers for your audio bits. Some containers are expected to always use certain codecs for your data; other containers are more flexible and can use any kind of codec. Core Audio supports many of the common codecs and file formats through Audio Conversion Services.

Codecs Supported by Core Audio

Here is a brief list and description of some of the audio codecs supported by Core Audio:

- *MPEG-1, Audio Layer 3 (MP3)*: The most well-known lossy[3] compression format. It originated from the audio part of the MPEG-1 motion video specification, known as Audio Layer 3. It took on a life of its own when people started using it just for audio files. Generally speaking, compression levels of about 11:1 can often be achieved, where most people are unable to distinguish the difference from the original source.

---

[2] *Endianness* describes the sequence order of how bytes are stored in computer memory. The term originates from the book *Gulliver's Travels*, where two political factions broke their eggs on different ends. The Big-Endians broke their eggs on the big end, and the Little-Endians broke their eggs on the small end. For our purposes, we don't need to go deep into the details of the different permutations of byte order, because we get to use high-level tools and APIs that just need us to pass the correct flags. But if you want to know more, there is a wealth of easy-to-find information on endianness, as it is a fundamental concept in computing.

[3] *Lossy* compression means that data is compressed in such a way that it is not possible to get back the exact same original bits when you decompress it. Thus, an audio sample may not sound exactly the same as the original. The reason you would do this is to get significantly better compression rates. Typically, lossy compression formats are biased/optimized to try to first lose the bits that most humans won't notice losing.

- *Advanced Audio Coding (AAC), MPEG-2 Part 7, MPEG-4 Part 3, MPEG-4*: The successor to MP3 developed by the MPEG group, best known as the default format of the iPod. Like its forefather MP3, it is a lossy compression format, but tends to offer better compression rates for about the same level of quality as MP3.

- *Apple Lossless*: Also known as Apple Lossless Audio Codec (ALAC) and Apple Lossless Encoder (ALE), a codec developed by Apple that is not lossy. It can achieve compression levels typically between 40% to 60%—much better than IMA-4 (described next), which typically gets only about 25%. However, this comes at the expense of needing more computational power.

- *IMA/ADPCM*: IMA (also known as IMA-4) stands for Interactive Multimedia Association. ADPCM stands for Adaptive Differential Pulse-Code Modulation. It was developed in the 1970s by Bell Labs for voice compression. It yields about a 4:1 compression ratio.

- *Adaptive Multi-Rate (AMR or AMR-NB)*: A compression format optimized for speech. It is widely used by the mobile phone standards, GSM and UMTS.

- *iLBC (internet Low Bitrate Codec)*: Another compression format optimized for speech. It is royalty-free and is a good candidate for Voice over IP (VoIP) applications.

- *μLaw and aLaw*: Compression algorithms used by digital telecommunication systems. μLaw is primarily used by systems in North America and Japan, while aLaw is used by systems in Europe.

File Formats Supported by Core Audio

Associated with the actual codecs are their file formats and extensions. Here is a quick list of the supported formats:

- *Audio Interchange File Format (AIFF)*: A linear PCM format used by Apple in the 1980s. Files have an *.aif* or *.aiff* extension. It is a big-endian–based format. There is also a variant called AIFF-C or AIFC, which is a compressed variant of AIFF. Various compression schemes can be applied to AIFC, including one interesting scheme Apple came up with to abuse the notion of compression and simply make a little-endian variation instead. However, these little-endian variants are rare to find in the wild, and the practice is discouraged.

- *Waveform Audio File Format (WAVE or WAV)*: The file container format from Microsoft. Files have a *.wav* extension. This format's most popular usage has been for storing linear PCM audio in little-endian byte order. This file format also supports compressed data that conforms to Microsoft's (legacy) Audio Compression Manager (ACM) codec.

- *MP3*: Often, people who compress their audio using the MP3 codec also use a file container that goes by the same name, MP3. (To be picky, MP3 is a streaming format, which people tend to also use as a file format.) Files have an *.mp3* extension. MP3 files typically are used in conjunction with a metadata container format called ID3.

- *MP4/M4A/3GPP/3GP2*: These containers are all based on the same ISO base media file format specified from MPEG-4 Part 12. Files have the extension *.mp4, .m4a, .3gp,* or *.3g2*. Though all derived from the same base format, each has subtle differences. And each container tends to be used to represent different codec encodings. For example, codecs using AAC sometimes use MP4 or M4A (or sometimes neither, using AAC instead). In contrast, Apple Lossless always uses M4A. AMR is found only in the 3G* flavors, and AC3 (Dolby Digital codec) is found only in MP4/M4A.

- *Advanced Audio Coding (AAC)/Audio Data Transport Stream (ADTS)/Audio Data Interchange Format (ADIF)*: Like MP3, audio compressed using the AAC codec may use a file container that sometimes casually goes by the same name. Files have an *.aac* extension. However, to be more picky, there is a file container format called ADIF, consisting of a single header followed by AAC data blocks. Alternatively, there is a streaming format called ADTS, and it may also be used as the container. These files may have the *.adts* extension instead.

- *AMR*: Like the MP3 codec and container, AMR-encoded audio may use a container named AMR. (AMR may often use the 3G* family of containers instead.) Files have an *.amr* extension.

- *Core Audio Format (CAF)*: A container format invented by Apple that can contain any type of format/codec. It has no size restrictions, and it has a lot of metadata fields, which can be useful if you want to store additional information that the native container doesn't support. Files have a *.caf* extension.

Using afconvert to Convert Between Formats

On your Mac OS X development system, a tool called afconvert is available to you to help you convert between file formats. You are encouraged to use this tool to convert your audio formats to something that is optimal for the iPhone and iPod touch.

Let's look at some examples:

- Convert a file into linear PCM, little-endian, 16-bit integer, and put it in a CAF format:

```
/usr/bin/afconvert -f caff -d LEI16 {INPUT} {OUTPUT}
```

- Convert a file into IMA-4 and put it in a CAF format:

```
/usr/bin/afconvert -f caff -d ima4 {INPUT} {OUTPUT}
```

- Convert a file into AAC and put it in an *.m4a* file at 128,000 bps:

```
/usr/bin/afconvert -f m4af -d aac {INPUT} {OUTPUT}
```

Hardware-Accelerated Codecs: Restricted and Unrestricted Codec Groups

In addition to the general-purpose CPU, the iPhone and iPod touch contain dedicated hardware optimized to decode certain audio codecs. Opting to use the special hardware with these specific codecs may offer great savings in CPU and battery consumption. And if the CPU is less burdened by decoding audio, there is more processing available for other aspects of your game. However, if you choose to use the special hardware, certain limitations are imposed on you, because this hardware is a finite and limited resource in itself. For example, the hardware currently has the capability to decode only one thing at a time. So you wouldn't be able to play two sounds simultaneously utilizing the special hardware.

The special hardware supports only certain codecs, which tend to be the most computationally expensive to process. The remaining codecs don't get hardware acceleration, typically because they are inexpensive enough to be processed with the normal CPU while still leaving enough processing power to do other things for your game.

Apple likes to break the codecs into two groups, which I will call *unrestricted* and *restricted*. Often, Apple refers to the restricted group as *compressed* and the unrestricted group as *uncompressed*, but these are misnomers, as many types in the unrestricted group are compressed. As already stated, the difference really is in how computationally expensive each type is to deal with.

The restricted group consists of the following formats:

- MP3
- AAC
- Apple Lossless

The remaining formats have low enough CPU requirements that they are considered unrestricted:

- Linear PCM
- IMA/ADPCM (IMA-4)
- AMR
- iLBC
- µLaw and aLaw

Prior to iPhone OS 3.0, Core Audio provided access to restricted formats only via hardware acceleration. Starting in iPhone OS 3.0, Core Audio provides a software decoder for the restricted formats, so it is possible to use the general CPU for all the formats. Now you can do things such as play one restricted format sound utilizing hardware acceleration, and another restricted format sound through the CPU. You could even try to play more than two simultaneous restricted format sounds, but you need to be careful about overtaxing your CPU.

For typical games, generally you want to avoid burdening the CPU with audio processing, so you can utilize the CPU for other aspects of your game. Thus, linear PCM and IMA-4 tend to be the most commonly used codecs on the iPhone and iPod touch. IMA-4 yields about a 4:1 compression ratio, and tends to give the best trade-off between size and CPU utilization. In addition, for games that include a custom soundtrack, since music tends to have large file sizes, background music may be encoded in a restricted codec and utilize hardware acceleration.

We will discuss how to use Audio Session Services to control access to hardware acceleration later in this chapter. In Chapter 12, we will discuss background music in more detail.

Codec and File Format Suggestions

So now that you've been exposed to an assortment of codecs and file formats, you might be wondering which ones to use. It is hard to generalize without knowing the specifics of your application, but I will try to offer some suggestions.

If you don't need to worry about simultaneously loading/decoding multiple audio files, and you don't mind lossy compression, AAC is a great option. It will save you disk space and make your application smaller for distribution. You do need to keep in mind that the hardware-accelerated decoder can handle only one restricted file at a time, so this scenario is best if you can ensure your application preloads all the audio samples while nothing else may be using the decoder. AAC is also a better option than MP3 because of royalty concerns. You may distribute AAC royalty-free, but MP3 distribution may require you to pay royalty fees.

If you cannot use a restricted compression format, then IMA-4 is probably your best option. It will get you the best compression without much more CPU cost than using completely raw PCM formats like WAV.

As for file containers, you have the option of putting everything in CAF. However, because I sometimes use non-Apple audio tools, I personally find using more native containers easier, because the CAF file format is not widely supported.

Now that you've been given an overview of Core Audio, it is time to dive into it. In the remainder of this chapter, we will focus on the native proprietary Core Audio APIs that will get you started playing short sounds. These include System Sound Services, AVFoundation, and the all-important Audio Session Services. These also happen to be the simplest and easiest to use APIs.

IPHONE OS VERSION DIFFERENCES

At the time of this writing, the latest iPhone OS version is 3.1.2. There are not many changes between 3.0 and 3.1.2, but there were very significant changes from 2.2.1 to 3.0. Here, I will assume you are using iPhone OS 3.0 or later. I will also take care to point out 3.1-only features.

While there is always a lot of fanfare about new frameworks and features in every new major OS release, Core Audio is a bit odd in that it underwent fairly significant behind-the-scenes improvements in the 3.0 release, without much noise or documentation. Some very significant limitations, such as being unable to decode AAC or MP3 formats with certain APIs, were lifted; missing APIs were filled in; behaviors regarding what needs to be done by the developer in interruption events were simplified in some areas; and simulator support continued to improve. So consider yourself warned if you are trying to use an older OS version.

See the following Apple documentation for more information regarding OS version changes:

- iPhone OS 2.2 to iPhone OS 3.0 API Differences
  (`http://developer.apple.com/iphone/library/releasenotes/Gen eral/iPhone30APIDiffs/index.html`)

- iPhone SDK Release Notes for iPhone OS 3.1
  (`http://developer.apple.com/iphone/library/releasenotes/Gen eral/RN-iPhoneSDK-3/index.html`)

Alerts and Vibration: Introducing System Sound Services

Using the System Sound Services API is the most basic way to produce a sound on a device. It can also be used to invoke a vibration on devices that support it. However, there are several important things to know about this API:

- Sounds may not be encoded in any of the restricted codec types discussed earlier (e.g., MP3, AAC, and Apple Lossless).

- Sounds played using System Sound Services are limited to a maximum duration of 30 seconds. (Ideally, Apple suggests the sounds should be less than 5 seconds.)

- System Sound Services is the exception to the rule about Audio Session Services in that System Sound Services is not subject to the configuration rules set up in your audio session.

- System Sound Services plays all sounds at the current system audio level and offers no volume control.

That said, System Sound Services provides a very small and easy-to-use API to play sounds. Like all sound APIs in Core Audio, it can play multiple sounds simultaneously, which some developers coming from other platforms may find surprising. For these reasons, System Sound Services has been a magnet for first-time iPhone developers trying to play sounds. However, I am going to try to discourage you from using this API for general sound effects.

The Case Against System Sound Services for General Sound Effects

The reason I recommend avoiding the use of System Sound Services to play sounds for your games is that this API works more like an alert API than it does a general sound effect API.

Consider that this API has only two functions for playing sound, and one of them has Alert in its name:

```
void AudioServicesPlayAlertSound(SystemSoundID system_sound_id)
void AudioServicesPlaySystemSound(SystemSoundID system_sound_id)
```

AudioServicesPlayAlertSound() is intended for playing an alert sound to let the user know something important has happened. In fact, on an iPhone set to silent mode, playing a sound will invoke a vibration. Consider the game Asteroids and a phone in silent mode. You probably don't want your phone to start vibrating every time a sound effect plays (e.g., a gun firing, an engine thrust, an asteroid exploding, or a UFO flying by). In a fast-paced game, the device will be vibrating nonstop—it's annoying and wears out the battery.

With the other System Sound Services function, AudioServicesPlaySystemSound(), you can optionally pass in a special constant (kSystemSoundID_Vibrate) as the parameter, which will invoke a vibration instead of playing a sound. Thus, you can see that this API is really intended for alerting the user.

Another limitation is that System Sound Services does not necessarily conform to your audio session rules, which may make it hard to keep the behavior of your audio based on this API in agreement with any other audio you might be using in conjunction with System Sound Services. This is the only sound API on the device that does not conform with Audio Session Services.

You might be wondering why I am making such a big deal of this. The reason stems from experience with developing on Mac OS X (the desktop). Many conventions help bring a consistent UI across all Mac applications, which, in turn, help provide a consistent user experience and make things more intuitive for users. In addition, assuming you use APIs and widgets as intended, Apple can tweak them in future versions of the operating system to make them better. But if you are using them in a nonstandard way, things may break or the metaphors may no longer work.

For example, imagine that you were developing a Mac application and decided to modify a Mac alert sheet to be some kind of decorative text-entry box because it happens to provide an easy way to present the application's icon. Now suppose that in a later operating system release, the alert sheet is modified to display a special alert icon instead, and the behavior is changed to e-mail the event to a network administrator. You don't want this icon or behavior, since you weren't using the alert sheet for actual alerts.

> **TIP:** I encourage you to read and take to heart Apple's Human Interface Guidelines. They are guidelines, not rules, but they are generally well thought out. Developers that "get it" typically develop great apps that users love, giving them a competitive edge.

As a final point, note that Apple doesn't really say anything about the latency of System Sound Services. It could be high or low, but the lack of a statement leaves the possibility open that the sound playback may take longer than you consider desirable. Consider a game object exploding. You would generally expect the explosion noise to start at the same time you start drawing the explosion graphics (excluding the possibility you are doing a speed-of-light versus speed-of-sound comparison). In my experiments, latency is low, but since Apple says nothing about this, it is technically free to change in future OS releases (though I would venture to say that this is unlikely).

In summary, I believe System Sound Services is an alert API and should be treated as such. And with plenty of other APIs to choose from to play sounds, there really isn't any loss in reserving this API for only alerts.

A System Sound Services Example

Now that I have properly discouraged you from using System Sound Services as a general sound effect API, I do want to emphasize that there are still legitimate uses a game might have for it, such as alerting a user that their network connection in a multiplayer game has suddenly been disconnected. Here, we will run through a simple example on how to use System Sound Services. This example will play an alert sound, play a system sound, and invoke a vibration.

> **NOTE:** The assumption for this book is that readers already have a basic knowledge of iPhone development—some experience with Objective-C, Xcode, and Interface Builder. For brevity, I omit explanations of the very basic material. You are encouraged to look at the supplied finished projects, as they may contain additional code or comments not explicitly discussed here.

A finished Xcode project called SystemSoundServices is provided for you. If you want to re-create this project from scratch, start by selecting the View-based Application template (see Figure 9–3), and name the project SystemSoundServices. I added the AudioToolbox.framework as an additional framework to link to, because System Sound Services uses the Audio Toolbox. (You may remove the CoreGraphics.framework because this example doesn't need it.) You will need to copy the two audio files found in the finished project into the Resources group (see Figure 9–4).

Figure 9–3. *A View-based Application template was used for this example.*

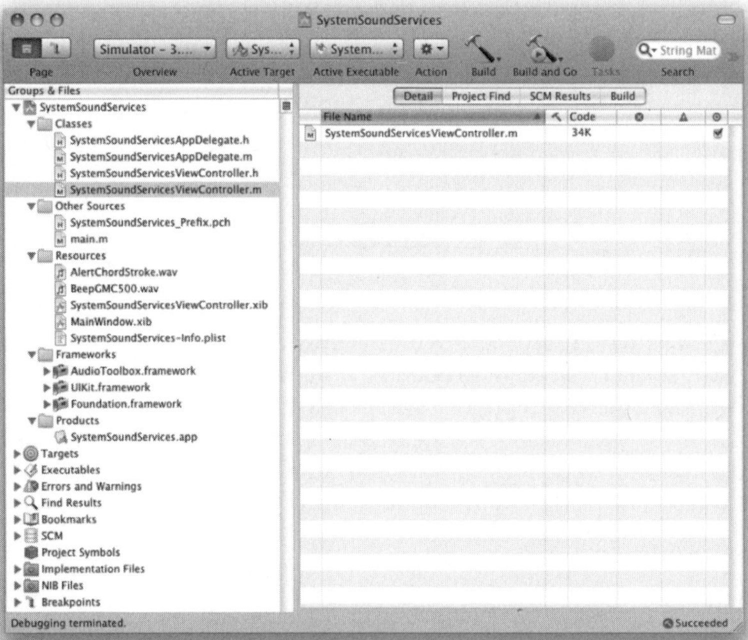

Figure 9–4. *The Xcode project with all the files and resources added*

In *SystemSoundServicesViewController.h*, we add the following:

```
#include <AudioToolbox/AudioToolbox.h>
```

We also add these three method declarations:

```
- (IBAction) playSystemSound;
- (IBAction) playAlertSound;
- (IBAction) vibrate;
```

Next, we create a very simple interface in Interface Builder, consisting of three buttons named Vibrate, Play System Sound, and Play Alert Sound. Wire them up to their corresponding events (see Figure 9–5).

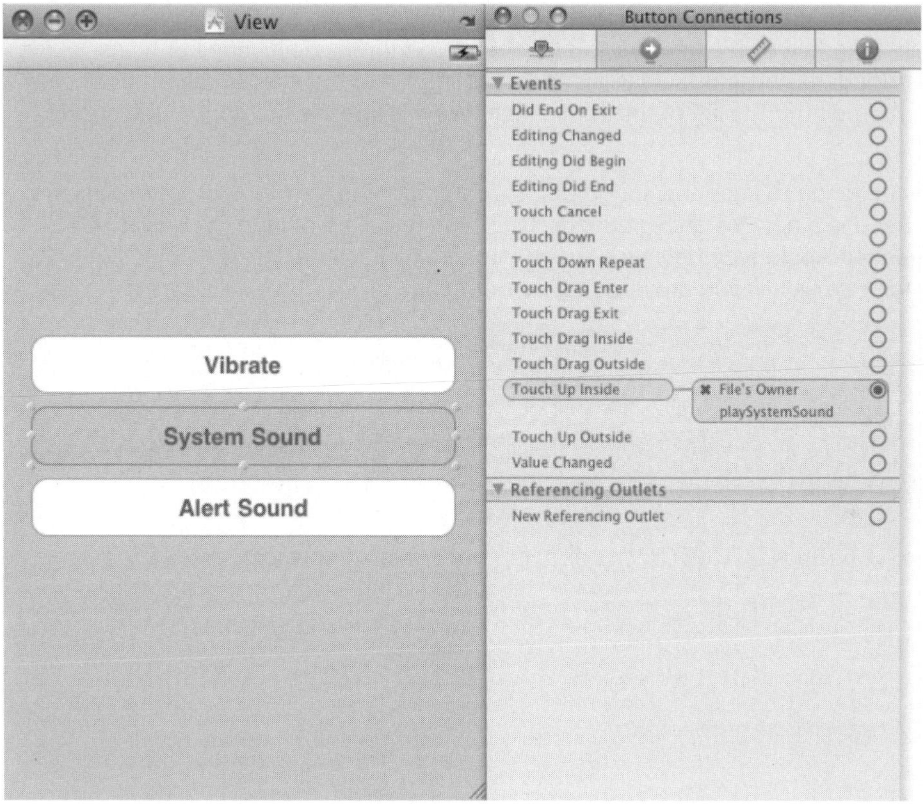

Figure 9–5. *Wiring up one of the three buttons*

Now that we have a test program ready to go, we just need to fill in the three methods to do something. So let's start with the easiest, which is `vibrate`.

Invoking vibration is easy because we don't need a sound file. To vibrate, we actually use the same method used to play a system sound: `AudioServicesPlaySystemSound()`. But instead of passing a sound as a parameter, we pass the special constant, `kSystemSoundID_Vibrate`. Add the following implementation to *SystemSoundServices ViewController.m*:

```
- (IBAction) vibrate
{
        AudioServicesPlaySystemSound(kSystemSoundID_Vibrate);
}
```

To play an actual sound, we just need to load a sound file and pass its identifier to AudioServicesPlaySystemSound() or AudioServicesPlayAlertSound().

Let's play an alert sound next. An alert sound does slightly different things, depending on which device you are using. On the iPhone and later iPod touches, it plays the specified sound that you pass in as a parameter. On the original iPod touch, it plays a short alert melody.

First, we need to load a sound. Typically, games like to load in resources before the actual game starts playing, in order to prevent any performance hiccups or stalls, which would disrupt game play. So, we will load the sound file at the start of the program and keep it in memory for the life of the application. We will free the memory at the end of the program.

Since we are going to keep the sound object around for the life of the program, the first thing we need is a new instance variable. The variable will be of type SystemSoundID, which is just an Apple type definition for an integer. You can declare an Objective-C 2.0 property for it as well, if you are into that sort of thing.

> **NOTE:** Don't forget to synthesize or implement the accessors in the implementation file if you are reproducing the project from scratch. In general, since these are boring lines, particularly synthesize, I will omit them for brevity in the book. However, they are in the finished code examples.

In *SystemSoundServicesViewController.h*, our code should now look like the following.

```
#import <UIKit/UIKit.h>
#include <AudioToolbox/AudioToolbox.h>

@interface SystemSoundServicesViewController : UIViewController
{
        SystemSoundID alertSoundID;
}

@property(nonatomic, assign) SystemSoundID alertSoundID;

- (IBAction) playSystemSound;
- (IBAction) playAlertSound;
- (IBAction) vibrate;

@end
```

Next, we want to load a sound file at the beginning of the program. So, we will add code to the viewDidLoad method in *SystemSoundServicesViewController.m*. AudioServicesCreateSystemSoundID() is the function we need to use to load a sound file and get back a SystemSoundID, which is used to identify the resource. The function takes two parameters: a CFURLRef that points to the location of the file, and a pointer to a SystemSoundID, which is used to return the ID value. So our code looks like this:

```
- (void) viewDidLoad
{
        [super viewDidLoad];

        // Get the sound file URL within the app bundle. This is autoreleased.
        NSURL* alert_sound_url = [NSURL fileURLWithPath:[[NSBundle mainBundle]
          pathForResource:@"AlertChordStroke" ofType:@"wav"]];

        // Create a system sound object representing the sound file
        AudioServicesCreateSystemSoundID(
                (CFURLRef)alert_sound_url,
                &alertSoundID
        );
}
```

First, we create an NSURL object that points to the location where the audio file is stored. Notice we use an NSURL instead of a CFURLRef. Keep in mind that Cocoa and Core Foundation objects are toll-free bridged,[4] so we can cast one to the other without any problems. Also notice that the method used to create the NSURL is also autoreleased so it will be freed at the end of the event loop. We do not need to keep the NSURL around for the life of the program; only the SystemSoundID needs to be kept.

Then we simply call AudioServicesCreateSystemSoundID() with the (type-casted) NSURL. We provide the reference to our alertSoundID instance variable so the returned SystemSoundID will be assigned directly to it.

Now that we have allocated a sound object, we should remember to free it. So let's release it in the dealloc method using AudioServicesDisposeSystemSoundID():

```
- (void) dealloc
{
        // Release the alert sound memory
        AudioServicesDisposeSystemSoundID(alertSoundID);
        [super dealloc];
}
```

----

[4] *Toll-free bridging* is a way to cast Objective-C objects to Core Foundation objects and vice versa. Its origins and reasons are somewhat complicated, relating back to when NeXT was acquired by Apple and the NeXT operating system became the foundation for Mac OS X. Since NeXT was Objective-C–centric, and Mac classic was C-centric, it was convenient to be able to pass pointers to objects between Apple's new C libraries (i.e., Core Foundation) and Objective-C libraries without actually needing to copy and convert data. Long story short, if you have a Cocoa/Objective-C class and a Core Foundation/C class with the same name (the only difference being the prefix of NS versus CF and the Ref suffix, e.g., NSString/CFStringRef), then the class is usually toll-free bridged, and you can just use a C-style cast to tell the compiler the types are actually the same. But beware, not all types are toll-free bridged; for example, NSBundle and CFBundleRef are not toll-free bridged. Apple's documentation is the authoritative source for this information. Apple's Carbon-Cocoa Integration Guide is a good reference.

Finally, we are ready to play the sound. With our sound file already loaded, it becomes another one-liner.

```
- (IBAction) playAlertSound
{
        AudioServicesPlayAlertSound(self.alertSoundID);
}
```

> **NOTE:** You might also consider freeing the sound memory in the `didReceiveMemoryWarning` method, but this would require you to check if the sound file is in memory before playing it, and loading it on demand if it is not already in memory.

Finally, let's play a system sound. We could just reuse our `alertSoundID` for the system sound, like this:

```
- (IBAction) playSystemSound
{
        AudioServicesPlaySystemSound(self.alertSoundID);
}
```

However, we are going to use a different sound. We could also just employ the same pattern we went through to create and use the alert sound, but instead, we are going to do something a little different to demonstrate another feature.

System Sound Services also provides an API that allows you to set up a callback that will be invoked immediately after your sound completes playing. So to demonstrate this API, rather than allocating a new sound resource that persists through the life of the program, we will load the resource on demand and release it when the sound finishes playing.

`AudioServicesAddSystemSoundCompletion()` is the function you use to set up a callback. You provide the `SystemSoundID` of the sound you want on which you want a callback to be invoked. You also provide the callback function you want invoked. Then, if the sound is played, your callback function will be invoked after the sound finishes playing. The function takes additional parameters to describe the run loop and mode you are using. We will just be using the defaults (by passing `NULL`), since we are making a standard Cocoa Touch application and using the standard Cocoa run loop. And like most callback functions, it allows you to pass in any pointer for user data. We will not need that parameter in this example, but for those not familiar with the pattern, a common thing to do is pass `self` when in Objective-C, so you can get a pointer to the instance of your class in the callback function.

First, we will define our custom callback function at the top of *SystemSoundServicesViewController.m*, before the `@implementation`, since this is just a C function, and not part of our class.

```
static void MySoundFinishedPlayingCallback(SystemSoundID sound_id, void* user_data)
{
        AudioServicesDisposeSystemSoundID(sound_id);
}
```

In our case, we just take the `SystemSoundID` that was given to us and release the sound resource.

Now let's implement our final playSystemSound method. The code should look very familiar to you, as it contains all the pieces you've already seen to load a sound resource and play it. The only difference is that now everything is done with local variables (not requiring instance variables), and we register a callback before we play the sound.

```
- (IBAction) playSystemSound
{
        // Get the sound file URL from the app bundle. (This is autoreleased.)
        NSURL* system_sound_url = [NSURL fileURLWithPath:[[NSBundle mainBundle]
        pathForResource:@"BeepGMC500" ofType:@"wav"]];
        SystemSoundID system_sound_id;

        // Create a system sound object representing the sound file
        AudioServicesCreateSystemSoundID(
                (CFURLRef)system_sound_url,
                &system_sound_id
        );

            // Register the sound completion callback.
            AudioServicesAddSystemSoundCompletion(
                system_sound_id,
                NULL, // uses the main run loop
                NULL, // uses kCFRunLoopDefaultMode
                MySoundFinishedPlayingCallback, // the name of custom callback function
                NULL // for user data, but we don't need to do that, so we just pass NULL
        );

        // Play the System Sound
        AudioServicesPlaySystemSound(system_sound_id);
}
```

For completeness, Apple also provides `AudioServicesRemoveSystemSoundCompletion(SystemSoundID inSystemSoundID)` to remove the completion callback for a `SystemSoundID`. Our program doesn't require this, so it's not demonstrated. But this function is there if you need it.

A Comment on Asynchronous Playback

An important thing to recognize is that the play APIs do not block when called. This means the program execution does not stop and wait for the sound to finish playing. Instead, the sound starts playing and the function returns immediately. Core Audio is doing the threading behind the scenes for you. This is true of all the play APIs in Core Audio, not just the ones in System Sound Services.

In general, you normally don't need to worry too much about the consequences of being asynchronous, particularly when Cocoa and Core Audio give you callbacks to let you know when events like the sound finished playing happened. However, it is still possible to create trouble for yourself, such as when trying to free memory from a currently playing sound. The behavior may differ depending on which API you are using, so you should always check the Apple documentation for further guidance.[5] Defensive programming, such as calling stop on a playing sound before deleting it, can avoid these problems.

Setting Policies for Your Audio: Introducing Audio Session Services

Unlike the other APIs in Core Audio, Audio Session Services is not directly about playing or recording audio, but about describing policies for how you want your application's audio to behave. Because of this, this topic is easy to overlook. But it is essential to getting your iPhone application to behave properly and as you users expect.

Here are some examples of audio policies:

- Do you want your application's sounds to be mixed with other applications such as iPod music playback, or should the other applications be silenced?

- Should your audio be silenced by the ring/silent switch?

- Should your audio continue playing when the screen is locked?

- How will your application respond to interruptions, such as a phone call?

- Do you need to do anything special on an audio route change (e.g., a user plugs in or unplugs a headset)?

Audio Session Services also allows you to make queries to the device your application is running on to find out the hardware characteristics. For example, you can discover the hardware sample rate, the current playback volume of the device, and whether audio input is available.

Audio Session Services is usually broken down into three components:

- *Categories*: The audio behavior rules for your application

- *Interruptions and property changes*: Notifications of when your audio is interrupted, when an interruption ends, and when a property like the hardware route changes, allowing you to respond

- *Hardware characteristics*: Things like whether an input device is available

---

[5] System Sound Services immediately stops playing the sound and frees it in this case (all without crashing), so this is not a problem here, assuming this is the behavior you actually want (i.e., maybe you want the sound to finish playing). But as another example, we will have a concurrency issue to deal with in Chapter 12 using an OpenAL extension.

Every application inherits a default audio session behavior. However, since every application has different needs, the chances are low that the default settings will be the appropriate behavior for your application, so you should explicitly set what you need.

iPhone OS 3.1 has six Audio Session Services categories, provided as constants for your code, as shown in Table 9–1. (Prior to iPhone OS 3.0, there were seven categories, but two have since been deprecated, and one more was introduced in OS 3.1.)

Table 9–1. *The Audio Session Services Categories*

Category (kAudioSessionCategory_ and AVAudioSessionCategory)	Allows Audio Mixing?	Obeys Ring/Silent Switch?	Description
AmbientSound	Yes	Yes	Good for games with sound effects but no music, so iPod audio can be mixed in. Also good for "play-along" style applications, such as a virtual music instrument that plays over iPod music.
SoloAmbientSound	No	Yes	Good for games that have both sound effects and music. Audio from other applications such as the iPod, will be silenced. (This is the default category starting in 2.2.)
MediaPlayback (AudioSession) Playback (AVAudioSession)	No Can be overridden with the property kAudioSessionProperty _OverrideCategoryMixW ithOthers	No	Good for media player applications such as an alternative iPod jukebox-like program or streaming Internet music player. Also good for musical instrument programs such as a virtual piano or ocarina. Audio will continue to play when the device is set to silent and when the screen locks. (This was the default prior to 2.2.)
RecordAudio (AudioSession) Record (AVAudioSession)	No	No	For recording audio only. It silences playback audio.

Category (kAudioSessionCategory_ and AVAudioSessionCategory)	Allows Audio Mixing?	Obeys Ring/Silent Switch?	Description
PlayAndRecord	No Can be overridden with the property kAudioSessionProperty _OverrideCategoryMixW ithOthers	No	For simultaneous recording and playback of audio, such as for VoIP applications.
AudioProcessing	No	N/A	Gives you access to hardware encoding/decoding without actually needing to play or record audio. Useful for things like converting audio files without actually playing them. (New to OS 3.1.)

Another important aspect to understand is that the "allow audio mixing" setting will decide whether hardware acceleration or the software decoder is used by default. If you select a category that does not allow audio mixing, the operating system will try to use hardware acceleration first when you attempt to use a restricted codec. Remember that the hardware accelerator can handle only one restricted file at a time, so Core Audio will fall back to software if the hardware accelerator is not available.

If you select a category that does allow audio mixing, the software codec will become the default. The reason is that the hardware decoding unit may be in use by another application such as the iPod music player. So choose your category carefully and/or pick the file formats you use in your application carefully.

Boilerplate Code and Procedures for Using Audio Session Services

We will not work through a complete example of using Audio Session Services by itself, because it is hard to prove that we actually accomplished anything without implementing something else to actually play audio. Don't worry—all the subsequent examples will use Audio Session Services, so you will have plenty of working code examples to play with by the end of the audio section of this book. But since you need to walk before you can run, I will show you some simple boilerplate code here.

To get started with audio sessions, there are three simple steps:

1. Initialize your audio session.

2. Set your audio session category.

3. Activate your audio session.

The minimal code example looks like this (ignoring error checking):

```
#include <AudioToolbox/AudioToolbox.h>
...
        AudioSessionInitialize(NULL, NULL, NULL, NULL); // step 1
        UInt32 session_category = kAudioSessionCategory_SoloAmbientSound;
        AudioSessionSetProperty(kAudioSessionProperty_AudioCategory,
            sizeof(session_category), &session_category); // step 2
        AudioSessionSetActive(true); // step 3
```

Audio Session Services is provided by the Audio Toolbox framework, so you must have the proper #include and link to the framework.

AudioSessionInitialize() takes four parameters. The first two are for the run loop and run loop mode. You may recognize these from the System Sound Services example. Passing in NULL will use the default run loop and mode. The next parameter is for a callback function that you want invoked when an interruption (e.g., phone call) starts or ends. The final parameter allows you to pass your user data to the callback function. So a slightly more typical example of this function might be as follows:

```
AudioSessionInitialize(NULL, NULL, MyInterruptionListenerCallback, self);
```

MyInterruptionListenerCallback is defined as follows:

```
void MyInterruptionListenerCallback(void* user_data, UInt32 interruption_state)
{
        id my_class_ptr = (id)user_data;

        // e.g. A phone call comes in...
        if(kAudioSessionBeginInterruption == interruption_state)
        {
                // Do something appropriate here...
                // Don't worry about deactivating the Audio Session.
                        // That was done automatically when the interruption started.
        }
        // e.g. The phone call was ignored...
        else if(kAudioSessionEndInterruption == interruption_state)
        {
                // Might be a good place to reactivate the Audio Session
                AudioSessionSetActive(true);
        }
}
```

What you actually do in your callback function will depend on which audio APIs you are using and the specific needs of your app.

For AudioSessionSetActive(), Apple encourages you to be a "good citizen" and set your audio session as active only when you are actually using audio. For example, for a voice recorder application, you would set your audio session as active only when actually recording. Then, right after you finish recording, you would deactivate your session. This gives Apple the opportunity to resume audio from another application that may want the resource, such as the iPod player. For games, however, chances are that your audio session will need to be active as long as your application is running.

Detecting Hardware and Getting Properties

Now that you have seen the basics for setting up a category for an audio session, let's look at the other components that make up Audio Session Services: hardware queries and route changes.

A common hardware query is to find out if there is an input device (e.g., microphone) available. Since the first-generation iPod touch lacks a microphone, and the second-generation iPod touch requires an external microphone attachment, it is possible that a microphone will not be available. The query looks like this:

```
UInt32 input_available = 0;
UInt32 the_size = sizeof(input_available);
AudioSessionGetProperty(kAudioSessionProperty_AudioInputAvailable, &the_size,
&input_available);
```

The value will be returned to the variable input_available. The variable will be set to 1 if input is available or 0 if no input is available. AudioSessionGetProperty() takes a key constant as the first parameter, the size of the return variable, and a pointer to the return value. This is a common pattern in Core Audio. Core Audio likes to use generic functions for *GetProperty() and *SetProperty() so they can be reused for different things. Since the API is C-based, this is achieved by passing pointers with size information and a key constant.

Audio Session Services provides a property listener callback API, which you can set to monitor property changes of specific supported types. As an example, we will set up a simple property listener that triggers if an input device comes or goes.

```
AudioSessionAddPropertyListener(kAudioSessionProperty_AudioInputAvailable,
MyPropertyListener, self);
```

MyPropertyListener is defined as follows:

```
void MyPropertyListener(void* user_data, AudioSessionPropertyID property_id,
    UInt32 data_size, const void* property_data)
{
        if(kAudioSessionProperty_AudioInputAvailable == property_id)
        {
                if(sizeof(UInt32) == data_size)
                {
                        UInt32 input_is_available = *(UInt32*)property_data;
                        if(input_is_available)
                        {
                        printf("Input is available\n");
                        }
                        else
                        {
                                printf("Input is not available\n");
                        }
                }
        }
}
```

Notice that the setup for a property listener callback is very similar to that of all the other callbacks you have seen so far.

AVFoundation, discussed in the next section, also includes a partial Objective-C interface for audio sessions. The API is fairly straightforward. Perhaps the most interesting difference is that rather than registering callback functions, AVFoundation uses a standard Cocoa delegate pattern, so you just need to implement the methods and set the delegate if you want the callbacks.

Easy Audio Playback in Objective-C with AVFoundation

For many years now, Cocoa programmers developing Mac OS X apps have wished for a friendly, Objective-C–based framework for Core Audio. Unfortunately, the wait continues on the desktop, but for iPhone OS, the dream is becoming realized, in the form of AVFoundation, introduced in iPhone OS 2.2.

AVFoundation first introduced the AVAudioPlayer class, which is a succinct and friendly API to play back audio. AVAudioPlayer doesn't care how long or short the file is, and handles all the different file formats supported by the device, including the compressed ones. (This is quite a contrast to all the limitations imposed with System Sound Services.)

In iPhone OS 3.0, Apple expanded AVFoundation to include AVAudioRecorder and AVAudioSession, which give Objective-C APIs to recording and Audio Session Services. For example, the boilerplate code presented in the previous section could actually be rewritten using the Objective-C API instead of the C API.

Using AVFoundation involves some trade-offs. Probably the most serious trade-off for games is that AVFoundation tends to have higher latency. AVAudioPlayer does contain a method called prepareToPlay, which will start preloading some buffers, which may help reduce the latency. But officially, Apple recommends OpenAL or the I/O unit if you need really low latency. The higher latency of AVFoundation may make it less suitable for fast-paced games that demand low-latency sound effects. However, AVFoundation may still be useful for background music, since the player probably won't notice if that music takes an additional second to start playing. And for games that don't demand very low latencies, AVFoundation may be the ideal framework.

We will walk through a simple example involving audio playback with AVFoundation. It will allow you to play up to two simultaneous files. It is very easy to imagine a game needing more than one sound at a time—for example, a weapon firing and an object being destroyed. But to add contrast to the System Sound Services example, we will play two long files, since AVAudioPlayer doesn't care about the length of the files. When might this happen in a game? Background music is usually long. And speech can also be long. You might have lengthy narration or dialogue, or maybe you have a tutorial with audio voice-over. In our example, we will play some music and speech together.

> **NOTE:** Apple has a pretty good developer example called avTouch, which you are encouraged to investigate. Apple's avTouch example has a considerable amount of code dedicated to the UI, especially showing off AVAudioPlayer's meter-level capabilities (i.e., current signal amplitude). Since your game will probably be more concerned with playing audio than visualizing it with Apple widgets, we will forgo a lot of the visual bells and whistles in our example, and instead demonstrate playing two sounds simultaneously. Apple's avTouch was written before the public release of the AVAudioSession class, which we will use in our example.

The completed Xcode project and source are available under the project name AVPlayback. We start off by creating a new Xcode project using the View-based Application template, naming it AVPlayback. We create a new Objective-C class called AVPlaybackSoundController, which gives us the .h and .m files. This is a nice way to keep the audio stuff separate from the view implementation. We add the two audio files to the project, and add AVFoundation.framework to the list of linked libraries (see Figure 9–6).

Figure 9–6. The complete Xcode project for the AVPlayback example

Next, to wire up stuff in Interface Builder, we add the following code to the *AVPlaybackViewController.h* file:

```
#import <UIKit/UIKit.h>

@class AVPlaybackSoundController;

@interface AVPlaybackViewController : UIViewController
{
        IBOutlet AVPlaybackSoundController* avPlaybackSoundController;
        IBOutlet UIBarButtonItem* playButton;
}

@property(nonatomic, retain) AVPlaybackSoundController* avPlaybackSoundController;

- (IBAction) playButtonPressed:(id)the_sender;
- (IBAction) rewindButtonPressed:(id)the_sender;
- (IBAction) fastForwardButtonPressed:(id)the_sender;


@end
```

In Interface Builder, using the *AVPlaybackViewController.xib* file, we create a simple interface, which is composed of a play/pause, rewind, and fast-forward buttons. We also add an NSObject to the *.xib* file and set its class to AVPlaybackSoundController, making sure to connect the outlet to the file's owner. This is the pointer that connects the view to our sound controller class. Figure 9–7 shows the raw interface, the UI elements, and the outlets and actions that wire up the buttons to our code.

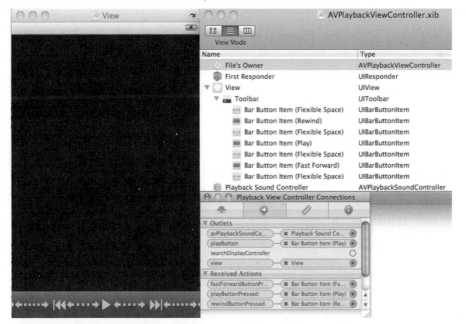

Figure 9–7. *The Interface Builder .xib for AVPlaybackViewController. The raw interface is on the left. The list showing all the UI elements that make up the interface is in the top right. The bottom-right panel shows some of the outlets and actions wired up to the controls.*

Next, in *AVPlaybackViewController.m*, we implement these three methods:

```
- (IBAction) playButtonPressed:(id)the_sender
{
        [self.avPlaybackSoundController playOrPauseSpeech];
}

- (IBAction) rewindButtonPressed:(id)the_sender
{
        [self.avPlaybackSoundController rewindSpeech];
}

- (IBAction) fastForwardButtonPressed:(id)the_sender
{
        [self.avPlaybackSoundController fastForwardSpeech];
}
```

This class does nothing except forward the messages to our sound controller. Now we are ready to implement our sound controller class.

In *AVPlaybackSoundController.h*, we start with the following:

```
#import <AVFoundation/AVFoundation.h>
#import <UIKit/UIKit.h>

@interface AVPlaybackSoundController : NSObject <AVAudioSessionDelegate,
AVAudioPlayerDelegate>
{
        AVAudioPlayer* avMusicPlayer;
        AVAudioPlayer* avSpeechPlayer;
}

@property(nonatomic, retain) AVAudioPlayer* avMusicPlayer;
@property(nonatomic, retain) AVAudioPlayer* avSpeechPlayer;

- (void) playOrPauseSpeech;
- (void) rewindSpeech;
- (void) fastForwardSpeech;


@end
```

Because we will be playing two files simultaneously, we need two separate instances of AVAudioPlayer: one for music and the other for speech. We also have three methods that are invoked when the play, rewind, and fast-forward buttons are tapped in the UI.

The only nonobvious thing in this header is that our class conforms to two protocols: AVAudioSessionDelegate and AVAudioPlayerDelegate. We are going to make our class the delegate of both our AVAudioSession and our AVAudioPlayers.

Now we will set up an audio session. Instead of using the C API for this example, we will use the Objective-C based AVAudioSession class.

```
#import "AVPlaybackSoundController.h"

#define SKIP_TIME_AMOUNT 5.0 // 5 seconds
#define MUSIC_VOLUME_REDUCTION 0.4 // 5 seconds
```

```objc
// Nameless category (class continuation) for declaring "private" (helper) methods.
@interface AVPlaybackSoundController ()
- (void) initAudioSession;
- (void) initMusicPlayer;
- (void) initSpeechPlayer;
@end

@implementation AVPlaybackSoundController

@synthesize avMusicPlayer;
@synthesize avSpeechPlayer;

 - (void) initAudioSession
{
        // Set up the audio session
        NSError* audio_session_error = nil;
        BOOL is_success = YES;

        // Set the category
                is_success = [[AVAudioSession sharedInstance] setCategory:AVAudioSession↵
                    CategoryPlayback error:&audio_session_error];
        if(!is_success || audio_session_error)
        {
                NSLog(@"Error setting Audio Session category: %@", [audio_session_error
                    localizedDescription]);
        }

        // Make this class the delegate so we can receive the interruption messages
        [[AVAudioSession sharedInstance] setDelegate:self];

        audio_session_error = nil;
        // Make the Audio Session active
        is_success = [[AVAudioSession sharedInstance] setActive:YES error:&audio_↵
            session_error];
        if(!is_success || audio_session_error)
        {
                NSLog(@"Error setting Audio Session active: %@", [audio_session_error
                    localizedDescription]);
        }
}
```

AVAudioSession is a singleton class. To get the instance, we invoke sharedInstance. In the C language API, you would initialize a session, set its category, and activate the session. Unlike with the C API, we don't have an explicit initialize, but we do have a delegate. The delegate takes the place of registering a callback function. The two methods, beginInterruption and endInterruption, will be invoked for interruptions in your delegate if you define them. AVAudioSession also invokes additional methods for category and property changes. You do not need to explicitly register callbacks, as is necessary with the C API.

We set the delegate to self so our class can handle these events. We can fill out a stub for the interruption functions and any other ones we care about, like this:

```objc
- (void) beginInterruption
{
        NSLog(@"AVAudioSession beginInterruption");
```

```
}
- (void) endInterruption
{
        NSLog(@"AVAudioSession endInterruption");
}
```

It turns out that for this example, we don't actually need these functions, because AVAudioPlayer also has delegate methods for interruptions. Since our needs are light in this example, it is more convenient to use the AVAudioPlayer delegate methods. We could have skipped defining and implementing these optional delegate methods for AVAudioSessionDelegate. However, just to demonstrate them, I have added simple implementations that call NSLog.

Next, we need to do is allocate the two instances of AVAudioPlayer.

```
- (void) initMusicPlayer
{
        NSError* file_error = nil;
        NSURL* file_url = [[NSURL alloc] initFileURLWithPath:[[NSBundle mainBundle]
                pathForResource:@"battle_hymn_of_the_republic" ofType:@"mp3"]
                isDirectory:NO];
        avMusicPlayer = [[AVAudioPlayer alloc] initWithContentsOfURL:file_url
            error:&file_error];
        if(!file_url || file_error)
        {
                NSLog(@"Error loading music file: %@", [file_error
                    localizedDescription]);
        }
        self.avMusicPlayer.delegate = self;
        self.avMusicPlayer.numberOfLoops = -1; // repeat infinitely
        [file_url release];
}

- (void) initSpeechPlayer
{
        NSError* file_error = nil;

        NSURL* file_url = [[NSURL alloc] initFileURLWithPath:[[NSBundle mainBundle]
                pathForResource:@"TheDeclarationOfIndependencePreambleJFK"
                ofType:@"caf"]
                isDirectory:NO];
        self.avSpeechPlayer = [[AVAudioPlayer alloc] initWithContentsOfURL:file_url
                error:&file_error];
        if(!file_url || file_error)
        {
                NSLog(@"Error loading speech file: %@", [file_error
                    localizedDescription]);
        }
        self.avSpeechPlayer.delegate = self;

        [file_url release];
}
```

Here are a few points to note about this example:

- The music file is left as an MP3, but the speech file was converted to IMA-4 and uses a *.caf* container. As noted earlier, hardware acceleration for AAC, MP3, and Apple Lossless can support only one file at a time. If you try playing two files encoded in these formats simultaneously, the device will be forced to decode in software, which is expensive for the CPU. Thus, you should generally not try to play more than one of these at a time.

- We set both players to use this class as the delegate.

- We set numberOfLoops to -1 for the music player. This will cause the music to repeat infinitely.

- If it is possible to make all your recordings the same sample rate, you may get better performance, as the system needs to do less mixing. My samples are recorded at different rates, so this is not the optimal situation.

Finally, to actually run this code, we call the preceding methods in awakeFromNib.

```
- (void) awakeFromNib
{
        [self initAudioSession];
        [self initMusicPlayer];
        [self initSpeechPlayer];

        [self.avMusicPlayer play];
}
```

We also start playing the music immediately, and expect the music to play continuously. The UI will control only the speech.

Next, let's implement the play/pause control for speech:

```
- (void) playOrPauseSpeech
{
        if([self.avSpeechPlayer isPlaying])
        {
                [self.avSpeechPlayer pause];
                self.avMusicPlayer.volume = 1.0;
        }
        else
        {
                [self.avSpeechPlayer play];
                self.avMusicPlayer.volume = MUSIC_VOLUME_REDUCTION;
        }
}
```

This is pretty straightforward. If the speech is playing, pause it; otherwise, start playing.

We do introduce one new trick here: We adjust the volume of the music. With System Sound Services, you cannot control volume outside the device's master volume. With AVAudioPlayer, there is a simple property that ranges from 0.0 to 1.0, which is independent of the device's master volume. So when we start playing speech, we immediately reduce the music volume to MUSIC_VOLUME_REDUCTION, which is defined as

0.4. This allows us to more clearly hear the speech, which continues to play at its own 1.0 volume level. When the speech pauses, we restore the music volume to 1.0.

There is a corner case of what happens when the speech finishes playing. We would like to restore the music volume back to maximum and rewind the speech, so when the user taps the play button again, the speech will start over. The AVAudioPlayerDelegate protocol provides audioDidFinishPlaying:successfully: to help us handle this case:

```
- (void) audioPlayerDidFinishPlaying:(AVAudioPlayer*)which_player
successfully:(BOOL)the_flag
{
        if(which_player == self.avSpeechPlayer)
        {
                // return volume of music back to max
                self.avMusicPlayer.volume = 1.0;
                // rewind the speech to the beginning for next time
                self.avSpeechPlayer.currentTime = 0.0;
        }
}
```

The successfully flag returns NO if playback stopped because of a decoding error, instead of naturally coming to the end of the sound.

To rewind, AVAudioPlayer has a property called currentTime. We just set the value to 0 to rewind.

Now we will implement rewind and fast forward:

```
- (void) rewindSpeech
{
        if(YES == self.avSpeechPlayer.isPlaying)
        {
                [self.avSpeechPlayer stop]; // pause seems to break things with seeking
                self.avSpeechPlayer.currentTime -= SKIP_TIME_AMOUNT;
                [self.avSpeechPlayer play];
        }
        else
        {
                self.avSpeechPlayer.currentTime -= SKIP_TIME_AMOUNT;
        }
}

- (void) fastForwardSpeech
{
        if(YES == self.avSpeechPlayer.isPlaying)
        {
                [self.avSpeechPlayer stop]; // pause seems to break things with seeking
                self.avSpeechPlayer.currentTime += SKIP_TIME_AMOUNT;
                [self.avSpeechPlayer play];
        }
        else
        {
                self.avSpeechPlayer.currentTime += SKIP_TIME_AMOUNT;
        }
}
```

SKIP_TIME_AMOUNT is defined as 5.0, which means 5 seconds. This way, each time the fast-forward or rewind button is pressed, the speech will skip by 5 seconds.

Lastly, let's look at audio session interruptions one more time. As stated earlier, each API has different requirements for handling and recovering from an interruption. AVAudioPlayer, following the classic Cocoa/Objective-C philosophy, requires the least from you. When an interruption occurs, AVAudioPlayer is automatically paused. It will remember the current position, so if an interruption ends, you may simply start playing again.

In our example, music is always playing, so we know we always need to resume playing. Speech, on the other hand, may or not be playing. Fortunately, both cases are easy to handle. The callback will be invoked only for players who were interrupted. If speech was not playing, the callback will not be invoked with the speech player instance. So, we can simply call play.

```
- (void) audioPlayerEndInterruption:(AVAudioPlayer*)which_player
{
        [which_player play];
}
```

FOURCC ERROR CODES

We have been skipping over the issues of error checking and error return codes. Usually, this is mundane and obvious stuff. However, if you've been looking carefully at the APIs, you may have noticed that Core Audio and some other lower-level frameworks in the operating system like to use the type OSStatus for their error results. OSStatus is a type definition to SInt32. If you've ever gotten an actual error and tried printing it out, you'll see something like 1718449215. And you'll gawk at it in frustration, asking, "What the heck does that mean?"

A very long time ago (back in the Mac Classic days), Apple devised a technique of using a sequence of 4 bytes to represent things, usually consisting of human-readable characters with mnemonic qualities (e.g., MPEG, H264, wht?, and prop). And its use has been adopted by other people and companies. For example, Microsoft uses it in DirectX. This technique is called Four-Character Code (FourCC or 4CC).

Unfortunately, when we get this code thrown back at us as an error, we have no idea what the raw number means. There are several techniques to map this raw number back into a FourCC form.

One way is to use the built-in Calculator app that comes with Mac OS X. Switch to programmer view (⌘3) or click the green zoom button in the top-left corner ("maximize" button for Windows people, though as you'll see, it does not really maximize). Select ASCII mode and Decimal mode (Dec on Leopard or 10 on Snow Leopard) in the UI. Then paste in the number. You'll see the FourCC version in the left-bottom area of the LCD readout. In the following example, you can see that 1718449215 maps to fmt?:

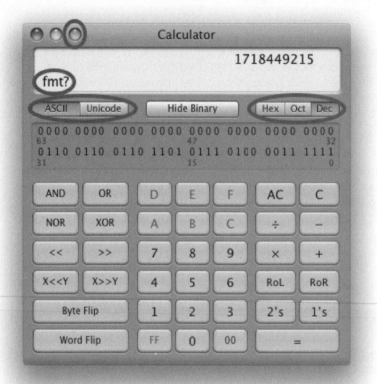

Now you can search through the headers for fmt?. For example, in the Core Audio supplied header *AudioConverter.h* file, I found that kAudioConverterErr_FormatNotSupported maps to this FourCC code.

You can also convert the code programmatically yourself. You may find something like this on the Internet:

```
int big_endian_error_code = CFSwapInt32HostToBig(error_code);
printf("%4.4s", (const char*)&big_endian_error_code);
```

Unfortunately, Apple isn't completely consistent about using FourCC for all error codes. Sometimes, the codes are meant to be raw base-10 numbers; sometimes, they are meant to be read in hexadecimal. So the preceding example may convert what you are not supposed to, and you'll get even more nonsense.

Apple has a function in some of their Core Audio examples called CAX4CCString, which converts error codes to a (printable) string and also handles the case of whether it should be converted to FourCC, decimal, or hexadecimal. Unfortunately, it is written in C++ (when I said function, I really meant C++ class). I personally hate having to switch languages and compilers when I don't really have to. If I'm working in pure C, I usually prefer to stay there. (ISO C99 and ISO C++98 don't always play nice together.) So, I have ported this class into a pure C function, as follows:

```
#include <stdint.h>
#include <ctype.h>
#include <stdio.h>
#include <arpa/inet.h>
//      Example usage:
```

```
//  printf("The error is: %s", FourCCToString(error_code));
const char* FourCCToString(int32_t error_code)
{
        static char return_string[16];
        uint32_t big_endian_code = htonl(error_code);
        char* big_endian_str = (char*)&big_endian_code;
        // see if it appears to be a 4-char-code
        if(isprint(big_endian_str[0])
                && isprint(big_endian_str[1])
                && isprint(big_endian_str[2])
                && isprint (big_endian_str[3]))
        {
                return_string[0] = '\'';
                return_string[1] = big_endian_str[0];
                return_string[2] = big_endian_str[1];
                return_string[3] = big_endian_str[2];
                return_string[4] = big_endian_str[3];
                return_string[5] = '\'';
                return_string[6] = '\0';
        }
        else if(error_code > -200000 && error_code < 200000)
        {
                // no, format it as an integer
                snprintf(return_string, 16, "%d", error_code);
        }
        else
        {
                // no, format it as an integer but in hex
                snprintf(return_string, 16, "0x%x", error_code);
        }
        return return_string;
}
```

This is a little verbose, just because I like clarity. I also use the POSIX function `htonl` instead of Core Foundation's `CFSwapInt32HostToBig`, because it makes the code a little more portable. (Apple has duplicate byte-swapping functions throughout many of its frameworks.)

However, unlike the C++ version, my version is not reentrant, because of my use of `static`, which could be a problem if this function is called concurrently in multithreaded code. Whether you care or not is up to you, your code base, and your usage patterns. You are, of course, free to use Apple's version if C++ makes sense for your own project. Or you could port it over to Objective-C if you are using Objective-C. (I recommend returning an autoreleased `NSString` to make it fire-and-forget like the C++ version, without resorting to using `static` like mine.)

A copy of this code is hidden away inside *AudioSessionSupport.c*, found in the Space Rocks! source code.

Mission Complete...but Our Princess Is in Another Castle!

You're great! You made it through the first of the four audio chapters. You now can play sound using the easiest APIs in Core Audio. If what you've learned so far can meet all your requirements for your game, then you could just move on to the networking section of the book.

However, if your games have high performance requirements or involve rich 3D environments, they will benefit greatly from using the other APIs covered in the next three chapters. We are also going to cover additional topics, such as playing music from the iPod library and using the microphone.

Some of the techniques in the upcoming chapters are more challenging and technical, but these other APIs offer you many more features and finer control than those presented in this chapter. There is a lot to cover, so you might want to rest here before moving on. And then take it slow, relax, and breathe. You can do it!

Chapter 10

Making Noise with OpenAL

OpenAL is a cross-platform industry standard for 3D sound. OpenAL stands for Open Audio Library. Technically, OpenAL is a general-purpose audio library and is flexible enough to be used in many types of applications that require sound, but the primary use of OpenAL tends to be in games.

OpenAL places a strong emphasis on performance for real-time multimedia applications and low latency, while providing an API that game programmers are comfortable with. For iPhone OS developers, Apple has recognized the benefits of these characteristics and has embraced OpenAL as part of Core Audio. Furthermore, Apple has been touting OpenAL as the API most game developers should use on iPhone OS.

The design of OpenAL is heavily influenced by OpenGL, which was covered in Chapters 6 through 8. OpenAL shares the same coordinate system as OpenGL, so it is relatively straightforward to describe object positions in both systems. OpenAL's API may look very familiar to OpenGL programmers, as it shares many similar conventions, such as the two-letter prefix (al/gl), the type identifiers in the suffix (e.g., 3, i, f, and v), and the use of Gen to denote functions that allocate memory, such as alGen* and glGen*. Like OpenGL, OpenAL is a state machine and has a polling-oriented design.[1]

OpenAL is a large topic, and we will be focusing on it in this and the next two chapters (although Chapter 12 will also present more Core Audio-specific APIs as well). But OpenAL is a small enough specification that it is actually possible to cover most of it reasonably in these three chapters.

---

[1] By *polling-oriented*, I mean that there are no callback functions that notify you events have happened, such as a sound has finished playing. In OpenAL, if you want to know the state of something, you must explicitly ask OpenAL for the information when you want to know it.

OpenAL Overview

Let's start with a quick look at what OpenAL provides and some background on OpenAL, so you can understand where it fits in the game programming picture.

What OpenAL Supports

OpenAL provides the following:

- Low-latency playback

- Automatic sound mixing for multiple simultaneous sounds

- Positional (a.k.a. spatial or 3D) audio

- Distance attenuation (sounds get fainter as objects become more distant)

- Doppler effect (pitches shift when objects travel towards or away from another)

- Audio input capturing

I am always a little surprised to hear people claim that OpenAL does things that it doesn't actually do. So, to be clear, here are some things OpenAL does not provide:

- Occlusion (objects can obstruct other objects so sound is blocked, absorbed, or reflected; for example, imagine listening to a speaker that has a door in front of it)

- Culling (removing objects from being played based on some criteria; for example, because they are really far away or because they are occluded)

- Environmental effects (reverb, filters, etc.; for example, you would expect some kind of echo if you shoot a gun inside a large, metallic tunnel)

- APIs to deal with various file formats (e.g., AAC, MP3, Ogg Vorbis, WAV, etc.)

Although the OpenAL specification does not provide these things, it is possible to implement them yourself and integrate them with your OpenAL code. Also, OpenAL has an extension mechanism that allows vendors to add functionality. However, iPhone OS currently supports only two extensions (covered in the "Submitting Sound Data to OpenAL Data Buffers" and "OpenAL Extensions for iPhone OS" sections of this chapter), neither of which includes the features on this list.

Some History of OpenAL

The description of OpenAL as "a cross-platform industry standard" might give people a certain impression of things. However, until recently, the actual history of OpenAL tends to paint a contradictory picture. While things are much better now, for many years, OpenAL was on life support. It was unclear that OpenAL would survive and even be remembered.

OpenAL started in 1998, with a few aborted attempts to create a standard. But the real origin of OpenAL centers around Loki Entertainment Software. That company ported commercial games to Linux, so having a cross-platform 3D audio API was beneficial. As an iPhone developer, you may not have heard of Loki, but commercial games on Linux were a big deal for the Linux community. Mac users also appreciate the idea of getting games onto other non-Windows computer platforms.

And also of possible interest to game developers (and players), there are at least two semi-recognizable names that came out of Loki. The first is Sam Lantinga, creator of the Simple DirectMedia Layer (SDL). SDL is a simple but powerful cross-platform open source library that does video, audio, input, and so on, and is perfectly suited for developing games. It has been ported to just about every platform out there. So if you ever see an amazing game port that runs on some obscure new mobile device, chances are it is using SDL. (There is even a fledgling port for iPhone OS as of this writing.) The second is Ryan Gordon (a.k.a. Icculus). He has been responsible for porting a great many commercial games to Linux and Mac, such as the Unreal Tournament series (and games using the Unreal Engine). Certainly, Mac games have been very hard to come by, so Mac gamers owe him a great deal. And for developers, he tends to leave a trail of open source libraries and utilities in his wake. He has also ported some other types of apps, such as Google Earth to Linux.

In 1999, Loki pursued a specification and a Linux implementation. Loki then started talking with Creative Labs, the company that dominated the Windows sound card market at the time, about standardizing the API and expanding the supported platforms. In 2000, the OpenAL 1.0 specification was released, and initial OpenAL-compliant libraries for Linux, Mac OS 8/9, Windows, and BeOS were shipped that same year.

But the next few years would not be kind to OpenAL. First, Loki Entertainment Software did not survive, and there was no longer a commercial organization backing the Linux development. Second, in this time period, Apple was making the transition to Mac OS X. Getting games was hard enough on the Mac, but now game publishers had to figure out which operating system to support. Apple was also on its deathbed according to many people, so developing for Macs, which was already a tiny market, was now fractured by the two operating systems, and probably not going to be around much longer anyway. So, there was little incentive to publish games on Mac. Without Linux and Mac, there didn't seem to be a strong need for a cross-platform audio API.

You might be wondering about the video game consoles. In this period, we saw the rise of Microsoft and Sony. Neither of them seemed to express any interest in OpenAL, nor did Nintendo or Sega. So, it would be left to the game developers or third parties to implement if they wanted it.

Creative Labs became the guardian of OpenAL and kept it alive. Creative Labs owns the trademark to OpenAL (see Figure 10-1) and hosts the web site.

Figure 10-1. *OpenAL is a registered trademark of Creative Labs, Inc.*

Creative Labs continued to write implementations and native drivers for their sound cards for OpenAL, and managed to get some games to adopt OpenAL. However, in the early years, many gamers complained about the bugginess of using OpenAL, and if games shipped with alternative audio back-end implementations, players would make sure to not use the OpenAL back end. Also during this period, the trend was to move away from hardware-accelerated sound cards to inexpensive integrated sound chips built into the motherboards, so it became less clear if Creative Labs would continue to invest in OpenAL.

Interestingly, the motherboard sound design did temporarily give rise to another implementation by Nvidia. As Nvidia expanded into the motherboard market, it created its own OpenAL implementation for Windows to work with its sound chipsets. But after a period of time, Nvidia seemed to abandon this implementation.

Meanwhile, Linux and Mac implementations were being supplied by the open source communities, but the number of people we are talking about usually could be counted on one hand. These implementations also had their own bugs and limitations, which made adoption challenging.

Finally, the biggest problem may have been in the OpenAL 1.0 specification itself. There were many places where the spec was not well defined, so every implementation behaved differently. Those that actually tried to make their programs cross-platform (such as myself) were in for a terrible shock. Assuming things worked at all, you might hear very different results. One of the more famous examples of this is the Doppler velocity value for the Doppler effect. The spec didn't say what this value was, so some implementations used unitless values of 1.0, while others used 343.3 (based on 343.3 meters per second, the speed of sound in air under certain conditions).

With all these problems, OpenAL's future was unclear. But several major events bolstered OpenAL. First, Apple decided to implement its own version of OpenAL and officially support it in the Mac OS X operating system. In 2005, Apple released Mac OS X 10.4 Tiger, which included OpenAL as an official framework. Unfortunately, this new OpenAL implementation exposed even more problems with the 1.0 spec. And, of course, as a new implementation, it had bugs itself. Fortunately, for game developers, Apple actually had open sourced its implementation. Apple encouraged developers to fix bugs directly in the OpenAL source and ship their games with their own patched version of OpenAL, if necessary.

Second, also in 2005, work began on a 1.1 revision to the OpenAL specification to fix all the problems. Led by Garin Hiebert from Creative Labs, the community pulled together to come up with a workable spec. (Unlike OpenGL, the community is not large enough to have an Architecture Review Board.) And in 2006, the 1.1 spec was completed.

Since then, all the OpenAL implementations have adopted 1.1 (or died). With the new spec, porting across the different implementations has become feasible. Creative Labs has expanded its implementations to include Xbox and Xbox 360, which is an interesting development. A new software-based implementation named OpenAL Soft has come into existence, and it has become the implementation for Linux, as well as for systems that use Open Sound System (OSS), which covers most of the Unix world. And it also has a DirectSound back end, so it offers an alternative implementation for Windows.

But of most interest to people reading this book for the iPhone-specific knowledge is that Apple has brought OpenAL to iPhone OS. I don't think I need to convince any of you how big of a market that opens for OpenAL. Unlike with Xbox or Windows, where the developer must opt in to using OpenAL instead of using a Microsoft native API, Apple has embraced OpenAL as the technology to use for games. Assuming that most iPhone and iPod touch users play games—and more than 50 million of these devices have already been sold of this writing[2]—iPhone and iPod touch may already comprise OpenAL's largest user base by far.

That said, the OpenAL developer community still remains small for the moment, judging by the traffic on the official OpenAL mailing list. And the list of significant names is still relatively short. When I first joined the mailing list, there were four people I typically dealt with: Garin Hiebert, who maintained the Creative Labs Windows implementation; Stephen Holmes, maintainer of the Nvidia Windows implementation; Ryan Gordon, a key maintainer/user of the Mac OS X version; and Joseph Valenzuela, who was the current expert on the Linux/Loki code base at the time. Since then, the names have changed, but not so much the size of the community. These include Daniel Peacock, who now maintains the Creative Labs implementation; Bob Aron, who originally implemented Apple's version; and Chris Robinson of OpenAL Soft. Of course, there are other important and influential people involved, but I already run the risk of offending someone by forgetting to list them, so I will stop here.[3]

---

[2] Apple announced it has sold more than 30 million iPhones and 20 million iPod touches at its media event in September 2009.

[3] To give a sense of how many people I left out, just for Apple's implementation, there is a whole list of people on the Core Audio team that helped bring OpenAL to Mac OS X. And the people who implemented the iPhone OS version are not necessarily the same ones who implemented the Mac OS X version. And this also omits the original Mac Classic/Carbonized version.

My Story and Goals for Audio Coverage

So, you might be wondering where I fit into this picture. I don't really. I was just an unfortunate hobbyist who picked up OpenAL 1.0 many years ago, hoping to embellish the cross-platform OpenGL-based projects I was working on at the time. Little did I realize the pain and suffering that would ensue due to the broken spec and defective implementations.

I was surprised to see that I was given an acknowledgment in the OpenAL 1.1 spec for providing my feedback and problems with the spec to Garin. And I was told by Bob Aron that I once owned the majority of the OpenAL bug list at Apple. I'm sure that has changed since then, though I still try to pester Bob every once in a while with a new bug. I'm joking, of course, but the moral is that you should file those bug reports. Believe me when I say they do fix things.

Somewhere along the way, I guess I've become somewhat of an expert on OpenAL. I've actually read the full spec multiple times (out of necessity due to all the problems I've had). I don't know about you, but I've never had to read the entire spec for anything else before. And I've actually dived into Apple's OpenAL source code multiple times, trying to understand things, fix bugs, or make improvements. I have worked with the other implementations of OpenAL as well.

My goal here is to introduce you to OpenAL, hoping to help you avoid the pain that I had to endure. With the 1.1 spec, things will be much more pleasant than my original experience, but I will attempt to draw attention to important areas that may still cause OpenAL developers problems.

In the original versions of my chapters, I omitted recounting my own experiences with OpenAL. My editor requested that I revise them to include more personal anecdotes. In doing so, most of my memories tended to dwell on the frustrations I've endured through the years, which in turn, manifested itself with a negative overtone in my early revision drafts. My wonderful reviewers pointed this out to me, and I have tried to revise the tone, because I don't want to give the impression that OpenAL is a bad technology—quite the contrary. I am a strong proponent of OpenAL. In fact, one of the primary reasons I agreed to contribute to this book is that I want to encourage more developers to try OpenAL. I felt passionately about trying to create something that might be akin to an authoritative, comprehensive introduction/how-to guide for OpenAL.

Despite my desire to evangelize OpenAL, I know I do no one any favors if I sugarcoat it, and fail to identify the problematic and difficult areas. So, I call them as I see them. I apologize if the tone of my chapters seems schizophrenic at times.

As of this writing, there are very few (if any) books that cover OpenAL in detail. So, it's possible that some readers will have purchased this book more for the information on OpenAL than for iPhone development. I have made an effort to accommodate those readers, while still giving iPhone developers everything they expect.

Since OpenAL is a cross-platform standard, most of the things I talk about apply to OpenAL on any platform. When there are significant variations between OpenAL implementations, I will bring attention to those issues, so non-iPhone developers and cross-platform developers will have the knowledge they need to make their applications work and portable. Additionally, a lot of the discussion about game engine design holds true regardless of platform.

However, since this is an iPhone book, the native languages are C and Objective-C, so the examples are coded in that. I urge the non-iPhone developers to not to be too dismissive of the information just because of Objective-C. Objective-C is a minimalistic superset of the C language, and it is very easy to learn. It tends to be a verbose and descriptive language, so even if you don't know it, you can generally read it pretty easily (think of it as pseudo code).

iPhone developers can rest assured that the information here has not been watered down at all. In fact, you will see interesting facts about Apple's specific implementation of OpenAL, as well as a couple of (advanced) Objective-C runtime techniques that you would be hard-pressed to find anywhere else.

Roadmap for the Audio Coverage

Because there are a lot of features to cover, I felt it would be better to introduce material as we need it, one element at a time, rather than front-loading all the information and risk overwhelming you. So, we will start by just trying to get basic sound effects playing. We will then go through an iterative process to improve the game and utilize more of the features OpenAL provides.

Because of the complementary nature of OpenGL and OpenAL, Ben Smith and I felt it was important to provide a unified code example for the book. So, for most of the audio section, we will continue to build on Space Rocks!, the example used in Chapters 7 and 8.

This chapter can be divided into three fundamental pieces:

- In the first part, we will start with just getting sound playback to work through OpenAL in the Space Rocks! game. We will just take the easiest and most direct path to get sound working, and ignore issues like good design and scalability in this first iteration.

- The next part of this chapter will go back and fill in a few more details that are important to know for any shipping application. We will also take this opportunity to embellish our Space Rocks! code a little more.

- In the final part of this chapter, we will identify the problems we inadvertently created by ignoring certain issues of software architecture. We will then go back and try to fix the deficiencies by creating a general design for our OpenAL-based audio engine.

The discussion in the final section might be considered unusual for a "beginning"-style book, but in practice, every OpenAL developer is ultimately challenged with these same issues. In my opinion, it would be derelict to not help new OpenAL developers through these issues, so I will take the plunge into discussing some design. This may be the hardest part of the entire audio section, as it isn't your standard technical how-to. But we'll get through it, and you'll be able to apply what you learned to all your future OpenAL projects.

Chapter 11 will ease up a bit and introduce all the cool 3D features OpenAL provides. We will add each 3D feature one by one to Space Rocks! and make our game really spiffy.

The audio section will conclude in Chapter 12, introducing streaming. Streaming is useful for music, speech, and audio recording. This chapter will also cover Core Audio-specific APIs, as well as what OpenAL provides. By the end, we will have a complete Space Rocks! implementation with 3D sound effects, music, and speech.

So let's jump into it.

Setting Up Basic Sound in OpenAL

These are the basic steps we need to get a minimal program working with OpenAL:

1. Set up an audio session (iPhone OS-specific; outside OpenAL).

2. Open a device.

3. Create a context.

4. Activate the context (make the context current).

5. Generate sound sources.

6. Generate data buffers.

7. Load sound data from files (outside OpenAL).

8. Submit sound data to OpenAL data buffers.

9. Attach data buffers to sound sources.

10. Play sound.

11. Shut down and clean up.

While this list may seem long, don't panic. Most of these steps map one to one with a function call, which makes it very simple. The longest step is loading the sound data, which requires us to go outside OpenAL.

As stated, we are going to continue working with the Space Rocks! game introduced in the OpenGL chapters. Our starting point will be the project named SpaceRocksAudioStartingPoint. This is based on the final version of Space Rocks! from Chapter 8. We will add our OpenAL code to this. For the completed version of the project for the first part of this chapter, see the project named SpaceRocksSoundInit1 for the full code. (You will need to copy the sound effects from this project if you want to follow along with the implementation described here.)

Our very first goal will be to play a sound effect when the player fires a weapon. We will play a laser sound effect every time the player fires a volley[4] (see Figure 10-2). To start with, we are going to ignore good design and scalability. We are going to hard-code things and put things in less than optimal places. This demonstration is just to show the bare minimum you need to play sound. Later, we will improve the design and refactor the code.

Figure 10-2. *We will play a wimpy laser sound effect when the ship's weapon is fired.*

In the Space Rocks! game, we will first add a new `OpenALSoundController` class, which we will design as a singleton. This pattern should be familiar to you, since it is already used in the Space Rocks! code.

This would also be a good time to add the OpenAL framework and the Audio Toolbox framework to the list of frameworks we link against.

Setting Up an Audio Session

The first step for iPhone OS developers is to set up an audio session in our init method. Non-iPhone OS developers can move on to the next section, "Opening a Device."

For now, we are just going to use the C-based boilerplate code as presented in the previous chapter. There are some details you need to know about for handling interruptions using OpenAL, but we will discuss those later. Right now, we just want to get up and playing.

---

[4] Are you wondering why I use a laser sound effect for something that looks like a missile? Sorry, it was an early production artifact. The early build I saw was the vector-line version, and I had not seen the source code yet, so I misinterpreted the thing as a laser. By the time I received the later builds and started integrating, I had already recorded the sound effects. We'll use a missile sound effect later in this book for the UFO missiles.

To keep things a little cleaner, I separated the code related to the audio session into two files: *AudioSessionSupport.h* and *AudioSessionSupport.c*. In these files, a function named InitAudioSession()wraps the boilerplate code from the previous chapter. If you are starting from scratch, create these two new files and add the following implementation to *AudioSessionSupport.c*. (And don't forget to add the forward declaration in *AudioSessionSupport.h*.)

```
#include <AudioToolbox/AudioToolbox.h>

bool InitAudioSession(UInt32 session_category,
    AudioSessionInterruptionListener interruption_callback, void* user_data)
{
    AudioSessionInitialize(NULL, NULL, interruption_callback, user_data);
    AudioSessionSetProperty(kAudioSessionProperty_AudioCategory,
        sizeof(session_category), &session_category);
    AudioSessionSetActive(true);
    return true;
}
```

> **NOTE:** The finished project has all this code implemented, plus some additional stuff, including error checking and helper functions. You may just want to work directly with the finished code.

In *OpenALSoundController.m*'s init method, we want to call our new function to initialize the audio session.

```
- (id) init
{
    self = [super init];
    if(nil != self)
    {
        InitAudioSession(kAudioSessionCategory_AmbientSound, NULL, NULL);
    }
    return self;
}
```

For now, we pass NULL for the last two parameters. We will revisit these parameters later, when we want to deal with audio session interruption callbacks.

Opening a Device

Now we are ready to interact with OpenAL directly. The first thing we need to do is open a device for output. (Also, it would be a good time to remember to add the #includes and link the OpenAL framework in your project. See the sidebar on how to #include OpenAL.)

So first, in *OpenALSoundController.h*, we will need a new instance variable to hold the OpenAL device pointer.

```
@interface OpenALSoundController : NSObject
{
    ALCdevice* openALDevice;
}
```

In *OpenALSoundController.m*, let's create a new method named initOpenAL, where we will put our initialization code to open a device. We should have our class's init method invoke this method immediately after we initialize the audio session. Then, in initOpenAL, we will open the device.

```
- (id) init
{
    self = [super init];
    if(nil != self)
    {
        InitAudioSession(kAudioSessionCategory_AmbientSound, NULL, NULL);
    }
    [self initOpenAL];
    return self;
}

- (void) initOpenAL
{
    openALDevice = alcOpenDevice(NULL);
}
```

We call the OpenAL function alcOpenDevice() with NULL as the parameter to open the default output device on the system and save the device pointer into a member variable.

Advanced OpenAL Tip: Specifying OpenAL Devices

We pass NULL to alcOpenDevice(), to specify we want the default device, which is determined by the operating system. In principle, the OpenAL specification allows you to pass a specific device identifier, to request a specific output device such as the headphones. But philosophically, Apple wants you to always use NULL here, because the device routing should be considered to be under the control of the user. The user is the one plugging in headphones or docking the device. It is the user's direct actions that control the device, so you, as the developer, are just along for the ride.

In addition, Apple's current desktop implementation of OpenAL actually ignores specific device requests and always opens the default device, so it is not unreasonable to assume that the iPhone OS implementation has a similar limitation. In fact, as of this writing, for iPhone OS 3.1, the behavior of alcGetString(NULL, ALC_DEFAULT_DEVICE_SPECIFIER) seems suspect, and the Audio Library Context (ALC) Enumeration Extension appears broken.[5]

---

[5] For more information about the lack of device enumeration support on Mac OS X and initial patch, see my blog entry at
http://playcontrol.net/ewing/jibberjabber/defective_core_audio_mac_os.htm
l.

> **NOTE:** OpenAL is divided into two header files: *al.h* and *alc.h*. *alc.h* is for all of the device- and context-related APIs. All functions use the prefix `alc`. *al.h* is for everything else (actual playing of sounds and positional stuff). All functions use the prefix `al`. Each has its own type definitions and its own error functions. Try not to accidentally use the wrong one for the API commands you are currently using. Even though OpenAL divides the APIs into two separate headers, for linking purposes, the library is still considered to be a single monolithic item, so you don't need to do anything special for the linking case.

HOW TO #INCLUDE OPENAL FOR CROSS-PLATFORM DEVELOPMENT

The OpenAL specification does not dictate where header files are located. This has led to diverging conventions for the different OpenAL implementations. Apple uses a Mac OS X (NeXT) style framework and puts its headers in the OpenAL framework. So you are expected to do this:

```
#include <OpenAL/al.h>
#include <OpenAL/alc.h>
```

Since the code examples in this book are iPhone-centric, this is adequate for us and what we use. But most of the Linux and other Unix distributions like to follow the same convention they use for OpenGL, where they put the headers in a subdirectory called GL. So for OpenAL, they use a subdirectory named AL, and use this convention:

```
#include <AL/al.h>
#include <AL/alc.h>
```

For their respective implementations, Creative Labs and Nvidia didn't like to put headers in any subdirectory. So they use this convention:

```
#include <al.h>
#include <alc.h>
```

So, the conventions depend on which implementation you are using and the packaging vendor, but often they are misconstrued as Mac OS X, Linux (or other non-Apple Unix flavors), and Windows.

If you want to write portable software, I encourage you to be very careful about how you might use preprocessor directives to describe the situation. For example, suppose you hard-code preprocessor directives to always do this:

```
#include <al.h>
#include <alc.h>
```

On Windows, you might find yourself in trouble if users are using OpenAL Soft on Windows and are following the `<AL/al.h>` convention. Or if some package maintainer decides to do something different, you will need to know about it. (For example, once upon a time, FreeBSD Ports did a very odd thing with SDL 1.2 and put everything thing in a subdirectory called SDL11.)

In the example code for this chapter, I have included a demonstration of how you would incorrectly[6] set up the include directive to be Apple/Windows/other. I don't recommend you do this for real code, but some readers may be unfamiliar with preprocessor macros, so these macros are in the code for those who wish to see. But note that my headers are not truly portable, because I use some Apple-specific types elsewhere in the header for convenience.

For real cross-platform code, I advocate doing this:

```
#include "al.h"
#include "alc.h"
```

(Incidentally, this is the same strategy SDL recommends for its headers.) Then I push the burden for detecting the correct path on the build system.

Micromanaging all the different build systems is a pain, which is why I also advocate an open source tool called CMake. It is led and maintained by a company called Kitware, which has a handful of big projects such as the Visualization ToolKit (VTK). CMake is a build system generator (or metabuild system). You write a script that describes the files you want to build in your project, and CMake will then generate projects for Xcode, Makefile, Visual Studio , KDevelop, Eclipse, and so on, so you can use your IDE of choice. I have already contributed an OpenAL module for CMake, so you can just use CMake's package mechanism to invoke it, as in FIND_PACKAGE(OpenAL).

You can learn more about CMake at http://www.cmake.org.

Creating a Context

Like OpenGL, OpenAL has the notion of a context. The context contains and keeps track of all the state you might set up, such as the positions of objects or the gain levels. You need at least one active context to get audio output working.

We need to add another instance variable to *OpenALSoundController.h* to hold the context pointer:

```
ALCcontext* openALContext;
```

In *OpenALSoundController.m*'s initOpenAL method, add the following line directly after the line we added to open the device in the previous step:

```
openALContext = alcCreateContext(openALDevice, 0);
```

We supply the opened device from the previous step as the first parameter. The second parameter is an optional attribute list, which allows you to give hints to OpenAL. There are five official attributes in the spec, and vendors are allowed to add their own.

Advanced Tip: Using Attribute Lists

In practice, many implementations ignore the hints, or it is hard to measure their effectiveness in performance. Apple's desktop implementation ignores all but the

---

[6] I settled for the incorrect version because I am not using CMake in this book and didn't want to confuse anyone by changing the header search paths in the Xcode/SpaceRocks project settings.

numbers for mono and stereo sources,[7] but they will dynamically increase the numbers when needed. So don't feel bad about skipping the attribute list.[8]

For completeness, a sample attribute list is set up like this:

```
ALCint attr_list[] = {
    ALC_FREQUENCY, 22050,
    ALC_REFRESH, 60,
    ALC_SYNC, AL_TRUE,
    ALC_MONO_SOURCES, 31,
    ALC_STEREO_SOURCES, 1,
    0
};
openALContext = alcCreateContext(openALDevice, attr_list);
```

> **NOTE:** Apple provides a separate extension to set the output mixing frequency rate, which is covered in the "OpenAL Extensions for iPhone OS" section later in this chapter.

Activating the Context

Since OpenAL is a stateful API, any OpenAL command is applied to the context that was last designated as the current context. Since we just created our context, we want to make sure that any OpenAL commands that we call are applied to our new context. To ensure this, add the following line to *OpenALSoundController.m*'s initOpenAL method, immediately after the line we added to create the context in the previous step:

```
alcMakeContextCurrent(openALContext);
```

We are now finished (except for cleanup) with the APIs from ALC. We will now move on to the core AL APIs.

---

[7] The defaults for Apple's Mac OS X implementation are 0 for ALC_MONO_SOURCES and 1 for ALC_STEREO_SOURCES. Apple's defaults generally do the right thing and will automatically/dynamically increase the number of mono and stereo sources as needed, so you will almost never need to set these values yourself. However, there is one corner case in the current implementation, which occurs if you need exactly 32 mono sources. Apple's implementation currently does not reclaim the single stereo source for mono use, so in this case, you would need to explicitly set ALC_MONO_SOURCES to 32 and ALC_STEREO_SOURCES to 0. However, Apple is free to change it implementation at any time, so this footnote may become out of date.

[8] For Creative Labs-based drivers, it is strongly recommended you set ALC_STEREO_SOURCES correctly if you intend to have more than one simultaneously playing stereo sound. An example of this would be cross-fading stereo music.

Generating Sound Sources

In OpenAL, a source is a resource that represents a point emitting sound. In addition to emitting sound, a source has a bunch of properties, such as position and velocity, to facilitate the 3D capabilities of the API. For now, we are concerned with only playing back a sound, so we will ignore all the other properties.

Again, we need to add another instance variable in *OpenALSoundController.h*:

```
ALuint outputSource;
```

And again, append the following line to `initOpenAL` in *OpenALSoundController.m*:

```
alGenSources(1, &outputSource);
```

In this call, the first parameter tells OpenAL how many sources we want to create. OpenAL will generate that many sources and return numeric identifiers (of type `ALuint`, which is an integer) for each source to the second parameter. In our case, we pass a reference to a single `ALuint`. But if you wanted to create multiple sources in one command, you could pass an array:

```
ALuint sources_array[32];
alGenSources(32, sources_array);
```

Keep in mind that we are responsible for releasing the sources when we are finished with them. But because creating a source is a memory allocation operation, and memory allocation is not necessarily an inexpensive operation, for performance and memory fragmentation reasons, most games will create all the sources in an initialization stage and reuse/recycle them.

There are limits on how many sources can be generated, as will be discussed in the "OpenAL Source Limits" section later in this chapter. Also note that unlike OpenGL, OpenAL does not specify what valid source ID values are. So it is possible that a source could be assigned the ID value 0, whereas in OpenGL, 0 is reserved. Do no assume 0 is an error value in OpenAL. Use `alGetError()` to detect errors (described later), and use `alIsSource(source_id)` to determine if a source ID is valid.

> **NOTE:** I personally dislike the fact that 0 is not reserved. It makes certain patterns much more cumbersome. Apparently, a lot of other developers have been bitten by this. Creative Labs used to return 0 as a valid ID, but so many developers just assumed 0 wasn't a valid ID, as in OpenGL, that Creative Labs changed its implementation to avoid this. As far as I know, with the current implementations out there, it is unlikely you will get 0 as a valid ID. (Here's a trivia fun fact: Apple's desktop version currently increments a counter starting at 2400, an implementation detail that could change at any time.) But for safety and correctness, I strongly advise that you avoid treating 0 as special. Many of us would like to see this fixed in a 1.2 spec if it ever comes around, and I no longer think there is any opposition to the idea.

Generating Data Buffers

A data buffer in OpenAL is analogous to a texture in OpenGL. We are required to allocate a piece of memory in OpenAL to hold the linear PCM data of the sound we want to play. We will refer to this buffer through an integer ID.

As in the previous step, we need another instance variable in *OpenALSoundController.h*:

```
ALuint laserOutputBuffer;
```

And append the following line to initOpenAL in *OpenALSoundController.m*:

```
alGenBuffers(1, &laserOutputBuffer);
```

> **NOTE:** While I complained about sources including 0 as legitimate ID numbers, buffers do not have this problem. Though technically the spec doesn't explicitly reserve 0 as a return value, other parts of the spec allow you to pass 0 (or AL_NONE) as a buffer identifier to signify a special operation; for example, detaching a buffer from a source. So effectively, 0 cannot be a valid buffer ID. Nonetheless, you should still use alGetError() and alIsBuffer() to determine if an ID is a valid buffer.

Loading Sound Data from Files

Like OpenGL, OpenAL is designed to be agnostic with respect to platforms, file formats, and so on. While this helps keep an API lean, the first stumbling block new OpenAL users tend to hit is figuring out how to load their audio file into OpenAL. As you've learned, OpenGL doesn't know anything about image file formats such as PNG and JPEG. To create a texture, you must go outside OpenGL to load the raw data into a buffer, and then submit the buffer telling OpenGL what the pixel format is. Similarly, to load a file with OpenAL, you must go outside OpenAL to load the raw PCM data into a buffer, and then submit the buffer telling OpenAL what the format is.

Thus, we must leave OpenAL to find something to help us load a file. There are three approaches we can take:

- Write our own file loader.
- Use a third-party library.
- Use a native platform library.

To support simple uncompressed formats like WAV files, it is not uncommon to see people (re)write this code themselves. However, compressed files are often desirable, so many developers turn to third-party libraries that support considerably more advanced features and compression.

For the iPhone and iPod touch, we will be leveraging Core Audio directly for our audio file needs. By doing so, we get many benefits: We don't use up more disk space, we get to use a highly optimized library that may get hardware acceleration, and Apple insulates us from many of the patent and royalty concerns.

Non-iPhone/Mac OS X developers will need to find another solution to load audio files. As stated, you could implement this yourself, but I recommend you look for third-party libraries. The sidebars on Ogg Vorbis and ALUT should be of particular interest to you. I am also fond of a third-party library called SDL_sound, created by Ryan Gordon.

A former engineering colleague of mine liked to joke about "side quests" in software development. More often than not, to accomplish your ultimate goal, you have to do something that seems completely different and unrelated to the ultimate goal. These are often time-consuming and arguably annoying, particularly when you really just want to focus on the main goal. So he always compared it to side quests in video games where you might need to go on some obscure path to get some magic bean, to enter some castle, to save some pet, to get some fur to be used in a magic potion, to cure some person's relative, to get a map to lead you to a weapon, to defeat a special enemy, who gives you a key, which unlocks a door to the part of the game you wanted to go to in the first place. (Why can't you just blow up the door with your bombs?)

Well, we are about to embark on a little side quest of our own, outside OpenAL, back to the enchanted land of the Audio Toolbox and use Extended Audio File Services. The (mini-game) goal is to load a file into a buffer into linear PCM format (because OpenAL understands only linear PCM). This file will use 16-bit native endian signed data, because we know that this is the optimal format for the iPhone/iPod touch. The loader will preserve whether the file is mono or stereo.

NOTE: With this generic code, if you want spatialized sound, you must supply mono files for the sounds that you want to spatialize. This is because OpenAL will not apply 3D effects to stereo sounds.

The basic algorithm is as follows:

- Open the file.

- Get some information about the file to carry over (e.g., sample rate and number of channels).

- Fill out an AudioStreamBasicDescription structure describing the output format we want, which includes things like linear PCM, 16-bit, native endian, and signed, as well as the things we want to carry over, such as the sample rate.

- Apply our output structure to the file reference so Core Audio knows what we want to convert to.

- Tell Core Audio to decode the file into a buffer.

While the algorithm is not too hard, Core Audio requires you to fill out numerous fields in structures and to use the generic Get/Set property APIs, which are somewhat tedious. If you are a bit overwhelmed by this Core Audio code, don't fret too much about it. This is a general file-loader function that can be used as a black box. You can just drop it into your OS X/OpenAL-based projects and never worry about the implementation details.

> **NOTE:** The code is in the completed example project (SpaceRocksSoundInit1), and many things are commented, so it will not be included here. See the functions MyGetExtAudioFileRef(), MyGetDataFromExtAudioRef(), and MyGetOpenALAudioDataAll() in *OpenALSupport.c.* MyGetExtAudioFileRef() is responsible for opening a file. MyGetDataFromExtAudioRef() will read some PCM data from the open file. MyGetOpenALAudioDataAll() is a convenience function that opens a file and puts the entire file into a single buffer of memory. It is built using the other two functions. The code is factored into three functions for code reuse. Right now, we wish to read in an entire file in a single shot via MyGetOpenALAudioDataAll(). This is acceptable for short sounds, but for long sounds, which take up a lot of memory, we will want to look at streaming (reading small chunks). Streaming will be addressed in Chapter 12.

Once we have our black box file-loading functions, we just need to use them. For now, we only need to use the convenience function MyGetOpenALAudioDataAll(). This will load an entire audio file and put it into a buffer of memory.

First, we need one more instance variable for the memory buffer in *OpenALSoundController.h*:

```
void* laserPcmData;
```

In *OpenALSoundController.m*, append the following lines to initOpenAL:

```
ALsizei data_size;
ALenum al_format;
ALsizei sample_rate;
NSURL* file_url = [[NSURL alloc] initFileURLWithPath:↵
    [[NSBundle mainBundle] pathForResource:@"laser1" ofType:@"wav"]];
laserPcmData = MyGetOpenALAudioDataAll((CFURLRef)file_url, &data_size, &al_format,↵
    &sample_rate);
[file_url release];
```

MyGetOpenALAudioData() will open the file and read all the data into a new memory buffer created by malloc. (Since the function uses malloc to create the buffer, we must remember to free the memory later.) The function returns the pointer to the buffer, which we store in our instance variable laserPcmData. The three parameters data_size, al_format, and sample_rate are filled in with the correct values by MyGetOpenALAudioData(), which will be used directly by OpenAL in the next step.

Since we read the entire file into a buffer, we don't need to keep the NSURL around, so we may release it immediately after we are finished calling MyGetOpenALAudioData().

OGG VORBIS

You may have heard of an audio compression format called Ogg Vorbis. Vorbis is a lossy audio codec comparable to MP3. Ogg is the file container format, and typically has the filename extension *.ogg* for audio files.

Ogg Vorbis offers comparable compression to MP3, but is patent and royalty free, with free/open source reference implementations (BSD license). Because of this, it is particularly popular in the open source world.

However, on a mobile device, fine-tuning the Ogg Vorbis implementation to your specific hardware—to be optimized for limited CPU, memory, and battery life—is not necessarily an easy undertaking. Leveraging native hardware decoding support may be off-limits to a third-party developer.

Still, Ogg Vorbis is worth a look. Learn more about it at `http://www.xiph.org`.

ABOUT ALUT

If you've ever done your own research into OpenAL, you may have encountered something called ALUT.

In the 1.0 days of OpenAL, most of the implementations also included their own OpenAL Utility ToolKit (ALUT). ALUT was influenced by the OpenGL Utility Toolkit (GLUT), and had the similar goal of trying to allow succinct demo programs to be created and help people new to OpenAL ramp up very quickly. Perhaps the most popular of the functions that ALUT provided was `alutLoadWAVFile`, as OpenAL is completely file format-agnostic (and many people didn't want to take the side quest of implementing the loader themselves).

ALUT was always intended to be a cleanly separated library from OpenAL, following the GLUT design. Unfortunately, there was no spec for ALUT, and every implementation of ALUT was incompatible. In addition, ALUT was often built directly into the OpenAL library, so the separation was not very clean.

When OpenAL 1.1 finally came around, the conscious decision to drop ALUT completely was made. But a third party came along and reimplemented a new open source version of a stand-alone ALUT (named freealut) to work with OpenAL 1.1. This in itself was not a bad thing, but the freealut developers made the deadly mistake of not completely renaming the function names. This dire decision led to havoc with Apple's Mac OS X (desktop) implementation of OpenAL.

When Apple made the transition from OpenAL 1.0 to 1.1, it did so within the 10.4 Tiger time frame, rather than waiting for a new operating system release. A big change like this within the same release is very unusual, but OpenAL 1.1 wasn't ratified until just after Tiger initially shipped, and 1.1 was a huge leap forward, solving many flaws in 1.0.

For perfectly legitimate and wise reasons, Apple does not want to break compatibility for existing shipping programs, especially when it is only a system update and not a new major operating system version. So Apple left the legacy ALUT symbols in its Open AL framework so programs would continue to run. But these legacy ALUT symbols clash with the new third-party implementation of ALUT because they share the same names, but have different parameters. Apple also removed the ALUT header files in its implementation, so unless you know what you're doing, you can't compile programs using Apple's legacy version of ALUT. This left ALUT pretty much completely unusable on Mac OS X, and probably hurt adoption of ALUT, since OpenAL is a relatively small community and Mac OS X is a large part of it.

The freealut implementation has since taken steps to fix the clashes by deprecating the problematic functions and using preprocessor macros for Apple to use the legacy signature. But now there are a new set of issues, particularly for iPhone and iPod touch development, despite the fact that ALUT legacy symbols are not an issue on iPhone OS. First, the ALUT design has a bias toward wanting to completely hide the alcContext from the user, while Apple is embracing the explicit use of the alcContext. But perhaps more significant is that freealut is under the LGPL license, and the iPhone SDK license terms forbid dynamic linking. This means closed source applications will not be able to comply with the freealut license terms. Because of these issues, it appears that ALUT and OS X will continue to be at odds.

Submitting Sound Data to OpenAL Data Buffers

Now that we have all our linear PCM data in a buffer, we need to get it into OpenAL. Using the buffer ID value we generated from alGenBuffers(), we can use alBufferData() to copy the PCM data into OpenAL memory.

Append the following to initOpenAL in *OpenALSoundController.m*:

```
alBufferData(laserOutputBuffer, al_format, laserPcmData, data_size, sample_rate);
free(laserPcmData);
laserPcmData = NULL;
```

OpenAL will copy the contents of laserPcmData into its own buffer of memory. Since OpenAL now has its own copy of the data, we no longer need to keep our copy around and are free to release it.

Advanced OpenAL Tip: The alBufferDataStatic Extension

You can skip this section if you care only about standardized OpenAL. However, those who really need to squeak the most performance out of their applications may be interested in Apple's alBufferDataStatic extension. (Creative Labs also offers this extension for their Xbox 360 SDK.) This extension allows OpenAL to use your PCM buffer directly, avoiding the memory copy to give all the data to OpenAL, so it may speed up your loading time.

> **NOTE:** When I attended Apple's iPhone Tech Talks in 2008, the alBufferDataStatic extension was one of the first things mentioned in relation to OpenAL. It was encouraged as a best practice (with a red X next to the standard alBufferData way of doing things and a green checkmark next to this extension). Since then, I think Apple may have backed off a little, emphasizing some of the sharp edges you can cut yourself with when using this extension.

There are several downsides to using this extension:

- As an extension, it is not necessarily portable to other OpenAL implementations.

- Because OpenAL is using your PCM buffer, you may not free it immediately, as we did in the alBufferData() case. You must remember to free it, but only after you are completely finished using OpenAL with it.

- If I were to be generous, I would say there are "concurrency issues." If I were less generous, I would say there is a race condition bug that can lead to crashing under certain circumstances. Whether this is really a bug or the "expected behavior" is a point of contention, but suffice it to say that extreme care is needed when using this extension.

We'll revisit these sharp edges in Chapter 12.

To use the extension, Apple suggests boilerplate code like the following. In a header file, add this:

```
typedef ALvoid AL_APIENTRY (*alBufferDataStaticProcPtr) (ALint buffer_id, ALenum
al_format, ALvoid* pcm_data, ALsizei buffer_size, ALsizei sample_rate);
ALvoid alBufferDataStatic(ALint buffer_id, ALenum al_format, ALvoid* pcm_data, ALsizei
buffer_size, ALsizei sample_rate);
```

In the implementation file, include the following code:

```
ALvoid alBufferDataStatic(ALint buffer_id, ALenum al_format, ALvoid* pcm_data, ALsizei
buffer_size, ALsizei sample_rate)
{
    static alBufferDataStaticProcPtr the_proc = NULL;
    if(NULL == the_proc)
    {
        the_proc = (alBufferDataStaticProcPtr) alGetProcAddress((const ALCchar*)
            "alBufferDataStatic");
    }

    if(NULL != the_proc)
    {
        the_proc(buffer_id, al_format, pcm_data, buffer_size, sample_rate);
    }

    return;
}
```

Then we simply change our alBufferData() code, and skip immediately, freeing our PCM buffer:

```
alBufferDataStatic(laserOutputBuffer, al_format, laserPcmData, data_size, sample_rate);
```

> **CAUTION:** If you are an astute observer, you may notice that the PCM data pointer is not `const` in the extension function, whereas it is `const` in the regular `alBufferData()` function. In my opinion, it should be `const`, but as long as it is not, Apple reserves the right to modify your data buffer. So be careful about using your PCM buffer for other things if you use this extension.

For demonstration purposes, the `alBufferDataStatic` extension is used in the completed example code.

CAN YOU RETRIEVE RAW PCM DATA BACK FROM OPENAL?

Many developers wonder if they can get the raw PCM data back from OpenAL. This would be convenient for things like drawing oscilloscopes or spectrum analyzers. The answer is no. The reason is that OpenAL was designed for performance, and thus OpenAL is free to mutilate the data you provide, if it will help performance in any way. This part of the spec was geared more toward vendors implementing hardware acceleration for OpenAL (such as Creative Labs). Requiring the spec to be able to return the original data created undue burden for these implementations.

For those now wondering how you would build an oscilloscope with OpenAL, the solution is inelegant: Keep your own copy of the data and run your own timers to infer where you are in the buffer. Yes, this is kind of painful. You might be able to skip the timers with streaming if you care less about accuracy. We'll do something kind of related in Chapter 12, so stay tuned.

Attaching a Data Buffer to a Sound Source

We now have both an OpenAL data buffer, which holds our sound data, and an OpenAL source, which can play sounds. The next step is to connect the two, so when we finally tell the sound source to play, it knows which sound data we want.

In the `initOpenAL` method in *OpenALSoundController.m*, append the following line:

```
alSourcei(outputSource, AL_BUFFER, laserOutputBuffer);
```

`alSourcei()` is a generic OpenAL API function that sets properties on OpenAL sources. The first parameter is the source ID of the source you want to manipulate. The second parameter is a constant that states what kind of operation you want to perform. In this case, we are connecting a buffer to our source. The final parameter is the buffer ID.

After we call this function, unless we make any more changes, any time we want to play this source, it will use this attached buffer. We do this in our `initOpenAL` method because, for this example, we don't plan to change sounds.

Playing Sound

We are finally ready to actually play a sound! We are going to write a method called `playLaser`, which will encapsulate this. This is not clean design, but convenient to quickly finish this example.

Create the following method in *OpenALSoundController.m*:

```
- (void) playLaser
{
    alSourcePlay(outputSource);
}
```

As you can see, playing the sound is quite easy. Just call the OpenAL API function alSourcePlay() with the source ID, and the sound will play.

So let's have this sound effect trigger every time the user fires a gun. We know that when the user presses the fire button, the code eventually instructs a new BBMissile object to be created. So, in *BBMissile.m*, add the following line at the end of the awake method:

```
[[OpenALSoundController sharedSoundController] playLaser];
```

Now if you build and run the game, when you press the fire button, you should hear the laser sound start playing.

Shutting Down and Cleaning Up

For correctness, we should also remember to clean up memory. Here's what we need to do:

- We generated an OpenAL source, so we must delete the source.

- We generated an OpenAL buffer, so we delete the buffer.

- We created a context, so we must destroy the context. Note that It is technically an error to destroy an active context, so you should set the current context to NULL first.

- We opened a device, so we must close the device.

- We allocated a buffer for PCM data, so we must free that data if we didn't do so earlier (such as in the case where alBufferDataStatic() is used instead of plain-old alBufferData()).

> **TIP:** Deleting sources before deleting buffers is good defensive programming, because attempting to delete a buffer that is still attached to a source is an error. This is a fairly common gotcha.

The natural place to put our cleanup code is in the dealloc method of our OpenALSoundController class. But for organizational purposes, let's encapsulate the OpenAL-specific code from anything else the class needs to do in its cleanup routine.[9]

---

[9] It also makes it convenient to implement the finalize method if you are using Objective-C garbage collection, say on (desktop) Mac OS X.

We'll create a helper method called `tearDownOpenAL` in `OpenALSoundController`. We'll make our dealloc method call `tearDownOpenAL`.

```
- (void) dealloc
{
    [self tearDownOpenAL];
    [super dealloc];
}

- (void) tearDownOpenAL
{
    alDeleteSources(1, &outputSource);
    alDeleteBuffers(1, &laserOutputBuffer);
    alcMakeContextCurrent(NULL);

    if(openALContext)
    {
        alcDestroyContext(openALContext);
        openALContext = NULL;
    }
    if(openALDevice)
    {
        alcCloseDevice(openALDevice);
        openALDevice = NULL;
    }

    if(laserPcmData)
    {
        free(laserPcmData);
        laserPcmData = NULL;
    }
}
```

NOTE: If you are using Apple's `alBufferDataStatic` extension, you are encouraged to check for OpenAL errors on `alDeleteBuffers` to determine if it is safe to free the raw PCM data. This will be discussed in Chapter 12.

Cow Launched!

Groovy! You have now played sound in OpenAL. There is a lot more to cover, but you've taken your first step into a larger world. This is the foundation on which we will build everything else.

Exposing Flaws and the Missing Details

Now we can push a little farther with sounds for our Space Rocks! game. Let's add some sound effects for exploding asteroids and engine thrust (see Figures 10-3, 10-4, and 10-5.) Again, we throw good design to the wind, with the intent of highlighting a few points and problems.

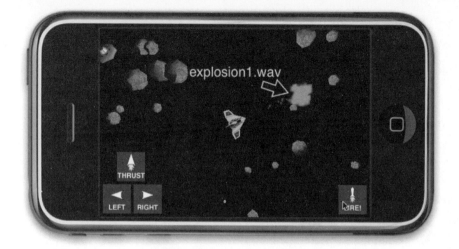

Figure 10-3. *A small, dense explosion sound played when small rocks are destroyed*

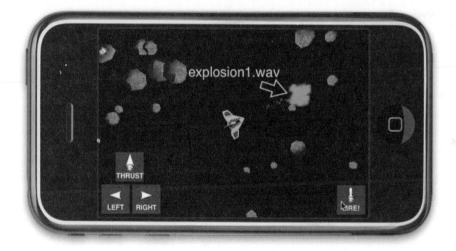

Figure 10-4. *A bigger, less dense explosion sound played when large rocks are destroyed*

Figure 10-5. *An engine thruster sound played when the player thrusts the ship*

Adding More Sounds

We will continue building on the game code that we've been working on up to this point. We will start in the OpenALSoundController class. If you would like, you may use SpaceRocksSoundInit1 as your starting point. The completed project for this part of the example is available in SpaceRocksSoundInit2.

First, we should generate a few more sources. We will generate a source for the exploding asteroids called outputSource2, and a source for the spaceship engine called outputSource3. We will also rename the old outputSource for the laser to outputSource1. Make sure to add/change the instance variables in *OpenALSoundController.h*, and then update initOpenAL in *OpenALSoundController.m*, where we previously generated the outputSource.

```
alGenSources(1, &outputSource);
alGenSources(1, &outputSource1);
alGenSources(1, &outputSource2);
alGenSources(1, &outputSource3);
```

Next, we will generate some buffers for the sound data. But let's get a little fancy and use two different explosion sounds. We will have a big explosion for breaking up a large asteroid and a small explosion for destroying a small asteroid. So, we will need a total of three more buffers, including the engine thrust sound. Again, add/change the instance variables in *OpenALSoundController.h* and then update initOpenAL in *OpenALSoundController.m*, where we previously generated the laserOutputBuffer.

```
alGenBuffers(1, &laserOutputBuffer);
alGenBuffers(1, &explosion1OutputBuffer);
alGenBuffers(1, &explosion2OutputBuffer);
alGenBuffers(1, &thrustOutputBuffer);
```

We also need to load the new sound files. Since we demonstrated the use of the alBufferDataStatic extension already, we will continue to use it for consistency. We add new code to the initOpenAL method to load the other sound files immediately after we load the laser file.

```
file_url = [[NSURL alloc] initFileURLWithPath:
    [[NSBundle mainBundle] pathForResource:@"explosion1" ofType:@"wav"]];
explosion1PcmData = MyGetOpenALAudioDataAll((CFURLRef)file_url, &data_size, &al_format,
    &sample_rate);
alBufferDataStatic(explosion1OutputBuffer, al_format, explosion1PcmData, data_size,
    sample_rate);
[file_url release];

file_url = [[NSURL alloc] initFileURLWithPath:
    [[NSBundle mainBundle] pathForResource:@"explosion2" ofType:@"wav"]];
explosion2PcmData = MyGetOpenALAudioDataAll((CFURLRef)file_url, &data_size, &al_format,
    &sample_rate);
alBufferDataStatic(explosion2OutputBuffer, al_format, explosion2PcmData, data_size,
    sample_rate);
[file_url release];

file_url = [[NSURL alloc] initFileURLWithPath:
    [[NSBundle mainBundle] pathForResource:@"thrust1" ofType:@"wav"]];
thrustPcmData = MyGetOpenALAudioDataAll((CFURLRef)file_url, &data_size, &al_format,
    &sample_rate);
alBufferDataStatic(thrustOutputBuffer, al_format, thrustPcmData, data_size,
    sample_rate);
[file_url release];
```

Finally, at the end of the initOpenAL method, we will set the thrust buffer to play on the thrust source, similar to what we did with the laser buffer. However, we will not set the explosion buffer, because we are going to dynamically change it depending on the situation.

```
alSourcei(outputSource1, AL_BUFFER, laserOutputBuffer);
alSourcei(outputSource3, AL_BUFFER, thrustOutputBuffer);
```

So let's deal with the explosions. Since they are sharing the same output source, we need to set the buffer to play immediately before we play the source. But there is a corner case: If the source is currently playing a sound, it is an OpenAL error to try to change the buffer. The source must be in a nonplaying or nonpaused state before trying to change the buffer. This may seem like a strange way to describe the requirement, but it is intentional. In OpenAL, every source has a current state called the AL_SOURCE_STATE. Valid states are AL_INITIAL, AL_STOPPED, AL_PLAYING, and AL_PAUSED. If a source has just been created, it has the state AL_INITIAL. The other states should be obvious. So to be in a nonplaying or nonpaused state means that the state must be either AL_STOPPED or AL_INITIAL. Changing the buffer when it is AL_PLAYING or AL_PAUSED will not work.

You can always stop playing the source by calling alSourceStop(). This is legal, whether or not the source is playing. But since this is a perfect opportunity to introduce some other OpenAL functionality, we will use another approach here. Rather than always calling alSourceStop(), we can query a source for various types of information using the alGetSource* functions. (There are different variants that end in different suffixes to handle different types, such as integer, float, and array.) In this case, we want the AL_SOURCE_STATE, which returns an integer value. So we use this:

```
ALint source_state = 0;
alGetSourcei(outputSource2, AL_SOURCE_STATE, &source_state);
```

If we find a playing or paused source, we will stop it. Then we will set the new buffer and start playing again.

Now, let's implement the play methods for the explosions in *OpenALSoundController.m*:

```
- (void) playExplosion1
{
    ALint source_state = 0;
    alGetSourcei(outputSource2, AL_SOURCE_STATE, &source_state);
    if(AL_PLAYING == source_state || AL_PAUSED == source_state)
    {
        alSourceStop(outputSource2);
    }
    alSourcei(outputSource2, AL_BUFFER, explosion1OutputBuffer);
    alSourcePlay(outputSource2);
}

- (void) playExplosion2
{
    ALint source_state = 0;
    alGetSourcei(outputSource2, AL_SOURCE_STATE, &source_state);
    if(AL_PLAYING == source_state || AL_PAUSED == source_state)
    {
        alSourceStop(outputSource2);
    }
    alSourcei(outputSource2, AL_BUFFER, explosion2OutputBuffer);
    alSourcePlay(outputSource2);
}
```

For engine thrust, we will do something a little different. Rather than just playing the sound and letting it end, we are going to loop the sound so it continues playing as long as the player is holding down thrust. To do this, we will use the alSource* functions, which are the setter counterparts to alGetSource*. The property we want for looping is AL_LOOPING. We will turn on looping immediately before we call the play function. So we will create another source for the engine sound. Add the following method to *OpenALSoundController.m*:

```
- (void) playThrust
{
    alSourcei(outputSource3, AL_LOOPING, AL_TRUE);
    alSourcePlay(outputSource3);
}
```

Then when the player stops thrusting, we call stopThrust. And although it's unnecessary for this particular example, we will disable looping after we stop playing. Again, add this to *OpenALSoundController.m*:

```
- (void) stopThrust
{
    alSourceStop(outputSource3);
    alSourcei(outputSource3, AL_LOOPING, AL_FALSE);
```

```
}
```

Now that we have all the back-end code in place, we need to hook it into the actual game. In the *BBRock.m*'s smash method, we will add the explosion sounds. Near the beginning of the method, where it is determined the rock has been smashed enough already and returns, we will invoke playExplosion1. Find the line:

```
if (smashCount >= 2) return;
```

Then add a line to invoke playExplosion1:

```
// if we have already been smashed once, then that is it
if (smashCount >= 2)
{
    [[OpenALSoundController sharedSoundController] playExplosion1];
    return;
}
```

Otherwise, we call playExplosion2. Add this line at the very end of the smash method:

```
[[OpenALSoundController sharedSoundController] playExplosion2];
```

In *BBSpaceShip.h*, we will need to add an instance variable called isThrusting of type BOOL to help us track whether the user is holding down the thrust, so we know when to call stopThrust. Then in *BBSpaceShip.m*, in the update method, directly after we get the forwardMagnitude, we can add the logic we need. Find this line:

```
if (forwardMag <= 0.0001) return; // we are not moving so return early
```

And replace it with the following:

```
if (forwardMag <= 0.0001)
{
    if(YES == isThrusting)
    {
        [[OpenALSoundController sharedSoundController] stopThrust];
    }
    isThrusting = NO;
    return; // we are not moving so return early
}
else
{
    if(NO == isThrusting)
    {
        [[OpenALSoundController sharedSoundController] playThrust];
    }
    isThrusting = YES;
}
```

Also, there is a corner case where the player dies while thrusting. In this case, we want to call stopThrust; otherwise, the looping would continue indefinitely. We want to make sure the method deadUpdate in *BBSpaceShip.m* calls stopThrust.

```
-(void)deadUpdate
{
    if ((particleEmitter.emitCounter <= 0) && (![particleEmitter activeParticles])) {
        // If we were thrusting, we better shut off the sound effect
        [[OpenALSoundController sharedSoundController] stopThrust];
        [[BBSceneController sharedSceneController] removeObjectFromScene:self];
```

```
        [[BBSceneController sharedSceneController] gameOver];
    }
}
```

Build and run your game, and you should now have different sounds for the various events.

> **TIP:** As an enhancement, you might want to ramp up the volume as the player holds down the thrust longer. To do this, you could set another property via alSourcei, called AL_GAIN. To actually implement this, you will need some additional code to keep track of how long the user has held down the thrust and how that translates to a gain value to use. A gain of 0.0 means no sound, and 1.0 is normal.
>
> ```
> alSourcei(outputSource3, AL_GAIN, current_gain);
> ```
>
> A similar idea is to introduce a weapon-charging mechanism that creates a bigger and louder bullet the longer you hold down the fire button. Then on button release, the weapon is discharged.

Problems to Notice

Now you have multiple sounds in your game, but you may notice some unpleasant things about it:

- The very first time you play a sound, you may experience a performance hiccup/stall.

- Having multiple firings before the first laser sound finishes cuts off the older sound and starts a new sound from the beginning.

- Having multiple explosions before the first sound finishes cuts off the previous explosion.

- There are no callback notifications for when a sound finishes playing.

Another shortcoming of the game in its current incarnation is that we did a poor job of allocating sound sources. We don't have enough sound sources to potentially play everything that needs to be simultaneously played, and idle sound sources are underutilized (i.e., the engine thrust source could be playing explosions when not thrusting).

We also did a poor job of loading files, because it is centralized in our generic controller. It might make more sense for each object subclass to dictate which files are needed. But in the latter case, we need a smarter system to avoid accidentally loading the same file multiple times and wasting memory.

Finally, the code is going to get harder to maintain because of the way we added sources and buffers.

Later in this chapter, we will try to address these problems and shortcomings. But before we get into that, there are a few more loose ends to cover.

OpenAL Error Checking

We skipped error checking for brevity in the previous examples, but you should know how it works.

When an error occurs within OpenAL, an error number is recorded. You may fetch this error value with a function provided by the OpenAL API, which then clears the error value that was recorded. If further errors occur before you fetch/clear the previous value, the existing error value will not be overwritten.

OpenAL divides error handling between its two different API parts: ALC and AL. Each has its own error function. For functions in *al.h*, you use `ALenum alGetError()`. For device-related functions, you use `ALCenum alcGetError(ALCDevice* device)`. You might also notice that each returns its own enum type, and the ALC version requires you pass the device as a parameter.

OpenAL also provides functions that will convert an error value into a string to make things a little less cryptic for you. Again, AL and ALC have their own functions: `alGetString()` and `alcGetString()`, where the latter requires the device as an additional parameter.

Because OpenAL retains the error code until you fetch and clear it, a typical strategy is to call `alGetError()` or `alcGetError()` immediately before the function you want to check gets called, with the sole purpose of clearing a possible old error. However, if you are consistently checking the error after every OpenAL function call, you shouldn't need to clear it.

In the case of ALC, error-checking code might look like this:

```
alcGetError(openALDevice); // Clear the error buffer
alcMakeContextCurrent(openALContext);
ALCenum alc_error = alcGetError(openALDevice);
if(ALC_NO_ERROR != alc_error)
{
    printf("OpenAL ALC error: %s\n", alcGetString(openALDevice, alc_error));
}
```

Here is an example from the AL side:

```
alGetError(); // Clear the error buffer
alSourcePlay(self.outputSource2);
ALenum al_error = alGetError(); // Get an error that may have occurred
if(AL_NO_ERROR != al_error)
{
    printf("OpenAL AL error occurred: %s\n", alGetString(al_error));
}
```

So, should you always do error checking? In general programming, most people say you should. But in OpenGL, which tends to be intimately tied to the hardware, there are real and significant performance issues with doing error checking. You can stall the OpenGL pipeline in the bad cases and cripple your performance. Since OpenAL was designed with the influences of OpenGL, and there are hardware-accelerated versions of OpenAL, it is reasonable to assume that there could be adverse performance penalties for using error checking. For iPhone OS, since it is a software implementation, the penalties are probably not that bad, so this may not be a strong argument for device-specific code.

Probably the best recommendation is to do the error checking, but wrap it in conditional preprocessor macros so it can be omitted from your final optimized releases. Generally speaking, you shouldn't ship a release build with OpenAL error checking compiled in it.

Almost all the errors returned by OpenAL can be entirely avoided by writing a correct OpenAL program in the first place. For the few errors that may be outside your ability control, but you still want to check,[10] such as in the case of AL_OUT_OF_MEMORY, you should try to avoid calling them in your tight inner game loops for performance reasons.

> **NOTE:** Personally, I am horribly inconsistent about error checking in OpenAL. I tend to avoid it until I encounter an actual error. And in OpenGL, I rarely do it at all. (Apple provides the OpenGL Profiler tool, which lets you look and break for errors at runtime. I wish it provided a counterpart for OpenAL!) It is easy to accumulate a lot of error-checking code and make your implementation much harder to read. (Notice I omit a lot of error checking in this book.) And then there is the laziness factor. But when you do encounter an error and haven't done error checking, it can be a pain to track down. (You may actually see me sneak in extra checks in later iterations of the examples of this book because I had to go back and add checks to hunt for errors I encountered.) Also, it helps to have the error checks in the code when you file a bug report with Apple.

Audio Session Interruptions

As iPhone OS developers, during an audio interruption such as an incoming phone call or alarm (see Figure 10-6), we have some requirements when we use OpenAL. Currently, Apple's developer examples shut down OpenAL on interruption, and then completely rebuild it. This means you must delete all buffers and sources, destroy the context, and close the device. Then to resume audio, you need to rebuild everything. Furthermore, you lose all your OpenAL state, which includes gain levels, looping, and the current playback position. So if you have a (long) sound that is in the middle of playing, you will lose its state, and it will be up to you to determine the current playback position and resume from there, if you care to do so.

---

[10] OpenAL vendors such as Apple sometimes introduce new, non-standardized errors through the OpenAL error mechanism to support some of their OpenAL extensions. You may need to test for errors when using extensions.

Figure 10-6. *A proper iPhone OS application must handle interruptions correctly.*

Fortunately, there is an easier way to handle audio session interruptions, starting in iPhone OS 3.0. We can use several OpenAL context functions, which Apple seems to have gotten to cooperate with the interruption system.

On a begin interruption event, we first call `alcSuspendContext()` on all our OpenAL contexts. This suspends all state processing in a context. Then we set the current context to `NULL` via `alcMakeContextCurrent()`. A suspended context should preserve all the existing state in the context. For example, a sound in the middle of playback will be frozen and then later resume when the context is unsuspended.[11]

On an end interruption event, we first reactivate the audio session. Then we undo what we did in the begin interruption stage; that is, we make a context current and resume processing on the contexts using `alcProcessContext()`.

Now is a good time to revisit how we initialized our audio session, which was the first thing we did in this chapter. First, we should implement a function to be our interruption callback function. In *OpenALSoundController.m*, we will add a new function before the line that starts as follows:

```
@implementation OpenALSoundController
```

---

[11] Apple's current OpenAL implementation is incorrect according to the OpenAL 1.1 spec. Apple's `alcSuspendContext` and `alcProcessContext` are actually no-ops, and the act of changing the current context suspends and resumes the context. From the Mac OS X source, it appears this was made as an accommodation to Doom 3 because it was relying on OpenAL 1.0 behavior and got caught in the transition to 1.1. But you should code these correctly, in case Apple fixes the implementation.

Technically, our function is not part of the OpenALSoundController class. We just
implement the function in this file because it is a convenient place to put it, since the
OpenALSoundController class is going to use the function.

The function implementation is as follows:

```
static void MyInterruptionCallback(void* user_data, UInt32 interruption_state)
{
    OpenALSoundController* openal_sound_controller = (OpenALSoundController*)user_data;
    if(kAudioSessionBeginInterruption == interruption_state)
    {
        alcSuspendContext(openal_sound_controller.openALContext);
        alcMakeContextCurrent(NULL);
    }
    else if(kAudioSessionEndInterruption == interruption_state)
    {
        OSStatus the_error = AudioSessionSetActive(true);
        if(noErr != the_error)
        {
            printf("Error setting audio session active! %d\n", the_error);
        }
        alcMakeContextCurrent(openal_sound_controller.openALContext);
        alcProcessContext(openal_sound_controller.openALContext);
    }
}
```

Next, we want to modify how we initialized our audio session. Recall that in
OpenALSoundController.m, we originally called InitAudioSession with the last two
arguments as NULL. Change this to the following:

```
- (id) init
{
    self = [super init];
    if(nil != self)
    {
        // Audio Session queries must be made after the session is set up
        InitAudioSession(kAudioSessionCategory_AmbientSound,
    MyInterruptionCallback, self);
        [self initOpenAL];
    }
    return self;
}
```

The second parameter is the function MyInterruptionCallback, which we just defined.
This will cause MyInterruptionCallback to be invoked when an interruption occurs. We
pass self as the third parameter, which is the instance of the OpenALSoundController. In
MyInterruptionCallback, this becomes the user_data parameter, and will allow us to
access properties and methods from OpenALSoundController. This will allow us to get
the OpenAL context and invoke the ALC commands we need to call.

With this code in place, we should now be able to handle audio interruptions.
Unfortunately, there is a potential corner case. Recall our looping sound effect for engine
thrust. If an interruption occurs while the user is thrusting, there is a race condition in our
code that will cause the incorrect thing to happen. The interruption will immediately call
our code to suspend the context and set it to NULL. This means the source is still in a

looping state. However, as the interruption comes in, the input system still responds to touches. So when the user releases the thrust button, it may very well be after the context has been suspended and set to NULL. This means the function call to stop looping the thrust source becomes a no-op, and we lose the event. When the game resumes, the thrust sound will resume its looping, even if the user isn't touching the thrust button.

The good news is that the user just needs to touch the thrust button again, and everything will start behaving as normal. The bad news is that there may not be a general, elegant system for handling this. The problem is not insurmountable, because there are work-arounds you can employ. You could explicitly reset all state attributes to default manually or tear down the entire OpenAL system and rebuild it. But this may not be what you want in the case where there is a non-user looping sound you want resumed on interruption end. You will need to consider how audio interruptions will affect your specific application states and how you wish to deal with them.

And, in general, you may want to add conditional checks before you call any AL functions, testing to see if you are in an interruption (or more specifically, have a valid OpenAL context). On iPhone OS, you will generate an OpenAL error if you try calling an AL function without a valid context. However, it generally won't crash your program, so if you forget the check, the consequences aren't terrible. (The next completed project example, SpaceRocksSoundResourceManager1, adds two lines to the preceding code to save the interruption state to a flag, so we can use that to do our checks. Look for the variable inInterruption.)

TESTING IPHONE INTERRUPTIONS

For all of you with an iPod touch or an iPhone without phone service, you might be wondering how to test an interruption. Unfortunately, the developer tools currently provide no way to simulate an interruption.

My solution is to use the alarm feature of the Clock application that comes with the device. When an alarm goes off, it triggers the same audio session begin interruption routine as an incoming phone call does. Acknowledging an alarm will then lead to the end interruption routine being invoked (see Figure 10-6). Keep in mind that unlike a phone call, there is no way that the user can "accept the phone call," which prevents the end interruption routine from ever happening.

Because there is overhead in getting your application launched and into the parts of your application you want to test, I usually set multiple alarms, so I don't need to keep quitting the application. Also, I set the first alarm to go off no sooner than 2 minutes from the time I am setting the alarm, because the clock granularity doesn't account for seconds (which means if you set it to the next minute, the alarm could go off sooner than you expect, because there are only a few seconds until the next minute flips). This sometimes results in getting the interruption before your program finishes launching.

Also, keep in mind that the interruption interface differs between the alarm and a phone call. A phone call completely overlaps or replaces the current interface, while the alarm overlays a dialog on top of your game. I have noticed that in the latter case, you still can interact with the game under certain conditions,[12] whereas interaction is not possible during a phone call.

OpenAL Extensions for iPhone OS

Two OpenAL extensions are currently available on iPhone OS. We have already discussed the `alBufferDataStatic` extension. The other extension is `MixerOutputRate`, which actually consists of two functions to let you query the current rate and set the rate:

```
alcMacOSXGetMixerOutputRate
alcMacOSXMixerOutputRate
```

By setting the mixer output rate, you may be able to increase the performance of your application. The trick is that you want to set the output rate to the same value as all your sound files. This will avoid any sample rate conversions that need to be done. So, if you make all your audio files 22,050 Hz, and you set the mixer output rate to the same value, you will avoid all unnecessary conversions and get optimal performance.

The ideal time to set this value is after you open the device, but before you create the context. Again, you will need to use the boilerplate code to find the extensions.

A demonstration of this has been snuck into the `SpaceRocksSoundInit2` example, just before the `alcContext` is created in *OpenALSoundController.m*, in the method `initOpenAL`. Chapter 12 provides general information about accessing OpenAL extensions.

> **NOTE:** I cheat for Apple in my boilerplate code. Apple's real headers use the wrong OpenAL type definitions. They use the AL type `ALdouble`, instead of the ALC type `ALCdouble`. Since this is a device-related function and is prefixed with `alc`, Apple should be consistent and use `ALCdouble`. In the grand scheme of things, it won't matter, since both types get mapped to the same thing. They also use `const` in front of primitive types, which I omit because it does nothing.

Performance Notes

To improve the performance of your iPhone apps, take advantage of the OpenAL extensions `alBufferDataStatic` and `alcMacOSXMixerOutputRate`. Remember that to get

---

[12] You must have a touch that is active and not release it. You can input additional touches. So in Space Rocks!, you may be thrusting or turning when the alarm hits. Don't release it, and then use other fingers to do stuff such as fire.

the most benefit from `alcMacOSXMixerOutputRate`, you should make all your audio files the same sample rate.

Additionally, iPhone OS has another function to let you set the preferred hardware sample rate on the device. Documentation for both `alcMacOSXMixerOutputRate` and `kAudioSessionProperty_ PreferredHardwareSampleRate` is almost nonexistent as of this writing, but my limited understanding of these settings is that the `alcMacOSXMixerOutputRate` affects the sampling rate of things mixed by the underlying 3DMixer Audio Unit, while the `kAudioSessionProperty_PreferredHardwareSampleRate` affects the final mixing rate that is output through your device via the Remote IO Audio Unit. Since you may have many (3D) OpenAL sources, you need to mix, setting the former will likely have a big impact on performance, as more things may need to be converted. If you mix APIs (for example, OpenAL with AVFoundation, as demonstrated in Chapter 12), you may notice a boost with the latter.

You may try setting both of these and see if you get a benefit. To use them, you should call these functions while the audio session is not active. The same rule about matching your sample rates for your files applies. (I sneak this code into the next completed project example, `SpaceRocksSoundResourceManager1`, in the `InitAudioSession()` function in *AudioSessionSupport.c*, but I do not discuss it further.)

```
Float64 preferred_sample_rate = 22050.0;
UInt32 the_size = sizeof(preferred_sample_rate);
AudioSessionSetProperty(kAudioSessionProperty_PreferredHardwareSampleRate, the_size,
    &preferred_sample_rate);
```

NOTE: Be aware that properties like `PreferredHardwareSampleRate` are best-effort functions. They may fail for reasons beyond your control. For example, the iPod music player may already be rendering at 44 kHz, which may prevent you from changing the rate. Check the error values if you want to know if the operations failed. And it will be up to you to decide what to do about it. For example, you may decide to continue, as there is nothing you can do about it anyway, or as an extreme, you may decide to abort the program.

Next, you may consider using lower-quality samples to get more performance. You will need to decide what trade-off to make between quality and performance (and memory). Often, iPhone developers use 22,050 Hz samples, rather than 44,100 Hz samples, because they are considered high enough quality.

On the subject of memory, remember that when you load your samples into an OpenAL buffer, this is uncompressed raw data. All the samples you load are consuming RAM. In the examples, we preload the samples and keep them resident for low-latency performance. But if you exhaust the amount of memory you have available, you may need to rethink your strategy.

The strategy usually employed is to load all the sound effects during the initialization phase. The assumption is that these sound effects are short and frequently used. On-demand loading and unloading would create latency you don't want, and may lead to bad memory fragmentation. However, for long sounds that are used infrequently and at predictable times (perhaps a transition at the end of a level), on-demand loading (possibly with streaming) may be a reasonable choice.

OpenAL Source Limits: "It's a Secret to Everybody"

This section covers a topic that most new OpenAL users aren't aware of. And this is a frustrating topic for anyone who has tried porting software across different OpenAL implementations. It's not a hard topic, but researching all the facts has been a challenge. Very few OpenAL developers I know of have spent a lot of time with the different OpenAL implementations, which means that there are very few people who can answer specific details about all the implementations. So get ready, you are about to learn a whole bunch of useful information that took me years to acquire.

On some OpenAL implementations, the maximum number of sources that can be generated is finite and small. The reason stems from both hardware design and performance. Some implementations, such as on Microsoft Windows using a Creative Labs sound card with hardware acceleration, resources may be directly mapped to hardware. As such, the number may be small depending on the device. And to complicate matters even further, it is also possible for resources to get dynamically diverted to handle other sound requirements, possibly from competing applications. This means you may not always be able to get the same number of sources you did in a previous run, or a source could just refuse to play and set an error.

For other OpenAL implementations, performance is the limiting consideration. Since simultaneous playback of multiple sources requires software mixing on the device, there will be a certain threshold where the mixing requirements overwhelm the CPU. Limits are one way of avoiding this scenario.

The OpenAL specification lacks the ability to query for a number of supported sources. (This is partly due to the difficulty of dealing with implementations that can dynamically divert resources away from your application.) Therefore, you generally need to know something about your target platform beforehand to pick an optimal number.

On iPhone OS, the maximum isn't documented. But as an experiment, you can look at the Apple's source code for the Mac OS X desktop implementation and also try generating sources yourself on iPhone OS. In the source code, there is a #define `AL_MAXSOURCES 256`. However, this check is made on only the number value passed to `alGenSources()`. So, you can generate only 256 sources per call to `alGenSources()`, but nothing is stopping you from making repeated calls to `alGenSources()` to get batches of 256 sources at a time.[13] If you try this yourself on your touch device, you

---

[13] This was probably not intended, and you should avoid doing this in production code.

can see you will get unique IDs back for each batch of 256. Requesting 257 in one shot will trigger an error.

However, Apple's implementation does make an additional distinction of how many sources you can generate versus how many sources you can simultaneously play. On Mac OS X, the default maximum is currently 64, but is customizable through the Apple extension `alcMacOSXMixerMaxiumumBusses` (and `alcMacOSXGetMixerMaxiumumBusses` to query). On iPhone OS, this extension is not available. Running some experiments, as of this writing, the number is 32—the default 31 mono sources plus 1 stereo source. (If you need 32 mono sources, you must set the attribute list for `alcCreateContext`.)

For the purposes of this book, we will assume a value of 32 sources to be a reasonably safe maximum for iPhone OS. Keep in mind that since Apple has not officially documented this number, this limit may change at any time. However, you might expect the number to at least catch up with the desktop as hardware and users and developers demand more sources.

For the cross-platform gurus who want a bottom value, the lowest number of sources I have personally encountered was eight on a Windows machine with an old, generic sound card back in the OpenAL 1.0 days. And, as a piece of trivia, the Loki implementation for Linux did not impose any limits on the number of sources. However, now in the 1.1 era, things have changed a little. Creative Labs provides both a generic software and a generic hardware driver configuration, in addition to native drivers for its own line of sound cards. The generic software driver configuration will give you 256 sources. The generic hardware configuration maps to DS3D buffers and requires a minimum of 16 sources. The hardware implementation caps out at 64 sources. Creative Labs native sound cards and drivers range from 60 to 128.

OpenAL Soft, which is cross-platform and software-based, is primarily the Linux implementation, but also works on Windows and some other platforms. It has picked up a little traction on Windows, because bundling in the OpenAL Soft implementation with an application is considered cleaner than requiring a separate Installer for the Creative Labs implementation. OpenAL Soft has a default of 256 sources, but this number can be overridden in a configuration file.

Table 10-1 summarizes the different values available for the different OpenAL implementations.

> **NOTE:** To my knowledge, all this information has never been consolidated in one single place before. So this is the first! I expect this material will find its way to the Internet some day, but take pride that you are among the first to see it.

Table 10-1. *OpenAL Source Limits on Different Platforms*

OpenAL Implementation	Maximum Number of Generated Sources	Maximum Number of Simultaneously Playing Sources
Apple Mac OS X	256	64

OpenAL Implementation	Maximum Number of Generated Sources	Maximum Number of Simultaneously Playing Sources
Apple iPhone OS	256	32 (unofficial)
Creative Labs Generic Software	256	256
Creative Labs Generic Hardware	16–64	16–64
Creative Labs Native Hardware	60–128	60–128
OpenAL Soft	256	256
Creative Labs SDK for Xbox	64	64
Creative Labs SDK for Xbox 360	128	128

Once OpenAL developers figure out the number of sources they will be dealing with, they may encounter a few additional problems:

- Generating a new source when you need it may cause performance hiccups, because memory allocation isn't necessarily a cheap operation. Generally, game events need low latency, and memory allocation may get in the way.

- If you are frequently allocating and deallocating objects as they come and go in the game, you increase the possibility of memory fragmentation, preventing you from allocating a new object when you need it.

- Many games have more game entities than sources for the life of the game. In this case, it is impractical to assign each game object a unique source.

The solution to these problems is to write a resource manager. It will essentially be a pool containing available sources and allowing objects to get a source when they need to play sounds. Then when the sound finishes, the source is returned to the pool.

Sound Resource Manager: Fixing the Design

To fix all the problems we have discussed so far, we will implement a resource management system. Sound resource managers can be designed many different ways, and easily get very complex. However, most games end up needing a resource manager for OpenAL to deal with the limited number of OpenAL sources. So, in the remainder of this chapter, we'll focus on creating a resource manager—after all, I wouldn't want to leave you stranded without knowing how to build this essential tool.

I don't claim that the design and code you are about to see are optimal. My intent is to give you an understanding of the basic issues involved and to make you aware of some of design challenges. Despite this, you may find that the finished results are good enough to be used, at the very least, in the first versions of your real games.

This section gets pretty involved, so you may want to take a break before starting it and take it slowly. Conceptually, it is not hard. But you need to keep track of a lot of state and detail to build a good resource manager.

> **NOTE:** You may have noticed my coding style differs from Ben's style in the previous chapters on OpenGL. Although Ben and I felt it exceptionally valuable to coordinate on a unified example, there are some clashes in the code. One of the more obvious things is that I haven't been namespacing (prefixing) my class names. For the new classes, I introduce for this example, you will see that I adopt some namespaces. Though interestingly, the OpenALSoundController class is almost stand-alone enough that you could take it as is for your own projects, so the lack of namespace may actually be a benefit to you.

Overview of the Resource Manager

Our resource management system will do the following:

- Load and cache files into a central database to avoid the same file from being loaded multiple times.

- Make sure all the file loading occurs before the game starts and not during it.

- Issue OpenAL sources to objects that need to play sounds and reclaim/recycle them when finished.

- Provide callbacks for sources that have finished playing.

In addition, we will introduce some support classes that will integrate more cleanly into the Space Rocks! design.

For a high-level preview of what we are going to do, see Figure 10-7. We will modify our OpenALSoundController class and make it the heart of the management system. The OpenALSoundController will contain two container data structures: an NSMutableDictionary to store loaded sound files and an NSMutableSet[14] to store OpenAL sources.

---

[14] A *set* is a type of data structure in programming that stores values without regard to order and without duplicates. NSSet and NSMutableSet are Cocoa classes that implement sets.

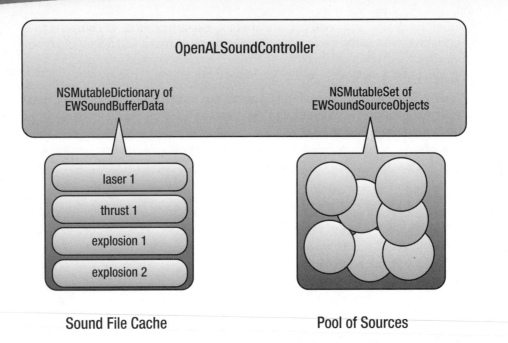

Figure 10-7. *The sound resource manager centers around the OpenALSoundController. The manager contains a file database (cache) system that maps file names to loaded buffers. The manager also contains a pool of OpenAL sources that can be fetched and recycled as needed.*

The NSMutableDictionary will act as a cache or file database for sound files. In the case where a file is needed in multiple places, we will have only one instance in memory, saving us from wasting memory on duplicated instances and wasting time reloading files we don't need to reload.

The NSMutableSet will store all the OpenAL sources we will use in our application. We will preallocate all the sources during the initialization of our program and place them in the set. When we need a source to play a sound, we will retrieve a source from the set. When we are finished with the source, we will put it back in the set (i.e., recycle it). Assuming we never need to play more simultaneous sounds than we have total number of sources, this recycling routine will give the illusion of an infinite supply of sources.

Because OpenAL sources and buffers are referred to by integer identifier numbers, not by Objective-C classes, we will introduce several wrapper classes to wrap our OpenAL data so we may store them in Cocoa data structures. These classes are EWSoundState, EWSoundSourceObject, and EWSoundBufferData.[15]

Lastly, we will add a callback notification system to OpenALSoundController to make it easy to get callbacks when a sound finishes playing.

---

[15] Chapter 11 introduces EWSoundListenerObject, which is a direct counterpart to EWSoundSourceObject. Chapter 12 introduces EWStreamBufferData, which is a counterpart to EWSoundBufferData.

We will continue coding from the project in SpaceRocksSoundInit2. For the completed project, look at SpaceRocksSoundResourceManager1.

Initial Cleanup

To start with, we are going to delete all the inelegant, hard-coded stuff we did in the previous steps. Our sound resource manager will replace this code.

OpenALSoundController.h should be reduced to the following:

```
#import <Foundation/Foundation.h>
#import <OpenAL/al.h>
#import <OpenAL/alc.h>

@interface OpenALSoundController : NSObject
{
    ALCdevice* openALDevice;
    ALCcontext* openALContext;
    ALuint outputSource1;
    ALuint outputSource2;
    ALuint outputSource3;

    ALuint laserOutputBuffer;
    ALuint explosion1OutputBuffer;
    ALuint explosion2OutputBuffer;
    ALuint thrustOutputBuffer;
    void* laserPcmData;
    void* explosion1PcmData;
    void* explosion2PcmData;
    void* thrustPcmData;
}

@property(nonatomic, assign) ALCdevice* openALDevice;
@property(nonatomic, assign) ALCcontext* openALContext;
@property(nonatomic, assign) ALuint outputSource1;
@property(nonatomic, assign) ALuint outputSource2;
@property(nonatomic, assign) ALuint outputSource3;
@property(nonatomic, assign) ALuint laserOutputBuffer;
@property(nonatomic, assign) ALuint explosion1OutputBuffer;
@property(nonatomic, assign) ALuint explosion2OutputBuffer;
@property(nonatomic, assign) ALuint thrustOutputBuffer;

+ (OpenALSoundController*) sharedSoundController;
- (void) initOpenAL;
- (void) tearDownOpenAL;


- (void) playLaser;
- (void) playExplosion1;
- (void) playExplosion2;
- (void) playThrust;
- (void) stopThrust;

@end
```

And *OpenALSoundController.m* should be reduced to the following:

```objectivec
#import "OpenALSoundController.h"
#include "AudioSessionSupport.h"
#include "OpenALSupport.h"

static void MyInterruptionCallback(void* user_data, UInt32 interruption_state)
{
    OpenALSoundController* openal_sound_controller = (OpenALSoundController*)user_data;
    if(kAudioSessionBeginInterruption == interruption_state)
    {
        alcSuspendContext(openal_sound_controller.openALContext);
        alcMakeContextCurrent(NULL);
    }
    else if(kAudioSessionEndInterruption == interruption_state)
    {
        OSStatus the_error = AudioSessionSetActive(true);
        if(noErr != the_error)
        {
            printf("Error setting audio session active! %d\n", the_error);
        }
        alcMakeContextCurrent(openal_sound_controller.openALContext);
        alcProcessContext(openal_sound_controller.openALContext);
    }
}


@implementation OpenALSoundController

@synthesize openALDevice;
@synthesize openALContext;
@synthesize outputSource1;
@synthesize outputSource2;
@synthesize outputSource3;
@synthesize laserOutputBuffer;
@synthesize explosion1OutputBuffer;
@synthesize explosion2OutputBuffer;
@synthesize thrustOutputBuffer;


// Singleton accessor.  this is how you should ALWAYS get a reference
// to the scene controller.  Never init your own.
+ (OpenALSoundController*) sharedSoundController
{
    static OpenALSoundController* shared_sound_controller;
    @synchronized(self)
    {
        if(nil == shared_sound_controller)
        {
            shared_sound_controller = [[OpenALSoundController alloc] init];
        }
        return shared_sound_controller;
    }
    return shared_sound_controller;
}

- (id) init
{
    self = [super init];
    if(nil != self)
```

```objc
    {
        // Audio Session queries must be made after the session is setup
        InitAudioSession(kAudioSessionCategory_AmbientSound, MyInterruptionCallback,
            self);
        [self initOpenAL];
    }
    return self;
}

- (void) initOpenAL
{
    openALDevice = alcOpenDevice(NULL);
    if(openALDevice != NULL)
    {
        // Use the Apple extension to set the mixer rate
        alcMacOSXMixerOutputRate(22050.0);

        // Create a new OpenAL Context
        // The new context will render to the OpenAL Device just created
        openALContext = alcCreateContext(openALDevice, 0);
        if(openALContext != NULL)
        {
            // Make the new context the Current OpenAL Context
            alcMakeContextCurrent(openALContext);
        }
        else
        {
            NSLog(@"Error, could not create audio context.");
            return;
        }
    }
    else
    {
        NSLog(@"Error, could not get audio device.");
        return;
    }

    alGenSources(1, &outputSource1);
    alGenSources(1, &outputSource2);
    alGenSources(1, &outputSource3);
    alGenBuffers(1, &laserOutputBuffer);
    alGenBuffers(1, &explosion1OutputBuffer);
    alGenBuffers(1, &explosion2OutputBuffer);
    alGenBuffers(1, &thrustOutputBuffer);

    ALsizei data_size;
    ALenum al_format;
    ALsizei sample_rate;
    NSURL* file_url;

    file_url = [[NSURL alloc] initFileURLWithPath:
        [[NSBundle mainBundle] pathForResource:@"laser1" ofType:@"wav"]];
    laserPcmData = MyGetOpenALAudioDataAll((CFURLRef)file_url, &data_size, &al_format,
&sample_rate);
    alBufferDataStatic(laserOutputBuffer, al_format, laserPcmData, data_size,
sample_rate);
    [file_url release];
```

```
    file_url = [[NSURL alloc] initFileURLWithPath:
        [[NSBundle mainBundle] pathForResource:@"explosion1" ofType:@"wav"]];
    explosion1PcmData = MyGetOpenALAudioDataAll((CFURLRef)file_url, &data_size,
&al_format, &sample_rate);
    alBufferDataStatic(explosion1OutputBuffer, al_format, explosion1PcmData, data_size,
sample_rate);
    [file_url release];

    file_url = [[NSURL alloc] initFileURLWithPath:
        [[NSBundle mainBundle] pathForResource:@"explosion2" ofType:@"wav"]];
    explosion2PcmData = MyGetOpenALAudioDataAll((CFURLRef)file_url,
        &data_size, &al_format, &sample_rate);
    alBufferDataStatic(explosion2OutputBuffer, al_format, explosion2PcmData, data_size,
sample_rate);
    [file_url release];

    file_url = [[NSURL alloc] initFileURLWithPath:
        [[NSBundle mainBundle] pathForResource:@"thrust1" ofType:@"wav"]];
    thrustPcmData = MyGetOpenALAudioDataAll((CFURLRef)file_url, &data_size, &al_format,
&sample_rate);
    alBufferDataStatic(thrustOutputBuffer, al_format, thrustPcmData, data_size,
sample_rate);
    [file_url release];

    alSourcei(self.outputSource1, AL_BUFFER, self.laserOutputBuffer);
    alSourcei(self.outputSource3, AL_BUFFER, self.thrustOutputBuffer);
}

- (void) tearDownOpenAL
{
    alSourceStop(outputSource1);
    alSourceStop(outputSource2);
    alSourceStop(outputSource3);
    alDeleteSources(1, &outputSource1);
    alDeleteSources(1, &outputSource2);
    alDeleteSources(1, &outputSource3);
    alDeleteBuffers(1, &laserOutputBuffer);
    alDeleteBuffers(1, &explosion1OutputBuffer);
    alDeleteBuffers(1, &explosion2OutputBuffer);
    alDeleteBuffers(1, &thrustOutputBuffer);

    alcMakeContextCurrent(NULL);
    if(openALContext)
    {
        alcDestroyContext(openALContext);
        openALContext = NULL;
    }
    if(openALDevice)
    {
        alcCloseDevice(openALDevice);
        openALDevice = NULL;
    }

    if(laserPcmData)
    {
        free(laserPcmData);
```

```
            laserPcmData = NULL;
    }
    if(explosion1PcmData)
    {
        free(explosion1PcmData);
        explosion1PcmData = NULL;
    }
    if(explosion2PcmData)
    {
        free(explosion2PcmData);
        explosion2PcmData = NULL;
    }
    if(thrustPcmData)
    {
        free(thrustPcmData);
        thrustPcmData = NULL;
    }

}

- (void) dealloc
{
    [self tearDownOpenAL];
    [super dealloc];
}

- (void) playLaser
{
    alSourcePlay(self.outputSource1);
}

- (void) playExplosion1
{
    // Note, loading a buffer on a playing or paused source is technically an error
    // and yields an AL error of AL_INVALID_OPERATION
    ALint source_state = 0;
    alGetSourcei(self.outputSource2, AL_SOURCE_STATE, &source_state);
    if(AL_PLAYING == source_state || AL_PAUSED == source_state)
    {
        alSourceStop(self.outputSource2);
    }
    alSourcei(self.outputSource2, AL_BUFFER, self.explosion1OutputBuffer);
    alSourcePlay(self.outputSource2);
}

- (void) playExplosion2
{
    ALint source_state = 0;
    alGetSourcei(self.outputSource2, AL_SOURCE_STATE, &source_state);
    if(AL_PLAYING == source_state || AL_PAUSED == source_state)
    {
        alSourceStop(self.outputSource2);
    }
    alSourcei(self.outputSource2, AL_BUFFER, self.explosion2OutputBuffer);
    alSourcePlay(self.outputSource2);
}
```

```
- (void) playThrust
{
    alSourcei(self.outputSource3, AL_LOOPING, AL_TRUE);
    alSourcePlay(self.outputSource3);
}

- (void) stopThrust
{
    alSourceStop(self.outputSource3);
    alSourcei(self.outputSource3, AL_LOOPING, AL_FALSE);
}
@end
```

Also, all the `BBSceneObject` classes that invoked the methods we just deleted from *OpenALSoundController* need to be cleaned up. For brevity, these deletions are omitted here. (Remember that the finished project `SpaceRocksSoundResourceManager1` has everything already cleaned up.)

The Sound File Database (Cache System)

We will start with loading a sound file. The algorithm is quite easy. We will use an `NSMutableDictionary` to hold our sound data keyed by the filenames. When we get a request to load a file, we check the dictionary to see if we already loaded the file. If so, we just return the data; otherwise, we load the file and add it to the dictionary.

First, we introduce a new class called `EWSoundBufferData`, which will encapsulate all the buffer data. One of the benefits of doing this is that it will let us hide some of the memory management details of using `alBufferData()` versus `alBufferDataStatic()`. We can easily switch our implementation if we chose to, without impacting the rest of the code.

Create *EWSoundBufferData.h* with the following code:

```
@interface EWSoundBufferData : NSObject
{
    ALuint openalDataBuffer;
    void* pcmDataBuffer;
    ALenum openalFormat;
    ALsizei dataSize;
    ALsizei sampleRate;
}

@property(nonatomic, assign, readonly) ALuint openalDataBuffer;

(void) bindDataBuffer:(void*)pcm_data_buffer
    withFormat:(ALenum)al_format
    dataSize:(ALsizei)data_size
    sampleRate:(ALsizei)sample_rate;

@end
```

`EWSoundBufferData` will call `alGenBuffer()` in its constructor and provide a read-only property for the outside to access.

Next, create *EWSoundBufferData.m*, with the following code:

```
#import "EWSoundBufferData.h"
#include "OpenALSupport.h"

#define USE_BUFFER_DATA_STATIC_EXTENSION

@implementation EWSoundBufferData
@synthesize openalDataBuffer;

- (id) init
{
    ALenum al_error;
    self = [super init];
    if(nil != self)
    {
        alGetError(); // clear errors
        alGenBuffers(1, &openalDataBuffer);
        al_error = alGetError();
        if(AL_NO_ERROR != al_error)
        {
            NSLog(@"Failed to generate OpenAL data buffer: %s", alGetString(al_error));
            [self release];
            return nil;
        }
    }
    return self;
}
```

We also provide one method that encapsulates `alBufferData` or `alBufferDataStatic`:

```
(void) bindDataBuffer:(void*)pcm_data_buffer
    withFormat:(ALenum)al_format
    dataSize:(ALsizei)data_size
    sampleRate:(ALsizei)sample_rate
{
    pcmDataBuffer = pcm_data_buffer;
    openalFormat = al_format;
    dataSize = data_size;
    sampleRate = sample_rate;
#ifdef USE_BUFFER_DATA_STATIC_EXTENSION
    alBufferDataStatic(openalDataBuffer, al_format, pcm_data_buffer, data_size,
        sample_rate);
#else
    alBufferData(openalDataBuffer, al_format, pcm_data_buffer, data_size, sample_rate);
    free(pcmDataBuffer);
    pcmDataBuffer = NULL;
#endif
}
```

We could probably eliminate the saving of the format, data size, and sample rate, since we never use it again. However, the information can be useful if you intend to do other things with the raw PCM data.

For convenience, I have added a preprocessor macro named USE_BUFFER_DATA_STATIC_EXTENSION at the top of *EWSoundBufferData.m* to make it easy to enable or disable this extension in the code. I have left it as enabled for this example.

Finally, for cleanup, we have the following:

```
- (void) dealloc
{
    if(alIsBuffer(openalDataBuffer))
    {
        alDeleteBuffers(1, &openalDataBuffer);
    }

    if(NULL != pcmDataBuffer)
    {
        free(pcmDataBuffer);
    }

    [super dealloc];
}
@end
```

Back in our `OpenALSoundController` class, we will add a new instance variable, `NSMutableDictionary* soundFileDictionary`, and a new method:

```
- (EWSoundBufferData*) soundBufferDataFromFileBaseName:(NSString*)sound_file_basename;
```

The `soundFileDictionary` will map base filenames, such as *laser1* to a `EWSoundBufferData` object, which wraps an OpenAL buffer containing the PCM data to the file. We place the `soundFileDictionary` in the `OpenALSoundController` because it is convenient to do so, since `OpenALSoundController` is a singleton that is globally accessible.

Allocate a new instance of the `soundFileDictionary` in *OpenALSoundController.m*'s init method, and release it in the `dealloc` method.

Next, implement the `soundBufferDataFromFileBaseName:` method. The method takes an `NSString*` parameter, which holds the base filename. So if the file is named *laser1.wav*, the base name is *laser1*, and the *.wav* is dropped. This is done for convenience, because the `NSURL initFileURLWithPath:ofType:` splits the base name and extension between the parameters.

To get a little clever and save us from needing to pass both the base name and extension, we will iterate through an array of known extensions and try to find the file.

After we get the file, we load the PCM data into an OpenAL buffer, as shown earlier in this chapter. Then we create a new `EWSoundBufferData` object and attach the PCM buffer to the OpenAL buffer using the method provided by `EWSoundBufferData`. Finally, we add the buffer to the dictionary.

```
- (EWSoundBufferData*) soundBufferDataFromFileBaseName:(NSString*)sound_file_basename
{
    ALsizei data_size;
    ALenum al_format;
    ALsizei sample_rate;
    NSURL* file_url = nil;

    // First make sure the file hasn't already been loaded.
    EWSoundBufferData* sound_data = [soundFileDictionary
        valueForKey:sound_file_basename];
```

```
    if(nil != sound_data)
    {
        return sound_data;
    }

    // Create a temporary array containing the file extensions we want to handle.
    // Note: This list is not exhaustive of all the types Core Audio can handle.
    NSArray* file_extension_array = [[NSArray alloc]
        initWithObjects:@"caf", @"wav", @"aac", @"mp3", @"aiff", @"mp4", @"m4a", nil];
    for(NSString* file_extension in file_extension_array)
    {
        // We need to first check to make sure the file exists.
        // NSURL's initFileWithPath:ofType will crash if the file doesn't exist.
        NSString* full_file_name = [NSString stringWithFormat:@"%@/%@.%@",
            [[NSBundle mainBundle] resourcePath], sound_file_basename, file_extension];
        if(YES == [[NSFileManager defaultManager] fileExistsAtPath:full_file_name])
        {
            file_url = [[NSURL alloc] initFileURLWithPath:
                [[NSBundle mainBundle] pathForResource:sound_file_basename
                    ofType:file_extension]];
            break;
        }
    }
    [file_extension_array release];

    if(nil == file_url)
    {
        NSLog(@"Failed to locate audio file with basename: %@", sound_file_basename);
        return nil;
    }

    void* pcm_data_buffer
        = MyGetOpenALAudioDataAll((CFURLRef)file_url, &data_size, &al_format,
            &sample_rate);
    [file_url release];
    if(NULL == pcm_data_buffer)
    {
        NSLog(@"Failed to load audio data from file: %@", sound_file_basename);
        return nil;
    }

    sound_data = [[EWSoundBufferData alloc] init];

    // Get the PCM data into the OpenAL buffer
    [sound_data bindDataBuffer:pcm_data_buffer withFormat:al_format
        dataSize:data_size sampleRate:sample_rate];

    // Put the data in a dictionary so we can find it by filename
    [soundFileDictionary setValue:sound_data forKey:sound_file_basename];
    return [sound_data autorelease];
}
```

Notice that this method has two different behaviors:

- If a sound file has not been loaded before (determined by whether the soundFileDictionary can find the buffer), this method will load the file and add it to the soundFileDictionary. It will then return an autoreleased instance of the EWSoundBufferData.

- If the sound file has been loaded before, this method just returns the EWSoundBufferData.

For optimal performance, we should try to load all the files before the game starts playing, so we can avoid "hiccups" during game play. Then during game play, when we need to actually play the sound, we get the fast path where the ready-to-go buffer is just returned from the soundFileDictionary. We will add an explicit loading stage a little later in this chapter.

OpenAL Source Management (Reserving and Recycling)

Next, we turn our attention to the code that formerly contained calls to alGenSources(). Instead of hard-coding OpenAL sources for explicit use purposes, such as one for a laser and another for an engine thrust, we will generate a pool of sources for general use. When we need a source, we will fetch a source from the pool, and when we are finished with it, we will return (recycle) it to the pool. Our storage container will be an NSMutableSet, because the order in which we use sources doesn't matter.

We will create all our sources in one shot in a C array, since OpenAL provides a convenient API for this. We will then use several instances of NSMutableSet to track whether the source is available. MAX_NUMBER_OF_ALSOURCES is defined as 32.

> NOTE: I also sneak in the alcMacOSXMixerOutputRate extension discussed earlier in this chapter while we're here. This is not related to resource management, but just an opportunity to add it to the code base.

Add the following instance variables to *OpenALSoundController.h*:

```
ALuint* allSourcesArray;
NSMutableSet* availableSourcesCollection;
NSMutableSet* inUseSourcesCollection;
NSMutableSet* playingSourcesCollection;
```

In *OpenALSoundController.m*, we introduce our new source management code at the end of the initOpenAL method.

```
- (void) initOpenAL
{
    openALDevice = alcOpenDevice(NULL);
    if(openALDevice != NULL)
    {
        // Use the Apple extension to set the mixer rate
        alcMacOSXMixerOutputRate(22050.0);

        // Create a new OpenAL context
```

```
        // The new context will render to the OpenAL device just created
        openALContext = alcCreateContext(openALDevice, 0);
        if(openALContext != NULL)
        {
            // Make the new context the current OpenAL context
            alcMakeContextCurrent(openALContext);
        }
        else
        {
            NSLog(@"Error, could not create audio context.");
            return;
        }
    }
    else
    {
        NSLog(@"Error, could not get audio device.");
        return;
    }

    allSourcesArray = (ALuint*)calloc(MAX_NUMBER_OF_ALSOURCES, sizeof(ALuint));

    alGenSources(MAX_NUMBER_OF_ALSOURCES, allSourcesArray);

    availableSourcesCollection = [[NSMutableSet alloc]
        initWithCapacity:MAX_NUMBER_OF_ALSOURCES];
    inUseSourcesCollection = [[NSMutableSet alloc]
        initWithCapacity:MAX_NUMBER_OF_ALSOURCES];
    playingSourcesCollection = [[NSMutableSet alloc]
        initWithCapacity:MAX_NUMBER_OF_ALSOURCES];

    for(NSUInteger i=0; i<MAX_NUMBER_OF_ALSOURCES; i++)
    {
        [availableSourcesCollection addObject:[NSNumber
            numberWithUnsignedInt:allSourcesArray[i] ]];
    }
}
```

You may be wondering why we have both inUseSourcesCollection and playingSourcesCollection. It could be argued that this is redundant, as you could design the system to always be playing a source if the source is in use. However, I want to make the distinction between a source that has been reserved for use but may not necessarily be playing and a source that has been reserved and is playing. (Note that I don't allow for playing sources that aren't reserved.) The reason for this will become clearer when we deal with streaming sources in Chapter 12. Streamed sources have different states, and it is sometimes easier to track them separately. So later, I would like to reserve sources for streaming, but not entangle them with our regular playback code.

Since I have talked about wanting to reserve sources for use, it is a good time to introduce the reserveSource: method. This method will remove an available source from the availableSourcesCollection and move it to the inUseSourcesCollection.

```
- (BOOL) reserveSource:(ALuint*)source_id
{
    NSNumber* source_number;
    if([availableSourcesCollection count] == 0)
    {
```

```
        // No available sources
        return NO;
    }

    source_number = [availableSourcesCollection anyObject];

    [inUseSourcesCollection addObject:source_number];
    // Remember to remove the object last or the object may be
    // destroyed before we finish changing the queues
    [availableSourcesCollection removeObject:source_number];

    *source_id = [source_number unsignedIntValue];
    return YES;
}
```

Since there is a possibility that we have exhausted all the available sources, we need to alert the calling function that there was no available source. Unfortunately, since the OpenAL 1.1 spec allows for any unsigned integer to be a source, we can't make up and return an invalid ID (such as 0) that allows us to identify the error condition. So, instead, we will return YES for successfully reserving a source, and NO for no available sources. Then we will return the source ID through a pointer parameter.

Conversely, we need a cleanup function to undo the reserveSource.

```
- (void) recycleSource:(ALuint)source_id
{
    NSNumber* source_number = [NSNumber numberWithUnsignedInt:source_id];

    // Remove from the inUse list
    [inUseSourcesCollection removeObject:source_number];

    // Add back to available sources list
    [availableSourcesCollection addObject:source_number];
}
```

Now we can take a look at the play and stop methods.

```
- (void) playSound:(ALuint)source_id
{
    // Trusting the source_id passed in is valid
    [playingSourcesCollection addObject:[NSNumber numberWithUnsignedInt:source_id]];
    alSourcePlay(source_id);
}

- (void) stopSound:(ALuint)source_id
{
    // Trusting the source_id passed in is valid
    alSourceStop(source_id);
    alSourcei(source_id, AL_BUFFER, AL_NONE); // detach the buffer from the source
    [playingSourcesCollection removeObject:[NSNumber numberWithUnsignedInt:source_id]];
    [self recycleSource:source_id];
}
```

In playSound:, notice that we finally add the source to the playingSourcesCollection. And in stopSound:, we stop, remove the source from the playingSourcesCollection, and then call recycleSource, which removes the source from the in-use collection and returns it to the available collection.

Now you may realize there is a big problem here. When playing sounds in OpenAL, we don't always call stop. The only time we ever call stop is to end the looping engine thrust noise. We played all other sounds until they end automatically. This means we don't have a way to recycle those sources, and we will lose them forever.

OpenAL does not have built-in callback event systems to let you know something happened. For better or worse, OpenAL is a polling-oriented API. So, the solution is to poll OpenAL and look for state changes. We can even construct our own callbacks, if desired. (We'll construct a callback system a little later in this chapter.)

To OpenALSoundController, we will add a new method called update, which should be called periodically. Since we already have a polling system in place to do our OpenGL animation among other things, it is not a big deal to add OpenAL to the mix.

Earlier, we used AL_SOURCE_STATE to determine if a source was playing or paused. We will use this again, but this time look for sources that are in the AL_STOPPED state. We will iterate through all the sources in the playingSourcesCollection. Any of these sources in the AL_STOPPED state means their playback has ended and we need to recycle them.

```
- (void) update
{
    NSMutableSet* items_to_be_purged_collection = [[NSMutableSet alloc]
        initWithCapacity:[playingSourcesCollection count]];
    for(NSNumber* current_number in playingSourcesCollection)
    {
        ALuint source_id = [current_number unsignedIntValue];
        ALenum source_state;
        alGetSourcei(source_id, AL_SOURCE_STATE, &source_state);
        if(AL_STOPPED == source_state)
        {
            alSourcei(source_id, AL_BUFFER, AL_NONE); // detach buffer from source
            // Because fast-enumeration is read-only on the enumerated container, we
            // must save the values to be deleted later
            [items_to_be_purged_collection addObject:current_number];
        }
    }

    for(NSNumber* current_number in items_to_be_purged_collection)
    {
        // Remove from the playing list
        [playingSourcesCollection removeObject:current_number];

        [self recycleSource:[current_number unsignedIntValue]];
    }

    [items_to_be_purged_collection release];
}
```

You might notice this line:

```
alSourcei(source_id, AL_BUFFER, AL_NONE);
```

This will detach the OpenAL buffer from the source. This is not absolutely necessary, but more of a safety precaution. In the event of a bug where some object retains the source

ID when it shouldn't and calls play, detaching the buffer will prevent any sound from playing. Otherwise, the previously attached sound will play. Now, there will still be a bug if something else was assigned the recycled source ID and set a new buffer, and the buggy object calls play. But, at the very least, you now know how to detach a buffer.

Finally, with the update method implemented, we need to make sure it is called every frame. If we go to *BBSceneController.m* and look at updateModel, we see it invokes update on all the scene objects. This seems like a good place to call our sound update.

```
- (void)updateModel
{
    // Simply call 'update' on all our scene objects
    [inputController updateInterface];
    [sceneObjects makeObjectsPerformSelector:@selector(update)];
    [[OpenALSoundController sharedSoundController] update];
    // Be sure to clear the events
    [inputController clearEvents];
}
```

Integration with Space Rocks!

We now have the core of our sound resource manager, but we still need to integrate it with the game. So we will take this opportunity to try to integrate better with the existing game design to make things cleaner than before.

First, it would be nice to have an object that could encapsulate an object's sound source state more cleanly. For this purpose, we will introduce a new class called EWSoundSourceObject. The fundamental idea is that every BBSceneObject is potentially an entity that can emit a single sound. The ship has its engine sound, every missile has its firing sound, and every asteroid has an explosion sound. So we will add EWSoundSourceObject as an instance variable to BBSceneObject, allowing all objects to emit a sound.

The most important property in EWSoundSourceObject is a source ID, which is negotiated with the sound resource manager. The class will have additional support methods as well.

The EWSoundSourceObject will also hold attributes such as the gain level. Any attribute that can be set on an OpenAL source using alSource* should be in here. But for reasons that will become more apparent in the next chapter (when I introduce the listener object), we will put some of these attributes in a parent class called EWSoundState. Our EWSoundSourceObject will inherit these attributes.

To start with, EWSoundState will have only one property, gainLevel. It has two methods, applyState and update, which are no-ops. They are intended to be overridden by the subclasses.

```
@interface EWSoundState : NSObject
{
    ALfloat gainLevel;
}
```

```
@property(nonatomic, assign) ALfloat gainLevel;

// Virtual functions which should be overridden by subclasses
- (void) applyState;
- (void) update;

@end


@interface EWSoundSourceObject : EWSoundState
{
    ALuint sourceID;
    BOOL hasSourceID;
    ALboolean audioLooping;
    ALfloat pitchShift;
}

@property(nonatomic, assign) ALuint sourceID;
@property(nonatomic, assign) BOOL hasSourceID;
@property(nonatomic, assign, getter=isAudioLooping) ALboolean audioLooping;
@property(nonatomic, assign) ALfloat pitchShift;

- (void) applyState;
- (void) update;

- (BOOL) playSound:(EWSoundBufferData*)sound_buffer_data;
- (void) stopSound;

@end
```

EWSoundSourceObject contains four instance variables. The sourceID will be issued from the sound resource manager when needed. Since there will be times when we don't have an issued source ID, we need a flag to tell us whether we have a legitimate source ID. The remaining two properties are for OpenAL attributes that don't belong in the parent class (for reasons that will become clearer in the next chapter). You have already been introduced to AL_LOOPING. AL_PITCH will shift the frequency of playback sound. The default value is 1.0. Every doubling of the pitch will shift up one octave. Every halving of the pitch will shift down one octave. A 0 is an illegal value. We won't be using this directly, but it's included for demonstration purposes. (Other properties are 3D-related and will be introduced in the next chapter.)

playSound: is probably the most interesting method here. It utilizes OpenALController's playSound: method, but this implementation acts as the bridge that connects the SceneObject system with the sound resource manager. Let's take a closer look at the implementation in *EWSoundSourceObject.m*:

```
- (BOOL) playSound:(EWSoundBufferData*)sound_buffer_data
{
    OpenALSoundController* sound_controller = [OpenALSoundController
sharedSoundController];
    ALuint buffer_id = sound_buffer_data.openalDataBuffer;
    ALuint source_id;
    BOOL is_source_available = [sound_controller reserveSource:&source_id];
    if(NO == is_source_available)
    {
```

```
        return NO;
    }

    self.sourceID = source_id;
    self.hasSourceID = YES;

    alSourcei(source_id, AL_BUFFER, buffer_id);
    [self applyState];
    [sound_controller playSound:source_id];

    return YES;
}
```

First, notice that the required parameter is an audio sample that you want to play. Part of the job of this method is to attach the audio buffer to the sound source so you play the correct sound.

Also notice that we reserve a source from the sound resource manager. Once we verify that we have a valid source, we save the source ID and set our internal flag so we know we have a valid source.

Lastly, before calling the sound controller's playSound: method, there is a call to applyState. Let's take a look at it:

```
- (void) applyState
{
    [super applyState];
    if(NO == self.hasSourceID)
    {
        return;
    }
    if([[OpenALSoundController sharedSoundController] inInterruption])
    {
        return;
    }
    alSourcef(self.sourceID, AL_GAIN, self.gainLevel);
    alSourcei(self.sourceID, AL_LOOPING, self.audioLooping);
    alSourcef(self.sourceID, AL_PITCH, self.pitchShift);
}
```

This method is important because it sets all the OpenAL attributes on the source ID we have been assigned. Since this source may have been used by other things, the source could have residual values from its last use. For example, we may want to play an asteroid explosion. However, imagine that the source was previously used for the engine noise, which was looping. The source may still have the looping state, and if we don't reset the value, we may get a looping explosion, which is not what we want. Applying the state on our newly issued source immediately before we start playing is critical to making sure the source has the correct values.

Also notice we have a check at the beginning of the method to make sure we have actually been issued a source. We don't want to accidentally apply a state to a source we used to own but has since been recycled and may be in use by something else.

Finally, we include a check for the interruption state to avoid calling these AL commands if there is no OpenAL context. The intent is that the game engine will be calling this method every frame. These frames might be called even during an audio interruption.

Now is a good time to introduce the update method. It just calls applyState.

```
- (void) update
{
    [super update];
    [self applyState];
}
```

It is intended that update be called every frame. The reason is that some values may change over time. For example, you may want to "animate" pitch or gain. Imagine a weapon-charging scenario. Hold down the fire button to make your weapon more powerful on discharge. Release the fire button to discharge your weapon. While you are doing this, you might consider gradually increasing the gain and the pitch so the weapon noise gets louder and higher pitched. Applying the state every frame is an easy way to make sure your OpenAL source stays in sync with the class's shadow values.[16]

To get update called every frame, we return to *BBSceneController.m* and add another line to updateModel, directly above where we added the sound controller update:

```
- (void)updateModel
{
    // simply call 'update' on all our scene objects
    [inputController updateInterface];
    [sceneObjects makeObjectsPerformSelector:@selector(update)];
    [[OpenALSoundController sharedSoundController] update];
    // be sure to clear the events
    [inputController clearEvents];
}
```

Finally, back in EWSoundSourceObject, stopSound is mostly a pass-through to the sound resource manager. The one thing to remember is to set hasSourceID to NO. And you should check to make sure hasSourceID is YES before passing through to stopSound.

Now again, you might notice the problem that we don't always call stop on our sources, so we can't set the hasSourceID to NO. It just so happens that we avoid this problem here, because our sound effects that play without calling stop are connected to objects that are destroyed and deleted from the system shortly after the sound effect starts playing. This means there is little chance of the source being applied an invalid set of attributes. However, this is not a good thing to rely on, and we should fix the problem. We fixed the last problem by polling. Our solution here needs the same information that was gathered from polling. So the problem is how to connect the AL_STOPPED detection discovered from polling to our EWSoundSourceObject, which exists outside the OpenALSoundController. The solution we will employ is callbacks.

---

[16] Setting the value every frame for values that you may not be using or haven't changed may not be the most efficient thing to do, and you may want to consider more optimized techniques.

SoundDidFinishPlaying Callbacks

Before I first got into OpenAL, I spent a lot of time with SDL_mixer, a satellite library of SDL that makes playing sound fairly simple. One thing this API provided was callbacks when sounds finished playing. I found that this system was very handy, and started building my code to depend on this information. Unfortunately at the time, I had latency problems with SDL_mixer on Windows. Also, it had two design flaws: it allowed for only one streaming channel, and the callbacks did not allow for passing user data with the C callbacks. So if you had classes you needed to act upon, you couldn't get at them without resorting to global variables. Because of these problems, I started looking at OpenAL. I was shocked to find that there were no callbacks in OpenAL.

Fortunately, even though OpenAL doesn't provide callbacks, that doesn't stop us from implementing our own. In our polling implementation, which searches for sound sources that have finished, we can create a callback event to happen right there when we discover a finished source.

To keep a clean separation between the OpenALSoundController and the EWSoundSourceObject, we can use generic constructs to connect the two. In C, we would do this with function pointers. But since this is an iPhone and iPod touch book, we can also do it in Objective-C using delegates. Since delegation is a common pattern in Cocoa and is much richer than a function pointer (since you get more language and compiler support, and can stuff anything you like in your objects), we will go the delegate route. Objective-C 2.0 introduces optional methods to protocols, which are the "new" and better way of setting up delegates, so we will embrace them, too.

> **TIP:** If you do use C function pointers for your own code, never omit the void* parameter for passing user data (also called *context*).

First, we set up a protocol for the callback. We can put this directly in *OpenALSoundController.h*:

```
@protocol EWSoundCallbackDelegate <NSObject>
@optional
- (void) soundDidFinishPlaying:(NSNumber*)source_number;
@end
```

Next, we add an instance variable and a property to the OpenALSoundController class for a delegate object that conforms to our protocol:

```
id<EWSoundCallbackDelegate> soundCallbackDelegate;

@interface OpenALSoundController : NSObject
{
    ...
    id<EWSoundCallbackDelegate> soundCallbackDelegate;
}
@property(nonatomic, assign) id<EWSoundCallbackDelegate> soundCallbackDelegate;
```

Modify the update method in the class to invoke the callback. We can put this immediately after we call recycleSource:

```
for(NSNumber* current_number in items_to_be_purged_collection)
{
    [self recycleSource:[current_number unsignedIntValue]];
    if([self.soundCallbackDelegate
respondsToSelector:@selector(soundDidFinishPlaying:)])
    {
        [self.soundCallbackDelegate soundDidFinishPlaying:current_number];
    }
}
```

Next, we need something to receive the callbacks. We will use BBSceneController because it has a list of all the SceneObjects. Once we get the event to the BBSceneController, it is easy to pass it on to all the SceneObjects. The first step is to make BBSceneController conform to the EWSoundCallbackDelegate protocol.

```
#import "OpenALSoundController.h"
@interface BBSceneController : NSObject <EWSoundCallbackDelegate> {
```

BBSceneController has not yet implemented an init method. We could try to reuse BBSceneController's loadScene method, but we really want a function that is called only once at the creation of the class instance. The problem with loadScene is it is called every time you start a new game (not just once per program run). So we will implement a new init method and use it to make BBSceneController the delegate of our sound controller.

```
- (id) init
{
    self = [super init];
    if(nil != self)
    {
        [[OpenALSoundController sharedSoundController] setSoundCallbackDelegate:self];
    }
    return self;
}
```

Then implement the delegate method in BBSceneController:

```
- (void) soundDidFinishPlaying:(NSNumber*)source_number
{
    [sceneObjects makeObjectsPerformSelector:@selector(soundDidFinishPlaying:)
        withObject:source_number];
}
```

Here, we just assume BBSceneObjects will always have a method called soundDidFinishPlaying. I am getting worn out by dealing with the indirection of delegates/function pointers, and I bet you are too by this point. So rather than introducing yet another level of indirection, let's be direct and require that BBSceneObjects implement a method by the same name. (We could give it a different name, but I think the name is descriptive.) Just don't confuse them. For this to work, we better add this to BBSceneObject:

```
- (void) soundDidFinishPlaying:(NSNumber*)source_number
{
    [self.soundSourceObject soundDidFinishPlaying:source_number];
}
```

Once again, we just assume EWSoundSourceObjects implements a method called soundDidFinishPlaying:, so we better implement that as well:

```
- (void) soundDidFinishPlaying:(NSNumber*)source_number
{
    if([source_number unsignedIntValue] == self.sourceID)
    {
        self.hasSourceID = NO;
    }
}
```

Finally, we can set hasSourceID to NO.

Here are a few things to note with this design:

- All living SceneObjects will receive the soundDidFinishPlaying callback message. So we check the parameter source ID value and compare it to our saved source ID value to see if the message is relevant to the particular receiver.

- Keep in mind that because many of our objects are destroyed before the sound completes, there is no guarantee that this callback will be invoked on the object that originated the sound.

- Also keep in mind that if we explicitly call stopSound: on a source, the callback will not be invoked. This is because we prevent the update method from knowing that a source ended by manually resetting the collection lists ourselves. This could easily be changed if you want the callback, but you'll need to think about whether this is really the behavior you want.

Potentially, there are other things you can do with the event callbacks. For example, you might chain a series of sound effects together, so that when one sound effect ends, you immediately start a second one. Or consider triggering events based on the end of sounds. Game over might be an interesting event to trigger based on the completion of a death sound or message. But you should be careful about basing critical events on sound completion. If the callback never fires because the sound doesn't finish in an expected way (e.g., due to an phone call interruption), you might never be able to trigger the critical event.

Final Integration Steps for Space Rocks!

We're almost there! Most of the infrastructure is in place. We just need to modify the individual SceneObjects to use the new stuff to load and play sounds (and delete the old code).

First, let's add our sound files to the *BBConfiguration.h* file. Remember that our loader method automatically guesses file extensions for us, so we just need the base filenames.

```
// laser1.wav
#define LASER1 @"laser1"
// explosion1.wav
#define EXPLOSION1 @"explosion1"
```

```
// explosion2.wav
#define EXPLOSION2 @"explosion2"
// thrust1.wav
#define THRUST1 @"thrust1"
```

Now let's move to *BBMissile.m*. First, we want to load the sound file. The engine doesn't currently provide an explicit loading stage for SceneObjects. Typically, we would consider loading the sound files in the init or awake method. But because sound files can take a long time to load, we might see an initial performance hiccup when we fire the very first missile in the game. (This was the performance hiccup I pointed out in the original version earlier in this chapter.)

We will introduce our own class method called loadResources for all BBSceneObjects, which we will invoke before we start the main game loop. Each BBSceneObject is free to load global resources that are shared between all instances of that object. In this case, it will be sound files, but you might consider loading other resources here, too, such as texture files and 3D model files. A sensible place to do this is in the init method of BBSceneController.

> **NOTE:** Veteran Cocoa programmers might be thinking of two class methods that might help: initialize and load. These class methods are invoked just once, no matter how many instances you have. And they are invoked before the first instance of the class is created. Unfortunately for us, initialize is still lazily called. In our missile case, it wouldn't be called until we tried to use the class for the first time, which is when the fire button is pressed—in the middle of game play. And load is called much too early for us to use.

But we are confronted with a small problem. We need to iterate through all BBSceneObject classes, which means the BBSceneObject class and all the subclasses of BBSceneObject. We could do this the hard way and hard-code every BBSceneObject class, and then manually invoke loadResources ourselves. But this is messy and error-prone, as we may introduce new classes to the game or refactor things.

Fortunately, there is a more elegant way to do this. But we need to take another side quest, this time to the Objective-C runtime system. We are going to utilize some of the dynamism of Objective-C to find all the BBSceneObject classes at runtime and invoke our loadResources class method on those classes. We will use programming techniques called *type introspection* and *reflection* to accomplish our goals.

Programmers with experience using a dynamic language—such as Objective-C, Java, C#, Python, or Lua—may find this approach obvious and elegant. But most OpenGL and OpenAL developers would never think to do something like this, because they are often tied to C or C++. (You will probably never see anything like this in another game programming book.) But this is a book on iPhone development, and we should take advantage of simple and elegant solutions that minimize code and errors whenever we can.

We are about to dive below Cocoa and deal directly with the Objective-C language and runtime, an area that even many experienced Cocoa programmers rarely explore. But relax. Our journey will be short and simple.

So first, we will add #import <objc/runtime.h> to the list of includes in
BBSceneController.m since we need to use some Objective-C runtime functions.

Next, we implement a new method called invokeLoadResources. The algorithm will be as
follows:

- Get a list of all the classes that exist.

- For each class in the list, find out if the class is a BBSceneObject or
  subclass.

- If found, call the loadResources class method.

To get the list of classes, we will use the Objective-C runtime function
objc_getClassList(). The function fills a buffer with all the classes and returns the
number of classes. We need to provide a buffer large enough to hold everything, so we
must call the function twice: the first time to figure out how large of a buffer to create,
and the second time to fill the buffer.

Then we iterate through the array of classes looking for BBSceneObject classes. NSObject
provides a class method called isSubclassOfClass:, which is exactly what we want to
use. But there is a slight gotcha: not all classes in the list are necessarily inherited from
NSObject. So we need to test to make sure the isSubclassOfClass: method actually
exists before we try using it. Another twist is that the method respondsToSelector: is
also an NSObject-provided method, so we can't use that either. The Objective-C runtime
provides class_respondsToSelector(), but it works only with instance methods, not
class methods, and isSubclassOfClass: is a class method. As a work-around, we use
the runtime function class_getClassMethod() to try to retrieve the isSubclassOfClass:
method directly. If we get a valid pointer, we know the method exists and it is safe to
invoke. And once we use the method, we will have our answer.

```
- (void) invokeLoadResources
{
    int number_of_classes;
    Class* list_of_classes = NULL;
    // Get the number of classes so we can create a buffer of the correct size
    number_of_classes = objc_getClassList(NULL, 0);
    if(number_of_classes <= 0)
    {
        return;
    }

    list_of_classes = malloc(sizeof(Class) * number_of_classes);
    number_of_classes = objc_getClassList(list_of_classes, number_of_classes);
    for(int i=0; i<number_of_classes; i++)
    {
        Class current_class = list_of_classes[i];
        if(class_getClassMethod(current_class, @selector(isSubclassOfClass:)))
        {
            if([current_class isSubclassOfClass:[BBSceneObject class]])
            {
                // We found a BBSceneObject
                if([current_class respondsToSelector:@selector(loadResources)])
                {
```

```
            objc_msgSend(current_class, @selector(loadResources));
        }
      }
    }
  }

  free(list_of_classes);
}
```

You might notice that we have an extra check to see if the class responds to `loadResources`. This is unnecessary if we implement a `loadResources` method in the parent `BBSceneObject` class for all to inherit. But if you don't do this, and decide to implement it as an optional protocol or informally require subclasses to implement it only if they use it, the extra check will avoid problems.

Also, instead of the traditional bracket invocation [`current_class loadResources`], you may notice the `objc_msgSend()`. Ultimately, the bracket notation is converted down to an `objc_msgSend()`, so it is the same exact call. We do this because the compiler will give an annoying warning with the brackets that the class may not respond to `loadResources`, since the compiler doesn't know what the class type is.

> **NOTE**: One of my astute reviewers asked a very good question. In the line that contains `malloc`, how many classes are we talking about, and is this something we can afford to do on an embedded device? I reviewed the numbers. In my final Space Rocks example, there are 1079 classes, and the size of `Class` is 4 bytes. So we are looking at 4316 bytes, which is tiny compared to the typical amounts of memory we use for resources like sounds and textures.

Finally, don't forget to invoke this method. We will do so in *BBSceneController*'s `init` method, which we added a little earlier:

```
- (id) init
{
    self = [super init];
    if(nil != self)
    {
        [[OpenALSoundController sharedSoundController] setSoundCallbackDelegate:self];
        [self invokeLoadResources];
    }
    return self;
}
```

This `loadResources` design works for a single-level game like Space Rocks!, but for larger games that may have separate levels, you want to load only the resources that you actually use; otherwise, you may exhaust your memory limits. This may mean needing to implement more fine-grained control within your `loadResources` method, as well as needing to implement finer-grain control on deciding which classes need to be loaded. You may find yourself back to manually managing lists of classes. But I hope that this example gives you some ideas on how reflection and dynamism can help you eliminate tedious and error-prone code.

Now we can add our `loadResources` class method to the `BBMissile` class. To load our sound file, we can use our convenience method in `EWSoundSourceObject`:

```
+ (void) loadResources
{
    [[OpenALSoundController sharedSoundController]
        soundBufferDataFromFileBaseName:LASER1];
}
```

And before in the awake method, we have this:

```
[[OpenALSoundController sharedSoundController] playLaser];
```

We can replace this line with the following line:

```
[self.soundSourceObject playSound:[EWSoundSourceObject soundBufferData:LASER1]];
```

We no longer need the hard-coded methods for playLaser, playExplosion*, and so on in the OpenALSoundController. This would be a good time to delete all those methods.

In *BBRock.m*, we follow the same `loadResources` pattern and the same replacement strategy as before, substituting the following lines in the obvious places:

```
+ (void) loadResources
{
    [[OpenALSoundController sharedSoundController]
        soundBufferDataFromFileBaseName:EXPLOSION1];
    [[OpenALSoundController sharedSoundController]
        soundBufferDataFromFileBaseName:EXPLOSION2];
}
```

```
[self.soundSourceObject playSound:
    [[OpenALSoundController sharedSoundController]
        soundBufferDataFromFileBaseName:EXPLOSION1]];
[self.soundSourceObject playSound:
    [[OpenALSoundController sharedSoundController]
        soundBufferDataFromFileBaseName:EXPLOSION2]];
```

Finally, in *BBSpaceShip.m*, we want to follow a similar loading and replacement strategy:

```
+ (void) loadResources
{
    [[OpenALSoundController sharedSoundController]
        soundBufferDataFromFileBaseName:THRUST1];
}
```

```
[self.soundSourceObject stopSound];
[self.soundSourceObject playSound:
    [[OpenALSoundController sharedSoundController]
        soundBufferDataFromFileBaseName:THRUST1]];
```

But we also need to set the looping property to `true` to make sure the sound loops. Since this sound always loops when we play it, we can set it just once in the awake method:

```
self.soundSourceObject.audioLooping = AL_TRUE;
```

Whew! You made it! Now when you play your game, it should be similar to before, but all the problems we identified, such as the hiccups on the first play and the multiple firings and explosions being cut off, should be fixed.

Handling When All Available Sources Are Exhausted

In the case where you do have more sounds to play than sources available, you need to develop some kind of policy. There are many different ways to handle this, and you must decide what makes the most sense for your application. Here are some possibilities:

- The easiest policy is not to play any new sounds. This is currently what our code does. However, it isn't very satisfying when a new asteroid explosion doesn't make a sound. (Fortunately for us, it is really hard to exhaust all our sources.)

- You could stop the oldest playing sounds and reallocate them for the new sounds. But again, you need to consider your application. In Space Rocks!, imagine if the engine thrust were the oldest playing sound. The user will probably notice that sound disappearing more than some distant asteroid explosion. And if you do reallocate a sound, you will need to consider how it will interact with a callback system such as soundDidFinishPlaying. If the system was being used in clever ways such as sound effect chaining, you will need to consider how a premature ending of a sound effect will affect things. You will also need to consider if you even want to fire the callback at all or cancel it. You might want to introduce a new callback for canceled events.

- You could use a policy based on distance. But imagine a little enemy UFO in the distance shooting at you. Even though it is farther away, it is arguably more important to hear than some other objects.

- You might attach priority values to sound events. A game designer can set these priority levels, and when culling needs to happen, you can eliminate the sounds that have the lowest priority levels. Note that you will still need a policy to figure out what to do in a tie.

Final Demo Embellishments

SpaceRocksSoundResourceManager2 includes some final embellishments (for this chapter) for your consideration.

First, we add a new explosion sound effect for when the spaceship is destroyed (see Figure 10-8) Then an example of using the soundDidFinishPlaying callbacks to trigger a game event has been added. On player death, instead of letting the ship death animation be the trigger to bring up the Game Over prompt, we change the program so the trigger is the playback end of the new death explosion sound (see Figure 10-9) Look for the changes in BBSpaceShip.

Figure 10-8. *A big, messy explosion sound with metallic debris is played when the ship is destroyed.*

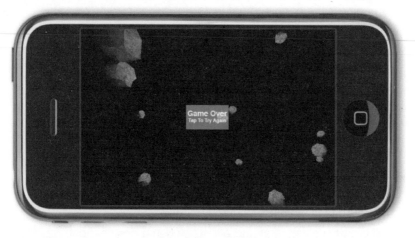

Figure 10-9. *Using the soundDidFinishPlaying callback system, we display the Game Over button after the spaceship explosion sound effect completes playback.*

We also add some sound effects to the UFO. It has a unique engine hum, which loops while the UFO is in the scene. Similar to the spaceship audio, we need to make sure the looping sound is terminated in various corner cases, such as when a new game is selected. The engine hum tends to overwhelm all the other sound effects, so we use the gainLevel property we defined to reduce the volume. There is also a new missile sound effect for the UFO's weapon[17] (see Figure 10-10). And the UFO will now make an

---

[17] The UFO and missile were fairly late additions to the engine upon my request to Ben because I needed some extra noise generators for the next chapter. This time, I was ready with a real missile sound to use, though ironically, the graphics for the alien-looking missile could probably use any sound, including my original wimpy laser.

explosion sound when destroyed. It shares the same explosion sound as the spaceship (see Figure 10-11). Look at the BBUFO class for changes.

Figure 10-10. *The UFO missile is given a missile launch sound effect, and the UFO now has an alien engine hum.*

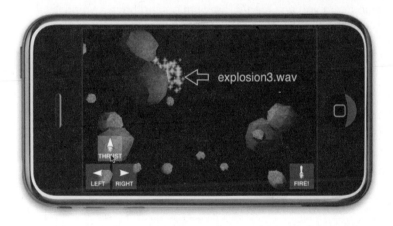

Figure 10-11. *The UFO reuses the same explosion sound as the spaceship when it is destroyed.*

Finally, we revisit the earlier audio interruption bug with the stuck engine sound. If you recall, the problem is that once the OpenAL context is disabled, any sound commands we run essentially become no-ops. This solution records the stopSound commands so they can be invoked later when the interruption has ended and we get back a valid OpenAL context.

There are many ways to record commands for later playback—some tedious and painful, and some too simplistic to scale as a general solution. This solution tries to be a little more clever and elegant, once again turning to the dynamism of Objective-C. This time, we stay at the Cocoa level instead of going down to the lower-level Objective-C runtime directly, and use NSInvocation to capture our Objective-C messages and store them in an NSMutableArray for later playback. For those unfamiliar with NSInvocation and this general idea, it is the same underlying principle and technology that allows the Cocoa's Undo Manager to work. Again, you will probably never see a technique like this applied to OpenGL or OpenAL in another book, so enjoy.

This demo applies the queue for both stopping and playing sounds. This could be further extended to other commands as well. Whether delayed commands for things like play make sense will depend on your application. (In our case, it is arguably questionable to queue a missile-firing sound when the missile could be long dead by the time the interruption ends, but this was done to demonstrate the technique.)

Look at OpenALSoundController and EWSoundSourceObject for the changes. More specifically, look at MyInterruptionCallback in OpenSoundController, and playSound:, stopSound, and the helper function CreateAutoreleasedInvocation in EWSoundSourceObject.

Save Point Reached

Congratulations! You made it to the end of this chapter. In this chapter, you were introduced to the concepts, history, and workings of OpenAL. We have taken on some of the more difficult issues in designing an OpenAL application and have a working example underway. We will continue to build on this code in the next two chapters.

3D Audio—Turning Noise into Game Sounds

Chapter 10 got a little heavy, but as I promised at the end of that chapter, things will lighten up in this chapter. We now get to apply 3D effects to our audio! No longer will we be making just a simple noise. We will be applying rich characteristics to the sounds that better represent the entities in your game.

To access 3D effects, we will be using OpenAL exclusively (as I noted in Chapter 10, I'm taking a mostly OpenAL-centric approach to my coverage of audio for iPhone games). This is not to say you couldn't implement 3D effects yourself without OpenAL, but OpenAL has already done a lot of the heavy lifting for you. OpenAL supports multiple properties to represent your sounds in 3D space. These are things like position, direction (or orientation), and velocity. In addition, OpenAL supports several distance-attenuation models.

We are going to walk through the complete feature list of 3D effects OpenAL provides out of the box, and apply them to Space Rocks! So without further ado, let's get started.

The Design of OpenAL: Sources, Buffers, and Listeners

OpenAL is designed around three fundamental object types (see Figure 11–1). You have already been introduced to the first two in the previous chapter.

The first object type is the buffer. As you have already seen, you give OpenAL buffers linear PCM data that contains your sounds. You can have a lot of different buffers, each to hold a different sound.

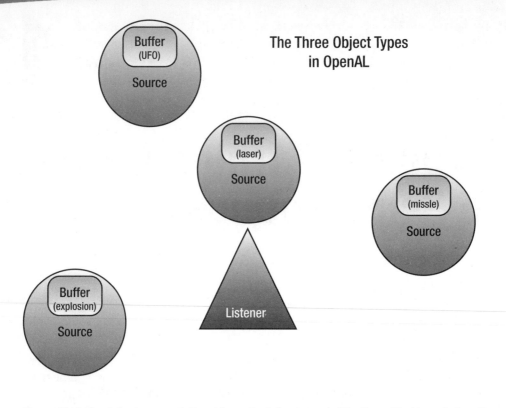

The Three Object Types
in OpenAL

Figure 11–1. *An abstract representation of Space Rocks! composed of the three object types in OpenAL: sources, buffers, and listeners. Imagine your ship is the listener. The sources around the ship map to game entity positions. Each playing source has a buffer attached to it which contains a particular sound effect.*

The second object type is the source. As you have seen, sources emit sound. You attach a specific buffer to a source so it emits the sound that you want. But there is more to them than that. Sources represent objects in 3D space, so they have a position value, a velocity value and other properties. You can think of a source as your noisemaking game entities. In fact, we already did this in the previous chapter by giving each BBSceneObject, such as our projectile weapons, its own EWSoundSourceObject that ultimately holds an OpenAL source when it is playing sounds. But we didn't apply any 3D properties to the sources. We will correct that omission in this chapter.

The third object type is the listener. Succinctly, you can think of the listener as "you" or "your head and ears." In OpenAL, the sources emit sounds, but for things like position to make any sense, they must be relative to something. Something must be able to hear the sounds. So the listener object is that something. Like sources, the listener also has 3D properties, such as position, velocity, and orientation. For example, in a game, if we place the listener in the center of a room facing north, and we place a radio (source) on the west wall of the room, it will sound like the radio is on your left. In the real world, assuming you have two speakers, left and right, OpenAL will render that sound so it comes out of only your left speaker. Similarly, in Figure 11–1, the source with the explosion sound that is to the left of the listener will come out on the left speaker.

Every OpenAL context provides exactly one listener. So, even though it was not mentioned, you have already implicitly created a listener in the previous chapter. You may think of the OpenAL context as holding all the listener's state, such as position and velocity values. While you have many buffers and sources, you can have only one active listener at a time, as you can have only one current context.

OpenAL provides a set of generic APIs to access properties of each of the three types. You've already been exposed to the API for sources. To reiterate, with sources, we have the generic family of functions to set a property on the source:

```
void alSourcef(ALuint source_id, ALenum parameter, ALfloat value );
void alSource3f(ALuint source_id, ALenum parameter, ALfloat value1, ALfloat value2,
ALfloat value3);
void alSourcefv(ALuint source_id, ALenum parameter, const ALfloat* values);
void alSourcei(ALuint source_id, ALenum parameter, ALint value);
void alSource3i(ALuint source_id, ALenum parameter, ALint value1, ALint value2, ALint
    value3);
void alSourceiv(ALuint source_id, ALenum parameter, const ALint* values);
```

The `parameter` is an OpenAL constant that represents a specific property you want to set, such as `AL_BUFFER` and `AL_LOOPING` (introduced in Chapter 10). There are multiple versions of the function because each is for a different type. As in OpenGL, f stands for float, v stands for array (or vector), 3 means three values, and i means integer.

For brevity, here is a condensed notation for the preceding set of functions:

```
alSource{f, 3f, fv, i, 3i, iv}(ALuint source_id, ALenum parameter, ...)
```

This notation will let me introduce similar sets of functions without needing to use up so much space.

To get property values, we have the generic family of functions:

```
alGetSource{f, 3f, fv, i, 3i, iv}(ALuint source_id, ALenum parameter, ...)
```

Similarly, for the listener, we have a parallel set of functions. Notice there is no ID value passed in, because the listener is implicitly inferred from the current active context.

```
alListener{f, 3f, fv, i, 3i, iv}(ALenum parameter, ...)
alGetListener{f, 3f, fv, i, 3i, iv}(ALenum parameter, ...)
```

Buffers also have these functions:

```
alBuffer{f, 3f, fv, i, 3i, iv}(ALuint buffer_id, ALenum parameter, ...)
alGetBuffer{f, 3f, fv, i, 3i, iv}(ALuint buffer_id, ALenum parameter, ...)
```

For generic things that don't apply to our three object types, but globally to the OpenAL system as a whole, OpenAL also offers the following generic functions:

```
void alGetBooleanv(ALenum parameter, ALboolean* data);
void alGetIntegerv(ALenum parameter, ALint* data);
void alGetFloatv(ALenum parameter, ALfloat* data);
void alGetDoublev(ALenum parameter, ALdouble* data);
ALboolean alGetBoolean(ALenum parameter);
ALint alGetInteger(ALenum parameter);
ALfloat alGetFloat(ALenum parameter);
ALdouble alGetDouble(ALenum parameter);
```

One example for these is to set and get values for the Doppler effect provided by OpenAL. We will talk about the Doppler effect later in the chapter.

Limits of 3D Audio in OpenAL

There are two important restrictions you need to be aware of if you want to use spatialized sound in OpenAL:

- You must use monaural (single-channel) buffers if you want them to be spatialized. If you provide a stereo sample, OpenAL will not spatialize it.

- You must have more than one speaker on your equipment if you want to actually hear positional sound. On the current models of the iPhone, your applications emit through only a single speaker when using the built-in speakers, so you will not be able to hear anything different with respect to the position property (not counting distance attenuation). On an iPhone or iPod touch, you should plug in headphones or external speakers if you want to fully hear all the effects OpenAL is applying.

OpenAL insulates you from the user's actual output equipment and configuration.[1] For example, you may have 2 speakers, but your friend has 7.1 speakers (as in a surround-sound setup). OpenAL doesn't give you access to this information. In the world of OpenAL, you are not supposed to care. The fundamental idea is that OpenAL and the underlying sound system are supposed to know how to spatialize sound correctly for your specific equipment.

So let's go back to our room example. You are still standing in the center of the room facing north with a radio on the wall directly west of you. You turn 90 degrees to the right. It is OpenAL's job to figure out that the noise should be heard coming from directly behind you, and then work with the underlying sound system to generate the noise to come out the right way for your equipment. Hypothetically in the ideal situation, on the system with 7.1 speakers (with a back-speaker configuration), the sound will come out of the back speaker.

Not all OpenAL implementations and underlying sound systems are able to support advanced speaker configurations. But as an end user of OpenAL, there is not much you can do about it, as the API isn't designed to give you direct access to control the individual speakers.

Integrating the Listener into Space Rocks!

The strategy for this chapter is to introduce each piece of functionality one at a time and keep building on top of the prior example until we have a full-featured game. But before

---

[1] There is a feature called device enumeration, but all you have are the names of devices, which could be anything.

we can start adding any properties, we need to do a bit of setup work to integrate a listener into Space Rocks! But don't worry, this will be easy. It is almost going to mirror how we handled source objects.

Creating the Listener Class

We will start by creating a new class to encapsulate the listener. We currently have a `EWSoundSourceObject` to encapsulate source objects. Let's create a new class called `EWSoundListenerObject` to complement it.

Do you remember that we made `EWSoundSourceObject` a subclass of `EWSoundState`? The reason is now revealed. There are some properties, such as gain level, that are common between sources and listeners. Why not share those commonalities by sharing a common parent class? So we will also make our `EWSoundListenerObject` a subclass of `EWSoundState`.

You might be thinking that we should do something extra because multiple sources are allowed, but there is only one listener per context. For simplicity, we are not going to worry about this issue. We will know to create only one instance of the listener in Space Rocks![2]

We will continue extending our code using the project `SpaceRocksSoundResourceManager2` from the end of the previous chapter as our starting position. The completed project for this next part of the example for implementing the listener is named `SpaceRocksOpenAL3D_0_Listener`.

Let's create the class. In *EWSoundListenerObject.h*, make `EWSoundListenerObject` a subclass of `EWSoundState`:

```
@interface EWSoundListenerObject : EWSoundState
{
}

@end
```

As with our `EWSoundSourceObject` from the previous chapter, we will expect to have two methods defined: `update` and `applyState`. The `update` method just calls `applyState`. This is also a good time to remind you that our `EWSoundState` parent class has the property `gainLevel`, which we implemented in `EWSoundSourceObject`. The OpenAL listener also supports the gain property (which is why we put it in the parent class), so let's take this opportunity to implement it in *EWSoundListenerObject.m*. The code is an almost identical mirror of `EWSoundSourceObject`. The only difference is that we need to use the `AL_GAIN` parameter, rather than `alSourcef`, to set the gain level on the listener.

---

[2] If we did want to handle this complexity, we might keep the OpenAL context associated with the listener as an instance variable in our listener class and check to see if our context is the current context before we try anything. Or we could go the other way and assume there is always only one context and make the class a singleton.

```
- (void) applyState
{
    [super applyState];
    if([[OpenALSoundController sharedSoundController] inInterruption])
    {
        return;
    }
    alListenerf(AL_GAIN, gainLevel);
}

- (void) update
{
    [super update];
    [self applyState];
}
```

And that's all we need for the basic infrastructure for the listener. But first, we want to integrate the use of our new listener class.

Picking the Designated Driver

We now come to a design decision point in our game. Who or what is going to be our listener in the game? Perhaps a clearer and more pointed version of this question is this: Where in the game world is our listener going to be located?

I think the most natural thing to do is to make our spaceship the listener, as in Figure 11–1. That means we put our "head and ears" where the spaceship is in the game. Thus, when the spaceship moves or turns, we move the listener with it. But we could make other choices. We could decide the listener is always in the dead center of the screen and never moves. This might actually seem very natural to the player. Or we could get creative and put the listener on the UFO or an asteroid. We could even make the listener a game selectable option, so it can be moved around. However, for this example, we will make the spaceship the listener, as it is easiest to conceptualize.

Now that we have chosen our designated listener, we need to integrate the code. If you recall, we gave every `BBSceneObject` an instance of `EWSoundSourceObject`. Well, let's follow that analogy and also add a `EWSoundListenerObject` to the `BBSpaceShip` class.

First, we add the new instance variable/property to the class in *BBSpaceShip.h*. Then we make sure to allocate a new instance of it at the end of *BBSpaceShip.m*'s awake method.

```
soundListenerObject = [[EWSoundListenerObject alloc] init];
```

Don't forget to release it in the `dealloc` method.

```
[soundListenerObject release];
```

Finally, add the following line to the end of *BBSpaceShip.m*'s update method. This will make sure the changes are applied at during every update loop.

```
[self.soundListenerObject update];
```

That's all there is to it. We have integrated the listener into Space Rocks!.

You may be wondering what the gain level does for the listener. You might think of it as the master volume control for OpenAL. By default, the listener gain is set to 1.0. If you changed it to 0.5, everything you hear will have its volumes cut by half. If you set it to 0.0, you will hear nothing. If you would like to experiment, try adding something like the following line right after you allocate the soundListenerObject at the end of the awake method:

```
soundListenerObject.gainLevel = 0.5;
```

We will not utilize our gainLevel property in Space Rocks!. For an example of the listener gain used as a master volume control, see the BasicOpenALStreaming example in the next chapter.

Adding Positions to Sounds

Now we are ready to add our very first 3D property: position. Both sources and the listener have position properties, so we need to implement them in both of our classes. We will continue from the project SpaceRocksOpenAL3D_0_Listener. The completed project for this example is named SpaceRocksOpenAL3D_1_Position. The end result for the example is illustrated in Figure11–2.

Figure 11–2. *With our spaceship as the listener, once we add positions to our sounds, the explosion should come from the front-left speaker, and the UFO sound should come from the front-right speaker, assuming some kind of surround-sound setup.*

Let's start in the parent class, EWSoundState. We will add a new instance variable to hold position values. We will use BBPoint, since it is perfect for this job—having x, y, and z coordinates works just as well for OpenAL as it does for OpenGL. Our class interface now looks like this:

```
#import <Foundation/Foundation.h>
#import <OpenAL/al.h>
#import "BBPoint.h"

@interface EWSoundState : NSObject
{
    ALfloat gainLevel;
```

```
    BBPoint objectPosition;
}

@property(nonatomic, assign) ALfloat gainLevel;
@property(nonatomic, assign) BBPoint objectPosition;

// virtual functions which should be overridden by subclasses
- (void) applyState;
- (void) update;

@end
```

Just to be explicit, we can initialize the value in the init method (though this is not really required):

```
- (id) init
{
    self = [super init];
    if(nil != self)
    {
        gainLevel = 1.0f;
        objectPosition = BBPointMake(0.0, 0.0, 0.0);
    }
    return self;
}
```

Now that we have a position value in the parent class, we need to make our subclasses utilize it so they can set the OpenAL positions for their sources and listener. In *EWSoundSourceObject.m*, add the following line to applyState, immediately after the line setting AL_GAIN, AL_LOOPING, and AL_PITCH:

```
alSource3f(sourceID, AL_POSITION, objectPosition.x, objectPosition.y, objectPosition.z);
```

> **NOTE:** You may have noticed I am accessing the instance variables directly instead of using the accessors, which is inconsistent with the other lines in this method. It is an optimization ploy. We are going to add a lot of these lines, and they are going to be called frequently, so we might need to save on the number of objc_msgSend method calls being invoked. If I were to go back and be consistent, I would remove the accessors from the other lines in this method. But I like showing this discrepancy because people new to Objective-C often forget that there is a subtle difference between using an accessor via dot notation and manipulating an instance variable directly.

Similarly, in *EWSoundListenerObject.m*, add this line in applyState after AL_GAIN is set:

```
alListener3f(AL_POSITION, objectPosition.x, objectPosition.y, objectPosition.z);
```

Since applyState is called on every game loop pass (frame), this causes the OpenAL positions to be set every pass.

Now we need to make sure objectPosition values stay in tandem with the actual scene objects they represent. So first, let's make sure the source positions stay in sync.

Let's go to BBSceneObject's update method. You might remember that we already added a line at the end of the update method to invoke the soundSourceObject's update method, which would in turn call its `applyState` and set our existing properties, such as `gainLevel` and `audioLooping`. Immediately before that line, we need to set the `soundSourceObject`'s position value so `applyState` can set the correct value. To do this, we can just copy the `BBSceneObject`'s translation value to our `soundSourceObject`'s value. It turns out that our coordinate system for `BBSceneObjects` is the same as the coordinate system for OpenAL. (This should be no surprise, as the `BBSceneObject` coordinate system was designed to work with OpenGL's coordinate system, and OpenGL and OpenAL are designed to use the same coordinate systems.)

The last two lines in `BBSceneObject`'s `update` method should look like these:

```
self.soundSourceObject.objectPosition = translation;
[self.soundSourceObject update];
```

Now let's update the listener position. To do that, we go to *BBSpaceShip.m* and modify the `update` method so the last two lines look like these:

```
self.soundListenerObject.objectPosition = translation;
[self.soundListenerObject update];
```

There is also a bug fix we need to apply. A little higher in the method, there is an early `return` statement in an `if` clause as an optimization. This will avoid updating our `soundListenerObject` if the method returns early, so we need to change this so it doesn't return early. We will just comment out the line. And to avoid any precision errors later in the code, let's explicitly set `forwardMag` to 0, since the threshold check considers small values to be 0.

```
if (forwardMag <= 0.0001)
{
    if(YES == isThrusting)
    {
        [self.soundSourceObject stopSound];
    }
    isThrusting = NO;
//  return; // we are not moving so return early
    forwardMag = 0.0;
    }
```

Handling Initial Positioning on Creation

There is one more thing we need to do, which is simple, but a little tedious. We currently have a corner-case bug where our source and listener classes do not have the correct position value on the initial creation. Right now, our code depends on the update loop to synchronize our sound objects with the actual values from the `BBSceneObject`. So it is possible for an object to start playing sound in the wrong position, and it won't be corrected until the update loop is reached.

The easiest place to fix this is in the `awake` method. And the best place to do this is in the `BBSceneObject`'s `awake` method so all the subclasses inherit the behavior. But there is a slight problem with that because not all the `BBSceneObject` subclasses call `[super awake]`. So, we need to refactor and fix all the code in the project to call `[super awake]` and implement `BBSceneObject`'s `awake` method to be as follows:

```
-(void)awake
{
    soundSourceObject.objectPosition = translation;
}
```

> **NOTE:** All the refactoring and implementation is already done in SpaceRocksOpenAL
> 3D_1_Position. Because there are a considerable number of line changes, and they have
> more to do with design implementation than audio, I encourage you to use this project instead of
> trying to reimplement all this yourself.

Finally, we need to handle the same corner case for the listener, so at the end of the BBSpaceShip's awake method, directly after we allocate the new object, we need to copy the position:

```
soundListenerObject      = [[EWSoundListenerObject alloc] init];
soundListenerObject.objectPosition = translation;
```

You now have enough code to actually try it. If you do, you might hear positional audio (provided you have headphones or external speakers). Wait for the UFO to come in. The engine noise should pan from your left speaker to the right speaker as it moves across the screen (see Figure 11–2).

But more likely, you will have a very hard time hearing the UFO. At best, the noise is generally really quiet when it first comes in, then gets louder as the UFO moves to the center, and then gets quiets as it moves away. This is because OpenAL has its distance attenuation feature enabled by default. Because we won't talk about distance attenuation until later in the chapter, let's just disable this feature for now.

Disabling Distance Attenuation

OpenAL provides a simple function to change the distance attenuation model, called alDistanceModel(ALenum distance_model). The distance attenuation models are covered in detail later in this chapter. For the curious, the default model is AL_INVERSE_DISTANCE_CLAMPED. To disable it, we just need to set the value to AL_NONE:

```
alDistanceModel(AL_NONE);
```

Let's create a setter and getter in our OpenALSoundController class:

```
- (void) setDistanceModel:(ALenum)distance_model
{
    alDistanceModel(distance_model);
}

- (ALenum) distanceModel
{
    ALint distance_model;
    distance_model = alGetInteger(AL_DISTANCE_MODEL);
    return (ALenum)distance_model;
}
```

Notice that there is no direct function to query the distance model. Instead, we use the generic alGet* functions to retrieve the value.

And let's make `BBSceneController` the controller of the distance model. In `BBSceneController`'s init method, we invoke our newly implemented `setDistanceModel` to turn off distance attenuation:

```
- (id) init
{
    self = [super init];
    if(nil != self)
    {
        [[OpenALSoundController sharedSoundController] setSoundCallbackDelegate:self];
        [self invokeLoadResources];
        [[OpenALSoundController sharedSoundController] setDistanceModel:AL_NONE];
    }
    return self;
}
```

That's all you need if you have a properly working implementation of OpenAL.

Working Around an alDistanceModelBug: Disabling Attenuation on a Per-Source Basis

Unfortunately, as of iPhone OS 3.1.2, it seems that setting the distance model to AL_NONE fails to disable distance attenuation.[3] So here, I'll show you another way to disable distance attenuation. Those not affected by the bug may want to read this section anyway, because it introduces another OpenAL source property called the rolloff factor.

The rolloff factor controls how quickly a sound attenuates as it gets farther away if you are using distance attenuation. Since this is a source property, you may set different rolloff factors on different sources. The OpenAL spec also says if you want to disable attenuation on a per-source basis, you can set the source's rolloff factor to 0.0. We will exploit this behavior to disable attenuation for our entire game, by setting the rolloff factors to 0.0 on all our sources.

Since this is just a source property, we are going to add a new instance variable to *EWSoundSourceObject.h*:

```
ALfloat rolloffFactor;
```

Declare a property for it for later convenience:

```
@property(nonatomic, assign) ALfloat rolloffFactor;
```

Don't forget to synthesize it.

In *EWSoundSourceObject.m*'s init method, we set the default value to 0.0:

---

[3] Apple's desktop implementation does work correctly. Interestingly, this is the only significant behavioral difference I've noticed between Apple's Mac and iPhone implementations of OpenAL (excluding capture, which is discussed in Chapter 12).

```
rolloffFactor = 0.0; // 0.0 disables attenuation
```

And in applyState, we make sure to set the source property:

```
alSourcef(sourceID, AL_ROLLOFF_FACTOR, rolloffFactor);
```

Now if you run the program, the positional audio should work without any attenuation being applied.[4] Whew!

Listener Orientation

The listener orientation represents the direction your "head and ears" are facing. Are you looking to the left? Are you looking right? Now remember that this is 3D space, so you might ask, "Is your head upside down"?

What do I mean by that last question? In the last example, our spaceship is looking toward the top of the screen. When the UFO first appears, it is on the left side of the screen and moves across to the right side. So we hear noise that originally starts by coming from the left speaker, and then moves to the right speaker as it crosses the field. But what if we turned our head 180 degrees to the left (more precisely, counterclockwise around the z axis), so we are looking toward the bottom of the screen? Now the sound of the UFO should start coming from the right speaker when it first appears and move to the left speaker as it crosses the field.

Now, let's reset. We are looking toward the top of the screen again. Let's imagine ourselves in the scene instead of a spaceship. Now do a headstand or bend forward and put your head between your legs so you are looking behind you (more precisely, spin 180 degrees around the x axis). You are facing the same direction as when we turned 180 degrees to the left, but the difference is that your head is now upside down. In this case, when the UFO comes, you hear it from your left ear instead of your right ear.

The point of the example was to illustrate that two vectors are needed to represent orientation. You need a direction, or at, vector that represents your line of sight, and an up vector to represent which way is up. As you can see from the two cases, even though both have the ship looking at the same direction, their orientation also makes a huge difference for determining which side the sound is on.

To properly set the two vectors in Space Rocks!, we need to examine our existing coordinate system. Next, we will review some math to help you understand and implement this correctly. Feel free to skip ahead if you know this already.

Right-Handed Coordinate Systems and the Right-Hand Rule

First, let's focus on determining the up vector. OpenGL and OpenAL use a right-handed coordinate system. In layman's terms, all this means is which way the z axis points if you

---

[4] I think I found another bug in the Apple implementation. Setting the Linear Distance model seems to ignore my rolloff factor = 0 disabling attempts.

have an x axis and a y axis. If you take your right hand, extend your thumb and index finger so it looks like a cocked gun, and then extend your middle finger so it is perpendicular to both your index finger and thumb, these fingers represent the axes you see in a right-handed coordinate system (see Figure 11–3). This is the right-hand rule.

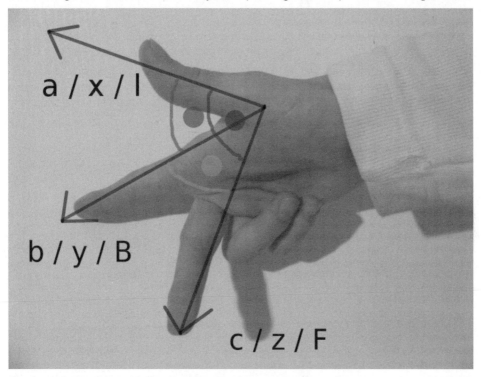

Figure 11–3. *The right-hand rule using three fingers to represent the x, y, and z axes. Picture by Abdull from Wikimedia Commons under the Creative Commons Attribution ShareAlike 3.0 License (http://commons.wikimedia.org/wiki/File:Rechte-hand-regel.jpg)*

Once you have your fingers in the correct position, the trick is to orient your hand so the axes line up with what you are trying to compare against. In Space Rocks!, if we spend a little time looking at the position values for all the objects, we see that x increases toward the right of the screen, and y increases toward the top of the screen. I like to point my middle finger to the right (x axis) and my thumb up (y axis), so that my index finger is pointing toward me. My index finger is pointing in the direction of the up vector, which is coming through the screen toward my body. Even though my hand is contorted, I like this convention because the common base case is to have the game-space axes match the computer-screen axes, where the x axis goes to the right and the y axis to goes up. This results in a gun-pointing-at-myself (shooting myself) position, which is something I could always easily remember for some strange reason.

If you got all that, then you can just move on to the next segment. But if you need more clarification, there is a variation of the right-hand rule for rotation called the right-hand grip rule that can be used as a substitute. Extend your palm with your thumb pointed up, as if to shake someone's hand, and then curl your fingers (see Figure 11–4). Your curled fingers point to the rotation direction. Your thumb is the vector.

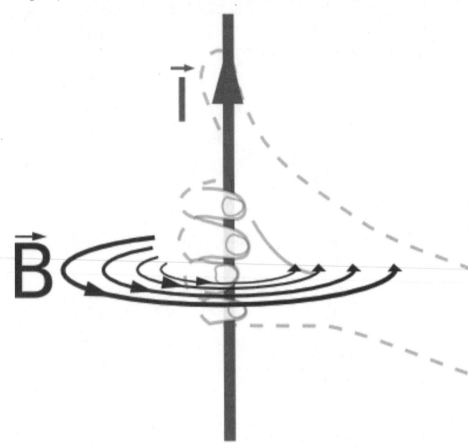

Figure 11–4. *The right-hand grip rule. Curl your fingers around the axis of rotation, and the thumb points in the direction of the up vector. This is often used in physics to find the direction of electric current (I) in a magnetic field (B), but we can also use it for audio purposes. Image from Wikimedia Commons under Public Domain (http://commons.wikimedia.org/wiki/File:Right_hand_rule.png)*

In physics, this would be used for torque and force, or magnetic fields and electric currents. In OpenGL, we often use it to figure out which way the normal vectors point when drawing a triangle. For OpenAL, we can also use it to find our up vector.

If we look at how we rotate the ship in the code, we find that the `rotation.z` instance variable in `BBSceneObject` contains an angle in degrees. The value increases as we turn counterclockwise in the game. Match your curled fingers to your screen so they go counterclockwise with the ship, and you'll see that your thumb points at you.

So we have systematically determined that our z axis points toward us when looking at the iPhone/iPod touch screen. Since we see the top of our spaceship (instead of the bottom), we know our ship's up orientation is aligned with the z axis. Since we also know our ship moves only in the x-y plane (because we have a 2D game), we can conclude that our listener's up vector needs to be <0.0, 0.0, 1.0>.

Unit Circle, Polar-to-Rectangular Coordinates, Phase Shifting, and Trigonometric Identities

This section's title may sound scary, especially if you hated high school math. But my intention is not to do a math lesson, but determine how to compute our listener's at vector. So I am going to zoom through this section and focus on just getting what we need.

Our problem is that we need to map our spaceship's BBSceneObject rotation.z value to the OpenAL listener coordinate system. Even though we know we are in a right-handed coordinate system, we have two obstacles:

- We have only an angle in degrees, and not a vector, so we need to convert.

- We need to determine where the origin of the rotation starts.

Let's start with the first problem.

First, I'm going to ask you to remember the unit circle, which is a way of converting angles to x and y coordinates (see Figure 11–5). This is exactly what we need to convert our rotation angle to a vector.

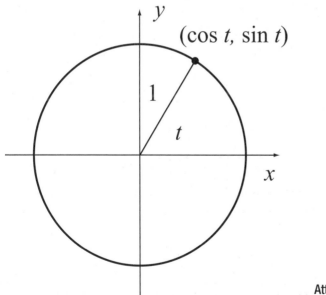

Attribution ShareAlike 3.0

Figure 11–5. *Unit circle with angles. By Gustavb from Wikimedia Commons under the Creative Commons License (http://commons.wikimedia.org/wiki/File:Unit_circle_angles.svg)*

The unit circle can be more generally expressed in terms of cosine and sine of an angle (see Figure 11–6).

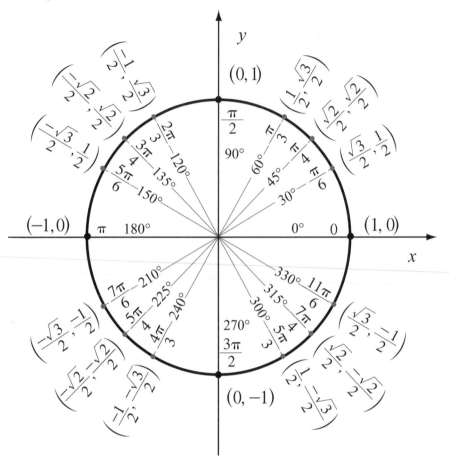

Figure 11–6. *Unit circle with cosine and sine. By Gustavb from Wikimedia Commons under the Creative Commons Attribution ShareAlike 3.0 License (http://commons.wikimedia.org/wiki/File:Unit_circle.svg)*

This leads us directly into polar-to-rectangular coordinate conversions. You can convert the angles to x and y values by these simple formulas:

$$x = r \cdot \cos(\theta)$$

$$y = r \cdot \sin(\theta)$$

Radius (r) is always 1 in the unit circle. Since we just need a direction vector, we are free to set r=1 to drop r out of the equation.

There, that wasn't so painful, right?

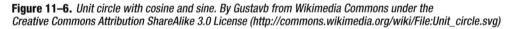

So all we need to do is drop in our angle (don't forget to convert from degrees to radians if you are using C math library functions), and we have our vector—well, almost. The second problem still needs to be solved.

The other problem is that our spaceship's starting orientation is different from the unit circle. Notice that when we start our game, for angle = 0, the ship is pointing toward the top of the screen (along the y axis). But the unit circle for angle = 0 points along the x axis (refer to Figure 11–6).

This means our spaceship is turned, or phase-shifted, by 90 degrees compared to the unit circle. So if we just plug into the above equations, our results will be wrong.

If you look at the x and y values around the unit circle in Figure 11–6, you'll notice that their magnitudes repeat around the circle, and it is only the positive and negative signs that change. I point this out to also remind you that cosine and sine are periodic (repeating) functions. (You can think of waveforms, too.) In fact, you can express sine in terms of cosine or vice versa, because they are essentially the same function, just shifted (based on the angle parameter).

This means that we can just look up a table of trigonometric identities (or derive it, if you really want to) to figure out what it means to phase-shift cosine and sine by 90 degrees to handle the fact that our spaceship starting orientation points along the y axis. This reveals the following useful identities:

$$\cos(\theta + 90°) = -\sin(\theta)$$

$$\sin(\theta + 90°) = \cos(\theta)$$

Substituting the identities into our original polar-to-rectangular conversion formulas, our equations change to the following:

$$x = -r \cdot \sin(\theta)$$

$$y = r \cdot \cos(\theta)$$

You can now breathe a big sigh of relief. Despite all those fancy math terms, we are left with two simple equations that we can drop directly into our source code.

Integration into Space Rocks!

Now we finally get to code. We are going to make the listener orientation match the spaceship orientation. So when the spaceship turns, the listener orientation will turn with it. For demonstration purposes, we will implement this, but you will need to decide whether it makes sense for your own game.

NOTE: I personally find the setup described here a little disorienting, because I tend to think of the orientation of the iPhone/iPod touch as the listener orientation and not the ship itself. If we used the accelerometer to rotate the ship so the ship always points up relative to the Earth and the device itself is rotated, I would be more onboard with the idea. But unfortunately, adding accelerometer support to Space Rocks! is a side quest too complicated for us to embark on given our time and space constraints for this book. So for demonstration purposes, ship orientation will have to do.

We will continue from the SpaceRocksOpenAL3D_1_Position project. The completed project for this example is named SpaceRocksOpenAL3D_2_Orientation.

In EWSoundListenerObject, we will add two BBPoint instance variables to represent our at and up vectors. OpenAL actually wants a six-element array, but I prefer to use two BBPoint values for our class.

Create an init method in *EWSoundListenerObject.m* so we can initialize the vectors with legal default values:

```
- (id) init
{
    self = [super init];
    if(nil != self)
    {
        atOrientation = BBPointMake(0.0f, 1.0f, 0.0f); // looking along Y
        upOrientation = BBPointMake(0.0f, 0.0f, 1.0f); // Z is up
    }
    return self;
}
```

Note that the up vector will never change, since we are in a 2D game and the up direction for the ship never changes.

In the applyState method, we set the value in OpenAL. Place it directly after the line where we set the AL_POSITION:

```
ALfloat orientation_array[6] = {
    atOrientation.x, atOrientation.y, atOrientation.z,
    upOrientation.x, upOrientation.y, upOrientation.z
};
alListenerfv(AL_ORIENTATION, orientation_array);
```

As I said, OpenAL wants a six-element array to set the listener orientation, so we must stuff our values in an array to hand it off.

Finally, to synchronize our listener value with BBSpaceShip's, in *BBSpaceShip.m*'s awake method, we add the following two lines to the very end of the method utilizing the equations presented in the previous section:

```
CGFloat radians = rotation.z/BBRADIANS_TO_DEGREES;
self.soundListenerObject.atOrientation = BBPointMake(-sinf(radians), cosf(radians),
0.0);
```

And in the update method, we can add the following line at the end of the method immediately before we call update on the soundListenerObject. The value of radians was already computed earlier in the same method.

```
self.soundListenerObject.atOrientation = BBPointMake(-sinf(radians), cosf(radians), 0.0);
```

Now run the program and try rotating your ship into different positions to see how it affects from which speaker sound emits. For fun, try re-creating the scenario in Figure 11–3.

Source Direction and Cones

While listeners have the property called orientation, sources have a similar property called direction. Direction is used in conjunction with another property called cones. Used together, these properties will allow you to constrain a sound to a particular direction. As an example, think of a person speaking into a megaphone/bullhorn. Anyone in front of the person speaking will hear what the person says. But anyone behind the person speaking will hear a greatly reduced sound, if anything at all.

In OpenAL, source direction has only one vector, unlike listener orientation, which has two vectors. OpenAL assumes that the sound emission is symmetric around the direction vector. So in our megaphone example, if the person speaking were to rotate the megaphone 180 degrees around the shaft axis (without changing the direction in which he was speaking), the sound emitted would be no different, even though the megaphone is upside down.

Inner Cone, Outer Cone, and Transitional Zone

Now hold on. Things might get a little tricky here. OpenAL provides not one, but two cones to play with per source: an inner cone and an outer cone. The inner cone is probably what you were thinking of when I first said cones. Any listener within this cone will play at its normal volume level.

In our megaphone example, if you (the listener) are standing directly in front of the person speaking into the megaphone (you are in the inner cone), you will hear the person speaking at his normal volume level. So think of an unpowered, nonamplified, acoustical bullhorn. OpenAL doesn't amplify sound.[5] Therefore, "full blast" is just normal sound.

The other important point is that OpenAL defines an outer cone. If the listener is outside both the inner and outer cone, the volume will play at a special gain level you can set, called the AL_CONE_OUTER_GAIN.

---

[5] The spec says implementations are free to amplify if you set the gain beyond 1.0, but the spec also says implementations are allowed to cap at 1.0 if they choose. This is to avoid clipping distortion.

This leaves the area between the inner cone and the outer cone, which is called the transitional zone. When a listener is inside this zone, the volume is interpolated between the inner cone gain level and the outer cone gain level.

Stare at the illustration in Figure 11–7 to try to make sense of what I just said. You may want to reread the above paragraphs a few times to see how that information matches with the diagram.

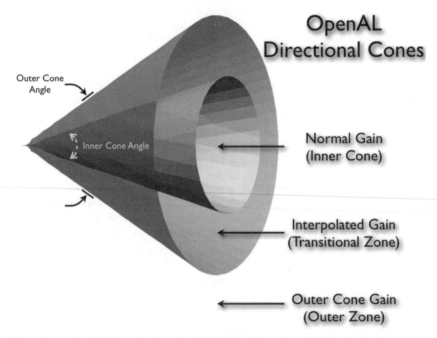

Figure 11–7. *OpenAL directional cones with their angles and zones labeled*

Continuing with our megaphone example, let's say you are standing directly behind the person with the megaphone and define this as part of the outer zone. Let's say the outer cone gain level is 0. This means you can't hear anything the person is saying. But if we say the outer cone gain level is 0.5, this means you hear the person at half volume. (You might conceptualize this as the ambient background sound.)

Finally, let's say you are standing next to the person speaking and define this as part of the transitional zone. The volume you hear will be somewhere between normal (full blast), and the outer cone gain level. So, for simplicity, we might say if the outer cone gain level is 0, and the normal gain is 1, you might hear the volume at 0.5 (though the actual value would be determined by the actual cone sizes you set).

Now that you have an understanding of OpenAL directional cones for sources, we should have an example of how to use them. For demonstration purposes, we will utilize the fact that the UFO spins. We will apply a directional cone to the UFO engine hum. When the inner cone is facing the spaceship, you will hear normal volume. As the inner cone spins away, you will hear the volume level decay. And, of course, it will spin back and the volume will increase again.

> **NOTE:** Cones seem to be a rather unused feature of OpenAL. I have to admit I had a hard time coming up with an example for Space Rocks! One of the more intuitive ideas I came up with was a cone-shaped tractor beam. When you are inside the tractor beam, you hear a louder noise than when you are outside the beam. But you need both a source and a listener to get involved to hear the difference, so I would need to have the UFO hit the spaceship with a tractor beam. Given the lack of time, lack of art assets to visualize this through OpenGL, and the lack of engine support for beam weapons, not to mention the complexity of explaining this, I have opted to do a much simpler example.

Implementation Time

Now it's time to implement source direction and cones in Space Rocks! We continue from SpaceRocksOpenAL3D_2_Orientation. The finished project for this example is named SpaceRocksOpenAL3D_3_DirectionCones.

In *EWSoundSourceObject.h*, we add the following instance variables:

```
BBPoint atDirection;
ALfloat coneInnerAngle;
ALfloat coneOuterAngle;
ALfloat coneOuterGain;
```

Also declare properties for these so we can access them outside the class later. Don't forget to synthesize them in the implementation.

```
@property(nonatomic, assign) ALfloat coneInnerAngle;
@property(nonatomic, assign) ALfloat coneOuterAngle;
@property(nonatomic, assign) ALfloat coneOuterGain;
```

In *EWSoundSourceObject.m*'s init method, let's set the values to the same values that OpenAL uses as the default. Note that if you want direction disabled, you set the vector to <0, 0, 0>. If you don't want either of the cones, you set the angle to 360.0, which means the sound goes in all directions. By default, OpenAL sets the outer cone gain to 0, so we will do the same.

```
- (id) init
{
    self = [super init];
    if(nil != self)
    {
        audioLooping = AL_FALSE;
        pitchShift = 1.0f;
        rolloffFactor = 0.0; // 0.0 disables attenuation
        atDirection = BBPointMake(0.0, 0.0, 0.0);
        coneInnerAngle = 360.0;
        coneOuterAngle = 360.0;
        coneOuterGain = 0.0;
    }
    return self;
}
```

And in *EWSoundSourceObject.m*'s `applyState` method, we set the source properties.

```
alSource3f(sourceID, AL_DIRECTION, atDirection.x, atDirection.y, atDirection.z);
alSourcef(sourceID, AL_CONE_INNER_ANGLE, coneInnerAngle);
alSourcef(sourceID, AL_CONE_OUTER_ANGLE, coneOuterAngle);
alSourcef(sourceID, AL_CONE_OUTER_GAIN, coneOuterGain);
```

We need to remember to keep the `soundSourceObject`'s direction in sync with the `BBSceneObject`'s `rotation.z` value. So we add the following two lines to *BBSceneObject.m*'s awake and update methods, directly after where we synchronized the object positions:

```
CGFloat angle_in_radians = rotation.z/BBRADIANS_TO_DEGREES;
soundSourceObject.atDirection = BBPointMake(-sinf(angle_in_radians),
cosf(angle_in_radians), 0.0);
```

Now let's actually use a directional cone. In *BBUFO.m*, we'll set some cone properties. In the awake method, immediately before the `playSound:` invocation, we can try these values:

```
self.soundSourceObject.coneInnerAngle = 90.0;
self.soundSourceObject.coneOuterAngle = 270.0;
self.soundSourceObject.coneOuterGain = 0.5;
```

At this point, try running the program and experience the noise change for yourself. When the UFO inner cone (90 degrees wide) is directed at the spaceship, you hear the loudest sound. When both the cones are directed away from the spaceship, you hear the least gain. If you want something really explicit, you can set the `coneOuterGain` value to 0, and experience the UFO noise turning off completely when it is facing away from the spaceship.

But now I'm going to advocate leaving the `coneOuterGain` value at 0.5, and then doing a cheap, but interesting trick.

In *BBSceneController.m*'s addUFO method, let's increase the `rotationalSpeed` of the UFO dramatically:

```
ufo.rotationalSpeed = BBPointMake(0.0, 0.0, 1000.0);
```

Now when you run the program, you will hear a pronounced oscillation in the sound effect because the UFO is spinning so fast. I think this is a neat little effect that goes well with our UFO, so I'm going to leave the fast spin rate set for the rest of the examples.

Velocity and the Doppler Effect

OpenAL also supports a velocity vector property. This is used in conjunction with the Doppler effect feature of OpenAL.

What is the Doppler effect? The classic example of the Doppler effect is a siren on an emergency vehicle. As the vehicle approaches you at high speed, you hear a higher-frequency noise than when the vehicle passes you and goes away, which is a lower-frequency noise. Applying this metaphor to the spaceship and UFO in our game, we get Figure 11–8 and Figure 11–9 to help visualize this effect.

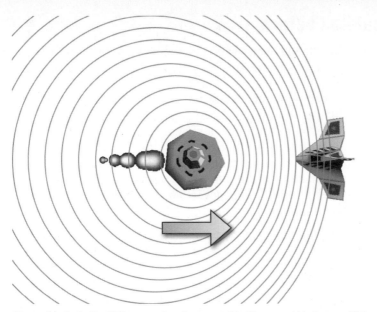

Figure 11–8. *As the UFO approaches the spaceship, the spaceship hears a higher-frequency noise. The circles representing sound wave crests bunch up near the spaceship. The distance between each circular wave (wavelength) is shorter. Shorter wavelengths mean you hear a higher frequency.*

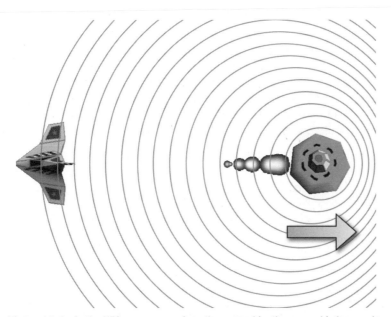

Figure 11–9. *As the UFO moves away from the spaceship, the spaceship hears a lower-frequency noise. The circles representing sound wave crests are spaced further apart around the spaceship as the UFO moves away. The distance between each circular wave (wavelength) is longer. Longer wavelengths mean you hear a lower frequency.*

Velocities and Scaling Factors

To use the Doppler effect in OpenAL, we need several things. First and foremost, the listener and the sound source need velocities. This brings up a subtle point. We have already been moving the positions of the objects in our game. So, does OpenAL automatically infer the velocities based on the changes in position? The answer is no. OpenAL requires you to explicitly set velocities as a separate property from position. But this is generally a good thing. Otherwise, you would need to work around corner cases such as when an object first materializes into the game, because the initial velocity is undefined. Another corner case to consider is if an object has a teleportation feature where it can instantly change to a new position. In this case, it may not make sense to have a pitch shift in frequency, which might imply extremely fast speed instead of teleportation.

An interesting side effect of setting the velocity properties separately from position is that you aren't obligated to portray realism. For example, perhaps for artistic reasons like a dream sequence or alternate reality, you decide you want to do the opposite of a real Doppler effect. When objects move toward the listener, maybe you decide you want a lower frequency instead of a higher one. Since OpenAL has separate properties for position and velocity, you can easily achieve this.

In addition to requiring velocities, OpenAL also provides two global scaling factors to let you manipulate how strong the Doppler effect is in your program:

- AL_DOPPLER_FACTOR is a simple scaling multiplier that makes the effect more exaggerated or muted.

- AL_SPEED_OF_SOUND indicates how fast sound travels in the units that you have been passing to OpenAL. For example, if your velocity units have all been in meters per second, then setting AL_SPEED_OF_SOUND to 343 (the default) might be a reasonable value.[6] But if your velocity units are in feet per second instead of meters per second, AL_SPEED_OF_SOUND should be 1125.

So without further ado, the formula OpenAL uses to compute the pitch shift is as follows:

$$frequency_{shifted} = frequency_{sample} \cdot \frac{SpeedOfSound - DopplerFactor \cdot velocity_{listener}}{SpeedOfSound - DopplerFactor \cdot velocity_{source}}$$

The formula solves for the shifted frequency, which is what you hear play through your speakers.

For you astute, mathematically inclined people out there, I need to clarify what $velocity_{listener}$ and $velocity_{source}$ really are, because the equation is slightly inaccurate for the sake of being more aesthetically pleasing. The velocities in this equation are not true vectors. Instead, each velocity is just a scalar (a simple float value). The values are

---

[6] 343 meters per second is the speed of sound in dry air.

the projection of each velocity projected onto the source-to-listener vector. What does this mean?

Imagine the UFO and the spaceship moving across the screen from left to right, parallel with each other, never getting closer to or farther from one another. No matter how fast they are moving, the pitch due to the Doppler effect will never change, because the Doppler effect happens only when the objects get closer or farther apart. So, we care only about the part of the velocity that travels along an imaginary line that connects the UFO and spaceship, which is the source-to-listener vector. The good news is that OpenAL automatically extracts the projected scalars from regular velocity vectors you provide, so you really don't need to worry about this detail. But the formula as a whole is presented to allow you to understand how changing all the factors impacts the results, because you will most likely be tweaking multiple values.

You may be wondering why you will be tweaking values, when OpenAL provides things that imply precision, such as precise-sounding factors like the speed of sound and unit systems like meters per second. In practice, more often than not, you will be filling these numbers in the equation by trial and error and experimentation, rather than mathematical rigor. Most game worlds are exaggerated and do not perfectly reflect reality. Frequently, distances are shorter and speeds are greater in game worlds to make things more exciting. Usually, this means needing to tweak things until they sound right.

Doppler Effect Example Time

Once again, it is example time. We will continue from the previous project, `SpaceRocksOpenAL3D_3_DirectionCones`. The finished project for this example is named `SpaceRocksOpenAL3D_4_VelocityDoppler`.

In *EWSoundState.h*, add a new instance variable for `objectVelocity` for the velocity vector:

`BBPoint objectVelocity;`

Initialize it in *EWSoundState.m*'s init method after `objectPosition` is initialized:

`objectVelocity = BBPointMake(0.0, 0.0, 0.0);`

In *EWSoundSourceObject.m*, apply it OpenAL in `applyState` after the lines following the directional cones we added in the previous section:

`alSource3f(sourceID, AL_VELOCITY, objectVelocity.x, objectVelocity.y, objectVelocity.z);`

In *EWSoundListenerObject.m*, do the same for the listener in `applyState` after the `AL_ORIENTATION` line:

`alListener3f(AL_VELOCITY, objectVelocity.x, objectVelocity.y, objectVelocity.z);`

OK, one minor surprise. The speed property is not in `BBSceneObject`, but in the subclass `BBMobileObject`. So, in *BBMobileObject.m*, synchronize the source velocities with the scene object, in its awake method, which must be created:

```
- (void) awake
{
```

```
    [super awake];
    soundSourceObject.objectVelocity = speed;
}
```

You may be wondering how I know that the speed vector used by the Space Rocks! game engine is going to map directly to OpenAL's notion of velocity without some scaling factor. The truth is that I don't know. But I thought I would try this first, and then tweak the Doppler factor and speed of sound values as appropriate.

In *OpenALSoundController.m*, we will implement accessors for these two parameters:

```
- (void) setDopplerFactor:(ALfloat)doppler_factor
{
    alDopplerFactor(doppler_factor);
}

- (ALfloat) dopplerFactor
{
    return alGetFloat(AL_DOPPLER_FACTOR);
}

- (void) setSpeedOfSound:(ALfloat)speed_of_sound
{
    alSpeedOfSound(speed_of_sound);
}

- (ALfloat) speedOfSound
{
        return alGetFloat(AL_SPEED_OF_SOUND);
}
```

In *OpenALSoundController.h*, declare the interfaces or properties so they can be used publicly without warnings. No synthesize is necessary, since we explicitly implemented them.

```
@property(nonatomic, assign) ALfloat dopplerFactor;
@property(nonatomic, assign) ALfloat speedOfSound;
```

Finally, let's use our accessors in *BBSceneController.m*'s init method after setDistanceModel. To start with, we will set the Doppler factor to 1.0 and the speed of sound to 343.3, which are the OpenAL defaults:

```
[[OpenALSoundController sharedSoundController] setDopplerFactor:1.0];
[[OpenALSoundController sharedSoundController] setSpeedOfSound:343.3];
```

As it turns out, I like how all our default values work for this instructional example. I think these values are strong enough that you can easily notice the Doppler effect being applied, but not too strong that everything becomes incomprehensible. But I encourage you to play with these parameters to see how they manipulate the effect.

Distance Attenuation

I saved this effect for last because I wanted to make sure you could clearly hear all the effects we applied in the prior steps.

Distance attenuation is simply making sounds become more silent as they move farther away. It is a big-sounding phrase for a very simple concept.

Attenuation Models

OpenAL provides six different built-in attenuation models that you can pick from to make distance attenuation seem more realistic or more artistic. The models are inverse, linear, exponential, and clamped versions of the aforementioned three models. (The default is Inverse Distance Clamped.) Clamped versions are the same as the nonclamped versions, except that for distances less than the reference distance, the gain is set (clamped) to 1. In addition, clamped versions also clamp distances to the maximum distance value if the distance exceeds that value.

The formulas and graphs are shown in the following sections. In all formulas, x represents the distance between the source and listener, and x≥0. Also note that OpenAL implementations are free to clamp gain values if the result exceeds hardware capabilities.

Inverse Distance

In the Inverse Distance model (see Figure 11–10), the gain decays quickly and then starts to level off as the distance gets greater. Smaller rolloff factors will reduce how quickly the gain drops. Reference distance shifts the curve to the right so that gain equals 1 at the reference distance. Note that even though the equation and graph allows gains greater than 1, OpenAL is free to clamp the maximum value at 1.

$$gain = \frac{ReferenceDistance}{ReferenceDistance + RolloffFactor \cdot (x - ReferenceDistance)}$$

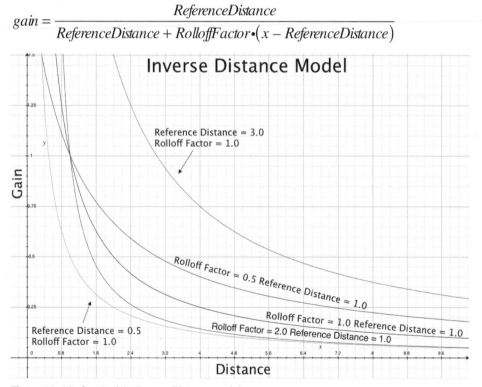

Figure 11–10. *Graph of the Inverse Distance model*

Inverse Distance Clamped

The Inverse Distance Clamped model (see Figure 11–11) behaves like the nonclamped model, except that gain greater than 1 is explicitly clamped. Also, there is a maximum distance parameter that prevents the gain from decaying any more beyond the designated distance.

$$gain = \begin{cases} 1 & 0 \leq x \leq ReferenceDistance \\ \dfrac{ReferenceDistance}{ReferenceDistance + RolloffFactor - (x - ReferenceDistance)} & ReferenceDistance < x < MaxDistance \\ \dfrac{ReferenceDistance}{ReferenceDistance + RolloffFactor - (MaxDistance - ReferenceDistance)} & x \geq MaxDistance \end{cases}$$

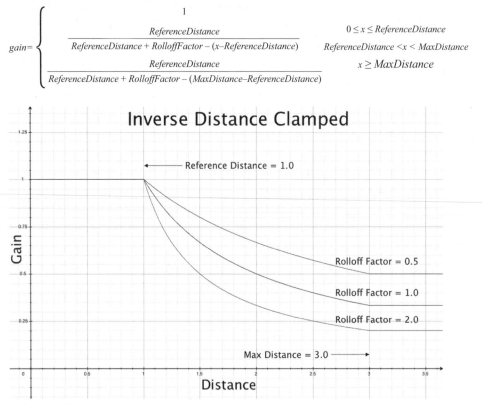

Figure 11–11. *Graph of the Inverse Distance Clamped model*

Linear Distance

The Linear Distance model (see Figure 11–12) makes the gain decay in a linear (straight-line) fashion. The reference distance value shifts the line so that the gain is 1 at the reference distance. Remember that OpenAL is free to clamp gain values greater than 1, even though the equation and graph allow for larger values.

$$gain = \begin{cases} 1 - RolloffFactor \cdot \dfrac{x - ReferenceDistance}{MaxDistance - ReferenceDistance} & 0 \leq x < MaxDistance \\ 1 - RolloffFactor & x \geq MaxDistance \end{cases}$$

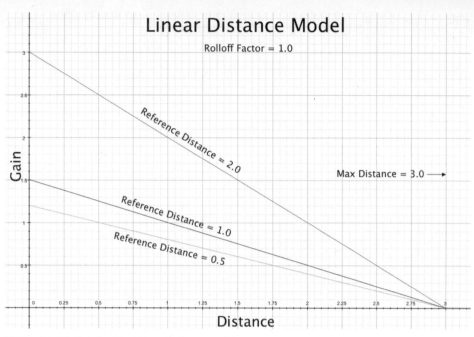

Figure 11–12. *Graph of the Linear Distance model*

Linear Distance Clamped

The Linear Distance Clamped model (see Figure 11–13) explicitly clamps gains greater than 1 to 1. From the graph, it is also more apparent that the reference distance is the trigger point for where the gain starts to decay. Comparing Figures 11–12 and 11–13, you can also see both the reference distance and the rolloff factor contribute to the slope of the line.

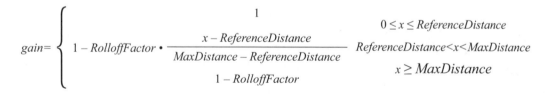

$$gain = \begin{cases} 1 & 0 \le x \le ReferenceDistance \\ 1 - RolloffFactor \cdot \dfrac{x - ReferenceDistance}{MaxDistance - ReferenceDistance} & ReferenceDistance < x < MaxDistance \\ 1 - RolloffFactor & x \ge MaxDistance \end{cases}$$

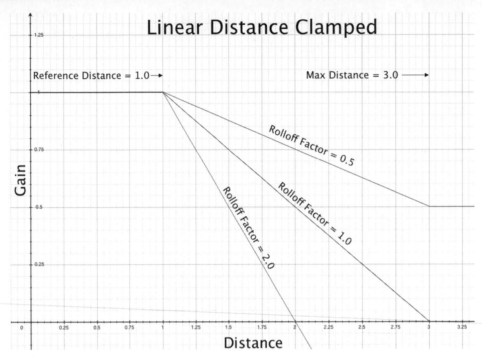

Figure 11–13. *Graph of the Linear Distance Clamped model*

Exponential Distance

You can tell that Exponential Distance model (see Figure 11–14) gets its name from the equation where there is an exponential value there. The curve exponentially drops based on the size of the rolloff factor. The reference distance shifts the curve so the gain is 1 where the reference distance is. Remember that OpenAL is free to clamp gain values greater than 1.

$$gain = \left(\frac{x}{ReferenceDistance}\right)^{-RolloffFactor}$$

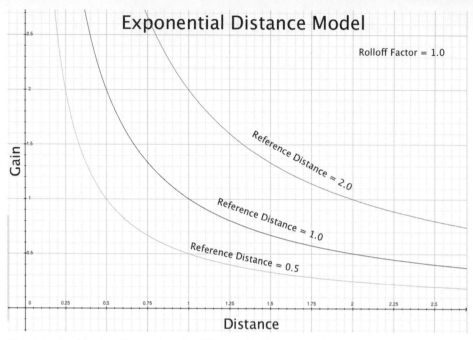

Figure 11–14. *Graph of the Exponential Distance model*

Exponential Distance Clamped

Like all the other clamped models, the Exponential Distance Clamped model (see Figure 11–15) explicitly clamps gains greater than 1 to 1. Gain decay stops when the maximum distance is reached. The rolloff factor affects the slope.

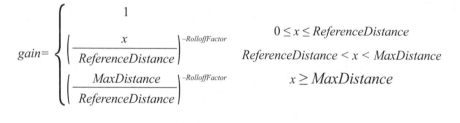

$$gain= \begin{cases} 1 & 0 \leq x \leq ReferenceDistance \\ \left(\dfrac{x}{ReferenceDistance} \right)^{-RolloffFactor} & ReferenceDistance < x < MaxDistance \\ \left(\dfrac{MaxDistance}{ReferenceDistance} \right)^{-RolloffFactor} & x \geq MaxDistance \end{cases}$$

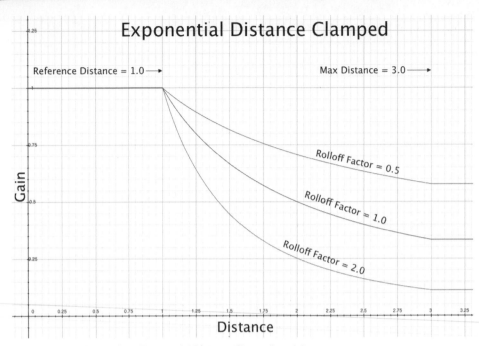

Figure 11–15. *Graph of the Exponential Distance Clamped model*

Distance Attenuation Parameters

So you might be asking, "Why do we need all these parameters?" and "What do they all mean?"

To answer the first question, the OpenAL 1.1 Specification and Reference gives an example of a jet and a clock. Imagine they are in the same location. The jet is obviously going to be louder than the clock, and the rate of volume decay over distance is going to be slower than the clock.

To compound matters, in your application, you are dealing with recorded PCM samples that are probably normalized. The volume levels of these recordings aren't going to reflect the power you hear in the real world. (Graphics people might think of this as a high dynamic range problem.)

As for what the parameters mean, the maximum distance is probably the most self-explanatory. Particularly for the clamped models, this value just specifies that you want to stop attenuating after you reach the maximum distance.

The rolloff factor basically specifies how fast the sound should decay. In the jet versus clock example, you probably want the jet sound to decay more slowly than the clock.

Reference distance is a difficult one to explain. The OpenAL Programmer's Guide defines it as "the distance under which the volume for the source would normally drop by half (before being influenced by the rolloff factor or AL_MAX_DISTANCE." However, I am not convinced this is an accurate description, or even useful.

The reference distance parameter has confused other people as well. The best explanation I've seen comes from Daniel Peacock. As I mentioned in Chapter 10, he is the current maintainer of the Creative Labs implementation of OpenAL. He is also one of the key authorities and guardians of OpenAL. He was kind enough to give me permission to quote a response he once gave on the OpenAL mailing list.

> *This is a confusing parameter—particularly because it has different behavior based on the distance model you select. In the ***_CLAMPED distance models, the distance between the source and the listener is always clamped between the AL_REFERENCE_DISTANCE and the AL_MAX_DISTANCE (i.e. the source can be no nearer than AL_REFERENCE_DISTANCE, and no further than AL_MAX_DISTANCE). The distance models without clamping do not impose any limits.*
>
> *After clamping the source-listener distance (if appropriate) … the AL_REFERENCE_DISTANCE term is plugged into the appropriate attenuation model and is used to calculate the source gain as attenuated by distance.*
>
> *The AL_REFERENCE_DISTANCE term in all the distance models is a way to indicate how loud a sound really is. Assuming that all the samples in the game are going to be (roughly) normalized, and they all have the same AL_REFERENCE_DISTANCE they would all attenuate over distance at the same rate and sound at the same level. This is clearly wrong if one of the samples is an explosion and one is a footstep. The explosion should be audible a long way off (so it might have a reference distance of 50) whereas the footsteps are much quieter and should not be audible from far away (so they might have a reference distance of 1 or 2).*

Picking a Distance Model

Now you might wonder how to pick a distance model. Typically, the Inverse or Inverse Clamped model is considered the most realistic of the group (not to imply it is actually realistic). It might be a prime choice for a first-person shooter game. Linear is considered the least realistic. I think linear might work well for a game like Space Rocks!. However, for our example, we will pick Inverse Clamped.

Another thing to notice is that the Inverse and Exponential models don't decay completely to 0. Consider a first-person shooter game in a large world. This means very distance objects may still make noise you can hear, which you may not expect. OpenAL doesn't support culling of any kind, so it is up to you to figure out how you want to handle really distant sounds and manually implement it.

You are encouraged to use the example project to play with the other models and parameters. The graphs and equations should help you pick a model and decide what to try to plug in for the values.

Back to Space Rocks!

Time to add distance attenuation to Space Rocks!. Again, by now you pretty much know the drill. We will continue from the previous project, SpaceRocksOpenAL3D_4_VelocityDoppler. The finished project for this example is named SpaceRocksOpenAL3D_5_DistanceAttenuation.

First, EWSoundSourceObject must support properties for rolloffFactor, referenceDistance, and maxDistance. We already added rolloffFactor from our earlier work-around to disable attenuation at the beginning of the chapter, so we are already partway there. So first, add the remaining two instance variables and properties to *EWSoundSourceObject.h* and remember to synthesize them in the implementation.

```
ALfloat rolloffFactor;
ALfloat referenceDistance;
ALfloat maxDistance;
```

```
@property(nonatomic, assign) ALfloat rolloffFactor;
@property(nonatomic, assign) ALfloat referenceDistance;
@property(nonatomic, assign) ALfloat maxDistance;
```

In *EWSoundSourceObject.m*, Initialize the defaults to match the OpenAL defaults in the init method:

```
rolloffFactor = 1.0; // 0.0 disables attenuation
referenceDistance = 1.0;
maxDistance = FLT_MAX;
```

Set the properties in applyState:

```
alSourcef(sourceID, AL_ROLLOFF_FACTOR, rolloffFactor);
alSourcef(sourceID, AL_REFERENCE_DISTANCE, referenceDistance);
alSourcef(sourceID, AL_MAX_DISTANCE, maxDistance);
```

In *BBSceneController.m*, change the distance model in init from AL_NONE to something else. For our example, we will use AL_INVERSE_DISTANCE_CLAMPED.

```
[[OpenALSoundController sharedSoundController]
setDistanceModel:AL_INVERSE_DISTANCE_CLAMPED];
```

Now it's time to actually set our three properties for our specific game needs. First, in BBSceneObject's init method, set the maxDistance immediately after we create the soundSourceObject:

```
soundSourceObject.maxDistance = 600.0;
```

The maximum size of our game field is approximately 600 units wide. It is unchanging, so we just hard-code this value here.

Finally, we need to go through every `BBSceneObject` subclass we have (for every object we care about) and set the `rolloffFactor` and `referenceDistance` properties to something that will work well with our attenuation model. The following are the values I picked. I encourage you to play with them and try other models.

- UFO: Attenuates, but a little more constant/consistent than other objects.

```
self.soundSourceObject.rolloffFactor = 0.5;
self.soundSourceObject.referenceDistance = 300.0;
```

- Rocks (asteroids): More attenuation than the UFO for depth (distance) perspective, but still loud enough to hear reasonably well from far away.

```
self.soundSourceObject.rolloffFactor = 1.0;
self.soundSourceObject.referenceDistance = 100.0;
```

- Spaceship laser (missile): Wimpy laser sound attenuates quickly.

```
self.soundSourceObject.rolloffFactor = 5.0;
self.soundSourceObject.referenceDistance = 50.0;
```

- UFO missile: Not as wimpy as the spaceship laser/missile, but does attenuate quickly. Notice as the missile gets close to your ship, it gets noticeably loud, which may be a good property to have for the player.

```
self.soundSourceObject.rolloffFactor = 3.0;
self.soundSourceObject.referenceDistance = 100.0;
```

PREPARING YOUR SOUND SAMPLES

There are a lot of things to consider when creating and editing your sound files for your game—too many to cover here. But to give you an idea, you might want to think about things like prenormalizing/balancing your sounds so volume levels for different samples overpower others. You might also want to think about and test how a sample will sound when looped if you need to deal with sounds that repeat.

As an example, for this book, I took some care in preparing the missile sample used in our game. Both the UFO and UFO missile are prime subjects for showing off our 3D effects, because they make long-duration noises and move gradually across the screen. Therefore, I wanted to put a little more effort into creating these effects. But usually, missile recordings already attenuate, because most test firings watch the missile from a stationary fixed point from which the missile moves away at a high speed. For our example, I wanted fairly constant burn amplitude so I could let OpenAL be the main driver of any attenuation you hear and avoid getting a double attenuation effect.

Figure 11–16 shows my modified missile launch waveform in GarageBand. The original waveform's amplitude dropped off toward zero much more quickly than what's pictured here. I modified the sample to try to keep it roughly constant, so any attenuation you hear in the game will be due to OpenAL's distance attenuation feature and not the original audio sample. As you can see, the waveform is mostly consistent (a little attenuation, but not too bad). There is a quick drop off at the end, just so it didn't end too abruptly. (Imagine the missile running out of fuel, I suppose.)

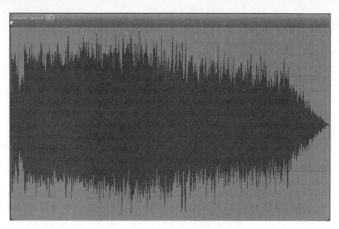

Figure 11–16. *Missile launch waveform in GarageBand*

On a related subject, you might be wondering about the tools that are available for editing audio files. I will suggest two:

- GarageBand by Apple (shown in Figure 11–16) ships as part of iLife with every new Mac. Assuming you are using a Mac, it should already be installed on your computer. GarageBand has a lot of features that go beyond just PCM files, which also means there tends to be more of a learning curve.

- Audacity (shown in Figure 11–17), containing the same missile waveform as in the GarageBand screenshot) is an open source (and free) cross-platform sound application for recording and editing sounds. I like using Audacity for a lot of simpler things. I also like using Audacity because I can run it on other platforms, which is convenient for cross-platform development. Check out Audacity at `http://audacity.sourceforge.net`.

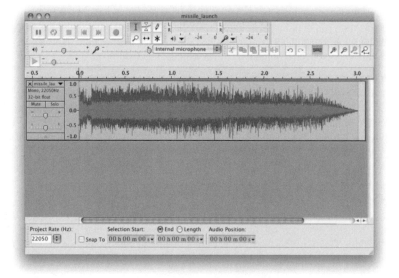

Figure 11–17. *Missile launch waveform in Audacity*

Using Relative Sound Properties to Selectively Disable 3D Effects

The final OpenAL property still to introduce is `AL_SOURCE_RELATIVE`. This property, when set to `AL_TRUE`, indicates that the position, velocity, direction, and cone properties of a source are to be interpreted relative to the listener position. By default, this is set to `AL_FALSE`.

Since it is easier to deal with absolute (nonrelative) values for our Space Rocks! engine, we haven't cared about changing the `AL_SOURCE_RELATIVE` property. However, this property can be exploited to accomplish something else that can be useful. We can abuse this property to effectively disable 3D effects on a per-source basis.

Now that we've added so much infrastructure into our engine, if we encounter a case where we don't want 3D effects applied on a single particular instance, we might have a mess trying to refactor the code to handle this case, particularly since many of these effects involve changes to both the source and listener.[7] But I will show you how to use the `AL_SOURCE_RELATIVE` property to accomplish this without too much pain. There is a certain irony about ending the chapter by disabling all the work we've done throughout this chapter, but *que sera, sera*.

The basic idea is simple. We enable the `AL_SOURCE_RELATIVE` property on the source that we want to not be spatialized, and then set all the source properties to values that make it appear that the source is moving in lockstep with the listener. This will give the illusion that 3D effects are off for the source. For example, with position, we set the position to <0, 0, 0>, which means it is at the same exact position of the listener. The code for this version is in `SpaceRocksOpenAL3D_6_SourceRelative`.

So let's begin undoing.

First, we add two new Boolean properties to `EWSoundSourceObject`. One is generically for `AL_SOURCE_RELATIVE`, just in case you want to use this property for its actual intended purpose. The other is explicitly for disabling 3D effects. In *EWSoundSourceObject.h*, add the instance variables and properties:

```
ALboolean sourceRelative;
BOOL positionalDisabled;
@property(nonatomic, assign, getter=isSourceRelative) ALboolean sourceRelative;
@property(nonatomic, assign, getter=isPositionalDisabled) BOOL positionalDisabled;
```

In *EWSoundSourceObject.m*, synthesize the properties, and in the `init` method, initialize these to `false`.

Next, the heart of this technique is just restructuring the `applyState` method in *EWSoundSourceObject.m* to check if the `positionalDisabled` flag is set, and setting different values if it is. The new code looks like this:

---

[7] You could make the sample stereo, but that has its own drawbacks.

```objc
- (void) applyState
{
    ALenum al_error;

    [super applyState];
    if(NO == self.hasSourceID)
    {
        return;
    }
    if([[OpenALSoundController sharedSoundController] inInterruption])
    {
        return;
    }
    alSourcef(self.sourceID, AL_GAIN, self.gainLevel);
    alSourcei(self.sourceID, AL_LOOPING, self.audioLooping);
    alSourcef(self.sourceID, AL_PITCH, self.pitchShift);

    if(YES == positionalDisabled)
    {
        // Disable positional sound

        // set to relative positioning so we can set everything to 0
        alSourcei(sourceID, AL_SOURCE_RELATIVE, AL_TRUE);
        // 0 to disable attenuation
        alSourcef(sourceID, AL_ROLLOFF_FACTOR, 0.0);
        // doesn't matter
        alSourcef(sourceID, AL_REFERENCE_DISTANCE, referenceDistance);
        // doesn't matter
        alSourcef(sourceID, AL_MAX_DISTANCE, maxDistance);

        alSource3f(sourceID, AL_POSITION, 0.0, 0.0, 0.0);
        alSource3f(sourceID, AL_DIRECTION, 0.0, 0.0, 0.0);
        alSourcef(sourceID, AL_CONE_INNER_ANGLE, 360.0);
        alSourcef(sourceID, AL_CONE_OUTER_ANGLE, 360.0);
        alSourcef(sourceID, AL_CONE_OUTER_GAIN, 0.0);
        alSource3f(sourceID, AL_VELOCITY, 0.0, 0.0, 0.0);
    }
    else
    {
        // set to relative positioning so we can set everything to 0
        alSourcei(sourceID, AL_SOURCE_RELATIVE, sourceRelative);
        alSourcef(sourceID, AL_ROLLOFF_FACTOR, rolloffFactor);
        alSourcef(sourceID, AL_REFERENCE_DISTANCE, referenceDistance);
        alSourcef(sourceID, AL_MAX_DISTANCE, maxDistance);

        alSource3f(sourceID, AL_POSITION,
            objectPosition.x, objectPosition.y, objectPosition.z);
        alSource3f(sourceID, AL_DIRECTION,
            atDirection.x, atDirection.y, atDirection.z);
        alSourcef(sourceID, AL_CONE_INNER_ANGLE, coneInnerAngle);
        alSourcef(sourceID, AL_CONE_OUTER_ANGLE, coneOuterAngle);
        alSourcef(sourceID, AL_CONE_OUTER_GAIN, coneOuterGain);
        alSource3f(sourceID, AL_VELOCITY, objectVelocity.x, objectVelocity.y,
objectVelocity.z);
    }
}
```

Finally, for our new property setters, we should explicitly implement them, instead of relying on synthesize, because we need to call `applyState` to make sure the change takes effect immediately.

```
- (void) setSourceRelative:(ALboolean)source_relative
{
    sourceRelative = source_relative;
    [self applyState];
}

- (void) setPositionalDisabled:(BOOL)positional_disabled
{
    positionalDisabled = positional_disabled;
    [self applyState];
}
```

And that's all there is to it. It's far easier to destroy than create, right?

In the code example, I do not go as far as to explicitly disable 3D for any specific objects (because we will continue building upon this code base in the next chapter, and I didn't want to deal with the forking situation). But I encourage you to play with it. I left a commented-out line in *BBUFO.m*'s awake method:

```
//      self.soundSourceObject.positionalDisabled = YES;
```

Achievement Unlocked: Use All OpenAL 3D Features

Congratulations! You are among the few elite that have seen and worked with all the official 3D features of OpenAL. Now it's just a matter of tweaking all those little parameters for your game. For additional reference, I highly recommend a great Apple developer example for Mac OS X that is included with Xcode called OpenALExample (once upon a time found in `file:///Developer/Examples/CoreAudio/Services/OpenALExample`, though with newer releases of Xcode, you may have to download it directly from Apple at `http://developer.apple.com/Mac/library/samplecode/OpenALExample/index.html`). It provides a Cocoa and OpenGL GUI to access all the properties we've talked about, so you can see how changing a value affects the outcome (see Figure 11–18). If you don't normally work on a Mac, but want to experiment with all the OpenAL properties, I highly recommend borrowing some time on a Mac and playing with this example.

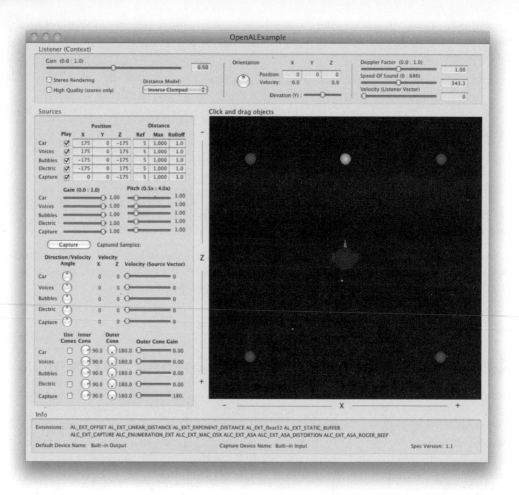

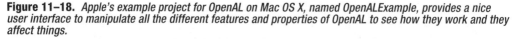

Figure 11–18. *Apple's example project for OpenAL on Mac OS X, named OpenALExample, provides a nice user interface to manipulate all the different features and properties of OpenAL to see how they work and they affect things.*

The next chapter discusses a topic that is mostly orthogonal to this chapter. However, the examples in the next chapter will build on the examples from this chapter and attempt to bring it all together. So get ready for the grand finale of the audio section.

Chapter 12

Streaming: Thumping, Pulse-Quickening Game Excitement

This is the longest chapter of the audio section, and may actually be the longest chapter of the entire book. But don't feel too discouraged, because the length is not related to the difficulty. We are going to cover multiple APIs, comparing their functionality to give you a better understanding of how they work. The goal is to help you select the API that accomplishes the most in the least amount of effort for your own game.

First, we will look at how you might use large audio files in your games. Then we will cover the Media Player framework, which allows you to access the iPod music library from within your application. We will walk through an example that lets the user construct a playlist from the iPod music library to be used as background music for Space Rocks!.

Next, we will move on to the more generic audio streaming APIs: AVFoundation, OpenAL, and Audio Queue Services. Using each of these APIs, we will repeat implementing background music for Space Rocks!. And in the OpenAL example, we will do sort of a grand finale and embellish the game by adding streaming speech and fully integrating it with the OpenAL capabilities we implemented in the previous two chapters.

Then we will turn our attention to audio capture. Once again, we will compare and contrast three APIs: Audio Queue Services, AVFoundation, and OpenAL.

Finally, we bring things full circle and close with some OpenGL and OpenAL optimization tips.

Music and Beyond

In the previous chapters, we focused on playing short sound effects. But what about longer things like music? Most games have background music, right?

For performance, we have been preloading all the audio files into RAM. But this isn't feasible for large audio files. A 44 kHz, 60-second stereo sample takes about 10MB of memory to hold (as linear PCM). For those wondering how to do the math:

$$\frac{44,100\ samples}{\sec ond} \cdot \frac{16\ bits}{sample} \cdot \frac{1\ byte}{8\ bits} \cdot 60\ seconds \cdot 2\ channels = 10,584,000\ bytes$$

Now, 10MB is a lot of RAM to use, particularly when we are listening to only a small piece of the 1-minute audio sample at any given moment. And on a RAM-limited device such as an iPhone, a more memory-efficient approach is critical if you hope to do anything else in your game, such as graphics.

In this chapter, we will look at APIs to help us deal with large amounts of audio data. Since the device we are talking about originates from a portable music player, it is only reasonable that iPhone OS provides special APIs to allow you to access the iPod music library. We will also look at the more general audio APIs that allow us to play our own bundled music. These general audio APIs are often referred to as *buffer-queuing* APIs or *streaming* APIs, because you continuously feed small chunks of data to the audio system. But I don't want you to get myopia for just music—these audio APIs are general purpose, and can handle other types of audio.

You might be thinking that you don't need anything beyond music in your game. However, there are other types of long-duration sounds that you may require. Speech is the most notable element. Speech can find many ways into games. Adventure games with large casts of characters with dialogue, such as the cult classic Star Control 2: The Ur-Quan Masters and the recently rereleased The Secret of Monkey Island (see Figures 12–1 and 12–2) are prime examples of games that make heavy use of both simultaneous music and speech throughout the entire game.

Figure 12–1. *The Secret of Monkey Island is a prime example of a game that has both music and speech. It's now available for iPhone OS!*

Figure 12–2. *In-game screenshot of The Secret of Monkey Island. Voice actors provide speech for the dialogue to enhance the quality of the game.*

It is also common for games to have an opening sequence that provides a narrator. And even action-oriented games need speech occasionally. Half-Life opened with an automated train tour guide talking to you as you descended into the compound, and you meet somewhat chatty scientists along the way. And for many people, the most memorable things from Duke Nukem 3D are the corny lines Duke says throughout the game.

Quick, arcade-style games may use streaming sound—perhaps for an opening or to tell you "game over"—because the sound is too infrequently used to be worth keeping resident. I recall seeing a port of Street Fighter 1 on the semi-obscure video game console TurboGrafx-16 with the CD-ROM drive add-on. To get the "Round 1 fight" and "<Character> wins" speeches, the console accessed the CD-ROM. The load times were hideously slow on this machine, so the game would pause multiple seconds to pull this dialogue. But the console had very limited memory, so the game developers decided not to preload these files. Whether they actually streamed them, I cannot say definitively, but they could have.

Games built around immersive environments that might not have a dedicated soundtrack still might need streaming. Imagine entering a room like a bar that has a TV, a radio, and a jukebox within earshot. You will be hearing all these simultaneously, and they are probably not short looping samples if they are going to be interesting.

You may remember my anecdote about SDL_mixer from Chapter 10, and how it ultimately led me to try OpenAL. My problem with SDL_mixer was it got tunnel vision on music. SDL_mixer made a strong distinction between sound effects (the short-duration sounds completely preloaded for performance) and music. SDL_mixer had a distinct API for dealing with music that was separate from sound effects. This in itself was not necessarily bad, but SDL_mixer made the assumption that you would only ever need one "music" channel. The problem I ran into was that I needed both speech and music. But speech was too long to be a "sound effect." Furthermore, at the time, SDL_mixer didn't support highly compressed audio such as MP3 for the nonmusic channel, which was one of the odd things about having a distinct API for music and sound effects. So SDL_mixer was pretty much a dead-end for my usage case without major hacking. This event scarred me for life, so I encourage you not to box yourself in by thinking too small.

And on that note, there is one final thing we will briefly address in this chapter that is related to streaming: audio input, also known as audio capture or audio recording. Audio capture also deals with continuous small chunks of data, but the difference is that it is coming from the audio system, rather than having you submit it to the audio system.

iPod Music Library (Media Player Framework)

iPhone OS 3.0 was the first version to let you access to the iPod music library programmatically via the Media Player framework. You can access songs, audiobooks, and podcasts from the user's iPod music library and play them in your application. This is one step beyond just setting the audio session to allow the user to mix in music from the iPod application (see Figure 12–3). This framework gives you ultimate authority over which songs are played. You can also present a media item picker so the user may change songs without quitting your application (and returning to the iPod application).

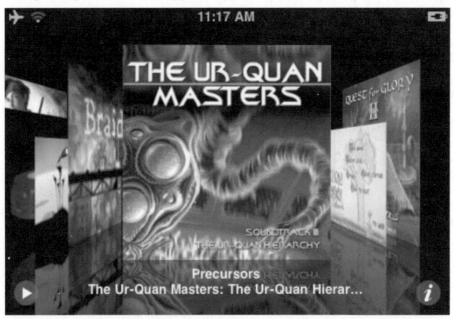

Figure 12–3. *The built-in iPod application in Cover Flow mode. Prior to iPhone OS 3.0, allowing your application to mix audio with the playing iPod application was the only way to let users play their own music in your application, albeit manually. Now with the Media Player framework, this can be accomplished more directly.*

> **NOTE:** The Media Player framework does not allow you to get direct access to the raw files or to the PCM audio data being played. There is also limited access to metadata. That means certain applications are not currently possible. Something as simple as a music visualizer really isn't possible because you can't analyze the PCM audio as it plays. And any game that hopes to analyze the music data, such as a beat/rhythm type of game, will not be able to access this data.

We will go through a short example. This example will probably be quite different from what you'll find in other books and documentation. Basic playback is quite simple, so there generally is an emphasis on building rich UIs to accompany your application. These include notifications to know when a song has changed (so you can update status text), how to search through collections to find songs that meet special criteria, and how to retrieve album artwork and display it in your app. But this is a game book, so we are going to take another approach.

Here, we are going to access the iPod library, present a media item picker, and play. The unique aspect is that we will use our existing Space Rocks! code and mix that in with our existing OpenAL audio that we used for sound effects.

First, you should make sure you have at least one song installed in your device's iPod library. (Production code should consider what to do in the case of an empty iPod library.) Also note that the iPhone simulator is currently not supported, so you must run this on an actual device.

Second, I want to remind you that we have been setting our audio session to `kAudioSessionCategory_AmbientSound` in the Space Rocks! code thus far. This allows mixing your application's audio with other applications. More specifically, this allows you to hear both your OpenAL sound effects and the iPod. (If you haven't already tried it, you might take a moment to go to the iPod application and start playing a song. Then start up Space Rocks! and hear the mixed sound for yourself.) When using the Media Player framework, you must continue to use the `AmbientSound` mode if you want to hear both your OpenAL sound effects and the Media Player framework audio.

Finally, we need to make a decision about how we want our media player to behave, as Apple gives us two options. Apple provides an application music player and an iPod music player. The iPod music player ties in directly to the built-in iPod music player application and shares the same state (e.g., shuffle and repeat modes). When you quit your application using this player, music still playing will continue to play. In contrast, the application music player gets its own state, and music will terminate when you quit your application. For this example, we will use the iPod music player, mostly because I find its seamless behavior with the built-in iPod player to be distinctive from the other streaming APIs we will be looking at later. Those who wish to use the application music player shouldn't fret about missing out. The programming interface is the same.

Playing iPod Music in Space Rocks!

We will continue building on Space Rocks! from the previous chapter, specifically, the project SpaceRocksOpenAL3D_6_SourceRelative. The completed project for this example is SpaceRocksMediaPlayerFramework.

To get started, we will create a new class named IPodMusicController to encapsulate the Media Player code. We also need to add the Media Player framework to the project.

Our IPodMusicController will be a singleton. It will encapsulate several convenience methods and will conform to the Apple's MPMediaPickerControllerDelegate so we can respond to the MPMediaPicker's delegate callback methods.

```
#import <UIKit/UIKit.h>
#import <MediaPlayer/MediaPlayer.h>

@interface IPodMusicController : NSObject <MPMediaPickerControllerDelegate>
{
}

+ (IPodMusicController*) sharedMusicController;
- (void) startApplication;
- (void) presentMediaPicker:(UIViewController*)current_view_controller;

@end
```

The startApplication method will define what we want to do when our application starts. So what do we want to do? Let's keep it fairly simple. We will get an iPod music player and start playing music if it isn't already playing.

Apple's MPMusicPlayerController class represents the iPod music player. It also uses a singleton pattern, which you've seen multiple times in previous chapters. For brevity, the implementation of the singleton accessor method is omitted here. See the finished example for the method named sharedMusicController.

Let's focus on the startApplication method.

```
- (void) startApplication
{
    MPMusicPlayerController* music_player = [MPMusicPlayerController iPodMusicPlayer];
    // Set or otherwise take iPod's current modes
    // [music_player setShuffleMode:MPMusicShuffleModeOff];
    // [music_player setRepeatMode:MPMusicRepeatModeNone];

    if(MPMusicPlaybackStateStopped == music_player.playbackState)
    {
        // Get all songs in the library and make them the list to play
        [music_player setQueueWithQuery:[MPMediaQuery songsQuery]];
        [music_player play];
    }
    else if(MPMusicPlaybackStatePaused == music_player.playbackState)
    {
        // Assuming that a song is already been selected to play
        [music_player play];
    }
    else if(MPMusicPlaybackStatePlaying == music_player.playbackState)
```

```
    {
        // Do nothing, let it continue playing
    }
    else
    {
        NSLog(@"Unhandled MPMusicPlayerController state: %d", music_player.playbackState);
    }
}
```

As you can see in the startApplication method, to get the iPod music player, we simply do this:

```
MPMusicPlayerController* music_player = [MPMusicPlayerController iPodMusicPlayer];
```

If we wanted to get the application music player instead, we would invoke this method instead:

```
MPMusicPlayerController* music_player = [MPMusicPlayerController
applicationMusicPlayer];
```

Optionally, we can set up some properties, such as the shuffle and repeat modes, like this:

```
[music_player setShuffleMode:MPMusicShuffleModeOff];
[music_player setRepeatMode:MPMusicRepeatModeNone];
```

We won't set them for this example, and instead rely on the iPod's current modes.

Next, we need to find some songs to play and start playing them. The MPMediaQuery class allows you to form queries for specific files. It also provides some convenient methods, which we will take advantage of to query for all songs contained in the library. The MPMusicPlayerController has a method called setQueueWithQuery, which will add the results of the query to the iPod's play queue. So by the end of it, we will construct a queue containing all of the songs in the library.

```
[music_player setQueueWithQuery:[MPMediaQuery songsQuery]];
```

Then to play, we just invoke play:

```
[music_player play];
```

But you can see from this method implementation that we get a little fancy. We have a large if-else block to detect whether the iPod is currently playing audio, using the MPMusicPlayerController's playbackState property. We can instruct the iPod to create a new queue only if it is not already playing audio. There are six different states: playing, paused, stopped, interrupted (e.g., phone call interruption), seeking forward, and seeking backward. For this example, we will concern ourselves with only the first three states.

> **TIP:** You may encounter the paused state more frequently than you might initially expect. This is because the iPod application doesn't have a stop button; it has only a pause button. Users who were playing music on their iPod and "stopped" it in the middle of a song are likely to be paused. You will encounter the stopped state if the user has just rebooted the device or let the iPod finish playing a playlist to completion. I separate the case for demonstration purposes, but for real applications, you may consider lumping stopped and paused into the same case, as the users may not remember they were in the middle of a song.

Now we need to invoke this method from Space Rocks! We will return to *BBSceneController.m* and add the following line to its init method:

```
[[IPodMusicController sharedMusicController] startApplication];
```

(Don't forget to #import "IPodMusicController.h" at the top of the file.)

Now, when the game loads, you should hear music playing from your iPod. And you should notice that the OpenAL audio still works. Congratulations!

> **NOTE:** MPMusicPlayerController has a volume property. However, this volume is the master volume control, so if you change the volume, it affects both the iPod music and the OpenAL audio in the same way. This may make volume balancing between the iPod and OpenAL very difficult—if not impossible—as you will have only fine-grained control over OpenAL gain levels, and not the iPod in isolation.

Adding a Media Item Picker

Now we will go one extra step and allow the user to build a list of songs from a picker (see Figures 12–4 and 12–5). Unfortunately, our Space Rocks! code really didn't intend us to do this kind of thing. So what you are about to see is kind of a hack. But I don't want to overwhelm you with a lot of support code to make this clean, as our focus is on the picker and music player.

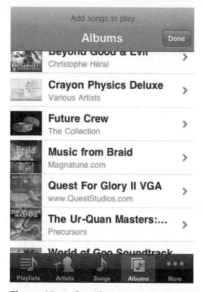

Figure 12–4. *Scrolling though the list of albums presented in the media item picker in the albums display mode showing my geeky but on-topic/game-related iPod music library.*

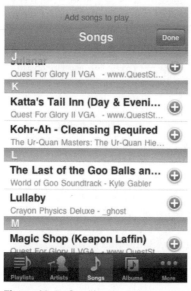

Figure 12–5. *Scrolling through the same media item picker in the songs display mode. Note the buttons on the right side of the table view list entries that allow you to add a song to the playlist you are constructing.*

As you might have noticed earlier, I listed a prototype in `IPodMusicController` for this method:

```
- (void) presentMediaPicker:(UIViewController*)current_view_controller;
```

We will write this method to encapsulate creating the picker and displaying it.

Apple provides a ready-to-use view controller subclass called `MPMediaPickerController`, which will allow you to pick items from your iPod library. Apple calls this the media item picker. It looks very much like the picker in the iPod application. One very notable difference, however, is that there is no Cover Flow mode with the media item picker.

Despite the shortcoming, we will use this class for our picker. Add the implementation for `presentMediaPicker` in *IPodMusicController.m*.

```
- (void) presentMediaPicker:(UIViewController*)current_view_controller
{
    MPMediaPickerController* media_picker = [[[MPMediaPickerController alloc]
     initWithMediaTypes:MPMediaTypeAnyAudio] autorelease];
    [media_picker setDelegate:self];
    [media_picker setAllowsPickingMultipleItems:YES];
    // For a message at the top of the view
    media_picker.prompt = NSLocalizedString(@"Add songs to play", "Prompt in media item
     picker");

        [current_view_controller presentModalViewController:media_picker animated:YES];
}
```

In the first line, we create a new `MPMediaPickerController`. It takes a mask parameter that allows you to restrict which media types you want to display in your picker. Valid values are `MPMediaTypeMusic`, `MPMediaTypePodcast`, `MPMediaTypeAudioBook`, and the convenience mask `MPMediaTypeAnyAudio`. We will use the latter, since the user may have been listening to a podcast or audiobook before starting Space Rocks!, and I don't see any reason to restrict it.

In the next line, we set the picker's delegate to `self`. Remember that earlier we made the `IPodMusicController` class conform to the `MPMediaPickerControllerDelegate` protocol. We will implement the delegate methods in this class shortly. Setting the delegate to `self` will ensure our delegate methods are invoked.

Next, we set an option on the picker to allow picking multiple items. This will allow the users to build a list of songs they want played, rather than just selecting a single song. This isn't that critical for our short game, but it is an option that you might want to use in your own games.

Then we set another option to show a text label at the very top of the picker. We will display the string `"Add songs to play"`. We set the `prompt` property with this string. You may have noticed the use of `NSLocalizedString`. In principle, when generating text programmatically, you should always think about localization. Since this is a Cocoa-level API, we can use Cocoa's localization support functions. Since we are not actually localizing this application, this is a little overkill, but it's here as a reminder to you to think about localization.

Now we are ready to display the media item picker. Notice that we passed in a parameter called `current_view_controller`. This represents our current active view controller. We want to push our media item picker view controller onto our active view controller, so we send the `presentModalViewController` message to our active view controller, with the media picker view controller as the parameter.

Next, let's implement the two delegate methods. The first delegate method is invoked after the user selects songs and taps Done. The second delegate method is invoked if the user cancels picking, (e.g., taps Done without selecting any songs).

```
#pragma mark MPMediaPickerControllerDelegate methods

- (void) mediaPicker:(MPMediaPickerController*)media_picker
didPickMediaItems:(MPMediaItemCollection*)item_collection
{
    MPMusicPlayerController* music_player = [MPMusicPlayerController iPodMusicPlayer];
    [music_player setQueueWithItemCollection:item_collection];
    [music_player play];

    [media_picker.parentViewController dismissModalViewControllerAnimated:YES];
}

- (void) mediaPickerDidCancel:(MPMediaPickerController *)media_picker
{
    [media_picker.parentViewController dismissModalViewControllerAnimated:YES];
}
```

The code in the first method should seem familiar, as it is almost the same as our `startApplication` code. We get the `iPodMusicController`, set the queue, and call `play`. Since this delegate method provides us the item collection, we use the `setQueueWithItemCollection` method instead of the query version. Lastly, in both functions, we remove the media picker item from the view controller so we can get back to the game.

That's the media item picker in a nutshell. Now we need to design a way for the user to bring up the picker. As I said, this is a hack. Rather than spending time trying to work in some new button, we will exploit the accelerometer and use a shake motion to be the trigger for bringing up a picker. (This also has the benefit of being kind of cool.) We will embark on another little side quest to accomplish this. (You might think that a better thing to do is shuffle the songs on shake, which you might like to try on your own.)

Shake It! (Easy Accelerometer Shake Detection)

In Chapter 3, you learned how to use the accelerometer. But we are going to spice things up and do something a little different. In iPhone OS 3.0, Apple introduced new APIs to make detecting shakes much easier:

```
- (void) motionBegan:(UIEventSubtype)the_motion withEvent:(UIEvent*)the_event;
- (void) motionEnded:(UIEventSubtype)the_motion withEvent:(UIEvent*)the_event;
- (void) motionCancelled:(UIEventSubtype)the_motion withEvent:(UIEvent*)the_event;
```

These were added into the `UIResponder` class, so you no longer need to access the accelerometer directly and analyze the raw accelerometer data yourself for common motions like shaking. Here, we will just use `motionBegan:withEvent:`.

Since this is part of the `UIResponder` class, we need to find the best place to add this code. This happens to be `BBInputViewController`, where we also handle all our touch events.

We will add the method and implement it as follows:

```
- (void) motionBegan:(UIEventSubtype)the_motion withEvent:(UIEvent *)the_event
{
    if(UIEventSubtypeMotionShake == the_motion)
    {
        [[IPodMusicController sharedMusicController] presentMediaPicker:self];
    }
}
```

This is very straightforward. We just check to make sure the motion is a shake event. If it is, we invoke our `presentMediaPicker:` method, which we just implemented. We pass `self` as the parameter because our `BBInputViewController` instance is the current active view controller to which we want to attach the picker.

For this code to actually work though, we need to do some setup. We need to implement three more methods for this class to make our `BBInputViewController` the first responder. Otherwise, the `motionBegan:withEvent:` method we just implemented will never be invoked. To do this, we drop in the following code:

```
- (BOOL) canBecomeFirstResponder
{
    return YES;
}

- (void) viewDidAppear:(BOOL)is_animated
{
    [self becomeFirstResponder];
    [super viewDidAppear:is_animated];
}

- (void) viewWillDisappear:(BOOL)is_animated
{
    [self resignFirstResponder];
    [super viewWillDisappear:is_animated];
}
```

Now you are ready to try it. Start up Space Rocks! and give the device a shake to bring up the picker. Select some songs and tap Done. You should hear the music change to your new selection. Shake it again and pick some other songs. Fun, eh? (Yes, pausing the game when presenting the media item picker would be a great idea, but since we currently lack a game pause feature, I felt that would be one side quest too far.)

This concludes our Media Player framework example. We will now move to general streaming APIs.

Audio Streaming

Audio streaming is the term I use to describe dealing with large audio data. Ultimately, the idea is to break down the audio into small, manageable buffers. Then in the playback case, you submit each small buffer to the audio system to play when it is ready to receive more data. This avoids needing to load the entire thing into memory at the same time and exhausting your limited amount of RAM.

The type of streaming I'm describing here is not the same as *network audio streaming*, which is often associated with things like Internet radio. With network audio streaming, the emphasis is on the *network* part. The idea is that you are reading in packets of data over the network and playing it. In principle, the audio streaming I am describing is pretty much the same idea, but lower level and only about the audio system. It doesn't really care where the data came from—it could be from the network, from a file, captured from a microphone, or dynamically generated from an algorithm.

While the concept is simple, depending on the API you use, preparing the buffers for use and knowing when to submit more data can be tedious. We will discuss three native APIs you can use for streaming: AVFoundation, OpenAL, and Audio Queue Services. Each has its own advantages and disadvantages.

AVFoundation is the easiest to use but the most limited in capabilities. OpenAL is lower-level, but more flexible than AVFoundation and can work seamlessly with all the cool OpenAL features we've covered in the previous two chapters. Audio Queue Services is at about the same level of difficulty as OpenAL, but may offer features and conveniences that OpenAL does not provide.

For applications that are not already using OpenAL already for nonstreaming audio, but need audio streaming capabilities that AVFoundation does not provide, Audio Queue Services is a compelling choice. But if your application is already using OpenAL for nonstreaming audio, the impedance mismatch between Audio Queue Services and OpenAL may cause you to miss easy opportunities to exploit cool things OpenAL can already do for you, such as spatializing your streaming audio (as demonstrated in this chapter).

AVFoundation-Based Background Music for Space Rocks!

Here's some good news: You already know how to play long files (stream) with AVAudioPlayer. We walked through an example in Chapter 9. AVAudioPlayer takes care of all the messy bookkeeping and threading, so you don't need to worry about it if you use this API.

There is more good news: iPhone OS allows you to use different audio APIs without jumping through hoops. We can take our Space Rocks! OpenAL-based application and add background music using AVAudioPlayer.

One thing to keep in mind is that you want to set the audio session only once (don't set it up in your AVFoundation code, and again in your OpenAL code). But interruptions must be handled for each API.

We will continue building on SpaceRocksOpenAL3D_6_SourceRelative from the previous chapter. (Note that this version does not include the changes we made for background music using the Media Player framework.) The completed project for this example is SpaceRocksAVFoundation. We will go through this very quickly, since you've already seen most of it in Chapter 9.

The Playback Sound Controller

As a baseline template, let's copy over our AVPlaybackSoundController class from Chapter 9 into the Space Rocks! project. We will then gut the code to remove the things we don't need. We will also add a few new methods to make it easier to integrate with Space Rocks! In truth, it would probably be just as easy to use Apple's AVAudioPlayer directly in the BBSceneController, but I wanted a separate place to put the interruption delegate callbacks to keep things clean.

Starting with the AVPlaybackSoundController header, let's delete all the old methods. Then delete the separate speech and music player. In its place, we'll create a generic "stream" player. The idea is that if the game needs multiple streams, we can instantiate multiple instances of this class. I suppose this makes this class less of a "controller," but oh well.

The class also conformed to the AVAudioSessionDelegate protocol. We will let the OpenAL controller class continue to set up and manage the audio session, so we can delete this, too. We need a way to specify an arbitrary sound file, so we'll make a new designated initializer called initWithSoundFile:, which takes an NSString* parameter. Finally, we'll add some new methods and properties to control playing, pausing, stopping, volume, and looping. The modified *AVPlaybackSoundController.h* file should look like this:

```
#import <AVFoundation/AVFoundation.h>
#import <UIKit/UIKit.h>

@interface AVPlaybackSoundController : NSObject <AVAudioPlayerDelegate>
{
    AVAudioPlayer* avStreamPlayer;
}

@property(nonatomic, retain) AVAudioPlayer* avStreamPlayer;
@property(nonatomic, assign) NSInteger numberOfLoops;
@property(nonatomic, assign) float volume;

- (id) initWithSoundFile:(NSString*) sound_file_basename;

- (void) play;
- (void) pause;
- (void) stop;

@end
```

In our implementation, we delete almost everything except the AVAudioPlayerDelegate methods. We will purge the audioPlayerDidFinishPlaying:successfully:-specific implementation though. We then just implement the new methods. Most of them are direct pass-throughs to AVAudioPlayer. The one exception is our new initializer. This code will create our new AVAudioPlayer instance. We also copy and paste the file-detection code we use from the OpenAL section to locate a file without requiring an extension. The new *AVPlaybackSoundController.m* file looks like this:

```objc
#import "AVPlaybackSoundController.h"

@implementation AVPlaybackSoundController

@synthesize avStreamPlayer;


- (id) initWithSoundFile:(NSString*)sound_file_basename
{
    NSURL* file_url = nil;
    NSError* file_error = nil;

    // Create a temporary array containing the file extensions we want to handle.
    // Note: This list is not exhaustive of all the types Core Audio can handle.
    NSArray* file_extension_array = [[NSArray alloc]
        initWithObjects:@"caf", @"wav", @"aac", @"mp3", @"aiff", @"mp4", @"m4a", nil];
    for(NSString* file_extension in file_extension_array)
    {
        // We need to first check to make sure the file exists;
        // otherwise NSURL's initFileWithPath:ofType will crash if the file doesn't exist
        NSString* full_file_name = [NSString stringWithFormat:@"%@/%@.%@",
            [[NSBundle mainBundle] resourcePath], sound_file_basename, file_extension];
        if(YES == [[NSFileManager defaultManager] fileExistsAtPath:full_file_name])
        {
            file_url = [[[NSURL alloc] initFileURLWithPath:[[NSBundle mainBundle]
                pathForResource:sound_file_basename ofType:file_extension]] autorelease];
            break;
        }
    }
    [file_extension_array release];

    if(nil == file_url)
    {
        NSLog(@"Failed to locate audio file with basename: %@", sound_file_basename);
        return nil;
    }

    self = [super init];
    if(nil != self)
    {
        avStreamPlayer = [[AVAudioPlayer alloc] initWithContentsOfURL:file_url
            error:&file_error];
        if(file_error)
        {
            NSLog(@"Error loading stream file: %@", [file_error localizedDescription]);
        }
        avStreamPlayer.delegate = self;
        // Optional: Presumably, the player will start buffering now instead of on play.
        [avStreamPlayer prepareToPlay];
    }
    return self;
}

- (void) play
{
    [self.avStreamPlayer play];
```

```objc
}

- (void) pause
{
    [self.avStreamPlayer pause];
}

- (void) stop
{
    [self.avStreamPlayer stop];
}

- (void) setNumberOfLoops:(NSInteger)number_of_loops
{
    self.avStreamPlayer.numberOfLoops = number_of_loops;
}

- (NSInteger) numberOfLoops
{
    return self.avStreamPlayer.numberOfLoops;
}

- (void) setVolume:(float)volume_level
{
    self.avStreamPlayer.volume = volume_level;
}

- (float) volume
{
    return self.avStreamPlayer.volume;
}

- (void) dealloc
{
    [avStreamPlayer release];
    [super dealloc];
}

#pragma mark AVAudioPlayer delegate methods

- (void) audioPlayerDidFinishPlaying:(AVAudioPlayer*)which_player
    successfully:(BOOL)the_flag
{
}

- (void) audioPlayerDecodeErrorDidOccur:(AVAudioPlayer*)the_player
    error:(NSError*)the_error
{
    NSLog(@"AVAudioPlayer audioPlayerDecodeErrorDidOccur: %@", [the_error
        localizedDescription]);
}

- (void) audioPlayerBeginInterruption:(AVAudioPlayer*)which_player
{
}

- (void) audioPlayerEndInterruption:(AVAudioPlayer*)which_player
```

```
{
    [which_player play];
  }
@end
```

We probably should do something interesting with `audioPlayerDidFinishPlaying:successfully:` to integrate it with the rest of the game engine, similar to what we did with the OpenAL resource manager. But since this example is concerned only with playing background music, which we will infinitely loop, we won't worry about that here.

Integration into Space Rocks!

Now for the integration. Remember to add `AVFoundation.framework` to the project so it can be linked. In *BBConfiguration.h*, we'll add our background music file. Prior to this point, I've been making my own sound effects, or in a few instances, finding public domain stuff on the Internet. But creating a good soundtrack exceeds my talents, and it is very hard to find one in the public domain or free for commercial use. Fortunately for us, Ben Smith got permission from the musician he used for Snowferno to reuse one of his soundtracks for Space Rocks! for our book. Please do not use this song for your own projects, as this permission does not extend beyond this book's example.

```
Attribution Credits:
Music by Michael Shaieb
© Copyright 2009 FatLab Music
From "Snowferno" for iPhone/iPod touch
```

Also, for demonstration purposes, I have compressed the soundtrack using AAC into an *.m4a* container file. This is to demonstrate that we can use restricted compression formats for our audio files in our game. Chapter 11 covered audio file formats. Remember that the hardware decoder can handle only one file in compression format at a time. While compressing it, I converted it down to 22 kHz to match all our other sample rates for performance. You'll find the file *D-ay-Z-ray_mix_090502.m4a* in the completed project. Make sure to add it to your project if you are following along.

Add this line to *BBConfiguration.h*:

```
#define BACKGROUND_MUSIC @"D-ay-Z-ray_mix_090502"
```

In *BBSceneController.h*, we're going to add a new instance variable:

```
@class AVPlaybackSoundController;

@interface BBSceneController : NSObject <EWSoundCallbackDelegate> {
    ...
    AVPlaybackSoundController* backgroundMusicPlayer;
}
```

In *BBSceneController.m*, we are going to create a new instance of the backgroundMusicPlayer in the init method. We want to use our background music file and set the player to infinitely loop. To avoid overwhelming all the other audio, we will reduce the volume of the music. Once this is all set up, we tell the player to play.

```
- (id) init
```

```
{
    self = [super init];
    if(nil != self)
    {
        SetPreferredSampleRate(22050.0);
        [[OpenALSoundController sharedSoundController] setSoundCallbackDelegate:self];
        [self invokeLoadResources];
        [[OpenALSoundController sharedSoundController]
            setDistanceModel:AL_INVERSE_DISTANCE_CLAMPED];
        [[OpenALSoundController sharedSoundController] setDopplerFactor:1.0];
        [[OpenALSoundController sharedSoundController] setSpeedOfSound:343.3];
        backgroundMusicPlayer = [[AVPlaybackSoundController alloc]
            initWithSoundFile:BACKGROUND_MUSIC];
        backgroundMusicPlayer.numberOfLoops = -1; // loop music
        backgroundMusicPlayer.volume = 0.5;
    }
    return self;
}
```

Conversely, in our dealloc method, we should remember to delete the player for good measure.

```
[backgroundMusicPlayer stop];
[backgroundMusicPlayer release];
```

And, of course, we need to actually start playing the music. We could do this in init, but the startScene method seems to be more appropriate. So add the following line there:

```
[backgroundMusicPlayer play];
```

Finally, in the audio session initialization code in our OpenALSoundController class, we should switch the mode from Ambient to Solo Ambient, because we are using an .m4a file for our background music, and we would like to minimize the burden on the CPU by using the hardware decoder. If we don't do this, the music will play using the software decoder, which will work but could significantly degrade the performance of Space Rocks!, since the game already pushes the CPU pretty hard, even without audio. And it doesn't make a lot of sense to keep using Ambient mode, which would allow mixing iPod music, now that we have our own soundtrack. Alternatively, we could avoid using a restricted compression format for our audio and not worry about this. But since we have an idle hardware decoding unit and can benefit from higher compression, we will exploit these capabilities. The remaining streaming examples will also switch to Solo Ambient for these same reasons.

Find our call to InitAudioSession in OpenALSoundController.m's init method, and change the first parameter to kAudioSessionCategory_SoloAmbientSound.

```
InitAudioSession(kAudioSessionCategory_SoloAmbientSound, MyInterruptionCallback, self,
PREFERRED_SAMPLE_OUTPUT_RATE);
```

Congratulations! Not only do you have background music, but you have also learned all the basic essential elements in creating a complete game solution with respect to audio. Many developers will often be satisfied here. They can play OpenAL sound effects and stream audio easily with AVFoundation.

But I encourage you to stick around for the next section on the OpenAL streaming solution. While it's more difficult, you'll continue to get features such as spatialized sound. You'll also be able to reuse more infrastructure, so things will integrate more smoothly, instead of having two disparate audio systems that don't really talk to each other. For example, we currently do nothing with AVAudioPlayer's audioPlayerDidFinishPlaying:successfully: method because we would have to think about how it would integrate with the rest of the system. We already defined all those behaviors for our OpenAL system, so there is less ambiguity on how we should handle it with OpenAL streaming.

OpenAL Buffer Queuing Introduction

Before we jump into the technical specifics of how OpenAL handles streaming, it may be a useful thought exercise to imagine how you might accomplish streaming with what you already know. Let's start with the three fundamental objects in OpenAL: buffers, sources, and listeners. Listeners are irrelevant to this discussion, so we can ignore them. It's going to come down to buffers and sources.

Conceptually, streaming is just playing small buffers sequentially. You use small buffers so you don't consume too much RAM trying to load a whole giant file.

To implement streaming with what you already know, you might try something like this (pseudo code):

```
while( StillHaveDataInAudioFile(music_file) )
{
    pcm_data = GetSmallBufferOfPCMDataFromFile(music_file);
    alBufferData(al_buffer, pcm_data, ...); // copy the data into a OpenAL buffer
    alSourcei(al_source, AL_BUFFER, al_buffer); // attach OpenAL Buffer to OpenAL source
    alSourcePlay(al_source);
    MagicFunctionThatWaitsForPlayingToStop();
}
```

In this pseudo code, we read a small chunk of data from a file, copy the data into OpenAL, and then play the data. Once the playback ends, we repeat the process until we have no more audio data.

In a theoretical world, this code could work. But in the real world, there is a fatal flaw of latency risk. Once the playback ends, you need to load the next chunk of data and then start playing it before the user perceives a pause in the playback. If you have a very fast, low-latency computer, you might get away with this, but probably not.

You could try to improve on this function by using a double-buffer technique (often employed in graphics). You would create two OpenAL buffers. While the source is playing, you could start reading and copying the next chunk of data. Then when the playback ends, you can immediately feed the source the next buffer. You still have a latency risk, in that you might not be able to call play fast enough, but your overall latency has been greatly reduced. To mitigate the case of being overloaded and falling behind, you could simply extend the number of buffers you attempt to preload. Instead of having two buffers, try ten or a hundred.

Fortunately, OpenAL solves this last remaining problem by providing several additional API functions that allow you to queue buffers to a playing (or stopped) source. That way, you don't need to worry about swapping the buffer at the perfect time and calling `play` to restart. OpenAL will do that on your behalf behind the scenes. This is a reasonably elegant design, in that you don't need to introduce any new object types. You remain with just buffers, sources, and listeners. Figure 12–6 illustrates how buffer queuing works in OpenAL.

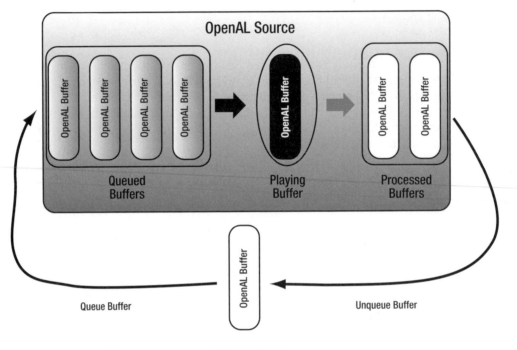

Figure 12–6. *The OpenAL buffer queuing life cycle. OpenAL allows you to queue OpenAL buffers on an OpenAL source. The source will play a buffer, and when finished, it will mark the buffer as processed. The source will then automatically start playing the next buffer in the queue. To keep the cycle going, you should reclaim the processed buffers, fill them with new audio data, and queue them again to the source. Note that you are permitted to have multiple OpenAL sources doing buffer queuing.*

That said, there is some grunt work and bookkeeping you must do. You will need to manage multiple buffers, and find opportune times to fill the buffers with new data and add them to the queue on your designated source(s). You are also required to unqueue[1] buffers from your source(s) when OpenAL is done with them (called *processed buffers*).

---

[1] The correct term may be *dequeue*, but the official OpenAL API uses the term *unqueue*, and you will see that term used in discussions out in the wild. Thus, I will continue to use the term *unqueue*.

Because there is enough going on, I felt it would be better to start with a simple isolated example before trying to integrate streaming into Space Rocks! We will start with a new project. The completed project for this example is called `BasicOpenALStreaming`. The project has a UI that is similar to the interface we constructed in Chapter 9 for `AVPlayback`, but even simpler (see Figure 12–7).

Figure 12–7. *The example project: BasicOpenALStreaming, which has a minimal UI*

In this example, we will just play music and forego the speech player. The play button will play and pause the music. For interest, we will add a volume slider. The volume slider is connected to the OpenAL listener gain, so we are using it like a master volume control.

All the important code is contained in the new class `OpenALStreamingController`. Much of this class should look very familiar to you, as it is mostly a repeat of the first OpenAL examples in Chapter 10 (i.e., initialize an audio session, create a source, and so on).

Initialization

Following the pattern we used for `OpenALSoundController` in Chapter 10, let's examine the changes we need to make for *OpenALStreamingController.m*'s initOpenAL method.

```
- (void) initOpenAL
{
    openALDevice = alcOpenDevice(NULL);
    if(openALDevice != NULL)
    {
```

```
        // Use the Apple extension to set the mixer rate
        alcMacOSXMixerOutputRate(44100.0);

        // Create a new OpenAL context
        // The new context will render to the OpenAL device just created
        openALContext = alcCreateContext(openALDevice, 0);
        if(openALContext != NULL)
        {
            // Make the new context the current OpenAL context
            alcMakeContextCurrent(openALContext);
        }
        else
        {
            NSLog(@"Error, could not create audio context.");
            return;
        }
    }
    else
    {
        NSLog(@"Error, could not get audio device.");
        return;
    }

    alGenSources(1, &streamingSource);
    alGenBuffers(MAX_OPENAL_QUEUE_BUFFERS, availableALBufferArray);
    availableALBufferArrayCurrentIndex = 0;

    // File is from Internet Archive Open Source Audio, US Army Band, public domain
    // http://www.archive.org/details/TheBattleHymnOfTheRepublic_993
    NSURL* file_url = [NSURL fileURLWithPath:[[NSBundle mainBundle]
        pathForResource:@"battle_hymn_of_the_republic" ofType:@"mp3"]];
    if(file_url)
    {
        streamingAudioRef = MyGetExtAudioFileRef((CFURLRef)file_url,
            &streamingAudioDescription);
    }
    else
    {
        NSLog(@"Could not find file!\n");
        streamingAudioRef = NULL;
    }

    intermediateDataBuffer = malloc(INTERMEDIATE_BUFFER_SIZE);
}
```

The only new/customized code is at the bottom of the method after the OpenAL context is initialized.

First, we create an OpenAL source, which we will use to play our music using `alGenSources`. Next, we create five OpenAL buffers using the array version of the function. The number of buffers was picked somewhat arbitrarily. We'll talk about picking the number a little later, but for now, just know that our program will have a maximum of five buffers queued at any one time.

Then we open the music file we are going to play. I am reusing the same file from the AVPlayback example in Chapter 9.

The first semi-new thing is that we call `MyGetExtAudioFileRef`. Recall that in our side quest in Chapter 10 when we loaded files into OpenAL using Core Audio, we deliberately broke up the function into three pieces, but we used only the third piece, `MyGetOpenALAudioDataAll`, which is built using the other two pieces. `MyGetOpenALAudioDataAll` loads the entire file into a buffer. But since we don't want to load the entire file for this streaming example, we need to use the two other pieces. The first piece, `MyGetExtAudioFileRef`, will just open the file using Core Audio (Extended File Services) and return a file handle (`ExtAudioFileRef`). We save this file reference in an instance variable, because we need to read the data from it later as we stream. We also have `streamingAudioDescription` as an instance variable, because we need to keep the audio description metadata around for the other function. (We'll get to the second piece a little later.)

Next, we allocate memory for a PCM buffer. This is memory we will have Extended File Services decode file data into so we can use it. I have hard-coded the buffer to be 32KB, which means this demo is going to stream audio data in 32,768-byte chunks at a time.

That concludes our initialization. Let's now go to the heart of the program, which is in the `animationCallback:` method in `OpenALStreamingController`. This is where all the important stuff happens.

Unqueuing

We need to do two things with OpenAL streaming: queue buffers to play and unqueue buffers that have finished playing (processed buffers). We will start with unqueuing (and reclaiming) the processed buffers. I like to do this first, because I can then turn around and immediately use that buffer again for the next queue.

First, OpenAL will let us query how many buffers have been processed using `alGetSourcei` with `AL_BUFFERS_PROCESSED`. In *OpenALStreamingController.m*'s `animationCallback:` method, we need to have the following:

```
ALint buffers_processed = 0;
alGetSourcei(streamingSource, AL_BUFFERS_PROCESSED, &buffers_processed);
```

Next, we can write a simple while loop to unqueue and reclaim each processed buffer, one at a time.[2] To actually unqueue a buffer, OpenAL provides the function `alSourceUnqueueBuffers`. You provide it the source you want to unqueue from, the number of buffers you want to unqueue, and a pointer to where the unqueued buffer IDs will be returned.

```
while(buffers_processed > 0)
{
    ALuint unqueued_buffer;
    alSourceUnqueueBuffers(streamingSource, 1, &unqueued_buffer);
```

---

[2] If you want to be clever, you can do it without the loop in one shot. Hint: not required but, C99 variable-length arrays might be fun/convenient to use here.

```
            availableALBufferArrayCurrentIndex--;
            availableALBufferArray[availableALBufferArrayCurrentIndex] = unqueued_buffer;

            buffers_processed--;
        }
```

We keep an array of available buffers so we can use them in the next step. We use the array like a stack, hence the incrementing and decrementing of the availableALBufferArrayCurrentIndex. Don't get too hung up on this part. Just consider it an opaque data structure. Because we're doing a minimalist example, I wanted to avoid using Cocoa data structures or introducing my own. The next example will not be minimalist.

Queuing

Now we are ready to queue a buffer. When we queue a buffer, we need to load a chunk of the data from the file, get the data into OpenAL, and queue it to the OpenAL source. We are going to queue only one buffer in a single function pass. The idea is that this function will be called repeatedly (30 times a second or so). The assumption is the function call rate will be faster than OpenAL can use up the buffer, so there will always be multiple buffers queued in a given moment, up to some maximum number of queue buffers that we define. For this example, MAX_OPENAL_QUEUE_BUFFERS is hard-coded as follows:

```
#define MAX_OPENAL_QUEUE_BUFFERS 5
```

We continue adding code to animationCallback: in *OpenALStreamingController.m*. The first thing we do is check to make sure we have available buffers to queue. If not, then we don't need to do anything.

```
if(availableALBufferArrayCurrentIndex < MAX_OPENAL_QUEUE_BUFFERS)
{
```

Once we establish we need to queue a new buffer, we do it.

```
    ALuint current_buffer = availableALBufferArray[availableALBufferArrayCurrentIndex];

    ALsizei buffer_size;
    ALenum data_format;
    ALsizei sample_rate;

    MyGetDataFromExtAudioRef(streamingAudioRef, &streamingAudioDescription,
        INTERMEDIATE_BUFFER_SIZE, &intermediateDataBuffer, &buffer_size,
        &data_format, &sample_rate);
    if(0 == buffer_size) // will loop music on EOF (which is 0 bytes)
    {
        MyRewindExtAudioData(streamingAudioRef);
        MyGetDataFromExtAudioRef(streamingAudioRef, &streamingAudioDescription,
            INTERMEDIATE_BUFFER_SIZE, &intermediateDataBuffer, &buffer_size,
            &data_format, &sample_rate);
    }
    alBufferData(current_buffer, data_format, intermediateDataBuffer, buffer_size,
        sample_rate);
    alSourceQueueBuffers(streamingSource, 1, &current_buffer);
```

```
availableALBufferArrayCurrentIndex++;
```

We use our MyGetDataFromExtAudioRef function (which is our second piece of the Core Audio file loader from Chapter 10) to fetch a chunk of data from our file. We provide the file handle and the audio description, which you can consider as opaque data types for Core Audio. We provide the buffer size and buffer to which we want the data copied. The function will return by reference the amount of data we actually get back, the OpenAL data format, and the sample rate. We can then feed these three items directly into alBufferData. We use alBufferData for simplicity in this example. For performance, we should consider using alBufferDataStatic, since this function is going to be called a lot, and we are going to be streaming in the middle of game play where performance is more critical. We will change this in the next example.

Finally, we call OpenAL's function alSourceQueueBuffers to queue the buffer. We specify the source, the number of buffers, and an array containing the buffer IDs.

There is a corner case handled in the preceding code. If we get 0 bytes back from MyGetDataFromExtAudioRef, it means we hit the end of the file (EOF). For this example, we want to loop the music, so we call our custom helper function MyRewindExtAudioData, which rewinds the file pointer to the beginning. We then grab the data again. If you were thinking you could use OpenAL's built-in loop functionality, this won't work. OpenAL doesn't have access to the full data anymore, since we broke everything into small pieces and unqueued the old data (the beginning of the file). We must implement looping ourselves.

Buffer Underrun

We've now queued the buffer, but there is one more step we may need to take. It could happen that we were not quick enough in queuing more data, and OpenAL ran out of data to play. If OpenAL runs out of data to play, it must stop playing. This makes sense, because OpenAL can't know whether we were too slow at queuing more data or we actually finished playing (and don't plan to loop). I call the case where we were too slow a *buffer underrun*.

To remedy the potential buffer underrun case, our task is to find out if the OpenAL source is still playing. If it is not playing, we need to determine if it is because of a buffer underrun or because we don't want to play (e.g., finished playing, wanted to pause, etc.).

We will use alGetSourcei to find the source state to figure out if we are not playing. Then we can use alGetSourcei to get the number of buffers queued to help determine if we are in a buffer underrun situation. (We will have one queued buffer now since we just added one in the last step.) Then we make sure the user didn't pause the player, which would be a legitimate reason for not playing even though we have buffers queued. If we determine we should, in fact, be playing, we simply call alSourcePlay.

```
ALenum current_playing_state;
alGetSourcei(streamingSource, AL_SOURCE_STATE, &current_playing_state);
// Handle buffer underrun case
if(AL_PLAYING != current_playing_state)
{
```

```
   ALint buffers_queued = 0;

   alGetSourcei(streamingSource, AL_BUFFERS_QUEUED, &buffers_queued);

   if(buffers_queued > 0 && NO == self.isStreamingPaused)
   {
       // Need to restart play
       alSourcePlay(streamingSource);
   }
}
```

Pausing

We use `alSourcePause` for the first time in this example. It probably behaves exactly as you think it does, so there is not much to say about it.

Fast Forwarding and Rewinding

You may be wondering why we removed the fast-forward and rewind buttons from the `AVPlayback` example. The reason is that seeking is more difficult with OpenAL streaming than it is with `AVAudioPlayer`.

OpenAL does have support for seeking. There are three different attributes you can use with `alSource*` and `alGetSource*`: `AL_SEC_OFFSET`, `AL_SAMPLE_OFFSET`, and `AL_BYTE_OFFSET`. These deal with the positions in seconds, samples, or bytes. With fully loaded buffers, seeking is pretty easy. But with streaming, you will need to do some additional bookkeeping.

The problem is that with streaming, OpenAL can seek only within the range of what is currently queued. If you seek to something that is outside that range, it won't work. In addition, you need to make sure your file handle is kept in sync with your seek request; otherwise, you will be streaming new data in at the wrong position. Thus, you really need to seek at the file level instead of the OpenAL level.

Generally, emptying the current queue and rebuffering it at the new position is the easiest solution. (If you don't empty the queue, you may have a lag between when the users requested a seek and when they actually hear it.) But, of course, as you've just emptied your queue and need to start over, you may have introduced some new latency issues. For this kind of application, probably no one will care though. For simplicity, this was omitted from the example. For the curious, notice that our `MyRewindExtAudioData` function wraps `ExtAudioFileSeek`. This is what you'll probably want to use to seek using Extended File Services.

Startup Number of Buffers and Filling the Queue

Recall that in this example, we fill only one buffer per update loop pass. This means the game loop must be run through at least five times before we can fill our queue to our designated maximum of `MAX_OPENAL_QUEUE_BUFFERS`. This brings up the question, "What is the best strategy for filling the queue?"

There are two extremes to consider. The first extreme is what we did in the example. We fill a single buffer and move on. The advantages of this strategy are that it is easy to implement and it has a cheap startup cost. It allows us to spread the buffer fill-up cost over a longer period of time. The disadvantage is that when we first start up, we don't have a safety net. We are particularly vulnerable to an untimely system usage spike that prevents us from being able to queue the next buffer in time.

The other extreme is that we fill up our queue to our designated maximum when we start playing. So, in this example, rather than filling just one buffer, we would fill up five buffers. While this gives us extra protection from starvation, we have a trade-off of a longer startup cost. This may manifest itself as a performance hiccup in the game if the startup cost is too great. For example, the player may fire a weapon that we tied to streaming. If we spend too much time up front to load more buffers, the user may perceive a delay between the time he touched the fire button and when the weapon actually seemed to fire in the game.

You will need to experiment to find the best pattern for you and your game. You might consider hybrids of the two extremes, where on startup, you queue two or three buffers instead of the maximum. You might also consider varying the buffer sizes and the number of buffers you queue based on metrics such as how empty the queue is or how taxed the CPU is. And, of course, multithreading/concurrency can be used, too.

How to Choose the Number and Size of Buffers

Finally, you may be wondering why we picked five buffers and made our buffers 32KB. This is somewhat of a guessing game. You generally need to find values that give good performance for your case. You are trying to balance different things.

The buffer size will affect how long it takes to load new data from the file. Larger buffers take more time. If you take too much time, you will starve the queue, because you didn't get data into the queue fast enough. In my personal experience, I have found 1KB to 64KB to be the range for buffer sizes. More typically, I tend to deal with 8KB to 32KB. Apple seems to like 16KB to 64KB. Some of Apple's examples include a CalculateBytesForTime function, which will dynamically decide the size based on some criteria. (It's worth a look.)

I also like powers of two because of a hard-to-reproduce bug I had way back with the Loki OpenAL implementation. When not using power-of-two buffer sizes, I had certain playback problems. That implementation is dead now, but the habit stuck with me. Some digital processing libraries, like for a Fast Fourier Transform (FFT), often prefer arrays in power-of-two sizes for performance reasons. So it doesn't hurt.[3]

---

[3] To be pedantic, buffer sizes must be an exact multiple of the sample frame size (or block alignment in Wave format terminology). As it turns out, powers of two always work for mono and stereo samples.

As for the number of buffers, you basically want enough to prevent buffer underruns. The more buffers you have queued, the less likely it will be that you deplete the queue before you can add more. However, if you have too many buffers, you are wasting memory. The point of streaming is to save memory. And, obviously, there is a relationship with the buffer size. Larger buffer sizes will last longer, so you need fewer buffers.

Also, you might think about the startup number of buffers. In our example, we queue only one buffer to start with. One consequence of that is we must make our buffer larger to avoid early starvation. If we had queued more buffers, the buffer size could be smaller.

OpenAL-Based Background Music for Space Rocks!

This is the moment you've been waiting for. Now that you understand OpenAL buffer queuing, let's integrate it into Space Rocks!, thereby completing our game engine.

We will again use SpaceRocksOpenAL3D_6_SourceRelative from the previous chapter as our starting point for this example. The completed project for this example is SpaceRocksOpenALStreaming1. (This version does not include the changes we made for background music using Media Player framework or AVFoundation. This will be an exclusively OpenAL project.)

The core changes will occur in two locations. We will need to add streaming support to our update loop in OpenALSoundController, and we need a new class to encapsulate our stream buffer data.

A New Buffer Data Class for Streaming

Let's start with the new class. We will name it EWStreamBufferData and create .h and .m files for it. The purpose of this class is analogous to the EWSoundBufferData class we made earlier, except it will be for streamed data.

```
@interface EWStreamBufferData : NSObject
{
    ALenum openalFormat;
    ALsizei dataSize;
    ALsizei sampleRate;
```

In Chapter 10, we implemented a central/shared database of audio files with soundFileDictionary and EWSoundBufferData. We will not be repeating that pattern with EWStreamBufferData. This is because it makes no sense to share streamed data. With fully loaded sounds, we can share the explosion sound between the UFO and the spaceship. But with streamed data, we can't do this because we have only a small chunk of the data in memory at any given time. So, in the case of the explosion sound, the spaceship might be starting to explode while the UFO is ending its explosion. Each needs a different buffer segment in the underlying sound file. For streamed data, if both the UFO and spaceship use the same file, they still need to have separate instances of EWStreamBufferData. Because of the differences between the two classes, I have opted to not make EWStreamBufferData a subclass of EWSoundBufferData. You could do this if you want, but you would need to modify the existing code to then be aware of the differences.

This class will contain the multiple OpenAL buffers needed for buffer queuing. In the previous example, we used five buffers. This time, we will use 32. (I'll explain the increase in buffers later.) We will use the alBufferDataStatic extension for improved performance, so we also need 32 buffers for raw PCM data.

```
#define EW_STREAM_BUFFER_DATA_MAX_OPENAL_QUEUE_BUFFERS 32
    ALuint openalDataBufferArray[EW_STREAM_BUFFER_DATA_MAX_OPENAL_QUEUE_BUFFERS];
    void* pcmDataBufferArray[EW_STREAM_BUFFER_DATA_MAX_OPENAL_QUEUE_BUFFERS];
```

We will also need to keep track of which buffers are queued and which are available. In the previous example, I apologized for being too minimalist for using a single C array. This time, we will use two NSMutableArrays for more clarity.

```
    NSMutableArray* availableDataBuffersQueue;
    NSMutableArray* queuedDataBuffersQueue;
```

This class will also contain the ExtAudioFileRef (file handle) to the audio file (and AudioStreamBasicDescription) so we can load data into the buffers from the file as we need it.

```
    ExtAudioFileRef streamingAudioRef;
    AudioStreamBasicDescription streamingAudioDescription;
```

We also have a few properties. We have a streamingPaused property in case we need to pause the audio, which will allow us to disambiguate from a buffer underrun, as in the previous example. (We will not actually pause the audio in our game.) We add audioLooping so it can be an option instead of hard-coded. And we add an atEOF property so we can record if we hit the end of file.

```
    BOOL audioLooping;
    BOOL streamingPaused;
    BOOL atEOF;
}
@property(nonatomic, assign, getter=isAudioLooping) BOOL audioLooping;
@property(nonatomic, assign, getter=isStreamingPaused) BOOL streamingPaused;
@property(nonatomic, assign, getter=isAtEOF) BOOL atEOF;
```

We will also add three methods:

```
+ (EWStreamBufferData*) streamBufferDataFromFileBaseName:(NSString*)sound_file_basename;
- (EWStreamBufferData*) initFromFileBaseName:(NSString*)sound_file_basename;
- (BOOL) updateQueue:(ALuint)streaming_source;
@end
```

The initFromFileBaseName: instance method is our designated initializer, which sets the file to be used for streaming. For convenience, we have a class method named streamBufferDataFromFileBaseName:, which ultimately does the same thing as initFromFileBaseName:, except that it returns an autoreleased object (as you would expect, following standard Cocoa naming conventions).

You might have noticed that this design contrasts slightly with the method soundBufferDataFromFileBaseName:, which we placed in OpenALSoundController instead of EWSoundBufferData. The main reason is that for EWSoundBufferData objects, we had a central database to allow resource sharing. Since OpenALSoundController is a singleton, it was convenient to put the central database there. EWStreamBufferData differs in that we won't have a central database. Since this class is relatively small, I thought we might take the opportunity to relieve the burden on OpenALSoundController. Ultimately, the two classes are going to work together, so it doesn't matter too much. But for symmetry, we will add a convenience method to OpenALSoundController named streamBufferDataFromFileBaseName:, which just calls the one in this class.

The updateQueue: method is where we are going to do most of the unqueuing and queuing work. We could do this in the OpenALSoundController, but as you saw, the code is a bit lengthy. So again, I thought I we might take the opportunity to relieve the burden on OpenALSoundController.

Finally, because we are using alBufferDataStatic, we want an easy way to keep our PCM buffer associated with our OpenAL buffer, particularly with our NSMutableArray queues. We introduce a helper class that just encapsulates both buffers so we know they belong together.

```
@interface EWStreamBufferDataContainer : NSObject
{
    ALuint openalDataBuffer;
    void* pcmDataBuffer;
}
@property(nonatomic, assign) ALuint openalDataBuffer;
@property(nonatomic, assign) void* pcmDataBuffer;
@end
```

In our initialization code for EWStreamBufferData, we need to allocate a bunch of memory: 32 OpenAL buffers (via alGenBuffers), 32 PCM buffers (via malloc), and 2 NSMutableArrays, which are going to mirror the buffer queue state by recording which buffers are queued and which are available. Let's first look at the code related to initialization:

```
@implementation EWStreamBufferData
@synthesize audioLooping;
@synthesize streamingPaused;
@synthesize atEOF;

- (void) createOpenALBuffers
{

    for(NSUInteger i=0; i<EW_STREAM_BUFFER_DATA_MAX_OPENAL_QUEUE_BUFFERS; i++)
    {
        pcmDataBufferArray[i] = malloc(EW_STREAM_BUFFER_DATA_INTERMEDIATE_BUFFER_SIZE);
    }

    alGenBuffers(EW_STREAM_BUFFER_DATA_MAX_OPENAL_QUEUE_BUFFERS, openalDataBufferArray);

    availableDataBuffersQueue = [[NSMutableArray alloc]
        initWithCapacity:EW_STREAM_BUFFER_DATA_MAX_OPENAL_QUEUE_BUFFERS];
```

```
        queuedDataBuffersQueue = [[NSMutableArray alloc]
            initWithCapacity:EW_STREAM_BUFFER_DATA_MAX_OPENAL_QUEUE_BUFFERS];

        for(NSUInteger i=0; i<EW_STREAM_BUFFER_DATA_MAX_OPENAL_QUEUE_BUFFERS; i++)
        {
            EWStreamBufferDataContainer* stream_buffer_data_container =
                [[EWStreamBufferDataContainer alloc] init];
            stream_buffer_data_container.openalDataBuffer = openalDataBufferArray[i];
            stream_buffer_data_container.pcmDataBuffer = pcmDataBufferArray[i];
            [availableDataBuffersQueue addObject:stream_buffer_data_container];
            [stream_buffer_data_container release];
        }
    }
}

- (id) init
{
    self = [super init];
    if(nil != self)
    {
        [self createOpenALBuffers];
    }
    return self;
}

- (EWStreamBufferData*) initFromFileBaseName:(NSString*)sound_file_basename
{
    self = [super init];
    if(nil != self)
    {
        [self createOpenALBuffers];

        NSURL* file_url = nil;

// Create a temporary array containing all the file extensions we want to handle.
// Note: This list is not exhaustive of all the types Core Audio can handle.
NSArray* file_extension_array = [[NSArray alloc]
  initWithObjects:@"caf", @"wav", @"aac", @"mp3", @"aiff", @"mp4", @"m4a", nil];
for(NSString* file_extension in file_extension_array)
{
    // We need to first check to make sure the file exists;
    // otherwise NSURL's initFileWithPath:ofType will crash if the file doesn't exist
    NSString* full_file_name = [NSString stringWithFormat:@"%@/%@.%@",
      [[NSBundle mainBundle] resourcePath], sound_file_basename, file_extension];
    if(YES == [[NSFileManager defaultManager] fileExistsAtPath:full_file_name])
    {
        file_url = [[NSURL alloc] initFileURLWithPath:[[NSBundle mainBundle]
          pathForResource:sound_file_basename ofType:file_extension]];
        break;
    }
}
[file_extension_array release];

if(nil == file_url)
{
    NSLog(@"Failed to locate audio file with basename: %@", sound_file_basename);
    [self release];
    return nil;
```

```
    }

    streamingAudioRef = MyGetExtAudioFileRef((CFURLRef)file_url,
        &streamingAudioDescription);
    [file_url release];
    if(NULL == streamingAudioRef)
    {
        NSLog(@"Failed to load audio data from file: %@", sound_file_basename);
        [self release];
        return nil;
    }
}

        return self;
}


+ (EWStreamBufferData*) streamBufferDataFromFileBaseName:(NSString*)sound_file_basename
{
        return [[[EWStreamBufferData alloc] initFromFileBaseName:sound_file_basename]
autorelease];
}
```

Let's examine the initFromFileBaseName: method. The first part of the method is just a copy-and-paste of our file-finding code that tries to guess file extensions. The following is the only important line in this function:

```
streamingAudioRef = MyGetExtAudioFileRef((CFURLRef)file_url,
&streamingAudioDescription);
```

This opens our file and returns the file handle and AudioStreamBasicDescription.

The streamBufferDataFromFileBaseName: convenience class method just invokes the initFromFileBaseName: instance method.

Finally, in the createOpenALBuffers method, the final for loop fills our availableDataBuffersQueue with our EWStramBufferDataContainer wrapper object. That way, it is easy to get at both the PCM buffer and OpenAL buffer from the array object.

You might be wondering why we have two arrays when the previous example had only one. With two arrays, we can easily know if a buffer is queued or available. We are doing a little extra work here by mirroring (or shadowing) the OpenAL state, but it's not much more work.

For correctness, we also should write our dealloc code:

```
- (void) dealloc
{
    [self destroyOpenALBuffers];

    if(streamingAudioRef)
    {
        ExtAudioFileDispose(streamingAudioRef);
    }

    [super dealloc];
}
```

```
- (void) destroyOpenALBuffers
{
    [availableDataBuffersQueue release];
    [queuedDataBuffersQueue release];

    alDeleteBuffers(EW_STREAM_BUFFER_DATA_MAX_OPENAL_QUEUE_BUFFERS,
        openalDataBufferArray);

    for(NSUInteger i=0; i<EW_STREAM_BUFFER_DATA_MAX_OPENAL_QUEUE_BUFFERS; i++)
    {
        free(pcmDataBufferArray[i]);
        pcmDataBufferArray[i] = NULL;
    }
}
```

There shouldn't be any surprises here, except that this class also keeps a file handle, so we need to remember to close the file handle if it is open.

The real meat of this class is the updateQueue: method. As I said, we are going to put all the stuff in the updateQueue update loop from the BasicOpenALStreaming example. This loop should look very familiar to you, as it is the same algorithm. For brevity, I won't reproduce the entire body of the code here, but it's included with the completed project example. However, we will zoom in on subsections of the method next.

Unqueue the Processed Buffers

As in the BasicOpenALStreaming example, let's start with unqueuing the processed buffers in the updateQueue method.

```
ALint buffers_processed = 0;
alGetSourcei(streaming_source, AL_BUFFERS_PROCESSED, &buffers_processed);
while(buffers_processed > 0)
{
    ALuint unqueued_buffer;
    alSourceUnqueueBuffers(streaming_source, 1, &unqueued_buffer);

    [availableDataBuffersQueue insertObject:[queuedDataBuffersQueue lastObject]
        atIndex:0];
    [queuedDataBuffersQueue removeLastObject];

    buffers_processed--;
}
```

Astute observers might notice that we do nothing with the unqueued_buffer we retrieve from OpenAL. This is because we are mirroring (shadowing) the OpenAL buffer queue with our two arrays, so we already know which buffer was unqueued.[4]

---

[4] I should mention that I have been bitten by OpenAL bugs where the buffer IDs returned were either wrong or in the wrong order. This is not supposed to happen, but if you are concerned, you might add an assert to verify the buffer IDs match.

Queue a New Buffer If Necessary

Continuing in updateQueue, let's queue a new buffer if we haven't gone over the number of queued buffers specified by our self-imposed maximum, which is 32 buffers. Since we have a data structure that holds all our available buffers, we can just check if the data structure has any buffers.

```
if([availableDataBuffersQueue count] > 0 && NO == self.isAtEOF)
{
    // Have more buffers to queue
    EWStreamBufferDataContainer* current_stream_buffer_data_container =
        [availableDataBuffersQueue lastObject];
    ALuint current_buffer = current_stream_buffer_data_container.openalDataBuffer;
    void* current_pcm_buffer = current_stream_buffer_data_container.pcmDataBuffer;

    ALenum al_format;
    ALsizei buffer_size;
    ALsizei sample_rate;

    MyGetDataFromExtAudioRef(streamingAudioRef, &streamingAudioDescription,
        EW_STREAM_BUFFER_DATA_INTERMEDIATE_BUFFER_SIZE,
        &current_pcm_buffer, &buffer_size, &al_format, &sample_rate);
    if(0 == buffer_size) // will loop music on EOF (which is 0 bytes)
    {
        if(YES == self.isAudioLooping)
        {
            MyRewindExtAudioData(streamingAudioRef);
            MyGetDataFromExtAudioRef(streamingAudioRef, &streamingAudioDescription,
                EW_STREAM_BUFFER_DATA_INTERMEDIATE_BUFFER_SIZE,
                &current_pcm_buffer, &buffer_size, &al_format, &sample_rate);
        }
        else
        {
            self.atEOF = YES;
        }
    }

    if(buffer_size > 0)
    {
        alBufferDataStatic(current_buffer, al_format, current_pcm_buffer, buffer_size,
            sample_rate);
        alSourceQueueBuffers(streaming_source, 1, &current_buffer);

        [queuedDataBuffersQueue insertObject:current_stream_buffer_data_container
            atIndex:0];
        [availableDataBuffersQueue removeLastObject];
```

There are just a few minor new things here. First, audio looping is now an option, so we have additional checks for atEOF. If we are at an EOF, we don't want to do anything. (We will have additional logic at the end of this function to determine what to do next if we do encounter EOF.) If we encounter EOF while fetching data, we record that in our instance variable, but only if we are not supposed to loop audio. If we are supposed to loop, we pretend we never hit EOF and just rewind the file.

The other minor thing is we now use alBufferDataStatic.

Handle a Buffer Underrun

Still in updateQueue, let's handle the buffer underrun case.

```
ALenum current_playing_state;
alGetSourcei(streaming_source, AL_SOURCE_STATE, &current_playing_state);
// Handle buffer underrun case
if(AL_PLAYING != current_playing_state)
{
    ALint buffers_queued = 0;
    alGetSourcei(streaming_source, AL_BUFFERS_QUEUED, &buffers_queued);
    if(buffers_queued > 0 && NO == self.isStreamingPaused)
    {
        // Need to restart play
        alSourcePlay(streaming_source);
    }
}
}
```

This code is essentially identical to the previous example.

Handle EOF and Finished Playing

The part to handle EOF and finished playing is new but simple. To end the updateQueue method, for convenience, this function will return YES if we discover that the source has finished playing its sound. (The OpenALSoundController will use this information later.) This requires two conditions:

- We must have encountered an EOF.

- The OpenAL source must have stopped playing.

Once we detect those two conditions, we just record the state so we can return it. We also add a repeat check for processed buffers, since typically, once it is detected that the sound is finished playing, this method will no longer be invoked for that buffer instance. This is a paranoid check. In theory, there is a potential race condition between OpenAL processing buffers and us trying to remove them. It is possible that once we pass the processed buffers check at the top of this method, OpenAL ends up processing another buffer while we are in the middle of the function. We would like to leave everything in a pristine state when it is determined that that we are finished playing, so we run the processed buffers check one last time and remove the buffers as necessary.

```
if(YES == self.isAtEOF)
{
    ALenum current_playing_state;

    alGetSourcei(streaming_source, AL_SOURCE_STATE, &current_playing_state);
    if(AL_STOPPED == current_playing_state)
    {
        finished_playing = YES;

        alGetSourcei(streaming_source, AL_BUFFERS_PROCESSED, &buffers_processed);
```

```
        while(buffers_processed > 0)
        {
            ALuint unqueued_buffer;
            alSourceUnqueueBuffers(streaming_source, 1, &unqueued_buffer);
            [availableDataBuffersQueue insertObject:[queuedDataBuffersQueue lastObject]
                atIndex:0];
            [queuedDataBuffersQueue removeLastObject];

            buffers_processed--;
        }
    }
  }

  return finished_playing;
}
```

Whew! You made it through this section. I hope that wasn't too bad, as you've already seen most of it before. Now we need to make some changes to the OpenALSoundController.

OpenALSoundController Changes

Since the OpenALSoundController is our centerpiece for all our OpenAL code, we need to tie in the stuff we just wrote with this class. There are only a few new methods we are going to introduce in OpenALSoundController:

```
- (EWStreamBufferData*) streamBufferDataFromFileBaseName:(NSString*)sound_file_basename;
- (void) playStream:(ALuint)source_id
streamBufferData:(EWStreamBufferData*)stream_buffer_data;
- (void) setSourceGain:(ALfloat)gain_level sourceID:(ALuint)source_id;
```

The method streamBufferDataFromFileBaseName: is just a pass-through to EWStreamBufferData's streamBufferDataFromFileBaseName:, which we add mostly for aesthetic reasons. This gives us symmetry with OpenALSoundController's soundBufferDataFromFileBaseName: method.

```
- (EWStreamBufferData*) streamBufferDataFromFileBaseName:(NSString*)sound_file_basename
{
    return [EWStreamBufferData streamBufferDataFromFileBaseName:sound_file_basename];
}
```

The setSourceGain: method is kind of a concession/hack. Prior to this, only our BBSceneObjects made sound. They all access their OpenAL source properties (such as gain) through EWSoundSourceObjects. But because we are focusing on background music, it doesn't make a lot of sense to have a BBSceneObject to play background music. So, this is a concession to let us set the volume level on our background music without needing the entire SceneObject infrastructure.

```
- (void) setSourceGain:(ALfloat)gain_level sourceID:(ALuint)source_id
{
    alSourcef(source_id, AL_GAIN, gain_level);
}
```

The playStream: method is the most important new method we add. This method will allow us to designate we are playing a stream instead of a preloaded sound. We could get really clever and try to unify everything into one play method, but this will keep things more straightforward for educational purposes.

We also need to go back and modify some existing methods to be aware of streams. Additionally, we will introduce some additional bookkeeping to manage our streams. Most important, we will introduce a new instance variable:

```
NSMutableDictionary* streamingSourcesDictionary;
```

In the initOpenAL method, allocate a new dictionary for this instance variable with the other collections. (And don't forget to release it in the tearDownOpenAL method.)

```
streamingSourcesDictionary = [[NSMutableDictionary alloc]
initWithCapacity:MAX_NUMBER_OF_ALSOURCES];
```

We will use this to track which sources are currently playing a stream, similar to how we tracked currently playing (preloaded) sounds. You may notice this is a dictionary instead of a set, which is different from what we did with preloaded sources. In this case, we also want access to the buffer that the source is currently playing. So when we go through our OpenALSoundController's update loop, we can call the updateQueue: method we wrote in the previous section. In the preloaded case, we didn't need to do anything with the buffer, so we didn't need access to the data. Thus, we could use an NSSet containing only sources. But our streamingSourcesDictionary will be keyed by source IDs, and the values will be EWStreamBufferData objects.

Now that you know where we are going with streamingSourcesDictionary, let's look at our new methods. The only one with new material here worth talking about is playStream:.

```
// Must call reserveSource to get the source_id
- (void) playStream:(ALuint)source_id
    streamBufferData:(EWStreamBufferData*)stream_buffer_data
{
    // Trusting the source_id passed in is valid
    [streamingSourcesDictionary setObject:stream_buffer_data
        forKey:[NSNumber numberWithUnsignedInt:source_id]];
    // updateQueue will automatically start playing
    [stream_buffer_data updateQueue:source_id];
}
```

This is a simple method because all the logic is elsewhere. It is just bookkeeping. First, we add our source and EWStreamBufferData to our streamingSourcesDictionary. Then we just call the updateQueue: method we implemented in the previous section to start playing. Recall that one pass of updateQueue: will queue a new buffer and then do buffer underrun detection. Since there will be a new buffer in the queue but the source is stopped (because we never started playing it), the code will consider this to be a buffer underrun situation and automatically start playing for us. How nice and elegant, right?

Now it's important that we enhance our update method to handle streams. It needs to do all the same stuff that the loop does for preloaded sources—detect finished playback, invoke callbacks, and recycle the sources. But it also needs to update the buffer queues for each playing stream. To update the buffer queues, we need to invoke updateQueue: on each EWStreamBufferData object. This will be very easy to implement.

In fact, it is almost a copy-and-paste of the existing code. At the bottom of the update method, add the following code:

```
NSMutableDictionary* streaming_items_to_be_purged_dictionary =
    [[NSMutableDictionary alloc] initWithCapacity:[streamingSourcesDictionary count]];
for(NSNumber* current_number in streamingSourcesDictionary)
{
    ALuint source_id = [current_number unsignedIntValue];
    EWStreamBufferData* stream_buffer_data =
      [streamingSourcesDictionary objectForKey:current_number];
    BOOL finished_playing = [stream_buffer_data updateQueue:source_id];
    if(YES == finished_playing)
    {
        [streaming_items_to_be_purged_dictionary setObject:stream_buffer_data
          forKey:current_number];
    }
}
for(NSNumber* current_number in streaming_items_to_be_purged_dictionary)
{
    [streamingSourcesDictionary removeObjectForKey:current_number];
    [self recycleSource:[current_number unsignedIntValue]];
    if([self.soundCallbackDelegate
        respondsToSelector:@selector(soundDidFinishPlaying:)])
    {
        [self.soundCallbackDelegate soundDidFinishPlaying:current_number];
    }
}
[streaming_items_to_be_purged_dictionary release];
```

As before with preloaded sources, we iterate through all the items in the collection and look for sources that have stopped playing. Notice that we use the return value of updateQueue: to determine if we stopped playing. We use this instead of querying the source directly because we don't want to accidentally interpret a buffer underrun condition as a finished playing situation. We already wrote all that logic in updateQueue:, and now we get to benefit from it.

Also notice that we kill two birds with one stone. In calling updateQueue: to find out if a source has finished playing, we are also updating the OpenAL buffer queue for the stream if it is not finished playing. (Don't you love how this is all coming together?)

And finally, when we do encounter a sound finished situation, we do what we did before: recycle the source and invoke our soundDidFinishedPlaying: delegate callback. Again, this all wonderfully coming together in an elegant manner. Even though we are talking about buffer streaming, it doesn't need to affect the behavior of the OpenAL sources. So when a source finishes playing, regardless of whether it is preloaded or loaded, you get (the same) callback notification. This means all our existing BBSceneObject code that listens for these callbacks doesn't need to change at all.

Now you can see why trying to deal with callbacks in our AVFoundation background music example would require some serious design decisions and possible significant code changes: AVFoundation callbacks don't match up with how our BBSceneObjects are using them.

Now that we're on a roll with respect to integration, there is one more easy thing we can try. Even though we have separate playSound: and playStream: methods, we can reuse the stopSound: method for both cases.

```
- (void) stopSound:(ALuint)source_id
{
    // Trusting the source_id passed in is valid
    alSourceStop(source_id);
    alSourcei(source_id, AL_BUFFER, AL_NONE); // detach the buffer from the source
    // Remove from the playingSourcesCollection or streamingSourcesDictionary,
    //no callback will be fired. Just try removing from both collections.
    //As far as I know, there is no problem trying to remove if it doesn't exist.
    [playingSourcesCollection removeObject:[NSNumber numberWithUnsignedInt:source_id]];
    [streamingSourcesDictionary removeObjectForKey:[NSNumber
        numberWithUnsignedInt:source_id]];
    [self recycleSource:source_id];
}
```

We are employing a trick here. Instead of first checking to see which collection the source is in, we just try to remove it from both. According to Apple's documentation on NSMutableDictionary, removing a key that does not exist does nothing. So it sounds like a safe operation. The documentation doesn't say anything about NSMutableSet, but I am going to assume they are consistent.

Also, notice this line:

```
alSourcei(source_id, AL_BUFFER, AL_NONE);
```

For preloaded sources, I said it was optional to detach the buffer, since we were just attaching new buffers when we needed the source again. But with buffer queuing, if we stop prematurely, we may still have queued buffers, and there is no API to remove those. Officially, from the spec, this line of code is how you clear all the buffers from a source.

Finally, as we leave OpenALSoundController, remember to change the audio session mode to kAudioSessionCategory_SoloAmbientSound in the init method in our call to InitAudioSession().

BBSceneController Integration

We're finally here. Now we get to try playing our music. Again, we will be using the music from FatLab Music, just as in the AVFoundation/Space Rocks! example.

Remember to add the #define to *BBConfiguration.h*:

```
// Music by Michael Shaieb
// © Copyright 2009 FatLab Music
// From "Snowferno" for iPhone/iPod Touch
#define BACKGROUND_MUSIC @"D-ay-Z-ray_mix_090502"
```

In BBSceneController, we are going to add two new instance variables:

```
EWStreamBufferData* backgroundMusicStreamBufferData;
ALuint backgroundMusicSourceID;
```

In the init method, let's load the sound file and tell it to loop:

```
backgroundMusicStreamBufferData = [[EWStreamBufferData alloc]
initFromFileBaseName:BACKGROUND_MUSIC];
backgroundMusicStreamBufferData.audioLooping = YES;
```

In the startScene method, let's reserve a source and start playing. (We also set the music's gain level here.)

```
BOOL source_available = [[OpenALSoundController sharedSoundController]
reserveSource:&backgroundMusicSourceID];
if(YES == source_available)
{
    [[OpenALSoundController sharedSoundController] setSourceGain:0.50
        sourceID:backgroundMusicSourceID];
    [[OpenALSoundController sharedSoundController] playStream:backgroundMusicSourceID
        streamBufferData:backgroundMusicStreamBufferData];
}
else
{
    NSLog(@"Unexpected Error: No AL source available for background music");
}
```

To clean up, in the dealloc method, we will stop playing and release the buffer.

```
[[OpenALSoundController sharedSoundController] stopSound:backgroundMusicSourceID];
[backgroundMusicStreamBufferData release];
```

That's it. You're ready to build and play. You can now pat yourself on the back. You have a fully capable OpenAL engine that can play sound effects and streams.

Analysis: Number of Buffers and Buffer Sizes

I promised to explain why we used 32 buffers and 16KB buffer sizes. This was a number I experimentally found to work well enough with Space Rocks! I don't claim this is optimal, but it is sufficient to get over one of our dangerous bottleneck points.

In our game engine design, we use NSTimer to trigger our game update loop, which the audio engine is tied to. The problem is that NSTimer operates on the main thread, so it can be blocked if we are busy doing other things. When you die and touch the game restart button, the engine reloads a whole bunch of things. This creates a bottleneck point.

On a first-generation iPhone, the reload time was sufficiently long that the music suffered a buffer underrun condition. While the game is loading, we are not able to queue more buffers, and with too few buffers, the audio system hit an underrun. This may be exacerbated by the fact that we don't guarantee the queue is always filled with the maximum number of buffers and it is a best-effort approach. On a first-generation iPhone, all the visual particle effects can tax the device pretty hard. Usually, the particle effects increase when the player dies, which may subsequently lead to starving the buffer queue because the CPU can't keep up with our desired update rate. By the time the game gets to the reload routine, there may be very few buffers remaining in the queue to endure the length of the reload routine time. Experimentally, I found 32 buffers at 16KB to be sufficient to be able to reload the game without encountering an underrun condition.[5]

Now 32 buffers at 16KB buffer sizes add up to arguably a lot of memory to use when the point of streaming was to minimize our memory footprint in a given moment.[6] When you begin memory tuning for your game, this should be one of the first areas to revisit. As a reference point to consider and shoot for, Daniel Peacock says he personally likes to use four buffers of 25 milliseconds. Buffer size is scaled based on the sample rate to fill 25 milliseconds.

There are other remedies you can try instead of increasing the number of buffers or sizes of the buffers. One approach is to identify the long blocking parts of your application and sprinkle some calls to queue more buffers throughout the routines. For example, in our reloading routine, we could try something aggressive and queue a buffer after every new BBRock we allocate.

Another solution is to use threads to update our OpenAL audio engine so it is not blocked. You could explicitly write your own multithreaded code. Alternatively. if you have access to another timer system like CADisplayLink on the iPhone or Core Video on the Mac (a high-priority timer running on an alternative thread that is guaranteed to fire in unison with your display's refresh rate), you could tie the OpenAL buffer updates to that. This is obviously a general statement to all OpenAL developers, not just iPhone developers, as this blocking problem may be an issue on all single-threaded engine designs. You will need to find a good system that works for you and your target platform(s).

And at the risk of stating the obvious, a very easy solution is to reduce the sample rate of your audio. A 44 kHz sample takes twice as much memory as a 22 kHz sample of the same duration. Another way to think of this is that you can fit twice as much play time in a single buffer using a 22 kHz sample as opposed to a 44 kHz sample.

Star Power Ready!

While we have just accomplished streaming (stereo) music, we've only scratched the surface of what the streaming part of our audio engine can do. So, we're not just going to leave it there. We will do one more short embellishment to give you an idea of what kind of audio power you now have.

OpenAL Speech for Space Rocks!

As I've said, streaming isn't just for music. And there is no reason to limit yourself to just one streaming source at a time.

We did a whole lot of work to set up OpenAL streaming. Now, let's reap the benefits. We will add a speech file to the game and spatialize that speech. You are going to see all

---

[5] The ideal number is between 20 and 32, but I didn't feel like testing them all.

[6] And if you have multiple streams, this amount of memory is per-stream.

the stuff we have done with OpenAL in the previous chapters come together in one little speech sound effect. Think of this as the grand finale!

This speech is going to be really cheesy. We'll have the little UFO taunt you with a "Game Over" message when you die (see Figure 12–8). Since the UFO moves (and we will be using a mono sound file), we just need to play the speech using the existing EWSoundSourceObject infrastructure we developed in the prior two chapters. In fact, we can just replace the UFO engine hum with the taunt and not even touch the spatialization code.

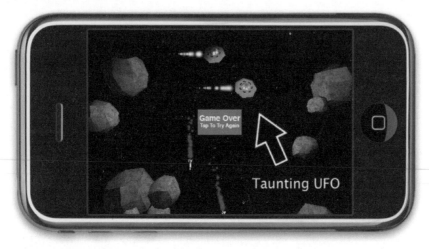

Figure 12–8. *We add a new UFO to taunt using spatialized streaming speech.*

The speech is a 6-second sample. Although it's shorter than what streaming is typically used for, it works for demonstration purposes, and is large enough that multiple buffers are needed to play the file. And for an infrequently used sound, streaming is not an unreasonable option.

The new audio file is called *gameover.caf*. It sings, "Game over. You're dead. You lose. Do not pass go."[7] I compressed it using IMA4. Because the background music is already using the hardware decoder, we want to make sure to avoid overburdening the system with playing a second restricted format. To match all our other sample rates, this file is encoded at 22,050 Hz. And, of course, it is mono so it can be spatialized.

We will continue building on SpaceRocksOpenALStreaming1. The completed project for this example is SpaceRocksOpenALStreaming2.

Add the #define to *BBConfiguration.h*:

```
#define GAME_OVER_SPEECH @"gameover"
```

---

[7] Did you know that Mac OS X ships with a voice synthesizer and there is a command-line tool called say to access it? Try typing this at the terminal: say -v Bad "Game Over You're Dead You Lose Do Not Pass Go".

EWSoundSourceObject: Finishing the implementation

Next, we should add some missing infrastructure to EWSoundSourceObject. We currently have a playSound: method in the class, but not a playStream: method. Let's add it.

```
- (BOOL) playStream:(EWStreamBufferData*)stream_buffer_data
{
    OpenALSoundController* sound_controller = [OpenALSoundController
        sharedSoundController];
    if(sound_controller.inInterruption)
    {
        NSInvocation* an_invocation =
            CreateAutoreleasedInvocation(self,@selector(playStream:),
            stream_buffer_data, nil);
        [sound_controller queueEvent:an_invocation];
        // Yes or No?
        return YES;
    }
    else
    {
        ALuint source_id;
        BOOL is_source_available = [sound_controller reserveSource:&source_id];
        if(NO == is_source_available)
        {
            return NO;
        }

        self.sourceID = source_id;
        self.hasSourceID = YES;
        [self applyState];
        [sound_controller playStream:source_id streamBufferData:stream_buffer_data];
    }
    return YES;
}
```

This code is essentially a copy-and-paste from playSound:, but is a little simpler, because we pass the buck and let the OpenALSoundController figure out how to attach and queue the buffers.

Now we're finished filling in the missing infrastructure. Wow, that was too easy.

BBSceneController: Adding a New UFO

Next, let's modify BBSceneController to create a taunting UFO on player death. We will change the gameOver method to add two new lines:

```
-(void)gameOver
{
    UFOCountDown = RANDOM_INT(500,800);
    [self addTauntUFO];
    [inputController gameOver];
}
```

First, we reset the UFOCountDown timer, because we want to minimize the chance of having two UFOs at the same time. Since the UFO has a noisy engine, we would like to increase the chances of hearing the speech clearly. (You might wait for the first UFO to pass before dying.) For simplicity, if there is a UFO already in the scene, we leave it alone. There is a small probability that the existing UFO could destroy our new taunting UFO with its missiles, but we're not going to worry about that. Consider it an Easter Egg.

Next, we call a new method called addTauntUFO to create the UFO.

```
-(void)addTauntUFO
{
    BBUFO * ufo = [[BBUFO alloc] init];
    // The UFO starts in the upper left and moves to the right
    ufo.translation = BBPointMake(-270.0, 60.0, 0.0);
    ufo.speed = BBPointMake(50.0, 0.0, 0.0);
    ufo.scale = BBPointMake(30, 30, 30.0);
    ufo.rotation = BBPointMake(-20.0, 0.0, 0.0);
    ufo.rotationalSpeed = BBPointMake(0.0, 0.0, 50.0);
    ufo.shouldTaunt = YES;
    [self addObjectToScene:ufo];
    [ufo release];
}
```

This is very similar to addUFO. We just change the speed and rotation for distinctiveness, and adjust the y position so it is lower on the screen. This is to avoid overlapping with the regular UFO if it is on the screen. We also set a new property called shouldTaunt to YES, placing it before addObjectToScene:. We want this property set before the UFO's awake method is called so the correct audio sample will be used.

And that's all we need to change in BBSceneController. This is way too easy. Now we only need to modify BBUFO to taunt.

UFO: Taunting and Callbacks

We will add the new Boolean property, shouldTaunt, to BBUFO. While we're here, let's add an ALuint for the tauntID. We will use this to save the OpenAL source ID that we are playing the taunt on for later use with a callback.

```
@interface BBUFO : BBMobileObject {
    BBParticleSystem * particleEmitter;
    NSInteger missileCountDown;
    BOOL destroyed;
    BOOL shouldTaunt;
    ALuint tauntID;
}
@property(nonatomic, assign) BOOL shouldTaunt;
```

After synthesizing the shouldTaunt property in the implementation, we modify the awake method to conditionally set the proper sound effect. If we are taunting, we load the *gameover* file as a stream. If we are not taunting, we load the engine sound as usual. (We could add a second source to the UFO to play both, but the engine is noisy, so this is fine.)

I want to reiterate that we could do this without touching a single 3D audio property, but the existing directional cone is going to make hearing the speech kind of difficult. So as a special case, we will disable the directional cones for taunting. (Perhaps it would have been better to subclass the UFO, but this is meant to be just a quick hack for demonstration purposes.)

```
    if(YES == self.shouldTaunt)
    {
        self.soundSourceObject.coneInnerAngle = 360.0;
        self.soundSourceObject.coneOuterAngle = 360.0;
        self.soundSourceObject.coneOuterGain = 0.0;
        self.soundSourceObject.rolloffFactor = 0.5;
        self.soundSourceObject.referenceDistance = 300.0;

        self.soundSourceObject.audioLooping = AL_FALSE;
        self.soundSourceObject.gainLevel = 1.0;

        EWStreamBufferData* game_over_speech =
          [[OpenALSoundController sharedSoundController]
          streamBufferDataFromFileBaseName:GAME_OVER_SPEECH];
        [self.soundSourceObject playStream:game_over_speech];
        tauntID = self.soundSourceObject.sourceID;
    }
    else
    {
        self.soundSourceObject.coneInnerAngle = 90.0;
        self.soundSourceObject.coneOuterAngle = 270.0;
        self.soundSourceObject.coneOuterGain = 0.50;
        self.soundSourceObject.rolloffFactor = 0.5;
        self.soundSourceObject.referenceDistance = 300.0;

        self.soundSourceObject.audioLooping = AL_TRUE;
        self.soundSourceObject.gainLevel = 0.3; // let's lower sound it's too loud
        [self.soundSourceObject playSound:
[[OpenALSoundController sharedSoundController]
        soundBufferDataFromFileBaseName:UFO_ENGINE]];
    }
```

With streaming, we need to remember to always turn off looping on the source, because we do looping in the buffer. In this case, we aren't looping at all, so both need to be off. We load the file and play it. And we save the source ID in taunt ID. We release the newly created buffer because we don't need it anymore. (The system will retain it as long as it is playing.)

In the dealloc method, let's make sure we stop the taunt. We could let it play to completion, but it makes more sense to kill the taunt if the player starts a new game.

```
if(AL_TRUE == self.soundSourceObject.audioLooping)
{
    [self.soundSourceObject stopSound];
}
// Additional check needed for taunt mode. Let's kill the speech if we are resetting
else if(YES == self.shouldTaunt)
{
    [self.soundSourceObject stopSound];
}
```

And that's it. We have a UFO that will taunt us! And this streaming speech will have all the same 3D effects that we applied to the engine hum. You can even hear the Doppler effect mess up the singing.

But let's now put the cherry on top. We will use the callback feature that we spent so much effort building in Chapter 10. When the UFO is finished speaking, we will do something very explicit so we know everything is working. We will have the UFO fire off a four-missile salvo to show off (see Figure 12–9). This will prove the callback system works!

> **NOTE:** In the last moments of this book production, Ben changed the artwork for the UFO missile at my request to make it more distinct for example purposes. So the image in Figure 12–9 is a little different from what you will see when running the program.

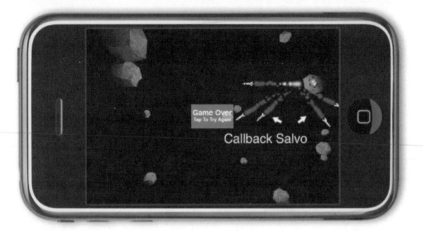

Figure 12–9. *Using the callback system we implemented in Chapter 10, we instruct the UFO to fire a four-missile salvo after the taunt.*

Let's implement the sound callback.

```
- (void) soundDidFinishPlaying:(NSNumber*)source_number
{
    [super soundDidFinishPlaying:source_number];

    if(YES == self.shouldTaunt && [source_number unsignedIntValue] == tauntID)
    {
        tauntID = 0;
        [self fireMissile];
        [self fireMissile];
        [self fireMissile];
        [self fireMissile];
    }
}
```

If we are taunting and get back the `tauntID` we saved, that means the source finished playing the taunt.

Build and run the game. With luck, everything will just work. Congratulations! You have completed the entire OpenAL engine. Yes, that was a lot of work, but you have everything! You have resource management, callbacks, 3D effects, and streaming—all working in tandem. In my opinion, this is much better than what we had in the

AVFoundation music integration example. And the Audio Queue Services solution discussed in the next section will have the same impedance mismatch as AVFoundation.

The alBufferDataStatic Crashing Bug

We have been using Apple's `alBufferDataStatic` extension, introduced in Chapter 10, to make audio streaming more efficient, but it has a nonobvious behavior that can cause your application to crash if you're not careful to work around it.

To refresh your memory, the `alBufferDataStatic` extension works by allowing you to provide a pointer to the raw PCM data for your audio for an OpenAL buffer. This is in contrast to the standard `alBufferData` command, which will copy the PCM data to the OpenAL buffer. The `alBufferDataStatic` extension gives an edge in performance because you avoid the memory copy. But as a trade-off, you must manage the memory for the PCM data yourself.

Managing the memory yourself entails two simple concepts:

- Remember to release the memory when you are completely finished with it so your program doesn't have any memory leaks.

- Do not destroy (or modify) the data while some other part of the system may be accessing it.

Let's begin with a basic example. We start playing a sound in OpenAL using a buffer created from the `alBufferDataStatic` extension. If we try to free the raw PCM buffer while OpenAL is still playing this sound, we will likely crash our program. So obviously, we shouldn't free our PCM buffers while OpenAL is using them. This seems easy enough.

Let's extend the example. As we just did in the previous example with the taunting UFO, we start playing a buffer and poll OpenAL until it stops playing (or explicitly stop the sound ourselves). When OpenAL tells us the AL_SOURCE_STATE is AL_STOPPED, we detach the OpenAL buffer from the source, delete the OpenAL buffer using `alDeleteBuffers()`, and then free the raw PCM buffer. On the surface, this seems reasonable and should work. But there is an implementation detail that we must contend with. Apple's OpenAL implementation may still be using the raw PCM buffer under the hood, even though it seemingly appears the system is done with the buffer. And if Apple is still using the buffer, our program will likely crash. Unfortunately, the UFO taunting example has created the perfect storm for this race condition.

Why did this race condition appear only now, in the UFO taunting example? Well, this is the first time we delete buffers immediately after they finish playing. Please be aware that this is not a bug specific to streaming. This could happen with preloaded sounds, too. With our preloaded sounds from Chapter 10 and our streaming background music, we didn't delete the buffers until shutdown, and the race condition didn't occur in those situations.

> **NOTE:** In my opinion, the `alBufferDataStatic` extension crashing problem is an Apple bug. If the OpenAL source has stopped playing (either by natural completion or by calling `alSourceStop()` explicitly), and the `AL_SOURCE_STATE` says it is `AL_STOPPED`, you wouldn't expect Apple to be still using the buffer. However, Apple contests my labeling of this as a bug and considers it the proper, expected behavior.

Apple's response to dealing with this issue is to check for an OpenAL error after you call `alDeleteBuffers()`, but before you free the PCM data. Apple claims to have overloaded the error mechanism for this case. Officially, the only thing the spec says is that `alDeleteBuffers` returns the error `AL_INVALID_NAME`. So Apple says it added a special case to let you know that the deletion of the buffer has failed, which you should use as an indicator of whether it is actually safe to free the PCM data. Unfortunately, this doesn't seem to work for me.

So you can experience this yourself, let's add it to Space Rocks! (These code changes are included as part of SpaceRocksOpenALStreaming2.) In *EWStreamBufferData.m*, modify the `destroyBuffers` method to look like the following:

```
- (void) destroyOpenALBuffers
{
    ALenum al_error = alGetError(); // clear errors
    [availableDataBuffersQueue release];
    [queuedDataBuffersQueue release];

    alDeleteBuffers(EW_STREAM_BUFFER_DATA_MAX_OPENAL_QUEUE_BUFFERS,
        openalDataBufferArray);
    al_error = alGetError();
    if(AL_NO_ERROR != al_error)
    {
        NSLog(@"EWStreamBufferData alDeleteBuffers error: %s", alGetString(al_error));
    }
#ifdef USE_BUFFER_DATA_STATIC_EXTENSION_FOR_STREAM
    for(NSUInteger i=0; i<EW_STREAM_BUFFER_DATA_MAX_OPENAL_QUEUE_BUFFERS; i++)
    {
        if(NULL != pcmDataBufferArray[i])
        {
            free(pcmDataBufferArray[i]);
            pcmDataBufferArray[i] = NULL;
        }
    }
#else
    if(NULL != pcmDataBuffer)
    {
        free(pcmDataBuffer);
        pcmDataBuffer = NULL;
    }
#endif
}
```

There are two things to notice:

- We added an `alGetError()` check after `alDeleteBuffers()`. If we encounter an error, we call `NSLog()` to report it. The code then continues as if nothing happened. In reality, we should do something special to avoid calling `free()` on the PCM buffer, but since I have never once seen this print an error when the program crashes, there doesn't seem to be much point in complicating the example.

- There is a new preprocessor macro named `USE_BUFFER_DATA_STATIC_EXTENSION_FOR_STREAM` to allow us to switch between using the `alBufferDataStatic` extension and disabling it. This macro is defined in *EWStreamBufferData.h*. Because I didn't want you to experience a crash the first time you ran this program, I have commented out the line in the code that accompanies this book.

To try to reproduce this problem, you should reactivate the line and recompile. Then run the game and destroy your ship to summon the taunting UFO. When the UFO stops speaking, the crashing bug has a chance of occurring. You may also tap the Try Again button while the UFO is in the middle of the taunt. This will immediately stop the playback and run the same cleanup code.[8] For me, doing this creates a fairly reliable reproducible demonstration of the bug (i.e., over 50% crash rate).

Work-Arounds

In the absence of `alGetError()` telling us anything useful, we must devise our own work-arounds. Since this is a race condition problem, a solution is to increase the amount of time between when the sound supposedly stops playing and when the buffer is deleted. A naive approach would be to add some commands that waste some time before we delete the buffer. For example, a simple call to `sleep()` or `usleep()` at the beginning of the `destroyOpenALBuffers` method might be sufficient for most cases. You will need to experimentally find the shortest amount of time that consistently avoids the crash. If you have more useful commands you can run instead of sleeping, that would be better. The time probably doesn't need to be long. I found that just adding a few `NSLog()` statements to debug this block of code increases the execution time enough to make a significant difference between crashing and not crashing. But the downside to this solution is that there are no guarantees that the delay time you pick will always be long enough. And if you pick too long of a time, the player may notice the delay while playing the game.

A less naive approach to increase the time between stop and deletion is to add another layer of indirection and create an event queue holding the buffers that need to be deleted at some future point. You could then revisit this queue at some arbitrarily long time later. When you get around to revisiting those buffers, you need to call `alDeleteBuffers()` again and check for an error again. If there is an error, you need to keep the buffers in the queue and try again later. Otherwise, you can finally delete the

---

[8] If the other UFO destroys the taunting UFO, this also triggers a stop and deletion of the buffers.

PCM buffer. There are two downsides to this solution. First, there is a lot more complexity. Second, if you are tight on memory, the resources waiting in the queue will not be useful to you until you finally free a queue item. However, this is probably the best work-around.

Finally, at the risk of stating the obvious, you could avoid using the extension, either entirely or just in cases where it is likely to bite you. For example. this race condition bug was not really an issue with just the sound effects and background music, so maybe you would single out short-lived sounds like the UFO taunting.

> **NOTE:** As I pointed out earlier, Creative Labs also supports the `alBufferDataStatic` extension for its Xbox and Xbox 360 implementations. Though I have not personally tested these implementations, I have been informed that their XAudio- and XAudio 2-based implementations do not suffer from the race condition as just described for Apple's implementation. So our original design implementation should just work as expected, and all the work-arounds we talked about in this section are irrelevant.

DESIGN IMPLICATIONS OF DEALLOCATION FAILURES

If we take a step back, we can observe that there are actually two problems with cleaning up after `alBufferDataStatic()`. One is that `alGetError()` doesn't work, which prevents programmers from synchronizing with `alDeleteBuffers()` correctly even if they tried. The more general and important problem, though, is that the `alDeleteBuffers()` behavior is contrary to good design/good practice in Objective-C, C++, and other languages that offer automatic resource management. For example, the standard C library function `free()` does not return a value and does not set any error flags. In Objective-C, `dealloc` (and `finalize`, too) is not designed to fail. And C++ destructors are not designed to fail either (e.g., never throw an exception in a destructor).

As you can see in our Objective-C based examples in this book, the natural and established memory programming convention/pattern has us release resources when we are finished with them. Then when reference counts go to 0, `dealloc` routines are invoked automatically and things are cleaned up. Violating this programming paradigm to deal with the possibility that you need to abort in `dealloc` has serious drawbacks for correctness, simplicity, and understandability as your code will no longer look like a standard Objective-C/Cocoa program. Furthermore, C++ has been gradually adopting a memory programming pattern that strongly resembles the Objective-C/Cocoa retain-and-release model, with things like Boost's `shared_ptr`, which has officially been adopted as part of the C++ spec in C++ TR1 and C++0X. So C++ is also impacted by this design.[9]

In the general case, you probably should give some thought and care in designing the programming patterns you use with `alBufferDataStatic()`.

---

[9] Bjarne Stroustrup, the creator of C++, has been advocating Resource Acquisition Is Initialization (RAII) for years.

Audio Queue Services Based Background Music for Space Rocks!

Even though we have just completed the entire audio engine with OpenAL, we're going to take a step back and take a look at a third potential API you can use: Audio Queue Services. With the introduction of AVFoundation and the fact that you can accomplish streaming through OpenAL, the case for using Audio Queue Services has grown weaker as of late. But there are features and conveniences that Audio Queue Services provides that the other two do not. Also, Audio Queue Services is currently the only way to access the full power of audio capturing, which is covered later in this chapter. Here, I will give you a brief introduction and example of using Audio Queue Services for background music.

According to Apple, Audio Queue Services is a "high-level" API for playing and recording audio. But according to most Cocoa developers, what is considered high level by the Core Audio team is typically infuriating and frustrating. (AVFoundation is the first API to ever buck that trend.) Audio Queue Services provides a C API, and using it is roughly about the same level of difficulty as what you just saw with OpenAL buffer queuing. In fact, it is pretty much the same design in that you are periodically unqueuing and queuing new buffers.

Perhaps the most significant difference between Audio Queue Services and OpenAL buffer queuing is that Audio Queue Services is callback-driven, whereas you need to poll in OpenAL. This means you get a nice, clean event to provide more data, instead of constantly asking the system if a queue has been processed. This also has an advantage in that there are fewer blocking issues. As you saw in our OpenAL example, if we were blocked from running our update loop (for example because we were preoccupied restarting the level and not running the update loop), then we risked starving the audio (buffer underrun). Audio Queue Services runs the callback on a separate thread, so blocking is not really an issue.[10]

As with all the Core Audio APIs, there is a lot of setting and getting of properties through generic functions and opaque types, which adds to the tedium of writing the code, but nothing you can't handle. So, if you are not already using OpenAL in your application and AVFoundation is not suitable, you might consider using Audio Queue Services. The callback-driven design might make things simpler to write. Also, Audio Queue Services has some fine-grained timing and synchronization features you can investigate if you're interested.

Apple has a pretty good example of how to use Audio Queue Services for playback in the "Playing Audio" section of the *Audio Queue Services Programming Guide*, found here:

```
http://developer.apple.com/documentation/MusicAudio/Conceptual/AudioQueue
ProgrammingGuide/AQPlayback/PlayingAudio.html#//apple_ref/doc/uid/TP40005
343-CH3-SW2
```

---

[10] Just don't spend too much time doing computation in the callback.

To give you a working project that you can play with, I have taken this example and integrated it in our Space Rocks! code. (This version does not include our changes for AVFoundation or OpenAL streaming.) I have left Apple's line-identifier comments intact, plus added explicit "Listing" markers so you can easily cross-reference with the Apple documentation.

Once again, this project is based on SpaceRocksOpenAL3D_6_SourceRelative from Chapter 11. The completed project for this example is SpaceRocksAudioQueueServices. See *AudioQueueServicesController.h* and *AudioQueueServicesController.m* for the code specific to Audio Queue Services.

We do need to make a few changes in this project:[11]

- A bit of refactoring was necessary to encapsulate it into a nice class for easy reuse in the game.

- The original example runs its own infinite run loop. This wasn't going to cut it, since we have a game loop to run, so this is changed to work with our application.

- We loop the audio, rather than letting it end, since we are going to use it for background music. (It might have been better to make looping an option, but I didn't want to overcomplicate the changes, and we would need to start thinking about callback notifications for sound finishing.)

- We add interruption support.

Let's examine two of the changes in a bit more detail: looping and interruptions.

Rewind and Looping

In the HandleOutputBuffer callback, the critical change is to reset the mCurrentPacket to 0. Being even more explicit, the fifth parameter to AudioFileReadPackets tells the function which packet to start reading from. In the rewind case, it is 0.

```
// New rewind code
pAqData->mCurrentPacket = 0; // reset counter
UInt32 numPackets = pAqData->mNumPacketsToRead;
    result = AudioFileReadPackets(
    pAqData->mAudioFile,
    false,
    &numBytesReadFromFile,
    pAqData->mPacketDescs,
    0,  // start at the beginning (packet #0)
    &numPackets,
    inBuffer->mAudioData);
```

---

[11] If you compare our example to Apple's original code, I may have also made a few tiny bug fixes in our version, though it's hard for me to say with certainty, since there was so much copy and paste to do, plus the changes that had to be integrated.

Audio Session Interruptions

Apple talks about interruptions in Technical Q&A QA1558, found here:

`http://developer.apple.com/iphone/library/qa/qa2008/qa1558.html`

The crux is that starting in iPhone OS 3.0, audio queues are paused automatically in an interruption, and you just need to resume (if appropriate) on the `endInterruption` event. But there is a major caveat. If you are using the hardware decoder, all bets are off, because the hardware decoder may not be able to restore its state for ambiguous reasons. Since we are using the hardware decoder for our music, we can't rely on this feature.[12] Thus, we must do it the pre-3.0 way by completely tearing down the audio queue on interruption and reloading it on `endInterruption`.

To accomplish the complete teardown and then restore the state, we must do the following:

- Stop the audio queue.
- Save the current `mCurrentPacket` value.
- Close the audio queue and file, and then clean up memory.

Then on `endInterruption`, we create a new audio queue using the same file.[13] We remember to set the `mCurrentPacket` to our saved value, and then start playing the queue. See the methods `beginInterruption` and `endInterruption` in *AudioQueueServicesController.m*.

A special change we need to make for Space Rocks! to handle interruptions is where we place the callback function. Originally, we had the `MyInterruptionCallback` function inside `OpenALSoundController`. The problem is that we need to handle interruptions for both OpenAL and audio queues, but they are in separate files that don't know about each other. So we move the callback and audio session initialization code to the *BBSceneController.m* file, since our scene controller needs to talk to both of these files to play sound and music. Note that we didn't have this problem with our AVFoundation/Space Rocks! integration because `AVAudioPlayer` has its own delegate callbacks that are invoked on interruption.

For more information about handling interruptions, see Apple's documentation entitled "Handling Audio Interruptions" which is part of the *Audio Sessions Programming Guide*, found here:

---

[12] I have independently verified that the audio queue may fail to resume with our program. It will not always fail to resume, but you probably don't want to rely on this unpredictable behavior.

[13] We save the file URL as an instance variable in the class so we can remember which file to reopen.

```
http://developer.apple.com/iphone/library/documentation/Audio/Conceptual/
AudioSessionProgrammingGuide/HandlingAudioInterruptions/HandlingAudioInte
rruptions.html#//apple_ref/doc/uid/TP40007875-CH11-SW11
```

Perfect Full Combo!

Marvelous! You have seen how to implement streaming playback in AVFoundation, OpenAL, and Audio Queue Services. It's now up to you to decide which API to use, based on features and simplicity that make the most sense for your own projects.

Incidentally, this marks the end of using Space Rocks! as an example for the book. But the fun isn't quite over yet. We are now going to move from playing back (streaming) sound to capturing sound.

Audio Capture

We are going to talk a little about reading (capturing) data from an audio input device such as a microphone. This could involve recording audio to save or archive of audio to some medium, such as a tape or file. But it also applies in cases when you don't want to save the data. You may just want to use it immediately as it comes in and throw it away. Maybe you are just forwarding the information over the network. Maybe you are using it to seed a random-number generator. Maybe you just want to detect the current frequency for a guitar tuner type app. Maybe you just want to measure the current amplitude for a decibel meter app. None of these examples require you to archive the data.

Of course, not all iPhone OS devices have microphone support. The first-generation iPod touch completely lacks a microphone, and the second-generation iPod touch has only an external add-on microphone. However, there are some really clever newer iPhone/iPod touch games that use microphone support. One such example is Ocarina by Smule, a clever app that transforms your iPhone into a musical instrument. This app has four virtual buttons you touch on the screen to simulate finger holes, and you blow into the microphone to play a musical note (see Figures 12–10 and 12–11).

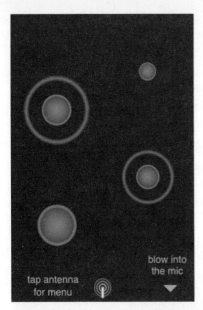

Figure 12–10. *The virtual music instrument app, Ocarina by Smule, makes interesting use of audio capture. Touch the virtual finger holes and blow into the microphone to generate a musical note.*

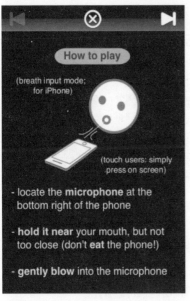

Figure 12–11. *The instruction page for Ocarina*

Here, I will give a brief overview of the capture APIs on iPhone OS, and then present a couple examples.

Audio Capture APIs

The same three frameworks that give us streaming playback also provide (streaming) capture:

- *AVFoundation*: AVFoundation introduced AVAudioRecorder as part of the API in 3.0. It provides a simple API in Objective-C for recording, as AVAudioPlayer does for playing. Unfortunately, this class has somewhat limited utility for games as it stands. Currently, it is geared toward recording to an audio file. So rather than pulling buffers into RAM, which you can immediately use, the buffers are written to a file. If you want to get at the data, you will need to open that file. We will run through a quick AVFoundation capturing example in the next section.

- *OpenAL*: OpenAL includes a capture API as part of the 1.1 spec. But here's the bad news: As of iPhone OS 3.1.2, Apple still has not finished implementing it. This means you cannot currently use OpenAL to capture your audio. Technically speaking, Apple's implementation does conform to the OpenAL 1.1 spec in that it provides the appropriate API functions in the headers and library, so you can compile and link your application successfully. But alas, when you try to actually open a capture device while running your program, the operation fails. Still, I feel you should have access to an example on how to use OpenAL capture, so I have implemented one (actually two). We will run through this example at the end of this chapter.

> **NOTE:** I don't know if or when Apple will finish implementing OpenAL capture. If you want it, I strongly recommend you file a bug report on it. (Apple counts how many people want a feature and uses that to help determine priorities, so duplicate bug reports are good.) I am personally optimistic Apple will finish implementing OpenAL capture support, but this not based on any special information. So, if you have an important project with a hard deadline, I wouldn't advise waiting for this feature.

- *Audio Queue Services*: If you need general-purpose capture support that can deal with buffers instead of just files, then Audio Queue Services is currently the only game in town[14] (until Apple finishes implementing OpenAL capture). Using Audio Queue Services for recording is very similar to playing, which was demonstrated in an example earlier in this chapter. Apple's *Audio Queue Services Programming Guide* contains a step-by-step guide for recording. So using your experience from the earlier section, you should be able to

---

[14] Not counting using audio units directly,

learn recording fairly easily. Also, you can refer to Apple's official iPhone SDK example called SpeakHere, which uses audio queues for recording.

> **NOTE:** Apple's SpeakHere example uses Objective-C++, which is basically C++ and Objective-C mixed together in peaceful coexistence. (File extensions are *.mm.*) If you don't know C++, don't worry too much. You should be able to make it through the example as the C++isms aren't too extreme. You might be wondering why Apple would do this for an instructional example, which really didn't need C++, meant for iPhone developers who are being encouraged to develop in C and Objective-C. I don't know the answer. But Cocoa developers will add this as another bullet point to their long list of grievances with the Core Audio group through the years. The Core Audio group definitely sticks out like a sore thumb at Apple, as it is one of the few groups to post public example code in C++. Incidentally, if you ever dig through the open source, Apple's OpenAL implementation is written in C++, even though it is publicly a C API. Presumably, the Core Audio implementation is also written in C++, though this is all private, behind-the-scenes stuff that doesn't affect us since we don't access the source code.

AVFoundation: File Recording with AVAudioRecorder

Our project is named `AVRecorder`. Structurally, this project looks very much like the `AVPlayback` project example in Chapter 9. This example will have an `AVAudioRecorder` instance to record audio to a file, and an `AVAudioPlayer` instance to play back that file. We will have a simple UI that contains two buttons: a record button and a play button (see Figure 12–12). To avoid having to draw art assets, we will use the camera button to represent the record button (I'm not going to win any design awards, for sure). For convenience, all the AVFoundation-related code will be restricted to one file, *AVRecorderSoundController*. The UI logic is restricted to the other files. Since you already know how to use `AVAudioPlayer`, we will focus on `AVAudioRecorder`.

To start with, we need to know if an input device is available. Audio Session Services provides a way to query this, and `AVAudioSession` wraps it in an Objective-C API. In our demo, we put up a simple `UIAlertView` to notify the user if we could not find an input device.

```
if(NO == [[AVAudioSession sharedInstance] inputIsAvailable])
{
    NSLog(@"%@", NSLocalizedString(@"No input device found", @"No input device
        found"));

    UIAlertView* alert_view = [[UIAlertView alloc]
        initWithTitle:NSLocalizedString(@"No input device found",
          @"No input device found")
        message:NSLocalizedString(@"We could not detect an input device.
          If you have an external microphone, plug it in.", @"Plug in your microphone")
        delegate:nil
        cancelButtonTitle:NSLocalizedString(@"OK", @"OK")
      otherButtonTitles:nil
```

```
    ];
    [alert_view show];
    [alert_view release];
}
```

Figure 12–12. *Our recording example project, AVRecorder*

In addition, we can listen for device changes using Audio Session Services. AVAudioSession provides a nice delegate callback to let us know the input device status has changed (i.e., someone plugged in or unplugged an external microphone).

```
- (void) inputIsAvailableChanged:(BOOL)is_input_available
{
    NSLog(@"AVAudioSession inputIsAvailableChanged:%d", is_input_available);
}
```

Speaking of delegate callbacks, AVAudioRecorder defines several callback methods, such as audioRecorderDidFinishRecording: and the usual stuff for interruptions. We make our class conform to this protocol and set the delegate to self in our example.

```
@interface AVRecorderSoundController : NSObject <AVAudioSessionDelegate,
AVAudioPlayerDelegate, AVAudioRecorderDelegate>
```

Next, there is a slight change in how we approach initializing an audio session in this example. In all our other examples, we set the audio session at the beginning of the program and never touched it again. In this example, we switch the audio session between recording and playback mode, depending on which we want to do at the moment. We also deactivate the audio session when our application is idle for good measure.

So when we are about to record, we set the following:

```
[[AVAudioSession sharedInstance] setCategory:AVAudioSessionCategoryRecord error:nil];
[[AVAudioSession sharedInstance] setActive:YES error:nil];
```

And when we are about to play, we set this:

[[AVAudioSession sharedInstance] setCategory:AVAudioSessionCategoryPlayback error:nil];
[[AVAudioSession sharedInstance] setActive:YES error:nil];

When idle, we disable the audio session:

[[AVAudioSession sharedInstance] setActive:NO error:nil];

For this example, we create a temporary file to store our recording. We make use of the Cocoa function NSTemporaryDirectory() to help us find the temporary directory to write to:

```
NSString* temp_dir = NSTemporaryDirectory();
NSString* recording_file_path = [temp_dir stringByAppendingString:
@"audio_recording.caf"];
NSURL* recording_file_url = [[NSURL alloc] initFileURLWithPath:recording_file_path];
```

To actually create the AVAudioRecorder, we just do this:

```
avRecorder = [[AVAudioRecorder alloc] initWithURL:recording_file_url
    settings:nil
    error:nil
];
```

Optionally, you can provide an NSDictionary containing settings for the recorder. There are a bunch of different options. Some of the more interesting ones are AVFormatIDKey, which lets you specify the compression format; AVEncoderAudioQualityKey, which specifies the quality level in terms of high, medium, low, and so on; and AVSampleRateKey, which dictates the sample rate.

Here's an example dictionary:

```
NSDictionary* record_settings = [[NSDictionary alloc]
  initWithObjectsAndKeys:
     [NSNumber numberWithDouble:8000.0], AVSampleRateKey,
     [NSNumber numberWithInt:kAudioFormatAppleLossless],
        AVFormatIDKey, // needs CoreAudioTypes.h
     [NSNumber numberWithInt:1], AVNumberOfChannelsKey, // mono
     [NSNumber numberWithInt:AVAudioQualityMax], AVEncoderAudioQualityKey,
     nil
];
```

There is a caveat about the sample rate. Your physical microphone may be much less capable than the sample rate you request. For example, the first-generation iPhone's built-in microphone can go up to only 8000 Hz. If you request 44,100 Hz, AVAudioRecorder might up-sample to meet your request, but you won't get any better quality, just a larger file.

If you want more information or control over your devices, Audio Session Services provides two properties that might be useful, which AVAudioSession also wraps:

- CurrentHardwareSampleRate: This is a read-only value, and will tell you the current rate of your device. One twist is that it is context-sensitive. If you are in recording mode, it will tell you about the input device. If you are in playback mode, it will tell you about the output device.

- PreferredHardwareSampleRate: You can set this if you want to try changing the rate. If you query this value, there is a possibility it will return 0.0, so be prepared for that.

According to Technical Q&A QA1631 (http://developer.apple.com/iphone/library/qa/qa2008/qa1631.html), you should deal with PreferredHardwareSampleRate when the audio session is not active. Conversely, you should query CurrentHardwareSampleRate when the audio session is active.

To record, you do this:

```
[self.avRecorder record];
```

Optionally, you can call the method prepareToRecord before recording. This will create the file for writing beforehand and try to do things to minimize latency when you do finally invoke record.

To stop recording, do this:

```
[self.avRecorder stop];
```

Interruptions will automatically pause your recording. On endInterruption, you can resume by calling record again.

That is AVAudioRecorder in a nutshell. It is a pretty easy-to-use API and closely mirrors AVAudioPlayer, so you shouldn't have any trouble learning it.

KEY-VALUE OBSERVING

Running the AVRecorder example, you might have noticed the buttons disable and enable appropriately. You can't start recording while playing back a file. And when playback finishes, the record button becomes reenabled.

You'll also notice that I completely separated our AVFoundation logic from the view (sans the UIAlert). I followed a typical model-view-controller (MVC) paradigm, where AVRecorderSoundController is the model (sorry for the naming confusion), UIButtons is the view, and AVRecorderViewController is the controller. This means our model class can't directly access the UIButtons to disable them, because it knows nothing about the view representation/implementation. Only the view controller knows anything about the buttons in this example. But the model class doesn't know anything about the view controller either, so it can't tell the view controller (for example) that playback just finished and it needs to reenable the record button. So how can this work?

The wrong thing to do would be to give the model a pointer back to the controller. This would be bad design (because it violates MVC principles) and kind of ugly. And polling would be even worse. Using the delegate's callbacks provided by AVFoundation would not be a bad idea, but I already used them up.

Designing some new delegates might be a possibility, but there is a much better solution, called key-value observing (KVO).

KVO is a Cocoa technology. Simply put, it lets you listen for when an object's value changes. To implement this, Apple does some wickedly cool tricks with the Objective-C dynamic runtime. But all you need to know is that when using KVO, you can get a change notification any time a value is changed using key-value coding (KVC).

KVO is a really interesting technology, as it makes keeping things that don't have explicit relationships in sync very easy. Apple takes this one step further on Mac OS X and introduces a technology called key-value binding (KVB). KVC, KVO, and KVB form *Cocoa bindings*. Cocoa bindings are a wonderful way to keep models and views in sync with little or no controller code.

I had not planned on using KVO in this book, but it was just too elegant of a solution to pass up. I wanted to give you the general idea, and maybe get you to think about other clever techniques for solving general problems when working on iPhone OS.

As for how our demo really works, it is quite easy. Our controller has a pointer to the model (AVRecorderSoundController). On startup, we have our controller register to listen for the "recording" and "playing" properties (keypaths) defined in the AVRecorderSoundController class, which we designed to keep track of the current recording and playing states for our class.

```
- (void) viewDidLoad
{
    // Use Key-Value-Observing (KVO) to listen for changes to the "model's" properties
    // so we know when to disable and enable our buttons.
    [self addObserver:self forKeyPath:@"avRecorderSoundController.recording"
        options:NSKeyValueObservingOptionNew context:NULL];

    [self addObserver:self forKeyPath:@"avRecorderSoundController.playing"
        options:NSKeyValueObservingOptionNew context:NULL];
}
```

Then we implement a special method named observeValueForKeyPath:ofObject:change:context: that is invoked whenever there is a change on the properties we are listening for. When the method is invoked, we find out which property was changed and act accordingly.

```
- (void)observeValueForKeyPath:(NSString*)key_path
    ofObject:(id)the_object
    change:(NSDictionary*)the_change
    context:(void*)the_context
{
    if([key_path isEqualToString:@"avRecorderSoundController.recording"])
    {
        //  NSLog(@"avRecorderSoundController.recording changed");
        if(YES == avRecorderSoundController.isRecording)
        {
            playButton.enabled = NO;
        }
        else
        {
            playButton.enabled = YES;
        }
    }
    else if([key_path isEqualToString:@"avRecorderSoundController.playing"])
    {
```

```
        // NSLog(@"avRecorderSoundController.playing changed");
        if(YES == avRecorderSoundController.isPlaying)
        {
            recordButton.enabled = NO;
        }
        else
        {
            recordButton.enabled = YES;
        }
    }
}
```

On cleanup, we say we want to stop listening for changes.

```
- (void) dealloc
{
    [self removeObserver:self forKeyPath:@"avRecorderSoundController.playing"];
    [self removeObserver:self forKeyPath:@"avRecorderSoundController.recording"];

    [super dealloc];
}
```

OpenAL: Capture Oscilloscope

So we're finally here. This is the last OpenAL (and last audio) example for the book. The example is an oscilloscope. It captures the data from the microphone and dumps it to the screen using OpenGL. In theory, if/when Apple finishes capture support, this example should just work.[15] See the project OpenALCaptureiPhone.

Meanwhile, since the example isn't a lot of fun when it doesn't work, I have ported it to Mac OS X (see Figure 12–13), in the project named OpenALCaptureMac. The OpenAL code is the same, with the slight exception of the setup, which needs to set up the audio session on iPhone OS. The OpenGL setup code is a little different, since I use NSOpenGLView instead of EAGLView.[16] And for interest, I demonstrate how to switch over from using NSTimer to Core Video's display link. On Mac OS X, the Core Video display link is a better way to produce timer callbacks, as the display link is guaranteed to fire in unison with your display's refresh rate. NSTimer is problematic because it may drift.

---

[15] Well, it may have some bugs, because I can't test it.

[16] One of these days, I should port it over to CAOpenGLLayer and use a layer hosting view to really modernize it for the latest Mac OS X state of the art.

NOTE: Those on iPhone OS should take notice that I just bashed how all the code in this book works, as we use NSTimer. In my first draft of this chapter, I resulted to dropping a lot of hints (without violating the NDA) encouraging you to look at the Mac OS X display link code, believing it was inevitable that a comparable technology would come to iPhone OS. Since then, Apple has released iPhone OS 3.1, which does contain an analogous technology called CADisplayLink. So I can now drop the pretense and tell you to go use it. I have ported the OpenALCaptureiPhone project to use it. (You may have noticed I also snuck in the CADisplayLink code to the BasicOpenALStreaming example. (Unfortunately, Apple's 3.1 release came too late for us to integrate this into the Space Rocks! game.) Apple's new default OpenGL templates also demonstrate it.

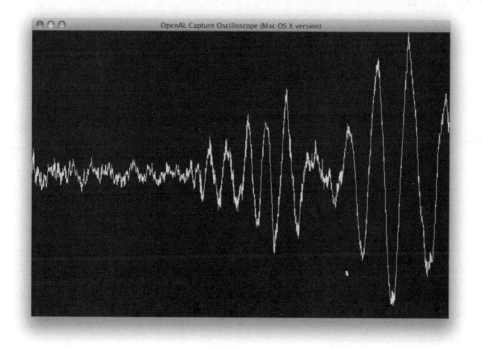

Figure 12–13. *OpenAL capture oscilloscope example for Mac OS X (because iPhone OS does not yet support OpenAL capture)*

USING THE OPENAL EXTENSION MECHANISM

As stated earlier, OpenAL has an extension mechanism to allow vendors to add features to their OpenAL implementations. As an end user of OpenAL, the OpenAL extension mechanism allows you to find out which extensions are available dynamically at runtime and use them. Being able to query for extensions at runtime is valuable for cases such as the vendor shipping a new extension in a future OpenAL release. You may want to maintain backward compatibility, so you need to be able to control whether you use the feature based on whether it is available to your end user.

For example, on iPhone OS, you need to worry about whether or not users upgraded their OS version, whether the new extension is available only on newer models, or whether the new extension may be constrained to specific device types like iPod touch. Rather than you needing to know all this information a-priori and hard-coding it into your application, it is much easier to just query OpenAL to find out if the extension is available. In addition, being able to dynamically query for extensions can help with cross-platform development, since there may be some extensions that are available on multiple platforms.

Four sets of API functions help you deal with OpenAL extensions. Each set is composed of two functions: one for ALC and the other is for AL. The first set is as follows:

```
const ALCchar* alcGetString(ALCdevice* deviceHandle, ALCenum param_name);
const ALchar* alGetString(ALenum param_name);
```

Here, param_name is ALC_EXTENSIONS for alcGetString(), or AL_EXTENSIONS for alGetString(). These functions will return a list of available extensions separated by spaces. For example, adding these two lines to our Space Rocks! engine prints the following:

```
printf("ALC_EXTENSIONS=%s\n", alcGetString(openALDevice, ALC_EXTENSIONS));
printf("AL_EXTENSIONS=%s\n", alGetString(AL_EXTENSIONS));
```

```
ALC_EXTENSIONS=ALC_EXT_CAPTURE ALC_ENUMERATION_EXT ALC_EXT_MAC_OSX
AL_EXTENSIONS=AL_EXT_OFFSET AL_EXT_LINEAR_DISTANCE AL_EXT_EXPONENT_DISTANCE
AL_EXT_STATIC_BUFFER
```

If you know the exact name of the extension you are looking for, this next set of functions will tell you if the extension is available.

```
ALCboolean alcIsExtensionPresent(const ALCdevice* device_handle, const ALCchar*
ext_name);
ALboolean alIsExtensionPresent(const ALchar* ext_name);
```

To get an actual function entry address for an extension, this set of functions is required:

```
void* alcGetProcAddress(const ALCdevice* device_handle, const ALchar* func_name);
void* alGetProcAddress(const ALchar* func_name);
```

You saw these functions in Chapter 10, such as in the boilerplate code for using the alBufferDataStatic extension. These functions will return NULL if the extension is not present. In principle, for maximum flexibility, the boilerplate code that was presented should have had additional code or support to deal with the case where the extension is not available. This could be done by surrounding the code with checks to al*IsExtensionPresent() and handling the different cases, or by doing some fallback case if the return pointer is NULL.

Lastly, there is a set of functions to get enum values:

```
ALCenum alcGetEnumValue(const ALCdevice* device_handle, const ALCchar* enum_name);
ALenum alGetEnumValue(const ALchar* enum_name);
```

Getting enum values can be important because a lot of OpenAL functions take enum values as parameters. What if you need a value that exists only as an extension and there is no constant defined in the headers?

You saw the example for al*GetProcAddress() in Chapter 10. As a slightly different example, a popular extension for OpenAL is support for 32-bit floating-point samples. For this book, we've been using 16-bit integers because the iPhone/iPod touch prefers that format. Other platforms may actually prefer 32-bit floating-point values.

For example, say we wanted to use 32-bit floating-point samples with `alBufferData()`. We have been using the enum value AL_FORMAT_MONO16 for mono samples, and AL_FORMAT_STEREO16 for stereo samples in our examples. We need a different enum value to represent mono and stereo 32-bit floating-point formats. For the 32-bit floating-point mono enum, say we happen to know the names of the extension and enum values we are seeking. The code snippet looks like this:

```
if(alIsExtensionPresent("AL_EXT_float32") == AL_TRUE)
{
    printf("Got AL_EXT_float32 extension");
    al_format = alGetEnumValue("AL_FORMAT_MONO_FLOAT32");
}


else
{
    printf("Don't have AL_EXT_float32 extension");
    al_format = AL_FORMAT_MONO16;
}
```

So how can we find out the names we're looking for? There is a web page that can help, located at `http://icculus.org/alextreg/`. Also, there is an OpenAL wiki being developed, which contains some of the extensions. See `http://connect.creativelabs.com/openal/OpenAL%20Wiki/Extensions.aspx`.

The Capture APIs

The OpenAL Capture API is pretty small. It consists of five functions:

```
ALCdevice* alcCaptureOpenDevice(const ALCchar* device_name, ALCuint sample_rate,
ALCenum al_format, ALCsizei buffer_size);
ALCboolean alcCaptureCloseDevice(ALCdevice* device_name);
void alcCaptureStart(ALCdevice* device_name);
void alcCaptureStop(ALCdevice* device_name);
void alcCaptureSamples(ALCdevice* device_name, ALCvoid* data_buffer, ALCsizei
    number_of_samples);
```

Open, close, start, and stop should be pretty obvious. The remaining function, `alcCaptureSamples`, is how you get PCM data back from the input device.

ALC Device Enumeration

To start with, you might consider checking to see if a capture device actually exists. You can use Audio Session Services to tell you this on iPhone, as in the preceding example. With pure OpenAL, you could just try opening the device, which might be the best way of doing it. You can also try the ALC enumeration system, which lets you get a list of devices and find out the name of the default device. There are separate flags for getting input devices and output devices.

> **NOTE:** The ALC enumeration system is still sometimes referred to as the Enumeration extension, but the OpenAL 1.1 spec formally adopted it and requires this to be supported. Incidentally, OpenAL Capture is in the same boat and is sometimes still called the Capture extension. But OpenAL Capture was officially adopted in the 1.1 spec, so it is no longer just an extension.

To be overzealous, you can check for the extension anyway (using the OpenAL extension mechanism). Then you can get the device name and list of devices. However, on iPhone OS as of this writing, the Enumeration extension seems to be broken. The extension returns true, but you get no device names back. (It fails on output devices, too.) So, you are better off just trying to open the device. But for interest, because dealing with a double NULL-terminated C array for string lists is probably something a lot of people aren't used to seeing, here is some sample code:

```
if(alcIsExtensionPresent(NULL, "ALC_ENUMERATION_EXT") == AL_TRUE)

{
    // Enumeration extension found
    printf("ALC_ENUMERATION_EXT available");

    const ALCchar* list_of_devices;
    const ALCchar* default_device_name;

    // Pass in NULL device handle to get list of devices
    default_device_name = alcGetString(NULL, ALC_CAPTURE_DEFAULT_DEVICE_SPECIFIER);

    // Devices contains the device names, separated by NULL
    // and terminated by two consecutive NULLs
    list_of_devices = alcGetString(NULL, ALC_CAPTURE_DEVICE_SPECIFIER);

    printf("Default capture device is %s\n", default_device_name);
    const ALCchar* device_string_walk = list_of_devices;
    int device_num = 0;
    do
    {

        printf(" * Capture Device %d: [%s].\n", device_num, device_string_walk);
        device_string_walk += strlen(device_string_walk)+1;
        device_num++;

    } while(device_string_walk[0] != '\0');
}
```

Capturing Audio

To actually open the device, we do this:[17]

---

[17] The example code actually wraps this in a helper function called InitOpenALCaptureDevice, but it boils down to this.

```
alCaptureDevice = alcCaptureOpenDevice(NULL, 22050, AL_FORMAT_MONO16, 32768);
```

The first parameter is a C string containing the device name, which can be obtained from alcGetString(), as shown in the previous code snippet. Or we can just pass NULL to open the default capture device as we do here.

The second parameter is the sample rate. We use 22 kHz here. (Optionally, you could query the currentHardwareSampleRate, as discussed earlier.) If the rate is higher than what your hardware can support, OpenAL generally up-samples.

The third parameter is the data format. We are telling it we want to get back the data as 16-bit mono. Other options include 8-bit and stereo. You've seen these same data formats before when dealing with alBufferData.

> **NOTE:** A data format extension supported by many OpenAL implementations is called
> AL_EXT_float32, which means implementations can support 32-bit floating-point samples. If
> your implementation supports it, you can get the format types for 32-bit floating-point mono and
> 32-bit floating-point stereo. Technically, the spec allows the capture device opening to fail with
> "supported" extension formats. The reason is that the extension may be supported only for
> output. But to my knowledge, most implementations that support the float extension support it
> with capture as well. Unfortunately, iPhone OS currently does not support this extension.

The last parameter is how large of a buffer you want OpenAL to reserve for holding audio data. The larger the buffer, the larger the window of samples you get to see. Note that with higher sample rates and larger data formats, you need a larger buffer to hold the same number of samples as you would with lower rates and smaller formats. For simplicity, I somewhat arbitrarily pick 32KB here.

So, if we don't get back NULL from this call, we have an open device. Unlike with OpenAL output, we don't set up a context. OpenAL capture does not have a context. In fact, the three OpenAL object types—sources, buffers, and listeners—do not make an appearance in the OpenAL Capture API. You deal with the device and PCM buffers directly. (If you want to take the PCM buffer and play it, then you can give it to an OpenAL buffer and play it on a source.)

Once we are ready to start capturing samples, we call the following method:

```
alcCaptureStart(alCaptureDevice);
```

Once again, we need to remember that OpenAL has a polling-oriented design. That means we need to constantly check if OpenAL has gotten more input data. In our update loop, we query OpenAL to find out how many samples it has collected (see *OpenALCaptureController.m*'s dataArray:maxArrayLength:getBytesPerSample). If we want the samples, we can retrieve them.

To find out how many samples OpenAL has collected, we do this:

```
ALCint number_of_samples = 0;
alcGetIntegerv(alCaptureDevice, ALC_CAPTURE_SAMPLES, 1, &number_of_samples);
```

Now we have some options. We can retrieve the PCM samples now, or we can wait until we accumulate more. In our demo program, we wait until we reach a certain threshold before we retrieve the data. This way, the rest of the code doesn't need to worry about always dealing with different amounts of data. One trade-off with this approach is latency. We have higher latency costs because we wait until we have a full buffer.

Finally, to retrieve the data, we do this:

```
alcCaptureSamples(alCaptureDevice, data_array, number_of_samples);
```

The variable `data_array` is the buffer where we want the OpenAL capture data to be copied, Once we retrieve the data, it will be removed from OpenAL's internal buffer. Also, keep in mind that the number of samples is not the same as the number of bytes. So we need to make sure the `data_array` we pass in is large enough to hold the number of samples we retrieve.

To compute the number of bytes needed for a given number of samples, the formula is as follows:

$$SizeInBytes = NumberOfSamples \cdot BlockAlignment$$

where:

$$BlockAlignment = NumberOfChannels \cdot \frac{BitsPerSample}{8}$$

or combined:

$$SizeInBytes = NumberOfSamples \cdot NumberOfChannels \cdot \frac{BitsPerSample}{8}$$

That's pretty much it. If you want to pause capturing, you can call this method:

```
alcCaptureStop(alCaptureDevice);
```

And to close the device, do this:

```
alcCloseDevice(alCaptureDevice);
```

So that is OpenAL capture in a nutshell. If you run the program on your Mac and your default input device is set to the internal microphone (go to System Preferences), you should just be able to make some noise and see the scope change.

This demo application does a few extracurricular activities that should be explained:

- The method `dataArray:maxArrayLength:getBytesPerSample` was done as a protocol. I wanted to keep the OpenGL and OpenAL code mostly separated for cleanliness. But since OpenGL needs the data from OpenAL to draw, I did it using a delegate pattern to keep things generic. In theory, something else other than OpenAL could conform to the protocol and generate the data for OpenGL without requiring drastic changes to the code.

- In the OpenGL side of the code, there is conversion for 16-bit integer to 32-bit float before the data is rendered in OpenGL. There are a couple of reasons for this, mostly centered on performance. First, once upon a time, Apple implied that you should be using floating-point values for vertices in OpenGL, as fixed-point values would have no performance benefits and would lose accuracy. However, Apple has since refined its documentation a little to suggest using the smallest data types you can get away with, because you may get some performance savings for having less overall data to send across the bus. But Apple says if you do any math computations, you should be using floating-point values. So, if you need to do any computations on the data you captured, such as FFT calculations, you are better off with floating-point values. To demonstrate, I included the conversion in the demo, even though we don't do any calculations here.

- As I already mentioned, the demo uses Core Video and the display link in the Mac OS X version. Look for the #define USE_COREVIDEO_TIMER in the code.

The OpenGL code itself demonstrates an OpenGL optimization technique, which is discussed in the next section.

Back to OpenGL

In a sense, we have come full circle with the OpenGL chapters. OpenAL audio capture is used to generate data for the visuals, which are implemented in OpenGL. But I use a slightly more advanced form of getting data to the GPU, called *vertex buffer objects*.

Vertex Buffer Objects

Currently, the way we draw using vertex arrays in OpenGL ES is generally inefficient. The problem is that we start with large amounts of data in the CPU and main system memory describing vertices, colors, normals, and texture coordinates, and we need to copy them to the GPU to draw. We do this every time we draw a frame. This can be a huge amount of data. And typically, memory bus speeds are slower than processor speeds, which present bottlenecks. In addition, a lot of our data is static (unchanging). The geometry of our spaceship never changes. Wouldn't it be better if we didn't need to keep sending this data across the bus? The answer is yes. OpenGL has a solution: the vertex buffer object (VBO), which among other things, gives you a way to specify if the data needs to change.

NOTE: A long time ago, OpenGL provided something called a display list, which offered a way of caching static geometry on the video card so you didn't need to keep sending it. One downside to the display list was that it could not be altered, so if you needed to change something, you had to destroy it and create a new one.

For this example, it is debatable whether we will see any performance gains since we are frequently changing the data. However, this demo does reuse the data until enough new capture data is accumulated, so there is a potential case for a performance boost. Also, with respect to performance on PowerVR chipsets, using VBOs may or may not lead to performance gains, depending on which model of chip you are using. This is also sensitive to driver implementations as well. But according to both Apple and PowerVR, you are encouraged to use VBOs for performance. PowerVR's recommendations go as far as to claim that while VBOs may not help your performance depending on the chip, it will also not hurt your performance. You can see these recommendations here:

```
http://www.imgtec.com/factsheets/SDK/PowerVR%20MBX.3D%20Application%20Dev
elopment%20Recommendations.1.0.67a.External.pdf
```

In addition, the word on the Internet is that the iPhone 3GS sees significant performance gains using VBOs, so the time to start looking at VBOs is now.

But the real reason I used VBOs was for educational purposes. Many OpenGL beginning tutorials depend on the glBegin/glVertex/glEnd paradigm, which is not in OpenGL ES and is being removed from OpenGL (proper). Since most people use OpenGL for performance, I felt it was worth the extra steps to demonstrate VBOs.

This demo shows how to change a VBO when you have streaming data. See the renderScene method in the OpenGL code for the interesting parts. Also, the color of the oscilloscope line will change to red when the VBO has just been changed. This will give you a sense of two things: how much we are reusing the data and how long it takes us to fill our OpenAL buffer (see Figure 12–14).

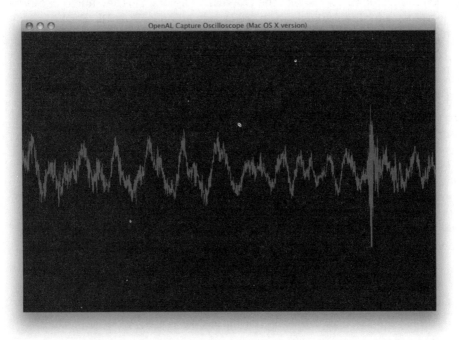

Figure 12–14. *The OpenAL capture oscilloscope turns red when the VBO is updated.*

TIP: For more details on using VBOs, see the tutorial on my web site (`http://playcontrol.net/ewing/jibberjabber/opengl_vertex_buffer_ob ject.html`). That demo uses static geometry. (And, by the way, static geometry is what all the models in Space Rocks! are using, so we would theoretically get a performance boost by using VBOs in our Space Rocks! code.)

Some Notes on OpenGL and OpenAL Optimization

Since I am on the topic of optimization, I'll close by mentioning a few thoughts I have on this topic, focusing on the similarities and differences between OpenGL and OpenAL.

First, the easiest optimization is to know what your underlying implementation uses as its native data format. This is true for OpenGL and OpenAL. OpenAL on the iPhone wants 16-bit little-endian signed integer data. Similarly in OpenGL, you want to pick a texture format the hardware is optimized to deal with. In OpenGL, you also want to think about packing your vertex arrays so the underlying types (vertices, colors, textures, and normals) are interleaved and word-aligned.

In OpenGL, one of the biggest guidelines is to avoid unnecessary state changes. Turing on and off texturing, loading new textures, changing colors, and so on all take their toll on OpenGL performance. In principle, this is true for OpenAL as well. However, particularly on the iPhone, where OpenAL is a software implementation, this tends to be less significant. You are mostly paying for function call overhead in the software case, which is far less disastrous as stalling and flushing the OpenGL pipeline.

Also in OpenGL is the notion of never using glGet*. Because OpenGL usually works on a separate processor (GPU) than the CPU, there is an amount of concurrency that can be achieved. But the use of glGet* creates sync points where the GPU and CPU must come together to get you the information you request. This will kill concurrency and result in poor performance. In OpenAL, it is mostly impossible to avoid using alGet*, as a lot of the API design requires you to ask for things. As you saw, we were constantly querying for the source state for resource management, callbacks, and buffer underruns. We had to query for the number of processed buffers. And we needed to query for the number of samples captured. But again, with software implementations, this is less of a problem. And the truth is that the video cards are far more sophisticated and tend to be more sensitive to these types of problems, as they are doing much more processing than the sound cards. (Face it, no one is talking about general-purpose computation on sound cards, a la OpenCL.)

In OpenGL, you typically shadow (mirror) state with your own variables to avoid using glGet. And often with OpenGL, people make even more elaborate libraries on top of their shadowing code to automatically coalesce and group state changes to minimize changes in the OpenGL state machine to maximize performance. OpenSceneGraph is an example of a third-party open source library that will sort out your OpenGL drawing order so it minimizes state changes (among other things). If you are going to build something like this for your own projects, you might consider including OpenAL state as well. Of course, you won't be able to reasonably mirror all things (e.g., the aforementioned source state, processed buffers, and samples captured), but you can get some things, like position and velocity. Whether you will see performance benefits or not is hard to say. Performance is tricky to talk about in generalities. But if you are already going to the effort of building it for your OpenGL stuff, it's probably not much more work to extend it to OpenAL and give it a try.

> **NOTE:** Hardware-based OpenAL implementations, such as ones using Creative Labs sound cards, are more likely to be affected and benefit from minimizing queries to the device and changing of state. For code you intend to share across multiple platforms, you may want to take this into account when designing your implementation. One piece of low-hanging fruit presented in this book is our polling-oriented design for callbacks and buffer queuing. Implementing a timer to fire approximately when you think a polling check is needed is a relatively simple thing to do. However, there is a caveat to be aware of with this approach. Be aware that sounds that have been shifted due to using AL_PITCH or Doppler play back at different speeds. A sound pitch shifted into a higher frequency plays faster than when you play it normally. And conversely, a sound pitch shifted into a lower frequency plays slower.

Another optimization often employed in OpenGL is (geometry) batching. For example, you might be drawing ten different objects and calling glDrawArrays ten times. Instead, you can combine all your objects into one giant array and call draw just once. In OpenAL, there is also a notion of batching, though it is a little different, and usually found only on Creative Labs hardware implementations. The motivation is that the hardware will dutifully recompute all the panning and attenuation properties as you set them. So, if you are in a single pass of an update loop and you change all the positions for your sources, as you set the new positions, everything is being recomputed. But then at the end of your loop, you get around to changing the listener position, and all the prior computations need to be invalidated and redone. Creative Lab's implementation of alcSuspendContext will allow the system to batch or coalesce OpenAL commands without doing the computation. Then calling alcProcessContext will resume processing and compute just the current values without wasting computation on all the intermediate/invalidated values. As I pointed out earlier, Apple's alcSuspendContext is a no-op, so don't expect this Creative Labs technique to work elsewhere.

The End of the Audio Road

Conglaturation !!! You have completed a great game(book). And prooved the justice of our culture. Now go and rest our heroes![18] A little tongue-in-cheek, bad video game ending humor here. It was a long road, and you've made it to the end!

You've seen the various different sound APIs and their strengths and weaknesses. And you've seen how OpenGL and OpenAL can work together to help create a compelling game. You should now be able to select the APIs that best suit your needs and have ideas on how you can utilize these technologies to help you make the best game possible.

The following are some additional references that may be of help to you.

For OpenAL, these resources are available:

- *The OpenAL 1.1 Specification and Reference*:
  http://connect.creativelabs.com/openal/Documentation/OpenA
  L%201.1%20Specification.pdf

- *The OpenAL Programmer's Guide*:
  http://connect.creativelabs.com/openal/Documentation/OpenA
  L_Programmers_Guide.pdf

- *The OpenAL home page*:
  http://connect.creativelabs.com/openal

Apple documentation includes these references:

- *Using Sound in iPhone OS*:
  http://developer.apple.com/iphone/library/documentation/iP
  hone/Conceptual/iPhoneOSProgrammingGuide/AudioandVideoTech
  nologies/AudioandVideoTechnologies.html#//apple_ref/doc/ui
  d/

- *Core Audio Overview*:
  http://developer.apple.com/iphone/library/documentation/Mu
  sicAudio/Conceptual/CoreAudioOverview/Introduction/Introdu
  ction.html

- *Audio Session Programming Guide*:
  http://developer.apple.com/iphone/library/documentation/Au
  dio/Conceptual/AudioSessionProgrammingGuide/Introduction/I
  ntroduction.html

- *Audio Queue Services Programming Guide*:
  http://developer.apple.com/iphone/library/documentation/Mu
  sicAudio/Conceptual/AudioQueueProgrammingGuide/Introductio
  n/Introduction.html

---

[18] From the infamous ending of the horrible game Ghostbusters on the NES, with bad grammar, spelling mistakes, etc. reproduced here.

I also suggest using the Apple Bug Reporter (http://bugreport.apple.com) to report bugs, request features, and request documentation enhancements.

For information about OpenGL performance, see *PowerVR 3D Application Development Recommendations* (http://www.imgtec.com/factsheets/SDK/PowerVR%20MBX.3D%20Application%20Development%20Recommendations.1.0.67a.External.pdf).

You can also find tutorials and information on my web site, PlayControl Software (http://playcontrol.net).

It's game over for me. Peter Bakhirev will join you next and teach you all about how to add networking to your game. <Free Play/Press Start>

See you next mission!

Chapter 13

Networking for iPhone Games: Introduction

Up until now, you have been learning about how to make iPhone games that look, sound, and feel great. In this and the next three chapters, we are going to make them even more engaging and fun. I am going to show you how to use the power of the iPhone SDK to turn your games from a solitary experience into something that will bring your players and their iPhones and iPod touches together.

In this chapter, we'll start with a quick overview of the frameworks and technologies that are involved in making applications talk to each other.

In Chapter 14, we'll build our first multiplayer game using the GameKit framework. In it, two players will go head-to-head over Bluetooth in real time in a remake of the classic game Pong.

Then, after whetting your appetite for connectivity, Chapter 15 takes a look at more sophisticated networking APIs, such as Bonjour and CFNetwork. We'll create a game that will let you invite all of your friends and family to participate in a math puzzle competition on your local wireless network or over Bluetooth.

Finally, if you decide to build games that transcend local networks and connect players from around the world over the Internet, Chapter 16 will give you some pointers about how to go about doing that.

And with that, it's time to meet the network.

Meet the Network

Besides having support for multitouch input, hardware-accelerated 3D and 2D graphics, and a robust audio toolkit, both the iPhone and iPod touch come equipped with excellent communication capabilities. Having all of those things together in one device makes for an ideal platform for creating multiplayer games. Before we dive into demonstrating how to actually make those, let's look at the technologies we'll be dealing with along the way.

Network Interfaces

iPhones and iPod touches have three ways to send and receive data, all of them utilizing radio frequencies:

■ *Wi-Fi (802.11 wireless networking standard)*: As of the writing of this book, all of the models of both devices can use this technology, giving them access to other devices on the same wireless networks and Internet connectivity via access points.

■ *Bluetooth*: This is a wireless protocol for exchanging data between devices over short distances. Even though Bluetooth support was included in the original iPhone, only starting with iPhone 3G and iPod touch second generation can Bluetooth be used to establish "personal area networks," allowing devices to connect to each other and exchange data using TCP/IP.

■ *Cellular data network*: By using a mobile phone service provider's infrastructure, iPhones are capable of connecting to the Internet using technologies such as GSM with EDGE, 3G, and so on.

These communication links are usually called *network interfaces*.

TCP/IP

When it comes to delivering information over network interfaces, the iPhone operating system relies on a set of rules for formatting, transmitting, and routing data known as TCP/IP, which stands for Transmission Control Protocol/Internet Protocol. Vast majority of computer networks in the world today use TCP/IP to ensure fast, safe, and reliable data delivery, including the biggest network of them all—the Internet.

Under the hood, TCP and IP are two different protocols that work together closely, but have different responsibilities. TCP ensures that packets of data are transmitted from one end to another in an orderly manner and without losses. IP, on the other hand, is concerned only with how to address and deliver each parcel of data. There are two major versions of IP: IPv4 and IPv6, with the former being more widespread as of the writing of this book.

In order to be able to specify where a particular transmission is going to or coming from, each device that uses TCP/IP networking must be assigned an *IP address*, which uniquely identifies the device on a particular network. In IPv4, IP addresses consist of four numbers, between 0 and 255, separated by dots (e.g., 192.168.1.56). It is possible for one device to be connected to several networks at once using different network interfaces, in which case it will have several different IP addresses. An example of such a configuration is shown in Figure 13–1.

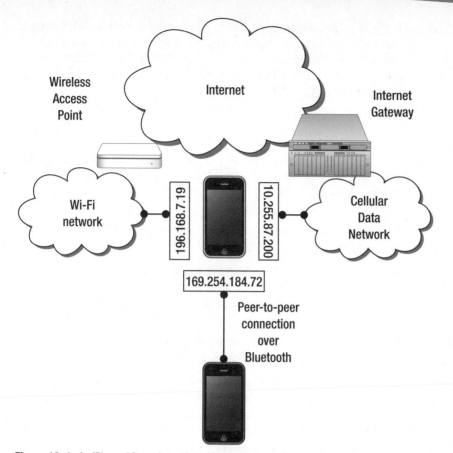

Figure 13–1. *An iPhone 3G can have three IP addresses assigned to it at the same time if each network interface is being used.*

One device can have several simultaneous but separate data exchanges happening over the same network. To be able to distinguish between those, TCP/IP has the notion of a *port*, which is identified by a number, from 0 to 65535. For example, whenever you visit a web site, by default, your browser knows to connect to port 80 on the web server, because that particular port number is reserved for data exchanges related to web content.

As a real-world analogy, think of post offices and mail delivery. Apartment buildings have street addresses, which correspond to devices having IP addresses. But that level of granularity might not be enough to deliver mail from one residence to another if we are talking about buildings with dozens or hundreds of apartments. Therefore, each apartment in a particular building has a number, which is analogous to port number in TCP/IP. Instead of piling all of the mail destined to a particular building in its lobby, envelopes and packages are distributed to mailboxes that belong to individual apartments, a system that makes for much more orderly delivery.

TCP/IP is actually a family of protocols, each of which plays a different role. We will be dealing with only a couple of them in the chapters to come. Depending on your choice of protocol, data delivery can be reliable but slower (TCP) or unreliable but faster (User Datagram Protocol, abbreviated to UDP). We will cover the differences between these two protocols in a bit more detail in Chapter 16.

Bonjour

Built on top of TCP/IP, Bonjour is a protocol that allows devices and applications to find each other on the network using names that map to IP addresses and port numbers. Here are some of the places where you might have seen this protocol in action:

- When you connect to a Wi-Fi network with other computers on it, names of some of those computers show up in your iTunes, and you are able to browse their libraries and play some of their music.

- When a friend comes over to your house and connects his laptop to your network, his computer's name suddenly shows up in your Finder, allowing you to drag and drop files in and out of some folders on his computer.

- When you need to connect to a remote printer on your company's network, its name magically appears without you needing to remember its IP address.

Bonjour treats all of these instances of iTunes, file-sharing destinations, and printers as *services* that have human-readable names and types. Instead of someone maintaining a centralized directory of services on a particular network, each service constantly advertises its existence on that network. Applications that want to use services of a particular type can listen for such advertisements, and discover the IP address and port for contacting each particular service.

iPhone SDK and Networking

TCP/IP and Bonjour are fairly complex protocols. However, as you have probably come to expect by now, the iPhone SDK comes with several tools that allow us to take advantage of the device's communication capabilities without needing to get our hands too dirty.

Sockets and Connections

When talking about sources or destinations of messages that get sent over a TCP/IP network, we will refer to sockets. A *socket* is an endpoint on the network, which represents a unique combination of IP address, port number, and transmission protocol (UDP or TCP). In iPhone OS, as in many other systems, sockets are resources that are managed by the operating system.

A *connection* is a logical link between two sockets (usually residing on different devices) that represents a separate data-exchange session.

BSD Socket API

Also known as *Berkeley sockets*, the BSD Socket API is the de facto standard when it comes to networking libraries for the C programming language. It gets its name from the version of Unix that first introduced this API: Berkeley Software Distribution. Today, you can find an implementation of this framework for nearly every operating system that has a C-based software development toolkit.

In iPhone SDK, Berkeley sockets is the lowest level networking API that developers can access. We won't be using it directly in this book (except for a couple of functions that aren't available otherwise). Rather, we will focus on more developer-friendly frameworks that Apple introduced in Mac and iPhone operating systems.

CFNetwork

CFNetwork framework is a nice Objective-C wrapper around Berkeley sockets that makes it easier to write networking code that plays nicely with other frameworks in the iPhone SDK. It provides developers with an implementation of the HTTP and FTP protocols, and eases the task of handling various TCP/IP network events by integrating sockets with run loops. You'll learn more about this framework in Chapter 15.

NSNetServices

NSNetServices is a group of classes that allow you to use Bonjour protocol to advertise and discover services. They are also covered in Chapter 15.

GameKit

In an attempt to advance multiplayer gaming, Apple decided to put together a framework that includes several tools that make the process of creating those kinds of games easier. The following are the two major features of this framework:

- *Peer-to-peer networking over Bluetooth*: This will come in handy when we are building a simple two-player game in Chapter 14.

- *Support for voice chat between two players*: Even though this feature isn't very useful in situations where the two participants are located right next to each other (connected via Bluetooth or a local wireless network), it can be a great capability to add to a game that is played over the Internet. We will talk about this feature briefly in Chapter 16.

In GameKit terminology, *peer* means "someone or something that we are exchanging data with." With a gaming twist, it can refer to an opponent or another player. We will also be talking about sessions. A *session* is a data exchange between two peers that gets established, goes on for some time, and then is terminated. Peer and session are similar to the notions of socket and connection.

> **NOTE:** GameKit uses TCP/IP to establish sessions and exchange data between peers, which theoretically means that you should be able to use any of the available network interfaces to communicate. In practice, the picture is a bit more complicated. iPhone OS 3.1 and higher can utilize both wireless (in some cases) and Bluetooth network interfaces to establish peer-to-peer connections, but iPhone OS 3.0 is limited to Bluetooth only. At the same time, the iPhone simulator also has support for GameKit peer-to-peer networking, but only via your computer's wireless or Ethernet connection, not via Bluetooth. This means that in order to test your GameKit-enabled game, you need to carefully consider which version of the iPhone OS is running and which communication channels to employ on each device that you are planning to use.

Summary

This chapter was meant to prepare you for what's to come in the next ones. So far, we have covered some of the basics of TCP/IP networks and briefly looked at the frameworks and libraries we will be dealing with in the next three chapters. By now, you should be hungry to see some code and to write some more games. Fire up your Xcode. It's time to play!

Chapter 14

Going Head to Head

In this chapter, you will learn how to create a game that lets two people play against each other using two iPhones or iPod touches. To accomplish this, we will use the GameKit framework, which allows iPhone apps to communicate using a wireless technology called Bluetooth.

Hello Pong!

A great place to begin our journey is the "Hello World" of computer games: Pong. It's a perfect example to use in this chapter for two reasons. If you have never played this game before, this is your chance to get acquainted with and be inspired by one of the great classics. And what's even more important, the simplicity of its rules allows us to avoid spending too much time on trying to understand the game mechanics, so we can focus on the networking aspects instead.

> **NOTE:** In Pong, each player controls a paddle, which is used to bounce the ball to the opposite side of the field. Your goal is to make your opponent miss the ball. Each time that happens, the ball gets moved to the center of the screen and the game begins again. In the original game, you got a point every time your opponent missed. For the sake of simplicity, we are going to skip that feature. However, I encourage you to be creative and expand the game to make it as interesting and engaging as possible. After all, that's what game development is all about.

We are going to start with a version of the game where you control one paddle and the computer controls the other, as shown in Figure 14–1. We will then gradually add code that lets you play against another human player. By the end of this chapter, you will be able to install a copy of the game on a friend's iPhone or iPod touch and finally determine which one of you is better at Pong by battling it out in front of a cheering crowd.

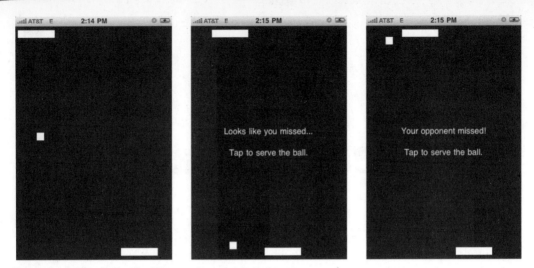

Figure 14–1. *Pong—visually, this game is as simple as they come.*

Download the source code that accompanies this book from the Apress web site, and unzip the archive to a folder on your computer. Locate the GKPong project and open it in Xcode. Run the game to get a better understanding of how it works and what it looks like.

Before we start changing it, let's quickly go through the classes that comprise this app:

- Paddle is responsible for loading the image of the Pong paddle and keeping track of the paddle's velocity and position.

- Ball encapsulates all of the logic for displaying and moving the ball on the screen.

- GKPongViewController is responsible for handling user input and managing the interactions between various views and game objects.

- GKPongAppDelegate doesn't do much work beyond displaying the main view right after the app launches.

What makes this game tick? Touch event handling implemented in GKPongViewController allows the player to control one of the paddles. The gameLoop method, which is executed approximately 30 times a second, is responsible for moving the ball and the other paddle.

Using Peer Picker to Find a Human Opponent

So, what did you think about competing against a computer? "Boring," you say? That's what I thought. Let's fix it by dismantling the very code that controls that other paddle, and adding the ability to find people around us who are also running GKPong and would like to play.

Instead of jumping into the game right away after tapping through the welcome screen, our player now needs to be presented with some UI that allows searching for an opponent. Luckily for us, Apple has already created a standardized UI that does exactly that. All we need to do is initialize an instance of GKPeerPickerController and put it up on the screen. This class is part of the GameKit framework, which needs to be added to our project: right-click Frameworks, select **Add ➤ Existing Frameworks**, and find *GameKit.framework*, which is usually located at /Developer/Platforms/ iPhoneOS.platform/Developer/SDKs/iPhoneOS3.1.sdk/System/Library/Frameworks/Game Kit.framework.

Let's go ahead and make the necessary changes to *GKPongViewController.m*:

```
#import "GKPongViewController.h"

#define INITIAL_BALL_SPEED 4.5
#define INITIAL_BALL_DIRECTION (0.3 * M_PI)

@implementation GKPongViewController

@synthesize gameLoopTimer;

- (void)processOneFrameComputerPlayer {
  float distance = ball.center.x - topPaddle.center.x;
  static const float kMaxComputerDistance = 10.0;

  if ( fabs(distance) > kMaxComputerDistance ) {
    distance = kMaxComputerDistance * (fabs(distance) / distance);
  }

  [topPaddle moveHorizontallyByDistance:distance inViewFrame:self.view.frame];
}

- (void)gameLoop {
  if ( gameState != gameStatePlaying ) {
    return;
  }
  [bottomPaddle processOneFrame];
  [topPaddle processOneFrame];
  [self processOneFrameComputerPlayer];
  [ball processOneFrame];
}

- (void)ballMissedPaddle:(Paddle*)paddle {
  if ( paddle == topPaddle ) {
    didWeWinLastRound = YES;
    gameState = gameStateWaitingToServeBall;
    [self showAnnouncement:@"Your opponent missed!\n\n
        Tap to serve the ball."];
  }
  else {
    didWeWinLastRound = NO;
    gameState = gameStateWaitingToServeBall;
    [self showAnnouncement:@"Looks like you missed...\n\n
        Tap to serve the ball."];
  }
}
```

```objc
- (void)touchesBegan:(NSSet *)touches withEvent:(UIEvent *)event {
  if ( gameState == gameStatePlaying ) {
    UITouch *touch = [[event allTouches] anyObject];
    paddleGrabOffset = bottomPaddle.center.x - [touch locationInView:touch.view].x;
  }
}

- (void)touchesMoved:(NSSet *)touches withEvent:(UIEvent *)event {
  if ( gameState == gameStatePlaying ) {
    UITouch *touch = [[event allTouches] anyObject];
    float distance = ([touch locationInView:touch.view].x + paddleGrabOffset) -
bottomPaddle.center.x;
    [bottomPaddle moveHorizontallyByDistance:distance inViewFrame:self.view.frame];
  }
}

- (void)touchesEnded:(NSSet *)touches withEvent:(UIEvent *)event {
  UITouch *touch = [[event allTouches] anyObject];

  if ( gameState == gameStateLaunched && touch.tapCount > 0 ) {
    [self hideAnnouncement];
    gameState = gameStatePlaying;
    [self startGame];
    gameState = gameStateLookingForOpponent;
    GKPeerPickerController *picker;
    picker = [[GKPeerPickerController alloc] init];
    picker.delegate = self;
    [picker show];
  }
  else if ( gameState == gameStateWaitingToServeBall && touch.tapCount > 0 ) {
    [self hideAnnouncement];
    gameState = gameStatePlaying;
    [self resetBall];
  }
}

- (void)peerPickerControllerDidCancel:(GKPeerPickerController *)picker {
  picker.delegate = nil;
  [picker autorelease];

  [self showAnnouncement:@"Welcome to GKPong!\n\n
      Please tap to begin."];
  gameState = gameStateLaunched;
}

- (void)startGame {
  topPaddle.center = CGPointMake(self.view.frame.size.width/2,
topPaddle.frame.size.height);
  bottomPaddle.center = CGPointMake(self.view.frame.size.width/2,
self.view.frame.size.height - bottomPaddle.frame.size.height);
  [self resetBall];

  [self.view addSubview:topPaddle.view];
  [self.view addSubview:bottomPaddle.view];
  [self.view addSubview:ball.view];
```

```objectivec
  self.gameLoopTimer = [NSTimer scheduledTimerWithTimeInterval:0.033 target:self
selector:@selector(gameLoop) userInfo:nil repeats:YES];
}

- (void)viewDidLoad {
  [super viewDidLoad];

  sranddev();

  announcementLabel = [[AnnouncementLabel alloc] initWithFrame:self.view.frame];
  announcementLabel.center = CGPointMake(announcementLabel.center.x,
announcementLabel.center.y - 23.0);

  topPaddle = [[Paddle alloc] init];
  bottomPaddle = [[Paddle alloc] init];

  ball = [[Ball alloc] initWithField:self.view.frame topPaddle:topPaddle
bottomPaddle:bottomPaddle];
  ball.delegate = self;

  [self showAnnouncement:@"Welcome to GKPong!\n\n
      Please tap to begin."];
  didWeWinLastRound = NO;
  gameState = gameStateLaunched;
}

- (void)showAnnouncement:(NSString*)announcementText {
  announcementLabel.text = announcementText;
  [self.view addSubview:announcementLabel];
}

- (void)hideAnnouncement {
  [announcementLabel removeFromSuperview];
}

- (void)resetBall {
  [ball reset];
  ball.center = CGPointMake(self.view.frame.size.width/2,
self.view.frame.size.height/2);
  ball.direction = INITIAL_BALL_DIRECTION + ((didWeWinLastRound)? 0: M_PI);
  ball.speed = INITIAL_BALL_SPEED;
}

- (void)dealloc {
  [topPaddle release];
  [bottomPaddle release];
  [ball release];
  [announcementLabel removeFromSuperview];
  [announcementLabel release];
  [gameLoopTimer invalidate];
  self.gameLoopTimer = nil;
  [super dealloc];
}
@end
```

In order to communicate user's actions to our application, peer picker needs a delegate that implements the GKPeerPickerControllerDelegate protocol. In our case, GKPongViewController takes on that responsibility.

Whenever the user dismisses the peer picker dialog by tapping the Cancel button, we would like to switch the view back to the welcome screen. We will do this by implementing the peerPickerControllerDidCancel: delegate method.

Also notice that we are keeping track of what the player is up to by changing the gameState variable. It is used throughout the code to determine the correct course of action whenever we need to respond to something that the user does. For example, we display peer picker in response to a tap on the screen only if gameState is equal to gameStateLaunched; that is, the welcome message is being shown.

Let's now make all of the necessary changes to *GKPongViewController.h*:

```
#import <UIKit/UIKit.h>
#import <GameKit/GameKit.h>
#import "Ball.h"
#import "Paddle.h"
#import "AnnouncementLabel.h"

typedef enum {
    gameStateLaunched,
    gameStateLookingForOpponent,
    gameStateWaitingToServeBall,
    gameStatePlaying
} GameState;

@interface GKPongViewController : UIViewController <BallDelegate> {
@interface GKPongViewController : UIViewController <BallDelegate,
GKPeerPickerControllerDelegate> {
    Paddle *topPaddle;
    Paddle *bottomPaddle;
    float paddleGrabOffset;

    Ball *ball;
    float initialBallDirection;

    AnnouncementLabel *announcementLabel;

    BOOL didWeWinLastRound;
    NSTimer *gameLoopTimer;
    GameState gameState;
}

@property (retain, nonatomic) NSTimer *gameLoopTimer;

- (void)showAnnouncement:(NSString*)announcementText;
- (void)hideAnnouncement;
- (void)startGame;
- (void)resetBall;
@end
```

What Does It Look Like?

Go ahead and fire up two instances of the game. Tap through the welcome screen in both apps, and you should see the peer picker. It will take a few moments for the devices to discover each other. Then you should be able to select your opponent on one device and confirm or decline the invitation to play on the other.

> **NOTE:** If you are using two iPhone OS devices to run the app, make sure to always redeploy the code to both of your test devices every time you want to run a new version of the game. That way, you won't run into strange problems that sometimes result from the fact that the two apps don't work the same way due to one of them being out of date. You can also use an iPhone OS device in conjunction with the iPhone simulator to run GKPong. Just make sure that both your computer and the iPhone/iPod touch are connected to the same wireless network, as mentioned in the previous chapter.

Figures 14–2 through 14–7 show what this sequence looks like on my second-generation iPod touch and iPhone 3G, called Petro iPod 2G and Petro 3G, respectively.

Figure 14–2. *The GKPong app has been launched. As soon as user taps the screen, the peer picker will appear.*

Figure 14–3. *The GameKit framework makes sure that Bluetooth is enabled before search for peers can begin.*

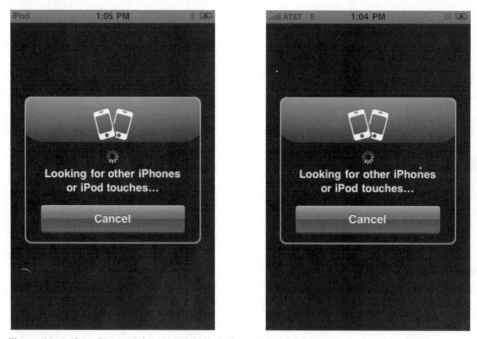

Figure 14–4. *Once Bluetooth is enabled, both devices start looking for peers.*

Figure 14–5. *After some time, devices detect each other's presence, and users are finally able to choose their opponent.*

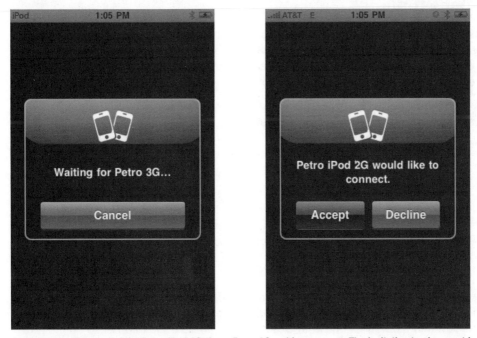

Figure 14–6. *The user of the Petro iPod 2G chose Petro 3G as his opponent. The invitation to play must be accepted by the other party before game can begin.*

Figure 14–7. *The user is notified when his invitation is declined.*

How Does It Work?

Are you curious as to what actually happens when the peer picker goes to work? If so, let's step back from the code for a moment and take a look behind the scenes. You don't necessarily need to understand this part before moving on to the next topic, so feel free to skip this section if you're not interested.

It turns out that GKPeerPickerController does quite a few things on our behalf. First and foremost, it advertises our application's presence to everyone who is in the vicinity and is willing to listen. That includes all other GameKit-enabled applications that are running on Bluetooth-capable iPhones or iPod touches located within a couple dozen feet from us and actively looking for peers.

There can be several different types of apps running at the same time, and the framework makes sure that our GKPong game is not going to accidentally discover and connect to a chess application, for example. In order to accomplish all of this, GameKit employs a networking protocol called Bonjour (introduced in the previous chapter and detailed in the next chapter), which was adopted to work over Bluetooth as of version 3.0 of the iPhone SDK.

Once a peer of the same type (another GKPong app) is found, the peer picker displays its name in the list of available opponents. As soon as the user taps that row, Bonjour does one last thing: It figures out what exactly needs to be done in order to connect to that device. When that is done, we can finally start exchanging data.

Making the Connection

Notice how nothing happens when you click the Accept button in our game? That's because we don't actually have any handling for it. Switch to *GKPongViewController.m* and add the following code:

```objc
#import "GKPongViewController.h"

#define INITIAL_BALL_SPEED 4.5
#define INITIAL_BALL_DIRECTION (0.3 * M_PI)

@implementation GKPongViewController

@synthesize gameLoopTimer;
@synthesize gkPeerID, gkSession;

- (void)gameLoop {
  if ( gameState != gameStatePlaying ) {
    return;
  }
  [bottomPaddle processOneFrame];
  [topPaddle processOneFrame];
  [ball processOneFrame];
}

- (void)ballMissedPaddle:(Paddle*)paddle {
  if ( paddle == topPaddle ) {
    didWeWinLastRound = YES;
    gameState = gameStateWaitingToServeBall;
    [self showAnnouncement:@"Your opponent missed!\n\n
      Tap to serve the ball."];
  }
  else {
    didWeWinLastRound = NO;
    gameState = gameStateWaitingToServeBall;
    [self showAnnouncement:@"Looks like you missed...\n\n
        Tap to serve the ball."];
  }
}

- (void)touchesBegan:(NSSet *)touches withEvent:(UIEvent *)event {
  if ( gameState == gameStatePlaying ) {
    UITouch *touch = [[event allTouches] anyObject];
    paddleGrabOffset = bottomPaddle.center.x - [touch locationInView:touch.view].x;
  }
}

- (void)touchesMoved:(NSSet *)touches withEvent:(UIEvent *)event {
  if ( gameState == gameStatePlaying ) {
    UITouch *touch = [[event allTouches] anyObject];
    float distance = ([touch locationInView:touch.view].x + paddleGrabOffset) -
bottomPaddle.center.x;
    [bottomPaddle moveHorizontallyByDistance:distance inViewFrame:self.view.frame];
  }
}

- (void)touchesEnded:(NSSet *)touches withEvent:(UIEvent *)event {
```

```
    UITouch *touch = [[event allTouches] anyObject];

  if ( gameState == gameStateLaunched && touch.tapCount > 0 ) {
    [self hideAnnouncement];
    gameState = gameStateLookingForOpponent;

    GKPeerPickerController *picker;
    picker = [[GKPeerPickerController alloc] init];
    picker.delegate = self;
    [picker show];
  }
  else if ( gameState == gameStateWaitingToServeBall && touch.tapCount > 0 ) {
    [self hideAnnouncement];
    gameState = gameStatePlaying;
    [self resetBall];
  }
}

- (void)peerPickerControllerDidCancel:(GKPeerPickerController *)picker {
        picker.delegate = nil;
  [picker autorelease];

  [self showAnnouncement:@"Welcome to GKPong!\n\n
      Please tap to begin."];
  gameState = gameStateLaunched;
}

- (void)peerPickerController:(GKPeerPickerController *)picker didConnectPeer:(NSString
*)peerID toSession:(GKSession *)session {
    self.gkPeerID = peerID;
    self.gkSession = session;

    [picker dismiss];
    picker.delegate = nil;
    [picker autorelease];
}

- (void)startGame {
  topPaddle.center = CGPointMake(self.view.frame.size.width/2,
topPaddle.frame.size.height);
  bottomPaddle.center = CGPointMake(self.view.frame.size.width/2,
self.view.frame.size.height - bottomPaddle.frame.size.height);
  [self resetBall];

  [self.view addSubview:topPaddle.view];
  [self.view addSubview:bottomPaddle.view];
  [self.view addSubview:ball.view];

  self.gameLoopTimer = [NSTimer scheduledTimerWithTimeInterval:0.033 target:self
selector:@selector(gameLoop) userInfo:nil repeats:YES];
}

- (void)viewDidLoad {
  [super viewDidLoad];

  sranddev();
```

```
    announcementLabel = [[AnnouncementLabel alloc] initWithFrame:self.view.frame];
    announcementLabel.center = CGPointMake(announcementLabel.center.x,
announcementLabel.center.y - 23.0);

    topPaddle = [[Paddle alloc] init];
    bottomPaddle = [[Paddle alloc] init];

    ball = [[Ball alloc] initWithField:self.view.frame topPaddle:topPaddle
bottomPaddle:bottomPaddle];
    ball.delegate = self;

    [self showAnnouncement:@"Welcome to GKPong!\n\n
        Please tap to begin."];
    didWeWinLastRound = NO;
    gameState = gameStateLaunched;
}

- (void)showAnnouncement:(NSString*)announcementText {
    announcementLabel.text = announcementText;
    [self.view addSubview:announcementLabel];
}

- (void)hideAnnouncement {
    [announcementLabel removeFromSuperview];
}

- (void)resetBall {
    [ball reset];
    ball.center = CGPointMake(self.view.frame.size.width/2,
self.view.frame.size.height/2);
    ball.direction = INITIAL_BALL_DIRECTION + ((didWeWinLastRound)? 0: M_PI);
    ball.speed = INITIAL_BALL_SPEED;
}

- (void)dealloc {
    [topPaddle release];
    [bottomPaddle release];
    [ball release];
    [announcementLabel removeFromSuperview];
    [announcementLabel release];
    [gameLoopTimer invalidate];
    self.gameLoopTimer = nil;
    [super dealloc];
}
@end
```

By calling peerPickerController:didConnectPeer:toSession, the picker tells its
delegate that it has found an opponent, or peer, identified by the string peerID, and that
a connection (also known as *session*) with that peer has been established. From this
point on, gkSession object is responsible for all of the communication between the two
players/applications.

Let's not forget to add the necessary declarations to *GKPongViewController.h*:

```
#import <UIKit/UIKit.h>
#import <GameKit/GameKit.h>
#import "Ball.h"
```

```
#import "Paddle.h"
#import "AnnouncementLabel.h"

typedef enum {
  gameStateLaunched,
  gameStateLookingForOpponent,
  gameStateWaitingToServeBall,
  gameStatePlaying
} GameState;

@interface GKPongViewController : UIViewController <BallDelegate,
GKPeerPickerControllerDelegate> {
  Paddle *topPaddle;
  Paddle *bottomPaddle;
  float paddleGrabOffset;

  Ball *ball;
  float initialBallDirection;

  AnnouncementLabel *announcementLabel;

  BOOL didWeWinLastRound;
  NSTimer *gameLoopTimer;
  GameState gameState;

  NSString *gkPeerID;
  GKSession *gkSession;
}

@property (retain, nonatomic) NSTimer *gameLoopTimer;
@property (retain, nonatomic) NSString *gkPeerID;
@property (retain, nonatomic) GKSession *gkSession;

- (void)showAnnouncement:(NSString*)announcementText;
- (void)hideAnnouncement;
- (void)startGame;
- (void)resetBall;
@end
```

Sending and Receiving Messages

Now that we found another player who is willing to interact with us, it's time to see what else goes into making a multiplayer game.

Whenever you play a game that's confined to one device, all movements and changes to in-game objects happen inside the same application's memory space. In GKPong, when a user touches the screen, we process that event and change the paddle's position accordingly. When the ball bounces off a paddle, we recalculate the ball's coordinates, speed, and direction, in addition to moving its image on the screen. If we are playing against a computer, no one else in the world needs to know anything about how those variables change.

Now, imagine that our friend Bob wants to play the game with us, and he will be using his own iPhone. Obviously, Bob would like to see our paddle move on his screen every time we move it on ours. The same is true for the ball—every time it bounces, both players need to see the change in the ball's trajectory as soon as possible.

One of the biggest challenges in designing multiplayer games is determining what information needs to be communicated between different instances of the app. You might be tempted to just send all of the data that you have as often as you can, but that would quickly overwhelm the device's communication channels and drain its battery. Therefore, we must carefully pick what information needs to be shared with our peer and what can be omitted. As we continue building the game, you will notice that this theme comes up again and again.

Let's take it one step at a time, starting with what happens when two people agree to play against each other.

Rolling the Dice

Think back to the original version of our application. Who tapped the screen to serve the ball every time a new round started? That's right—the human player. But now that we have not one but two human players, who will get to go first? That's easy—whoever loses a round gets to start the next one. But what if we haven't played a single round yet? In real-world sports, they sometimes toss a coin to determine who is going to start the match. That sounds like a good way to resolve the question (if the coin is fair, that is). In our case, a random-number generator can serve the same purpose. And so, we are going to play a mini game that will determine who gets to kick off the Pong match. Instead of being a coin toss, it's more akin to rolling dice. Figure 14–8 shows what that algorithm looks like.

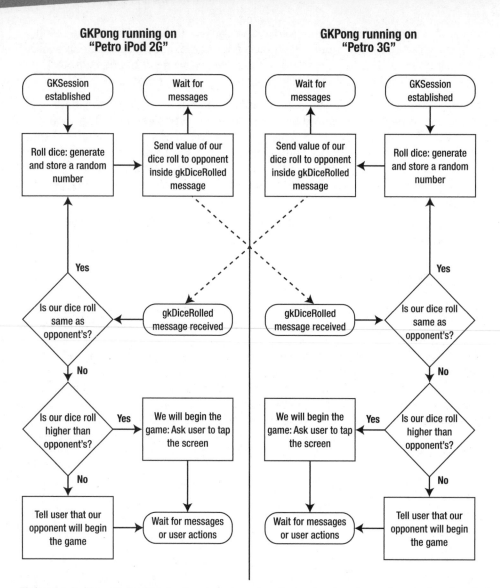

Figure 14–8. *Dice roll algorithm involves two apps generating and exchanging random numbers in order to determine who will start the game. This diagram comes into play after user of the Petro 3G iPhone accepts the invitation to play.*

Keep in mind that we can't actually start playing Pong before we figure out which player will kick off the match. Therefore, rolling the dice is the first thing that needs to happen after the connection is established. Let's open *GKPongViewController.m* and add the following code:

```
#import "GKPongViewController.h"

#define INITIAL_BALL_SPEED 4.5
#define INITIAL_BALL_DIRECTION (0.3 * M_PI)
```

```
enum {
  gkMessageDiceRolled
};

@implementation GKPongViewController

@synthesize gameLoopTimer;
@synthesize gkPeerID, gkSession;

- (void)gameLoop {
  if ( gameState != gameStatePlaying ) {
    return;
  }
  [bottomPaddle processOneFrame];
  [topPaddle processOneFrame];
  [ball processOneFrame];
}

- (void)ballMissedPaddle:(Paddle*)paddle {
  if ( paddle == topPaddle ) {
    didWeWinLastRound = YES;
    gameState = gameStateWaitingToServeBall;
    [self showAnnouncement:@"Your opponent missed!\n\n
        Tap to serve the ball."];
  }
  else {
    didWeWinLastRound = NO;
    gameState = gameStateWaitingToServeBall;
    [self showAnnouncement:@"Looks like you missed...\n\n
        Tap to serve the ball."];
  }
}

- (void)touchesBegan:(NSSet *)touches withEvent:(UIEvent *)event {
  if ( gameState == gameStatePlaying ) {
    UITouch *touch = [[event allTouches] anyObject];
    paddleGrabOffset = bottomPaddle.center.x - [touch locationInView:touch.view].x;
  }
}

- (void)touchesMoved:(NSSet *)touches withEvent:(UIEvent *)event {
  if ( gameState == gameStatePlaying ) {
    UITouch *touch = [[event allTouches] anyObject];
    float distance = ([touch locationInView:touch.view].x + paddleGrabOffset) -
bottomPaddle.center.x;
    [bottomPaddle moveHorizontallyByDistance:distance inViewFrame:self.view.frame];
  }
}

- (void)touchesEnded:(NSSet *)touches withEvent:(UIEvent *)event {
  UITouch *touch = [[event allTouches] anyObject];

  if ( gameState == gameStateLaunched && touch.tapCount > 0 ) {
    [self hideAnnouncement];
    gameState = gameStateLookingForOpponent;
```

```
        GKPeerPickerController *picker;
        picker = [[GKPeerPickerController alloc] init];
        picker.delegate = self;
        [picker show];
    }
    else if ( gameState == gameStateWaitingToServeBall && touch.tapCount > 0 ) {
        [self hideAnnouncement];
        gameState = gameStatePlaying;
        [self resetBall];
    }
}

- (void)peerPickerControllerDidCancel:(GKPeerPickerController *)picker {
        picker.delegate = nil;
    [picker autorelease];

    [self showAnnouncement:@"Welcome to GKPong!\n\n
        Please tap to begin."];
    gameState = gameStateLaunched;
}

- (void)diceRolled {
    NSMutableData *data = [NSMutableData dataWithCapacity:1+sizeof(int)];
    char messageType = gkMessageDiceRolled;
    [data appendBytes:&messageType length:1];
    myDiceRoll = rand();
    [data appendBytes:&myDiceRoll length:sizeof(int)];


    [gkSession sendDataToAllPeers:data withDataMode:GKSendDataReliable error:nil];
}

- (void)peerPickerController:(GKPeerPickerController *)picker didConnectPeer:(NSString
*)peerID toSession:(GKSession *)session {
    self.gkPeerID = peerID;
    self.gkSession = session;
    [gkSession setDataReceiveHandler:self withContext:NULL];

    [picker dismiss];
    picker.delegate = nil;
    [picker autorelease];

    gameState = gameStateRollingDice;
    [self diceRolled];
}

- (void)receiveData:(NSData *)data fromPeer:(NSString *)peer inSession:(GKSession
*)session context:(void *)context {
    const char *incomingPacket = (const char *)[data bytes];
    char messageType = incomingPacket[0];


    switch (messageType) {
      case gkMessageDiceRolled: {
        int peerDiceRoll = *(int *)(incomingPacket + 1);
```

```
      if ( peerDiceRoll == myDiceRoll ) {
        [self diceRolled];
        return;
      }
      else if ( myDiceRoll > peerDiceRoll ) {
        [self showAnnouncement:@"The game is about to begin.\n\n
            Tap to serve the ball!"];
        gameState = gameStateWaitingToServeBall;
        didWeWinLastRound = NO;
      }
      else {
        [self showAnnouncement:@"The game is about to begin.\n\n
            Waiting for the opponent..."];
        gameState = gameStateWaitingForOpponentToServeBall;
        didWeWinLastRound = YES;
      }


      [self startGame];
      break;
    }
  }
}

- (void)startGame {
  topPaddle.center = CGPointMake(self.view.frame.size.width/2,
topPaddle.frame.size.height);
  bottomPaddle.center = CGPointMake(self.view.frame.size.width/2,
self.view.frame.size.height - bottomPaddle.frame.size.height);
  [self resetBall];

  [self.view addSubview:topPaddle.view];
  [self.view addSubview:bottomPaddle.view];
  [self.view addSubview:ball.view];

  self.gameLoopTimer = [NSTimer scheduledTimerWithTimeInterval:0.033 target:self
selector:@selector(gameLoop) userInfo:nil repeats:YES];
}

- (void)viewDidLoad {
  [super viewDidLoad];

  sranddev();

  announcementLabel = [[AnnouncementLabel alloc] initWithFrame:self.view.frame];
  announcementLabel.center = CGPointMake(announcementLabel.center.x,
announcementLabel.center.y - 23.0);

  topPaddle = [[Paddle alloc] init];
  bottomPaddle = [[Paddle alloc] init];

  ball = [[Ball alloc] initWithField:self.view.frame topPaddle:topPaddle
bottomPaddle:bottomPaddle];
  ball.delegate = self;

  [self showAnnouncement:@"Welcome to GKPong!\n\n
```

```
      Please tap to begin."];
   didWeWinLastRound = NO;
   gameState = gameStateLaunched;
}

- (void)showAnnouncement:(NSString*)announcementText {
   announcementLabel.text = announcementText;
   [self.view addSubview:announcementLabel];
}

- (void)hideAnnouncement {
   [announcementLabel removeFromSuperview];
}

- (void)resetBall {
   [ball reset];
   ball.center = CGPointMake(self.view.frame.size.width/2,
self.view.frame.size.height/2);
   ball.direction = INITIAL_BALL_DIRECTION + ((didWeWinLastRound)? 0: M_PI);
   ball.speed = INITIAL_BALL_SPEED;
}

- (void)dealloc {
   [topPaddle release];
   [bottomPaddle release];
   [ball release];
   [announcementLabel removeFromSuperview];
   [announcementLabel release];
   [gameLoopTimer invalidate];
   self.gameLoopTimer = nil;
   [super dealloc];
}
@end
```

The new diceRolled method does two things: comes up with a random number, and then sends that number over to our opponent. Whenever we want to send some data using GKSession, we first need to pack it into NSData object. We are using NSMutableData in order to make the process of putting our message together a bit easier:

```
NSMutableData *data = [NSMutableData dataWithCapacity:1+sizeof(int)];
```

We are anticipating that this is not the only kind of message that we'll be sending to our opponent. Therefore, we are introducing a notion of message type, which is an enum that will help us figure out what to do with a particular message when it arrives.

```
char messageType = gkMessageDiceRolled;
[data appendBytes:&messageType length:1];
```

We also need to actually roll the dice, store the resulting value for later use, and include it in the network message:

```
 myDiceRoll = rand();
[data appendBytes:&myDiceRoll length:sizeof(int)];
```

After we put the message together in this way, it will look something like Figure 14–9.

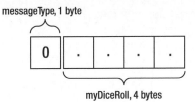

myDiceRoll, 4 bytes

Figure 14–9. *The resulting "dice rolled" message is 5 bytes long. The body of the message is an integer that contains the value of our dice roll.*

Finally, we are ready to ship it out. Since our app might not function correctly if the message is dropped, we are asking for a guaranteed delivery by specifying GKSendDataReliable:

```
[gkSession sendDataToAllPeers:data withDataMode:GKSendDataReliable error:nil];
```

Now, look back at how we initialized the NSMutableData object. See that dataWithCapacity part? This is a bit of an optimization on our part. We know exactly how much data will be sent, even before we start putting the message together: it's 1 byte for the messageType and sizeof(int) bytes for the one integer that we want to include. By using dataWithCapacity, we are telling NSMutableData how much memory we will need in advance, therefore possibly avoiding unnecessary memory allocations later on. Strictly speaking, this step might not be entirely necessary for such a small amount of memory. This is just an example of an optimization that you might want to think about when working on your own apps.

Let's go through the other changes that we made to the code just now. First, whenever a new connection is established, we want to make sure that any messages that arrive via that session are delivered directly to us. We tell GKSession that GKPongViewController is responsible for handling the incoming data:

```
[gkSession setDataReceiveHandler:self withContext:NULL];
```

Whenever the data does arrive, GKSession will attempt to call the receiveData:fromPeer:inSession:context method on the object that was designated as the handler. It is then up to us to make sense of that data. Remember how we put our "dice roll" message together? The first byte indicated the type. Keep in mind that we will have more kinds of messages in the future. That's why we are putting the switch/case statement in from the very beginning:

```
- (void)receiveData:(NSData *)data fromPeer:(NSString *)peer inSession:(GKSession
*)session context:(void *)context {
  const char *incomingPacket = (const char *)[data bytes];
  char messageType = incomingPacket[0];

  switch (messageType) {
    case gkMessageDiceRolled: {
```

If the message is indeed of type gkMessageDiceRolled, we will try to extract the value of our opponent's dice roll by interpreting the group of bytes that comes after the message type byte as an integer:

```
      int peerDiceRoll = *(int *)(incomingPacket + 1);
```

If you aren't too sure what that line means, here is an expanded version:

```
const char *bytesAfterMessageType = incomingPacket + 1;
int *peerDiceRollPointer = (int *)bytesAfterMessageType;
int peerDiceRoll = *peerDiceRollPointer;
```

We need to resolve possible ties. If both players come up with the same value, we roll the dice again, by calling `diceRolled`:

```
if ( peerDiceRoll == myDiceRoll ) {
  [self diceRolled];
  return;
}
```

Note that by the time this code gets called, the `myDiceRoll` variable will already contain results of our own dice roll attempt, because `diceRolled` is guaranteed to be called before `receiveData:fromPeer:inSession:context`. Think about why that is.

If we happen to win this mini game of dice, we get to serve the ball first. If not, we will wait for the opponent to do so. Once that is settled, we are finally ready to start the game:

```
else if ( myDiceRoll > peerDiceRoll ) {
  [self showAnnouncement:@"The game is about to begin.\n\n
      Tap to serve the ball!"];
  gameState = gameStateWaitingToServeBall;
  didWeWinLastRound = NO;
}
else {
  [self showAnnouncement:@"The game is about to begin.\n\n
      Waiting for the opponent..."];
  gameState = gameStateWaitingForOpponentToServeBall;
  didWeWinLastRound = YES;
}

[self startGame];
```

Before compiling, don't forget to modify *GKPongViewController.h* accordingly:

```
#import <UIKit/UIKit.h>
#import <GameKit/GameKit.h>
#import "Ball.h"
#import "Paddle.h"
#import "AnnouncementLabel.h"

typedef enum {
  gameStateLaunched,
  gameStateLookingForOpponent,
  gameStateRollingDice,
  gameStateWaitingForOpponentToServeBall,
  gameStateWaitingToServeBall,
  gameStatePlaying
} GameState;

@interface GKPongViewController : UIViewController <BallDelegate,
GKPeerPickerControllerDelegate> {
  Paddle *topPaddle;
  Paddle *bottomPaddle;
  float paddleGrabOffset;
```

```
    Ball *ball;
    float initialBallDirection;

    AnnouncementLabel *announcementLabel;

    BOOL didWeWinLastRound;
    NSTimer *gameLoopTimer;
    GameState gameState;

    NSString *gkPeerID;
    GKSession *gkSession;

    int myDiceRoll;
}

@property (retain, nonatomic) NSTimer *gameLoopTimer;
@property (retain, nonatomic) NSString *gkPeerID;
@property (retain, nonatomic) GKSession *gkSession;

- (void)showAnnouncement:(NSString*)announcementText;
- (void)hideAnnouncement;
- (void)startGame;
- (void)resetBall;
@end
```

Congratulations! If this chapter were a hill, we would be at the top of it right now. From this point on, the going should get easier. Make sure to go back and review any material that might seem a little fuzzy.

This is a good spot to take a break. Come back when you are ready to continue.

Ready...Set...Go!

Let's try to run the app in its current state and figure out what else needs to be done. It seems like our dice rolling is working, so one of the players gets to start the match by tapping the screen. But the other player never finds out that the game has actually begun, and his screen just keeps saying, "Waiting for opponent...." Well, if you think about it, it's not really surprising, since we don't have any code that would notify our opponent that the ball has been served. In order to fix that, let's edit *GKPongViewController.m* and create a new message type:

```
enum {
  gkMessageDiceRolled,
  gkMessageBallServed
};
```

When is it a good time to send such a message to our peer? Whenever we tap the screen to begin the game, of course:

```
- (void)touchesEnded:(NSSet *)touches withEvent:(UIEvent *)event {
  UITouch *touch = [[event allTouches] anyObject];

  if ( gameState == gameStateLaunched && touch.tapCount > 0 ) {
    [self hideAnnouncement];
```

```
        gameState = gameStateLookingForOpponent;

        GKPeerPickerController *picker;
        picker = [[GKPeerPickerController alloc] init];
        picker.delegate = self;
        [picker show];
    }
    else if ( gameState == gameStateWaitingToServeBall && touch.tapCount > 0 ) {
        [self hideAnnouncement];
        gameState = gameStatePlaying;
        [self resetBall];

        char messageType = gkMessageBallServed;
        [gkSession sendDataToAllPeers:[NSData dataWithBytes:&messageType length:1]
withDataMode:GKSendDataReliable error:nil];
    }
}
```

In addition, we also need to interpret and process the message when it comes in:

```
- (void)receiveData:(NSData *)data fromPeer:(NSString *)peer inSession:(GKSession
*)session context:(void *)context {
    const char *incomingPacket = (const char *)[data bytes];
    char messageType = incomingPacket[0];

    switch (messageType) {
        case gkMessageDiceRolled: {
            int peerDiceRoll = *(int *)(incomingPacket + 1);
            if ( peerDiceRoll == myDiceRoll ) {
                [self diceRolled];
                return;
            }
            else if ( myDiceRoll > peerDiceRoll ) {
                [self showAnnouncement:@"The game is about to begin.\n\n
                    Tap to serve the ball!"];
                gameState = gameStateWaitingToServeBall;
                didWeWinLastRound = NO;
            }
            else {
                [self showAnnouncement:@"The game is about to begin.\n\n
                    Waiting for the opponent..."];
                gameState = gameStateWaitingForOpponentToServeBall;
                didWeWinLastRound = YES;
            }

            [self startGame];
            break;
        }

        case gkMessageBallServed:
            didWeWinLastRound = YES;
            [self resetBall];
            [self hideAnnouncement];
            gameState = gameStatePlaying;
            break;
    }
}
```

At this point, you might be wondering how the ball knows to start or stop moving without us calling any kind of a stop or start method. The mechanism is quite simple: As soon as the dice roll is executed and we call `startGame`, a timer is scheduled. This timer starts calling the gameLoop method 30 times a second or so. In turn, gameLoop calls [ball processOneFrame], which makes the ball recalculate and update its position; however, this happens only if our `gameState` variable is equal to `gameStatePlaying`. That's why whenever we change the value of `gameState` to something else, the objects on the screen stop moving. When we set it to `gameStatePlaying`, the game comes alive again.

Hits and Misses

Launch the game. If we've done everything right, the ball should be getting served correctly now, on both screens. But we still have a problem: Whenever the ball misses or bounces off our paddle, the other player doesn't know about it, and the game gets out of sync until the next time the ball is served. By now, you should have a pretty good idea about how to correct this. Let's first handle the easier of the two cases: communicating when the ball misses our paddle.

GKPongViewController.m needs a few changes, such as a new message type:

```
enum {
  gkMessageDiceRolled,
  gkMessageBallServed,
  gkMessageBallMissed
};
```

Since all of the ball-movement processing happens inside of a class called `Ball`, how does `GKPongViewController` know when the ball misses one of the paddles? Why, through delegation, of course! `ballMissedPaddle:` is called, and that's how we find out. Let's also tell our peer about it:

```
- (void)ballMissedPaddle:(Paddle*)paddle {
  if ( paddle == topPaddle ) {
    didWeWinLastRound = YES;
    gameState = gameStateWaitingToServeBall;
    [self showAnnouncement:@"Your opponent missed!\n\n
        Tap to serve the ball."];
  }
  else {
    didWeWinLastRound = NO;
    gameState = gameStateWaitingToServeBall;
    [self showAnnouncement:@"Looks like you missed...\n\n
        Tap to serve the ball."];
    char messageType = gkMessageBallMissed;
    [gkSession sendDataToAllPeers:[NSData dataWithBytes:&messageType length:1]
withDataMode:GKSendDataReliable error:nil];
  }
}
```

And last, but not least, we process the incoming message:

```
- (void)receiveData:(NSData *)data fromPeer:(NSString *)peer inSession:(GKSession
*)session context:(void *)context {
  const char *incomingPacket = (const char *)[data bytes];
```

```
char messageType = incomingPacket[0];

switch (messageType) {
  case gkMessageDiceRolled: {
    int peerDiceRoll = *(int *)(incomingPacket + 1);
    if ( peerDiceRoll == myDiceRoll ) {
      [self diceRolled];
      return;
    }
    else if ( myDiceRoll > peerDiceRoll ) {
      [self showAnnouncement:@"The game is about to begin.\n\n
          Tap to serve the ball!"];
      gameState = gameStateWaitingToServeBall;
      didWeWinLastRound = NO;
    }
    else {
      [self showAnnouncement:@"The game is about to begin.\n\n
          Waiting for the opponent..."];
      gameState = gameStateWaitingForOpponentToServeBall;
      didWeWinLastRound = YES;
    }

    [self startGame];
    break;
  }

  case gkMessageBallServed:
    didWeWinLastRound = YES;
    [self resetBall];
    [self hideAnnouncement];
    gameState = gameStatePlaying;
    break;

  case gkMessageBallMissed:
    didWeWinLastRound = YES;
    [self showAnnouncement:@"You won the last round!\n\n
        Waiting for the opponent..."];
    gameState = gameStateWaitingForOpponentToServeBall;
    break;
  }
}
```

That was easy enough—a little too easy, in fact. Something doesn't feel right. Take a look at the `ballMissedPaddle:` method again. We seem to still be trying to detect and handle the case when our ball flies past the paddle that's located at the top of the screen, which is our local representation of the opponent's paddle. Why would we need to do that if we just added the code that makes our peer tell us when the ball misses their paddle?

Also notice that we still didn't add the code that communicates our peer's paddle position changes to us, which means that at any given point in time, we cannot be certain where our opponent's paddle is. This, in turn, means that the code that tries to detect whether or not the ball flew past the paddle located on the top of the screen might produce incorrect results. This leaves us with only one sure way to find out about our opponent's failures to bounce the ball back to us: listen for gkMessageBallMissed messages.

The two pieces of code that we are about to remove do, of course, make sense if both paddles are under our complete control, as was the case when we were playing against a computer.

Let's get rid of that conditional statement:

```
- (void)ballMissedPaddle:(Paddle*)paddle {
    if ( paddle == topPaddle ) {
        didWeWinLastRound = YES;
        gameState = gameStateWaitingToServeBall;
        [self showAnnouncement:@"Your opponent missed!\n\n
            Tap to serve the ball."];
    }
    else {
        didWeWinLastRound = NO;
        gameState = gameStateWaitingToServeBall;
        [self showAnnouncement:@"Looks like you missed...\n\n
            Tap to serve the ball."];
        char messageType = gkMessageBallMissed;
        [gkSession sendDataToAllPeers:[NSData dataWithBytes:&messageType length:1]
withDataMode:GKSendDataReliable error:nil];
    }
}
```

Let's also remove the logic that is responsible for actually detecting the miss. It's located in *Ball.m*:

```
- (void)processOneFrame {
    // Recalculate our position
    CGPoint ballPosition = view.center;

    ballPosition.x -= speed * cos(direction);
    ballPosition.y -= speed * sin(direction);
    view.center = ballPosition;

    // Are we hitting the wall on the right?
    if ( ballPosition.x >= (fieldFrame.size.width - view.frame.size.width/2) ) {
        if ( !alreadyBouncedOffWall ) {
            self.direction = M_PI - direction;
            alreadyBouncedOffWall = YES;
        }
    }
    // Are we hitting the wall on the left?
    else if ( ballPosition.x <= view.frame.size.width/2 ) {
        if ( !alreadyBouncedOffWall ) {
            self.direction = M_PI - direction;
            alreadyBouncedOffWall = YES;
        }
    }
    else {
        alreadyBouncedOffWall = NO;
    }

    // If we have moved out of the bouncing zone, reset "already bounced" flag
```

```
    if ( alreadyBouncedOffPaddle && ballPosition.y + view.frame.size.height/2 <
bottomPaddle.frame.origin.y &&
        ballPosition.y - view.frame.size.height/2 > topPaddle.frame.origin.y +
topPaddle.frame.size.height) {
        alreadyBouncedOffPaddle = NO;
    }

    // Are we moving past bottom paddle?
    if ( ballPosition.y + view.frame.size.height/2 >= (bottomPaddle.frame.origin.y) && !
alreadyBouncedOffPaddle ) {
        // Bounce or miss?
        if ( ballPosition.x + view.frame.size.width/2 > bottomPaddle.frame.origin.x &&
            ballPosition.x - view.frame.size.width/2 < bottomPaddle.frame.origin.x +
bottomPaddle.frame.size.width ) {
            [self bounceBallOffPaddle:bottomPaddle];
        }
        else {
            // We missed the paddle
            [delegate ballMissedPaddle:bottomPaddle];
        }
    }

    // Are we moving past top paddle?
    if ( ballPosition.y - view.frame.size.height/2 <= topPaddle.frame.origin.y +
topPaddle.frame.size.height && ! alreadyBouncedOffPaddle ) {
        // Bounce or miss?
        if ( ballPosition.x + view.frame.size.width/2 > topPaddle.frame.origin.x &&
            ballPosition.x - view.frame.size.width/2 < topPaddle.frame.origin.x +
topPaddle.frame.size.width ) {
            [self bounceBallOffPaddle:topPaddle];
        }
        else {
            // We missed the paddle
            [delegate ballMissedPaddle:topPaddle];
        }
    }
}
```

That does it for the "ball missed" case. What happens when the ball bounces? We need to go through a similar process there, with one caveat: As things stand right now, the ball handles the bounces but doesn't tell GKPongViewController when they happen. Let's add another method to the BallDelegate protocol, located in *Ball.h*:

```
@protocol BallDelegate
- (void)ballMissedPaddle:(Paddle*)paddle;
- (void)ballBounced;
@end
```

And add the code to call the new delegate method, also located in *Ball.m*:

```
- (void)processOneFrame {
    // Recalculate our position
    CGPoint ballPosition = view.center;

    ballPosition.x -= speed * cos(direction);
    ballPosition.y -= speed * sin(direction);
    view.center = ballPosition;
```

```
    // Are we hitting the wall on the right?
    if ( ballPosition.x >= (fieldFrame.size.width - view.frame.size.width/2) ) {
      if ( !alreadyBouncedOffWall ) {
        self.direction = M_PI - direction;
        alreadyBouncedOffWall = YES;
      }
    }
    // Are we hitting the wall on the left?
    else if ( ballPosition.x <= view.frame.size.width/2 ) {
      if ( !alreadyBouncedOffWall ) {
        self.direction = M_PI - direction;
        alreadyBouncedOffWall = YES;
      }
    }
    else {
      alreadyBouncedOffWall = NO;
    }

    // If we have moved out of the bouncing zone, reset "already bounced" flag
    if ( alreadyBouncedOffPaddle && ballPosition.y + view.frame.size.height/2 <
bottomPaddle.frame.origin.y &&
        ballPosition.y - view.frame.size.height/2 > topPaddle.frame.origin.y +
topPaddle.frame.size.height) {
      alreadyBouncedOffPaddle = NO;
    }

    // Are we moving past bottom paddle?
    if ( ballPosition.y + view.frame.size.height/2 >= (bottomPaddle.frame.origin.y) && !
alreadyBouncedOffPaddle ) {
      // Bounce or miss?
      if ( ballPosition.x + view.frame.size.width/2 > bottomPaddle.frame.origin.x &&
          ballPosition.x - view.frame.size.width/2 < bottomPaddle.frame.origin.x +
bottomPaddle.frame.size.width ) {
        [self bounceBallOffPaddle:bottomPaddle];
        [delegate ballBounced];
      }
      else {
        // We missed the paddle
        [delegate ballMissedPaddle:bottomPaddle];
      }
    }
}
```

Now that GKPongViewController possesses all of the necessary information, let's share some of it with our peer.

Add the following code to *GKPongViewController.m*:

```
enum {
  gkMessageDiceRolled,
  gkMessageBallServed,
  gkMessageBallMissed,
  gkMessageBallBounced
};

typedef struct {
  CGPoint position;
```

```
    float direction;
    float speed;
} BallInfo;

@implementation GKPongViewController

@synthesize gameLoopTimer;
@synthesize gkPeerID, gkSession;

- (void)gameLoop {
  if ( gameState != gameStatePlaying ) {
    return;
  }
  [bottomPaddle processOneFrame];
  [topPaddle processOneFrame];
  [ball processOneFrame];
}

- (void)ballMissedPaddle:(Paddle*)paddle {
  didWeWinLastRound = NO;
  gameState = gameStateWaitingToServeBall;
  [self showAnnouncement:@"Looks like you missed...\n\n
      Tap to serve the ball."];

  char messageType = gkMessageBallMissed;
  [gkSession sendDataToAllPeers:[NSData dataWithBytes:&messageType length:1]
withDataMode:GKSendDataReliable error:nil];
}

- (void)ballBounced {
  NSMutableData *data = [NSMutableData dataWithCapacity:1+sizeof(BallInfo)];
  char messageType = gkMessageBallBounced;
  [data appendBytes:&messageType length:1];


  BallInfo message;
  message.position = ball.center;
  message.direction = ball.direction;
  message.speed = ball.speed;
  [data appendBytes:&message length:sizeof(BallInfo)];

  [gkSession sendDataToAllPeers:data withDataMode:GKSendDataReliable error:nil];
}
```

Scroll down and add another block of code:

```
- (void)receiveData:(NSData *)data fromPeer:(NSString *)peer inSession:(GKSession
*)session context:(void *)context {
  const char *incomingPacket = (const char *)[data bytes];
  char messageType = incomingPacket[0];

  switch (messageType) {
    case gkMessageDiceRolled: {
      int peerDiceRoll = *(int *)(incomingPacket + 1);
      if ( peerDiceRoll == myDiceRoll ) {
        [self diceRolled];
        return;
```

```
    }
    else if ( myDiceRoll > peerDiceRoll ) {
      [self showAnnouncement:@"The game is about to begin.\n\n
          Tap to serve the ball!"];
      gameState = gameStateWaitingToServeBall;
      didWeWinLastRound = NO;
    }
    else {
      [self showAnnouncement:@"The game is about to begin.\n\n
          Waiting for the opponent..."];
      gameState = gameStateWaitingForOpponentToServeBall;
      didWeWinLastRound = YES;
    }

    [self startGame];
    break;
  }

  case gkMessageBallServed:
    didWeWinLastRound = YES;
    [self resetBall];
    [self hideAnnouncement];
    gameState = gameStatePlaying;
    break;

  case gkMessageBallMissed:
    didWeWinLastRound = YES;
    [self showAnnouncement:@"You won the last round!\n\n
        Waiting for the opponent..."];
    gameState = gameStateWaitingForOpponentToServeBall;
    break;

  case gkMessageBallBounced: {
    BallInfo peerBallInfo = *(BallInfo *)(incomingPacket + 1);
    ball.direction = peerBallInfo.direction + M_PI;
    ball.speed = peerBallInfo.speed;
    ball.center = CGPointMake(self.view.frame.size.width - peerBallInfo.position.x,
self.view.frame.size.height - peerBallInfo.position.y);
    break;
    }
  }
}
```

These latest modifications follow the same pattern that we've applied before:

- Define a new message type.

- Whenever an event that interests us happens, send a message of the new type to our peer.

- Make sure to properly handle incoming messages of the new type.

There is one slight deviation, however. In order to make constructing the network message easier, we are adding a new struct that will hold all of the variables that are necessary to accurately describe the position, speed, and direction of the ball after it bounces off our paddle.

```
typedef struct {
  CGPoint position;
  float direction;
  float speed;
} BallInfo;
```

Now, instead of adding several variables to the NSMutableData one by one, we can add everything in one shot, without needing to worry about their order:

```
- (void)ballBounced {
  NSMutableData *data = [NSMutableData dataWithCapacity:1+sizeof(BallInfo)];
  char messageType = gkMessageBallBounced;
  [data appendBytes:&messageType length:1];

  BallInfo message;
  message.position = ball.center;
  message.direction = ball.direction;
  message.speed = ball.speed;
  [data appendBytes:&message length:sizeof(BallInfo)];

  [gkSession sendDataToAllPeers:data withDataMode:GKSendDataReliable error:nil];
}
```

It also makes our life a little easier on the message-processing end. We can access parts of the structure by their names instead of needing to juggle pointers. The code comes out much cleaner:

```
case gkMessageBallBounced: {
      BallInfo peerBallInfo = *(BallInfo *)(incomingPacket + 1);
      ball.direction = peerBallInfo.direction + M_PI;
      ball.speed = peerBallInfo.speed;
      ball.center = CGPointMake(self.view.frame.size.width - peerBallInfo.position.x,
self.view.frame.size.height - peerBallInfo.position.y);
      break;
    }
```

A side question for you to think about: Why can't we use the values sent to us by our peer without first changing them in particular ways (see ball.direction and ball.center in the preceding code)?

Let's step back for a moment. Why does the peer have to send us all of the updated variables instead of just telling us the fact that the ball has bounced and letting us calculate the rest? The answer is exactly the same as it was when we asked the question about detecting the ball misses locally versus waiting for gkMessageBallMissed messages: We might not have enough information to correctly calculate the outcome of the bounce at any given point in time.

For example, in order to make the game a bit more realistic, we have some code in there that continuously calculates the velocity of the paddle and uses that value whenever the paddle comes in contact with the ball and we need to calculate trajectory of bounce. And as far as our opponent's paddle is concerned, we don't really have up-to-date velocity information at this point. And even after we add the code to receive and process our peer paddle's movements, such an approach wouldn't necessarily work. You'll see why shortly.

The Paddle Comes Alive

Our game is almost there. The ball bounces correctly now, and the misses seem to get registered pretty accurately. But it still doesn't work quite right, since the paddle located on the top of the screen never moves—it looks like we are simply bouncing the ball against a wall.

Let's write a bit more code to make it right. Open *GKPongViewController.m* and add the new message type:

```
enum {
  gkMessageDiceRolled,
  gkMessageBallServed,
  gkMessageBallMissed,
  gkMessageBallBounced,
  gkMessagePaddleMoved
};
```

Next, let's compose and send the message to our peer:

```
- (void)paddleMoved {
  NSMutableData *data = [NSMutableData dataWithCapacity:1+sizeof(int)+sizeof(float)];
  char messageType = gkMessagePaddleMoved;
  [data appendBytes:&messageType length:1];
  myLastPaddleUpdateID++;
  [data appendBytes:&myLastPaddleUpdateID length:sizeof(int)];
  float x = bottomPaddle.center.x;
  [data appendBytes:&x length:sizeof(float)];


  [gkSession sendDataToAllPeers:data withDataMode:GKSendDataUnreliable error:nil];
}

- (void)touchesBegan:(NSSet *)touches withEvent:(UIEvent *)event {
  if ( gameState == gameStatePlaying ) {
    UITouch *touch = [[event allTouches] anyObject];
    paddleGrabOffset = bottomPaddle.center.x - [touch locationInView:touch.view].x;
  }
}

- (void)touchesMoved:(NSSet *)touches withEvent:(UIEvent *)event {
  if ( gameState == gameStatePlaying ) {
    UITouch *touch = [[event allTouches] anyObject];
    float distance = ([touch locationInView:touch.view].x + paddleGrabOffset) -
bottomPaddle.center.x;

    float previousX = bottomPaddle.center.x;
    [bottomPaddle moveHorizontallyByDistance:distance inViewFrame:self.view.frame];
    if ( bottomPaddle.center.x != previousX ) {
      [self paddleMoved];
    }
  }
}
```

And finally, let's not forget to process the message when it comes in:

```
- (void)receiveData:(NSData *)data fromPeer:(NSString *)peer inSession:(GKSession
*)session context:(void *)context {
  const char *incomingPacket = (const char *)[data bytes];
  char messageType = incomingPacket[0];

  switch (messageType) {
    case gkMessageDiceRolled: {
      int peerDiceRoll = *(int *)(incomingPacket + 1);
      if ( peerDiceRoll == myDiceRoll ) {
        [self diceRolled];
        return;
      }
      else if ( myDiceRoll > peerDiceRoll ) {
        [self showAnnouncement:@"The game is about to begin.\n\n
            Tap to serve the ball!"];
        gameState = gameStateWaitingToServeBall;
        didWeWinLastRound = NO;
      }
      else {
        [self showAnnouncement:@"The game is about to begin.\n\n
            Waiting for the opponent..."];
        gameState = gameStateWaitingForOpponentToServeBall;
        didWeWinLastRound = YES;
      }

      [self startGame];
      break;
    }

    case gkMessageBallServed:
      didWeWinLastRound = YES;
      [self resetBall];
      [self hideAnnouncement];
      gameState = gameStatePlaying;
      break;

    case gkMessageBallMissed:
      didWeWinLastRound = YES;
      [self showAnnouncement:@"You won the last round!\n\n
          Waiting for the opponent..."];
      gameState = gameStateWaitingForOpponentToServeBall;
      break;

    case gkMessageBallBounced: {
      BallInfo peerBallInfo = *(BallInfo *)(incomingPacket + 1);
      ball.direction = peerBallInfo.direction + M_PI;
      ball.speed = peerBallInfo.speed;
      ball.center = CGPointMake(self.view.frame.size.width - peerBallInfo.position.x,
self.view.frame.size.height - peerBallInfo.position.y);
      break;
    }

    case gkMessagePaddleMoved: {
      int paddleUpdateID = *(int *)(incomingPacket + 1);
      if ( paddleUpdateID <= peerLastPaddleUpdateID ) {
        return;
      }
```

```
      peerLastPaddleUpdateID = paddleUpdateID;

      float x = *(float *)(incomingPacket + 1 + sizeof(int));
      topPaddle.center = CGPointMake(self.view.frame.size.width - x,
topPaddle.center.y);
      break;
    }
  }
}

- (void)startGame {
  topPaddle.center = CGPointMake(self.view.frame.size.width/2,
topPaddle.frame.size.height);
  bottomPaddle.center = CGPointMake(self.view.frame.size.width/2,
self.view.frame.size.height - bottomPaddle.frame.size.height);
  [self resetBall];

  myLastPaddleUpdateID = 0;
  peerLastPaddleUpdateID = 0;

  [self.view addSubview:topPaddle.view];
  [self.view addSubview:bottomPaddle.view];
  [self.view addSubview:ball.view];

  self.gameLoopTimer = [NSTimer scheduledTimerWithTimeInterval:0.033 target:self
selector:@selector(gameLoop) userInfo:nil repeats:YES];
}
```

Once again, the idea is pretty straightforward: Every time our paddle changes its position due to touch events, we send the updated position over to our peer so that it can be reflected on his screen. (Keep in mind that we don't let the paddle move off visible part of the application window completely, which means that sometimes we must leave the object stationary, even though the player is still dragging her finger across the screen.)

```
    float previousX = bottomPaddle.center.x;
    [bottomPaddle moveHorizontallyByDistance:distance inViewFrame:self.view.frame];
    if ( bottomPaddle.center.x != previousX ) {
      [self paddleMoved];
    }
```

But the way we are sending the position updates is a bit different from the other messages that we've been using so far. We are using GKSendDataUnreliable, as opposed to GKSendDataReliable data mode:

```
- (void)paddleMoved {
  NSMutableData *data = [NSMutableData dataWithCapacity:1+sizeof(int)+sizeof(float)];
  char messageType = gkMessagePaddleMoved;
  [data appendBytes:&messageType length:1];
  myLastPaddleUpdateID++;
  [data appendBytes:&myLastPaddleUpdateID length:sizeof(int)];
  float x = bottomPaddle.center.x;
  [data appendBytes:&x length:sizeof(float)];

  [gkSession sendDataToAllPeers:data withDataMode:GKSendDataUnreliable error:nil];
}
```

What we are telling `GKSession` here is that we don't really care whether or not this message gets delivered to the other side. It might get there, or it might not. It might also get delivered out of order, which means that if we send message A followed by message B, there is a possibility that our peer will see message B first and then message A. Or one of those messages might not arrive at all. In the worst case, neither message A nor message B will get there.

You might be wondering why would we want to use such a sloppy delivery method. Why don't we care about our data being transmitted safely and reliably? Why don't we use same delivery method that we've used before? What's so different about this particular kind of message? The answer to all of those questions consists of two parts.

First of all, reliable delivery of packets is an expensive operation. Instead of just sending one packet and moving on to the next, we now must wait for a confirmation that the data arrived safely to the other side. We must also be prepared to retransmit the message in case we aren't sure that the delivery happened successfully. All of that takes time. In a game where objects can move fairly often, usage of such an expensive transmission method might lead to performance problems.

The other part of the answer is that we don't really rely on the paddle position updates for anything important. Even if one of the messages doesn't arrive, we will most likely receive another one in the future—whenever the paddle moves again. The worst thing that can happen is the user noticing the opponent's paddle moving a bit erratically. And even that is not such a big deal. More than half of the time, our players will focus their eyes on the ball; otherwise, it would be pretty darn difficult to bounce it. Think about what would happen if gkMessageDiceRolled, gkMessageBallServed. or gkMessageBallBounced didn't arrive successfully. Such failure would result in a disconnected gaming experience, where the two players might see very different things on their respective screens. By comparison, missing one or two paddle position updates every so often is a small issue.

This is a vast and interesting topic that can easily consume a chapter all by itself. But the bottom line is that we are using the fastest possible delivery method for sending data that is not very important to guaranteeing our game play experience.

As I mentioned before, whenever `GKSendDataUnreliable` is used, messages can get lost, but they also can arrive out of order. Think about what this means for the paddle position updates. As you're moving your finger from right to left, your peer is constantly getting updates as to the new position of my paddle, and the object gets redrawn on their screen accordingly. If everything is going fine, paddle's X coordinate is always increasing. Even if some messages are lost, all that means is that the paddle object pauses briefly, and then resumes its movement after fresh packets arrive. But whenever a message is delayed and arrives later than the ones that were sent after it, as far as receiving end is concerned, the information that that message contains is already out of date. If our peer did move the paddle on the screen in response to that message, it would have jumped backward, as depicted in Figure 14–10.

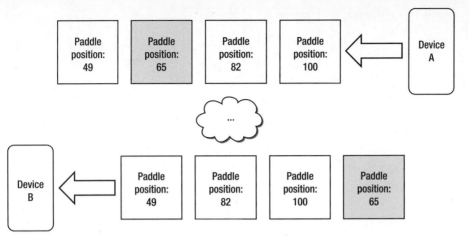

Figure 14–10. *Device A sends out "Paddle position: 65" after "Paddle position: 49," but the order gets mixed up during unreliable transmission. This results in device B recording that paddle jumped from position 100 to 65, which could produce a confusing, erratic animation.*

What is a good way to protect our app from this? Changing the data mode to "reliable" would certainly fix this issue, but the cost of that solution is more than we are willing to pay. The approach that we are going to take is to drop the outdated packets. Each message will carry a sequence number in it. Every time a message is sent, the sequence number is incremented:

```
myLastPaddleUpdateID++;
[data appendBytes:&myLastPaddleUpdateID length:sizeof(int)];
```

Whenever we receive a message with a sequence number lower than the last one, we discard it:

```
int paddleUpdateID = *(int *)(incomingPacket + 1);
if ( paddleUpdateID <= peerLastPaddleUpdateID ) {
  return;
}
peerLastPaddleUpdateID = paddleUpdateID;
```

In order to avoid reusing sequence numbers and getting out of sync with our peer, we will reset them every time we start playing the game:

```
myLastPaddleUpdateID = 0;
peerLastPaddleUpdateID = 0;
```

Now, messages that arrive late will get ignored, as seen in Figure 14–11.

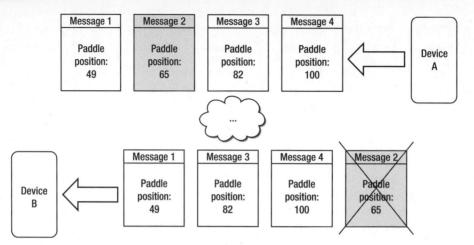

Figure 14–11. *It is easy to discard outdated messages, since each message now carries a sequence number. Here, device B will no longer render the paddle jumping incorrectly from position 100 to 65.*

The game is now fully functional. However, we can't call it a finished product just yet. We need to take care of one more thing.

Game Over: Handling Disconnects

Run the game once again. This time, observe what happens when one player closes the app while his opponent keeps on playing. That's right—nothing happens. The other app doesn't really do anything about it and keeps on running, completely oblivious. Sure, you and your opponent are very likely to be right next to each other and are perfectly capable of communicating whenever one of you exits the game (the limited range of Bluetooth won't let you roam too far apart). But the game should still detect and appropriately handle such scenario.

It turns out that we can ask GKSession to let us know when our peer gets disconnected, by providing a delegate. This gives us a chance to notify the player that the game is over and go back to the welcome screen. Let's make GKPongViewController implement the GKSessionDelegate protocol and add the necessary handler.

Modify *GKPongViewController.h* first:

```
@interface GKPongViewController : UIViewController <BallDelegate,
    GKPeerPickerControllerDelegate> {
    GKPeerPickerControllerDelegate, GKSessionDelegate> {
```

Then switch to *GKPongViewController.m* and add the following code:

```
- (void)peerPickerController:(GKPeerPickerController *)picker
    didConnectPeer:(NSString *)peerID toSession:(GKSession *)session {

    self.gkPeerID = peerID;
    self.gkSession = session;
    [gkSession setDataReceiveHandler:self withContext:NULL];
    gkSession.delegate = self;
```

```
        [picker dismiss];
        picker.delegate = nil;
        [picker autorelease];

        gameState = gameStateRollingDice;
        [self diceRolled];
    }

- (void)session:(GKSession *)session peer:(NSString *)peerID
    didChangeState:(GKPeerConnectionState)state {


    if ( [gkPeerID isEqualToString:peerID] && state == GKPeerStateDisconnected ) {
        UIAlertView *alertView = [[UIAlertView alloc] initWithTitle:@"Disconnection"
            message:@"Your opponent seems to have disconnected. Game is over."
            delegate:self cancelButtonTitle:@"Ok" otherButtonTitles:nil];
        [alertView show];


        [gkSession disconnectFromAllPeers];
        gkSession.delegate = nil;
        self.gkSession = nil;
        self.gkPeerID = nil;


        [bottomPaddle.view removeFromSuperview];
        [topPaddle.view removeFromSuperview];
        [ball.view removeFromSuperview];
        [gameLoopTimer invalidate];


        [self showAnnouncement:@"Welcome to GKPong!\n\nPlease tap to begin."];
        gameState = gameStateLaunched;
    }
}
```

Let's go through the changes that we just implemented. First, whenever our peer gets disconnected, we let our player know by displaying a pop-up message. Then we must make sure that our GKSession object is cleaned up and released.

Before we can return to the welcome screen, both paddles and the ball get removed from the view. Also, in order to prevent CPU from doing unnecessary work while there is no game being played, we stop the gameLoopTimer. It will be scheduled again the next time startGame gets called.

Summary

Well, what do you think about the transformation that our little app just went through? We started with a game that was confined to one device, and gave it the ability to communicate with other copies of itself, turning the player's gaming experience from solitary and mechanical into social and competitive.

In the process, you learned how to use GameKit to establish Bluetooth connections between apps and allow them to exchange messages. As you probably realized by now, there is a lot more that happens behind those simple method calls that deliver your data or create sessions.

Once you are sure that you have a pretty good handle on everything that we just did, feel free to move on to the next chapter. There, we will dive deeper into the networking frameworks, and you'll learn how to create more complex multiplayer games.

Let's also not forget to enjoy the fruits of our labor. So, what are you waiting for? Call your friends—it's time to play Pong!

Chapter 15

Party Time

Being able to play a computer game with or against one other human is definitely an improvement over going at it alone. But wouldn't it be better if we could invite even more of our friends to participate? That's exactly what we are going to do in this chapter. You will learn how to use sockets, streams, and Bonjour to create games that several people can play at once over Bluetooth or a local Wi-Fi network.

8 x 3 = ?

Just as in the previous chapter, we need to pick a game idea to implement before we can plunge into coding. This time we want as many people as possible playing together, coming and going as they please without interrupting the game play—like a real party that you might throw at your house. Pong is limited to two players due to how its playing field is configured. It would be very difficult to extend it to meet our criteria without turning it into something that doesn't even look like Pong anymore.

Fortunately, a whole class of games fit the bill perfectly. Let's call this category "trivia games." In our case, instead of answering questions about longest rivers, tallest mountains, and French monarchs, we will have players try to solve arithmetic puzzles faster than everyone else, in a game called TwentyFour.

In each round of TwentyFour, you are given four random numbers between 1 and 9. Your goal is to use addition, subtraction, multiplication, or division to combine all of those numbers into an expression that results in 24. Whoever finishes this task first wins the round, and the game starts again. For example, suppose you got the numbers 8, 9, 2, and 5. The simplest solution is to add all the numbers together. But you can also go another way: start with 5 – 2 = 3, followed by 9 / 3 = 3, and finally 8 x 3 = 24. Here is another example: 2, 4, 6, and 3. One of the answers is 4 x 6 x (3 – 2). Can you spot another one?

Starting Point

For the sake of saving some time, we are going to start with a functioning version of the game and gradually add multiplayer features to it, just as we did with GKPong. If you haven't already downloaded the project archive for this book, now would be a good time to do so. After you download and unpack the source code, locate the project called TwentyFour and open it in Xcode. Build and run it. You will notice that the interface has already been set up to accommodate more than one player, as shown in Figures 15–1 through 15–4. Go ahead and play a few games.

AT&T E
3:56 PM
Welcome to TwentyFour!
Please enter your name:
Petro
space
return

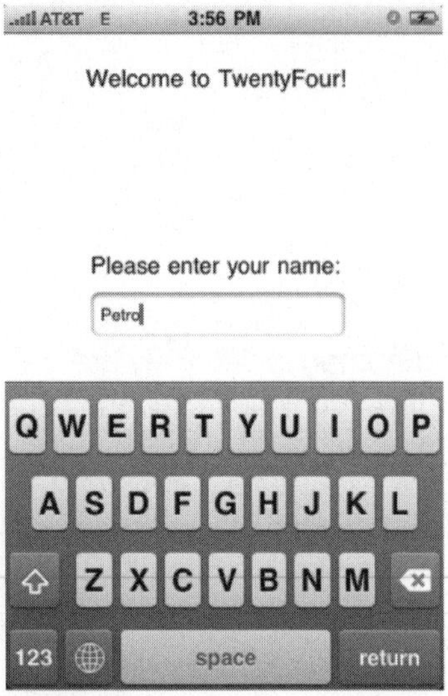

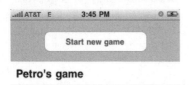

Figure 15–1. *Welcome: Players need to introduce themselves before being allowed to play TwentyFour.*

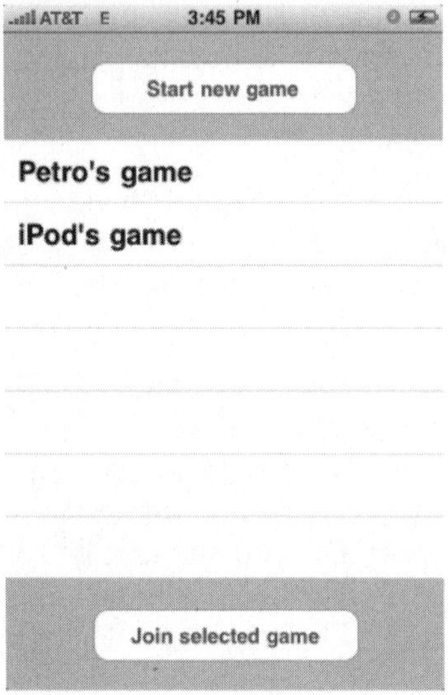

AT&T E
3:45 PM
Start new game
Petro's game
iPod's game
Join selected game

Figure 15–2. *Lobby: It's simple and to the point.*

Figure 15–3. *Game: Solve arithmetic puzzles by tapping buttons.*

Figure 15–4. *Results: Get the feeling for how you stack up against the competition.*

Let's walk through its source code and see how the various classes work together, starting with the view controllers. Each one has a corresponding Interface Builder *.xib* file and is responsible for managing its respective view:

- `WelcomeViewController` greets the player and asks for the player's name.

- `LobbyViewController` allows the player to start a new game or join one that was started by someone else. In the initial version of the app, only the former option is available.

- `TwentyFourViewController` is the most complex of them all, as it deals with the UI for the actual game.

- `ResultsViewController` takes care of displaying the results of each round. Right now, you will not see any other names besides your own appear there, because the multiplayer logic is not implemented yet.

- `WaitingViewController` is the simplest one. It's a half-transparent overlay with a rotating activity indicator in the center. We will be using it later on.

We also have two classes that are not derived from `UIViewController`:

- `TwentyFourAppDelegate` deals with switching the views around and managing the overall flow of the application.

- `GameController` keeps track of several aspects of the game logic, such as timing of rounds, making up puzzles, and processing results.

Where Are We Going?

Before embarking on this exciting journey, we need to get some clarity about what is it that we want to see in the final version of the app. Let's imagine how we would play this game in the real world, and then attempt to turn that concept into something that we can implement in software.

First, we get a whole bunch of people in one room. Since we want everyone to compete on equal terms, we need to make sure that all the players get the same challenge to work on and the same amount of time to find the solution. This means that someone must be appointed to make up the numbers, distribute them to players, collect answers, and keep track of time. We will call this person the *host*. The flow will look something like this:

- The host comes up with a set of four random numbers and writes them on pieces of paper, one copy for each player.

- The host distributes these challenges to each player. Players are not allowed to look at the numbers until they are given a signal by the host.

- The host gives a signal for the players to start solving the challenge, and starts the clock, giving each competitor 100 seconds to find a solution and submit an answer.

- The players try to find a solution to the challenge. On the piece of paper they were given, they write their answer, along with their name, and hand it back to the host. Any competitors who can't find the solution write "I give up."

- Whenever the host collects an answer from one of the players, the host writes down how long it took that player to find the solution.

- After 100 seconds, the host collects answers (or lack thereof) from any remaining players and declares the round to be over.

- The host arranges all answers in the order of how long it took to produce them, from fastest to slowest, and declares a winner.

- The game begins all over again.

These rules might be a bit too bureaucratic for a game that you would play at a real party. It is better to think of this as an algorithm. All we need to do now is translate some of the concepts into software requirements, and we are good to go.

Instead of a real room, we will have virtual rooms. Each player can decide whether she wants to join an existing room or create a new one. Of course, we won't be putting our numbers or answers on paper. This will be done using the iPhone UI and whatever networking tools are available in the SDK. Finally, we will offload to the computer such boring tasks of generating random numbers, keeping track of time, and tabulating answers.

Now that we know what we want, let's talk about how we will go about making it happen.

What's in the Structure?

Take another look at the list of steps in the previous section. Notice that it would be pretty difficult to implement this game without having a separation between the host and players. In the course of a round, the two kinds of participants have distinctly different responsibilities: The host controls the flow of the game, and the players are there to enjoy the ride. Contrast that with Pong, where it is possible to play without putting someone in charge of the game.

What does all this mean in terms of how we should implement the multiplayer logic? When it comes to designing software that utilizes networking, developers often encounter just such a division of responsibilities between modules—one is in charge, and all others follow orders. Chances are that you have heard the name of this design idea before: the *client/server model*. You encounter it every time you use a browser, which is a *client*, to connect to a web *server*. Our game will use the same model of interaction. In order to avoid confusion, from this point on, I will use the term *player* to refer to users of our app. *Client* will refer to the part of our application that allows players to join rooms and enjoy the game of TwentyFour. *Server* refers to our implementation of the host.

Let's list responsibilities of these two components to get a better idea of the differences between them:

The server will do the following:

- Create a game room and allow clients to join it.

- Whenever a new player joins, update the player list accordingly and notify all other clients about it.

- Whenever a player leaves, update the player list accordingly and notify all other clients about it.

- Come up with challenges.

- Tell clients what the challenge is.

- Collect answers from clients.

- Make sure that game rounds don't go over the allotted time.

- Tabulate the results.

- Announce the results to clients.

The client will do the following:

- Find out what game rooms are available and allow the player to select and join a room.

- Upon receiving a challenge from the server, present it to the player.

- Allow the player to enter answers to challenges and submit them to the server.

- Whenever the player decides to leave the game, notify the server about it.

- Upon receiving results of the round from the server, present them to the player.

Keep in mind that we don't want any of our players to explicitly perform the tasks of the host from the "real-world" version of the game—that's what computers (or, in our case, iPhones and iPod touches) are for. Whenever a player decides to create a new room, that player will be able to play in it along with everyone else—instead of shuffling papers and checking the clock—and a server object will be created to take on the host's responsibilities for that room. The final structure will look something like the diagram in Figure 15–5.

Notice that the picture in Figure 15–5 includes a few instances of a connection. As you will remember from the GKPong example, communication between applications doesn't "just happen." Before any of the other good stuff can take place, we need a component that will make sure that clients can talk to the server and vice versa.

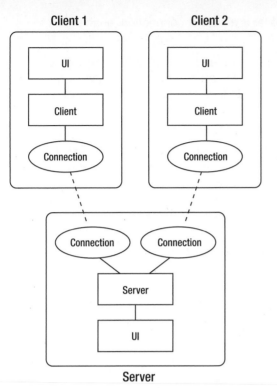

Figure 15–5. *Clients communicate with the server via network connections.*

Making Connections

A word of warning: This and the next part of the chapter will be the most complex. Strictly speaking, you don't need to understand every last detail of what's included here. However, if you are curious as to what makes networking applications tick, this is your chance to peek under the hood.

If you took the time to carefully read the previous chapter, it will be easier to make sense of the material that follows. We will talk about two things that we have dealt with before, but didn't cover in detail: socket connections and socket servers.

The code that we are about to write will not be game-specific. In fact, you can use same classes as part of any other application that needs to communicate over a network. In the process, some things will seem a bit abstract, but I promise you that all of it will start falling into place soon. For now, just hang on tight.

Introducing the Connection and Stream Objects

A connection is an object that allows us to exchange data bidirectionally with another party over a network. For example, the GKSession object that we used in Chapter 14 to enable two GKPong apps to talk to each other is a kind of connection, enabling us to exchange data bidirectionally over Bluetooth.

But we won't be using `GKSession` in this chapter. Instead, we will be dealing with a networking framework that GameKit itself is built on top of (at least partially): CFNetwork. This will give us a great opportunity to look at what goes on behind the scenes and get our hands dirty in some fairly low-level code.

If you want to get anything done on a network, you will most likely need to use sockets, which were introduced in Chapter 13. Usually, it takes quite a bit of code to use such a primitive but very powerful construct on its own. Luckily for us, Apple engineers made it possible to pair sockets with another entity that makes our life easier: *streams*. A stream is an object through which you can transmit data in one direction, guaranteeing that the bytes that you send will come out on the other end in the same order as they were entered. There are two kinds of streams:

- You can read data from *input* (also known as *read*) streams.
- You can write data into *output* (also known as *write*) streams.

In the SDK, you will find these under `NSInputStream` and `NSOutputStream`, respectively.

By itself, a stream is just a buffer that temporarily holds data before or after its transmission. In order to actually deliver data somewhere meaningful, streams need to be tied to something, like a file, a memory location, or a socket.

It turns out that the `NSStream` framework already implements so much of the functionality that we require that we don't even need to interact with sockets directly, except for when we implement the aforementioned socket server. So, don't be surprised if you don't see many references to socket objects in the following code.

Keep in mind that each stream can send bytes in only one direction. Therefore, if we want to implement bidirectional data exchange, we will need a pair of streams: one for input and one for output.

Let's create a new class called `Connection`. Here is what *Connection.h* will look like:

```
#import <Foundation/Foundation.h>

@class Connection;

@protocol ConnectionDelegate
- (void)connectionClosed:(Connection*)connection;
@end

@interface Connection : NSObject {
  NSInputStream *inputStream;
  NSMutableData *incomingDataBuffer;
  int nextMessageSize;
  BOOL outputStreamWasOpened;
  NSOutputStream *outputStream;
  NSMutableData *outgoingDataBuffer;
  id<ConnectionDelegate> delegate;
  id userInfo;
}
```

```
@property (nonatomic, retain) NSInputStream *inputStream;
@property (nonatomic, retain) NSOutputStream *outputStream;
@property (nonatomic, retain) id<ConnectionDelegate> delegate;
@property (nonatomic, retain) id userInfo;

- (id)initWithNativeSocketHandle:(CFSocketNativeHandle)nativeSocketHandle;
- (id)initWithInputStream:(NSInputStream*)istr outputStream:(NSOutputStream*)ostr;

- (BOOL)connect;
- (void)close;
@end
```

Before exploring what some of these variables do, let's go through *Connection.m*. We will look at it in five parts: Initialization, closing and cleanup, reading data, writing data, and handling stream events. In order to get the whole listing, concatenate all five parts into one file (or get the final version from the project archive).

Connection Initialization

Here's the first part of *Connection.m*, which handles initialization:

```
#import "Connection.h"
#import <CFNetwork/CFSocketStream.h>

@implementation Connection

@synthesize delegate, userInfo;
@synthesize inputStream, outputStream;

- (id)initWithNativeSocketHandle:(CFSocketNativeHandle)nativeSocketHandle {
  CFReadStreamRef readStream;
  CFWriteStreamRef writeStream;
  CFStreamCreatePairWithSocket(kCFAllocatorDefault, nativeSocketHandle,
      &readStream, &writeStream);

  self.inputStream = (NSInputStream*)readStream;
  self.outputStream = (NSOutputStream*)writeStream;
  return self;
}

- (id)initWithInputStream:(NSInputStream*)istr outputStream:(NSOutputStream*)ostr {
  self.inputStream = istr;
  self.outputStream = ostr;
  return self;
}

- (BOOL)connect {
  if ( !inputStream || !outputStream ) {
    return NO;
  }

  incomingDataBuffer = [[NSMutableData alloc] init];
  outgoingDataBuffer = [[NSMutableData alloc] init];

  CFReadStreamSetProperty((CFReadStreamRef)inputStream,
```

```
    kCFStreamPropertyShouldCloseNativeSocket, kCFBooleanTrue);
CFWriteStreamSetProperty((CFWriteStreamRef)outputStream,
    kCFStreamPropertyShouldCloseNativeSocket, kCFBooleanTrue);

inputStream.delegate = self;
[inputStream scheduleInRunLoop:[NSRunLoop currentRunLoop]
    forMode:NSDefaultRunLoopMode];
outputStream.delegate = self;
[outputStream scheduleInRunLoop:[NSRunLoop currentRunLoop]
    forMode:NSDefaultRunLoopMode];

outputStreamWasOpened = NO;
nextMessageSize = -1;

[inputStream open];
[outputStream open];
return YES;
}
```

We are anticipating that our connection will get initialized in two ways:

■ When initWithNativeSocketHandle: is called, we receive a value
    called nativeSocketHandle, which is a data type that the operating
    system uses to refer to open files and sockets. This means that the
    actual socket connection will already be established elsewhere.

■ On the other hand, some other part of the code might have already
    done the work of binding a socket to a pair of streams. In that case, it
    will call initWithInputStream:outputStream: to create a connection.

We will use both of these initialization methods later on.

The next step in opening a connection is to properly initialize the input and output
streams. That's what happens inside the connect method. Here, we have a chance to
configure the behavior of the connection to our liking. For example, whenever we decide
to close our streams, we want the underlying socket connection to also be terminated.
We also need to provide each stream with a delegate that will be notified about
significant events in the stream's life cycle. We will cover events in detail later on.

Let's move on to the next part of *Connection.m*.

Closing and Cleanup

The second part of *Connection.m*, which handles closing and cleanup, looks like this:

```
- (void)close {
  [inputStream removeFromRunLoop:[NSRunLoop currentRunLoop]
      forMode:NSDefaultRunLoopMode];
  [inputStream close];
  inputStream.delegate = nil;

  [outputStream removeFromRunLoop:[NSRunLoop currentRunLoop]
      forMode:NSDefaultRunLoopMode];
  [outputStream close];
  outputStream.delegate = nil;
```

```
}

- (void)dealloc {
  self.delegate = nil;
  self.userInfo = nil;
  inputStream.delegate = nil;
  self.inputStream = nil;
  outputStream.delegate = nil;
  self.outputStream = nil;

  [incomingDataBuffer release];
  [outgoingDataBuffer release];

  [super dealloc];
}
```

This part is fairly straightforward. Whenever we want to terminate the connection, we call the close method, which reverses what we did in connect.

Oh, and you should be fairly familiar with what dealloc does by now.

Reading Data

Next up is the third part of *Connection.m*, which is the section that reads data:

```
- (void)processIncomingData:(NSData*)data {
}

- (void)readFromStreamIntoIncomingBuffer {
  uint8_t buf[1024];
  while( [inputStream hasBytesAvailable] ) {
    NSInteger bytesRead = [inputStream read:buf maxLength:sizeof(buf)];
    if ( bytesRead > 0 ) {
      [incomingDataBuffer appendBytes:buf length:bytesRead];
    }
    else {
      if ( [inputStream streamStatus] == NSStreamStatusAtEnd ) {
        break;
      }
      else {
        [self close];
        [delegate connectionClosed:self];
        return;
      }
    }
  }

  while( YES ) {
    if ( nextMessageSize == -1 ) {
      if ( [incomingDataBuffer length] >= sizeof(int) ) {
        memcpy(&nextMessageSize, [incomingDataBuffer bytes], sizeof(int));
        NSRange r = {0, sizeof(int)};
        [incomingDataBuffer replaceBytesInRange:r withBytes:nil length:0];
      }
      else {
        break;
```

```
      }
   }

   if ( [incomingDataBuffer length] >= nextMessageSize ) {
      NSData* raw = [NSData dataWithBytes:[incomingDataBuffer bytes]
         length:nextMessageSize];
      [self processIncomingData:raw];
      NSRange r = {0, nextMessageSize};
      [incomingDataBuffer replaceBytesInRange:r withBytes:NULL length:0];
      nextMessageSize = -1;
   }
   else {
      break;
   }
   }
   }
}
```

This is probably the most complicated piece of code that you will encounter in this chapter. Before trying to understand what is going on here, let's talk about how data actually gets packaged and shipped over.

Imagine a conveyor belt that transports goods from a warehouse to a shipping facility, where they get put into boxes and sent to customers. Let's say someone purchased a book. Right after that, another order came in—this time for a digital camera and some batteries. It was followed by an order for five DVDs. Warehouse employees could just pile up all those items on the belt and send them on their merry way. But how will the person on the receiving end know what to do with all those things? Does she put them all in one box and ship it out? Does she need to separate them? One way to avoid the guessing game is to place a simple order description on the belt before sending the actual goods. It should give the shipping facility employees enough information to sort the items into boxes correctly.

Our socket stream is similar to a conveyor belt. It transports bytes from one end to the other. It is up to the sender to include some instructions that will help the receiver make sense of the never-ending stream of bytes. One way to go about it is to agree that every group of bytes that constitutes a "message" will be preceded by another group of 4 bytes (enough to hold a variable of type int) that tells the receiver the length of the incoming message. Such a structure will look something like this:

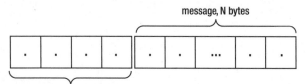

N = message length, 4 bytes

Now let's go over the method called readFromStreamIntoIncomingBuffer step by step. We start by trying to read as much data from the input stream as possible:

```
uint8_t buf[1024];
while( [inputStream hasBytesAvailable] ) {
   NSInteger bytesRead = [inputStream read:buf maxLength:sizeof(buf)];
```

If data is available, we place it in a temporary buffer. Otherwise, we try to figure out why the read operation failed, which could be because we exhausted the stream and must wait for more data to arrive. In case an error occurs, we simply close the connection and let the outside world know about it:

```
if ( bytesRead > 0 ) {
  [incomingDataBuffer appendBytes:buf length:bytesRead];
}
else {
  if ( [inputStream streamStatus] == NSStreamStatusAtEnd ) {
    break;
  }
  else {
    [self close];
    [delegate connectionClosed:self];
    return;
  }
}
}
```

At this point, all of the bytes that we took off the conveyor belt should be in our temporary buffer, and we now need to sort them into messages. First, we try to find the 4 bytes that will tell us the message's length. Note that sizeof(int) is equal to 4:

```
while( YES ) {
  if ( nextMessageSize == -1 ) {
    if ( [incomingDataBuffer length] >= sizeof(int) ) {
      memcpy(&nextMessageSize, [incomingDataBuffer bytes], sizeof(int));
      NSRange r = {0, sizeof(int)};
      [incomingDataBuffer replaceBytesInRange:r withBytes:nil length:0];
    }
    else {
      break;
    }
  }
```

We need to be careful not to process the same data over and over again. That's why we remove the first 4 bytes from the buffer by calling replaceBytesInRange:withBytes:length: immediately after copying them into nextMessageSize. Now that we know how long the next message is, we will try to extract that many bytes from the buffer using the same copy-then-remove technique. But keep in mind that we might not have all of the bytes available to us yet. If that's the case, we will keep whatever data we have so far in incomingDataBuffer (which is an instance variable, and it isn't destroyed when we exit this method). Whenever a new batch of bytes arrives, we will come back and try to finish putting together the message. However, if we do have a complete message, we will go on to process it by calling processIncomingData::

```
if ( [incomingDataBuffer length] >= nextMessageSize ) {
    NSData* raw = [NSData dataWithBytes:[incomingDataBuffer bytes]
        length:nextMessageSize];
    [self processIncomingData:raw];
    NSRange r = {0, nextMessageSize};
    [incomingDataBuffer replaceBytesInRange:r withBytes:NULL length:0];
    nextMessageSize = -1;
```

```
      }
      else {
        break;
      }
    }
  }
}
```

Note that we don't yet have the logic to process the actual messages. That's because we still are not sure what they will contain. We will come back to this a bit later in the chapter.

That does it for the reading part. What about writing?

Writing Data

The fourth part of *Connection.m* takes care of writing data:

```
- (void)writeOutgoingBufferToStream {
  if ( [outgoingDataBuffer length] == 0 || !outputStreamWasOpened ) {
    return;
  }
  if ( ! [outputStream hasSpaceAvailable] ) {
    return;
  }

  NSInteger bytesWritten = [outputStream write:[outgoingDataBuffer bytes]
      maxLength:[outgoingDataBuffer length]];

  if ( bytesWritten == -1 ) {
    if ( [outputStream streamStatus] == NSStreamStatusClosed ||
        [outputStream streamStatus] == NSStreamStatusError ) {
      [self close];
      [delegate connectionClosed:self];
    }
    return;
  }

  NSRange r = {0, bytesWritten};
  [outgoingDataBuffer replaceBytesInRange:r withBytes:nil length:0];
}
```

By the time this method is called, we should already have our messages stored in outgoingDataBuffer, packaged and ready to be shipped out. (We will add the part that actually composes messages later.) At this point, all we need to do is write as many bytes as we can into the outputStream. The stream has a finite amount of storage space available, and, depending on how many bytes we want to send out, it might not be able to accommodate all of our data at once. For example, if we want to send 100 bytes, but the output stream has space for only 75 bytes, we need to hang on to the remaining 25 bytes and wait for an event that will tell us that more data can be sent. Meanwhile, the 75 bytes that did go out need to be removed from our outgoing buffer, which is done by calling replaceBytesInRange:withBytes:length:.

That was simple enough. Now let's look at the last part.

Handling Stream Events

The final part of *Connection.m* handles stream events:

```
- (void)stream:(NSStream *)theStream handleEvent:(NSStreamEvent)streamEvent {
    if ( theStream == inputStream && streamEvent & NSStreamEventHasBytesAvailable ) {
        [self readFromStreamIntoIncomingBuffer];
    }

    if ( theStream == outputStream && streamEvent & NSStreamEventHasSpaceAvailable ) {
        [self writeOutgoingBufferToStream];
    }

    if ( theStream == outputStream && streamEvent & NSStreamEventOpenCompleted ) {
        outputStreamWasOpened = YES;
        [self writeOutgoingBufferToStream];
    }

    if ( streamEvent & (NSStreamEventErrorOccurred|NSStreamEventEndEncountered)) {
        [self close];
        [delegate connectionClosed:self];
    }
}

@end
```

Remember that during initialization, we designated self to be the delegate for both inputStream and outputStream. From that point on, whenever the operating system has anything important to tell the world about what is happening with one of those streams, we will be the first ones to know about it. Any time that happens, stream:handleEvent: will be called, giving us a chance to react. Whenever data arrives via the input stream, we will try to read it by calling readFromStreamIntoIncomingBuffer. If the output stream has room for more bytes to be written, we will take that opportunity and execute writeOutgoingBufferToStream. And if one of the streams reports an error, we will take as a sign that it's time to terminate the connection.

So, how does iPhone OS know to send these events to the delegate? That happens because we scheduled our streams to be processed by something called a *run loop*. Think of it as the main loop of the application that processes everything from user's taps on the screen, to timers, to miscellaneous UI and socket events. Using a run loop allows us to tell the operating system, "Wake me up if something important happens, I'm interested in one of the following events…," instead of needlessly waiting around for things to do. As a result, we can save some CPU cycles and battery power, which is especially important on a small device like an iPhone.

The Complete Picture

Voila! We can now read and write data over a network using sockets. The Connection class consists of a few components that work together, which means that we can benefit from having a diagram that should be worth at least a couple dozen words (see Figure 15–6).

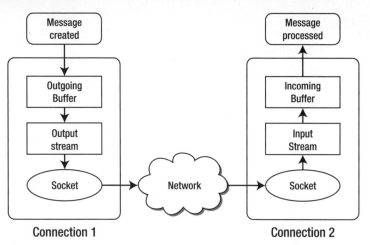

Figure 15–6. *Each message must make a number of hops before it reaches its destination.*

This all sounds great. But how do we actually establish these connections?

Socket Servers

Have you ever moored a boat? You know, where you stand aboard the vessel, throw a rope ashore, and someone ties it down? What if no one were available to catch that rope, and you couldn't really get to the shore yourself? That's right—you would be adrift, floating around without a connection to dry land. Having a rope is not enough; you need some way to fasten it.

Establishing a network connection between two applications is just like mooring a boat: One side initiates the connection (throws the rope), and the other side (the server) recognizes the request, performs all the steps necessary to establish the connection, and sends back an acknowledgment (ties down the rope).

In order to get some help with the boat, we need to know to whom to throw the rope. The same goes for socket connections: We need to uniquely identify the endpoint on the network with which we would like to establish communication. And what's more, something needs to be listening for our connection request on that other end. Fortunately, the operating system developers at Apple have already done most of the hard work for us, and all we need to know is which part of the iPhone SDK to use to make this happen. It turns out that CFNetwork framework includes everything that's required to both listen and respond to socket connection requests.

The SocketServer Class

It's time to create a new class. Let's call it SocketServer. Open *SocketServer.h* and put the following code there:

```
#import <Foundation/Foundation.h>
```

```
@class Connection;

@protocol SocketServerDelegate
- (void)socketServerStarted;
- (void)socketServerDidNotStart;
- (void)newClientConnected:(Connection*)connection;
@end

@interface SocketServer : NSObject {
  CFSocketRef listeningSocket;
  uint16_t listeningPort;
  NSNetService *netService;
  NSString *serverName;
  id<SocketServerDelegate> delegate;
  BOOL serverStarted;
}

@property (nonatomic, retain) NSNetService *netService;
@property (nonatomic, retain) NSString *serverName;
@property (nonatomic, retain) id<SocketServerDelegate> delegate;

- (BOOL)start;
- (void)stop;
@end
```

Just as we did with Connection class, we will look at the implementation file in parts, which will give us a chance to discuss each piece separately. We will cover how to create a server, how to announce its existence to the world, how to terminate the server, and how we control its life cycle (starting and stopping). Open *SocketServer.m*, and let's begin.

Socket Server Initialization

In the first part of *SocketServer.m*, we create the socket server:

```
#include <sys/socket.h>
#include <netinet/in.h>
#include <unistd.h>
#include <CFNetwork/CFSocketStream.h>
#import "SocketServer.h"
#import "Connection.h"

@implementation SocketServer

@synthesize serverName, netService;
@synthesize delegate;

static void serverAcceptCallback(CFSocketRef socket, CFSocketCallBackType type,
    CFDataRef address, const void *data, void *info) {
  SocketServer *server = (SocketServer*)info;
  if ( type != kCFSocketAcceptCallBack ) {
    return;
  }
  CFSocketNativeHandle handle = *(CFSocketNativeHandle*)data;
  Connection *connection = [[[Connection alloc]
      initWithNativeSocketHandle:handle] autorelease];
```

```
    if ( [connection connect] ) {
        [server.delegate newClientConnected:connection];
    }
}

- (BOOL)createServer {
    CFSocketContext socketCtxt = {0, self, NULL, NULL, NULL};
    listeningSocket = CFSocketCreate(kCFAllocatorDefault, PF_INET, SOCK_STREAM,
        IPPROTO_TCP, kCFSocketAcceptCallBack, (CFSocketCallBack)&serverAcceptCallback,
        &socketCtxt);
    if ( listeningSocket == NULL ) {
        return NO;
    }

    int existingValue = 1;
    setsockopt( CFSocketGetNative(listeningSocket),
        SOL_SOCKET, SO_REUSEADDR, (void *)&existingValue,
        sizeof(existingValue));

    struct sockaddr_in socketAddress;
    memset(&socketAddress, 0, sizeof(socketAddress));
    socketAddress.sin_len = sizeof(socketAddress);
    socketAddress.sin_family = AF_INET;
    socketAddress.sin_port = 0;
    socketAddress.sin_addr.s_addr = htonl(INADDR_ANY);

    NSData *socketAddressData =
        [NSData dataWithBytes:&socketAddress length:sizeof(socketAddress)];
    if ( CFSocketSetAddress(listeningSocket,
        (CFDataRef)socketAddressData) != kCFSocketSuccess ) {
        if ( listeningSocket != NULL ) {
            CFRelease(listeningSocket);
            listeningSocket = NULL;
        }
        return NO;
    }

    NSData *socketAddressActualData =
        [(NSData *)CFSocketCopyAddress(listeningSocket) autorelease];
    struct sockaddr_in socketAddressActual;
    memcpy(&socketAddressActual, [socketAddressActualData bytes],
        [socketAddressActualData length]);
    listeningPort = ntohs(socketAddressActual.sin_port);

    CFRunLoopRef currentRunLoop = CFRunLoopGetCurrent();
    CFRunLoopSourceRef runLoopSource =
        CFSocketCreateRunLoopSource(kCFAllocatorDefault, listeningSocket, 0);
    CFRunLoopAddSource(currentRunLoop, runLoopSource, kCFRunLoopCommonModes);
    CFRelease(runLoopSource);

    return YES;
}
```

That's one dense-looking piece of code, if you ask me. Fortunately, we don't need to cover most of it in great detail, but it would still be good to understand the general flow.

Take a look at the very first function, serverAcceptCallback(). Once we configure our server, the operating system will execute this piece of code whenever another application decides to initiate a connection to us. Whenever that happens, we will create a Connection object and pass it to our delegate, which is responsible for handling whatever happens after that.

Also note that serverAcceptCallback() mixes both C and Objective-C. That's because we are dealing with CFNetwork there, which is not an Objective-C framework (unlike Cocoa Touch and others, where class names start with NS), which means that we need to use C to do some of the work.

The second method, createServer, requires a bit more explanation. We will go through it step by step. First of all, we need to create a socket. There are a whole lot of configuration options here, most of which we are not interested in right now. The important bit is that this is where we designate serverAcceptCallback to be responsible for handling connection requests. The only other two things that you might want to know is that we will be using the TCP protocol (the IPPROTO_TCP flag) and that the same socket will be used multiple times to accept as many connections as possible (the SO_REUSEADDR flag):

```
CFSocketContext socketCtxt = {0, self, NULL, NULL, NULL};
listeningSocket = CFSocketCreate(kCFAllocatorDefault, PF_INET, SOCK_STREAM,
  IPPROTO_TCP, kCFSocketAcceptCallBack, (CFSocketCallBack)&serverAcceptCallback,
  &socketCtxt);
if ( listeningSocket == NULL ) {
  return NO;
}

int existingValue = 1;
setsockopt( CFSocketGetNative(listeningSocket),
  SOL_SOCKET, SO_REUSEADDR, (void *)&existingValue,
  sizeof(existingValue));
```

But it turns out that this particular socket does not yet have a network address associated with it, which is why we need to bind it to one. Here, we are asking the operating system to allow us to listen for connection requests that come from any network that our device is connected to (the INADDR_ANY flag), and we are leaving it up to the networking subsystem to find a free port for us to listen on (socketAddress.sin_port = 0):

```
struct sockaddr_in socketAddress;
memset(&socketAddress, 0, sizeof(socketAddress));
socketAddress.sin_len = sizeof(socketAddress);
socketAddress.sin_family = AF_INET;
socketAddress.sin_port = 0;
socketAddress.sin_addr.s_addr = htonl(INADDR_ANY);

NSData *socketAddressData =
  [NSData dataWithBytes:&socketAddress length:sizeof(socketAddress)];
if ( CFSocketSetAddress(listeningSocket,
    (CFDataRef)socketAddressData) != kCFSocketSuccess ) {
  if ( listeningSocket != NULL ) {
    CFRelease(listeningSocket);
    listeningSocket = NULL;
```

```
    }
    return NO;
  }
```

In order for others to establish connections to our server, we will need to tell them exactly which endpoint we are listening on, which means that we need to know which port the operating system assigned to us. That's what happens here:

```
NSData *socketAddressActualData =
    [(NSData *)CFSocketCopyAddress(listeningSocket) autorelease];
struct sockaddr_in socketAddressActual;
memcpy(&socketAddressActual, [socketAddressActualData bytes],
    [socketAddressActualData length]);
listeningPort = ntohs(socketAddressActual.sin_port);
```

And last, but not least, we need to add our listening socket to the run loop in order for the operating system to notify us about new connection requests:

```
CFRunLoopRef currentRunLoop = CFRunLoopGetCurrent();
CFRunLoopSourceRef runLoopSource =
    CFSocketCreateRunLoopSource(kCFAllocatorDefault, listeningSocket, 0);
CFRunLoopAddSource(currentRunLoop, runLoopSource, kCFRunLoopCommonModes);
CFRelease(runLoopSource);

return YES;
}
```

The work that we have done just now gives us the ability to catch the rope and tie it down to some stationary object ashore. But how will the world know to throw the rope to us? That's what the next part is about.

Publishing via Bonjour

In the second part of *SocketServer.m*, we let the world know about our server:

```
- (BOOL)publishService {
  netService = [[NSNetService alloc]
      initWithDomain:@"" type:@"_twentyfour._tcp."
      name:serverName port:listeningPort];
  if (self.netService == nil)
    return NO;
  [self.netService scheduleInRunLoop:[NSRunLoop currentRunLoop]
      forMode:NSRunLoopCommonModes];
  [self.netService setDelegate:self];
  [self.netService publish];
  return YES;
}

- (void)netServiceDidPublish:(NSNetService*)sender {
  if ( sender != self.netService ) {
    return;
  }
  if ( serverStarted ) {
    return;
  }
  serverStarted = YES;
```

```
    [delegate socketServerStarted];
}
```

One of Apple's strengths is its ability to take useful but complex technologies and make them easy to use. And we are looking at a great example of one such technology in action. `NSNetService` is an implementation of the Bonjour protocol, which was introduced in Chapter 13. The best part is that we don't need to understand exactly what happens behind the scenes in order to use it.

In `publishService`, all we need to do is pass a few configuration parameters, such as the type of our server, to distinguish it from other applications (`"_twentyfour._tcp."`), the server's name, and on which port we can be contacted. As before, the run loop will take care of notifying us of important events via delegation.

Once we `publish` the service, the operating system will try to tell the world about our app. If it succeeds, `netServiceDidPublish:` will be called. As soon as that happens, our server will be fully operational and ready to accept connections.

Starting and Stopping

The final part of *SocketServer.m* deals with controlling the server:

```
- (void)terminateServer {
  if ( listeningSocket != nil ) {
    CFSocketInvalidate(listeningSocket);
    CFRelease(listeningSocket);
    listeningSocket = nil;
    listeningPort = 0;
  }
}

- (void) unpublishService {
  if ( self.netService ) {
    [self.netService stop];
    [self.netService removeFromRunLoop:[NSRunLoop currentRunLoop]
        forMode:NSRunLoopCommonModes];
    self.netService = nil;
  }
}

- (void)netService:(NSNetService*)sender didNotPublish:(NSDictionary*)errorDict {
  if ( sender != self.netService ) {
    return;
  }
  [self terminateServer];
  [self unpublishService];
  [delegate socketServerDidNotStart];
}

- (BOOL)start {
  if ( ! [self createServer] ) {
    return NO;
  }
  if ( ! [self publishService] ) {
    [self terminateServer];
```

```
    return NO;
  }
  return YES;
}

- (void)stop {
  serverStarted = NO;
  [self terminateServer];
  [self unpublishService];
}

- (void)dealloc {
  self.netService = nil;
  self.serverName = nil;
  self.delegate = nil;

  [super dealloc];
}
@end
```

As much as we would like to keep the server running for as long as we can, sometimes we need to shut it down. Here, we are simply undoing the setup procedure. We need to be able to shut down the listening socket in terminateServer, which will prevent any further connections from being accepted. In unpublishService, we ask Bonjour to stop telling everyone about the server.

But we also need to handle the case when Bonjour wasn't able to announce anything in the first place, for whatever reason. That's when netService:didNotPublish: will get called, giving us a chance to release whatever resources the server was taking up.

The start and stop methods allow users of the SocketServer class to control it. For instance, we don't want anyone calling createServer and publishService directly, because they might do it in a wrong order. That's why we are encapsulating it in a separate start method.

Finding Servers via Bonjour

While we have our eyes on the networking part of the app, let's implement one more important component. We can now advertise our server on the network, but there is no code to look for servers and connect to them. Remember how LobbyViewController already has a table view that we can fill with a list of games? Let's write that part now. Open *LobbyViewController.h* and add the following code to it:

```
#import <UIKit/UIKit.h>

@interface LobbyViewController : UIViewController <UITableViewDataSource> {
  UITableView *gameList;
  NSMutableArray *games;
  NSNetServiceBrowser *netServiceBrowser;
  NSNetService *selectedGame;
}
@property (nonatomic, retain) IBOutlet UITableView* gameList;
@property (nonatomic, retain) NSNetServiceBrowser *netServiceBrowser;
```

```
@property (nonatomic, retain) NSNetService *selectedGame;
- (IBAction)startNewGame;
- (IBAction)joinSelectedGame;
@end
```

Here, we are introducing an array that will contain servers that we find on the network, a Bonjour-related object that will let us search for those servers, and a variable that will reference whichever server the user selects from the list. Switch to *LobbyViewController.m* and let's see these in action, in two parts.

Looking for Servers

The first part of *LobbyViewController.m* deals with looking for servers:

```
#import "LobbyViewController.h"
#import "TwentyFourAppDelegate.h"

@implementation LobbyViewController

@synthesize gameList;
@synthesize gameList, netServiceBrowser, selectedGame;

- (void)viewDidLoad {
  netServiceBrowser = [[NSNetServiceBrowser alloc] init];
  netServiceBrowser.delegate = self;
  games = [[NSMutableArray alloc] init];
}

- (void)viewDidAppear:(BOOL)animated {
  [games removeAllObjects];
  [gameList reloadData];
  [netServiceBrowser searchForServicesOfType:@"_twentyfour._tcp." inDomain:@""];
  [super viewDidAppear:animated];
}

- (void)viewDidDisappear:(BOOL)animated {
  [netServiceBrowser stop];
  [super viewDidDisappear:animated];
}

- (void)netServiceBrowser:(NSNetServiceBrowser *)netServiceBrowser
    didFindService:(NSNetService *)netService moreComing:(BOOL)moreServicesComing {
  if ( ! [games containsObject:netService] ) {
    [games addObject:netService];
  }
  if ( !moreServicesComing ) {
    [gameList reloadData];
  }
}

- (void)netServiceBrowser:(NSNetServiceBrowser *)netServiceBrowser
    didRemoveService:(NSNetService *)netService
    moreComing:(BOOL)moreServicesComing {
```

```
    [games removeObject:netService];
    if ( !moreServicesComing ) {
      [gameList reloadData];
    }
  }

- (NSInteger)tableView:(UITableView *)tableView numberOfRowsInSection:
    (NSInteger)section {
  return 0;
  return [games count];
}

- (UITableViewCell *)tableView:(UITableView *)tableView
    cellForRowAtIndexPath:(NSIndexPath *)indexPath {
  static NSString* gameListIdentifier = @"gameListIdentifier";

  UITableViewCell *cell = (UITableViewCell *)[tableView
      dequeueReusableCellWithIdentifier:gameListIdentifier];
  if (cell == nil) {
    cell = [[[UITableViewCell alloc] initWithFrame:CGRectZero
        reuseIdentifier:gameListIdentifier] autorelease];
  }
  NSNetService* server = [games objectAtIndex:indexPath.row];
  cell.textLabel.text = [server name];
  return nil;
  return cell;
}
```

NSNetServiceBrowser allows you to search, or *browse*, for services that were published by NSNetService, just as we did in *SocketServer.m*. In order to get relevant results, we need to specify the type of servers that we are seeking. In our case, the type is equal to the string value @"_twentyfour._tcp.", because that's what we specified when the server was advertised.

We would like the search to start whenever the view becomes visible, and cease when the screen is showing something else. Hence, we have the call to NSNetServiceBrowser's searchForServicesOfType:inDomain: in viewDidAppear:, and the corresponding stop in viewDidDisappear:. Avoiding unnecessary searches while the user isn't looking at this particular view allows us to save some CPU cycles and reduce the amount of data we are sending over the network, which is a fairly power-intensive operation.

Whenever the Bonjour subsystem finds something of interest, it will notify us by calling the appropriate delegate methods:

- netServiceBrowser:didFindService:moreComing: lets us know that a new service was found.

- netServiceBrowser:didRemoveService:moreComing: is executed whenever a service is removed and is no longer being advertised.

Note the moreServicesComing Boolean flag. Whenever several services are added or removed at the same time, corresponding delegate methods will be called once for each entry. However, you might want to refresh the table view only after processing all the entries, to avoid flickering and unnecessary refreshing of the list. This flag will let you know whether or not you should expect more updates in the immediate future.

We are keeping the server list in a variable called *games*, which is being used as a source of rows for the table view.

Connecting to Servers

The remainder of *LobbyViewController.m* handles connecting to a server:

```
- (IBAction)startNewGame {
  [[TwentyFourAppDelegate getInstance] startNewGame];
}

- (IBAction)joinSelectedGame {
  NSIndexPath *currentRow = [gameList indexPathForSelectedRow];
  if ( currentRow == nil ) {
    return;
  }

  [[TwentyFourAppDelegate getInstance] showWaitingScreen];

  self.selectedGame = [games objectAtIndex:currentRow.row];
  selectedGame.delegate = self;
  [selectedGame resolveWithTimeout:5.0];
}

- (void)netService:(NSNetService *)sender didNotResolve:(NSDictionary *)errorDict {
  if ( sender != selectedGame ) {
    return;
  }

  [[TwentyFourAppDelegate getInstance] hideWaitingScreen];

  [selectedGame stop];
  selectedGame.delegate = nil;
  self.selectedGame = nil;

  UIAlertView *alert = [[UIAlertView alloc] initWithTitle:@"Error"
      message:@"Selected game is not available" delegate:nil
      cancelButtonTitle:@"Ok" otherButtonTitles:nil];
  [alert show];
  [alert release];
}

- (void)netServiceDidResolveAddress:(NSNetService *)sender {
  if ( sender != selectedGame ) {
    return;
  }

  [[TwentyFourAppDelegate getInstance] hideWaitingScreen];
```

```
    NSInputStream *inputStream;
    NSOutputStream *outputStream;
    if ( ! [selectedGame getInputStream:&inputStream outputStream:&outputStream]) {
      UIAlertView *alert = [[UIAlertView alloc] initWithTitle:@"Error"
          message:@"Could not connect to selected game" delegate:nil
          cancelButtonTitle:@"Ok" otherButtonTitles:nil];
      [alert show];
      [alert release];
      [selectedGame stop];
      selectedGame.delegate = nil;
      self.selectedGame = nil;
      return;
    }

    [selectedGame stop];
    selectedGame.delegate = nil;
    self.selectedGame = nil;

    Connection *connection = [[[Connection alloc] initWithInputStream:inputStream
        outputStream:outputStream] autorelease];

    [[TwentyFourAppDelegate getInstance] connectToGame:connection];
}

- (void)dealloc {
  self.gameList = nil;
  self.netServiceBrowser = nil;
  self.selectedGame = nil;
  [games release];
  games = nil;
  [super dealloc];
}
@end
```

Now that the server list is visible, our users are free to pick which server they would like to play on by selecting one of the entries and tapping the "Join selected game" button. As soon as that happens, joinSelectedGame is called, and our code springs into action once again.

In order to connect to the selected server, we need to retrieve a few bits of information about it, such as its network address and on which port it's listening. In Bonjour lingo, this process is called *resolving the service*. But it cannot happen immediately, because it involves actually reaching out to the service in question over the network and querying it. By specifying a timeout of 5 seconds in the call to resolveWithTimeout:, we are setting a deadline for Bonjour to get back to us with or without results. In the meantime, we will put up an activity indicator on the screen to let the user know that something is happening. We do this by calling TwentyFourAppDelegate's showWaitingScreen, which displays WaitingViewController's half-transparent view on top of the LobbyViewController.

If Bonjour fails to resolve the service within the specified amount of time, it will let us know by calling netService:didNotResolve:. At that point, we can't really do much besides letting the user know that something went wrong by displaying an alert view.

We should also not forget to hide the temporary activity indicator at this point. Usually, Bonjour does a pretty good job of keeping the list of services current, but every once in a while, you might see a ghost entry that points to a server that no longer exists. If you try to resolve such service, it will fail, of course.

If the service is resolved, `netServiceDidResolveAddress:` will be called, giving us a chance to actually open a connection to that particular server. As I noted earlier, the `NSNetService` class was designed by Apple engineers to be as easy to use as possible. To this end, they already included a method that tries to initiate a socket connection based on the service's address and port information, and tie a pair of streams to it: `getInputStream:outputStream:`. We are using it here to keep the code shorter, but if you feel like doing a bit more work, you can accomplish the same thing by accessing the service's connection information via `NSNetService`'s `hostName` and `port` methods, and passing that information into `NSStream`'s `getStreamsToHost:port:inputStream:outputStream:` method.

In any case, we should end up with a pair of streams that are attached to a socket. This is the second time that we get to create an instance of the `Connection` class that we wrote a little while ago. Only this time, instead of passing a native socket handle, we are using input and output streams that were generously created for us by `NSNetService`.

Final Details

How is this connection going to be used? Frankly, we don't know yet, since we don't have the multiplayer logic fleshed out right now. All we know is that some class somewhere will need it to send and receive data. `TwentyFourAppDelegate` seems to be aware of every component of our app, which makes it a good candidate for the role of a traffic cop of sorts. It seems to be as good a place as any to send our connection, and find a good use for it later. Let's open *TwentyFourAppDelegate.h* and declare a new method, called `connectToGame::`

```
#import <UIKit/UIKit.h>
#import "Connection.h"
#import "GameController.h"

@class TwentyFourViewController;
@class WelcomeViewController;
@class LobbyViewController;
@class ResultsViewController;
@class WaitingViewController;

@interface TwentyFourAppDelegate : NSObject <UIApplicationDelegate,
    GameControllerDelegate> {
  UIWindow *window;
  NSString* playerName;
  TwentyFourViewController *tfViewController;
  WelcomeViewController *welcomeViewController;
  LobbyViewController *lobbyViewController;
  ResultsViewController *resultsViewController;
  WaitingViewController *waitingViewController;
```

```
    GameController *gameController;
}

@property (nonatomic, retain) IBOutlet UIWindow *window;
@property (nonatomic, retain) NSString *playerName;
@property (nonatomic, retain) IBOutlet TwentyFourViewController *tfViewController;
@property (nonatomic, retain) IBOutlet WelcomeViewController *welcomeViewController;
@property (nonatomic, retain) IBOutlet LobbyViewController *lobbyViewController;
@property (nonatomic, retain) IBOutlet ResultsViewController *resultsViewController;
@property (nonatomic, retain) IBOutlet WaitingViewController *waitingViewController;

+ (TwentyFourAppDelegate*)getInstance;
- (void)playerNameEntered:(NSString*)name;
- (void)startNewGame;
- (void)submitResultFailure:(NSString*)reason;
- (void)submitResultSuccess:(float)seconds;
- (void)exitGame;
- (void)showWaitingScreen;
- (void)hideWaitingScreen;
- (void)connectToGame:(Connection*)connection;

@end
```

For the time being, let's leave the body of the method, located in *TwentyFourAppDelegate.m*, empty:

```
#import "TwentyFourAppDelegate.h"
#import "TwentyFourViewController.h"
#import "WelcomeViewController.h"
#import "LobbyViewController.h"
#import "ResultsViewController.h"
#import "WaitingViewController.h"

@implementation TwentyFourAppDelegate

@synthesize window;
@synthesize playerName;
@synthesize tfViewController, welcomeViewController, lobbyViewController;
@synthesize resultsViewController, waitingViewController;

- (void)submitResultFailure:(NSString*)reason {
  [gameController submitResultFailure:reason];
}

- (void)submitResultSuccess:(float)seconds {
  [gameController submitResultSuccess:seconds];
}

- (void)startRoundWithChallenge:(NSArray*)challenge secondsToPlay:(float)seconds {
  [tfViewController startRoundWithChallenge:challenge secondsToPlay:seconds];
  [window addSubview:tfViewController.view];
  [resultsViewController.view removeFromSuperview];
}

- (void)updateGameStatus:(NSString*)status {
  resultsViewController.labelStatus.text = status;
}
```

```objc
- (void)updateGameResults:(NSArray*)results {
    resultsViewController.results = results;
    [resultsViewController.tableResults reloadData];
}

- (void)playerNameEntered:(NSString*)name {
    self.playerName = name;
    [window addSubview:lobbyViewController.view];
    [welcomeViewController.view removeFromSuperview];
}

- (void)showWaitingScreen {
    [window addSubview:waitingViewController.view];
    [window bringSubviewToFront:waitingViewController.view];
}

- (void)hideWaitingScreen {
    [waitingViewController.view removeFromSuperview];
}

- (void)startNewGame {
    [self showWaitingScreen];
    GameController *game = [[GameController alloc] init];
    game.delegate = self;
    [game startWithPlayerName:playerName];
    gameController = game;
}

- (void)connectToGame:(Connection*)connection {
}

- (void)gameControllerStarted {
    [self hideWaitingScreen];
    [lobbyViewController.view removeFromSuperview];
}

- (void)gameControllerDidNotStart {
    [self hideWaitingScreen];

    [gameController release];
    gameController = nil;

    UIAlertView *alert = [[UIAlertView alloc] initWithTitle:@"Error"
        message:@"Could not start/join game." delegate:nil cancelButtonTitle:@"Ok"
        otherButtonTitles:nil];
    [alert show];
    [alert release];
}

- (void)exitGame {
    [gameController stop];
    gameController.delegate = nil;
    [gameController release];
    gameController = nil;
    [window addSubview:lobbyViewController.view];
    [tfViewController.view removeFromSuperview];
}
```

```
- (void)showGameResultsScreen {
  [window addSubview:resultsViewController.view];
  [tfViewController.view removeFromSuperview];
}

- (void)gameControllerTerminated {
  UIAlertView *alert = [[UIAlertView alloc] initWithTitle:@"Error"
      message:@"Game has been terminated." delegate:nil cancelButtonTitle:@"Ok"
      otherButtonTitles:nil];
  [alert show];
  [alert release];

  [gameController release];
  gameController = nil;
  [window addSubview:lobbyViewController.view];
  [tfViewController stopRound];
  [tfViewController.view removeFromSuperview];
}

- (void)applicationDidFinishLaunching:(UIApplication *)application {
  sranddev();
  [window addSubview:welcomeViewController.view];
  [window makeKeyAndVisible];
}

+ (TwentyFourAppDelegate*)getInstance {
  return (TwentyFourAppDelegate*)[UIApplication sharedApplication].delegate;
}

- (void)dealloc {
  [tfViewController release];
  [welcomeViewController release];
  [lobbyViewController release];
  [resultsViewController release];
  [waitingViewController release];
  [gameController release];
  self.playerName = nil;
  [window release];
  [super dealloc];
}
@end
```

Congratulations! At this point, you have learned quite a bit: how to use sockets and streams; listen for network connection requests; and advertise, discover, and connect to servers. Given these tools, you can create a variety of interesting applications. Now is a good time to take a break, as we still have quite a bit of work ahead of us.

Implementing the Game Client

We have spent a lot of time working on the networking infrastructure, and we are now in the position to start taking full advantage of it. As I mentioned earlier, we have two major components that need to be communicating with each other: a game server and a game client. We can pick either one to be implemented first. We are going to start with the client, since it is the simpler of the two. In a sense, we are saving best for last!

Let's review the responsibilities we decided to assign to the client part:

- Find out what game rooms are available and allow a player to select and join a room.

- Upon receiving a challenge from the server, present it to the player.

- Allow a player to enter answers to challenges and submit them to the server.

- Upon receiving results of the round from the server, present them to the player.

- Whenever a player decides to leave the game, notify the server about it.

For the client, it turns out that we have already implemented the logic to discover and connect to game rooms (we have been calling them *game servers*) inside `LobbyViewController`, which addresses the first point. As for the remaining client functionality, we need to look at the structure of the existing application in order to find the right places to hook into.

Tracing the Logic

Let's look at which classes are currently responsible for starting a new game round, collecting the player's answer, and coming up with final results. Keep in mind that right now the game doesn't do any significant tallying of results, since we have only one player, who always wins. Single-player flow is shown in Figure 15–7. In order to better understand what's going on, try cross-checking it with the corresponding source files in Xcode.

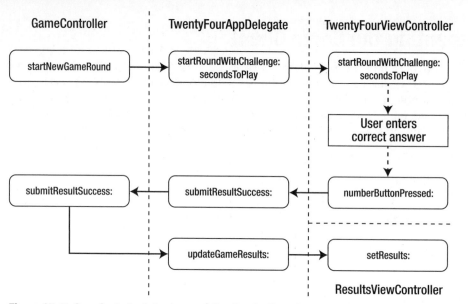

Figure 15–7. *GameController is in charge of directing the flow of the game. TwentyFourAppDelegate is simply passing messages around. TwentyFourViewController is responsible for the UI.*

For the multiplayer version, we need to move most of the decision-making over to the server, which includes coming up with challenges and aggregating results, leaving the client to be the go-between for the game UI and the server. What's the best way to accomplish that? After all is said and done, we probably want the flow to look something like the diagram shown in Figure 15–8.

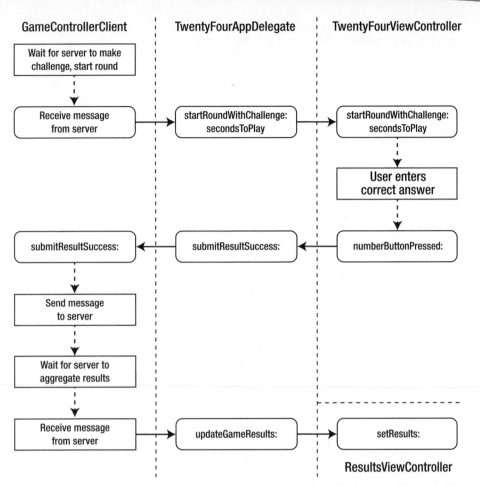

Figure 15–8. *GameControllerClient is responsible for communicating with the server. The rest of the app doesn't need to know about it, as the interfaces stay the same.*

Notice how the middle and the right columns don't change. That's because the current version of the game has been deliberately constructed to contain all of the important logic in one spot and allow for the changes that we are looking to make to be contained to the smallest number of source files possible. We don't need to touch any of the view controllers, and TwentyFourAppDelegate will require only minor modifications. We will need to replace our current GameController class with another one that has an ability to communicate with the server by using a Connection object. Instead of rewriting GameController, we'll use it as a base, and override some of the methods. By the time we are finished with the client, you'll see why such an approach makes sense.

Choosing the Network Message Format

Figure 15–8 contains a few boxes that say "Send message to server" and "Receive message from server." But if you look at the Connection class, you will see that we still don't have any methods there that allow us to send and receive messages. Remember that we decided to leave that part for later. Well, now is the time to make the decision about what our messages will look like.

We were faced with the same problem when implementing GKPong in the previous chapter. There, we decided to pack data into byte arrays in a particular way for each message type. The final messages came out short, and the message-building code was fairly efficient, which is important for a real-time game that requires frequent communications. The downside is that the format turned out to be fairly rigid, requiring us to add a block of somewhat arcane code for each new type of message that we wanted to send. In other words, we traded flexibility for efficiency.

With TwentyFour, we are going to try something different. We can afford to sacrifice some performance in exchange for a more flexible message format. This will allow us to expand and tweak the game without needing to spend too much time making up new message types.

In general, network message construction involves two steps:

■ Create an object or a structure in memory that represents the message, and fill it with values.

■ Turn that object into an array of bytes.

For GKPong, we did both of those ourselves, by hand, so to speak. This time around, we will try to use existing tools to do some coding. In particular, the second step can be implemented using a class called NSKeyedArchiver, which automatically encodes objects into byte arrays. Whenever you need to turn the resulting block of data back into an object, you use NSKeyedUnarchiver. Both of these are part of the Foundation framework.

To accomplish the first step, we need to find a fitting data structure. Arrays aren't very convenient, since you need to remember which index corresponds to which value. It would be great if we could access values by name, which would make the code easier to understand. What does that remind you of? NSDictionary, of course! We can store and look up values using string literals and not worry about in which order to store values.

Let's implement it. Whenever a message is received, we will pass it on to the delegate via connection:receivedMessage:. In order to send a message, we need to call the new sendMessage: method. Open *Connection.h* and add the method definitions:

```
#import <Foundation/Foundation.h>

@class Connection;

@protocol ConnectionDelegate
```

```
- (void)connectionClosed:(Connection*)connection;
- (void)connection:(Connection*)connection receivedMessage:(NSDictionary*)message;
@end

@interface Connection : NSObject {
  NSInputStream *inputStream;
  NSMutableData *incomingDataBuffer;
  int nextMessageSize;
  BOOL outputStreamWasOpened;
  NSOutputStream *outputStream;
  NSMutableData *outgoingDataBuffer;
  id<ConnectionDelegate> delegate;
  id userInfo;
}

@property (nonatomic, retain) NSInputStream *inputStream;
@property (nonatomic, retain) NSOutputStream *outputStream;
@property (nonatomic, retain) id<ConnectionDelegate> delegate;
@property (nonatomic, retain) id userInfo;

- (id)initWithNativeSocketHandle:(CFSocketNativeHandle)nativeSocketHandle;
- (id)initWithInputStream:(NSInputStream*)istr outputStream:(NSOutputStream*)ostr;

- (BOOL)connect;
- (void)close;
- (void)sendMessage:(NSDictionary*)message;
@end
```

Back when we wrote *Connection.m*, we left one of the methods empty, in anticipation of implementing it later. Switch to *Connection.m* and add the following code to processIncomingData::

```
- (void)processIncomingData:(NSData*)data {
  NSDictionary* message = [NSKeyedUnarchiver unarchiveObjectWithData:data];
  [delegate connection:self receivedMessage:message];
}
```

Then add the new sendMessage: method immediately after writeOutgoingBufferToStream:

```
- (void)writeOutgoingBufferToStream {
  if ( [outgoingDataBuffer length] == 0 || !outputStreamWasOpened ) {
    return;
  }
  if ( ! [outputStream hasSpaceAvailable] ) {
    return;
  }

  NSInteger bytesWritten = [outputStream write:[outgoingDataBuffer bytes]
      maxLength:[outgoingDataBuffer length]];

  if ( bytesWritten == -1 ) {
    if ( [outputStream streamStatus] == NSStreamStatusClosed ||
        [outputStream streamStatus] == NSStreamStatusError ) {
      [self close];
      [delegate connectionClosed:self];
    }
```

```
      return;
    }

    NSRange r = {0, bytesWritten};
    [outgoingDataBuffer replaceBytesInRange:r withBytes:nil length:0];
}

- (void)sendMessage:(NSDictionary*)message {
    NSData* rawMessage = [NSKeyedArchiver archivedDataWithRootObject:message];
    int messageLength = [rawMessage length];
    [outgoingDataBuffer appendBytes:&messageLength length:sizeof(int)];
    [outgoingDataBuffer appendData:rawMessage];
    [self writeOutgoingBufferToStream];
}
```

Now that we have given the Connection class a language to speak, it's time to make our app talk.

Making It Talk

Create a new class called GameControllerClient. Your *GameControllerClient.h* file should look like this:

```
#import <Foundation/Foundation.h>
#import "GameController.h"
#import "Connection.h"

@interface GameControllerClient : GameController <ConnectionDelegate> {
    Connection *gameServerConnection;
    BOOL isFullyConnected;
}
@property (nonatomic, retain) Connection *gameServerConnection;
- (void)startWithConnection:(Connection*)connection playerName:(NSString*)name;
@end
```

Now, switch over to *GameControllerClient.m* and fill in the implementation:

```
#import "GameControllerClient.h"

@implementation GameControllerClient

@synthesize gameServerConnection;

- (void)startWithConnection:(Connection*)connection playerName:(NSString*)name {
    self.playerName = name;
    self.gameServerConnection = connection;
    gameServerConnection.delegate = self;
    if ( ! [gameServerConnection connect] ) {
        self.gameServerConnection = nil;
        [delegate gameControllerDidNotStart];
        return;
    }
    isFullyConnected = NO;
    [gameServerConnection sendMessage:
        [NSDictionary dictionaryWithObjectsAndKeys:playerName, @"handshake", nil]];
}
```

```objc
- (void)submitResultSuccess:(float)seconds {
  [gameServerConnection sendMessage:
      [NSDictionary dictionaryWithObjectsAndKeys:[NSNumber numberWithFloat:seconds],
      @"resultSuccess", nil]];
}

- (void)submitResultFailure:(NSString*)reason {
  [gameServerConnection sendMessage:
      [NSDictionary dictionaryWithObjectsAndKeys:reason, @"resultFailure", nil]];
}

- (void)connection:(Connection*)connection receivedMessage:(NSDictionary*)message {
  if ( [message objectForKey:@"results"] ) {
    [delegate updateGameResults:[message objectForKey:@"results"]];
    if ( !isFullyConnected ) {
      [delegate gameControllerStarted];
      [delegate showGameResultsScreen];
      isFullyConnected = YES;
    }
  }

  if ( [message objectForKey:@"startRound"] ) {
    if ( !isFullyConnected ) {
      [delegate gameControllerStarted];
      isFullyConnected = YES;
    }
    [delegate startRoundWithChallenge:[message objectForKey:@"startRound"]
        secondsToPlay:[[message objectForKey:@"time"] floatValue]];
  }

  if ( [message objectForKey:@"status"] ) {
    [delegate updateGameStatus:[message objectForKey:@"status"]];
  }
}

- (void)stop {
  if ( !isFullyConnected ) {
    [delegate gameControllerDidNotStart];
  }
  [gameServerConnection close];
  gameServerConnection.delegate = nil;
  isFullyConnected = NO;
}

- (void)connectionClosed:(Connection*)connection {
  if ( connection != gameServerConnection ) {
    return;
  }
  if ( !isFullyConnected ) {
    [delegate gameControllerDidNotStart];
  }
  else {
    [delegate gameControllerTerminated];
  }
  gameServerConnection.delegate = nil;
  isFullyConnected = NO;
```

```
}

- (void)dealloc {
    self.gameServerConnection = nil;
    [super dealloc];
}
@end
```

Let's break it down. In startWithConnection:playerName:, we begin by initializing a controller with a Connection object and the name of our player. In order for the server to correctly maintain a list of participants, each client will need to introduce itself whenever it connects. So, we agree to include the "handshake" key in the very first message that is sent, with its value set as our player's name. The server won't need any more information from us at this point, so having only one entry in the dictionary is sufficient. We expect to receive a reply to this message at some point in the future, which will tell us that the connection has been fully established. In the meantime, we will keep isFullyConnected set to NO.

The two methods submitResultSuccess: and submitResultFailure: were originally introduced in GameController, and we are overriding them here. In the original version, each answer was turned into a list of results that contained one element, which was then fed back to the ResultsViewController (as was shown in Figure 15–7). Now we simply send the answer to the server and have it take care of aggregating the results (shown in the top part of Figure 15–8).

Whenever we receive a message from the server, connection:receivedMessage: is called. Here, we take the message apart and try to interpret its contents:

```
if ( [message objectForKey:@"results"] ) {
  [delegate updateGameResults:[message objectForKey:@"results"]];
  if ( !isFullyConnected ) {
    [delegate gameControllerStarted];
    [delegate showGameResultsScreen];
    isFullyConnected = YES;
  }
}
```

Whenever the incoming message includes the key "results", we take it as a cue to update ResultsViewController (shown in the bottom part of Figure 15–8). If this is a reply to our handshake, we consider ourselves to be fully connected. At this point, we want to let our delegate know that we are in business by calling gameControllerStarted, because it might have put up an activity indicator on the screen while waiting for the connection to be established, and we don't want it to be hanging there forever. Another key that we check for is called "startRound".

```
if ( [message objectForKey:@"startRound"] ) {
  if ( !isFullyConnected ) {
    [delegate gameControllerStarted];
    isFullyConnected = YES;
  }
  [delegate startRoundWithChallenge:[message objectForKey:@"startRound"]
      secondsToPlay:[[message objectForKey:@"time"] floatValue]];
}
```

Whenever we receive such message, we know that it's time to kick off the next game round. We expect the message to contain two values of interest: an array of numbers that represents the challenge and a number of seconds that the player has to come up with an answer before the round is over. Here, we see the real power of NSKeyedArchiver, which is able to encode a whole tree of objects, which point to other objects, which point to other objects, and so on. After being turned from a byte array into a dictionary, the "startRound" message will look something like this:

NSDictionary	
startRound	NSArray
time	100.0

NSArray
8
9
2
5

The line of text on the bottom of the results view is used to keep players informed about how the game is progressing, and to warn them whenever a new round start is imminent. The server can control what that text shows by sending a "status" key:

```
if ( [message objectForKey:@"status"] ) {
  [delegate updateGameStatus:[message objectForKey:@"status"]];
}
```

That's it for the connection:receivedMessage method. The rest of the methods deal with closing connections and deallocating memory.

Hooking It Up

Finally, we need to actually plug our new class into the app. Remember that LobbyViewController is responsible for displaying which servers are available and allowing the user to pick one. As soon as that happens, TwentyFourAppDelegate's connectToGame: is called. At that point, GameControllerClient should be instantiated and given control over the connection to the server. Let's do that now. Open *TwentyFourAppDelegate.m* and add the following code:

```
- (void)startNewGame {
  [self showWaitingScreen];

  GameController *game = [[GameController alloc] init];
  game.delegate = self;
  [game startWithPlayerName:playerName];

  gameController = game;
}

- (void)connectToGame:(Connection*)connection {
  [self showWaitingScreen];
```

```
GameControllerClient *game = [[GameControllerClient alloc] init];
game.delegate = self;
[game startWithConnection:connection playerName:playerName];

    gameController = game;
}
```

If you try to build the project now, you will get a compilation error at this point. Make sure to import *GameControllerClient.h* at the top of *TwentyFourAppDelegate.m*.

Notice how remarkably similar `startNewGame` and `connectToGame:` are. Depending on what the user wants to do, we instantiate the appropriate type of game controller, and the rest of the code stays exactly the same. This is an excellent example of using inheritance to change the behavior of an existing class. If the app is constructed correctly, the UI code doesn't really need to know whether the game is being played in a stand-alone mode or a server is involved. Such an approach increases reusability of the code, which is A Good Thing!

Implementing the Game Server

The server is the brain behind our little multiplayer game. It's the glue that makes the whole thing work together. Let's review the list of everything that we want the server to do:

- Create a game room and allow clients to join it.
- Whenever a new player joins, update the player list accordingly and notify all other clients about it.
- Whenever a player leaves, update the player list accordingly and notify all other clients about it.
- Come up with challenges.
- Tell clients what the challenge is.
- Collect answers from clients.
- Make sure that game rounds don't go over the allotted time.
- Tabulate the results.
- Announce the results to the clients.

Some of the functionality already exists, and it will simply get moved around. But there are several pieces of code that we need to write from scratch. Let's begin with the ability to manage player lists.

Managing Players

Up until now, we have dealt with one player, and life has been simple. Each round ended with a list of results that contained only one entry. Unfortunately, those days are over. We now need to store more information, which requires some more coding.

As usual, you should understand what is it that we are trying to achieve before writing more code. For example, what does it mean for the server to "tabulate results"? Ideally, whenever a user is presented with results of a particular round, the list of players should be sorted so that the player who answered in the shortest amount of time appears at the top. If some player gave up, it should be clearly indicated, and that player's name should appear after the names of those players who came up with an answer. The same is true for players who failed to solve the challenge because time ran out. In other words, we want our ResultsViewController's view to look like the one in Figure 15–4.

This means that we will probably need an array that contains objects that describe players, and a way to sort that array according to the rules we've established. We know that each player has a name, and we know the amount of time it took the player to submit the answer. In case players don't come up with an answer, we also need a variable that will explain the reason for failure (they either gave up or ran out of time).

This is enough to start writing some code. Let's introduce a new class called Player. In *Player.h*, we want to have the following declarations:

```
#import <Foundation/Foundation.h>

@interface Player : NSObject {
  NSString *name;
  NSString *status;
  float lastResult;
  BOOL isPlaying;
}

@property (nonatomic, retain) NSString *name;
@property (nonatomic, retain) NSString *status;
@property (nonatomic, assign) float lastResult;
@property (nonatomic, assign) BOOL isPlaying;

- (void)startPlayingWithStatus:(NSString*)status;
- (void)setDidntAnswerLastRound;
- (BOOL)didAnswerLastRound;
- (NSComparisonResult)compare:(Player*)anotherPlayer;
- (NSString*)describeResult;
@end
```

We are budgeting in a couple of convenience methods here that will come in handy a bit later. Now, switch over to *Player.m* and add the following:

```
#import "Player.h"

@implementation Player

@synthesize name, status, lastResult, isPlaying;

- (void)startPlayingWithStatus:(NSString*)s {
```

```
    self.status = s;
    lastResult = MAXFLOAT;
    isPlaying = YES;
}

- (void)setDidntAnswerLastRound {
    lastResult = MAXFLOAT;
}

- (BOOL)didAnswerLastRound {
    return (lastResult != MAXFLOAT);
}

- (NSComparisonResult)compare:(Player*)anotherPlayer {
    if ( ![self didAnswerLastRound] && [anotherPlayer didAnswerLastRound] ) {
      return NSOrderedDescending;
    }
    else if ( [self didAnswerLastRound] && ![anotherPlayer didAnswerLastRound] ) {
      return NSOrderedAscending;
    }
    else if ( ![self didAnswerLastRound] && ![anotherPlayer didAnswerLastRound] ) {
      return [name localizedCaseInsensitiveCompare:anotherPlayer.name];
    }
    else {
      if ( lastResult > anotherPlayer.lastResult ) {
        return NSOrderedDescending;
      }
      else if ( lastResult < anotherPlayer.lastResult ) {
        return NSOrderedAscending;
      }
      else {
        return NSOrderedSame;
      }
    }
}

- (NSString*)describeResult {
    if ( lastResult != MAXFLOAT ) {
      return [NSString stringWithFormat:@"%@: %.2f seconds", name, lastResult];
    }
    else {
      return [NSString stringWithFormat:@"%@: %@", name, status];
    }
}

- (void)dealloc {
    self.name = nil;
    self.status = nil;
    [super dealloc];
}

@end
```

Let's take a closer look at the method called compare:. Such methods are sometimes called *comparators*. You usually don't execute comparators directly, but instead supply them as arguments to sorting methods, which use them to figure out relative positions of two objects of the same type in an array. The sorting algorithm will proceed to call this method on each pair of elements that it needs to compare, and it will adjust the order of the list based on the return value. In our case, we will use this method to sort lists of players based on whether or not they submitted their answers and how fast they did so:

```
if ( ![self didAnswerLastRound] && [anotherPlayer didAnswerLastRound] ) {
  return NSOrderedDescending;
}
else if ( [self didAnswerLastRound] && ![anotherPlayer didAnswerLastRound] ) {
  return NSOrderedAscending;
}
else if ( ![self didAnswerLastRound] && ![anotherPlayer didAnswerLastRound] ) {
  return [name localizedCaseInsensitiveCompare:anotherPlayer.name];
}
```

Here, we want players who did submit correct responses to be placed above those that didn't (returning NSOrderedDescending will make anotherPlayer be placed before self in the list). The ones who failed to answer should be sorted by their names in an alphabetic order. Likewise, players who answered in a shorter amount of time should be placed above those who took longer:

```
else {
  if ( lastResult > anotherPlayer.lastResult ) {
    return NSOrderedDescending;
  }
  else if ( lastResult < anotherPlayer.lastResult ) {
    return NSOrderedAscending;
  }
  else {
    return NSOrderedSame;
  }
}
```

The next method, describeResult:, is responsible for coming up with a textual description of the player's round results—that's where the contents of the table view cells in Figure 15–4 come from.

Laying It Out

Now that we finally have all building blocks in place, let's implement the server. I will list the complete source code for the new class, and then we will go over it step by step to cover everything that needs explaining.

Create a new class called GameControllerServer. Open *GameControllerServer.h* and add the following:

```
#import <Foundation/Foundation.h>
#import "GameController.h"
#import "SocketServer.h"
#import "Player.h"
#import "Connection.h"

@interface GameControllerServer : GameController <SocketServerDelegate,
    ConnectionDelegate> {
  SocketServer *server;
```

```
    NSMutableSet *connections;
    NSMutableSet *connectedPlayers;
    Player *myPlayer;

    NSTimeInterval roundLength;
    NSDate *timeRoundStarted;
    NSMutableArray *challenge;
    BOOL isPlaying;
}

@property (nonatomic, retain) NSMutableArray *challenge;
@property (nonatomic, retain) NSDate *timeRoundStarted;
@property (nonatomic, retain) Player *myPlayer;
@end
```

And here is the source for *GameControllerServer.m*:

```
#import "GameControllerServer.h"

@interface GameControllerServer ()
- (void)handleNewPlayer:(NSString*)name connection:(Connection*)connection;
- (void)startNewGameRound;
- (void)checkIfRoundShouldStop;
- (void)handleResultSuccess:(Connection*)connection seconds:(NSNumber*)seconds;
- (void)handleResultFailure:(Connection*)connection reason:(NSString*)reason;
- (void)tabulateResults;
- (void)broadcastMessage:(NSDictionary*)message;
@end

@implementation GameControllerServer

@synthesize challenge, timeRoundStarted, myPlayer;

- (void)startWithPlayerName:(NSString*)name {

    server = [[SocketServer alloc] init];
    server.serverName = [NSString stringWithFormat:@"%@'s game", name];
    server.delegate = self;
    connections = [[NSMutableSet alloc] init];
    connectedPlayers = [[NSMutableSet alloc] init];

    if ( ! [server start] ) {
        [self socketServerDidNotStart];
        return;
    }

    Player *player = [[Player alloc] init];
    player.name = name;
    self.myPlayer = player;
    [connectedPlayers addObject:player];
    [player release];
}

- (void)socketServerStarted {
    [delegate gameControllerStarted];
    [self startNewGameRound];
}
```

```objc
- (void)socketServerDidNotStart {
  [delegate gameControllerDidNotStart];
  server.delegate = nil;
  [server release];
  server = nil;
}

- (void)newClientConnected:(Connection*)connection {
  connection.userInfo = nil;
  connection.delegate = self;
  [connections addObject:connection];
}

- (void)connection:(Connection*)connection receivedMessage:(NSDictionary*)message {
  if ( [message objectForKey:@"handshake"] && connection.userInfo == nil ) {
    [self handleNewPlayer:[message objectForKey:@"handshake"]
        connection:connection];
    return;
  }
  if ( [message objectForKey:@"resultSuccess"] ) {
    [self handleResultSuccess:connection
        seconds:[message objectForKey:@"resultSuccess"]];
    return;
  }
  if ( [message objectForKey:@"resultFailure"] ) {
    [self handleResultFailure:connection
        reason:[message objectForKey:@"resultFailure"]];
    return;
  }
}

- (void)handleNewPlayer:(NSString*)name connection:(Connection*)connection {
  Player *player = [[Player alloc] init];
  player.name = name;
  [player setDidntAnswerLastRound];

  float timeLeft = roundLength + [timeRoundStarted timeIntervalSinceNow];
  if ( isPlaying && timeLeft > 20.0 ) {
    [player startPlayingWithStatus:@"New player, guessing..."];
    [connection sendMessage:[NSDictionary dictionaryWithObjectsAndKeys:
        challenge, @"startRound",
        [NSNumber numberWithFloat:timeLeft], @"time", nil]];
  }
  else {
    player.status = @"Just joined, itching to play!";
    player.isPlaying = NO;
  }

  connection.userInfo = player;
  [connectedPlayers addObject:player];
  [self tabulateResults];

  if ( isPlaying ) {
    [connection sendMessage:[NSDictionary dictionaryWithObjectsAndKeys:
        @"Waiting for answers...", @"status", nil]];
  }
  else {
```

```
      [connection sendMessage:[NSDictionary dictionaryWithObjectsAndKeys:
          @"Next round will start shortly...", @"status", nil]];
    }
}

- (void)connectionClosed:(Connection*)connection {
  id player = connection.userInfo;
  connection.userInfo = nil;
  connection.delegate = nil;
  [connections removeObject:connection];

  if ( player ) {
    [connectedPlayers removeObject:player];
    [player release];
    [self tabulateResults];
    [self checkIfRoundShouldStop];
  }
}

- (void)startNewGameRound {
  isPlaying = YES;
  roundLength = 100.0;
  self.timeRoundStarted = [NSDate date];
  self.challenge = [self makeNewChallenge];

  [connectedPlayers makeObjectsPerformSelector:
      @selector(startPlayingWithStatus:) withObject:@"Still guessing..."];

  [self broadcastMessage:[NSDictionary dictionaryWithObjectsAndKeys:
      challenge, @"startRound",
      [NSNumber numberWithFloat:roundLength], @"time",
      @"Waiting for answers...", @"status", nil]];
  [delegate startRoundWithChallenge:challenge secondsToPlay:roundLength];
  [delegate updateGameStatus:@"Waiting for answers..."];

  [self tabulateResults];

  if ( nextRoundTimer ) {
    [nextRoundTimer invalidate];
  }
  self.nextRoundTimer = [NSTimer scheduledTimerWithTimeInterval:roundLength+2.0
      target:self selector:@selector(stopGameRound) userInfo:nil repeats:NO];
}

- (void)checkIfRoundShouldStop {
  if ( !isPlaying ) {
    return;
  }
  NSEnumerator *enumerator = [connectedPlayers objectEnumerator];
  Player *player;
  while ((player = (Player*)[enumerator nextObject])) {
    if ( player.isPlaying ) {
      return;
    }
  }
  isPlaying = NO;
  [nextRoundTimer setFireDate:[NSDate date]];
```

```objc
}

- (void)stopGameRound {
  [self broadcastMessage:[NSDictionary dictionaryWithObjectsAndKeys:
      @"Next round will start shortly...", @"status", nil]];
  [delegate updateGameStatus:@"Next round will start shortly..."];
  if ( nextRoundTimer ) {
    [nextRoundTimer invalidate];
  }
  self.nextRoundTimer = [NSTimer scheduledTimerWithTimeInterval:10.0
      target:self selector:@selector(startNewGameRound) userInfo:nil repeats:NO];
}

- (void)stop {
  if ( nextRoundTimer ) {
    [nextRoundTimer invalidate];
  }
  server.delegate = nil;
  [server stop];
  [connections makeObjectsPerformSelector:@selector(close)];
  [connections release];
  connections = nil;
}

- (void)handleResultSuccess:(Connection*)connection seconds:(NSNumber*)seconds {
  Player *player = connection.userInfo;
  if ( player ) {
    player.lastResult = [seconds floatValue];
    player.isPlaying = NO;
    [self tabulateResults];
    [self checkIfRoundShouldStop];
  }
}

- (void)handleResultFailure:(Connection*)connection reason:(NSString*)reason {
  Player *player = connection.userInfo;
  if ( player ) {
    [player setDidntAnswerLastRound];
    player.status = reason;
    player.isPlaying = NO;
    [self tabulateResults];
    [self checkIfRoundShouldStop];
  }
}

- (void)submitResultSuccess:(float)seconds {
  myPlayer.lastResult = seconds;
  myPlayer.isPlaying = NO;
  [self tabulateResults];
  [self checkIfRoundShouldStop];
}

- (void)submitResultFailure:(NSString*)reason {
  [myPlayer setDidntAnswerLastRound];
  myPlayer.status = reason;
  myPlayer.isPlaying = NO;
  [self tabulateResults];
```

```
    [self checkIfRoundShouldStop];
}

- (void)tabulateResults {
    NSArray *results = [[connectedPlayers allObjects]
        sortedArrayUsingSelector:@selector(compare:)];
    NSMutableArray *textResults = [NSMutableArray arrayWithCapacity:[results count]];
    for( int ndx = 0; ndx < [results count]; ndx++ ) {
        Player *p = [results objectAtIndex:ndx];
        [textResults addObject:[p describeResult]];
    }

    [self broadcastMessage:[NSDictionary dictionaryWithObjectsAndKeys:
        textResults, @"results", nil]];
    [delegate updateGameResults:textResults];
}

- (void)broadcastMessage:(NSDictionary*)message {
    [connections makeObjectsPerformSelector:
        @selector(sendMessage:) withObject:message];
}

- (void)dealloc {
    server.delegate = nil;
    [server release];
    [connections release];
    [connectedPlayers release];
    self.myPlayer = nil;
    self.timeRoundStarted = nil;
    self.challenge = nil;
    [super dealloc];
}

@end
```

Initialization

The `startWithPlayerName:` method does all of the setup. We allocate two mutable sets that will hold live connections to the server, and `Player` objects that describe all of the players who are playing. The direct user of our app is also considered to be one of the players.

> **NOTE:** What is an `NSMutableSet` and why are we using it instead of, say, an array? The official definition of a set is "an unordered collection of distinct elements." You can also think of it as a bag of items. Arrays contain elements in order, and the order is not important to us at the moment. Plus, sets do provide a performance benefit sometimes, which isn't too big of a deal in this particular app, but is pretty cool nevertheless. If you ask a set to check whether or not a particular element is a member, it takes less CPU time to do so than with an array. If you wanted to remove an element from an array, you would need to know its index to get the best performance. We don't want to be dealing with indexes, which means that the array would need to scan all of the elements to locate the one we are removing; a set can perform such removal faster.

In order to allow others to connect to us, we create a socket server. If it starts up successfully, we can begin playing the game. Otherwise, we let the delegate know that something went wrong.

Players Joining and Leaving

Whenever a client connects to our socket server, the `newClientConnected:` delegate method will be called. At that point, we store the connection in the set, therefore retaining it and preventing it from being deallocated.

But we don't consider the connection to be fully established until we receive a handshake, which we check for in the `connection:receivedMessage:` delegate method, which is called whenever a message comes from one of the connected clients. The other two keys that we recognize tell us about whether or not that particular player found a correct answer to a challenge. Instead of processing it on the spot, we call helper methods, which we will cover a bit later.

Whenever a handshake does come in, it gets processed by the `handleNewPlayer:connection:` helper method. Before we can do anything, a `Player` object needs to be created:

```
- (void)handleNewPlayer:(NSString*)name connection:(Connection*)connection {
  Player *player = [[Player alloc] init];
  player.name = name;
  [player setDidntAnswerLastRound];
```

After that, we face a dilemma: If a player joins the game in the middle of a round, should we let her play or should we make her wait until the next round starts? I'm a big proponent of keeping players engaged at all times, unless it creates confusion. We are happy to throw a new player right in the thick of things, unless there isn't really enough time left in the round for the player to have a fair chance of finding a solution. (How would you feel if I teased you with a problem and gave you only few brief seconds to think about it, let alone punch in the answer?)

The way we calculate remaining time might seem a bit counterintuitive at first. Why would we be adding the two values instead of subtracting one from the other?

```
  float timeLeft = roundLength + [timeRoundStarted timeIntervalSinceNow];
```

But keep in mind that since `timeRoundStarted` points to a moment in the past when the current round started, `timeIntervalSinceNow` will return a negative value, as per the documentation for `NSDate`.

If we have more than 20 seconds left in this round, the new player is free to participate, and we immediately send a `"startRound"` message, which will cause that client to update its UI accordingly. Otherwise, that player will need to wait for the next round to begin before getting a chance to compete:

```
  if ( isPlaying && timeLeft > 20.0 ) {
    [player startPlayingWithStatus:@"New player, guessing..."];
    [connection sendMessage:[NSDictionary dictionaryWithObjectsAndKeys:
        challenge, @"startRound",
```

```
                    [NSNumber numberWithFloat:timeLeft], @"time", nil]];
  }
  else {
    player.status = @"Just joined, itching to play!";
    player.isPlaying = NO;
  }
```

Whenever a message arrives from one of the clients, we definitely know which connection it came through, because we are passed a Connection object along with the message itself (take a look at connection:receivedMessage: again). But we also need to know which Player object each connection is associated with in order to process game results correctly. To make our lives easier, the Connection class includes a property called userInfo of type id, which allows us to assign anything we want to it. When a new Player object is created, we immediately associate it with the connection, in addition to inserting it into the set that holds all of our players:

```
  connection.userInfo = player;
  [connectedPlayers addObject:player];
```

Now that we have a new player, we want everyone to know about her. Calling tabulateResults will cause an updated list of results (that includes our new participant) to be distributed to all the clients:

```
  [self tabulateResults];
```

We want to keep the new player informed about what's going on in the game as much as possible, which is why we are sending a "status" message at the very end of the method. The isPlaying variable tells us whether a game is in progress or we are between rounds right now:

```
  if ( isPlaying ) {
    [connection sendMessage:[NSDictionary dictionaryWithObjectsAndKeys:
        @"Waiting for answers...", @"status", nil]];
  }
  else {
    [connection sendMessage:[NSDictionary dictionaryWithObjectsAndKeys:
        @"Next round will start shortly...", @"status", nil]];
  }
}
```

Everyone who joins the game will inevitably leave at some point. We face this fact of life every time that a client connection is closed and the connectionClosed: delegate method is called. Here, we simply reverse the setup that was done in newClientConnected: and handleNewPlayer:connection:.

Starting and Stopping Game Rounds

The next group of methods is responsible for controlling the game flow and creating challenges for players to solve. The startNewGameRound method consists of three parts.

First, it sets up various variables that describe the state of the game:

```
- (void)startNewGameRound {
  isPlaying = YES;
```

```
roundLength = 100.0;
self.timeRoundStarted = [NSDate date];
self.challenge = [self makeNewChallenge];
```

At this point, we also need to reset that state of all participating Player objects, which is done by calling the startPlayingWithStatus: method on every one of them:

```
[connectedPlayers makeObjectsPerformSelector:
    @selector(startPlayingWithStatus:) withObject:@"Still guessing..."];
```

Second, we need to send a "startRound" message to all of the connected players, and update our local UI (you might recognize those two delegate method calls from the original GameController implementation):

```
[self broadcastMessage:[NSDictionary dictionaryWithObjectsAndKeys:
    challenge, @"startRound",
    [NSNumber numberWithFloat:roundLength], @"time",
    @"Waiting for answers...", @"status", nil]];
[delegate startRoundWithChallenge:challenge secondsToPlay:roundLength];
[delegate updateGameStatus:@"Waiting for answers..."];
```

Once again, in order to keep everyone updated on the last list of players and their status, we rebuild and resend aggregate results. All of the players will have their status appear as "Still guessing...":

```
[self tabulateResults];
```

The final part of the method ensures that roughly 100 seconds from now, at the latest, the round will be stopped, by scheduling a timer that will call stopGameRound:

```
if ( nextRoundTimer ) {
  [nextRoundTimer invalidate];
}
self.nextRoundTimer = [NSTimer scheduledTimerWithTimeInterval:roundLength+2.0
    target:self selector:@selector(stopGameRound) userInfo:nil repeats:NO];
}
```

But the round might actually be over sooner. If we run out of players who are still thinking about the solution, we don't really want to wait for the full 100 seconds to elapse. That's what checkIfRoundShouldStop is for. In it, we use a handy object called an *enumerator* to check every Player object in our set to see if that player is still guessing:

```
NSEnumerator *enumerator = [connectedPlayers objectEnumerator];
Player *player;
while ((player = (Player*)[enumerator nextObject])) {
  if ( player.isPlaying ) {
    return;
  }
}
```

Every time we ask for nextObject, the enumerator will pick out a new object from the set and return it to us, and we can then inspect it. Whenever we run out of objects, nil will be returned, terminating the loop. Keep in mind that this is a read-only operation, as it doesn't modify the contents of the set.

If we go through all of the players without finding anyone who has yet to submit an answer, the round is officially over. Instead of letting nextRoundTimer fire whenever it was originally scheduled to do so, we will force it to fire immediately by resetting its `fireDate` to "now":

```
isPlaying = NO;
[nextRoundTimer setFireDate:[NSDate date]];
```

Two things happen when `stopGameRound` gets called. First, we tell everyone that the next round will start soon by sending a "status" message to connected players and calling a delegate method to update our own UI:

```
[self broadcastMessage:[NSDictionary dictionaryWithObjectsAndKeys:
    @"Next round will start shortly...", @"status", nil]];
[delegate updateGameStatus:@"Next round will start shortly..."];
```

Then we schedule `nextRoundTimer` to fire again in 10 seconds, and to call `startNewGameRound` this time:

```
if ( nextRoundTimer ) {
  [nextRoundTimer invalidate];
}
self.nextRoundTimer = [NSTimer scheduledTimerWithTimeInterval:10.0
    target:self selector:@selector(startNewGameRound) userInfo:nil repeats:NO];
```

In this way, we create a loop in which `startNewGameRound` and `stopGameRound` take turns being called, guaranteeing that the game keeps running until the app shuts down or the player who is hosting this particular game server decides to leave (at which point, `stop` will be called, giving us a chance to break the timer chain and do some cleanup).

And how does this sequence get set in motion? If you go back to the "Initialization" section, you'll notice that the very first time `startNewGameRound` gets called is right at the point where our socket server gets the go-ahead—in `socketServerStarted`. If you drew a picture of the game's life cycle, it would look something like Figure 15–9.

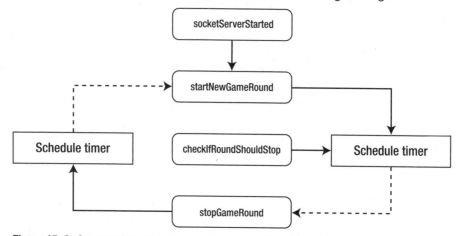

Figure 15–9. *A new socket server is created as soon as the game begins. From that point on, we use timers to start and stop game rounds. This loop will continue until the player decides to quit the game.*

Collecting and Processing Answers

As we are going through the code, keep in mind that besides serving clients that are connected to us over the network, we also have a player who uses the same app on which the game server is running to play the game. During each round, solutions to the challenge might come from two different directions, and we must process them both. That's why we have two sets of result-processing methods:

- `handleResultSuccess:seconds:` and `handleResultFailure:reason:` are invoked by `connection:receivedMessage:` to handle answers that come from remote players.

- `submitResultSuccess:` and `submitResultFailure:` handle our local participant.

The only difference between the two is how they get their hands on the `Player` object.

Whenever a player comes up with the correct solution, we record how long it took her to give the answer, mark that particular player as "no longer playing in this round," and retabulate and redistribute results:

```
player.lastResult = [seconds floatValue];
player.isPlaying = NO;
[self tabulateResults];
```

This is also a good time to see if we have finally collected all of the answers and can stop the round:

```
[self checkIfRoundShouldStop];
```

If the answer is wrong, we use the `Player` object's `status` property to record the reason why it was incorrect. If you search through *TwentyFourViewController.m* for mentions of `submitResultFailure`, you'll see that wrong answers come in two flavors: a player either runs out of time or gives up.

How do we tabulate the results? It turns out to be a relatively easy task. First, we turn the `connectedPlayers` set into an array and sort it using the comparator that we created as part of the `Player` class:

```
NSArray *results = [[connectedPlayers allObjects]
    sortedArrayUsingSelector:@selector(compare:)];
```

But we are only interested in our results list containing the textual description of each result, not a whole `Player` object. To accomplish that, we insert `NSStrings` that describe each player's result into another array:

```
NSMutableArray *textResults = [NSMutableArray arrayWithCapacity:[results count]];
for( int ndx = 0; ndx < [results count]; ndx++ ) {
  Player *p = [results objectAtIndex:ndx];
  [textResults addObject:[p describeResult]];
}
```

After we have our list, it is distributed to all of our connected clients. To keep everything in sync, we also update our local UI via a delegate method:

```
[self broadcastMessage:[NSDictionary dictionaryWithObjectsAndKeys:
    textResults, @"results", nil]];
[delegate updateGameResults:textResults];
```

Hooking It Up

Now that we have the final piece, it's time to complete the puzzle. Let's start the game server whenever a user taps the "Start new game" button in the lobby view. Switch over to *TwentyFourAppDelegate.m*. Write an `import` statement for *GameControllerServer.h* at the top of the file, and then modify `startNewGame` to use our new server class:

```
- (void)startNewGame {
  [self showWaitingScreen];

  GameController *game = [[GameController alloc] init];
  GameControllerServer *game = [[GameController alloc] init];
  game.delegate = self;
  [game startWithPlayerName:playerName];

  gameController = game;
}
```

How's that for surgical precision?

Summary

This chapter was a pretty intense ride. Not only did we need to cover how to use sockets and connections, but we also had to pay close attention to how the game logic itself is laid out in order to keep the code manageable and reuse as much of it as possible.

Whenever you develop a game from scratch, it pays off to think about it as a multiplayer game from the very beginning, even if you don't have any plans (yet) to take it there. Such an approach imposes a certain order on the code that you'll be writing, and makes you think about your app as a set of coupled components, rather than a monolith that will be very difficult to debug when you need to come back to it in a couple months.

Chapter 16

Connecting with the Outside World

We have covered a lot in the previous two chapters. In fact, you should now know enough to build a wide range of applications that utilize networking APIs to connect to each other. But so far, we have been talking about games that can be played only by people whose iPhones and iPod touches are connected to the same wireless networks, or that are located within several feet of each other, reachable by Bluetooth. In some cases, you can dismiss these limitations as not very significant—after all, having an interactive gaming session with other human beings that share the same physical space could be classified as "the ultimate social experience." However, as the world is getting more and more connected, there remain fewer excuses that justify leaving your players around the world disconnected from one another.

If you agree with the basic premise that "everything and everyone want to be connected," then you'll want to know what it takes to bring your already-networked games online, or add some social elements to your still-solitary applications. This chapter provides a brief introduction to using the Internet to enhance your users' gaming experience.

Challenges

To make this exercise less abstract, let's examine what would it take to add online game play capabilities to the games that we created in Chapters 14 and 15: GKPong and TwentyFour. How can the iPhone SDK help us here? And is there anything that the SDK can't do for us in this regard? What are some of the challenges that we will be facing in our quest to bring these games online?

Au Revoir, Bonjour!

The first casualty of such a transition is Bonjour—the technology that we learned to love and respect, and the one that makes it easy for us to find opponents and discover game servers. The reason is quite simple: Currently, due to the way Bonjour is designed, developers can't use it outside local networks. Even though there are some ways to make Bonjour operate over the Internet, as we've seen Apple do with MobileMe and Back to My Mac, such work-arounds seem too complicated to be practical for game developers.

Although the situation might change in the future, as of right now, Bonjour is pretty much useless for online multiplayer games. For a game like TwentyFour, this means replacing the mechanism that allows us to look for servers to connect to.

NOTE: If you need your game to have both a local and online options, you will still want to use NSNetServices for the local part, in addition to whatever needs to be done for online game play to work.

No GameKit Peer-to-Peer for You!

Losing Bonjour also means losing the peer-to-peer capabilities of GameKit, since the latter heavily relies on the former to discover peers and figure out how to establish sessions

Given that all of the networking aspects of GKPong are based on this functionality, it means that we would need to rewrite quite a bit of that game.

Server, interrupted

Imagine playing a game of TwentyFour with a bunch of friends. You launch the app on your iPhone, tap "Start new game," and tell everyone to join in. You are in the middle of a round, desperately trying to figure out the answer. Suddenly, your iPhone starts ringing—it's your mom calling. As soon as you take the call, your game is terminated. What happens to all of the players? They get disconnected and kicked back out into the lobby, of course. Now, this would be unfortunate. But, given that all your friends are in the same room—and perfectly capable of arranging another game while you are on the phone—it's not such a big issue.

Now suppose that this game is being played online, and you have several people from around the world connected to the server running on your iPhone (isn't technology wonderful?). In that case, disconnecting all of them at once would make the players feel a lot worse, since it would happen without a warning, and you wouldn't be able to easily tell them, "It's my mom. I'll be right back."

What does this tell us? In order to be usable online, a game server, like the one built into TwentyFour, needs to be a lot more reliable and available than what we can get out of an app running on a device with a limited battery life, and subject to the availability of 3G or a Wi-Fi signal.

For a game like GKPong, this is not such a big issue. Whenever there are only two players, if one of them gets distracted, the whole game is effectively over, even if the game server remains available. The other opponent simply doesn't have anyone to play against. But this doesn't mean that we can get away with not introducing a centralized server in this case. Remember that we no longer have Bonjour to play matchmaker for us. We'll need to replace it with some sort of a game server whose "contact information" is known to both clients beforehand.

Lag

Slow communication is one of the more serious issues facing online multiplayer game developers, and it's the one that you cannot really remove; you can only code around it. Simply stated, it takes time for packets to travel over the Internet. How much time they will spend in transit depends on several variables, such as connection speed on both the sender's and receiver's end, and distance between the two peers. A more technical term to describe the amount of time that it takes a message to get from one end to another is *latency*.

It takes a typical GKPong message only a few milliseconds to travel from one iPhone to another via Bluetooth. But as soon as you start sending data over the Internet, expect it to take at least ten times as long on a broadband connection, and even longer over a cellular data connection. Whenever high latency starts negatively impacting gaming experience by making game play feel slow or unresponsive, players start complaining of "lag."

Real-time games like GKPong usually suffer a lot more from lag issues than games like TwentyFour, where other players don't expect to see results of their actions as soon as they happen. It's not a problem if your answer arrives a second later—it will still be counted. In GKPong, however, due to the way we chose to implement it, if the gkMessageBallBounced message spends any significant time traveling from my iPod touch to yours, you will start seeing the ball jittering and going out of bounds before bouncing back.

If you are interested in learning more about how to go about solving problems related to high latency in online games, look for materials related to "lag compensation in multiplayer games."

> **TIP:** One crude way to simulate lag in your games is to schedule messages to be sent out in the future instead of immediately whenever you need to communicate something. Since you don't want to make your overall application sluggish by "sleeping," use NSObject's performSelector:withObject:afterDelay: to postpone execution of methods responsible for sending out messages.

It's All Greek to Me...

Remember how we used NSKeyedArchiver and NSKeyedUnarchiver to make TwentyFour apps exchange messages with each other? It was possible because both sides were able to encode and decode variables using the algorithm implemented by those two classes, in exactly the same way, every time. It was easy because both sides were created using the same iPhone SDK, and we were guaranteed consistency. However, once you decide to use different platforms for different sections of your app (i.e., iPhone game clients connecting to a game server that's running on Linux), you must deal with a possibility that you won't have an implementation of NSKeyedArchiver and NSKeyedUnarchiver algorithms for a particular platform that you want to use.

One common solution to this problem is to use standard, well-defined ways to format your data, such as XML, JavaScript Object Notation (JSON), and the like. You can typically find libraries that will take care of handling the low-level details of encoding and decoding for you, no matter which programming language you choose.

Another way to go about it is to "roll your own," just as we did with GKPong. You can make up your own format, and make sure that you can handle composition and parsing of messages on both the server and client end. Both approaches have their positives and negatives. Make sure to do your research before plunging into the deep end.

> **CAUTION:** When dealing with cross-platform networking code, make sure to pay attention to the byte order. It's generally a good idea to convert your data to big-endian or network order before transmission. Third-party libraries usually take care of this for you, but if you do decide to come up with your own, this is something that you should keep in mind. For more information, look up "Endianness" on Wikipedia.

And a Bunch More

Once your game leaves the confines of a local network and enters rough waters of the Internet, your list of things to pay attention to will grow quite substantially. I have covered some of the challenges already, Here are a few more:

- *Security*: Now that your game will be accessible to so many more people, you will want to make sure that it is protected against those who are looking to cause trouble. This includes securing your server computers and making sure that it won't be easy for players to cheat.

- *Scalability*: This is a fancy word for being able to handle the demand. Popular iPhone games can get hundreds of thousands of players. Can your server handle that many? Even if you don't get that many, prepare to deal with spikes in usage when your game becomes available for sale or a favorable review appears and people rush to try it out.

■ *Monitoring*: When something goes wrong with your servers, as happens from time to time, make sure that you are the first one to find out about it. Don't wait for your players to e-mail you a "Your game doesn't work" message, or, even worse, leave bad reviews in the App Store because they just downloaded the game and it cannot connect to the server.

Basics of Online Game Play

Even though it might feel like we just got told to fight a war twice the size with an army half of what it used to be, all is not lost. Don't let the list of challenges set you back. Problems like these have existed for as long as games have been around, and all of them can be addressed if you put in enough effort. In an online multiplayer gaming project, the stakes are higher, but so is the potential payoff, both in terms of player engagement and popularity of your app.

Let's start with simple things. As far as the game client goes, we still have CFNetwork on our side. We just need to figure out how to build a game server and where to run it.

Keep in mind that we are talking about real-time (shooters, racing, and so on) and turn-based (card or board) games here.

Client/Server Games

The vast majority of multiplayer games use the client/server model. In an iPhone game that's running over a local network, you typically bundle a server into the game app itself, just as we did with TwentyFour. However, an online game would have a dedicated piece of game server software running somewhere on a computer that's connected to the Internet. The network structure of a typical online game server setup is shown in Figure 16–1.

Online game servers can be written in a variety of languages—any language that gives you the ability to accept and establish sockets connections will do. For performance reasons, many developers choose to go with C-based languages. Usually, this comes down to using the tools that you know versus learning new ones or finding people with skills that complement your own.

Where do you run such a server? There are a couple of considerations here:

■ You need a computer that your game clients can contact from the Internet.

■ Given how popular iPhone games can get, you need a computer (or a group of computers) that is powerful enough to handle a lot of connections.

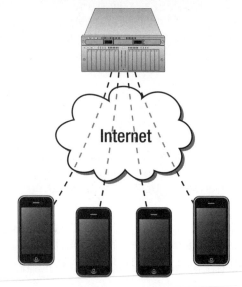

Game server application running on Mac OS X, Linus etc

Internet

Game client app running on iPhones and iPod Touches

Figure 16–1. *A game running on an iPhone is connected via the Internet to a central server, which takes on all of the responsibilities that our little TwentyFour server did, and then some. Typically, connections stay open for the whole duration of the gaming session, allowing bidirectional exchange of messages.*

The typical answer here is to find a company that specializes in hosting services and to pay to rent or lease computers located in that company's data centers. They will typically be powerful and connected enough to handle an online multiplayer game server that has a small-to-medium-sized player base.

Connecting to a Game Server Without Bonjour

In terms of code on the client side, you can reuse the vast majority of the `Connection` class that we created in Chapter 15. Instead of asking `NSNetService` to create a pair of streams that will then be used to communicate with the server, you'll need to establish a connection to the game server explicitly, using the server's hostname (or IP address) and port number.

If you are interested in having this functionality in your other apps or games, I have a few more lines of code for you. Load the TwentyFour project from Chapter 15, open *Connection.h*, and add a method with the following signature:

```
- (id)initWithHostName:(NSString*)hostName portNumber:(int)portNumber;
```

Now, somewhere in *Connection.m*, add the implementation:

```
- (id)initWithHostName:(NSString*)hostName portNumber:(int)portNumber {
```

```
CFReadStreamRef readStream;
CFWriteStreamRef writeStream;
CFStreamCreatePairWithSocketToHost(NULL, (CFStringRef)hostName, portNumber,
    &readStream, &writeStream);
self.inputStream = (NSInputStream*)readStream;
self.outputStream = (NSOutputStream*)writeStream;
return self;
}
```

This method is very similar to the `initWithNativeSocketHandle:` method that we created earlier, but instead of pairing streams with a native socket handle, we are instructing the operating system to create a socket based on the hostname and port number. Note that the actual connection will not be opened until you call `Connection`'s connect method.

Peer-to-Peer Games

If you lift the hood of the GameKit framework and look at the internals of `GKSession`, you'll find that it mostly uses Bonjour to find peers, and a networking protocol called UDP to exchange data between peers. What makes UDP different from TCP (which we used in TwentyFour) is that it doesn't have a notion of a connection. You simply specify which IP address and port you want to send a bunch of bytes to, and the operating system tries to deliver the data for you. When using UDP, the networking layer does not guarantee that your packets will be delivered or in what order they will get there. If you want to transmit data reliably, you need to implement an algorithm that will do so. (Does this remind you of `GKSendDataReliable` versus `GKSendDataUnreliable`?)

It should come as no surprise that you, too, can use UDP in your apps, via CFNetwork. In theory, you can use it to reimplement GKPong to be playable online. And since Bonjour is not available, you'll need a centralized server that will allow your peers to find each other. The basic structure of a peer-to-peer setup is illustrated in Figure 16–2.

In practice, there are quite a few issues with using UDP over the Internet to implement online peer-to-peer games—most of them having to do with bypassing firewalls and ensuring that peers can connect to each other. This is the main reason why a lot of developers decide to go with a client/server option instead, which is simpler but might result in additional latency.

> **TIP:** If you want to learn more about designing peer-to-peer networking protocols using UDP, make sure to pick up a copy of *iPhone Cool Projects* (Apress, 2009) and read Chapter 2, entitled "Mike Ash's Deep Dive into Peer-to-Peer Networking."

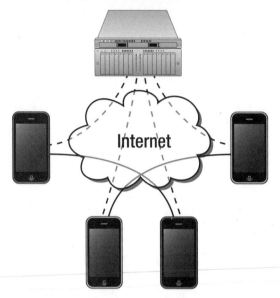

Game server application
running on Mac OS X, Linus etc

Game client app
running on iPhones and iPod Touches

Figure 16–2. *Game clients use a centralized server to find peers, but then communicate with each other directly, allowing for lower latency.*

Something About Reinventing the Wheel

At this point, you might be wondering, "Hasn't all this been done before? Do I really have to do this all myself, from scratch?" Unless you find low-level network programming interesting and are willing to invest some time into getting it right, it could be quite painful to use tools like CFNetwork directly. That's why you might want to look at the libraries and toolkits other developers have created that could be of use to you.

As of this book's writing, CocoaAsyncSocket (`http://code.google.com/p/cocoaasyncsocket/`) is considered to be one of the best third-party networking libraries to use for iPhone and/or Mac OS X development. With this library, you don't need to worry about a lot of low-level details. However, just as with any other tool that you pick up, you need to learn how to use it effectively. The API is more complex than GameKit, but it's also more powerful. Luckily, it does come with some documentation and a couple of examples.

Then there is enet (`http://enet.bespin.org`), a "thin, simple and robust communication layer on top of UDP." If you do need a replacement for GKSession's miraculous ability to mix and match reliable and unreliable packet delivery, enet can do it for you. Also, because it's a platform-independent framework, you can write both an iPhone game client and, say, a Linux game server, using the same library. Of course, you will need some time to learn the ropes, as usual. Also, enet is written in C, which means that you won't get to interact with classes, but will need to deal in functions and data structures, much as we needed to do when using the CFNetwork directly. But don't let these seeming inconveniences stop you from creating something great. According to Phil Hassey, the author of the award-winning real-time strategy game Galcon, the multiplayer part of that game was written using enet, and "it worked out-of-the-box."

Like a Drop in the Ocean

There is a whole lot more to building successful online multiplayer games than I can cover here. But by now, you should have a pretty good idea of how to go about it.

If you are serious about exploring this topic further, a good place to get advice and additional information is forums where game developers hang out, such as GameDev.net (http://www.gamedev.net/community/forums). For more iPhone- and Mac OS X-oriented game development, check out the iPhone Dev SDK forum (http://iphonedevsdk.com/forum/iphone-sdk-game-development) and iDevGames.com (http://idevgames.com/forum).

Making Games More Social

What if you have a game that can't really be called multiplayer—does that mean that your players are doomed to forever feeling isolated? Of course not! There are many different ways of using networking frameworks to give your game's audience a sense of connectedness and belonging. I will introduce some of these techniques in the rest of this chapter.

Sharing High Scores Online

One of the best ways to keep your players engaged with the game is to constantly give them something to strive for. For example, you can allow them to compete with each other via an online leaderboard. Implementing something like this requires having a central server, but the infrastructure is not as complex as what is required for online play, so it can be done faster and cheaper. Plus, it works for any game that awards points to players, making it one of the most basic and accessible techniques for bringing social interactions into games.

Usually, you store the scores on a central server that game clients can connect to via the Internet. Data transfer can be done via HTTP, which is the best tool to use in these circumstances. The iPhone SDK has several classes that implement this protocol for you. Take a look at NSURLRequest and NSURLConnection, and the sample code that demonstrates their use.

On the server side, you'll need several components:

- A server computer that will run all this. If you already have a web site, using the same server would be a good starting point.

- A place to store the scores, usually a database, such as MySQL or PostgreSQL.

- A web server that will accept clients' requests (that is, if you do decide to go with HTTP). A typical choice for web server software is Apache.

- A script running inside of the web server. This script will handle communication with the clients and interact with the database. This part can be implemented in a myriad of programming languages.

A sketch of what the resulting infrastructure might look like is shown in Figure 16–3.

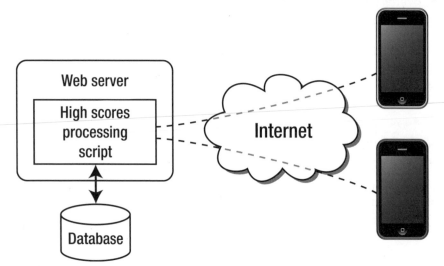

Figure 16–3. *All of the data is stored on the server. Clients submit scores when players get awarded some, and fetch them when players want to see the leaderboard.*

When it comes time to present the high-score table, depending on how fast you want to implement this functionality and how integrated with your app you want the high-score table to look, you have a few options:

- Request the list of scores from the server and display each entry in the list as a cell inside a UITableView.

- Have the server construct and send back an HTML file that will contain a nicely formatted high-score table, which can then be rendered on the iPhone by a UIWebView.

- Request the list of scores from the server and have the client turn it into an HTML file that can be rendered by a UIWebView.

- Fetch scores from the server and render them on the screen using custom routines and UI elements. Let your imagination and graphics design requirements show you the way here.

> **TIP:** For a detailed walk-through of how to implement an online leaderboard in your own game, with source code included, check out Chapter 2 of *iPhone Games Projects* (Apress, 2009), titled "Responsive Social Gaming with RESTful Web Services," by PJ Cabrera.

Chasing Ghosts

Once you start sharing scores, why not use the same infrastructure to allow players to record and share whole game-play performances, allowing others to replay them and compete, as if in real time? Think of a racing game. Instead of chasing a car controlled by another player over the network in real time, you could be trying to beat a car that simply follows a path recorded during a gaming session that was played by you or someone else earlier. Usually, those cars are displayed half-transparently, giving you a feeling that you are competing against a ghost. This idea can apply to several gaming genres, not just racing.

Here, instead of (or, typically, in addition to) submitting and fetching high scores, you upload and download files that contain game-play data that can be used to re-create actions taken by another player, or even the same one, in the game.

A great example of this feature can be seen in an iPhone game called DrawRace by Redlynx Ltd.

Chatting

Another great way to bring people together is to let them talk to one another. Here you have two options: text and voice.

The easiest way to implement text chat is with a client/server model, where clients send messages to and receive messages from chat rooms via a central server. When it comes to the chat protocol, you can either pick an existing one, like XMPP (also known as Jabber) or create your own. Both approaches have their positive and negative aspects. Jabber is fairly complex but powerful, allowing you to take advantage of server software that has been written already (check out an open source Jabber server implementation called Openfire at `http://www.igniterealtime.org/projects/openfire/index.jsp`). Making something from scratch, arguably, involves more coding and debugging, but could be easier to control and extend.

One of the interesting new features that was introduced in iPhone SDK 3.0 is the ability to establish a voice chat session between two iPhone apps. It works over Bluetooth and Wi-Fi. If you want to allow players to chat over the Internet, you will again need a central server that will allow chat participants to find each other, and to initialize the voice chat connection. For more information, search the Xcode documentation for `GKVoiceChat`.

Summary

Whew! We have covered a lot of ground in these four chapters on networking. You should now know how to create iPhone games that can be played over Bluetooth using GameKit, in addition to utilizing CFNetwork and Bonjour to connect players via local Wi-Fi network—and it's not a small feat! In addition to all of that, if you decide to open the doors for gamers from all over the world to compete, you should have a pretty good idea of where to begin.

Network programming is an exciting topic, from both technical and business perspectives. There is no doubt that, everything else being equal, social games attract more players and retain participants for longer periods of time—allowing you, the game developer, to be more successful.

Chapter 17

Putting It All Together: Now Comes the Fun Part

You have now been introduced to and familiarized with all the basic aspects of iPhone game development. It's time to take your preferred tools out of the graphics, sound, and networking compartments of your new toolbox, and break ground on your own amazing iPhone game. This last chapter will make sure you're pointed in the right direction before starting out.

What We've Covered

A quick review of all the subjects and technologies touched on in the previous chapters will help you narrow down exactly which ones you'll need to use in your game. Most of what we've covered falls into one of three general categories: graphics, sound, and networking.

Chapters 3 through 5 covered basic 2D graphics, including UIKit, Quartz, and Core Animation. Consider these technologies if your game won't need to display and animate large numbers of game elements at a time, and you don't need the raw power and flexibility of OpenGL. Getting up and running can be especially quick using Interface Builder to create and lay out views and menus.

Chapters 6 through 8 were also graphics-related, focusing on the use of OpenGL ES. If you plan on developing a game with 3D graphics, a lot of fast animation, tons of particles, or other special effects, OpenGL ES is the right choice for you. However, even if you decide to use OpenGL ES, you may want to take advantage of the other 2D frameworks for components like menus and other GUI elements.

Now that you've decided how to render your graphics, it's time to think about your game's audio. While some people may not consider audio as important as graphics, never underestimate the value sound can bring to an interactive experience. Chapters 9 through 12 presented a wealth of choices for adding audio to your iPhone game. We covered the basics of playing short sound effects, giving your game a soundtrack, and even 3D positional audio, if you're striving for a truly immersive experience best enjoyed through headphones.

That brings us to the third and final section of our toolbox, networking tools. The vast majority of iPhone games take advantage of being on a network-connected device in one way or another. Chapters 13 through 16 outlined the different networking frameworks available for use in your game. If your game calls for real-time multiplayer capabilities, either local or global, everything you've learned about GameKit, Bonjour, and sockets will come in handy. If your game isn't multiplayer, you can still use what you learned in this book to add elements like online leaderboards to your game.

Some Game Design Tips

While game design is certainly part of game development, we've focused primarily on the technical aspects of game design, since this book is aimed at programmers. The App Store has enabled smaller and smaller development teams to create games, which means those team members end up wearing more and more hats. One- or two-man teams, absent a dedicated designer or producer, have created some of the most successful iPhone games. If you fall into this category and plan on designing the game yourself, you can find plenty of resources to learn more about the specifics of iPhone game and UI design, such as *iPhone Games Projects* by PJ Cabrera *et al* (Apress, 2009) and *iPhone User Interface Design Projects* by Joachim Bondo *et al* (Apress, 2009).

The following are a few general tips for iPhone game designers:

- *Keep it simple*: Many games begin as grandiose, ambitious designs without an honest evaluation of the man-hours it will take to complete such a design. The first game developed on any platform plays an important role as a learning experience. It provides a way to get your hands dirty and become familiar with any limitations or features it may have. Keeping your game design simple will get your game to the App Store quicker, and may make it more popular with the more casual mobile gaming audience.

- *Be original*: With more than 100,000 apps available from the App Store, there is no shortage of copycat games. Customers are spread thinly over all iPhone games, and your customer base will be spread even thinner if you try competing in a crowded group of highly similar games. If you do wish to make yet another tower-defense, line-drawing, or match-three game, be sure find a way to differentiate or improve on existing games to help yours stand out from the crowd. Design a high-quality original game, and people might soon be trying to copy your creation, spawning an entirely new genre of iPhone game in the process!

- *Show everyone*: From the earliest possible stage of development, show your game to as many people as possible. Feedback on your game from people not involved in its development is invaluable. Try to don a thick skin and take people's opinions to heart, whether those opinions are good or bad. A game's interface or mechanic can be incredibly obvious to the designer, while confusing or frustrating to a newcomer. Issues like these are much better off solved before a game appears on the App Store.

Wrapping It Up

You've been given the foundation needed for a great iPhone game. It is now up to you to decide its shape and fill in the details. You've joined the ranks of one of the largest and fastest growing communities of developers. If you get stuck on anything along the way, chances are good that a fellow developer has already figured out a solution. Getting to know some fellow developers and participating in online iPhone communities can be especially helpful.

Now comes the especially fun and rewarding part: bringing the black glass canvas in the palm of your hand to life. Perhaps someday soon, thousands of people will be carrying your game in their pockets, everywhere they go.

Index

F

∎ M

You Need the Companion eBook

Your purchase of this book entitles you to buy the companion PDF-version eBook for only $10. Take the weightless companion with you anywhere.

We believe this Apress title will prove so indispensable that you'll want to carry it with you everywhere, which is why we are offering the companion eBook (in PDF format) for $10 to customers who purchase this book now. Convenient and fully searchable, the PDF version of any content-rich, page-heavy Apress book makes a valuable addition to your programming library. You can easily find and copy code—or perform examples by quickly toggling between instructions and the application. Even simultaneously tackling a donut, diet soda, and complex code becomes simplified with hands-free eBooks!

Once you purchase your book, getting the $10 companion eBook is simple:

❶ Visit **www.apress.com/promo/tendollars/**.

❷ Complete a basic registration form to receive a randomly generated question about this title.

❸ Answer the question correctly in 60 seconds, and you will receive a promotional code to redeem for the $10.00 eBook.

Apress®
THE EXPERT'S VOICE™

233 Spring Street, New York, NY 10013

Offer valid through 8/10.